The Editor

MICHAEL PATRICK GILLESPIE is Professor of English at Florida International University. He is the author of *Oscar Wilde and the Poetics of Ambiguity*, *Branding Oscar Wilde*, *The Aesthetics of Chaos: Nonlinear Thinking and Contemporary Literary Criticism*, *Inverted Volumes Improperly Arranged: James Joyce and His Trieste Library*, *Reading the Book Himself: Narrative Strategies in the Works of James Joyce*, *The Aesthetics of Chaos*, *The Myth of an Irish Cinema*, *James Joyce and the Exilic Imagination*, *Reading William Kennedy*, and *Film Appreciation through Genres*. His other edited works include the Norton Critical Edition of *The Importance of Being Earnest*, *James Joyce and the Fabrication of an Irish Identity*, and *Joyce through the Ages: A Non-Linear View*.

A NORTON CRITICAL EDITION

Oscar Wilde

THE PICTURE OF DORIAN GRAY

AUTHORITATIVE TEXTS

BACKGROUNDS

REVIEWS AND REACTIONS

CRITICISM

THIRD EDITION

Edited by

MICHAEL PATRICK GILLESPIE
FLORIDA INTERNATIONAL UNIVERSITY

W · W · NORTON & COMPANY · *New York* · *London*

W. W. Norton & Company has been independent since its founding in 1923, when William Warder Norton and Mary D. Herter Norton first published lectures delivered at the People's Institute, the adult education division of New York City's Cooper Union. The firm soon expanded its program beyond the Institute, publishing books by celebrated academics from America and abroad. By midcentury, the two major pillars of Norton's publishing program—trade books and college texts—were firmly established. In the 1950s, the Norton family transferred control of the company to its employees, and today—with a staff of five hundred and hundreds of trade, college, and professional titles published each year—W. W. Norton & Company stands as the largest and oldest publishing house owned wholly by its employees.

Manufacturing by Maple Press
Book design by Antonina Krass
Production manager: Stephen Sajdak

ISBN: 978-0-393-69687-5 (pbk.)

W. W. Norton & Company, Inc., 500 Fifth Avenue, New York, N. Y. 10110
www.wwnorton.com
W. W. Norton & Company Ltd., 15 Carlisle Street, London W1D 3BS

3 4 5 6 7 8 9 0

Dedicated to the Memory of Vincent J. Gillespie
1953–2005
Son, brother, husband, father, friend

Contents

Criticism

Preface

In a letter composed on February 12, 1894, and sent to Ralph Payne, who had written to praise *The Picture of Dorian Gray*, Oscar Wilde neatly summarizes his relations to the central characters and gently mocks simplistic reactions to them through a series of concise analogies. "I am so glad you like that strange coloured book of mine: it contains much of me in it. Basil Hallward is what I think I am: Lord Henry what the world thinks me: Dorian what I would like to be— in other ages perhaps" (*The Letters of Oscar Wilde*, 352). While the passage from his letter catches the tone of Wilde's insouciant wit and sly self-deprecation, it also neatly suggests a number of elements central to an understanding of the novel.

Even allowing for his irrepressible flamboyance, Wilde certainly came very close to the mark in relating how diverse perceptions of his own nature inform conceptions of the characters in his novel. For all its originality, *The Picture of Dorian Gray* takes up themes of aesthetics, sensuality, and personal independence that Wilde had explored in lectures and in writings for over a decade before the book appeared. The novel, however, enjoys the distinction of allowing for extended discussions of all of those themes and of providing a relatively safe venue for elaborating upon a broad range of indulgences at which previous expressions could only hint.

Though Edward Carson, who prosecuted Wilde for immoral acts in 1895 (see pp. 381–89), sought to make the book a manifesto of Wilde's hedonistic lifestyle, I think it more accurate to see it as a rigorous examination of the limitations of the aesthetic views that had come to shape his art. *The Picture of Dorian Gray* articulates, without offering a clear resolution, the conflict that arises as a result of the struggle within an individual's nature between the impulse toward self-gratification and the sense of guilt that is a consequence of acting upon that inclination.

Nonetheless, one can understand, if not sympathize with, Carson's inclination to collapse fact and fiction. All of Wilde's writing has an intensely personal tone to it, and the issues of art, imagination, and sensuality outlined in the novel were at the time unsettled in Wilde's own life. *The Picture of Dorian Gray* merely provides greater space than heretofore available for a wide-ranging exposition of his interests and concerns. Though the consequent aesthetic and ethical issues that arise in the narrative may seem daunting, one can come to a solid understanding of the novel by keeping in mind a few fundamental concepts.

The Trinitarian description that he favors in his February 12th letter neatly captures the way Wilde's life informed both the composition and perception of the work. The tension among the probity of Basil Hallward, the immorality of Lord Henry, and the unabashed self-indulgence of Dorian combine to echo the author's conflicting feelings during this period, evident in any biographical account of him. At the same time, the similarities can prove to be a trap for hasty readers who seek to interpret the work by simply imposing Wilde and their impressions of him on the central characters of the novel. In fact, *The Picture of Dorian Gray* presents a complex view of the conflicted interrelation between fantasy and fact that characterized Wilde's world and his writings, and it presents contemporary readers with the challenge of forming understandings without mistaking Wilde for his characters.

Of course, Wilde did much to encourage this blurring of distinctions. From the time of his permanent move from Oxford to London in 1879, flamboyance had characterized his approach to the world. With a single-minded determination, Wilde made himself a public personality well before he had gained prominence as a writer. Indeed, for much of the 1880s his determined advocacy of "art for art's sake" seemed as much self-parody as sincere assertion of belief.

When *The Picture of Dorian Gray* appeared, however, its narrative went beyond the flummery often characterizing his public performances. Its discourse demanded that points of view Wilde had previously thrown out casually at dinner parties or alluded to obliquely in public lectures now be given full and sustained scrutiny. Further, its sustained tone of intellectual rigor—evident in Lord Henry Wotton's explanation in Chapter Two of New Hedonism—insisted that equally serious attention be paid to Wilde as its author.

Taking Oscar Wilde seriously was a new proposition for late-Victorian London. He had already gained notoriety as a journalist, critic, and short story writer, but *The Picture of Dorian Gray* offered readers the first substantial piece of evidence of Wilde's far-ranging creative ability. Although much of the dialogue features the same style of repartee that made Wilde such a desirable dinner guest and many of the descriptions have the same fascination with excess that punctuated his poems and public lectures, the content of the novel lays out serious consideration of ethical issues relating to the movement from the nineteenth century's fixation upon society to the twentieth century's celebration of the individual. Critics may debate

whether *The Picture of Dorian Gray* stands as the first English
Modernist novel, but few will disagree that it touches on the same
issue—the role that one should allow social institutions in shaping
an individual's character—that writers like James Joyce, D. H. Law-
rence, and Virginia Woolf would minutely explore in the next quarter century.

Wilde could make these great thematic strides because he relied
on stylistic forms he had been practicing to perfection for a decade.
The narrative of his novel builds on the strengths of his earlier
work—a fascination for detail, a love of paradox, and a deft sense of
humor. This allows its content to go well beyond the scope of any
previous writing. Both in novella and novel form, the story of Dorian
Gray explores with great sensitivity the relation of art to morality,
the impact of hedonism, and the inescapability of spiritual questions. Wilde pursues these topics without turning the book into a
polemic because his formal writing skills give him the ability to
engage ideas without seeming to assume a didactic mode.

The duality exercised in the form and content stands as the key
to the novel's lasting success. In publishing *The Picture of Dorian
Gray* Wilde showed himself capable of much more than a flippant
response to the world. His representations of the major characters
demonstrate a keen sensitivity to human appetites, human needs,
and most of all, human weaknesses. At the same time, Wilde refuses
to recapitulate the standard pieties or received wisdoms of his
Victorian contemporaries. Instead, *The Picture of Dorian Gray*
shows an author determined to explore the contradictory elements
of human nature.

Not surprisingly, the boldness of his ideas created a great deal of
consternation among a number of readers and reviewers who saw
the first version of Dorian Gray's story in novella form in *Lippincott's Magazine* in June 1890. As the excerpts from contemporane-
ous reviews reprinted in this edition attest, the apparent open
advocacy of a lifestyle based solely upon gratification—the New
Hedonism expounded by Lord Henry—was more than many could
bear. Despite the death of Dorian at the end of the tale, the self-
indulgence in which he had partaken over the course of the narrative maddened some readers. (One is reminded of the observation
that Puritans disapproved of bearbaiting not because of the suffering endured by the animal but because of the enjoyment experienced
by the audience.)

The events leading to the composition of *The Picture of Dorian
Gray* gave little indication of the impact it would produce. In the fall
of 1889, J. Marshall Stoddart, the American editor of *Lippincott's
Magazine*, traveled to England. Stoddart previously had met Wilde
in 1882 while the latter was touring America, and at a dinner party

in London Stoddart persuaded Wilde and Arthur Conan Doyle to contribute novella length works to the magazine. (Doyle subsequently sent Stoddart his second Sherlock Holmes adventure, "The Sign of Four.") Wilde initially proposed that *Lippincott's* use a story that he had already written, "The Fisherman and His Soul," but Stoddart rejected the idea. Wilde wrote to Stoddart on December 17, 1889, that he had "invented a new story which is better than 'The Fisherman and His Soul' and I am quite ready to set to work at once on it" (*The Letters of Oscar Wilde*, 251).

Wilde sent the initial version of the work to Stoddart early in 1890. As the manuscript, held by the Clark Library, attests, Stoddart did not hesitate to excise portions that he felt would be too graphic for his readers' sensibilities. (A full discussion of the first manuscript appears in the Donald L. Lawler essay in this collection.) Stoddart apparently had a good idea of the taste of American readers. The novella appeared in the July 1890 issue of *Lippincott's*. The issue in which it appeared quickly sold out, and American critics praised the work as a modern morality tale. That was not the case in England, however, where a number of reviewers excoriated the work. A lively debate, lasting into the fall, took place in the columns of various newspapers between Wilde and his supporters on one hand and hostile reviewers on the other.

Although Wilde steadfastly defended his work, the criticism did in fact have an impact on his revisions when he rewrote it as a full-length novel. In its expanded form, published by Ward, Lock & Company in 1891, *The Picture of Dorian Gray* retains its essential narrative elements. However, Wilde made modifications that present some of his more daring ideas in a less direct fashion and he included a Preface that addresses through aphoristic statements the charges of immorality leveled against the novella. Individual readers can judge the effect of these changes. (To facilitate comparison, the original *Lippincott's* version immediately follows the expanded text of *The Picture of Dorian Gray* in this Norton Critical Edition.) However, one cannot dispute that the novel, as we now have it, has exercised a powerful impact upon its readers for well over a century.

In organizing this Norton Critical Edition, I have tried to provide a sampling of the aesthetic world that informed Wilde's creative efforts. Selections from Joris-Karl Huysmans and Walter Pater provide glimpses of the writings that shaped Wilde's views, and portions of two of Wilde's essays offer clear articulations of his adaptation and application. Likewise, an extensive selection of responses to the novella's appearance shows not only the public perception of the work but also Wilde's sense of what his writing aimed at.

The criticism gathered here reflects the range of approaches that offer effective methods for understanding Wilde's novel. The section begins with Joseph Carroll, who offers a revised view of the impact of sexuality on our readings based on Darwinian theory. Nils Clausson assesses the impact of cross-genre perspectives of the narrative. Emily Eells reminds us of the impact of recent literary antecedents on Wilde. Michael Patrick Gillespie sees a post-Modern slant to the absence of values in the narrative. Richard Haslam challenges recent work emphasizing Wilde's credentials as an Irish writer. Donald Lawler traces the evolution of the work's composition. And Ellen Scheible links Wilde's aesthetics to a critique of imperialism. While these selections cannot exhaust possibilities for reading, they do underscore the variety of approaches that can produce a satisfying understanding of the novel.

Many people have contributed to this project, and I realize that to a great extent whatever success it enjoys relates directly to their efforts. No one has done more to shape this volume than my editors at Norton: Carol Bemis, Rachel Goodman, and Thea Goodrich. Their enthusiasm, energy, and trust have been invaluable. Their sound judgments have saved me from numerous false steps, and their warm support has made working on this edition a pleasure. There may still be shortcomings here that even they could not find, but the value of this book comes to a large degree from their careful scrutiny. I also wish to thank the staff at the Clark Library, Maneck Daruwala, John Espy, A. Nicholas Fargnoli, Kenneth Furton, Paula Gillespie, Merlin Holland, Tim Machan, Michael McKinney, Asher Milbauer, Joan Navarre, Albert Rivero, Mary Jane Rochelson, David Rose, Heather Russell, Sara Schepis, Joan Sommers, the staff of the Florida International University Library, and the Inter-Library Loan staff at Marquette University.

A Note on the Texts

The Picture of Dorian Gray first appeared as a novella of over fifty thousand words. It was published in the July 1890 issue of *Lippincott's Monthly*. The revised and expanded novel-length version was printed by Ward, Lock & Company in April 1891 and sold for six shillings. This was the same company that bound the British edition of *Lippincott's* magazine. A new printing was called for in October 1895, by which time the publisher had become Ward, Lock & Bowden. The novel was not reprinted again until 1901, the year following Wilde's death, by Charles Carrington, a slightly disreputable English publisher of pornographic literature in Paris, who, following Wilde's bankruptcy in 1895, had acquired the rights in expectation that profit was to be made from the scandal surrounding the novel, which figured prominently in Wilde's famous trials. Robert Ross, as executor of the Wilde estate, eventually reacquired the rights to the novel. Since that time, the novel has never been out of print.

In the March 1891 edition of Frank Harris's *Fortnightly Review* Wilde published "A Preface to 'Dorian Gray.'" It consisted of twenty-three aphorisms, written by Wilde in response to the criticisms made of the *Lippincott's Dorian Gray* (see "Reviews and Reactions," pp. 357–73). By the time Ward, Lock & Company brought out the novel-length version in April, Wilde had added a new aphorism to the Preface ("No artist is ever morbid. The artist can express everything") and had divided the original ninth aphorism (beginning "The nineteenth century dislike of Realism . . .") to make a final total of twenty-five aphorisms.

As in the first Norton Critical Edition of *The Picture of Dorian Gray*, this volume reprints the texts of the original 1890 *Lippincott's* novella and the revised and expanded version into the novel published by Ward, Lock & Company in 1891. These were the only two versions prepared for and seen through publication by the author. The revised version of 1891, representing Wilde's final intentions, here appears ahead of the *Lippincott's* text of 1890. Obvious typographical errors have been silently emended. With that exception, this edition reproduces the settings, including Wilde's punctuation, of the 1891 edition.

The Texts of
THE PICTURE OF
DORIAN GRAY

The Preface[1]

The artist is the creator of beautiful things.

To reveal art and conceal the artist is art's aim.

The critic is he who can translate into another manner or a new material his impression of beautiful things.

The highest as the lowest form of criticism is a mode of autobiography.

Those who find ugly meanings in beautiful things are corrupt without being charming. This is a fault.

Those who find beautiful meanings in beautiful things are the cultivated. For these there is hope.

They are the elect to whom beautiful things mean only Beauty.

There is no such thing as a moral or an immoral book. Books are well written, or badly written. That is all.

The nineteenth century dislike of Realism is the rage of Caliban seeing his own face in a glass.

The nineteenth century dislike of Romanticism is the rage of Caliban not seeing his own face in a glass.

The moral life of man forms part of the subject-matter of the artist, but the morality of art consists in the perfect use of an imperfect medium.

No artist desires to prove anything. Even things that are true can be proved.

No artist has ethical sympathies. An ethical sympathy in an artist is an unpardonable mannerism of style.

No artist is ever morbid. The artist can express everything.

Thought and language are to the artist instruments of an art.

Vice and Virtue are to the artist materials for an art.

From the point of view of form, the type of all the arts is the art of the musician. From the point of view of feeling, the actor's craft is the type.

All art is at once surface and symbol.

Those who go beneath the surface do so at their peril.

Those who read the symbol do so at their peril.

It is the spectator, and not life, that art really mirrors.

---

1. Wilde's preface to *Dorian Gray* appeared in Frank Harris's *Fortnightly Review* several months before the second edition of the novel. It seems to have three aims. The first is to take weapons out of the hands of the critics who had attacked the *Lippincott's Magazine* edition of *Dorian Gray* by anticipating some of the charges likely to be made against it. The second intent is to respond to some of the criticism made of the magazine edition. In so doing, Wilde was to repeat the major points of his aesthetic creed at the time (and to anticipate the main line of his defense of *Dorian Gray* at the trials). The third intention is expressed in the tone and manner of the epigrams, which anticipate those Wilde published in 1894 under the title "Phrases and Philosophies for the Use of the Young" in *The Chameleon*, an Oxford undergraduate journal.

Diversity of opinion about a work of art shows that the work is new, complex, and vital.

When critics disagree the artist is in accord with himself.

We can forgive a man for making a useful thing as long as he does not admire it. The only excuse for making a useless thing is that one admires it intensely.

All art is quite useless.

OSCAR WILDE

The Picture of Dorian Gray
(1891)

Chapter I

The studio was filled with the rich odour of roses, and when the light summer wind stirred amidst the trees of the garden there came through the open door the heavy scent of the lilac, or the more delicate perfume of the pink-flowering thorn.[1]

From the corner of the divan of Persian saddle-bags on which he was lying, smoking, as was his custom, innumerable cigarettes, Lord Henry Wotton could just catch the gleam of the honey-sweet and honey-coloured blossoms of a laburnum,[2] whose tremulous branches seemed hardly able to bear the burden of a beauty so flame-like as theirs; and now and then the fantastic shadows of birds in flight flitted across the long tussore-silk[3] curtains that were stretched in front of the huge window, producing a kind of momentary Japanese effect, and making him think of those pallid jade-faced painters of Tokio[4] who, through the medium of an art that is necessarily immobile, seek to convey the sense of swiftness and motion. The sullen murmur of the bees shouldering their way through the long unmown grass, or circling with monotonous insistence round the dusty gilt horns of the straggling woodbine,[5] seemed to make the stillness more

1. The exotic decor is a reproduction of Charles Ricketts's studio in London, where Wilde was a frequent visitor. Ricketts (1866–1931), an artist and printer, may have been the original for Basil Hallward. He designed the title page and binding for *Dorian Gray* and for many other Wilde volumes.
2. A small tree or shrub bearing clusters of yellow flowers.
3. A coarse brown silk from India.
4. In Wilde's "Decay of Lying," Vivian's prescription for anyone desiring a true Japanese effect is not to go to Tokyo but to "stay at home and steep yourself in the work of certain Japanese artists, and then when you have absorbed the spirit of their style, and caught their imaginative manner of vision, you will go some afternoon and sit in the park . . . and if you cannot see an absolutely Japanese effect there, you will not see it anywhere."
5. A name for various plants of a climbing habit; in early use (later only dial.), convolvulus and ivy; now chiefly (*U.S.*) the Virginia Creeper *Ampelopsis quinquefolia*, and the West Indian *Ipomœa tuberosa* (Spanish Woodbine). *esp.* The common honeysuckle, *Lonicera Periclymenum*, a climbing shrub with pale yellow fragrant flowers; also extended to other species, as the N. American *L. grata* [OED].

oppressive. The dim roar of London was like the bourdon[6] note of a distant organ.

In the centre of the room, clamped to an upright easel, stood the full-length portrait of a young man of extraordinary personal beauty, and in front of it, some little distance away, was sitting the artist himself, Basil Hallward, whose sudden disappearance some years ago caused, at the time, such public excitement, and gave rise to so many strange conjectures.

As the painter looked at the gracious and comely form he had so skilfully mirrored in his art, a smile of pleasure passed across his face, and seemed about to linger there. But he suddenly started up, and, closing his eyes, placed his fingers upon the lids, as though he sought to imprison within his brain some curious dream from which he feared he might awake.

"It is your best work, Basil, the best thing you have ever done," said Lord Henry, languidly. "You must certainly send it next year to the Grosvenor.[7] The Academy[8] is too large and too vulgar. Whenever I have gone there, there have been either so many people that I have not been able to see the pictures, which was dreadful, or so many pictures that I have not been able to see the people, which was worse. The Grosvenor is really the only place."

"I don't think I shall send it anywhere," he answered, tossing his head back in that odd way that used to make his friends laugh at him at Oxford. "No: I won't send it anywhere."

Lord Henry elevated his eyebrows, and looked at him in amazement through the thin blue wreaths of smoke that curled up in such fanciful whorls from his heavy opium-tainted cigarette.[9] "Not send it anywhere? My dear fellow, why? Have you any reason? What odd chaps you painters are! You do anything in the world to gain a reputation. As soon as you have one, you seem to want to throw it away.

6. A low, reverberating sound, as the bass stop of an organ.
7. A Bond Street art gallery established by the painter Sir Coutts Lindsay in May 1877 as an alternative to the galleries of the Royal Academy. It came to be known as the "Temple of the Aesthetic" and was parodied by Gilbert and Sullivan in *Patience* as the "greenery-yallery, Grosvenor Gallery" because of its dominant color keys. Wilde had done reviews of exhibits there in the late 1870s and early 1880s and shared Lord Henry's opinion of its worth.
8. The Royal Academy of Arts (an honorary society of painters, architects, and sculptors founded in 1768) represented the art establishment of the day.
9. Wilde gave many of his own habits and much of his own background to the three main characters, each of whom represents, alternately, idealized, true-to-life, and extreme views of their creator. Thus, Wilde attended Oxford as did Basil and smoked Egyptian, opium-tainted cigarettes as did Henry. However, there is little doubt that Wilde drew his characters from others as well. Basil combines qualities of Ricketts and his friend Charles H. Shannon (1863–1937), who shared lodgings with him in Chelsea. Shannon designed the bindings for Wilde's plays. He and Ricketts edited the *Dial* from 1889 to 1897. Lord Henry may have a touch of the painter James McNeill Whistler (1834–1903) in him and much of Wilde, but critical consensus makes Lord Ronald Sutherland-Gower (1845–1916) the leading candidate as the inspiration for Lord Henry. Gower knew Wilde at Oxford, and the two were intimates in the 1870s and 1880s.

It is silly of you, for there is only one thing in the world worse than being talked about, and that is not being talked about. A portrait like this would set you far above all the young men in England, and make the old men quite jealous, if old men are ever capable of any emotion."

"I know you will laugh at me," he replied, "but I really can't exhibit it. I have put too much of myself into it."

Lord Henry stretched himself out on the divan and laughed.

"Yes, I knew you would; but it is quite true, all the same."

"Too much of yourself in it! Upon my word, Basil, I didn't know you were so vain; and I really can't see any resemblance between you, with your rugged strong face and your coal-black hair, and this young Adonis,[1] who looks as if he was made out of ivory and rose-leaves. Why, my dear Basil, he is a Narcissus,[2] and you—well, of course you have an intellectual expression, and all that. But beauty, real beauty, ends where an intellectual expression begins. Intellect is in itself a mode of exaggeration, and destroys the harmony of any face. The moment one sits down to think, one becomes all nose, or all forehead, or something horrid. Look at the successful men in any of the learned professions.[3] How perfectly hideous they are! Except, of course, in the Church.[4] But then in the Church they don't think. A bishop keeps on saying at the age of eighty what he was told to say when he was a boy of eighteen, and as a natural consequence he always looks absolutely delightful. Your mysterious young friend, whose name you have never told me, but whose picture really fascinates me, never thinks. I feel quite sure of that. He is some brainless, beautiful creature, who should be always here in winter when we have no flowers to look at, and always here in summer when we want something to chill our intelligence. Don't flatter yourself, Basil: you are not in the least like him."

"You don't understand me, Harry," answered the artist. "Of course I am not like him. I know that perfectly well. Indeed, I should be sorry to look like him. You shrug your shoulders? I am telling you the truth. There is a fatality about all physical and intellectual distinction, the sort of fatality that seems to dog through history the faltering steps of kings. It is better not to be different from one's fellows. The ugly and the stupid have the best of it in this world.

---

1. In Greek mythology, a youth of extraordinary good looks, beloved of Aphrodite, killed by a wild boar.
2. In classical mythology, the youth who spurned the love of the nymph Echo, causing her death. His punishment was to fall in love with his own reflected image and pine away until death, at which moment he was transformed into the narcissus flower.
3. Any profession that one studies at a university in order to pursue the desired occupation.
4. An abbreviated reference to the Church of England. During the Protestant Reformation it repudiated the supremacy of the Pope, and instead asserted that of the secular Sovereign over all persons and in all causes, ecclesiastical as well as temporal, in his dominions.

They can sit at their ease and gape at the play. If they know nothing of victory, they are at least spared the knowledge of defeat. They live as we all should live, undisturbed, indifferent, and without disquiet. They neither bring ruin upon others, nor ever receive it from alien hands. Your rank and wealth, Harry; my brains, such as they are— my art, whatever it may be worth; Dorian Gray's good looks—we shall all suffer for what the gods have given us, suffer terribly."

"Dorian Gray? Is that his name?" asked Lord Henry, walking across the studio towards Basil Hallward.

"Yes, that is his name. I didn't intend to tell it to you."

"But why not?"

"Oh, I can't explain. When I like people immensely I never tell their names to any one. It is like surrendering a part of them. I have grown to love secrecy. It seems to be the one thing that can make modern life mysterious or marvellous to us. The commonest thing is delightful if one only hides it. When I leave town now I never tell my people where I am going. If I did, I would lose all my pleasure. It is a silly habit, I dare say, but somehow it seems to bring a great deal of romance into one's life. I suppose you think me awfully foolish about it?"

"Not at all," answered Lord Henry, "not at all, my dear Basil. You seem to forget that I am married, and the one charm of marriage is that it makes a life of deception absolutely necessary for both parties. I never know where my wife is, and my wife never knows what I am doing. When we meet—we do meet occasionally, when we dine out together, or go down to the Duke's—we tell each other the most absurd stories with the most serious faces. My wife is very good at it— much better, in fact, than I am. She never gets confused over her dates, and I always do. But when she does find me out, she makes no row at all. I sometimes wish she would; but she merely laughs at me."

"I hate the way you talk about your married life, Harry," said Basil Hallward, strolling towards the door that led into the garden. "I believe that you are really a very good husband, but that you are thoroughly ashamed of your own virtues. You are an extraordinary fellow. You never say a moral thing, and you never do a wrong thing.[5] Your cynicism is simply a pose."

"Being natural is simply a pose, and the most irritating pose I know," cried Lord Henry, laughing; and the two young men went out into the garden together, and ensconced themselves on a long bamboo seat that stood in the shade of a tall laurel bush. The sunlight slipped over the polished leaves. In the grass, white daisies were tremulous.

---

5. This may be an echo of John Wilmot's (earl of Rochester) epitaph for Charles II: "Here lies a Great and Mighty King / Whose Promise none rely'd on; / He never said a Foolish Thing? / Nor ever did a Wise One" (*Dorian Gray*, Murray 239).

After a pause, Lord Henry pulled out his watch. "I am afraid I must be going, Basil," he murmured, "and before I go, I insist on your answering a question I put to you some time ago."

"What is that?" said the painter, keeping his eyes fixed on the ground.

"You know quite well."

"I do not, Harry."

"Well, I will tell you what it is. I want you to explain to me why you won't exhibit Dorian Gray's picture. I want the real reason."

"I told you the real reason."

"No, you did not. You said it was because there was too much of yourself in it. Now, that is childish."

"Harry," said Basil Hallward, looking him straight in the face, "every portrait that is painted with feeling is a portrait of the artist, not of the sitter. The sitter is merely the accident, the occasion. It is not he who is revealed by the painter; it is rather the painter who, on the coloured canvas, reveals himself. The reason I will not exhibit this picture is that I am afraid that I have shown in it the secret of my own soul."

Lord Henry laughed. "And what is that?" he asked.

"I will tell you," said Hallward; but an expression of perplexity came over his face.

"I am all expectation, Basil," continued his companion, glancing at him.

"Oh, there is really very little to tell, Harry," answered the painter; "and I am afraid you will hardly understand it. Perhaps you will hardly believe it."

Lord Henry smiled, and, leaning down, plucked a pink-petalled daisy from the grass, and examined it. "I am quite sure I shall understand it," he replied, gazing intently at the little golden white-feathered disk, "and as for believing things, I can believe anything, provided that it is quite incredible."

The wind shook some blossoms from the trees, and the heavy lilac-blooms, with their clustering stars, moved to and fro in the languid air. A grasshopper began to chirrup by the wall, and like a blue thread a long thin dragon-fly floated past on its brown gauze wings. Lord Henry felt as if he could hear Basil Hallward's heart beating, and wondered what was coming.

"The story is simply this," said the painter after some time. "Two months ago I went to a crush[6] at Lady Brandon's. You know we poor artists have to show ourselves in society from time to time, just to remind the public that we are not savages. With an evening coat and a white tie, as you told me once, anybody, even a stock-broker, can

6. A crowded social gathering.

gain a reputation for being civilized. Well, after I had been in the room about ten minutes, talking to huge overdressed dowagers and tedious Academicians, I suddenly became conscious that some one was looking at me. I turned half-way round, and saw Dorian Gray for the first time. When our eyes met, I felt that I was growing pale. A curious sensation of terror came over me. I knew that I had come face to face with some one whose mere personality was so fascinating that, if I allowed it to do so, it would absorb my whole nature, my whole soul, my very art itself. I did not want any external influence in my life. You know yourself, Harry, how independent I am by nature. I have always been my own master; had at least always been so, till I met Dorian Gray. Then—but I don't know how to explain it to you. Something seemed to tell me that I was on the verge of a terrible crisis in my life. I had a strange feeling that Fate had in store for me exquisite joys and exquisite sorrows. I grew afraid, and turned to quit the room. It was not conscience that made me do so: it was a sort of cowardice. I take no credit to myself for trying to escape."

"Conscience and cowardice are really the same things, Basil. Conscience is the trade-name of the firm.[7] That is all."

"I don't believe that, Harry, and I don't believe you do either. However, whatever was my motive—and it may have been pride, for I used to be very proud—I certainly struggled to the door. There, of course, I stumbled against Lady Brandon. 'You are not going to run away so soon, Mr. Hallward?' she screamed out. You know her curiously shrill voice?"[8]

"Yes; she is a peacock in everything but beauty," said Lord Henry, pulling the daisy to bits with his long, nervous fingers.

"I could not get rid of her. She brought me up to Royalties, and people with Stars and Garters,[9] and elderly ladies with gigantic tiaras and parrot noses. She spoke of me as her dearest friend. I had only met her once before, but she took it into her head to lionize me. I believe some picture of mine had made a great success at the time, at least had been chattered about in the penny newspapers, which is the nineteenth-century standard of immortality. Suddenly I found myself face to face with the young man whose personality had so strangely stirred me. We were quite close, almost touching. Our eyes met again. It was reckless of me, but I asked Lady Brandon

---

7. An epigram revised from its earlier form in Wilde's 1883 play, *The Duchess of Padua*, Act 1: "Conscience is but the name which cowardice / Fleeing from battle scrawls upon its shield" (*Complete Works* 569).
8. Some critics haves asserted that the cameo of Lady Brandon is based in part on Wilde's mother, Lady Jane Wilde, a writer and supporter of Irish revolution in her youth. She was known for her salons in Dublin and later, in reduced circumstances, in London. However, Wilde's devotion to her makes it doubtful that he would present such a satirical critique here and in the dialogue that follows.
9. The Order of the Garter was the highest of all English knightly orders. Stars and "orders and ribbons" (below) refer to insignia of English orders of knighthood.

to introduce me to him. Perhaps it was not so reckless, after all. It was simply inevitable. We would have spoken to each other without any introduction. I am sure of that. Dorian told me so afterwards. He, too, felt that we were destined to know each other."

"And how did Lady Brandon describe this wonderful young man?" asked his companion. "I know she goes in for giving a rapid *précis*[1] of all her guests. I remember her bringing me up to a truculent and red-faced old gentleman covered all over with orders and ribbons, and hissing into my ear, in a tragic whisper which must have been perfectly audible to everybody in the room, the most astounding details. I simply fled. I like to find out people for myself. But Lady Brandon treats her guests exactly as an auctioneer treats his goods. She either explains them entirely away, or tells one everything about them except what one wants to know."

"Poor Lady Brandon! You are hard on her, Harry!" said Hallward, listlessly.

"My dear fellow, she tried to found a *salon*,[2] and only succeeded in opening a restaurant. How could I admire her?[3] But tell me, what did she say about Mr. Dorian Gray?"

"Oh, something like, 'Charming boy—poor dear mother and I absolutely inseparable. Quite forget what he does—afraid he—doesn't do anything—oh, yes, plays the piano—or is it the violin, dear Mr. Gray?' Neither of us could help laughing, and we became friends at once."

"Laughter is not at all a bad beginning for a friendship, and it is far the best ending for one," said the young lord, plucking another daisy.

Hallward shook his head. "You don't understand what friendship is, Harry," he murmured—"or what enmity is, for that matter. You like every one; that is to say, you are indifferent to every one."

"How horribly unjust of you!" cried Lord Henry, tilting his hat back, and looking up at the little clouds that, like ravelled skeins of glossy white silk, were drifting across the hollowed turquoise of the summer sky. "Yes; horribly unjust of you. I make a great difference between people. I choose my friends for their good looks, my acquaintances for their good characters, and my enemies for their good intellects. A man cannot be too careful in the choice of his enemies. I have not got one who is a fool. They are all men of some intellectual power, and consequently they all appreciate me. Is that very vain of me? I think it is rather vain."

---

1. A summary.
2. The reception-room of a Parisian lady of fashion; hence, a reunion of notabilities at the house of such a lady; also, a similar gathering in other capitals [*OED*].
3. A quip Wilde had once directed at the poet Marc-André Raffalovich (1865–1934), thereby inciting the latter's enmity.

"I should think it was, Harry. But according to your category I must be merely an acquaintance."

"My dear old Basil, you are much more than an acquaintance."

"And much less than a friend. A sort of brother, I suppose?"

"Oh, brothers! I don't care for brothers. My elder brother won't die, and my younger brothers seem never to do anything else."

"Harry!" exclaimed Hallward, frowning.

"My dear fellow, I am not quite serious. But I can't help detesting my relations. I suppose it comes from the fact that none of us can stand other people having the same faults as ourselves. I quite sympathize with the rage of the English democracy against what they call the vices of the upper orders. The masses feel that drunkenness, stupidity, and immorality should be their own special property, and that if any one of us makes an ass of himself he is poaching on their preserves. When poor Southwark got into the Divorce Court,[4] their indignation was quite magnificent. And yet I don't suppose that ten per cent of the proletariat[5] live correctly."

"I don't agree with a single word that you have said, and, what is more, Harry, I feel sure you don't either."

Lord Henry stroked his pointed brown beard, and tapped the toe of his patent-leather boot with a tasselled ebony cane. "How English you are Basil! That is the second time you have made that observation. If one puts forward an idea to a true Englishman—always a rash thing to do—he never dreams of considering whether the idea is right or wrong. The only thing he considers of any importance is whether one believes it oneself. Now, the value of an idea has nothing whatsoever to do with the sincerity of the man who expresses it. Indeed, the probabilities are that the more insincere the man is, the more purely intellectual will the idea be, as in that case it will not be coloured by either his wants, his desires, or his prejudices. However, I don't propose to discuss politics, sociology, or metaphysics with you. I like persons better than principles, and I like persons with no principles better than anything else in the world.[6] Tell me more about Mr. Dorian Gray. How often do you see him?"

"Every day. I couldn't be happy if I didn't see him every day. He is absolutely necessary to me."

---

4. The Court for Divorce and Matrimonial Causes, established in 1857, took over the jurisdiction for hearing such cases from the church courts. At that time, men could obtain divorce by proving a wife committed adultery, but women could obtain one only after proving cruelty or desertion, in addition to their husband's adultery. In 1923, women were allowed to use the same grounds for divorce as men. In 1969, "irretrievable breakdown" became the test for divorce.
5. That class of the community which is dependent on daily labor for subsistence, and has no reserve or capital; the indigent wage-earners; sometimes extended to include all wage-earners; working men, the laboring classes.
6. "And I like . . . world" added in the 1891 edition. See notes to the *Lippincott's* edition.

"How extraordinary! I thought you would never care for anything but your art."

"He is all my art to me now," said the painter, gravely. "I sometimes think, Harry, that there are only two eras of any importance in the world's history. The first is the appearance of a new medium for art, and the second is the appearance of a new personality for art also. What the invention of oil-painting was to the Venetians, the face of Antinous[7] was to late Greek sculpture, and the face of Dorian Gray will some day be to me. It is not merely that I paint from him, draw from him, sketch from him. Of course, I have done all that. But he is much more to me than a model or a sitter. I won't tell you that I am dissatisfied with what I have done of him, or that his beauty is such that Art cannot express it. There is nothing that Art cannot express, and I know that the work I have done, since I met Dorian Gray, is good work, is the best work of my life. But in some curious way—I wonder will you understand me?—his personality has suggested to me an entirely new manner in art, an entirely new mode of style. I see things differently, I think of them differently. I can now recreate life in a way that was hidden from me before. 'A dream of form in days of thought':[8]—who is it who says that? I forget; but it is what Dorian Gray has been to me. The merely visible presence of this lad—for he seems to me little more than a lad, though he is really over twenty—his merely visible presence—ah! I wonder can you realize all that that means? Unconsciously he defines for me the lines of a fresh school, a school that is to have in it all the passion of the romantic spirit, all the perfection of the spirit that is Greek.[9] The harmony of soul and body—how much that is! We in our madness have separated the two, and have invented a realism that is vulgar, an ideality that is void. Harry! if you only knew what Dorian Gray is to me! You remember that landscape of mine, for which Agnew[1] offered me such a huge price, but which I would not part with? It is one of the best things I have ever done. And why is it so? Because, while I was painting it, Dorian Gray sat beside me. Some subtle influence passed from him to me, and for the first time in my life I saw in the plain woodland the wonder I had always looked for, and always missed."

"Basil, this is extraordinary! I must see Dorian Gray."

---

7. A beloved companion of the Roman emperor Hadrian, and an ideal of manly grace and beauty. He is the first of a series of gay men out of history alluded to in the text.

8. "A dream of form in days of thought" is from "To a Greek Girl" by poet Austin Dobson.

9. Basil's aestheticism is an ideal combination of the teaching of critics John Ruskin (1819–1900; "all the passion of the romantic spirit") and Walter Pater (1839–1894; "all the perfection of the spirit that is Greek"). Both taught Wilde at Oxford in the 1870s.

1. Thomas Agnew & Sons was privately sold in 2013, and now the art dealership operates as Agnews in St. James's Place, London.

Hallward got up from the seat, and walked up and down the garden. After some time he came back. "Harry," he said, "Dorian Gray is to me simply a motive in art. You might see nothing in him. I see everything in him. He is never more present in my work than when no image of him is there. He is a suggestion, as I have said, of a new manner. I find him in the curves of certain lines, in the loveliness and subtleties of certain colours. That is all."

"Then why won't you exhibit his portrait?" asked Lord Henry.

"Because, without intending it, I have put into it some expression of all this curious artistic idolatry, of which, of course, I have never cared to speak to him. He knows nothing about it. He shall never know anything about it. But the world might guess it; and I will not bare my soul to their shallow, prying eyes. My heart shall never be put under their microscope.[2] There is too much of myself in the thing, Harry—too much of myself!"

"Poets are not so scrupulous as you are. They know how useful passion is for publication. Nowadays a broken heart will run to many editions."

"I hate them for it," cried Hallward. "An artist should create beautiful things, but should put nothing of his own life into them. We live in an age when men treat art as if it were meant to be a form of autobiography. We have lost the abstract sense of beauty. Some day I will show the world what it is; and for that reason the world shall never see my portrait of Dorian Gray."

"I think you are wrong, Basil, but I won't argue with you. It is only the intellectually lost who ever argue. Tell me, is Dorian Gray very fond of you?"

The painter considered for a few moments. "He likes me," he answered after a pause; "I know he likes me. Of course I flatter him dreadfully. I find a strange pleasure in saying things to him that I know I shall be sorry for having said. As a rule, he is charming to me, and we sit in the studio and talk of a thousand things. Now and then, however, he is horribly thoughtless, and seems to take a real delight in giving me pain. Then I feel, Harry, that I have given away my whole soul to some one who treats it as if it were a flower to put in his coat, a bit of decoration to charm his vanity, an ornament for a summer's day."

"Days in summer, Basil, are apt to linger," murmured Lord Henry. "Perhaps you will tire sooner than he will. It is a sad thing to think of, but there is no doubt that Genius lasts longer than Beauty. That accounts for the fact that we all take such pains to over-educate

---

2. An echo of writer Algernon Swinburne's satirical rebuttal to his critics, titled "Under the Microscope" (1872), in which he also defended Dante Gabriel Rossetti and other Pre-Raphaelites from charges of excessive sensuality and immorality.

ourselves. In the wild struggle for existence, we want to have something that endures, and so we fill our minds with rubbish and facts, in
the silly hope of keeping our place. The thoroughly well-informed
man—that is the modern ideal. And the mind of the thoroughly
well-informed man is a dreadful thing. It is like a bric-à-brac shop,
all monsters and dust, with everything priced above its proper value.
I think you will tire first, all the same. Some day you will look at
your friend, and he will seem to you to be a little out of drawing, or
you won't like his tone of colour, or something. You will bitterly
reproach him in your own heart, and seriously think that he has
behaved very badly to you. The next time he calls, you will be perfectly cold and indifferent. It will be a great pity, for it will alter you.
What you have told me is quite a romance, a romance of art one
might call it, and the worst of having a romance of any kind is that
it leaves one so unromantic."

"Harry, don't talk like that. As long as I live, the personality of
Dorian Gray will dominate me. You can't feel what I feel. You change
too often."

"Ah, my dear Basil, that is exactly why I can feel it. Those who are
faithful know only the trivial side of love: it is the faithless who know
love's tragedies." And Lord Henry struck a light on a dainty silver
case, and began to smoke a cigarette with a self-conscious and satisfied air, as if he had summed up the world in a phrase.[3] There was a
rustle of chirruping sparrows in the green lacquer leaves of the ivy,
and the blue cloud-shadows chased themselves across the grass like
swallows. How pleasant it was in the garden! And how delightful
other people's emotions were!—much more delightful than their
ideas, it seemed to him. One's own soul, and the passions of one's
friends—those were the fascinating things in life. He pictured to
himself with silent amusement the tedious luncheon that he had
missed by staying so long with Basil Hallward. Had he gone to his
aunt's, he would have been sure to have met Lord Goodbody there,
and the whole conversation would have been about the feeding of the
poor, and the necessity for model lodging-houses. Each class would
have preached the importance of those virtues, for whose exercise
there was no necessity in their own lives. The rich would have spoken on the value of thrift, and the idle grown eloquent over the dignity of labour. It was charming to have escaped all that! As he
thought of his aunt, an idea seemed to strike him. He turned to Hallward, and said, "My dear fellow, I have just remembered."

"Remembered what, Harry?"

"Where I heard the name of Dorian Gray."

3. A statement Wilde later applied to himself in an 1897 letter written in prison and
known as *De Profundis* (*Letters* 466).

"Where was it?" asked Hallward, with a slight frown.

"Don't look so angry, Basil. It was at my aunt, Lady Agatha's. She told me she had discovered a wonderful young man, who was going to help her in the East End,[4] and that his name was Dorian Gray. I am bound to state that she never told me he was good-looking. Women have no appreciation of good looks; at least, good women have not. She said that he was very earnest, and had a beautiful nature. I at once pictured to myself a creature with spectacles and lank hair, horribly freckled, and tramping about on huge feet. I wish I had known it was your friend."

"I am very glad you didn't, Harry."

"Why?"

"I don't want you to meet him."

"You don't want me to meet him?"

"No."

"Mr. Dorian Gray is in the studio, sir," said the butler, coming into the garden.

"You must introduce me now," cried Lord Henry, laughing.

The painter turned to his servant, who stood blinking in the sunlight. "Ask Mr. Gray to wait, Parker: I shall be in in a few moments." The man bowed, and went up the walk.

Then he looked at Lord Henry. "Dorian Gray is my dearest friend," he said. "He has a simple and a beautiful nature. Your aunt was quite right in what she said of him. Don't spoil him. Don't try to influence him. Your influence would be bad. The world is wide, and has many marvellous people in it. Don't take away from me the one person who gives to my art whatever charm it possesses: my life as an artist depends on him. Mind, Harry, I trust you." He spoke very slowly, and the words seemed wrung out of him almost against his will.

"What nonsense you talk!" said Lord Henry, smiling, and, taking Hallward by the arm, he almost led him into the house.

Chapter II

As they entered they saw Dorian Gray.[1] He was seated at the piano, with his back to them, turning over the pages of a volume of

4. A notorious slum section of London containing the dock district. It was the scene of many charitable enterprises and was often mentioned in connection with the work of the Christian Socialists and the Salvation Army.
1. John Espey proposes an etymology for "Dorian" from "Doric," with the implied association to "Greek or masculine love" (38). See John Espey, "Resources for Wilde Studies at the Clark Library," *Oscar Wilde, Two Approaches: Papers Read at a Clark Library Seminar, April 17, 1976,* ed. Richard Ellmann and John Espey (Los Angeles: William Andrew Clark Memorial Library, 1977).

Schumann's "Forest Scenes."[2] "You must lend me these, Basil," he cried. "I want to learn them. They are perfectly charming."

"That entirely depends on how you sit to-day, Dorian."

"Oh, I am tired of sitting, and I don't want a life-sized portrait of myself," answered the lad, swinging round on the music-stool in a wilful, petulant manner. When he caught sight of Lord Henry, a faint blush coloured his cheeks for a moment, and he started up. "I beg your pardon, Basil, but I didn't know you had any one with you."

"This is Lord Henry Wotton, Dorian, an old Oxford friend of mine. I have just been telling him what a capital sitter you were, and now you have spoiled everything."

"You have not spoiled my pleasure in meeting you, Mr. Gray," said Lord Henry, stepping forward and extending his hand. "My aunt has often spoken to me about you. You are one of her favourites, and, I am afraid, one of her victims also."

"I am in Lady Agatha's black books at present," answered Dorian, with a funny look of penitence. "I promised to go to a club in Whitechapel[3] with her last Tuesday, and I really forgot all about it. We were to have played a duet together—three duets, I believe. I don't know what she will say to me. I am far too frightened to call."

"Oh, I will make your peace with my aunt. She is quite devoted to you. And I don't think it really matters about your not being there. The audience probably thought it was a duet. When Aunt Agatha sits down to the piano she makes quite enough noise for two people."

"That is very horrid to her, and not very nice to me," answered Dorian, laughing.

Lord Henry looked at him. Yes, he was certainly wonderfully handsome, with his finely-curved scarlet lips, his frank blue eyes, his crisp gold hair. There was something in his face that made one trust him at once. All the candour of youth was there, as well as all youth's passionate purity. One felt that he had kept himself unspotted from the world.[4] No wonder Basil Hallward worshipped him.

---

2. Pastoral piano music by composer Robert Schumann (1810–1856), whose melodic, romantic, and intricate compositions were highly esteemed by aesthetes.

3. A district of London bordering on the East End, where service and volunteer clubs served the poor. Whitechapel contained the Jewish ghetto, especially Polish and European Jews, and Chinatown. It was described at the time as "grubby but not unprosperous." General William Booth began the Salvation Army in Whitechapel in 1865. Several of the Jack the Ripper murders occurred in Whitechapel in 1888.

4. "Unspotted from the world" is a direct quote from the New Testament, James 1:27, in the King James version of the Bible, the form with which Wilde would have been most familiar. This idealized male image exactly corresponds to the forged painting in Wilde's 1889 short story "The Portrait of Mr. W. H." and to the appearance of many of Wilde's friends and intimates, most notably R. H. Sherard, a friend and future biographer; John Gray, the poet; and Wilde's lover Lord Alfred Douglas. The last correspondence reflects perhaps Wilde's conception of male beauty rather than a specific model since he did not meet Lord Alfred until two months after the novel-length version of *The Picture of Dorian Gray* appeared in print.

"You are too charming to go in for philanthropy, Mr. Gray—far too charming." And Lord Henry flung himself down on the divan, and opened his cigarette-case.

The painter had been busy mixing his colours and getting his brushes ready. He was looking worried, and when he heard Lord Henry's last remark he glanced at him, hesitated for a moment, and then said, "Harry, I want to finish this picture to-day. Would you think it awfully rude of me if I asked you to go away?"

Lord Henry smiled, and looked at Dorian Gray. "Am I to go, Mr. Gray?" he asked.

"Oh, please don't, Lord Henry. I see that Basil is in one of his sulky moods; and I can't bear him when he sulks. Besides, I want you to tell me why I should not go in for philanthropy."

"I don't know that I shall tell you that, Mr. Gray. It is so tedious a subject that one would have to talk seriously about it. But I certainly shall not run away, now that you have asked me to stop. You don't really mind, Basil, do you? You have often told me that you liked your sitters to have some one to chat to."

Hallward bit his lip. "If Dorian wishes it, of course you must stay. Dorian's whims are laws to everybody, except himself."

Lord Henry took up his hat and gloves. "You are very pressing, Basil, but I am afraid I must go. I have promised to meet a man at the Orleans.[5] Good-bye, Mr. Gray. Come and see me some afternoon in Curzon Street.[6] I am nearly always at home at five o'clock. Write to me when you are coming. I should be sorry to miss you."

"Basil," cried Dorian Gray, "if Lord Henry Wotton goes I shall go too. You never open your lips while you are painting, and it is horribly dull standing on a platform and trying to look pleasant. Ask him to stay. I insist upon it."

"Stay, Harry, to oblige Dorian, and to oblige me," said Hallward, gazing intently at his picture. "It is quite true, I never talk when I am working, and never listen either, and it must be dreadfully tedious for my unfortunate sitters. I beg you to stay."

"But what about my man at the Orleans?"

The painter laughed. "I don't think there will be any difficulty about that. Sit down again, Harry. And now, Dorian, get up on the platform, and don't move about too much, or pay any attention to what Lord Henry says. He has a very bad influence over all his friends, with the single exception of myself."

---

5. A London club on King Street decorated with sporting scenes. The marquess of Queensberry, Wilde's nemesis, was a member (see p. 356).
6. In Mayfair, east of Hyde Park, south of Berkeley Square, and north of Green Park. All the London streets mentioned in *Dorian Gray* may be found on a surveyor's map of the city. Basil, Lord Henry, and Dorian all live in or near Mayfair, which remains a fashionable district of London.

Dorian Gray stepped up on the dais, with the air of a young Greek martyr, and made a little *moue*[7] of discontent to Lord Henry, to whom he had rather taken a fancy. He was so unlike Basil. They made a delightful contrast. And he had such a beautiful voice. After a few moments he said to him, "Have you really a very bad influence, Lord Henry? As bad as Basil says?"

"There is no such thing as a good influence, Mr. Gray. All influence is immoral—immoral from the scientific point of view."[8]

"Why?"

"Because to influence a person is to give him one's own soul. He does not think his natural thoughts, or burn with his natural passions. His virtues are not real to him. His sins, if there are such things as sins, are borrowed. He becomes an echo of some one else's music, an actor of a part that has not been written for him. The aim of life is self-development. To realize one's nature perfectly—that is what each of us is here for. People are afraid of themselves, nowadays. They have forgotten the highest of all duties, the duty that one owes to one's self. Of course they are charitable. They feed the hungry, and clothe the beggar. But their own souls starve, and are naked. Courage has gone out of our race. Perhaps we never really had it. The terror of society, which is the basis of morals, the terror of God, which is the secret of religion—these are the two things that govern us. And yet—"

"Just turn your head a little more to the right, Dorian, like a good boy," said the painter, deep in his work, and conscious only that a look had come into the lad's face that he had never seen there before.

"And yet," continued Lord Henry, in his low, musical voice, and with that graceful wave of the hand that was always so characteristic of him, and that he had even in his Eton[9] days, "I believe that if one man were to live out his life fully and completely, were to give form to every feeling, expression to every thought, reality to every dream—I believe that the world would gain such a fresh impulse of joy that we would forget all the maladies of mediaevalism, and return to the Hellenic ideal[1]—to something finer, richer, than the Hellenic ideal, it may be. But the bravest man amongst us is afraid

---

7. A pouting grimace.
8. This scientific view combines Darwinism, especially Darwin's theories about child development, and the psychology of William James and the new psychoanalytic schools in Germany and Austria, all of which are bound together in this novel, in Wilde's speculative thinking at the time, and in the Decadent Movement.
9. The most prestigious public school in England. English public schools are equivalent to U.S. private schools.
1. In this *raisonneur* speech, Henry outlines a philosophy remarkably similar to that expressed by Wilde as his own in *De Profundis*. Some of it, at least, is based on Wilde's interpretation of Pater. The tradition in art that Pater called the "Hellenic Ideal" reached from Classical antiquity to the present. It was the ideal of beauty of form combined with sensuous appeal of both subject and treatment. Henry's version of the ideal is Wilde's variation, emphasizing Aestheticism and hedonism.

of himself. The mutilation of the savage has its tragic survival in the self-denial that mars our lives. We are punished for our refusals. Every impulse that we strive to strangle broods in the mind, and poisons us. The body sins once, and has done with its sin, for action is a mode of purification. Nothing remains then but the recollection of a pleasure, or the luxury of a regret. The only way to get rid of a temptation is to yield to it. Resist it, and your soul grows sick with longing for the things it has forbidden to itself, with desire for what its monstrous laws have made monstrous and unlawful. It has been said that the great events of the world take place in the brain. It is in the brain, and the brain only, that the great sins of the world take place also. You, Mr. Gray, you yourself, with your rose-red youth and your rose-white boyhood, you have had passions that have made you afraid, thoughts that have filled you with terror, day-dreams and sleeping dreams whose mere memory might stain your cheek with shame—"

"Stop!" faltered Dorian Gray, "stop! you bewilder me. I don't know what to say. There is some answer to you, but I cannot find it. Don't speak. Let me think. Or, rather, let me try not to think."

For nearly ten minutes he stood there, motionless, with parted lips, and eyes strangely bright. He was dimly conscious that entirely fresh influences were at work within him. Yet they seemed to him to have come really from himself. The few words that Basil's friend had said to him—words spoken by chance, no doubt, and with wilful paradox in them—had touched some secret chord that had never been touched before, but that he felt was now vibrating and throbbing to curious pulses.

Music had stirred him like that. Music had troubled him many times. But music was not articulate. It was not a new world, but rather another chaos, that it created in us. Words! Mere words! How terrible they were! How clear, and vivid, and cruel! One could not escape from them. And yet what a subtle magic there was in them! They seemed to be able to give a plastic form to formless things, and to have a music of their own as sweet as that of viol or of lute. Mere words! Was there anything so real as words?[2]

Yes; there had been things in his boyhood that he had not understood. He understood them now. Life suddenly became fiery-coloured to him. It seemed to him that he had been walking in fire. Why had he not known it?

With his subtle smile, Lord Henry watched him. He knew the precise psychological moment when to say nothing. He felt intensely

2. Another Pater echo, this time from his posthumously published novel *Gaston de Latour*. Lord Henry's remark on p. 21, "Nothing can cure the soul but the senses, just as nothing can cure the senses but the soul," recalls a doctrine expounded by Pater in *Marius the Epicurean* (1885) and earlier by William Blake.

interested. He was amazed at the sudden impression that his words had produced, and, remembering a book that he had read when he was sixteen, a book which had revealed to him much that he had not known before, he wondered whether Dorian Gray was passing through a similar experience.[3] He had merely shot an arrow into the air. Had it hit the mark? How fascinating the lad was!

Hallward painted away with that marvellous bold touch of his, that had the true refinement and perfect delicacy that in art, at any rate comes only from strength. He was unconscious of the silence.

"Basil, I am tired of standing," cried Dorian Gray, suddenly. "I must go out and sit in the garden. The air is stifling here."

"My dear fellow, I am so sorry. When I am painting, I can't think of anything else. But you never sat better. You were perfectly still. And I have caught the effect I wanted—the half-parted lips, and the bright look in the eyes. I don't know what Harry has been saying to you, but he has certainly made you have the most wonderful expression. I suppose he has been paying you compliments. You mustn't believe a word that he says."

"He has certainly not been paying me compliments. Perhaps that is the reason that I don't believe anything he has told me."

"You know you believe it all," said Lord Henry, looking at him with his dreamy, languorous eyes. "I will go out to the garden with you. It is horribly hot in the studio. Basil, let us have something iced to drink, something with strawberries in it."

"Certainly, Harry. Just touch the bell, and when Parker comes I will tell him what you want. I have got to work up this background, so I will join you later on. Don't keep Dorian too long. I have never been in better form for painting than I am to-day. This is going to be my masterpiece. It is my masterpiece as it stands."

Lord Henry went out to the garden, and found Dorian Gray burying his face in the great cool lilac-blossoms, feverishly drinking in their perfume as if it had been wine. He came close to him, and put his hand upon his shoulder. "You are quite right to do that," he murmured. "Nothing can cure the soul but the senses, just as nothing can cure the senses but the soul."

The lad started and drew back. He was bare-headed, and the leaves had tossed his rebellious curls and tangled all their gilded threads. There was a look of fear in his eyes, such as people have when they are suddenly awakened. His finely-chiselled nostrils quivered, and some hidden nerve shook the scarlet of his lips and left them trembling.

---

3. Wilde often spoke of such an influence in his own life but never revealed the book in question.

"Yes," continued Lord Henry, "that is one of the great secrets of life—to cure the soul by means of the senses, and the senses by means of the soul. You are a wonderful creation. You know more than you think you know, just as you know less than you want to know."

Dorian Gray frowned and turned his head away. He could not help liking the tall, graceful young man who was standing by him. His romantic olive-coloured face and worn expression interested him. There was something in his low, languid voice that was absolutely fascinating. His cool, white, flower-like hands, even, had a curious charm. They moved, as he spoke, like music, and seemed to have a language of their own. But he felt afraid of him, and ashamed of being afraid. Why had it been left for a stranger to reveal him to himself? He had known Basil Hallward for months, but the friendship between them had never altered him. Suddenly there had come some one across his life who seemed to have disclosed to him life's mystery. And, yet, what was there to be afraid of? He was not a schoolboy or a girl. It was absurd to be frightened.

"Let us go and sit in the shade," said Lord Henry. "Parker has brought out the drinks, and if you stay any longer in this glare you will be quite spoiled, and Basil will never paint you again. You really must not allow yourself to become sunburnt. It would be unbecoming."[4]

"What can it matter?" cried Dorian Gray, laughing, as he sat down on the seat at the end of the garden.

"It should matter everything to you, Mr. Gray."

"Why?"

"Because you have the most marvellous youth, and youth is the one thing worth having."

"I don't feel that, Lord Henry."

"No, you don't feel it now. Some day, when you are old and wrinkled and ugly, when thought has seared your forehead with its lines, and passion branded your lips with its hideous fires, you will feel it, you will feel it terribly. Now, wherever you go, you charm the world. Will it always be so? . . . You have a wonderfully beautiful face, Mr. Gray. Don't frown. You have. And Beauty is a form of Genius—is higher, indeed, than Genius, as it needs no explanation. It is of the great facts of the world, like sunlight, or spring-time, or the reflection in dark waters of that silver shell we call the moon. It cannot be questioned. It has its divine right of sovereignty. It makes princes of those who have it. You smile? Ah! when you have lost it you won't smile. . . . People say sometimes that Beauty is only superficial. That

---

4. Paul Fussell chronicles the twentieth-century change in English attitudes toward tanning in his book *Abroad: British Literary Traveling between the Wars* (New York: Oxford UP, 1980).

may be so. But at least it is not so superficial as Thought is. To me, Beauty is the wonder of wonders. It is only shallow people who do not judge by appearances. The true mystery of the world is the visible, not the invisible. . . . Yes, Mr. Gray, the gods have been good to you. But what the gods give they quickly take away. You have only a few years in which to live really, perfectly, and fully. When your youth goes, your beauty will go with it, and then you will suddenly discover that there are no triumphs left for you, or have to content yourself with those mean triumphs that the memory of your past will make more bitter than defeats. Every month as it wanes brings you nearer to something dreadful. Time is jealous of you, and wars against your lilies and your roses. You will become sallow, and hollow-cheeked, and dull-eyed. You will suffer horribly. . . . Ah! realize your youth while you have it. Don't squander the gold of your days, listening to the tedious, trying to improve the hopeless failure, or giving away your life to the ignorant, the common, and the vulgar. These are the sickly aims, the false ideals, of our age. Live! Live the wonderful life that is in you! Let nothing be lost upon you. Be always searching for new sensations. Be afraid of nothing. . . . A new Hedonism[5]—that is what our century wants. You might be its visible symbol. With your personality there is nothing you could not do. The world belongs to you for a season. . . . The moment I met you I saw that you were quite unconscious of what you really are, of what you really might be. There was so much in you that charmed me that I felt I must tell you something about yourself. I thought how tragic it would be if you were wasted. For there is such a little time that your youth will last—such a little time. The common hill-flowers wither, but they blossom again. The laburnum will be as yellow next June as it is now. In a month there will be purple stars on the clematis, and year after year the green night of its leaves will hold its purple stars. But we never get back our youth. The pulse of joy that beats in us at twenty, becomes sluggish. Our limbs fail, our senses rot. We degenerate into hideous puppets, haunted by the memory of the passions of which we were too much afraid, and the exquisite temptations that we had not the courage to yield to. Youth! Youth! There is absolutely nothing in the world but youth!"[6]

Dorian Gray listened, open-eyed and wondering. The spray of lilac fell from his hand upon the gravel. A furry bee came and buzzed

5. One can trace old hedonism back to the teaching of ancient Greek philosopher Aristippus, foregrounding pleasure as the chief end of human action. Lord Henry's new hedonism offers an aesthetic refinement, privileging the acquisition of new sensations. The philosophy as practiced by Dorian Gray might have been described better as a new antinomianism. Dorian sees himself absolved by the portrait from the effects of a life of self-indulgence.

6. Henry's speech reflects Wilde's own synthesis of Pater, Matthew Arnold (worship of youth and fear of declining powers), Whistler (superiority of art to nature), Blake, and assorted French geniuses from Théophile Gautier to Joris-Karl Huysmans.

round it for a moment. Then it began to scramble all over the oval stellated globe of the tiny blossoms. He watched it with that strange interest in trivial things that we try to develop when things of high import make us afraid, or when we are stirred by some new emotion for which we cannot find expression, or when some thought that terrifies us lays sudden siege to the brain and calls on us to yield. After a time the bee flew away. He saw it creeping into the stained trumpet of a Tyrian convolvulus.[7] The flower seemed to quiver, and then swayed gently to and fro.

Suddenly the painter appeared at the door of the studio, and made staccato signs for them to come in. They turned to each other, and smiled.

"I am waiting," he cried. "Do come in. The light is quite perfect, and you can bring your drinks."

They rose up, and sauntered down the walk together. Two green-and-white butterflies fluttered past them, and in the pear-tree at the corner of the garden a thrush began to sing.

"You are glad you have met me, Mr. Gray," said Lord Henry, looking at him.

"Yes, I am glad now. I wonder shall I always be glad?"

"Always! That is a dreadful word. It makes me shudder when I hear it. Women are so fond of using it. They spoil every romance by trying to make it last for ever. It is a meaningless word, too. The only difference between a caprice and a life-long passion is that the caprice lasts a little longer."

As they entered the studio, Dorian Gray put his hand upon Lord Henry's arm. "In that case, let our friendship be a caprice," he murmured, flushing at his own boldness, then stepped up on the platform and resumed his pose.

Lord Henry flung himself into a large wicker arm-chair, and watched him. The sweep and dash of the brush on the canvas made the only sound that broke the stillness, except when, now and then, Hallward stepped back to look at his work from a distance. In the slanting beams that streamed through the open doorway the dust danced and was golden. The heavy scent of the roses seemed to brood over everything.

After about a quarter of an hour Hallward stopped painting, looked for a long time at Dorian Gray, and then for a long time at the picture, biting the end of one of his huge brushes, and frowning. "It is quite finished," he cried at last, and stooping down he wrote his name in long vermilion letters[8] on the left-hand corner of the canvas.

7. The convolvulus, or bindweed, is native to Mediterranean limestone hills, and its presence in Basil's garden underscores the Edenic overtones of the scene.
8. James McNeill Whistler (1834–1903), American artist and friend of Wilde, would often sign his paintings in vermilion.

Lord Henry came over and examined the picture. It was certainly a wonderful work of art, and a wonderful likeness as well.

"My dear fellow, I congratulate you most warmly," he said. "It is the finest portrait of modern times. Mr. Gray, come over and look at yourself."

The lad started, as if awakened from some dream. "Is it really finished?" he murmured, stepping down from the platform.

"Quite finished," said the painter. "And you have sat splendidly to-day. I am awfully obliged to you."

"That is entirely due to me," broke in Lord Henry. "Isn't it, Mr. Gray?"

Dorian made no answer, but passed listlessly in front of his picture and turned towards it. When he saw it he drew back, and his cheeks flushed for a moment with pleasure. A look of joy came into his eyes, as if he had recognized himself for the first time. He stood there motionless and in wonder, dimly conscious that Hallward was speaking to him, but not catching the meaning of his words. The sense of his own beauty came on him like a revelation. He had never felt it before. Basil Hallward's compliments had seemed to him to be merely the charming exaggerations of friendship. He had listened to them, laughed at them, forgotten them. They had not influenced his nature. Then had come Lord Henry Wotton with his strange panegyric on youth, his terrible warning of its brevity. That had stirred him at the time, and now, as he stood gazing at the shadow of his own loveliness, the full reality of the description flashed across him. Yes, there would be a day when his face would be wrinkled and wizen, his eyes dim and colourless, the grace of his figure broken and deformed. The scarlet would pass away from his lips, and the gold steal from his hair. The life that was to make his soul would mar his body. He would become dreadful, hideous, and uncouth.

As he thought of it, a sharp pang of pain struck through him like a knife, and made each delicate fibre of his nature quiver. His eyes deepened into amethyst, and across them came a mist of tears. He felt as if a hand of ice had been laid upon his heart.

"Don't you like it?" cried Hallward at last, stung a little by the lad's silence, not understanding what it meant.

"Of course he likes it," said Lord Henry. "Who wouldn't like it? It is one of the greatest things in modern art. I will give you anything you like to ask for it. I must have it."

"It is not my property, Harry."

"Whose property is it?"

"Dorian's, of course," answered the painter.

"He is a very lucky fellow."

"How sad it is!" murmured Dorian Gray, with his eyes still fixed upon his own portrait. "How sad it is! I shall grow old, and horrible, and dreadful. But this picture will remain always young. It will never be older than this particular day of June. . . . If it were only the other way! If it were I who was to be always young, and the picture that was to grow old! For that—for that—I would give everything! Yes, there is nothing in the whole world I would not give! I would give my soul for that!"

"You would hardly care for such an arrangement, Basil," cried Lord Henry, laughing. "It would be rather hard lines on your work."

"I should object very strongly, Harry," said Hallward.

Dorian Gray turned and looked at him. "I believe you would, Basil. You like your art better than your friends. I am no more to you than a green bronze figure. Hardly as much, I dare say."

The painter stared in amazement. It was so unlike Dorian to speak like that. What had happened? He seemed quite angry. His face was flushed and his cheeks burning.

"Yes," he continued, "I am less to you than your ivory Hermes or your silver Faun.[9] You will like them always. How long will you like me? Till I have my first wrinkle, I suppose. I know, now, that when one loses one's good looks, whatever they may be, one loses every-thing. Your picture has taught me that. Lord Henry Wotton is per-fectly right. Youth is the only thing worth having. When I find that I am growing old, I shall kill myself."

Hallward turned pale, and caught his hand. "Dorian! Dorian!" he cried, "don't talk like that. I have never had such a friend as you, and I shall never have such another. You are not jealous of material things, are you?—you who are finer than any of them!"

"I am jealous of everything whose beauty does not die. I am jeal-ous of the portrait you have painted of me. Why should it keep what I must lose? Every moment that passes takes something from me, and gives something to it. Oh, if it were only the other way! If the pic-ture could change, and I could be always what I am now! Why did you paint it? It will mock me some day—mock me horribly!" The hot tears welled into his eyes; he tore his hand away, and, flinging him-self on the divan, he buried his face in the cushions, as though he was praying.

"This is your doing, Harry," said the painter, bitterly.

Lord Henry shrugged his shoulders. "It is the real Dorian Gray—that is all."

"It is not."

"If it is not, what have I to do with it?"

"You should have gone away when I asked you," he muttered.

---

9. A lustful rural demigod, portrayed as half-human with goat's legs. Fauns were deities of farmers and shepherds. *Hermes:* A son of Zeus, wing-footed messenger of the gods, and inventor of the lyre. His Latin name is Mercury.

"I stayed when you asked me," was Lord Henry's answer.

"Harry, I can't quarrel with my two best friends at once, but between you both you have made me hate the finest piece of work I have ever done, and I will destroy it. What is it but canvas and colour? I will not let it come across our three lives and mar them."

Dorian Gray lifted his golden head from the pillow, and with pallid face and tear-stained eyes looked at him, as he walked over to the deal painting-table that was set beneath the high curtained window. What was he doing there? His fingers were straying about among the litter of tin tubes and dry brushes, seeking for something. Yes, it was for the long palette-knife, with its thin blade of lithe steel. He had found it at last. He was going to rip up the canvas.

With a stifled sob the lad leaped from the couch, and, rushing over to Hallward, tore the knife out of his hand, and flung it to the end of the studio. "Don't, Basil, don't!" he cried. "It would be murder!"

"I am glad you appreciate my work at last, Dorian," said the painter, coldly, when he had recovered from his surprise. "I never thought you would."

"Appreciate it? I am in love with it, Basil. It is part of myself. I feel that."

"Well, as soon as you are dry, you shall be varnished, and framed, and sent home. Then you can do what you like with yourself." And he walked across the room and rang the bell for tea. "You will have tea, of course, Dorian? And so will you, Harry? Or do you object to such simple pleasures?"

"I adore simple pleasures," said Lord Henry. "They are the last refuge of the complex. But I don't like scenes, except on the stage. What absurd fellows you are, both of you! I wonder who it was defined man as a rational animal.[1] It was the most premature definition ever given. Man is many things, but he is not rational. I am glad he is not, after all: though I wish you chaps would not squabble over the picture. You had much better let me have it, Basil. This silly boy doesn't really want it, and I really do."

"If you let any one have it but me, Basil, I shall never forgive you!" cried Dorian Gray; "and I don't allow people to call me a silly boy."

"You know the picture is yours, Dorian. I gave it to you before it existed."

"And you know you have been a little silly, Mr. Gray, and that you don't really object to being reminded that you are extremely young."

"I should have objected very strongly this morning, Lord Henry."

"Ah! this morning! You have lived since then."

---

1. This definition of man, which predates Plato, was best known in the Latin formula *ratio animalis*. Although discredited in nearly every age, it has perversely survived to the present on the strength of tradition and style. Lord Henry's critique echoes that of Jonathan Swift in *Gulliver's Travels* (1726).

There came a knock at the door, and the butler entered with a laden tea-tray and set it down upon a small Japanese table. There was a rattle of cups and saucers and the hissing of a fluted Georgian urn. Two globe-shaped china dishes were brought in by a page. Dorian Gray went over and poured out the tea. The two men sauntered languidly to the table, and examined what was under the covers.

"Let us go to the theatre to-night," said Lord Henry. "There is sure to be something on, somewhere. I have promised to dine at White's,[2] but it is only with an old friend, so I can send him a wire to say that I am ill, or that I am prevented from coming in consequence of a subsequent engagement. I think that would be a rather nice excuse: it would have all the surprise of candour."

It is such a bore putting on one's dress-clothes," muttered Hallward. "And, when one has them on, they are so horrid."

"Yes," answered Lord Henry, dreamily, "the costume of the nineteenth century is detestable. It is so somber, so depressing. Sin is the only real colour-element left in modern life."

"You really must not say things like that before Dorian, Harry."

"Before which Dorian? The one who is pouring out tea for us, or the one in the picture?"

"Before either."

"I should like to come to the theatre with you, Lord Henry," said the lad.

"Then you shall come; and you will come too, Basil, won't you?"

"I can't, really. I would sooner not. I have a lot of work to do."

"Well, then, you and I will go alone, Mr. Gray."

"I should like that awfully."

The painter bit his lip and walked over, cup in hand, to the picture. "I shall stay with the real Dorian," he said, sadly.

"Is it the real Dorian?" cried the original of the portrait, strolling across to him. "Am I really like that?"

"Yes; you are just like that."

"How wonderful, Basil!"

"At least you are like it in appearance. But it will never alter," sighed Hallward. "That is something."

"What a fuss people make about fidelity!" exclaimed Lord Henry. "Why, even in love it is purely a question for physiology. It has nothing to do with our own will. Young men want to be faithful, and are not; old men want to be faithless, and cannot: that is all one can say."[3]

---

2. On St. James's Street, one of the older, established London clubs, known as a sporting and gambling club for the gentry. The then Prince of Wales, later King Edward VII, was a member.
3. Lord Henry underlines his view of the irreconcilable conflict of the will allied with conscience against the appetites and instincts perceived as forces of necessity. At least

"Don't go to the theatre to-night, Dorian," said Hallward. "Stop and dine with me."

"I can't, Basil."

"Why?"

"Because I have promised Lord Henry Wotton to go with him."

"He won't like you the better for keeping your promises. He always breaks his own. I beg you not to go."

Dorian Gray laughed and shook his head.

"I entreat you."

The lad hesitated, and looked over at Lord Henry, who was watching them from the tea-table with an amused smile.

"I must go, Basil," he answered.

"Very well," said Hallward; and he went over and laid down his cup on the tray. "It is rather late, and, as you have to dress, you had better lose no time. Good-bye, Harry. Good-bye, Dorian. Come and see me soon. Come to-morrow."

"Certainly."

"You won't forget?"

"No, of course not," cried Dorian.

"And . . . Harry!"

"Yes, Basil?"

"Remember what I asked you, when we were in the garden this morning."

"I have forgotten it."

"I trust you."

"I wish I could trust myself," said Lord Henry, laughing. "Come, Mr. Gray, my hansome[4] is outside, and I can drop you at your own place. Good-bye, Basil. It has been a most interesting afternoon."

As the door closed behind them, the painter flung himself down on a sofa, and a look of pain came into his face.

Chapter III[1]

At half-past twelve next day Lord Henry Wotton strolled from Curzon Street[2] over to the Albany[3] to call on his uncle, Lord Fermor, a genial if somewhat rough-mannered old bachelor, whom the outside

---

that is the way it appeared manifested in Darwinism and its corollaries to contemporary observers such as Wilde.

4. A hired horse-drawn cab.

1. This marks the first of five new chapters when Wilde expanded his novella into a novel.

2. A fashionable area of central London, just to the east of Hyde Park and to the north of Green Park.

3. The building, once the former Piccadilly residence of the Duke of York, second son of George III, was converted into elegant private apartments in 1802 and is still regarded as one of the most exclusive addresses in London. Among its distinguished residents have been poet Lord Byron, historian Thomas Babington Macaulay, and novelist

world called selfish because it derived no particular benefit from
him, but who was considered generous by Society as he fed the
people who amused him. His father had been our ambassador at
Madrid when Isabella was young, and Prim[4] unthought of, but had
retired from the Diplomatic Service in a capricious moment of
annoyance on not being offered the Embassy at Paris, a post to which
he considered that he was fully entitled by reason of his birth, his
indolence, the good English of his dispatches, and his inordinate
passion for pleasure. The son, who had been his father's secretary, had
resigned along with his chief, somewhat foolishly as was thought at
the time, and on succeeding some months later to the title, had set
himself to the serious study of the great aristocratic art of doing
absolutely nothing. He had two large town houses, but preferred
to live in chambers[5] as it was less trouble, and took most of his meals
at his club. He paid some attention to the management of his col-
lieries in the Midland counties,[6] excusing himself for this taint of
industry on the ground that the one advantage of having coal was
that it enabled a gentleman to afford the decency of burning wood
on his own hearth.[7] In politics he was a Tory, except when the Tories
were in office, during which period he roundly abused them for
being a pack of Radicals.[8] He was a hero to his valet,[9] who bullied
him, and a terror to most of his relations, whom he bullied in turn.
Only England could have produced him, and he always said that the
country was going to the dogs. His principles were out of date, but
there was a good deal to be said for his prejudices.

When Lord Henry entered the room, he found his uncle sitting
in a rough shooting coat, smoking a cheroot[1] and grumbling over

---

Matthew G. ("Monk") Lewis. Ernest Worthing of Wilde's comic play *The Importance
of Being Earnest* has his London residence there in apartment B.4.
4. Isabella and Prim were two figures in nineteenth-century Spanish politics. Queen Isabella
   II (1830–1904) reigned from 1843 to 1868. Both her accession to the throne and her
   abdication were engineered by soldier-statesman Juan Prim (1814–1870), whose career
   included military honors, titles, imprisonment, exile in England, and finally assassination.
5. I.e., Lord Fermor lived in rented rooms and leased his two townhouses.
6. The Midland counties are noted for mining and heavy industry, with Birmingham as
   the industrial hub. Midlands was also renowned hunt country and the site, in Nottinghamshire, of Sherwood Forest.
7. An oblique allusion to the view that a gentleman did not acquire money through trade
   or commerce.
8. Associated with the Liberal party, led by William Gladstone, and favored social reform
   policies. But "Radicals" also referred to the "Philosophical Radicals" of an earlier generation, whose economic and social theories descended from Adam Smith, Jeremy
   Bentham, and Thomas Malthus. *Tories:* More commonly referred to as conservatives
   in the later nineteenth century, Tories were led by Benjamin Disraeli and generally
   supported the policies of the Crown and the growth of the Empire.
9. A variation on the eighteenth-century phrase "Il n'ya point de héros pour son valet de
   chambre" [No man is a hero to his valet], attributed to Mme. A.-M. Bigot de Cornuel in
   an August 13, 1728, letter written by Mlle. Aïssé.
1. A cigar originally made in Southern India or Manila. This sort being truncated at both
   ends, the name was extended to all cigars with the two extremities cut off square, as
   distinguished from the ordinary cigar, which has one end pointed.

The Times.[2] "Well, Harry," said the old gentleman, "what brings you out so early? I thought you dandies never got up till two, and were not visible till five."

"Pure family affection, I assure you, Uncle George. I want to get something out of you."

"Money, I suppose," said Lord Fermor, making a wry face. "Well, sit down and tell me all about it. Young people, nowadays, imagine that money is everything."

"Yes," murmured Lord Henry, settling his button-hole[3] in his coat; "and when they grow older they know it. But I don't want money. It is only people who pay their bills who want that, Uncle George, and I never pay mine. Credit is the capital of a younger son, and one lives charmingly upon it. Besides, I always deal with Dartmoor's tradesmen,[4] and consequently they never bother me. What I want is information: not useful information, of course; useless information."

"Well, I can tell you anything that is in an English Blue-book,[5] Harry, although those fellows nowadays write a lot of nonsense. When I was in the Diplomatic,[6] things were much better. But I hear they let them in now by examination. What can you expect? Examinations, sir, are pure humbug from beginning to end. If a man is a gentleman, he knows quite enough, and if he is not a gentleman, whatever he knows is bad for him."

"Mr. Dorian Gray does not belong to Blue-books, Uncle George," said Lord Henry, languidly.

"Mr. Dorian Gray? Who is he?" asked Lord Fermor, knitting his bushy white eyebrows.

"That is what I have come to learn, Uncle George. Or rather, I know who he is. He is the last Lord Kelso's[7] grandson. His mother was a Devereux, Lady Margaret Devereux. I want you to tell me about his mother. What was she like? Whom did she marry? You have known nearly everybody in your time, so you might have known her. I am very much interested in Mr. Gray at present. I have only just met him."

---

2. *The London Times*, the most popular and well-respected newspaper at the time.
3. A flower worn through the lapel buttonhole: hence the popular name. Throughout the manuscript, Wilde alternates the spelling between "buttonhole" and "button-hole."
4. Dartmoor is an area in the southwest of England and consequently quite far from London, so Lord Henry is joking that tradesmen have too far to travel to pursue their bills with him.
5. Parliamentary reports: the most memorable treated social abuses in the nineteenth century.
6. The British Diplomatic Service. Prior to 1856 (when examinations were instituted), the main criterion for admission to the BDS was genealogy rather than merit.
7. Kelso is a place in Scotland and the family seat of Sir George Brisbane Scott-Douglas, whom Wilde visited and considered "a type of old fashioned propriety" (*Letters* 273n). Wilde habitually named his characters after places and his fictitious places after friends and acquaintances. Lord Henry's name comes from Wotton-under-Edge in Gloucestershire, near the home of More Adey, Wilde's friend.

"Kelso's grandson!" echoed the old gentleman—"Kelso's grandson! . . . Of course . . . I knew his mother intimately. I believe I was at her christening. She was an extraordinarily beautiful girl, Margaret Devereux, and made all the men frantic by running away with a penniless young fellow, a mere nobody, sir, a subaltern in a foot regiment, or something of that kind. Certainly. I remember the whole thing as if it happened yesterday. The poor chap was killed in a duel at Spa a few months after the marriage. There was an ugly story about it. They said Kelso got some rascally adventurer, some Belgian brute, to insult his son-in-law in public, paid him, sir, to do it, paid him, and that the fellow spitted his man as if he had been a pigeon. The thing was hushed up, but, egad, Kelso ate his chop alone at the club for some time afterwards. He brought his daughter back with him, I was told, and she never spoke to him again. Oh, yes; it was a bad business. The girl died too, died within a year. So she left a son, did she? I had forgotten that. What sort of boy is he? If he is like his mother he must be a good-looking chap."

"He is very good-looking," assented Lord Henry.

"I hope he will fall into proper hands," continued the old man. "He should have a pot of money waiting for him if Kelso did the right thing by him. His mother had money too. All the Selby property came to her, through her grandfather. Her grandfather hated Kelso, thought him a mean dog. He was, too. Came to Madrid once when I was there. Egad, I was ashamed of him. The Queen used to ask me about the English noble who was always quarrelling with the cabmen about their fares. They made quite a story of it. I didn't dare show my face at Court for a month. I hope he treated his grandson better than he did the jarvies."[8]

"I don't know," answered Lord Henry. "I fancy that the boy will be well off. He is not of age yet. He has Selby, I know. He told me so. And . . . his mother was very beautiful?"

"Margaret Devereux was one of the loveliest creatures I ever saw, Harry. What on earth induced her to behave as she did, I never could understand. She could have married anybody she chose. Carlington was mad after her. She was romantic, though. All the women of that family were. The men were a poor lot, but, egad! the women were wonderful. Carlington went on his knees to her. Told me so himself. She laughed at him, and there wasn't a girl in London at the time who wasn't after him. And by the way, Harry, talking about silly marriages, what is this humbug your father tells me about Dartmoor wanting to marry an American? Ain't English girls good enough for him?"

8. Cabdrivers.

"It is rather fashionable to marry Americans just now, Uncle George."

"I'll back English women against the world, Harry," said Lord Fermor, striking the table with his fist.

"The betting is on the Americans."

"They don't last, I am told," muttered his uncle.

"A long engagement exhausts them, but they are capital at a steeplechase.[9] They take things flying. I don't think Dartmoor has a chance."

"Who are her people?" grumbled the old gentleman. "Has she got any?"

Lord Henry shook his head. "American girls are as clever at concealing their parents, as English women are at concealing their past," he said, rising to go.

"They are pork-packers, I suppose?"

"I hope so, Uncle George, for Dartmoor's sake. I am told that pork-packing is the most lucrative profession in America, after politics."[1]

"Is she pretty?"

"She behaves as if she was beautiful. Most American women do. It is the secret of their charm."[2]

"Why can't these American women stay in their own country? They are always telling us that it is the Paradise for women."

"It is. That is the reason why, like Eve, they are so excessively anxious to get out of it," said Lord Henry. "Good-bye, Uncle George. I shall be late for lunch, if I stop any longer. Thanks for giving me the information I wanted. I always like to know everything about my new friends, and nothing about my old ones."

"Where are you lunching, Harry?"

"At Aunt Agatha's. I have asked myself and Mr. Gray. He is her latest *protégé*."

"Humph! tell your Aunt Agatha, Harry, not to bother me any more with her charity appeals. I am sick of them. Why, the good woman thinks that I have nothing to do but to write cheques for her silly fads."

---

9. An obstacle (horse) race run over a measured course. Henry uses the reference to play off his uncle's metaphor.

1. Wilde had visited America in 1882–83 and again the following year. He knew enough about America to understand the punning connection between "pork-packing" (with the same connotations as "pork barrel") and politics suggested here, but the reference is primarily aimed at nouveau riche Americans who had made their money through commerce.

2. Wilde canceled the following in manuscript (MS) for this added chapter: "'Clever?' / 'So clever that if Dartmoor doesn't propose to her before the end of the week, she is quite certain to propose to him.' / 'He hasn't got a chance, then?' / 'I don't think so.'"

"All right, Uncle George, I'll tell her, but it won't have any effect. Philanthropic people lose all sense of humanity. It is their distinguishing characteristic."

The old gentleman growled approvingly, and rang the bell for his servant. Lord Henry passed up the low arcade into Burlington Street, and turned his steps in the direction of Berkeley Square.[3]

So that was the story of Dorian Gray's parentage. Crudely as it had been told to him, it had yet stirred him by its suggestion of a strange, almost modern romance. A beautiful woman risking everything for a mad passion. A few wild weeks of happiness cut short by a hideous, treacherous crime. Months of voiceless agony, and then a child born in pain. The mother snatched away by death, the boy left to solitude and the tyranny of an old and loveless man. Yes; it was an interesting background. It posed the lad, made him more perfect as it were. Behind every exquisite thing that existed, there was something tragic. Worlds had to be in travail, that the meanest flower might blow.[4] . . . And how charming he had been at dinner the night before, as with startled eyes and lips parted in frightened pleasure he had sat opposite to him at the club, the red candleshades staining to a richer rose the wakening wonder of his face. Talking to him was like playing upon an exquisite violin. He answered to every touch and thrill of the bow. . . . There was something terribly enthralling in the exercise of influence. No other activity was like it. To project one's soul into some gracious form, and let it tarry there for a moment; to hear one's own intellectual views echoed back to one with all the added music of passion and youth; to convey one's temperament into another as though it were a subtle fluid or a strange perfume: there was a real joy in that—perhaps the most satisfying joy left to us in an age so limited and vulgar as our own, an age grossly carnal in its pleasures, and grossly common in its aims. . . . He was a marvellous type, too, this lad, whom by so curious a chance he had met in Basil's studio, or could be fashioned into a marvellous type, at any rate. Grace was his, and the white purity of boyhood, and beauty such as old Greek marbles kept for us. There was nothing that one could not do with him. He could be made a Titan[5] or a toy. What a pity it was that such beauty was destined to fade! . . . And Basil? From a psychological point of view, how interesting he was! The new manner in art, the fresh mode of looking at life, suggested so strangely by the merely visible presence of

3. Regarded then as the finest square in London.
4. The phrase evokes the famous line from William Wordsworth's "Ode: Intimations of Immortality from Recollections of Early Childhood": "the meanest flower that blows can give / Thoughts that do often lie too deep for tears."
5. One of the twelve giant gods and goddesses of Greek mythology, children of Uranus and Gaea, and, after them, the earliest of the gods.

one who was unconscious of it all; the silent spirit that dwelt in dim woodland, and walked unseen in open field, suddenly showing herself, Dryad-like[6] and not afraid, because in his soul who sought for her there had been wakened that wonderful vision to which alone are wonderful things revealed; the mere shapes and patterns of things becoming, as it were, refined, and gaining a kind of symbolical value, as though they were themselves patterns of some other and more perfect form whose shadow they made real: how strange it all was! He remembered something like it in history. Was it not Plato, that artist in thought, who had first analyzed it? Was it not Buonarrotti[7] who had carved it in the coloured marbles of a sonnet-sequence? But in our own century it was strange. . . . Yes; he would try to be to Dorian Gray what, without knowing it, the lad was to the painter who had fashioned the wonderful portrait. He would seek to dominate him—had already, indeed, half done so. He would make that wonderful spirit his own. There was something fascinating in this son of Love and Death.

Suddenly he stopped, and glanced up at the houses. He found that he had passed his aunt's some distance, and, smiling to himself, turned back.[8] When he entered the somewhat sombre hall, the butler told him that they had gone in to lunch. He gave one of the footmen his hat and stick, and passed into the dining-room.

"Late as usual, Harry," cried his aunt, shaking her head at him.

He invented a facile excuse, and having taken the vacant seat next to her, looked round to see who was there. Dorian bowed to him shyly from the end of the table, a flush of pleasure stealing into his cheek. Opposite was the Duchess of Harley, a lady of admirable good-nature and good temper, much liked by every one who knew her, and of those ample architectural proportions that in women who are not Duchesses are described by contemporary historians as stoutness. Next to her sat, on her right, Sir Thomas Burdon, a Radical member of Parliament, who followed his leader in public life, and in private life followed the best cooks, dining with the Tories, and thinking with the Liberals, in accordance with a wise and well-known rule. The post on her left was occupied by Mr. Erskine of Treadley, an old gentleman of considerable charm and culture, who had fallen, however, into bad habits of silence, having, as he explained once to Lady Agatha, said everything that he had to say before he was thirty. His own neighbour was Mrs. Vandeleur, one of his aunt's oldest friends, a perfect saint amongst women, but so

6. Dryads were nymphs of woods and trees in Greek mythology.
7. Originally appeared as Buonarotti, a typo for Michelangelo Buonarrotti (1475–1564), the Italian Renaissance master, who was a painter, sculptor, and poet.
8. Wilde canceled the MS reading: "and wondering if he, like Basil, was going to be always wrapped in dream."

dreadfully dowdy that she reminded one of a badly bound hymn-book. Fortunately for him she had on the other side Lord Faudel, a most intelligent middle-aged mediocrity, as bald[9] as a Ministerial statement in the House of Commons,[1] with whom she was conversing in that intensely earnest manner which is the one unpardonable error, as he remarked once himself, that all really good people fall into, and from which none of them ever quite escape.

"We are talking about poor Dartmoor, Lord Henry," cried the Duchess, nodding pleasantly to him across the table. "Do you think he will really marry this fascinating young person?"

"I believe she has made up her mind to propose to him, Duchess."

"How dreadful!" exclaimed Lady Agatha. "Really, some one should interfere."

"I am told, on excellent authority, that her father keeps an American dry-goods store," said Sir Thomas Burdon, looking supercilious.

"My uncle has already suggested pork-packing Sir Thomas."

"Dry-goods! What are American dry-goods?"[2] asked the Duchess, raising her large hands in wonder, and accentuating the verb.

"American novels," answered Lord Henry, helping himself to some quail.

The Duchess looked puzzled.

"Don't mind him, my dear," whispered Lady Agatha. "He never means anything that he says."

"When America was discovered," said the Radical member, and he began to give some wearisome facts. Like all people who try to exhaust a subject, he exhausted his listeners. The Duchess sighed, and exercised her privilege of interruption. "I wish to goodness it never had been discovered at all!" she exclaimed. "Really, our girls have no chance nowadays. It is most unfair."

"Perhaps, after all, America never has been discovered," said Mr. Erskine; "I myself would say that it had merely been detected."

"Oh! but I have seen specimens of the inhabitants," answered the Duchess, vaguely. "I must confess that most of them are extremely pretty. And they dress well, too. They get all their dresses in Paris. I wish I could afford to do the same."

"They say that when good Americans die they go to Paris," chuckled Sir Thomas, who had a large wardrobe of Humour's cast-off clothes.

"Really! And where do bad Americans go to when they die?" inquired the Duchess.

---

9. The pun on blunt and unadorned leaves the reader to decide if the description is of Lord Faudel's appearance or demeanor.
1. The lower house of the Parliament of Great Britain. Unlike the House of Lords, the upper house, it is made up of elected representatives.
2. American dry goods are textiles, clothes, notions, and the like. British dry goods, meaning groceries not liquid, would refer chiefly to produce, especially grains.

"They go to America," murmured Lord Henry.

Sir Thomas frowned. "I am afraid that your nephew is prejudiced against that great country," he said to Lady Agatha. "I have travelled all over it, in cars provided by the directors, who, in such matters, are extremely civil. I assure you that it is an education to visit it."

"But must we really see Chicago in order to be educated?" asked Mr. Erskine, plaintively. "I don't feel up to the journey."

Sir Thomas waved his hand. "Mr. Erskine of Treadley has the world on his shelves. We practical men like to see things, not to read about them. The Americans are an extremely interesting people.

They are absolutely reasonable. I think that is their distinguishing characteristic. Yes, Mr. Erskine, an absolutely reasonable people. I assure you there is no nonsense about the Americans."

"How dreadful!" cried Lord Henry. "I can stand brute force, but brute reason is quite unbearable. There is something unfair about its use. It is hitting below the intellect."

"I do not understand you," said Sir Thomas, growing rather red.

"I do, Lord Henry," murmured Mr. Erskine, with a smile.

"Paradoxes are all very well in their way . . ." rejoined the Baronet.

"Was that a paradox?" asked Mr. Erskine. "I did not think so. Perhaps it was. Well, the way of paradoxes is the way of truth. To test Reality we must see it on the tight-rope. When the Verities become acrobats we can judge them."[3]

"Dear me!" said Lady Agatha, "how you men argue! I am sure I never can make out what you are talking about. Oh! Harry, I am quite vexed with you. Why do you try to persuade our nice Mr. Dorian Gray to give up the East End? I assure you he would be quite invaluable. They would love his playing."

"I want him to play to me," cried Lord Henry, smiling, and he looked down the table and caught a bright answering glance.

"But they are so unhappy in Whitechapel," continued Lady Agatha.

"I can sympathize with everything, except suffering," said Lord Henry, shrugging his shoulders. "I cannot sympathize with that. It is too ugly, too horrible, too distressing. There is something terribly morbid in the modern sympathy with pain. One should sympathize with the colour, the beauty, the joy of life. The less said about life's sores the better."

"Still, the East End is a very important problem," remarked Sir Thomas, with a grave shake of the head.

"Quite so," answered the young lord. "It is the problem of slavery, and we try to solve it by amusing the slaves."

---

3. Wilde added "Paradoxes are all . . . judge them" to the margin of the MS.

The politician looked at him keenly. "What change do you propose, then?" he asked.

Lord Henry laughed. "I don't desire to change anything in England except the weather," he answered. "I am quite content with philosophic contemplation. But, as the nineteenth century has gone bankrupt through an over-expenditure of sympathy, I would suggest that we should appeal to Science to put us straight. The advantage of the emotions is that they lead us astray, and the advantage of Science is that it is not emotional."

"But we have such grave responsibilities," ventured Mrs. Vandeleur, timidly.

"Terribly grave," echoed Lady Agatha.

Lord Henry looked over at Mr. Erskine. "Humanity takes itself too seriously. It is the world's original sin. If the caveman had known how to laugh, History would have been different."

"You are really very comforting," warbled the Duchess. "I have always felt rather guilty when I came to see your dear aunt, for I take no interest at all in the East End. For the future I shall be able to look her in the face without a blush."

"A blush is very becoming, Duchess," remarked Lord Henry.

"Only when one is young," she answered. "When an old woman like myself blushes, it is a very bad sign. Ah! Lord Henry, I wish you would tell me how to become young again."

He thought for a moment. "Can you remember any great error that you committed in your early days, Duchess?" he asked, looking at her across the table.

"A great many, I fear," she cried.

"Then commit them over again," he said, gravely. "To get back one's youth, one has merely to repeat one's follies."

"A delightful theory!" she exclaimed. "I must put it into practice."

"A dangerous theory!" came from Sir Thomas's tight lips. Lady Agatha shook her head, but could not help being amused. Mr. Erskine listened.

"Yes," he continued, "that is one of the great secrets of life. Nowadays most people die of a sort of creeping common sense, and discover when it is too late that the only things one never regrets are one's mistakes."

A laugh ran round the table.

He played with the idea, and grew wilful; tossed it into the air and transformed it; let it escape and recaptured it; made it iridescent with fancy, and winged it with paradox. The praise of folly,[4] as he went on, soared into a philosophy, and Philosophy herself became

4. The allusion is to Erasmus's *In Praise of Folly* (1511). This scene has been noted especially by Wilde's biographers as illustrative of Wilde's best table-talk manner.

young, and catching the mad music of Pleasure, wearing, one might fancy, her wine-stained robe and wreath of ivy, danced like a Bacchante over the hills of life, and mocked the slow Silenus for being sober.[5] Facts fled before her like frightened forest things. Her white feet trod the huge press at which wise Omar sits,[6] till the seething grape-juice rose round her bare limbs in waves of purple bubbles, or crawled in red foam over the vat's black, dripping, sloping sides. It was an extraordinary improvisation. He felt that the eyes of Dorian Gray were fixed on him, and the consciousness that amongst his audience there was one whose temperament he wished to fascinate, seemed to give his wit keenness, and to lend colour to his imagination. He was brilliant, fantastic, irresponsible. He charmed his listeners out of themselves, and they followed his pipe laughing. Dorian Gray never took his gaze off him, but sat like one under a spell, smiles chasing each other over his lips, and wonder growing grave in his darkening eyes.

At last, liveried in the costume of the age, Reality entered the room in the shape of a servant to tell the Duchess that her carriage was waiting. She wrung her hands in mock despair. "How annoying!" she cried. "I must go. I have to call for my husband at the club, to take him to some absurd meeting at Willis's Rooms,[7] where he is going to be in the chair. If I am late he is sure to be furious, and I couldn't have a scene in this bonnet. It is far too fragile. A harsh word would ruin it. No, I must go, dear Agatha. Good-bye, Lord Henry, you are quite delightful, and dreadfully demoralizing. I am sure I don't know what to say about your views. You must come and dine with us some night. Tuesday? Are you disengaged Tuesday?"

"For you I would throw over anybody, Duchess," said Lord Henry, with a bow.

"Ah! that is very nice, and very wrong of you," she cried; "so mind you come;" and she swept out of the room, followed by Lady Agatha and the other ladies.

When Lord Henry had sat down again,[8] Mr. Erskine moved round, and taking a chair close to him, placed his hand upon his arm.

"You talk books away," he said; "why don't you write one?"

---

5. A leader of the satyrs and a notoriously drunken follower of Bacchus (god of wine and fertility) in Roman mythology. *Bacchante:* Maenads, female worshipers of Bacchus whose orgiastic rites were performed in the wild.

6. The Persian poet-astronomer whose work was immortalized in English by Edward FitzGerald's rendering of *The Rubaiyat of Omar Khayyam,* a poem much admired by the Decadents. Omar drank wine to forget the pangs of both mortality and his loss of faith in God.

7. Formerly Almack's Assembly Rooms, a club in King Street frequented by Wilde. It was in the eighteenth century one of the most fashionable clubs for ladies and gentlemen.

8. Wilde canceled the MS reading: "he poured himself a glass of green Chartreuse and asked the butler for a light."

"I am too fond of reading books to care to write them, Mr. Erskine. I should like to write a novel certainly, a novel that would be as lovely as a Persian carpet and as unreal. But there is no literary public in England for anything except newspapers, primers, and encyclopædias. Of all people in the world the English have the least sense of the beauty of literature."

"I fear you are right," answered Mr. Erskine. "I myself used to have literary ambitions, but I gave them up long ago. And now, my dear young friend, if you will allow me to call you so, may I ask if you really meant all that you said to us at lunch?"

"I quite forget what I said," smiled Lord Henry. "Was it all very bad?"

"Very bad indeed. In fact I consider you extremely dangerous, and if anything happens to our good Duchess we shall all look on you as being primarily responsible. But I should like to talk to you about life. The generation into which I was born was tedious. Some day, when you are tired of London, come down to Treadley, and expound to me your philosophy of pleasure over some admirable Burgundy I am fortunate enough to possess."

"I shall be charmed. A visit to Treadley would be a great privilege. It has a perfect host, and a perfect library."

"You will complete it," answered the old gentleman, with a courteous bow. "And now I must bid good-bye to your excellent aunt. I am due at the Athenæum.[9] It is the hour when we sleep there."

"All of you, Mr. Erskine?"

"Forty of us, in forty arm-chairs. We are practising for an English Academy of Letters."

Lord Henry laughed, and rose. "I am going to the Park," he cried.

As he was passing out of the door Dorian Gray touched him on the arm. "Let me come with you," he murmured.

"But I thought you had promised Basil Hallward to go and see him," answered Lord Henry.

"I would sooner come with you; yes, I feel I must come with you. Do let me. And you will promise to talk to me all the time? No one talks so wonderfully as you do."

"Ah! I have talked quite enough for to-day," said Lord Henry, smiling. "All I want now is to look at life. You may come and look at it with me, if you care to."

---

9. The leading literary club of London, located in the prestigious street of Pall Mall.

Chapter IV[1]

One afternoon, a month later, Dorian Gray was reclining in a luxurious arm-chair, in the little library of Lord Henry's house in Mayfair.[2] It was, in its way, a very charming room, with its high panelled
wainscoting of olive-stained oak, its cream-coloured frieze and ceiling of raised plaster-work, and its brickdust felt carpet strewn with
silk long-fringed Persian rugs. On a tiny satin-wood table stood a
statuette by Clodion,[3] and beside it lay a copy of "Les Cent Nouvelles," bound for Margaret of Valois by Clovis Eve,[4] and powdered
with the gilt daisies that Queen had selected for her device. Some
large blue china jars and parrot-tulips were ranged on the mantel-
shelf, and through the small leaded panes of the window streamed
the apricot-coloured light of a summer day in London.

Lord Henry had not yet come in. He was always late on principle,
his principle being that punctuality is the thief of time. So the lad
was looking rather sulky, as with listless fingers he turned over the
pages of an elaborately-illustrated edition of "Manon Lescaut"[5] that
he had found in one of the bookcases. The formal monotonous ticking of the Louis Quatorze clock[6] annoyed him. Once or twice he
thought of going away.

At last he heard a step outside, and the door opened. "How late
you are, Harry!" he murmured.

"I am afraid it is not Harry, Mr. Gray," answered a shrill voice.

He glanced quickly round, and rose to his feet. "I beg your pardon.
I thought—"

"You thought it was my husband. It is only his wife. You must let
me introduce myself. I know you quite well by your photographs. I
think my husband has got seventeen of them."

"Not seventeen, Lady Henry?"

"Well, eighteen, then. And I saw you with him the other night at
the Opera." She laughed nervously as she spoke, and watched him

1. This was chapter 3 in the *Lippincott's Magazine* edition.
2. The well-to-do area bounded by Park-lane, Piccadilly, Bond-street, and Brook-street.
   Lord Henry's library bears a striking resemblance in several details to Wilde's library
   in his Tite Street, Chelsea, home.
3. Claude Michel Clodion (1738–1814) was specially noted for his antique subjects.
4. A French bookbinder and illustrator (1565–1635) for the royal court, remembered as
   the designer of the "fanfare" style of bindery decoration admired by the Aesthetes. "*Les
   Cent Nouvelles*": A collection of bawdy French tales (1462), perennially a favorite of
   illustrators and collectors and prized for its spirit of pleasant indecency. *Margaret of
   Valois* (1553–1615): Married to French king Henry of Navarre, and as notorious for her
   dissolute behavior as she was renowned for her beauty.
5. Novel (1731) by Abbé de Prevost, the theme of which is the struggle between romantic
   love and self-indulgence. It was considered scandalous by the Victorians, who judged
   nearly all French novels too graphic.
6. A clock designed in the baroque manner of the period of Louis XIV of France
   (1638–1715).

with her vague forget-me-not eyes. She was a curious woman, whose dresses always looked as if they had been designed in a rage and put on in a tempest. She was usually in love with somebody, and, as her passion was never returned, she had kept all her illusions. She tried to look picturesque, but only succeeded in being untidy. Her name was Victoria, and she had a perfect mania for going to church.

"That was at 'Lohengrin,'[7] Lady Henry, I think?"

"Yes; it was at dear 'Lohengrin.' I like Wagner's music better than anybody's. It is so loud that one can talk the whole time without other people hearing what one says. That is a great advantage: don't you think so, Mr. Gray?"

The same nervous staccato laugh broke from her thin lips, and her fingers began to play with a long tortoise-shell paper-knife.

Dorian smiled, and shook his head: "I am afraid I don't think so, Lady Henry. I never talk during music—at least, during good music. If one hears bad music, it is one's duty to drown it in conversation."

"Ah! that is one of Harry's views, isn't it, Mr. Gray? I always hear Harry's views from his friends. It is the only way I get to know of them. But you must not think I don't like good music. I adore it, but I am afraid of it. It makes me too romantic. I have simply worshipped pianists—two at a time, sometimes, Harry tells me. I don't know what it is about them. Perhaps it is that they are foreigners. They all are, ain't they? Even those that are born in England become foreigners after a time, don't they? It is so clever of them, and such a compliment to art. Makes it quite cosmopolitan, doesn't it? You have never been to any of my parties, have you, Mr. Gray? You must come. I can't afford orchids, but I share no expense in foreigners. They make one's rooms look so picturesque. But here is Harry!—Harry, I came in to look for you, to ask you something—I forget what it was—and I found Mr. Gray here. We have had such a pleasant chat about music. We have quite the same ideas. No; I think our ideas are quite different. But he has been most pleasant. I am so glad I've seen him."

"I am charmed, my love, quite charmed," said Lord Henry, elevating his dark crescent-shaped eyebrows and looking at them both with an amused smile. "So sorry I am late, Dorian. I went to look after a piece of old brocade in Wardour Street,[8] and had to bargain for hours for it. Nowadays people know the price of everything, and the value of nothing."[9]

"I am afraid I must be going," exclaimed Lady Henry, breaking an awkward silence with her silly sudden laugh. "I have promised to

---

7. *Lohengrin,* an opera by Richard Wagner (1813–1883), was first performed in 1850. It was based on one of the Grail cycle stories, that of Lohengrin, Knight of the Swan.
8. Famous for antique shops.
9. This epigram originally appeared in Wilde's play *Lady Windermere's Fan* near the end of Act 3 as Lord Darlington's definition to Cecil Graham of a cynic.

drive with the Duchess. Good-bye, Mr. Gray. Good-bye, Harry. You are dining out, I suppose? So am I. Perhaps I shall see you at Lady Thornbury's."

"I dare say, my dear," said Lord Henry, shutting the door behind her, as, looking like a bird of paradise that had been out all night in the rain, she flitted out of the room, leaving a faint odour of frangipani.[1] Then he lit a cigarette, and flung himself down on the sofa.

"Never marry a woman with straw-coloured hair, Dorian," he said, after a few puffs.

"Why, Harry?"

"Because they are so sentimental."

"But I like sentimental people."

"Never marry at all, Dorian. Men marry because they are tired; women, because they are curious: both are disappointed."

"I don't think I am likely to marry, Harry. I am too much in love. That is one of your aphorisms. I am putting it into practice, as I do everything that you say."

"Who are you in love with?" asked Lord Henry, after a pause.

"With an actress," said Dorian Gray, blushing.

Lord Henry shrugged his shoulders. "That is a rather commonplace *début*."

"You would not say so if you saw her, Harry."

"Who is she?"

"Her name is Sibyl Vane."

"Never heard of her."

"No one has. People will some day, however. She is a genius."

"My dear boy, no woman is a genius. Women are a decorative sex. They never have anything to say, but they say it charmingly. Women represent the triumph of matter over mind, just as men represent the triumph of mind over morals."

"Harry, how can you?"

"My dear Dorian, it is quite true. I am analysing women at present, so I ought to know. The subject is not so abstruse as I thought it was. I find that, ultimately, there are only two kinds of women, the plain and the coloured. The plain women are very useful. If you want to gain a reputation for respectability, you have merely to take them down to supper. The other women are very charming. They commit one mistake, however. They paint in order to try and look young. Our grandmothers painted in order to try and talk brilliantly. *Rouge and esprit*[2] used to go together. That is all over now. As long as a woman can look ten years younger than her own daughter,

---

1. A perfume derived from the Plumeria flower.
2. A combination of beauty and wit (literally, makeup and liveliness of mind). Compare this to Max Beerbohm's argument in "A Defense of Cosmetics," in *The Yellow Book* 1 (April 1894): 65–82.

she is perfectly satisfied. As for conversation, there are only five women in London worth talking to, and two of these can't be admitted into decent society. However, tell me about your genius. How long have you known her?"

"Ah! Harry, your views terrify me."

"Never mind that. How long have you known her?"

"About three weeks."

"And where did you come across her?"

"I will tell you, Harry; but you mustn't be unsympathetic about it. After all, it never would have happened if I had not met you. You filled me with a wild desire to know everything about life. For days after I met you, something seemed to throb in my veins. As I lounged in the park, or strolled down Piccadilly, I used to look at every one who passed me and wonder, with a mad curiosity, what sort of lives they led. Some of them fascinated me. Others filled me with terror. There was an exquisite poison in the air. I had a passion for sensations. . . . Well, one evening about seven o'clock, I determined to go out in search of some adventure. I felt that this grey, monstrous London of ours, with its myriads of people, its sordid sinners, and its splendid sins, as you once phrased it, must have something in store for me. I fancied a thousand things. The mere danger gave me a sense of delight. I remembered what you had said to me on that wonderful evening when we first dined together, about the search for beauty being the real secret of life. I don't know what I expected, but I went out and wandered eastward, soon losing my way in a labyrinth of grimy streets and black, grassless squares. About half-past eight I passed by an absurd little theatre, with great flaring gas-jets and gaudy play-bills. A hideous Jew, in the most amazing waist-coat I ever beheld in my life, was standing at the entrance, smoking a vile cigar. He had greasy ringlets, and an enormous diamond blazed in the centre of a soiled shirt. 'Have a box, my Lord?' he said, when he saw me, and he took off his hat with an air of gorgeous servility. There was something about him, Harry, that amused me. He was such a monster. You will laugh at me, I know, but I really went in and paid a whole guinea for the stage-box. To the present day I can't make out why I did so; and yet if I hadn't—my dear Harry, if I hadn't, I should have missed the greatest romance of my life. I see you are laughing. It is horrid of you!"

"I am not laughing, Dorian; at least I am not laughing at you. But you should not say the greatest romance of your life. You should say the first romance of your life. You will always be loved, and you will always be in love with love. A *grande passion* is the privilege of people who have nothing to do. That is the one use of the idle classes of a country. Don't be afraid. There are exquisite things in store for you. This is merely the beginning."

"Do you think my nature so shallow?" cried Dorian Gray angrily.

"No; I think your nature so deep."

"How do you mean?"

"My dear boy, the people who love only once in their lives are really the shallow people. What they call their loyalty, and their fidelity, I call either the lethargy of custom or their lack of imagination. Faithfulness is to the emotional life what consistency is to the life of the intellect—simply a confession of failure. Faithfulness! I must analyse it some day. The passion for property is in it. There are many things that we would throw away if we were not afraid that others might pick them up. But I don't want to interrupt you. Go on with your story."

"Well, I found myself seated in a horrid little private box, with a vulgar drop-scene[3] staring me in the face. I looked out from behind the curtain, and surveyed the house. It was a tawdry affair, all Cupids and cornucopias, like a third-rate wedding-cake. The gallery and pit were fairly full, but the two rows of dingy stalls were quite empty, and there was hardly a person in what I suppose they called the dress-circle.[4] Women went about with oranges and ginger-beer, and there was a terrible consumption of nuts going on."

"It must have been just like the palmy days of the British Drama."

"Just like, I should fancy, and very depressing. I began to wonder what on earth I should do, when I caught sight of the play-bill. What do you think the play was, Harry?"

"I should think 'The Idiot Boy, or Dumb but Innocent.'[5] Our fathers used to like that sort of piece, I believe. The longer I live, Dorian, the more keenly I feel that whatever was good enough for our fathers is not good enough for us. In art, as in politics, *les grand-pères ont toujours tort.*"[6]

"This play was good enough for us, Harry. It was 'Romeo and Juliet.' I must admit that I was rather annoyed at the idea of seeing Shakespeare done in such a wretched hole of a place. Still, I felt interested, in a sort of way. At any rate, I determined to wait for the first act. There was a dreadful orchestra, presided over by a young Hebrew who sat at a cracked piano, that nearly drove me away, but at last the drop-scene was drawn up, and the play began. Romeo

---

3. A stage curtain on which a scene or design has been painted. At the time, scenes were usually stylized landscapes or gardens.
4. Gallery seats are the cheapest in the theater, usually furthest from the stage. The pit is located in the ground floor, behind the stalls. The stalls are ground floor seats at the front of the theater. The dress circle is a circular row of seats in a theater, usually the gallery next above the floor. The spectators seated there were originally expected to be in dress clothes.
5. The title is Wilde's parody of a type of rustic melodrama that still appealed to lower-class audiences in the 1890s but that had reached the peak of its appeal in the mid-nineteenth century, inspired, perhaps, by the novels of Walter Scott and the philosopher-rustics of William Wordsworth poems. A play, *The Idiot of the Mill,* may have inspired the mocking title (*Dorian Gray,* Murray 241).
6. Grandfathers are always wrong (French): a most un-Victorian sentiment.

was a stout elderly gentleman, with corked eyebrows, a husky tragedy voice, and a figure like a beer-barrel. Mercutio was almost as
bad. He was played by the low-comedian, who had introduced gags
of his own and was on most friendly terms with the pit. They were
both as grotesque as the scenery, and that looked as if it had come
out of a country-booth. But Juliet! Harry, imagine a girl, hardly seventeen years of age, with a little flower-like face, a small Greek
head with plaited coils of dark-brown hair, eyes that were violet wells
of passion, lips that were like the petals of a rose. She was the loveliest thing I had ever seen in my life.[7] You said to me once that
pathos left you unmoved, but that beauty, mere beauty, could fill
your eyes with tears. I tell you, Harry, I could hardly see this girl for
the mist of tears that came across me. And her voice—I never heard
such a voice. It was very low at first, with deep mellow notes, that
seemed to fall singly upon one's ear. Then it became a little louder,
and sounded like a flute or a distant hautbois.[8] In the garden-scene
it had all the tremulous ecstasy that one hears just before dawn when
nightingales are singing. There were moments, later on, when it had
the wild passion of violins. You know how a voice can stir one. Your
voice and the voice of Sibyl Vane are two things that I shall never
forget. When I close my eyes, I hear them, and each of them says
something different. I don't know which to follow. Why should I not
love her? Harry, I do love her. She is everything to me in life. Night
after night I go to see her play. One evening she is Rosalind, and
the next evening she is Imogen.[9] I have seen her die in the gloom of
an Italian tomb, sucking the poison from her lover's lips.[1] I have
watched her wandering through the forest of Arden, disguised as a
pretty boy in hose and doublet and dainty cap. She has been mad,
and has come into the presence of a guilty king, and given him
rue to wear, and bitter herbs to taste of. She has been innocent, and
the black hands of jealousy have crushed her reed-like throat. I have
seen her in every age and in every costume. Ordinary women never
appeal to one's imagination. They are limited to their century. No
glamour ever transfigures them. One knows their minds as easily as
one knows their bonnets. One can always find them. There is no
mystery in any of them. They ride in the Park in the morning, and
chatter at tea-parties in the afternoon. They have their stereotyped

---

7. In a letter to Lillie Langtry, famous beauty and actress (December 1883), Wilde
   announced his intention to marry "a beautiful girl called Constance Lloyd, a grave,
   slight, violet-eyed little Artemis, with great coils of heavy brown hair which make her
   flower-like head droop like a blossom" (*Letters* 154).
8. An oboe.
9. The daughter of Cymbeline in Shakespeare's play of the same name. *Rosalind*: The
   heroine of Shakespeare's *As You Like It*.
1. Thus Juliet dies, but in *Hamlet* 3.1.155–56, Ophelia complains, "And I, of ladies most
   deject and wretched / That suck'd the honey of his music vows."

smile, and their fashionable manner. They are quite obvious. But an actress! How different an actress is! Harry! why didn't you tell me that the only thing worth loving is an actress?"

"Because I have loved so many of them, Dorian."

"Oh, yes, horrid people with dyed hair and painted faces."

"Don't run down dyed hair and painted faces. There is an extraordinary charm in them, sometimes," said Lord Henry.

"I wish now I had not told you about Sibyl Vane."

"You could not have helped telling me, Dorian. All through your life you will tell me everything you do."

"Yes, Harry, I believe that is true. I cannot help telling you things. You have a curious influence over me. If I ever did a crime, I would come and confess it to you. You would understand me."

"People like you—the wilful sunbeams of life—don't commit crimes, Dorian. But I am much obliged for the compliment, all the same. And now tell me—reach me the matches, like a good boy: thanks—what are your actual relations with Sibyl Vane?"

Dorian Gray leaped to his feet, with flushed cheeks and burning eyes. "Harry! Sibyl Vane is sacred!"

"It is only the sacred things that are worth touching, Dorian," said Lord Henry, with a strange touch of pathos in his voice. "But why should you be annoyed? I suppose she will belong to you some day.[2] When one is in love, one always begins by deceiving one's self, and one always ends by deceiving others. That is what the world calls a romance. You know her, at any rate, I suppose?"

"Of course I know her. On the first night I was at the theatre, the horrid old Jew[3] came round to the box after the performance was over, and offered to take me behind the scenes and introduce me to her. I was furious with him, and told him that Juliet had been dead for hundreds of years, and that her body was lying in a marble tomb in Verona. I think, from his blank look of amazement, that he was under the impression that I had taken too much champagne, or something."

"I am not surprised."

"Then he asked me if I wrote for any of the newspapers. I told him I never even read them. He seemed terribly disappointed at that, and confided to me that all the dramatic critics were in a conspiracy against him, and that they were every one of them to be bought."

"I should not wonder if he was quite right there. But, on the other hand, judging from their appearance, most of them cannot be at all expensive."

---

2. One of J. M. Stoddart's substitutions made in the magazine edition and retained here. The Clark typescript (TS) originally read "She will be your mistress someday."

3. The casual anti-Semitism of this remark makes it all the more offensive to thoughtful readers, though unfortunately such observations would rarely have been criticized in the late-Victorian society represented in the novel.

"Well, he seemed to think they were beyond his means," laughed Dorian. "By this time, however, the lights were being put out in the theatre, and I had to go. He wanted me to try some cigars that he strongly recommended. I declined. The next night, of course, I arrived at the place again. When he saw me he made me a low bow, and assured me that I was a munificent patron of art. He was a most offensive brute, though he had an extraordinary passion for Shakespeare. He told me once, with an air of pride, that his five bankruptcies were entirely due to 'The Bard,' as he insisted on calling him. He seemed to think it a distinction."

"It was a distinction, my dear Dorian—a great distinction. Most people become bankrupt through having invested too heavily in the prose of life. To have ruined one's self over poetry is an honour. But when did you first speak to Miss Sibyl Vane?"

"The third night. She had been playing Rosalind. I could not help going round. I had thrown her some flowers, and she had looked at me; at least I fancied that she had. The old Jew was persistent. He seemed determined to take me behind, so I consented. It was curious my not wanting to know her, wasn't it?"

"No; I don't think so."

"My dear Harry, why?"

"I will tell you some other time. Now I want to know about the girl."

"Sibyl? Oh, she was so shy, and so gentle. There is something of a child about her. Her eyes opened wide in exquisite wonder when I told her what I thought of her performance, and she seemed quite unconscious of her power. I think we were both rather nervous. The old Jew stood grinning at the doorway of the dusty greenroom,[4] making elaborate speeches about us both, while we stood looking at each other like children. He would insist on calling me 'My Lord,' so I had to assure Sibyl that I was not anything of the kind. She said quite simply to me, 'You look more like a prince. I must call you Prince Charming.'"

"Upon my word, Dorian, Miss Sibyl knows how to pay compliments."

"You don't understand her, Harry. She regarded me merely as a person in a play. She knows nothing of life. She lives with her mother, a faded tired woman who played Lady Capulet[5] in a sort of magenta dressing-wrapper on the first night, and looks as if she had seen better days."

"I know that look. It depresses me," murmured Lord Henry, examining his rings.

---

4. A reception room and lounge for performers in a theater.
5. Juliet's mother in *Romeo and Juliet*.

"The Jew wanted to tell me her history, but I said it did not interest me."

"You were quite right. There is always something infinitely mean about other people's tragedies."

"Sibyl is the only thing I care about. What is it to me where she came from? From her little head to her little feet, she is absolutely and entirely divine. Every night of my life I go to see her act, and every night she is more marvellous."

"That is the reason, I suppose, that you never dine with me now. I thought you must have some curious romance on hand. You have; but it is not quite what I expected."

"My dear Harry, we either lunch or sup together every day, and I have been to the Opera with you several times," said Dorian, opening his blue eyes in wonder.

"You always come dreadfully late."

"Well, I can't help going to see Sibyl play," he cried, "even if it is only for a single act. I get hungry for her presence; and when I think of the wonderful soul that is hidden away in that little ivory body, I am filled with awe."

"You can dine with me to-night, Dorian, can't you?"

He shook his head. "To-night she is Imogen," he answered, "and to-morrow night she will be Juliet."

"When is she Sibyl Vane?"

"Never."

"I congratulate you."

"How horrid you are! She is all the great heroines of the world in one. She is more than an individual. You laugh, but I tell you she has genius. I love her, and I must make her love me. You, who know all the secrets of life, tell me how to charm Sibyl Vane to love me! I want to make Romeo jealous. I want the dead lovers of the world to hear our laughter, and grow sad. I want a breath of our passion to stir their dust into consciousness, to wake their ashes into pain. My God, Harry, how I worship her!" He was walking up and down the room as he spoke. Hectic spots of red burned on his cheeks. He was terribly excited.

Lord Henry watched him with a subtle sense of pleasure. How different he was not from the shy, frightened boy he had met in Basil Hallward's studio! His nature had developed like a flower, had borne blossoms of scarlet flame. Out of its secret hiding-place had crept his Soul, and Desire had come to meet it on the way.

"And what do you propose to do?" said Lord Henry, at last.

"I want you and Basil to come with me some night and see her act. I have not the slightest fear of the result. You are certain to acknowledge her genius. Then we must get her out of the Jew's hands. She is bound to him for three years—at least for two years and eight months—from the present time. I shall have to pay him something, of course. When all that is settled, I shall take a West End[6] theatre and bring her out properly. She will make the world as mad as she has made me."

"That would be impossible, my dear boy."

"Yes, she will. She has not merely art, consummate art-instinct, in her, but she has personality also; and you have often told me that it is personalities, not principles, that move the age."

"Well, what night shall we go?"

"Let me see. To-day is Tuesday. Let us fix to-morrow. She plays Juliet to-morrow."

"All right. The Bristol[7] at eight o'clock; and I will get Basil."

"Not eight, Harry, please. Half-past six. We must be there before the curtain rises. You must see her in the first act, where she meets Romeo."

"Half-past six! What an hour! It will be like having a meat-tea,[8] or reading an English novel. It must be seven. No gentleman dines before seven. Shall you see Basil between this and then? Or shall I write to him?"

"Dear Basil! I have not laid eyes on him for a week. It is rather horrid of me, as he has sent me my portrait in the most wonderful frame, specially designed by himself, and, though I am a little jealous of the picture for being a whole month younger than I am, I must admit that I delight in it. Perhaps you had better write to him. I don't want to see him alone. He says things that annoy me. He gives me good advice."

Lord Henry smiled. "People are very fond of giving away what they need most themselves. It is what I call the depth of generosity."

"Oh, Basil is the best of fellows, but he seems to me to be just a bit of a Philistine. Since I have known you, Harry, I have discovered that."

"Basil, my dear boy, puts everything that is charming in him into his work. The consequence is that he has nothing left for life but his prejudices, his principles, and his common sense. The only artists I have ever known, who are personally delightful, are bad artists. Good artists exist simply in what they make, and consequently are perfectly uninteresting in what they are. A great poet, a really great poet, is the most unpoetical of all creatures. But inferior poets are absolutely fascinating. The worse their rhymes are, the more picturesque they look. The mere fact of having published a book of second-rate sonnets makes a man quite irresistible. He lives the poetry that he cannot write. The others write the poetry that they dare not realize."

---

6. Area in central London noted, then and now, for its concentration of theaters.
7. A luxury hotel near the Ritz in Piccadilly.
8. A tea at which meat is served, also called "high tea."

"I wonder is that really so, Harry?" said Dorian Gray, putting some perfume on his handkerchief out of a large, gold-topped bottle that stood on the table. "It must be, if you say it. And now I am off. Imogen is waiting for me. Don't forget about to-morrow. Good-bye."

As he left the room, Lord Henry's heavy eyelids drooped, and he began to think. Certainly few people had ever interested him so much as Dorian Gray, and yet the lad's mad adoration of some one else caused him not the slightest pang of annoyance or jealousy. He was pleased by it. It made him a more interesting study. He had been always enthralled by the methods of natural science, but the ordinary subject-matter of that science had seemed to him trivial and of no import. And so he had begun by vivisecting himself, as he had ended by vivisecting others. Human life—that appeared to him the one thing worth investigating. Compared to it there was nothing else of any value. It was true that as one watched life in its curious crucible of pain and pleasure, one could not wear over one's face a mask of glass, nor keep the sulphurous fumes from troubling the brain and making the imagination turbid with monstrous fancies and mis-shapen dreams. There were poisons so subtle that to know their properties one had to sicken of them. There were maladies so strange that one had to pass through them if one sought to understand their nature. And, yet, what a great reward one received! How wonderful the whole world became to one! To note the curious hard logic of passion, and the emotional coloured life of the intellect—to observe where they met, and where they separated, at what point they were in unison, and at what point they were at discord—there was a delight in that! What matter what the cost was? One could never pay too high a price for any sensation.

He was conscious—and the thought brought a gleam of pleasure into his brown agate eyes—that it was through certain words of his, musical words said with musical utterance, that Dorian Gray's soul had turned to this white girl[9] and bowed in worship before her. To a large extent the lad was his own creation. He had made him premature. That was something. Ordinary people waited till life disclosed to them its secrets, but to the few, to the elect, the mysteries of life were revealed before the veil was drawn away. Sometimes this was the effect of art, and chiefly of the art of literature, which dealt immediately with the passions and the intellect. But now and then a complex personality took the place and assumed the office of art, was indeed, in its way, a real work of art, Life having its elaborate masterpieces, just as poetry has, or sculpture, or paintings.

9. A reference to Whistler's 1862 painting of that name, on which Swinburne based his poem "Before the Mirror," in *Poems and Ballads* (1866).

Yes, the lad was premature. He was gathering his harvest while it was yet spring. The pulse and passion of youth were in him, but he was becoming self-conscious. It was delightful to watch him. With his beautiful face, and his beautiful soul, he was a thing to wonder at. It was no matter how it all ended, or was destined to end. He was like one of those gracious figures in a pageant or a play, whose joys seem to be remote from one, but whose sorrows stir one's sense of beauty, and whose wounds are like red roses.

Soul and body, body and soul—how mysterious they were! There was animalism[1] in the soul, and the body had its moments of spirituality. The senses could refine, and the intellect could degrade. Who could say where the fleshly impulse ceased, or the psychical impulse began? How shallow were the arbitrary definitions of ordinary psychologists! And yet how difficult to decide between the claims of the various schools! Was the soul a shadow seated in the house of sin? Or was the body really in the soul, as Giordano Bruno[2] thought? The separation of spirit from matter was a mystery, and the union of spirit with matter was a mystery also.

He began to wonder whether we could ever make psychology so absolute a science that each little spring of life would be revealed to us. As it was, we always misunderstood ourselves, and rarely understood others. Experience was of no ethical value. It was merely the name men gave to their mistakes. Moralists had, as a rule, regarded it as a mode of warning, had claimed for it a certain ethical efficacy in the formation of character, had praised it as something that taught us what to follow and showed us what to avoid. But there was no motive power in experience. It was as little of an active cause as conscience itself. All that it really demonstrated was that our future would be the same as our past, and that the sin we had done once, and with loathing, we would do many times, and with joy.

It was clear to him that the experimental method was the only method by which one could arrive at any scientific analysis of the passions; and certainly Dorian Gray was a subject made to his hand, and seemed to promise rich and fruitful results. His sudden mad love for Sibyl Vane was a psychological phenomenon of no small interest. There was no doubt that curiosity had much to do with it, curiosity and the desire for new experiences; yet it was not a simple but rather a very complex passion. What there was in it of the purely sensuous instinct of boyhood had been transformed by the workings

---

1. Animal activity, physical exercise and enjoyment, but it can be taken as mere animal enjoyment, sensuality.
2. Proponent of the new astronomy of Copernicus and an advocate of freedom of thought. Bruno (1548–1600) was put to death by the Roman Inquisition, largely as the result of his attacks on orthodox Aristotelianism. Pater wrote an essay on Bruno, which appeared in *The Fort-nightly Review* (August 1889); Wilde would have known it. Bruno has been a cultural hero of writers and intellectuals since the mid-nineteenth century.

of the imagination, changed into something that seemed to the lad himself to be remote from sense, and was for that very reason all the more dangerous. It was the passions about whose origin we deceived ourselves that tyrannized most strongly over us. Our weakest motives were those of whose nature we were conscious. It often happened that when we thought we were experimenting on others we were really experimenting on ourselves.

While Lord Henry sat dreaming on these things, a knock came to the door, and his valet entered, and reminded him it was time to dress for dinner. He got up and looked out into the street. The sunset had smitten into scarlet gold the upper windows of the houses opposite. The panes glowed like plates of heated metal. The sky above was like a faded rose. He thought of his friend's young fiery-coloured life, and wondered how it was all going to end.

When he arrived home, about half-past twelve o'clock, he saw a telegram lying on the hall table. He opened it, and found it was from Dorian Gray. It was to tell him that he was engaged to be married to Sibyl Vane.

Chapter V[1]

"Mother, mother, I am so happy!" whispered the girl, burying her face in the lap of the faded, tired-looking woman who with back turned to the shrill intrusive light, was sitting in the one arm-chair that their dingy sitting-room contained. "I am so happy!" she repeated, "and you must be happy too!"

Mrs. Vane winced, and put her thin bismuth-whitened hands[2] on her daughter's head. "Happy!" she echoed, "I am only happy, Sibyl, when I see you act. You must not think of anything but your acting. Mr. Isaacs has been very good to us, and we owe him money."

The girl looked up and pouted. "Money, mother?" she cried, "what does money matter? Love is more than money."

"Mr. Isaacs has advanced us fifty pounds to pay off our debts, and to get a proper outfit for James. You must not forget that, Sibyl. Fifty pounds is a very large sum.[3] Mr. Isaacs has been most considerate."

"He is not a gentleman, mother, and I hate the way he talks to me," said the girl, rising to her feet, and going over to the window.

"I don't know how we could manage without him," answered the elder woman, querulously.

1. The second of the new chapters written for the revised edition.
2. Bismuth, a whitening agent in paints and cosmetics, is still used in the theater, especially by mimes and clowns.
3. In 2018, £50 from 1891 was worth around £6,170 or about $7,840 using the retail price index as the benchmark.

Sibyl Vane tossed her head and laughed. "We don't want him any more, mother. Prince Charming[4] rules life for us now." Then she paused. A rose shook in her blood, and shadowed her cheeks. Quick breath parted the petals of her lips. They trembled. Some southern wind of passion swept over her, and stirred the dainty folds of her dress. "I love him," she said simply.

"Foolish child! foolish child!" was the parrot-phrase flung in answer. The waving of crooked, false-jewelled fingers gave grotesqueness to the words.

The girl laughed again. The joy of a caged bird was in her voice. Her eyes caught the melody, and echoed it in radiance: then closed for a moment, as though to hide their secret. When they opened, the mist of a dream had passed across them.

Thin-lipped wisdom spoke at her from the worn chair, hinted at prudence, quoted from that book of cowardice whose author apes the name of common sense. She did not listen. She was free in her prison of passion.[5] Her prince, Prince Charming, was with her. She had called on Memory to remake him. She had sent her soul to search for him, and it had brought him back. His kiss burned again upon her mouth. Her eyelids were warm with his breath.

Then Wisdom altered its method and spoke of espial and discovery. This young man might be rich. If so, marriage should be thought of. Against the shell of her ear broke the waves of worldly cunning. The arrows of craft shot by her. She saw the thin lips moving, and smiled.

Suddenly she felt the need to speak. The wordy silence troubled her. "Mother, mother," she cried, "why does he love me so much? I know why I love him. I love him because he is like what Love himself should be. But what does he see in me? I am not worthy of him. And yet—why, I cannot tell—though I feel so much beneath him, I don't feel humble. I feel proud, terribly proud. Mother, did you love my father as I love Prince Charming?"

The elder woman grew pale beneath the coarse powder that daubed her cheeks, and her dry lips twitched with a spasm of pain. Sibyl rushed to her, flung her arms round her neck, and kissed her. "Forgive me, mother. I know it pains you to talk about our father. But it only pains you because you loved him so much. Don't look so sad. I am as happy to-day as you were twenty years ago. Ah! let me be happy for ever!"

"My child, you are far too young to think of falling in love. Besides, what do you know of this young man? You don't even know his name.

4. Dorian's performance as Sibyl's Prince Charming is a cruel reversal of the fairy tale prince; Sibyl's fate is similarly reversed.
5. An allusion to the theme of Richard Lovelace's poem "To Althea from Prison" (1642), with another reversal of roles of lover/beloved.

The whole thing is most inconvenient, and really, when James is going away to Australia[6] and I have so much to think of, I must say that you should have shown more consideration. However, as I said before, if he is rich . . ."

"Ah! mother, mother, let me be happy!"

Mrs. Vane glanced at her, and with one of those false theatrical gestures that so often become a mode of second nature to a stage-player, clasped her in her arms. At this moment the door opened, and a young lad with rough brown hair came into the room. He was thick-set of figure, and his hands and feet were large, and somewhat clumsy in movement. He was not so finely bred as his sister.[7] One would hardly have guessed the close relationship that existed between them. Mrs. Vane fixed her eyes on him, and intensified her smile. She mentally elevated her son to the dignity of an audience. She felt sure that the *tableau*[8] was interesting.

"You might keep some of your kisses for me, Sibyl, I think," said the lad, with a good-natured grumble.

"Ah! but you don't like being kissed, Jim," she cried. "You are a dreadful old bear." And she ran across the room and hugged him.

James Vane looked into his sister's face with tenderness. "I want you to come out with me for a walk, Sibyl. I don't suppose I shall ever see this horrid London again. I am sure I don't want to."

"My son, don't say such dreadful things," murmured Mrs. Vane, taking up a tawdry theatrical dress, with a sigh, and beginning to patch it. She felt a little disappointed that he had not joined the group. It would have increased the theatrical picturesqueness of the situation.

"Why not, mother? I mean it."

"You pain me, my son. I trust you will return from Australia in a position of affluence. I believe there is no society of any kind in the Colonies, nothing that I would call society; so when you have made your fortune you must come back and assert yourself in London."

"Society!" muttered the lad. "I don't want to know anything about that. I should like to make some money to take you and Sibyl off the stage. I hate it."

"Oh, Jim!" said Sibyl, laughing, "how unkind of you! But are you really going for a walk with me? That will be nice! I was afraid you were going to say good-bye to some of your friends—to Tom Hardy, who gave you that hideous pipe, or Ned Langton, who makes fun of

---

6. Although Australia had been designated as a British penal colony since 1788, by the late 1800s it had become a prime destination of fortune hunters and low-income Britons. Gold had been discovered there in 1823, thus inciting a gold rush.
7. The physical appearance of James Vane appears to owe a good deal to the appearance of Willie, Oscar Wilde's older brother.
8. A striking theatrical arrangement of persons in a frozen dramatic pose, very popular with theatergoers of the times.

you for smoking it. It is very sweet of you to let me have your last afternoon. Where shall we go? Let us go to the Park."[9]

"I am too shabby," he answered, frowning. "Only swell[1] people go to the Park."

"Nonsense, Jim," she whispered, stroking the sleeve of his coat.

He hesitated for a moment. "Very well," he said at last, "but don't be too long dressing." She danced out of the door. One could hear her singing as she ran upstairs. Her little feet pattered overhead.

He walked up and down the room two or three times. Then he turned to the still figure in the chair. "Mother, are my things ready?" he asked.

"Quite ready, James," she answered, keeping her eyes on her work. For some months past she had felt ill at ease when she was alone with this rough, stern son of hers. Her shallow secret nature was troubled when their eyes met. She used to wonder if he suspected anything. The silence, for he made no other observation, became intolerable to her. She began to complain. Women defend themselves by attacking, just as they attack by sudden and strange surrenders. "I hope you will be contented, James, with your sea-faring life," she said. "You must remember that it is your own choice. You might have entered a solicitor's[2] office. Solicitors are a very respectable class, and in the country often dine with the best families."

"I hate offices, and I hate clerks," he replied. "But you are quite right. I have chosen my own life. All I say is, watch over Sibyl. Don't let her come to any harm. Mother, you must watch over her."

"James, you really talk very strangely. Of course I watch over Sibyl."

"I hear a gentleman comes every night to the theatre, and goes behind to talk to her. Is that right? What about that?"

"You are speaking about things you don't understand, James. In the profession we are accustomed to receive a great deal of most gratifying attention. I myself used to receive many bouquets at one time. That was when acting was really understood. As for Sibyl, I do not know at present whether her attachment is serious or not. But there is no doubt that the young man in question is a perfect gentleman. He is always most polite to me. Besides, he has the appearance of being rich, and the flowers he sends are lovely."

"You don't know his name, though," said the lad harshly.

"No," answered his mother, with a placid expression in her face. "He has not yet revealed his real name. I think it is quite romantic of him. He is probably a member of the aristocracy."

---

9. Hyde Park.
1. Fashionable and wealthy.
2. In the English court system, this refers to one properly qualified and formally admitted to practice as a law agent in any court. Solicitors commonly instruct barristers, who then argue cases.

James Vane bit his lip. "Watch over Sibyl, mother," he cried, "watch over her."

"My son, you distress me very much. Sibyl is always under my special care. Of course, if this gentleman is wealthy, there is no reason why she should not contract an alliance with him. I trust he is one of the aristocracy. He has all the appearance of it, I must say. It might be a most brilliant marriage for Sibyl. They would make a charming couple. His good looks are really quite remarkable; everybody notices them."

The lad muttered something to himself, and drummed on the window-pane with his coarse fingers. He had just turned round to say something, when the door opened, and Sibyl ran in.

"How serious you both are!" she cried. "What is the matter?"

"Nothing," he answered. "I suppose one must be serious sometimes. Good-bye, mother; I will have my dinner at five o'clock. Everything is packed, except my shirts, so you need not trouble."

"Good-bye, my son," she answered, with a bow of strained stateliness.

She was extremely annoyed at the tone he had adopted with her, and there was something in his look that had made her feel afraid.

"Kiss me, mother," said the girl. Her flower-like lips touched the withered cheek, and warmed its frost.

"My child! my child!" cried Mrs. Vane, looking up to the ceiling in search of an imaginary gallery.

"Come, Sibyl," said her brother, impatiently. He hated his mother's affectations.

They went out into the flickering wind-blown sunlight, and strolled down the dreary Euston Road.[3] The passers-by glanced in wonder at the sullen, heavy youth, who, in coarse, ill-fitting clothes, was in the company of such a graceful, refined-looking girl. He was like a common gardener walking with a rose.

Jim frowned from time to time when he caught the inquisitive glance of some stranger. He had that dislike of being stared at which comes on geniuses late in life, and never leaves the commonplace. Sibyl, however, was quite unconscious of the effect she was producing. Her love was trembling in laughter on her lips. She was thinking of Prince Charming, and, that she might think of him all the more, she did not talk of him, but prattled on about the ship in which Jim was going to sail, about the gold he was certain to find, about the wonderful heiress whose life he was to save from the wicked,

3. Three great rail terminals in Euston Road helped turn the district into the site of flophouses, pawnshops, second-hand dealers, brothels, and cheap theaters. The giant Doric granite portal of Euston Road was symbolic of the commercial gateway to the city.

red-shirted bushrangers.[4] For he was not to remain a sailor, or a supercargo, or whatever he was going to be. Oh, no! A sailor's existence was dreadful. Fancy being cooped up in a horrid ship, with the hoarse, hump-backed waves trying to get in, and a black wind blowing the masts down, and tearing the sails into long screaming ribands! He was to leave the vessel at Melbourne, bid a polite good-bye to the captain, and go off at once to the gold-fields. Before a week was over he was to come across a large nugget of pure gold, the largest nugget that had ever been discovered, and bring it down to the coast in a waggon guarded by six mounted policemen. The bushrangers were to attack them three times, and be defeated with immense slaughter. Or, no. He was not to go to the gold-fields at all. They were horrid places, where men got intoxicated, and shot each other in bar-rooms, and used bad language. He was to be a nice sheep-farmer, and one evening, as he was riding home, he was to see the beautiful heiress being carried off by a robber on a black horse, and give chase, and rescue her. Of course she would fall in love with him, and he with her, and they would get married, and come home, and live in an immense house in London. Yes, there were delightful things in store for him. But he must be very good, and not lose his temper, or spend his money foolishly. She was only a year older than he was, but she knew so much more of life. He must be sure, also, to write to her by every mail, and to say his prayers each night before he went to sleep. God was very good, and would watch over him. She would pray for him too, and in a few years he would come back quite rich and happy.

The lad listened sulkily to her, and made no answer. He was heart-sick at leaving home.

Yet it was not this alone that made him gloomy and morose. Inexperienced though he was, he had still a strong sense of the danger of Sibyl's position. This young dandy who was making love to her could mean her no good. He was a gentleman, and he hated him for that, hated him through some curious race-instinct for which he could not account, and which for that reason was all the more dominant within him. He was conscious also of the shallowness and vanity of his mother's nature, and in that saw infinite peril for Sibyl and Sibyl's happiness. Children begin by loving their parents; as they grow older they judge them; sometimes they forgive them.

His mother! He had something on his mind to ask of her, something that he had brooded on for many months of silence. A chance phrase that he had heard at the theatre, a whispered sneer that had reached his ears one night as he waited at the stage-door, had set loose

---

4. The slang designation for an escaped convict who took refuge in the Australian "bush" and subsisted by robbery.

a train of horrible thoughts. He remembered it as if it had been the lash of a hunting-crop across his face. His brows knit together into a wedge-like furrow, and with a twitch of pain he bit his under-lip.

"You are not listening to a word I am saying, Jim," cried Sibyl, "and I am making the most delightful plans for your future. Do say something."

"What do you want me to say?"

"Oh! that you will be a good boy, and not forget us," she answered, smiling at him.

He shrugged his shoulders. "You are more likely to forget me, than I am to forget you, Sibyl."

She flushed. "What do you mean, Jim?" she asked.

"You have a new friend, I hear. Who is he? Why have you not told me about him? He means you no good."

"Stop, Jim!" she exclaimed. "You must not say anything against him. I love him."

"Why, you don't even know his name," answered the lad. "Who is he? I have a right to know."

"He is called Prince Charming. Don't you like the name. Oh! you silly boy! you should never forget it. If you only saw him, you would think him the most wonderful person in the world. Some day you will meet him: when you come back from Australia. You will like him so much. Everybody likes him, and I . . . love him. I wish you could come to the theatre to-night. He is going to be there, and I am to play Juliet. Oh! how I shall play it! Fancy, Jim, to be in love and play Juliet! To have him sitting there! To play for his delight! I am afraid I may frighten the company, frighten or enthrall them. To be in love is to surpass one's self. Poor dreadful Mr. Isaacs will be shouting 'genius' to his loafers at the bar. He has preached me as a dogma; to-night he will announce me as a revelation. I feel it. And it is all his, his only, Prince Charming, my wonderful lover, my god of graces. But I am poor beside him. Poor? What does that matter? When poverty creeps in at the door, love flies in through the window. Our proverbs want re-writing. They were made in winter, and it is summer now; spring-time for me, I think, a very dance of blossoms in blue skies."

"He is a gentleman," said the lad, sullenly.

"A Prince!" she cried, musically. "What more do you want?"

"He wants to enslave you."

"I shudder at the thought of being free."

"I want you to beware of him."

"To see him is to worship him, to know him is to trust him."

"Sibyl, you are mad about him."

She laughed, and took his arm. "You dear old Jim, you talk as if you were a hundred. Some day you will be in love yourself. Then you will know what it is. Don't look so sulky. Surely you should be glad to think that, though you are going away, you leave me happier than I have ever been before. Life has been hard for us both, terribly hard and difficult. But it will be different now. You are going to a new world, and I have found one. Here are two chairs; let us sit down and see the smart people go by."

They took their seats amidst a crowd of watchers. The tulip-beds across the road flamed like throbbing rings of fire. A white dust, tremulous cloud of orris-root[5] it seemed, hung in the panting air. The brightly-coloured parasols danced and dipped like monstrous butterflies.

She made her brother talk of himself, his hopes, his prospects. He spoke slowly and with effort. They passed words to each other as players at a game pass counters. Sibyl felt oppressed. She could not communicate her joy. A faint smile curving that sullen mouth was all the echo she could win. After some time she became silent. Suddenly she caught a glimpse of golden hair and laughing lips, and in an open carriage with two ladies Dorian Gray drove past.

She started to her feet. "There he is!" she cried.

"Who?" said Jim Vane.

"Prince Charming," she answered, looking after the victoria.[6]

He jumped up, and seized her roughly by the arm. "Show him to me. Which is he? Point him out. I must see him!" he exclaimed; but at that moment the Duke of Berwick's four-in-hand[7] came between, and when it had left the space clear, the carriage had swept out of the Park.

"He is gone," murmured Sibyl, sadly. "I wish you had seen him."

"I wish I had, for as sure as there is a God in heaven, if he ever does you any wrong, I shall kill him."

She looked at him in horror. He repeated his words. They cut the air like a dagger. The people round began to gape. A lady standing close to her tittered.

"Come away, Jim; come away," she whispered. He followed her doggedly, as she passed through the crowd. He felt glad at what he had said.

When they reached the Achilles Statue[8] she turned round. There was pity in her eyes that became laughter on her lips. She shook her head at him. "You are foolish, Jim, utterly foolish; a bad-tempered boy, that is all. How can you say such horrible things? You don't

---

5. Used as a perfume, it has the scent of violets.
6. A light, low, four-wheeled carriage having a collapsible hood, with seats (usually) for two persons and an elevated seat in front for the driver.
7. A vehicle with four horses, driven by one person.
8. A giant nude bronze statue by Sir Richard Westmacott, based on a Roman figure in Cavallo, Italy; erected by the Ladies of England in 1822 to commemorate the Duke of Wellington's victories. James and Sibyl are now near the southeast corner of Hyde Park.

know what you are talking about. You are simply jealous and unkind. Ah! I wish you would fall in love. Love makes people good, and what you said was wicked."

"I am sixteen," he answered, "and I know what I am about. Mother is no help to you. She doesn't understand how to look after you. I wish now that I was not going to Australia at all. I have a great mind to chuck the whole thing up. I would, if my articles[9] hadn't been signed."

"Oh, don't be so serious, Jim. You are like one of the heroes of those silly melodramas mother used to be so fond of acting in. I am not going to quarrel with you. I have seen him, and oh! to see him is perfect happiness. We won't quarrel. I know you would never harm any one I love, would you?"

"Not as long as you love him, I suppose," was the sullen answer.

"I shall love him for ever!" she cried.

"And he?"

"For ever, too!"

"He had better."

She shrank from him. Then she laughed and put her hand on his arm. He was merely a boy.

At the Marble Arch they hailed an omnibus,[1] which left them close to their shabby home in the Euston Road. It was after five o'clock, and Sibyl had to lie down for a couple of hours before acting. Jim insisted that she should do so. He said that he would sooner part with her when their mother was not present. She would be sure to make a scene, and he detested scenes of every kind.

In Sibyl's own room they parted. There was jealousy in the lad's heart, and a fierce murderous hatred of the stranger who, as it seemed to him, had come between them. Yet, when her arms were flung round his neck, and her fingers strayed through his hair, he softened, and kissed her with real affection. There were tears in his eyes as he went downstairs.

His mother was waiting for him below. She grumbled at his unpunctuality, as he entered. He made no answer, but sat down to his meagre meal. The flies buzzed round the table, and crawled over the stained cloth. Through the rumble of omnibuses, and the clatter of street-cabs, he could hear the droning voice devouring each minute that was left to him.

After some time, he thrust away his plate, and put his head in his hands. He felt that he had a right to know. It should have been told

9. An employment contract to serve on shipboard.
1. A large public horse-drawn vehicle carrying passengers by road, running on a fixed route and typically requiring the payment of a fare. *Marble Arch:* A triumphal single arch modeled after that of Titus in Rome and located at the northeast entrance to Hyde Park.

to him before, if it was as he suspected. Leaden with fear, his mother watched him. Words dropped mechanically from her lips. A tattered lace handkerchief twitched in her fingers. When the clock struck six, he got up, and went to the door. Then he turned back, and looked at her. Their eyes met. In hers he saw a wild appeal for mercy. It enraged him.

"Mother, I have something to ask you," he said. Her eyes wandered vaguely about the room. She made no answer. "Tell me the truth. I have a right to know. Were you married to my father?"

She heaved a deep sigh. It was a sigh of relief. The terrible moment, the moment that night and day, for weeks and months, she had dreaded, had come at last, and yet she felt no terror. Indeed in some measure it was a disappointment to her. The vulgar directness of the question called for a direct answer. The situation had not been gradually led up to. It was crude. It reminded her of a bad rehearsal.

"No," she answered, wondering at the harsh simplicity of life.

"My father was a scoundrel then!" cried the lad, clenching his fists.

She shook her head. "I knew he was not free. We loved each other very much. If he had lived, he would have made provision for us. Don't speak against him, my son. He was your father, and a gentleman. Indeed he was highly connected."

An oath broke from his lips. "I don't care for myself," he exclaimed, "but don't let Sibyl. . . . It is a gentleman, isn't it, who is in love with her, or says he is? Highly connected, too, I suppose."

For a moment a hideous sense of humiliation came over the woman. Her head drooped. She wiped her eyes with shaking hands. "Sibyl has a mother," she murmured; "I had none."

The lad was touched. He went towards her, and stooping down he kissed her. "I am sorry if I have pained you by asking about my father," he said, "but I could not help it. I must go now. Good-bye. Don't forget that you will have only one child now to look after, and believe me that if this man wrongs my sister, I will find out who he is, track him down, and kill him like a dog. I swear it."

The exaggerated folly of the threat, the passionate gesture that accompanied it, the mad melodramatic words, made life seem more vivid to her. She was familiar with the atmosphere. She breathed more freely, and for the first time for many months she really admired her son. She would have liked to have continued the scene on the same emotional scale, but he cut her short. Trunks had to be carried down, and mufflers[2] looked for. The lodging-house drudge bustled in and out. There was the bargaining with the cabman. The moment was lost in vulgar details. It was with a renewed

---

2. A wrap or scarf (frequently of wool or silk) worn around the neck for warmth.

feeling of disappointment that she waved the tattered lace handkerchief from the window, as her son drove away. She was conscious
that a great opportunity had been wasted. She consoled herself by
telling Sibyl how desolate she felt her life would be, now that she
had only one child to look after. She remembered the phrase. It had
pleased her. Of the threat she said nothing. It was vividly and dramatically expressed. She felt that they would all laugh at it some day.

Chapter VI[1]

I suppose you have heard the news, Basil?" said Lord Henry that evening, as Hallward was shown into a little private room at the Bristol
where dinner had been laid for three.

"No, Harry," answered the artist, giving his hat and coat to the
bowing waiter. "What is it? Nothing about politics, I hope? They
don't interest me. There is hardly a single person in the House of
Commons worth painting; though many of them would be the better for a little whitewashing."

"Dorian Gray is engaged to be married," said Lord Henry, watching him as he spoke.

Hallward started, and then frowned. "Dorian engaged to be married!" he cried. "Impossible!"

"It is perfectly true."

"To whom?"

"To some little actress or other."

"I can't believe it. Dorian is far too sensible."

"Dorian is far too wise not to do foolish things now and then, my
dear Basil."

"Marriage is hardly a thing that one can do now and then, Harry."

"Except in America," rejoined Lord Henry, languidly. "But I didn't
say he was married. I said he was engaged to be married. There is a
great difference. I have a distinct remembrance of being married,
but I have no recollection at all of being engaged. I am inclined to
think that I never was engaged."

"But think of Dorian's birth, and position, and wealth. It would
be absurd for him to marry so much beneath him."[2]

"If you want to make him marry this girl tell him that, Basil. He
is sure to do it, then. Whenever a man does a thoroughly stupid
thing, it is always from the noblest motives."

1. This was chapter 4 in the *Lippincott's Magazine* edition.
2. Basil is speaking in terms of social class rather than moral character.

"I hope the girl is good, Harry. I don't want to see Dorian tied to some vile creature, who might degrade his nature and ruin his intellect."

"Oh, she is better than good—she is beautiful," murmured Lord Henry, sipping a glass of vermouth and orange-bitters. "Dorian says she is beautiful; and he is not often wrong about things of that kind. Your portrait of him has quickened his appreciation of the personal appearance of other people. It has had that excellent effect, amongst others. We are to see her to-night, if that boy doesn't forget his appointment."

"Are you serious?"

"Quite serious, Basil. I should be miserable if I thought I should ever be more serious than I am at the present moment."

"But do you approve of it, Harry?" asked the painter, walking up and down the room, and biting his lip. "You can't approve of it, possibly. It is some silly infatuation."

"I never approve, or disapprove, of anything now. It is an absurd attitude to take towards life. We are not sent into the world to air our moral prejudices. I never take any notice of what common people say, and I never interfere with what charming people do. If a personality fascinates me, whatever mode of expression that personality selects is absolutely delightful to me. Dorian Gray falls in love with a beautiful girl who acts Juliet, and proposes to marry her. Why not? If he wedded Messalina[3] he would be none the less interesting. You know I am not a champion of marriage. The real drawback to marriage is that it makes one unselfish. And unselfish people are colourless. They lack individuality. Still, there are certain temperaments that marriage makes more complex. They retain their egotism, and add to it many other egos. They are forced to have more than one life. They become more highly organized, and to be highly organized is, I should fancy, the object of man's existence. Besides, every experience is of value, and, whatever one may say against marriage, it is certainly an experience. I hope that Dorian Gray will make this girl his wife, passionately adore her for six months, and then suddenly become fascinated by some one else. He would be a wonderful study."

"You don't mean a single word of all that, Harry; you know you don't. If Dorian Gray's life were spoiled, no one would be sorrier than yourself. You are much better than you pretend to be."

Lord Henry laughed. "The reason we all like to think so well of others is that we are all afraid for ourselves. The basis of optimism is sheer terror. We think that we are generous because we credit our

---

3. Empress of Rome, wife of Claudius, put to death in 48 CE for gross indecency and treason.

neighbour with the possession of those virtues that are likely to be a benefit to us. We praise the banker that we may overdraw our account, and find good qualities in the highwayman in the hope that he may spare our pockets. I mean everything that I have said. I have the greatest contempt for optimism. As for a spoiled life, no life is spoiled but one whose growth is arrested. If you want to mar a nature, you have merely to reform it. As for marriage, of course that would be silly, but there are other and more interesting bonds between men and women. I will certainly encourage them. They have the charm of being fashionable. But here is Dorian himself. He will tell you more than I can."

"My dear Harry, my dear Basil, you must both congratulate me!" said the lad, throwing off his evening cape with its satin-lined wings, and shaking each of his friends by the hand in turn. "I have never been so happy. Of course it is sudden: all really delightful things are. And yet it seems to me to be the one thing I have been looking for all my life." He was flushed with excitement and pleasure, and looked extraordinarily handsome.

"I hope you will always be very happy, Dorian," said Hallward, "but I don't quite forgive you for not having let me know of your engagement. You let Harry know."

"And I don't forgive you for being late for dinner," broke in Lord Henry, putting his hand on the lad's shoulder, and smiling as he spoke. "Come, let us sit down and try what the new *chef* here is like, and then you will tell us how it all came about."

"There is really not much to tell," cried Dorian, as they took their seats at the small round table. "What happened was simply this. After I left you yesterday evening, Harry, I dressed, had some dinner at that little Italian restaurant in Rupert Street, you introduced me to, and went down at eight o'clock to the theatre. Sibyl was playing Rosalind. Of course, the scenery was dreadful, and the Orlando absurd. But Sibyl! You should have seen her! When she came on in her boy's clothes she was perfectly wonderful. She wore a moss-coloured velvet jerkin[4] with cinnamon sleeves, slim brown cross-gartered hose, a dainty little green cap with a hawk's feather caught in a jewel, and a hooded cloak lined with dull red. She had never seemed to me more exquisite. She had all the delicate grace of that Tanagra figurine that you have in your studio,[5] Basil. Her hair clustered round her face like dark leaves round a pale rose. As for her

---

4. A vest. Rosalind is disguised as a boy, Ganymede, for much of *As You Like It*. Many of the Shakespeare allusions are to plays in which disguises conceal the true sex of the character: in most instances, young women are disguised as young men. The charade is further complicated because boys played all the female roles in Shakespeare's theater.
5. Wilde admired Tanagra statuettes on his early trips to Greece and kept one in the library of his Tite Street house. They were molded out of red clay.

acting—well, you shall see her to-night. She is simply a born artist.
I sat in the dingy box absolutely enthralled. I forgot that I was in
London and in the nineteenth century. I was away with my love in
a forest that no man had ever seen. After the performance was over
I went behind, and spoke to her. As we were sitting together, suddenly there came into her eyes a look that I had never seen there
before. My lips moved towards hers. We kissed each other. I can't
describe to you what I felt at that moment. It seemed to me that all
my life had been narrowed to one perfect point of rose-coloured joy.
She trembled all over, and shook like a white narcissus. Then she
flung herself on her knees and kissed my hands. I feel that I should
not tell you all this, but I can't help it. Of course our engagement is
a dead secret. She has not even told her own mother. I don't know
what my guardians will say. Lord Radley is sure to be furious. I don't
care. I shall be of age in less than a year, and then I can do what I
like. I have been right, Basil, haven't I, to take my love out of poetry,
and to find my wife in Shakespeare's plays? Lips that Shakespeare
taught to speak have whispered their secret in my ear. I have had
the arms of Rosalind around me, and kissed Juliet on the mouth."

"Yes, Dorian, I suppose you were right," said Hallward, slowly.

"Have you seen her to-day?" asked Lord Henry.

Dorian Gray shook his head. "I left her in the forest of Arden, I
shall find her in an orchard in Verona."[6]

Lord Henry sipped his champagne in a meditative manner. "At
what particular point did you mention the word marriage, Dorian?
And what did she say in answer? Perhaps you forgot all about it."

"My dear Harry, I did not treat it as a business transaction, and I
did not make any formal proposal. I told her that I loved her, and
she said she was not worthy to be my wife. Not worthy! Why, the
whole world is nothing to me compared with her."

"Women are wonderfully practical," murmured Lord Henry,—
"much more practical than we are. In situations of that kind we
often forget to say anything about marriage, and they always
remind us."

Hallward laid his hand upon his arm. "Don't, Harry. You have
annoyed Dorian. He is not like other men. He would never bring
misery upon any one. His nature is too fine for that."

Lord Henry looked across the table. "Dorian is never annoyed
with me," he answered. "I asked the question for the best reason possible, for the only reason, indeed, that excuses one for asking any
question—simple curiosity. I have a theory that it is always the
women who propose to us, and not we who propose to the women.

6. That is, Sibyl performed in *As You Like It* the previous night and will act in *Romeo and
Juliet* tonight.

Except, of course, in middle-class life. But then the middle classes are not modern."

Dorian Gray laughed, and tossed his head. "You are quite incorrigible, Harry; but I don't mind. It is impossible to be angry with you. When you see Sibyl Vane you will feel that the man who could wrong her would be a beast, a beast without a heart. I cannot understand how any one can wish to shame the thing he loves. I love Sibyl Vane. I want to place her on a pedestal of gold, and to see the world worship the woman who is mine. What is marriage? An irrevocable vow. You mock at it for that. Ah! don't mock. It is an irrevocable vow that I want to take. Her trust makes me faithful, her belief makes me good. When I am with her, I regret all that you have taught me. I become different from what you have known me to be. I am changed, and the mere touch of Sibyl Vane's hand makes me forget you and all your wrong, fascinating, poisonous, delightful theories."

"And those are . . . ?" asked Lord Henry, helping himself to some salad.

"Oh, your theories about life, your theories about love, your theories about pleasure. All your theories, in fact, Harry."

"Pleasure is the only thing worth having a theory about," he answered, in his slow, melodious voice. "But I am afraid I cannot claim my theory as my own. It belongs to Nature, not to me. Pleasure is Nature's test, her sign of approval. When we are happy we are always good, but when we are good we are not always happy."

"Ah! but what do you mean by good?" cried Basil Hallward.

"Yes," echoed Dorian, leaning back in his chair, and looking at Lord Henry over the heavy clusters of purple-lipped irises that stood in the centre of the table, "what do you mean by good, Harry?"

"To be good is to be in harmony with one's self," he replied, touching the thin stem of his glass with his pale, fine-pointed fingers. "Discord is to be forced to be in harmony with others. One's own life—that is the important thing. As for the lives of one's neighbours, if one wishes to be a prig[7] or a Puritan, one can flaunt one's moral views about them, but they are not one's concern. Besides, Individualism has really the higher aim. Modern morality consists in accepting the standard of one's age. I consider that for any man of culture to accept the standard of his age is a form of the grossest immorality."

"But, surely, if one lives merely for one's self, Harry, one pays a terrible price for doing so?" suggested the painter.

"Yes, we are overcharged for everything nowadays. I should fancy that the real tragedy of the poor is that they can afford nothing but

7. Someone who cultivates or affects a propriety of culture, learning, or morals that offends or bores others; a conceited or self-important and didactic person.

self-denial. Beautiful sins, like beautiful things, are the privilege of the rich."

"One has to pay in other ways but money."

"What sort of ways, Basil?"

"Oh! I should fancy in remorse, in suffering, in . . . well, in the consciousness of degradation."

Lord Henry shrugged his shoulders. "My dear fellow, mediæval art is charming, but mediæval emotions are out of date. One can use them in fiction, of course. But then the only things that one can use in fiction are the things that one has ceased to use in fact. Believe me, no civilized man ever regrets a pleasure, and no uncivilized man ever knows what a pleasure is."

"I know what pleasure is," cried Dorian Gray. "It is to adore some one."

"That is certainly better than being adored," he answered, toying with some fruits. "Being adored is a nuisance. Women treat us just as Humanity treats its gods. They worship us, and are always bothering us to do something for them."

"I should have said that whatever they ask for they had first given to us," murmured the lad, gravely. "They create Love in our natures. They have a right to demand it back."

"That is quite true, Dorian," cried Hallward.

"Nothing is ever quite true," said Lord Henry.

"This is," interrupted Dorian. "You must admit, Harry, that women give to men the very gold of their lives."

"Possibly," he sighed, "but they invariably want it back in such very small change. That is the worry. Women, as some witty Frenchman once put it, inspire us with the desire to do masterpieces, and always prevent us from carrying them out."

"Harry, you are dreadful! I don't know why I like you so much."

"You will always like me, Dorian," he replied. "Will you have some coffee, you fellows?—Waiter, bring coffee, and *fine-champagne*,[8] and some cigarettes. No: don't mind the cigarettes; I have some. Basil, I can't allow you to smoke cigars. You must have a cigarette. A cigarette is the perfect type of a perfect pleasure. It is exquisite, and it leaves one unsatisfied. What more can one want? Yes, Dorian, you will always be fond of me. I represent to you all the sins you have never had the courage to commit."

"What nonsense you talk, Harry!" cried the lad, taking a light from a fire-breathing silver dragon that the waiter had placed on the table. "Let us go down to the theatre. When Sibyl comes on the stage you will have a new ideal of life. She will represent something to you that you have never known."

---

8. A brandy liqueur rather than a type of champagne.

"I have known everything," said Lord Henry, with a tired look in his eyes, "but I am always ready for a new emotion. I am afraid, however, that, for me at any rate, there is no such thing. Still, your wonderful girl may thrill me. I love acting. It is so much more real than life. Let us go. Dorian, you will come with me. I am so sorry, Basil, but there is only room for two in the brougham.[9] You must follow us in a hansom."

They got up and put on their coats, sipping their coffee standing. The painter was silent and preoccupied. There was a gloom over him. He could not bear this marriage, and yet it seemed to him to be better than many other things that might have happened. After a few minutes, they all passed downstairs. He drove off by himself, as had been arranged, and watched the flashing lights of the little brougham in front of him. A strange sense of loss came over him. He felt that Dorian Gray would never again be to him all that he had been in the past. Life had come between them. . . . His eyes darkened, and the crowded, flaring streets became blurred to his eyes. When the cab drew up at the theatre, it seemed to him that he had grown years older.

Chapter VII[1]

For some reason or other, the house was crowded that night, and the fat Jew manager who met them at the door was beaming from ear to ear with an oily, tremulous smile. He escorted them to their box with a sort of pompous humility, waving his fat jewelled hands, and talking at the top of his voice. Dorian Gray loathed him more than ever. He felt as if he had come to look for Miranda and had been met by Caliban.[2] Lord Henry, upon the other hand, rather liked him. At least he declared he did, and insisted on shaking him by the hand, and assuring him that he was proud to meet a man who had discovered a real genius and gone bankrupt over a poet. Hallward amused himself with watching the faces in the pit. The heat was terribly oppressive, and the huge sunlight[3] flamed like a monstrous dahlia with petals of yellow fire. The youths in the gallery had taken off their coats and waistcoats and hung them over the side. They talked to each other across the theatre, and shared their oranges with the tawdry girls who sat beside them. Some women were

9. A closed, boxlike carriage with a driver's seat outside in front, synonymous with luxurious appointments.
1. This was chapter 5 in the *Lippincott's Magazine* edition.
2. Miranda is the daughter of Prospero, and Caliban is their reluctant savage servant in Shakespeare's *The Tempest*.
3. A skylight.

laughing in the pit. Their voices were horribly shrill and discordant. The sound of the popping of corks came from the bar.

"What a place to find one's divinity in!" said Lord Henry.

"Yes!" answered Dorian Gray. "It was here I found her, and she is divine beyond all living things. When she acts you will forget everything. These common, rough people, with their coarse faces and brutal gestures, become quite different when she is on the stage. They sit silently and watch her. They weep and laugh as she wills them to do. She makes them as responsive as a violin. She spiritualizes them, and one feels that they are of the same flesh and blood as one's self."

"The same flesh and blood as one's self! Oh, I hope not!"[4] exclaimed Lord Henry, who was scanning the occupants of the gallery through his opera-glass.

"Don't pay any attention to him, Dorian," said the painter. "I understand what you mean, and I believe in this girl. Any one you love must be marvellous, and any girl who has the effect you describe must be fine and noble. To spiritualize one's age—that is something worth doing.[5] If this girl can give a soul to those who have lived without one, if she can create the sense of beauty in people whose lives have been sordid and ugly, if she can strip them of their selfishness and lend them tears for sorrows that are not their own, she is worthy of all your adoration, worthy of the adoration of the world. This marriage is quite right. I did not think so at first, but I admit it now. The gods made Sibyl Vane for you. Without her you would have been incomplete."

"Thanks, Basil," answered Dorian Gray, pressing his hand. "I knew that you would understand me. Harry is so cynical, he terrifies me. But here is the orchestra. It is quite dreadful, but it only lasts for about five minutes. Then the curtain rises, and you will see the girl to whom I am going to give all my life, to whom I have given everything that is good in me."

A quarter of an hour afterwards, amidst an extraordinary turmoil of applause, Sibyl Vane stepped on to the stage. Yes, she was certainly lovely to look at—one of the loveliest creatures, Lord Henry thought, that he had ever seen. There was something of the fawn in her shy grace and startled eyes. A faint blush, like the shadow of a rose in a mirror of silver, came to her cheeks as she glanced at the crowded, enthusiastic house. She stepped back a few paces, and her

---

4. Lord Henry's repetition of Basil's phrase was added when Wilde revised the novella into a novel and recalls one of Wilde's epigrams in his essay "The Decay of Lying": "In point of fact what is interesting about people in good society . . . is the mask that each of them wears, not the reality that lies behind the mask. It is a humiliating confession, but we are all of us made out of the same stuff."

5. An allusion to an important theme in the 1855 novel *Marius the Epicurean* by Walter Pater.

lips seemed to tremble. Basil Hallward leaped to his feet and began to applaud. Motionless, and as one in a dream, sat Dorian Gray, gazing at her. Lord Henry peered through his glasses, murmuring, "Charming! charming!"

The scene was the hall of Capulet's house, and Romeo in his pilgrim's dress had entered with Mercutio and his other friends. The band, such as it was, struck up a few bars of music, and the dance began. Through the crowd of ungainly, shabbily-dressed actors, Sibyl Vane moved like a creature from a finer world. Her body swayed, while she danced, as a plant sways in the water. The curves of her throat were the curves of a white lily. Her hands seemed to be made of cool ivory.

Yet she was curiously listless. She showed no sign of joy when her eyes rested on Romeo. The few words she had to speak—

> Good pilgrim, you do wrong your hand too much,
>   Which mannerly devotion shows in this;
> For saints have hands that pilgrims' hands do touch,
>   And palm to palm is holy palmers' kiss—[6]

with the brief dialogue that follows, were spoken in a thoroughly artificial manner. The voice was exquisite, but from the point of view of tone it was absolutely false. It was wrong in colour. It took away all the life from the verse. It made the passion unreal.

Dorian Gray grew pale as he watched her. He was puzzled and anxious. Neither of his friends dared to say anything to him. She seemed to them to be absolutely incompetent. They were horribly disappointed.

Yet they felt that the true test of any Juliet is the balcony scene of the second act. They waited for that. If she failed there, there was nothing in her.

She looked charming as she came out in the moonlight. That could not be denied. But the staginess of her acting was unbearable, and grew worse as she went on. Her gestures became absurdly artificial. She over-emphasized everything that she had to say. The beautiful passage—

> Thou knowest the mask of night is on my face,
> Else would a maiden blush bepaint my cheek
> For that which thou hast heard me speak to-night—[7]

was declaimed with the painful precision of a school-girl who has been taught to recite by some second-rate professor of elocution. When she leaned over the balcony and came to those wonderful lines—

6. *Romeo and Juliet* 1.5.97–100.
7. *Romeo and Juliet* 2.2.85–87.

> *Although I joy in thee,*
> *I have no joy of this contract to-night:*
> *It is too rash, too unadvised, too sudden;*
> *Too like the lightning, which doth cease to be*
> *Ere one can say, "It lightens." Sweet, good-night!*
> *This bud of love by summer's ripening breath*
> *May prove a beauteous flower when next we meet—*[8]

she spoke the words as though they conveyed no meaning to her. It was not nervousness. Indeed, so far from being nervous, she was absolutely self-contained. It was simply bad art. She was a complete failure.

Even the common, uneducated audience of the pit and gallery lost their interest in the play. They got restless, and began to talk loudly and to whistle. The Jew manager, who was standing at the back of the dress-circle, stamped and swore with rage. The only person unmoved was the girl herself.

When the second act was over there came a storm of hisses, and Lord Henry got up from his chair and put on his coat. "She is quite beautiful, Dorian," he said, "but she can't act. Let us go."

"I am going to see the play through," answered the lad, in a hard, bitter voice. "I am awfully sorry that I have made you waste an evening, Harry. I apologize to you both."

"My dear Dorian, I should think Miss Vane was ill," interrupted Hallward. "We will come some other night."

"I wish she were ill," he rejoined. "But she seems to me to be simply callous and cold. She has entirely altered. Last night she was a great artist. This evening she is merely a commonplace, mediocre actress."

"Don't talk like that about any one you love, Dorian. Love is a more wonderful thing than Art."

"They are both simply forms of imitation," remarked Lord Henry. "But do let us go. Dorian, you must not stay here any longer. It is not good for one's morals to see bad acting. Besides, I don't suppose you will want your wife to act. So what does it matter if she plays Juliet like a wooden doll? She is very lovely, and if she knows as little about life as she does about acting, she will be a delightful experience. There are only two kinds of people who are really fascinating— people who know absolutely everything, and people who know absolutely nothing. Good heavens, my dear boy, don't look so tragic! The secret of remaining young is never to have an emotion that is unbecoming. Come to the club with Basil and myself. We will smoke cigarettes and drink to the beauty of Sibyl Vane. She is beautiful. What more can you want?"

8. *Romeo and Juliet* 2.2.116–22.

"Go away, Harry," cried the lad. "I want to be alone. Basil, you must go. Ah! can't you see that my heart is breaking?" The hot tears came to his eyes. His lips trembled, and, rushing to the back of the box, he leaned up against the wall, hiding his face in his hands.

"Let us go, Basil," said Lord Henry with a strange tenderness in his voice; and the two young men passed out together.

A few moments afterwards the footlights flared up, and the curtain rose on the third act. Dorian Gray went back to his seat. He looked pale, and proud, and indifferent. The play dragged on, and seemed interminable. Half of the audience went out, tramping in heavy boots, and laughing. The whole thing was a *fiasco*. The last act was played to almost empty benches. The curtain went down on a titter, and some groans.

As soon as it was over, Dorian Gray rushed behind the scenes into the greenroom. The girl was standing there alone, with a look of triumph on her face. Her eyes were lit with an exquisite fire. There was a radiance about her. Her parted lips were smiling over some secret of their own.

When he entered, she looked at him, and an expression of infinite joy came over her. "How badly I acted to-night, Dorian!" she cried.

"Horribly!" he answered, gazing at her in amazement—horribly! It was dreadful. Are you ill? You have no idea what it was. You have no idea what I suffered."

The girl smiled. "Dorian," she answered, lingering over his name with long-drawn music in her voice, as though it were sweeter than honey to the red petals of her mouth—"Dorian, you should have understood. But you understand now, don't you?"

"Understand what?" he asked, angrily.

"Why I was so bad to-night. Why I shall always be bad. Why I shall never act well again."

He shrugged his shoulders. "You are ill, I suppose. When you are ill you shouldn't act. You make yourself ridiculous. My friends were bored. I was bored."

She seemed not to listen to him. She was transfigured with joy. An ecstasy of happiness dominated her.

"Dorian, Dorian," she cried, "before I knew you, acting was the one reality of my life. It was only in the theatre that I lived. I thought that it was all true. I was Rosalind one night, and Portia the other. The joy of Beatrice was my joy, and the sorrows of Cordelia were mine also.[9] I believed in everything. The common people who acted with me seemed to me to be godlike. The painted scenes were my

---

9. All Shakespearean characters: Portia is the heroine of *The Merchant of Venice,* Beatrice of *Much Ado about Nothing,* and Cordelia of *King Lear.* Taken together, they would represent a good test of an actress's range.

world. I knew nothing but shadows, and I thought them real. You came—oh, my beautiful love!—and you freed my soul from prison. You taught me what reality really is. To-night, for the first time in my life, I saw through the hollowness, the sham, the silliness of the empty pageant in which I had always played. To-night, for the first time, I became conscious that the Romeo was hideous, and old, and painted, that the moonlight in the orchard was false, that the scenery was vulgar, and that the words I had to speak were unreal, were not my words, were not what I wanted to say. You had brought me something higher, something of which all art is but a reflection. You had made me understand what love really is. My love! my love! Prince Charming! Prince of life! I have grown sick of shadows.[1] You are more to me than all art can ever be. What have I to do with the puppets of a play? When I came on to-night, I could not understand how it was that everything had gone from me. I thought that I was going to be wonderful. I found that I could do nothing. Suddenly it dawned on my soul what it all meant. The knowledge was exquisite to me. I heard them hissing, and I smiled. What could they know of love such as ours? Take me away, Dorian—take me away with you, where we can be quite alone. I hate the stage. I might mimic a passion that I do not feel, but I cannot mimic one that burns me like fire. Oh, Dorian, Dorian, you understand now what it signifies? Even if I could do it, it would be profanation for me to play at being in love. You have made me see that."

He flung himself down on the sofa, and turned away his face. "You have killed my love," he muttered.

She looked at him in wonder, and laughed. He made no answer. She came across to him, and with her little fingers stroked his hair. She knelt down and pressed his hands to her lips. He drew them away, and a shudder ran through him.

Then he leaped up, and went to the door. "Yes," he cried, "you have killed my love. You used to stir my imagination. Now you don't even stir my curiosity. You simply produce no effect. I loved you because you were marvellous, because you had genius and intellect, because you realized the dreams of great poets and gave shape and substance to the shadows of art. You have thrown it all away. You are shallow and stupid. My God! how mad I was to love you! What a fool I have been! You are nothing to me now. I will never see you again. I will never think of you. I will never mention your name. You don't know what you were to me, once. Why, once . . . Oh, I can't bear to think of it! I wish I had never laid eyes upon you! You have spoiled the romance of my life. How little you can know of love, if you say it mars your art! Without your art you are nothing. I would have made

1. A direct allusion to Alfred, Lord Tennyson's poem "The Lady of Shalott" (1842).

you famous, splendid, magnificent. The world would have worshipped you, and you would have borne my name. What are you now? A third-rate actress with a pretty face."

The girl grew white, and trembled. She clenched her hands together, and her voice seemed to catch in her throat. "You are not serious, Dorian?" she murmured. "You are acting."

"Acting! I leave that to you. You do it so well," he answered, bitterly.

She rose from her knees, and, with a piteous expression of pain in her face, came across the room to him. She put her hand upon his arm, and looked into his eyes. He thrust her back. "Don't touch me!" he cried.

A low moan broke from her, and she flung herself at his feet, and lay there like a trampled flower. "Dorian, Dorian, don't leave me!" she whispered. "I am so sorry I didn't act well. I was thinking of you all the time. But I will try—indeed, I will try. It came so suddenly across me, my love for you. I think I should never have known it if you had not kissed me—if we had not kissed each other. Kiss me again, my love. Don't go away from me. I couldn't bear it. Oh! don't go away from me. My brother . . . No; never mind. He didn't mean it. He was in jest. . . . But you, oh! can't you forgive me for to-night? I will work so hard, and try to improve. Don't be cruel to me because I love you better than anything in the world. After all, it is only once that I have not pleased you. But you are quite right, Dorian. I should have shown myself more of an artist. It was foolish of me; and yet I couldn't help it. Oh, don't leave me, don't leave me." A fit of passionate sobbing choked her. She crouched on the floor like a wounded thing, and Dorian Gray, with his beautiful eyes, looked down at her, and his chiselled lips curled in exquisite disdain. There is always something ridiculous about the emotions of people whom one has ceased to love. Sibyl Vane seemed to him to be absurdly melodramatic. Her tears and sobs annoyed him.

"I am going," he said at last, in his calm, clear voice. "I don't wish to be unkind, but I can't see you again. You have disappointed me."

She wept silently, and made no answer, but crept nearer. Her little hands stretched blindly out, and appeared to be seeking for him. He turned on his heel, and left the room. In a few moments he was out of the theatre.

Where he went to he hardly knew. He remembered wandering through dimly-lit streets, past gaunt black-shadowed archways and evil-looking houses. Women with hoarse voices and harsh laughter had called after him. Drunkards had reeled by cursing, and chattering to themselves like monstrous apes. He had seen grotesque children huddled upon door-steps, and heard shrieks and oaths from gloomy courts.

As the dawn was just breaking he found himself close to Covent Garden.[2] The darkness lifted, and, flushed with faint fires, the sky hollowed itself into a perfect pearl. Huge carts filled with nodding lilies rumbled slowly down the polished empty street. The air was heavy with the perfume of the flowers, and their beauty seemed to bring him an anodyne for his pain. He followed into the market, and watched the men unloading their waggons. A white-smocked carter[3] offered him some cherries. He thanked him, wondered why he refused to accept any money for them, and began to eat them listlessly. They had been plucked at midnight, and the coldness of the moon had entered into them. A long line of boys carrying crates of striped tulips, and of yellow and red roses, defiled in front of him, threading their way through the huge jade-green piles of vegetables. Under the portico, with its grey sun-bleached pillars, loitered a troop of draggled bareheaded girls, waiting for the auction to be over. Others crowded round the swinging doors of the coffee-house in the Piazza. The heavy cart-horses slipped and stamped upon the rough stones, shaking their bells and trappings. Some of the drivers were lying asleep on a pile of sacks. Iris-necked, and pink-footed, the pigeons ran about picking up seeds.

After a little while, he hailed a hansom, and drove home. For a few moments he loitered upon the doorstep, looking round at the silent Square[4] with its blank close-shuttered windows, and its staring blinds. The sky was pure opal now, and the roofs of the houses glistened like silver against it. From some chimney opposite a thin wreath of smoke was rising. It curled, a violet riband, through the nacre-coloured air.[5]

In the huge gilt Venetian lantern, spoil of some Doge's barge[6] that hung from the ceiling of the great oak-panelled hall of entrance, lights were still burning from three flickering jets: thin blue petals of flame they seemed, rimmed with white fire. He turned them out, and, having thrown his hat and cape on the table, passed through the library towards the door of his bedroom, a large octagonal chamber on the ground floor that, in his new-born feeling for luxury, he had just had decorated for himself, and hung with some curious Renaissance tapestries that had been discovered stored in a disused

2. The site of this famous theater is near Trafalgar Square, an area rich in literary and theatrical history; it was also the location of open-air markets. Wilde wrote a remarkably similar scene in his story "Lord Arthur Savile's Crime." In George Bernard Shaw's 1931 play *Pygmalion*, Professor Henry Higgins first meets Eliza Doolittle when she is selling flowers in the market.
3. One who drives a cart.
4. Grosvenor Square, where Dorian had his London residence, is located in the heart of Mayfair. Wilde lived nearby on Charles Street prior to his marriage.
5. Nacre is mother-of-pearl.
6. The Doge is elected chief magistrate of the Venetian Republic.

attic at Selby Royal.[7] As he was turning the handle of the door, his eye fell upon the portrait Basil Hallward had painted of him. He started back as if in surprise. Then he went on into his own room, looking somewhat puzzled. After he had taken the buttonhole out of his coat, he seemed to hesitate. Finally he came back, went over to the picture, and examined it. In the dim arrested light that struggled through the cream-coloured silk blinds, the face appeared to him to be a little changed. The expression looked different. One would have said that there was a touch of cruelty in the mouth. It was certainly strange.

He turned round, and, walking to the window, drew up the blind. The bright dawn flooded the room, and swept the fantastic shadows into dusky corners, where they lay shuddering. But the strange expression that he had noticed in the face of the portrait seemed to linger there, to be more intensified even. The quivering, ardent sunlight showed him the lines of cruelty round the mouth as clearly as if he had been looking into a mirror after he had done some dreadful thing.

He winced, and, taking up from the table an oval glass framed in ivory Cupids, one of Lord Henry's many presents to him, glanced hurriedly into its polished depths. No line like that warped his red lips. What did it mean?

He rubbed his eyes, and came close to the picture, and examined it again. There were no signs of any change when he looked into the actual painting, and yet there was no doubt that the whole expression had altered. It was not a mere fancy of his own. The thing was horribly apparent.

He threw himself into a chair, and began to think. Suddenly there flashed across his mind what he had said in Basil Hallward's studio the day the picture had been finished. Yes, he remembered it perfectly. He had uttered a mad wish that he himself might remain young, and the portrait grow old; that his own beauty might be untarnished, and the face on the canvas bear the burden of his passions and his sins; that the painted image might be seared with the lines of suffering and thought, and that he might keep all the delicate bloom and loveliness of his then just conscious boyhood. Surely his wish had not been fulfilled? Such things were impossible. It seemed monstrous even to think of them. And, yet, there was the picture before him, with the touch of cruelty in the mouth.

Cruelty! Had he been cruel? It was the girl's fault, not his. He had dreamed of her as a great artist, had given his love to her because he had thought her great. Then she had disappointed him. She had been shallow and unworthy. And, yet, a feeling of infinite regret came over him, as he thought of her lying at his feet sobbing like a little child.

7. Dorian's country estate.

He remembered with what callousness he had watched her. Why had he been made like that? Why had such a soul been given to him? But he had suffered also. During the three terrible hours that the play had lasted, he had lived centuries of pain, æon upon æon of torture. His life was well worth hers. She had marred him for a moment, if he had wounded her for an age. Besides, women were better suited to bear sorrow than men. They lived on their emotions. They only thought of their emotions. When they took lovers, it was merely to have some one with whom they could have scenes. Lord Henry had told him that, and Lord Henry knew what women were. Why should he trouble about Sibyl Vane? She was nothing to him now.

But the picture? What was he to say of that? It held the secret of his life, and told his story. It had taught him to love his own beauty. Would it teach him to loathe his own soul? Would he ever look at it again?

No; it was merely an illusion wrought on the troubled senses. The horrible night that he had passed had left phantoms behind it. Suddenly there had fallen upon his brain that tiny scarlet speck that makes men mad. The picture had not changed. It was folly to think so.

Yet it was watching him, with its beautiful marred face and its cruel smile. Its bright hair gleamed in the early sunlight. Its blue eyes met his own. A sense of infinite pity, not for himself, but for the painted image of himself, came over him. It had altered already, and would alter more. Its gold would wither into grey. Its red and white roses would die. For every sin that he committed, a stain would fleck and wreck its fairness. But he would not sin. The picture, changed or unchanged, would be to him the visible emblem of conscience. He would resist temptation. He would not see Lord Henry any more—would not, at any rate, listen to those subtle poisonous theories that in Basil Hallward's garden had first stirred within him the passion for impossible things. He would go back to Sibyl Vane, make her amends, marry her, try to love her again. Yes, it was his duty to do so. She must have suffered more than he had. Poor child! He had been selfish and cruel to her. The fascination that she had exercised over him would return. They would be happy together. His life with her would be beautiful and pure.

He got up from his chair, and drew a large screen right in front of the portrait, shuddering as he glanced at it. "How horrible!" he murmured to himself, and he walked across to the window and opened it. When he stepped out on to the grass, he drew a deep breath. The fresh morning air seemed to drive away all his sombre passions. He thought only of Sibyl. A faint echo of his love came back to him. He repeated her name over and over again. The birds that were singing in the dew-drenched garden seemed to be telling the flowers about her.

Chapter VIII[1]

It was long past noon when he awoke. His valet had crept several times on tiptoe into the room to see if he was stirring, and had wondered what made his young master sleep so late. Finally his bell sounded, and Victor came in softly with a cup of tea, and a pile of letters, on a small tray of old Sèvres china,[2] and drew back the olive-satin curtains, with their shimmering blue lining, that hung in front of the three tall windows.

"Monsieur has well slept this morning," he said, smiling.

"What o'clock is it, Victor?" asked Dorian Gray, drowsily.

"One hour and a quarter, Monsieur."

How late it was! He sat up, and, having sipped some tea, turned over his letters. One of them was from Lord Henry, and had been brought by hand that morning. He hesitated for a moment, and then put it aside. The others he opened listlessly. They contained the usual collection of cards, invitations to dinner, tickets for private views, programmes of charity concerts, and the like, that are showered on fashionable young men every morning during the season. There was a rather heavy bill, for a chased silver Louis-Quinze[3] toilet-set, that he had not yet had the courage to send on to his guardians, who were extremely old-fashioned people and did not realize that we live in an age when unnecessary things are our only necessities; and there were several very courteously worded communications from Jermyn Street[4] money-lenders offering to advance any sum of money at a moment's notice and at the most reasonable rates of interest.

After about ten minutes he got up, and, throwing on an elaborate dressing-gown of silk-embroidered cashmere wool, passed into the onyx-paved bathroom. The cool water refreshed him after his long sleep. He seemed to have forgotten all that he had gone through. A dim sense of having taken part in some strange tragedy came to him once or twice, but there was the unreality of a dream about it.

As soon as he was dressed, he went into the library and sat down to a light French breakfast,[5] that had been laid out for him on a small round table close to the open window. It was an exquisite day. The warm air seemed laden with spices. A bee flew in, and buzzed

---

1. This was chapter 6 in the *Lippincott's Magazine* edition.
2. An elegant French porcelain made in Sèvres, a Paris suburb, since the eighteenth century.
3. Describes the rococo style popular in mid-eighteenth-century France during the reign of Louis XV, denoting elegance, fantasy, and luxury. *Chased:* A piece ornamented with embossed work or engraved in relief.
4. Located in the city of Westminster in London, close to Piccadilly Circus.
5. Probably coffee and pastry or toast.

round the blue-dragon bowl that, filled with sulphur-yellow roses, stood before him. He felt perfectly happy.

Suddenly his eye fell on the screen that he had placed in front of the portrait, and he started.

"Too cold for Monsieur?" asked his valet, putting an omelette on the table. "I shut the window?"

Dorian shook his head. "I am not cold," he murmured.

Was it all true? Had the portrait really changed? Or had it been simply his own imagination that had made him see a look of evil where there had been a look of joy? Surely a painted canvas could not alter? The thing was absurd. It would serve as a tale to tell Basil some day. It would make him smile.

And, yet, how vivid was his recollection of the whole thing! First in the dim twilight, and then in the bright dawn, he had seen the touch of cruelty round the warped lips. He almost dreaded his valet leaving the room. He knew that when he was alone he would have to examine the portrait. He was afraid of certainty. When the coffee and cigarettes had been brought and the man turned to go, he felt a wild desire to tell him to remain. As the door was closing behind him he called him back. The man stood waiting for his orders. Dorian looked at him for a moment. "I am not at home to any one, Victor," he said, with a sigh. The man bowed and retired.

Then he rose from the table, lit a cigarette, and flung himself down on a luxuriously-cushioned couch that stood facing the screen. The screen was an old one, of gilt Spanish leather, stamped and wrought with a rather florid Louis-Quatorze[6] pattern. He scanned it curiously, wondering if ever before it had concealed the secret of a man's life.

Should he move it aside, after all? Why not let it stay there? What was the use of knowing.? If the thing was true, it was terrible. If it was not true, why trouble about it? But what if, by some fate or deadlier chance, eyes other than his spied behind, and saw the horrible change? What should he do if Basil Hallward came and asked to look at his own picture? Basil would be sure to do that. No; the thing had to be examined, and at once. Anything would be better than this dreadful state of doubt.

He got up, and locked both doors. At least he would be alone when he looked upon the mask of his shame. Then he drew the screen aside, and saw himself face to face. It was perfectly true. The portrait had altered.

As he often remembered afterwards, and always with no small wonder, he found himself at first gazing at the portrait with a feeling

---

6. The china decoration is named for Louis XIV of France (1638–1715), called "The Sun King," who reigned seventy-two years. The pattern referenced was a border registered under that name by Spode, England's oldest pottery company, in December 1844.

of almost scientific interest. That such a change should have taken place was incredible to him. And yet it was a fact. Was there some subtle affinity between the chemical atoms, that shaped themselves into form and colour on the canvas, and the soul that was within him? Could it be that what that soul thought, they realized?—that what it dreamed, they made true? Or was there some other, more terrible reason? He shuddered, and felt afraid, and, going back to the couch, lay there, gazing at the picture in sickened horror.

One thing, however, he felt that it had done for him. It had made him conscious how unjust, how cruel, he had been to Sibyl Vane. It was not too late to make reparation for that. She could still be his wife. His unreal and selfish love would yield to some higher influence, would be transformed into some nobler passion, and the portrait that Basil Hallward had painted of him would be a guide to him through life, would be to him what holiness is to some, and conscience to others, and the fear of God to us all. There were opiates for remorse, drugs that could lull the moral sense to sleep. But here was a visible symbol of the degradation of sin. Here was an everpresent sign of the ruin men brought upon their souls.

Three o'clock struck, and four, and the half-hour rang its double chime, but Dorian Gray did not stir. He was trying to gather up the scarlet threads of life, and to weave them into a pattern; to find his way through the sanguine labyrinth of passion through which he was wandering. He did not know what to do, or what to think. Finally, he went over to the table and wrote a passionate letter to the girl he had loved, imploring her forgiveness, and accusing himself of madness. He covered page after page with wild words of sorrow, and wilder words of pain. There is a luxury in self-reproach. When we blame ourselves we feel that no one else has a right to blame us. It is the confession, not the priest, that gives us absolution. When Dorian had finished the letter, he felt that he had been forgiven.

Suddenly there came a knock to the door, and he heard Lord Henry's voice outside. "My dear boy, I must see you. Let me in at once. I can't bear your shutting yourself up like this."

He made no answer at first, but remained quite still. The knocking still continued, and grew louder. Yes, it was better to let Lord Henry in, and to explain to him the new life he was going to lead, to quarrel with him if it became necessary to quarrel, to part if parting was inevitable. He jumped up, drew the screen hastily across the picture, and unlocked the door.

"I am so sorry for it all, Dorian," said Lord Henry, as he entered. "But you must not think too much about it."

"Do you mean about Sibyl Vane?" asked the lad.

"Yes, of course," answered Lord Henry, sinking into a chair, and slowly pulling off his yellow gloves. "It is dreadful, from one point of view, but it was not your fault. Tell me, did you go behind and see her, after the play was over?"

"Yes."

"I felt sure you had. Did you make a scene with her?"

"I was brutal, Harry—perfectly brutal. But it is all right now. I am not sorry for anything that has happened. It has taught me to know myself better."

"Ah, Dorian, I am so glad you take it in that way! I was afraid I would find you plunged in remorse, and tearing that nice curly hair of yours."

"I have got through all that," said Dorian, shaking his head, and smiling. "I am perfectly happy now. I know what conscience is, to begin with. It is not what you told me it was. It is the divinest thing in us. Don't sneer at it, Harry, any more—at least not before me. I want to be good. I can't bear the idea of my soul being hideous."

"A very charming artistic basis for ethics, Dorian! I congratulate you on it. But how are you going to begin?"

"By marrying Sibyl Vane."

"Marrying Sibyl Vane!" cried Lord Henry, standing up, and looking at him in perplexed amazement. "But, my dear Dorian—"

"Yes, Harry, I know what you are going to say. Something dreadful about marriage. Don't say it. Don't ever say things of that kind to me again. Two days ago I asked Sibyl to marry me. I am not going to break my word to her. She is to be my wife."

"Your wife! Dorian! . . . Didn't you get my letter? I wrote to you this morning, and sent the note down, by my own man."

"Your letter? Oh, yes, I remember. I have not read it yet, Harry. I was afraid there might be something in it that I wouldn't like. You cut life to pieces with your epigrams."

"You know nothing then?"

"What do you mean?"

Lord Henry walked across the room, and, sitting down by Dorian Gray, took both his hands in his own, and held them tightly. "Dorian," he said, "my letter—don't be frightened—was to tell you that Sibyl Vane is dead."

A cry of pain broke from the lad's lips, and he leaped to his feet, tearing his hands away from Lord Henry's grasp. "Dead! Sibyl dead! It is not true! It is a horrible lie! How dare you say it?"

"It is quite true, Dorian," said Lord Henry, gravely. "It is in all the morning papers. I wrote down to you to ask you not to see any one till I came. There will have to be an inquest, of course, and you must not be mixed up in it. Things like that make a man fashionable in Paris. But in London people are so prejudiced. Here, one should never make one's *début* with a scandal. One should reserve that to give an interest to one's old age. I suppose they don't know your name at the theatre? If they don't, it is all right. Did any one see you going round to her room? That is an important point."

Dorian did not answer for a few moments. He was dazed with horror. Finally he stammered, in a stifled voice, "Harry, did you say an inquest? What did you mean by that? Did Sibyl—? Oh, Harry, I can't bear it! But be quick. Tell me everything at once."

"I have no doubt it was not an accident, Dorian, though it must be put in that way to the public. It seems that as she was leaving the theatre with her mother, about half-past twelve or so, she said she had forgotten something upstairs. They waited some time for her, but she did not come down again. They ultimately found her lying dead on the floor of her dressing-room. She had swallowed something by mistake, some dreadful thing they use at theatres. I don't know what it was, but it had either prussic acid or white lead in it. I should fancy it was prussic acid, as she seems to have died instantaneously."

"Harry, Harry, it is terrible!" cried the lad.

"Yes; it is very tragic, of course, but you must not get yourself mixed up in it. I see by *The Standard*[7] that she was seventeen. I should have thought she was almost younger than that. She looked such a child, and seemed to know so little about acting. Dorian, you mustn't let this thing get on your nerves. You must come and dine with me, and afterwards we will look in at the Opera. It is a Patti[8] night, and everybody will be there. You can come to my sister's box. She has got some smart women with her."

"So I have murdered Sibyl Vane," said Dorian Gray, half to himself—"murdered her as surely as if I had cut her little throat with a knife. Yet the roses are not less lovely for all that. The birds sing just as happily in my garden. And to-night I am to dine with you, and then go on to the Opera, and sup somewhere, I suppose, afterwards. How extraordinarily dramatic life is! If I had read all this in a book, Harry, I think I would have wept over it. Somehow, now that it has happened actually, and to me, it seems far too wonderful for tears. Here is the first passionate love-letter I have ever written in my life. Strange, that my first passionate love-letter should have been addressed to a dead girl. Can they feel, I wonder, those white silent people we call the dead? Sibyl! Can she feel, or know, or listen? Oh, Harry, how I loved her once! It seems years ago to me now. She was everything to me. Then came that dreadful night—was it really only last night?—when she played so badly, and my heart almost broke. She explained it all to me. It was terribly pathetic. But I was not moved a bit. I thought her shallow. Suddenly something happened

---

7. A politically conservative London morning newspaper.
8. Adelina Patti (1843–1919) was one of the most popular operatic sopranos of the period. Her performances were legendary.

that made me afraid. I can't tell you what it was, but it was terrible. I said I would go back to her. I felt I had done wrong. And now she is dead. My God! my God! Harry, what shall I do? You don't know the danger I am in, and there is nothing to keep me straight. She would have done that for me. She had no right to kill herself. It was selfish of her."

"My dear Dorian," answered Lord Henry, taking a cigarette from his case, and producing a gold-latten[9] matchbox, "the only way a woman can ever reform a man is by boring him so completely that he loses all possible interest in life. If you had married this girl you would have been wretched. Of course you would have treated her kindly. One can always be kind to people about whom one cares nothing. But she would have soon found out that you were absolutely indifferent to her. And when a woman finds that out about her husband, she either becomes dreadfully dowdy, or wears very smart bonnets that some other woman's husband has to pay for. I say nothing about the social mistake, which would have been abject, which, of course, I would not have allowed, but I assure you that in any case the whole thing would have been an absolute failure."

"I suppose it would," muttered the lad, walking up and down the room, and looking horribly pale. "But I thought it was my duty. It is not my fault that this terrible tragedy has prevented my doing what was right. I remember your saying once that there is a fatality about good resolutions—that they are always made too late. Mine certainly were."

"Good resolutions are useless attempts to interfere with scientific laws. Their origin is pure vanity. Their result is absolutely *nil*. They give us, now and then, some of those luxurious sterile emotions that have a certain charm for the weak. That is all that can be said for them. They are simply cheques that men draw on a bank where they have no account."

"Harry," cried Dorian Gray, coming over and sitting down beside him, "why is it that I cannot feel this tragedy as much as I want to? I don't think I am heartless. Do you?"

"You have done too many foolish things during the last fortnight to be entitled to give yourself that name, Dorian," answered Lord Henry, with his sweet, melancholy smile.

The lad frowned. "I don't like that explanation, Harry," he rejoined, "but I am glad you don't think I am heartless. I am nothing of the kind. I know I am not. And yet I must admit that this thing that has happened does not affect me as it should. It seems to me to be simply like a wonderful ending to a wonderful play. It has all the terrible beauty of a Greek tragedy, a tragedy in which I took a great part, but by which I have not been wounded."

9. Gold-plated or -foiled.

"It is an interesting question," said Lord Henry, who found an exquisite pleasure in playing on the lad's unconscious egotism—"an extremely interesting question. I fancy that the true explanation is this. It often happens that the real tragedies of life occur in such an inartistic manner that they hurt us by their crude violence, their absolute incoherence, their absurd want of meaning, their entire lack of style. They affect us just as vulgarity affects us. They give us an impression of sheer brute force, and we revolt against that. Sometimes, however, a tragedy that possesses artistic elements of beauty crosses our lives. If these elements of beauty are real, the whole thing simply appeals to our sense of dramatic effect. Suddenly we find that we are no longer the actors, but the spectators of the play. Or rather we are both. We watch ourselves, and the mere wonder of the spectacle enthralls us. In the present case, what is it that has really happened? Some one has killed herself for love of you. I wish that I had ever had such an experience. It would have made me in love with love for the rest of my life. The people who have adored me—there have not been very many, but there have been some—have always insisted on living on, long after I had ceased to care for them, or they to care for me. They have become stout and tedious, and when I meet them they go in at once for reminiscences. That awful memory of woman! What a fearful thing it is! And what an utter intellectual stagnation it reveals! One should absorb the colour of life, but one should never remember its details. Details are always vulgar."

"I must sow poppies[1] in my garden," sighed Dorian.

"There is no necessity," rejoined his companion. "Life has always poppies in her hands. Of course, now and then things linger. I once wore nothing but violets all through one season, as a form of artistic mourning for a romance that would not die. Ultimately, however, it did die. I forget what killed it. I think it was her proposing to sacrifice the whole world for me. That is always a dreadful moment. It fills one with the terror of eternity. Well—would you believe it?—a week ago, at Lady Hampshire's, I found myself seated at dinner next the lady in question, and she insisted on going over the whole thing again, and digging up the past, and raking up the future. I had buried my romance in a bed of asphodel.[2] She dragged it out again, and assured me that I had spoiled her life. I am bound to state that she ate an enormous dinner, so I did not feel any anxiety. But what a lack of taste she showed! The one charm of the past is that it is the past. But women never know when the curtain has fallen. They

---

1. Poppies symbolize forgetfulness and drugged sleep. Wilde changed this from "poppy" in *Lippincott's Magazine*. Flower symbolism, a familiar language to Victorians, is known today almost exclusively by florists.
2. Asphodel symbolizes death and the underworld.

always want a sixth act, and as soon as the interest of the play is entirely over they propose to continue it. If they were allowed their own way, every comedy would have a tragic ending, and every tragedy would culminate in a farce. They are charmingly artificial, but they have no sense of art. You are more fortunate than I am. I assure you, Dorian, that not one of the women I have known would have done for me what Sibyl Vane did for you. Ordinary women always console themselves. Some of them do it by going in for sentimental colours. Never trust a woman who wears mauve, whatever her age may be, or a woman over thirty-five who is fond of pink ribbons. It always means that they have a history. Others find a great consolation in suddenly discovering the good qualities of their husbands. They flaunt their conjugal felicity in one's face, as if it were the most fascinating of sins. Religion consoles some. Its mysteries have all the charm of a flirtation, a woman once told me; and I can quite understand it. Besides, nothing makes one so vain as being told that one is a sinner. Conscience makes egotists of us all.[3] Yes; there is really no end to the consolations that women find in modern life. Indeed, I have not mentioned the most important one."

"What is that, Harry?" said the lad, listlessly.

"Oh, the obvious consolation. Taking some one else's admirer when one loses one's own. In good society that always whitewashes a woman. But really, Dorian, how different Sibyl Vane must have been from all the women one meets! There is something to me quite beautiful about her death. I am glad I am living in a century when such wonders happen. They make one believe in the reality of the things we all play with, such as romance, passion, and love."

"I was terribly cruel to her. You forget that."

"I am afraid that women appreciate cruelty, downright cruelty, more than anything else. They have wonderfully primitive instincts. We have emancipated them, but they remain slaves looking for their masters, all the same. They love being dominated. I am sure you were splendid. I have never seen you really and absolutely angry, but I can fancy how delightful you looked. And, after all, you said something to me the day before yesterday that seemed to me at the time to be merely fanciful, but that I see now was absolutely true, and it holds the key to everything."

"What was that, Harry?"

"You said to me that Sibyl Vane represented to you all the heroines of romance—that she was Desdemona one night, and Ophelia the other; that if she died as Juliet, she came to life as Imogen."

---

3. This is a variation of Hamlet's lament "Thus conscience doth make cowards of us all" (*Hamlet* 3.1.84).

"She will never come to life again now," muttered the lad, burying his face in his hands.

"No, she will never come to life. She has played her last part. But you must think of that lonely death in the tawdry dressing-room simply as a strange lurid fragment from some Jacobean tragedy, as a wonderful scene from Webster, or Ford, or Cyril Tourneur.[4] The girl never really lived, and so she has never really died. To you at least she was always a dream, a phantom that flitted through Shakespeare's plays and left them lovelier for its presence, a reed through which Shakespeare's music sounded richer and more full of joy. The moment she touched actual life, she marred it, and it marred her, and so she passed away. Mourn for Ophelia, if you like. Put ashes on your head because Cordelia was strangled. Cry out against Heaven because the daughter of Brabantio died.[5] But don't waste your tears over Sibyl Vane. She was less real than they are."

There was a silence. The evening darkened in the room. Noiselessly, and with silver feet, the shadows crept in from the garden. The colours faded wearily out of things.

After some time Dorian Gray looked up. "You have explained me to myself, Harry," he murmured, with something of a sigh of relief. "I felt all that you have said, but somehow I was afraid of it, and I could not express it to myself. How well you know me! But we will not talk again of what has happened. It has been a marvellous experience. That is all. I wonder if life has still in store for me anything as marvellous."

"Life has everything in store for you, Dorian. There is nothing that you, with your extraordinary good looks, will not be able to do."

"But suppose, Harry, I became haggard, and old, and wrinkled? What then?"

"Ah, then," said Lord Henry, rising to go—"then, my dear Dorian, you would have to fight for your victories. As it is, they are brought to you. No, you must keep your good looks. We live in an age that reads too much to be wise, and that thinks too much to be beautiful. We cannot spare you. And now you had better dress, and drive down to the club. We are rather late, as it is."

"I think I shall join you at the Opera, Harry. I feel too tired to eat anything. What is the number of your sister's box?"

"Twenty-seven, I believe. It is on the grand tier. You will see her name on the door. But I am sorry you won't come and dine."

4. John Webster, John Ford, and Cyril Tourneur were English playwrights whose works dramatized passion and violence. They flourished during the Jacobean period (during the reign of James I of England, in the early seventeenth century).
5. Lord Henry refers to the death of Desdemona in Shakespeare's *Othello*.

"I don't feel up to it," said Dorian, listlessly. "But I am awfully obliged to you for all that you have said to me. You are certainly my best friend. No one has ever understood me as you have."

"We are only at the beginning of our friendship, Dorian," answered Lord Henry, shaking him by the hand. "Good-bye. I shall see you before nine-thirty, I hope. Remember, Patti is singing."

As he closed the door behind him, Dorian Gray touched the bell, and in a few minutes Victor appeared with the lamps and drew the blinds down. He waited impatiently for him to go. The man seemed to take an interminable time over everything.

As soon as he had left, he rushed to the screen and drew it back. No; there was no further change in the picture. It had received the news of Sibyl Vane's death before he had known of it himself. It was conscious of the events of life as they occurred. The vicious cruelty that marred the fine lines of the mouth had, no doubt, appeared at the very moment that the girl had drunk the poison, whatever it was. Or was it indifferent to results? Did it merely take cognizance of what passed within the soul? He wondered, and hoped that some day he would see the change taking place before his very eyes, shuddering as he hoped it.

Poor Sibyl! what a romance it had all been! She had often mimicked death on the stage. Then Death himself had touched her, and taken her with him. How had she played that dreadful last scene? Had she cursed him, as she died? No; she had died for love of him, and love would always be a sacrament to him now. She had atoned for everything, by the sacrifice she had made of her life. He would not think any more of what she had made him go through, on that horrible night at the theatre. When he thought of her, it would be as a wonderful tragic figure sent on to the world's stage to show the supreme reality of Love. A wonderful tragic figure? Tears came to his eyes as he remembered her childlike look and winsome fanciful ways and shy tremulous grace. He brushed them away hastily, and looked again at the picture.

He felt that the time had really come for making his choice. Or had his choice already been made? Yes, life had decided that for him—life, and his own infinite curiosity about life. Eternal youth, infinite passion, pleasures subtle and secret, wild joys and wilder sins—he was to have all these things. The portrait was to bear the burden of his shame: that was all.

A feeling of pain crept over him as he thought of the desecration that was in store for the fair face on the canvas. Once, in boyish mockery of Narcissus he had kissed, or feigned to kiss, those painted lips that now smiled so cruelly at him. Morning after morning he had sat before the portrait wondering at its beauty, almost enamoured of it, as it seemed to him at times. Was it to alter now with every mood to which he yielded? Was it to become a monstrous and loathsome thing, to be hidden away in a locked room, to be shut out from the sunlight that had so often touched to brighter gold the waving wonder of its hair? The pity of it! the pity of it![6]

For a moment he thought of praying that the horrible sympathy that existed between him and the picture might cease. It had changed in answer to a prayer; perhaps in answer to a prayer it might remain unchanged. And, yet, who, that knew anything about Life, would surrender the chance of remaining always young, however fantastic that chance might be, or with what fateful consequences it might be fraught? Besides, was it really under his control? Had it indeed been prayer that had produced the substitution? Might there not be some curious scientific reason for it all? If thought could exercise its influence upon a living organism, might not thought exercise an influence upon dead and inorganic things? Nay, without thought or conscious desire, might not things external to ourselves vibrate in unison with our moods and passions, atom calling to atom in secret love or strange affinity? But the reason was of no importance. He would never again tempt by a prayer any terrible power. If the picture was to alter, it was to alter. That was all. Why inquire too closely into it?

For there would be a real pleasure in watching it. He would be able to follow his mind into its secret places. This portrait would be to him the most magical of mirrors. As it had revealed to him his own body, so it would reveal to him his own soul. And when winter came upon it, he would still be standing where spring trembles on the verge of summer. When the blood crept from its face, and left behind a pallid mask of chalk with leaden eyes, he would keep the glamour of boyhood. Not one blossom of his loveliness would ever fade. Not one pulse of his life would ever weaken. Like the gods of the Greeks, he would be strong, and fleet, and joyous. What did it matter what happened to the coloured image on the canvas? He would be safe. That was everything.

He drew the screen back into its former place in front of the picture, smiling as he did so, and passed into his bedroom, where his valet was already waiting for him. An hour later he was at the Opera, and Lord Henry was leaning over his chair.

6. Key words of Othello's remark to Iago in *Othello* 4.1.195–96.

Chapter IX[1]

As he was sitting at breakfast next morning, Basil Hallward was shown into the room.

"I am so glad I have found you, Dorian," he said gravely. "I called last night, and they told me you were at the Opera. Of course I knew that was impossible. But I wish you had left word where you had really gone to. I passed a dreadful evening, half afraid that one tragedy might be followed by another. I think you might have telegraphed for me when you heard of it first. I read of it quite by chance in a late edition of *The Globe*,[2] that I picked up at the club. I came here at once, and was miserable at not finding you. I can't tell you how heart-broken I am about the whole thing. I know what you must suffer. But where were you? Did you go down and see the girl's mother? For a moment I thought of following you there. They gave the address in the paper. Somewhere in the Euston Road, isn't it? But I was afraid of intruding upon a sorrow that I could not lighten. Poor woman! What a state she must be in! And her only child, too! What did she say about it all?"

"My dear Basil, how do I know?" murmured Dorian Gray, sipping some pale-yellow wine from a delicate gold-beaded bubble of Venetian glass, and looking dreadfully bored. "I was at the Opera. You should have come on there. I met Lady Gwendolen, Harry's sister, for the first time. We were in her box. She is perfectly charming; and Patti sang divinely. Don't talk about horrid subjects. If one doesn't talk about a thing, it has never happened. It is simply expression, as Harry says, that gives reality to things. I may mention that she was not the woman's only child. There is a son, a charming fellow, I believe. But he is not on the stage. He is a sailor, or something. And now, tell me about yourself and what you are painting."

"You went to the Opera?" said Hallward, speaking very slowly, and with a strained touch of pain in his voice. "You went to the Opera while Sibyl Vane was lying dead in some sordid lodging? You can talk to me of other women being charming, and of Patti singing divinely, before the girl you loved has even the quiet of a grave to sleep in? Why, man, there are horrors in store for that little white body of hers!"

"Stop, Basil! I won't hear it!" cried Dorian leaping to his feet. "You must not tell me about things. What is done is done. What is past is past."

"You call yesterday the past?"

---

1. This was chapter 7 in the *Lippincott's Magazine* edition.
2. An evening newspaper, also read by Sherlock Holmes.

"What has the actual lapse of time got to do with it? It is only shallow people who require years to get rid of an emotion. A man who is master of himself can end a sorrow as easily as he can invent a pleasure. I don't want to be at the mercy of my emotions. I want to use them, to enjoy them, and to dominate them."

"Dorian, this is horrible! Something has changed you completely. You look exactly the same wonderful boy who, day after day, used to come down to my studio to sit for his picture. But you were simple, natural, and affectionate then. You were the most unspoiled creature in the whole world. Now, I don't know what has come over you. You talk as if you had no heart, no pity in you. It is all Harry's influence. I see that."

The lad flushed up, and, going to the window, looked out for a few moments on the green, flickering, sun-lashed garden. "I owe a great deal to Harry, Basil," he said, at last—"more than I owe to you. You only taught me to be vain."

"Well, I am punished for that, Dorian—or shall be some day."

"I don't know what you mean, Basil," he exclaimed, turning round. "I don't know what you want. What do you want?"

"I want the Dorian Gray I used to paint," said the artist, sadly.

"Basil," said the lad, going over to him, and putting his hand on his shoulder, "you have come too late. Yesterday when I heard that Sibyl Vane had killed herself—"

"Killed herself! Good heavens! is there no doubt about that?" cried Hallward, looking up at him with an expression of horror.

"My dear Basil! Surely you don't think it was a vulgar accident? Of course she killed herself."

The elder man buried his face in his hands. "How fearful," he muttered, and a shudder ran through him.

"No," said Dorian Gray, "there is nothing fearful about it. It is one of the great romantic tragedies of the age. As a rule, people who act lead the most commonplace lives. They are good husbands, or faithful wives, or something tedious. You know what I mean—middle-class virtue, and all that kind of thing. How different Sibyl was! She lived her finest tragedy. She was always a heroine. The last night she played—the night you saw her—she acted badly because she had known the reality of love. When she knew its unreality, she died, as Juliet might have died. She passed again into the sphere of art. There is something of the martyr about her. Her death has all the pathetic uselessness of martyrdom, all its wasted beauty. But, as I was saying, you must not think I have not suffered. If you had come in yesterday at a particular moment—about half-past five, perhaps, or a quarter to six—you would have found me in tears. Even Harry, who was here, who brought me the news, in fact, had no idea what I was going through. I suffered immensely. Then it passed away.

I cannot repeat an emotion. No one can, except sentimentalists. And you are awfully unjust, Basil. You come down here to console me. That is charming of you. You find me consoled, and you are furious. How like a sympathetic person! You remind me of a story Harry told me about a certain philanthropist who spent twenty years of his life in trying to get some grievance redressed, or some unjust law altered—I forget exactly what it was. Finally he succeeded, and nothing could exceed his disappointment. He had absolutely nothing to do, almost died of *ennui*,[3] and became a confirmed misanthrope. And besides, my dear old Basil, if you really want to console me, teach me rather to forget what has happened, or to see it from a proper artistic point of view. Was it not Gautier who used to write about *la consolation des arts*?[4] I remember picking up a little vellum-covered book in your studio one day and chancing on that delightful phrase. Well, I am not like that young man you told me of when we were down at Marlow[5] together, the young man who used to say that yellow satin could console one for all the miseries of life. I love beautiful things that one can touch and handle. Old brocades, green bronzes, lacquer-work, carved ivories, exquisite surroundings, luxury pomp, there is much to be got from all these. But the artistic temperament that they create, or at any rate reveal, is still more to me. To become the spectator of one's own life, as Harry says, is to escape the suffering of life. I know you are surprised at my talking to you like this. You have not realized how I have developed. I was a schoolboy when you knew me. I am a man now. I have new passions, new thoughts, new ideas. I am different, but you must not like me less. I am changed, but you must always be my friend. Of course I am very fond of Harry. But I know that you are better than he is. You are not stronger—you are too much afraid of life—but you are better. And how happy we used to be together! Don't leave me, Basil, and don't quarrel with me. I am what I am. There is nothing more to be said."

The painter felt strangely moved. The lad was infinitely dear to him, and his personality had been the great turning-point in his art. He could not bear the idea of reproaching him any more. After all, his indifference was probably merely a mood that would pass away. There was so much in him that was good, so much in him that was noble.

"Well, Dorian," he said at length, with a sad smile, "I won't speak to you again about this horrible thing, after to-day. I only trust your

---

3. Weariness of spirit (French).
4. Théophile Gautier (1811–1872), French poet and novelist, one of the founders of Aestheticism in Europe and originator of the phrase "art for art's sake."
5. A historic town on the River Thames, about thirty miles west of London.

name won't be mentioned in connection with it. The inquest is to take place this afternoon. Have they summoned you?"

Dorian shook his head, and a look of annoyance passed over his face at the mention of the word "inquest." There was something so crude and vulgar about everything of the kind. "They don't know my name," he answered.

"But surely she did?"

"Only my Christian name,[6] and that I am quite sure she never mentioned to any one. She told me once that they were all rather curious to learn who I was, and that she invariably told them my name was Prince Charming. It was pretty of her. You must do me a drawing of Sibyl, Basil. I should like to have something more of her than the memory of a few kisses and some broken pathetic words."

"I will try and do something, Dorian, if it would please you. But you must come and sit to me yourself again. I can't get on without you."

"I can never sit to you again, Basil. It is impossible!" he exclaimed, starting back.

The painter stared at him. "My dear boy, what nonsense!" he cried. "Do you mean to say you don't like what I did of you? Where is it? Why have you pulled the screen in front of it? Let me look at it. It is the best thing I have ever done. Do take the screen away, Dorian. It is simply disgraceful of your servant hiding my work like that. I felt the room looked different as I came in."

"My servant has nothing to do with it, Basil. You don't imagine I let him arrange my room for me? He settles my flowers for me sometimes—that is all. No; I did it myself. The light was too strong on the portrait."

"Too strong! Surely not, my dear fellow? It is an admirable place for it. Let me see it." And Hallward walked towards the corner of the room.

A cry of terror broke from Dorian Gray's lips, and he rushed between the painter and the screen. "Basil," he said, looking very pale, "you must not look at it. I don't wish you to."

"Not look at my own work! you are not serious. Why shouldn't I look at it?" exclaimed Hallward, laughing.

"If you try to look at it, Basil, on my word of honour I will never speak to you again as long as I live. I am quite serious. I don't offer any explanation, and you are not to ask for any. But, remember, if you touch this screen, everything is over between us."

Hallward was thunderstruck. He looked at Dorian Gray in absolute amazement. He had never seen him like this before. The lad was actually pallid with rage. His hands were clenched, and the

6. One's first, or given, name.

pupils of his eyes were like disks of blue fire. He was trembling all over.

"Dorian!"

"Don't speak!"

"But what is the matter? Of course I won't look at it if you don't want me to," he said, rather coldly, turning on his heel, and going over towards the window. "But, really, it seems rather absurd that I shouldn't see my own work, especially as I am going to exhibit it in Paris in the autumn. I shall probably have to give it another coat of varnish before that, so I must see it some day, and why not to-day?"

"To exhibit it! You want to exhibit it?" exclaimed Dorian Gray, a strange sense of terror creeping over him. Was the world going to be shown his secret? Were people to gape at the mystery of his life? That was impossible. Something—he did not know what—had to be done at once.

"Yes; I don't suppose you will object to that. Georges Petit is going to collect all my best pictures for a special exhibition in the Rue de Sèze,[7] which will open the first week in October. The portrait will only be away a month. I should think you could easily spare it for that time. In fact, you are sure to be out of town. And if you keep it always behind a screen, you can't care much about it."

Dorian Gray passed his hand over his forehead. There were beads of perspiration there. He felt that he was on the brink of a horrible danger. "You told me a month ago that you would never exhibit it," he cried. "Why have you changed your mind? You people who go in for being consistent have just as many moods as others have. The only difference is that your moods are rather meaningless. You can't have forgotten that you assured me most solemnly that nothing in the world would induce you to send it to any exhibition. You told Harry exactly the same thing." He stopped suddenly, and a gleam of light came into his eyes. He remembered that Lord Henry had said to him once, half seriously and half in jest, "If you want to have a strange quarter of an hour, get Basil to tell you why he won't exhibit your picture. He told me why he wouldn't, and it was a revelation to me." Yes, perhaps Basil, too, had his secret. He would ask him and try.

"Basil," he said, coming over quite close, and looking him straight in the face, "we have each of us a secret. Let me know yours, and I shall tell you mine. What was your reason for refusing to exhibit my picture?"

The painter shuddered in spite of himself. "Dorian, if I told you, you might like me less than you do, and you would certainly laugh

---

7. Petit founded a popular gallery there in 1882, famous for its association with the French Impressionist painters.

at me. I could not bear your doing either of those two things. If you wish me never to look at your picture again, I am content. I have always you to look at. If you wish the best work I have ever done to be hidden from the world, I am satisfied. Your friendship is dearer to me than any fame or reputation."

"No, Basil, you must tell me," insisted Dorian Gray. "I think I have a right to know." His feeling of terror had passed away, and curiosity had taken its place. He was determined to find out Basil Hallward's mystery.

"Let us sit down, Dorian," said the painter, looking troubled. "Let us sit down. And just answer me one question. Have you noticed in the picture something curious?—something that probably at first did not strike you, but that revealed itself to you suddenly?"

"Basil!" cried the lad, clutching the arms of his chair with trembling hands, and gazing at him with wild startled eyes.

"I see you did. Don't speak. Wait till you hear what I have to say. Dorian, from the moment I met you, your personality had the most extraordinary influence over me. I was dominated, soul, brain, and power by you. You became to me the visible incarnation of that unseen ideal whose memory haunts us artists like an exquisite dream. I worshipped you. I grew jealous of every one to whom you spoke. I wanted to have you all to myself. I was only happy when I was with you. When you were away from me you were still present in my art. . . . Of course I never let you know anything about this. It would have been impossible. You would not have understood it. I hardly understood it myself. I only knew that I had seen perfection face to face, and that the world had become wonderful to my eyes— too wonderful, perhaps, for in such mad worships there is peril, the peril of losing them, no less than the peril of keeping them. . . . Weeks and weeks went on, and I grew more and more absorbed in you. Then came a new development. I had drawn you as Paris in dainty armour, and as Adonis with huntsman's cloak and polished boar-spear. Crowned with heavy lotus-blossoms you had sat on the prow of Adrian's barge,[8] gazing across the green turbid Nile. You had leant over the still pool of some Greek woodland, and seen in the water's silent silver the marvel of your own face. And it had all been what art should be, unconscious, ideal, and remote. One day, a fatal day I sometimes think, I determined to paint a wonderful portrait of you as you actually are, not in the costume of dead ages, but in your own dress and in your own time. Whether it was the Realism[9] of the method, or the mere wonder of your own personality,

8. Antinous, male companion of the emperor Hadrian (here Adrian) of Rome, drowned in the Nile in 130 CE, presumably off one of the emperor's ornately decorated barges.
9. Close resemblance to what is real; fidelity of representation, rendering the precise details of the real thing or scene. In reference to art and literature, sometimes used as

thus directly presented to me without mist or veil, I cannot tell. But I know that as I worked at it, every flake and film of colour seemed to me to reveal my secret. I grew afraid that others would know of my idolatry. I felt, Dorian, that I had told too much, that I had put too much of myself into it. Then it was that I resolved never to allow the picture to be exhibited. You were a little annoyed; but then you did not realize all that it meant to me. Harry, to whom I talked about it, laughed at me. But I did not mind that. When the picture was finished, and I sat alone with it, I felt that I was right. . . . Well, after a few days the thing left my studio, and as soon as I had got rid of the intolerable fascination of its presence it seemed to me that I had been foolish in imagining that I had seen anything in it, more than that you were extremely good-looking and that I could paint. Even now I cannot help feeling that it is a mistake to think that the passion one feels in creation is ever really shown in the work one creates. Art is always more abstract than we fancy. Form and colour tell us of form and colour—that is all. It often seems to me that art conceals the artist far more completely than it ever reveals him. And so when I got this offer from Paris I determined to make your portrait the principal thing in my exhibition. It never occurred to me that you would refuse. I see now that you were right. The picture cannot be shown. You must not be angry with me, Dorian, for what I have told you. As I said to Harry, once, you are made to be worshipped."

Dorian Gray drew a long breath. The colour came back to his cheeks, and a smile played about his lips. The peril was over. He was safe for the time. Yet he could not help feeling infinite pity for the painter who had just made this strange confession to him, and wondered if he himself would ever be so dominated by the personality of a friend. Lord Henry had the charm of being very dangerous. But that was all. He was too clever and too cynical to be really fond of. Would there ever be some one who would fill him with a strange idolatry? Was that one of the things that life had in store?

"It is extraordinary to me, Dorian," said Hallward, "that you should have seen this in the portrait. Did you really see it?"

"I saw something in it," he answered, "something that seemed to me very curious."

"Well, you don't mind my looking at the thing now?"

Dorian shook his head. "You must not ask me that, Basil. I could not possibly let you stand in front of that picture."

"You will some day, surely?"

---

a term of commendation, when precision and vividness of detail are regarded as a merit, and sometimes unfavorably contrasted with idealized description or representation. It has often been used with the implication that the details are of an unpleasant or sordid character.

"Never."

"Well, perhaps you are right. And now good-bye, Dorian. You have been the one person in my life who has really influenced my art. Whatever I have done that is good, I owe to you. Ah! you don't know what it cost me to tell you all that I have told you."

"My dear Basil," said Dorian, "what have you told me? Simply that you felt that you admired me too much. That is not even a compliment."

"It was not intended as a compliment. It was a confession. Now that I have made it, something seems to have gone out of me. Perhaps one should never put one's worship into words."

"It was a very disappointing confession."

"Why, what did you expect, Dorian? You didn't see anything else in the picture, did you? There was nothing else to see?"

"No; there was nothing else to see. Why do you ask? But you mustn't talk about worship. It is foolish. You and I are friends, Basil, and we must always remain so."

"You have got Harry," said the painter, sadly.

"Oh, Harry!" cried the lad, with a ripple of laughter. "Harry spends his days in saying what is incredible, and his evenings in doing what is improbable. Just the sort of life I would like to lead. But still I don't think I would go to Harry if I were in trouble. I would sooner go to you, Basil."

"You will sit to me again?"

"Impossible!"

"You spoil my life as an artist by refusing, Dorian. No man comes across two ideal things. Few come across one."

"I can't explain it to you, Basil, but I must never sit to you again. There is something fatal about a portrait. It has a life of its own. I will come and have tea with you. That will be just as pleasant."

"Pleasanter for you, I am afraid," murmured Hallward, regretfully. "And now good-bye. I am sorry you won't let me look at the picture once again. But that can't be helped. I quite understand what you feel about it."

As he left the room, Dorian Gray smiled to himself. Poor Basil! How little he knew of the true reason! And how strange it was that, instead of having been forced to reveal his own secret, he had succeeded, almost by chance, in wresting a secret from his friend! How much that strange confession explained to him! The painter's absurd fits of jealousy, his wild devotion, his extravagant panegyrics, his curious reticences—he understood them all now, and he felt sorry. There seemed to him to be something tragic in a friendship so coloured by romance.

He sighed, and touched the bell. The portrait must be hidden away at all costs. He could not run such a risk of discovery again. It had been mad of him to have allowed the thing to remain, even for an hour, in a room to which any of his friends had access.

Chapter X[1]

When his servant entered, he looked at him steadfastly, and wondered if he had thought of peering behind the screen. The man was quite impassive, and waited for his orders. Dorian lit a cigarette, and walked over to the glass and glanced into it. He could see the reflection of Victor's face perfectly. It was like a placid mask of servility. There was nothing to be afraid of, there. Yet he thought it best to be on his guard.

Speaking very slowly, he told him to tell the housekeeper that he wanted to see her, and then to go to the frame-maker and ask him to send two of his men round at once. It seemed to him that as the man left the room his eyes wandered in the direction of the screen. Or was that merely his own fancy?

After a few moments, in her black silk dress, with old-fashioned thread mittens on her wrinkled hands, Mrs. Leaf[2] bustled into the library. He asked her for the key of the schoolroom.

"The old schoolroom, Mr. Dorian?" she exclaimed. "Why, it is full of dust. I must get it arranged, and put straight before you go into it. It is not fit for you to see, sir. It is not, indeed."

"I don't want it put straight, Leaf. I only want the key."

"Well, sir, you'll be covered with cobwebs if you go into it. Why, it hasn't been opened for nearly five years, not since his lordship died."

He winced at the mention of his grandfather. He had hateful memories of him. "That does not matter," he answered. "I simply want to see the place—that is all. Give me the key."

"And here is the key, sir," said the old lady, going over the contents of her bunch with tremulously uncertain hands. "Here is the key. I'll have it off the bunch in a moment. But you don't think of living up there, sir, and you so comfortable here?"

"No, no," he cried, petulantly. "Thank you, Leaf. That will do."

She lingered for a few moments, and was garrulous over some detail of the household. He sighed, and told her to manage things as she thought best. She left the room, wreathed in smiles.

As the door closed, Dorian put the key in his pocket, and looked round the room. His eye fell on a large purple satin coverlet heavily

---

1. This was chapter 8 in the *Lippincott's Magazine* edition.
2. Wilde revised this and the following page heavily from the novella, greatly reducing the importance of "poor old Leaf" from the rich vignette of the original to a faded remnant.

embroidered with gold, a splendid piece of late seventeenth-century Venetian work that his grandfather had found in a convent near Bologna. Yes, that would serve to wrap the dreadful thing in. It had perhaps served often as a pall for the dead. Now it was to hide something that had a corruption of its own, worse than the corruption of death itself—something that would breed horrors and yet would never die. What the worm was to the corpse, his sins would be to the painted image on the canvas. They would mar its beauty, and eat away its grace. They would defile it, and make it shameful. And yet the thing would still live on. It would be always alive.

He shuddered, and for a moment he regretted that he had not told Basil the true reason why he had wished to hide the picture away. Basil would have helped him to resist Lord Henry's influence, and the still more poisonous influences that came from his own temperament. The love that he bore him—for it was really love—had nothing in it that was not noble and intellectual. It was not that mere physical admiration of beauty that is born of the senses, and that dies when the senses tire. It was such love as Michel Angelo had known, and Montaigne, and Winckelmann, and Shakespeare himself.[3] Yes, Basil could have saved him. But it was too late now. The past could always be annihilated. Regret, denial, or forgetfulness could do that. But the future was inevitable. There were passions in him that would find their terrible outlet, dreams that would make the shadow of their evil real.

He took up from the couch the great purple-and-gold texture that covered it, and, holding it in his hands, passed behind the screen. Was the face on the canvas viler than before? It seemed to him that it was unchanged; and yet his loathing of it was intensified. Gold hair, blue eyes, and rose-red lips—they all were there. It was simply the expression that had altered. That was horrible in its cruelty. Compared to what he saw in it of censure or rebuke, how shallow Basil's reproaches about Sibyl Vane had been!—how shallow, and of what little account! His own soul was looking out at him from the canvas and calling him to judgement. A look of pain came across him, and he flung the rich pall over the picture. As he did so, a knock came to the door. He passed out as his servant entered.

"The persons are here, Monsieur."

He felt that the man must be got rid of at once. He must not be allowed to know where the picture was being taken to. There was

---

3. The passage has both aesthetic and erotic implications. Michel Montaigne (1533–1592), French essayist, and Johann Winckelmann (1717–1768), German archeologist and art historian, two of Wilde's cultural heroes, were believed to be homosexuals, as were Michelangelo and, some allege, Shakespeare. Wilde wrote in nearly identical terms in "The Portrait of Mr. W. H." and gave an eloquent defense of "the love that dare not speak its name" at his second trial.

something sly about him, and he had thoughtful, treacherous eyes. Sitting down at the writing-table, he scribbled a note to Lord Henry, asking him to send him round something to read, and reminding him that they were to meet at eight-fifteen that evening.

"Wait for an answer," he said, handing it to him, "and show the men in here."

In two or three minutes there was another knock, and Mr. Hubbard himself, the celebrated frame-maker of South Audley Street,[4] came in with a somewhat rough-looking young assistant. Mr. Hubbard was a florid, red-whiskered little man, whose admiration for art was considerably tempered by the inveterate impecuniosity of most of the artists who dealt with him. As a rule, he never left his shop. He waited for people to come to him. But he always made an exception in favour of Dorian Gray. There was something about Dorian that charmed everybody. It was a pleasure even to see him.

"What can I do for you, Mr. Gray?" he said, rubbing his fat freckled hands. "I thought I would do myself the honour of coming round in person. I have just got a beauty of a frame, sir. Picked it up at a sale. Old Florentine. Came from Fonthill,[5] I believe. Admirably suited for a religious subject, Mr. Gray."

"I am so sorry you have given yourself the trouble of coming round, Mr. Hubbard. I shall certainly drop in and look at the frame—though I don't go in much at present for religious art—but to-day I only want a picture carried to the top of the house for me. It is rather heavy, so I thought I would ask you to lend me a couple of your men."

"No trouble at all, Mr. Gray. I am delighted to be of any service to you. Which is the work of art, sir?"

"This," replied Dorian, moving the screen back. "Can you move it, covering and all, just as it is? I don't want it to get scratched going upstairs."

"There will be no difficulty, sir," said the genial frame-maker, beginning, with the aid of his assistant, to unhook the picture from the long brass chains by which it was suspended. "And, now, where shall we carry it to, Mr. Gray?"

---

4. A street in Mayfair, near Hyde Park. *Mr. Hubbard:* "Mr. Ashton" in the magazine edition. In *In Good Company* (London: Lane, 1917), pp. 212–13, Coulson Kernahan, the Ward, Lock & Company editor with whom Wilde worked in preparing the novel version, gives the following account of a hoax Wilde played on him over the name change. He reports receiving a telegram from Wilde in Paris: "Terrible blunder in book, coming back specially. Stop all proofs! Wilde." Wilde arrived at the office apparently distracted: "'Ashton is a gentleman's name,' he spoke brokenly and wrung his hands as if in anguish, 'and I've given it—God forgive me—to a tradesman! It must be changed to Hubbard. Hubbard positively smells of the tradesman.'"
5. William Beckford, author of *Vathek* (1786), a Gothic novel much admired by Byron, built a suitably Gothic mansion in Fonthill Wood, in Wiltshire. The frame would have come from the auction of Fonthill furnishings at Christie's Auction House in 1822.

"I will show you the way, Mr. Hubbard, if you will kindly follow me. Or perhaps you had better go in front. I am afraid it is right at the top of the house. We will go up by the front staircase, as it is wider."

He held the door open for them, and they passed out into the hall and began the ascent. The elaborate character of the frame had made the picture extremely bulky, and now and then, in spite of the obsequious protests of Mr. Hubbard, who had the true tradesman's spirited dislike of seeing a gentleman doing anything useful, Dorian put his hand to it so as to help them.

"Something of a load to carry, sir," gasped the little man, when they reached the top landing. And he wiped his shiny forehead.

"I am afraid it is rather heavy," murmured Dorian, as he unlocked the door that opened into the room that was to keep for him the curious secret of his life and hide his soul from the eyes of men.

He had not entered the place for more than four years—not, indeed, since he had used it first as a play-room when he was a child, and then as a study when he grew somewhat older. It was a large, well-proportioned room, which had been specially built by the last Lord Kelso for the use of the little grandson whom, for his strange likeness to his mother, and also for other reasons, he had always hated and desired to keep at a distance. It appeared to Dorian to have but little changed. There was the huge Italian *cassone*,[6] with its fantastically-painted panels and its tarnished gilt mouldings, in which he had so often hidden himself as a boy. There the satinwood bookcase filled with his dog-eared schoolbooks. On the wall behind it was hanging the same ragged Flemish tapestry where a faded king and queen were playing chess in a garden, while a company of hawkers rode by, carrying hooded birds on their gauntleted wrists. How well he remembered it all! Every moment of his lonely childhood came back to him as he looked round. He recalled the stainless purity of his boyish life, and it seemed horrible to him that it was here the fatal portrait was to be hidden away. How little he had thought, in those dead days, of all that was in store for him!

But there was no other place in the house so secure from prying eyes as this. He had the key, and no one else could enter it. Beneath its purple pall, the face painted on the canvas could grow bestial, sodden, and unclean. What did it matter? No one could see it. He himself would not see it. Why should he watch the hideous corruption of his soul? He kept his youth—that was enough. And, besides, might not his nature grow finer, after all? There was no reason that the future should be so full of shame. Some love might come across his life, and purify him, and shield him from those sins that seemed

6. A large, ornamented Italian chest of the Renaissance.

to be already stirring in spirit and in flesh—those curious unpictured sins whose very mystery lent them their subtlety and their
charm. Perhaps, some day, the cruel look would have passed away
from the scarlet sensitive mouth, and he might show to the world
Basil Hallward's masterpiece.

No; that was impossible. Hour by hour, and week by week, the
thing upon the canvas was growing old. It might escape the hideousness of sin, but the hideousness of age was in store for it. The
cheeks would become hollow or flaccid. Yellow crow's feet would
creep round the fading eyes and make them horrible. The hair would
lose its brightness, the mouth would gape or droop, would be foolish or gross, as the mouths of old men are. There would be the wrinkled throat, the cold, blue-veined hands, the twisted body, that he
remembered in the grandfather who had been so stern to him in his
boyhood. The picture had to be concealed. There was no help for it.

"Bring it in, Mr. Hubbard, please," he said, wearily, turning round.
"I am sorry I kept you so long. I was thinking of something else."

"Always glad to have a rest, Mr. Gray," answered the frame-maker,
who was still gasping for breath. "Where shall we put it, sir?"

"Oh, anywhere. Here: this will do. I don't want to have it hung
up. Just lean it against the wall. Thanks."

"Might one look at the work of art, sir?"

Dorian started. "It would not interest you, Mr. Hubbard," he said,
keeping his eye on the man. He felt ready to leap upon him and fling
him to the ground if he dared to lift the gorgeous hanging that concealed the secret of his life. "I shan't trouble you any more now. I am
much obliged for your kindness in coming round."

"Not at all, not at all, Mr. Gray. Ever ready to do anything for you,
sir." And Mr. Hubbard tramped downstairs, followed by the assistant, who glanced back at Dorian with a look of shy wonder in his
rough uncomely face. He had never seen any one so marvellous.

When the sound of their footsteps had died away, Dorian locked
the door, and put the key in his pocket. He felt safe now. No one
would ever look upon the horrible thing. No eye but his would ever
see his shame.

On reaching the library he found that it was just after five o'clock,
and that the tea had been already brought up. On a little table of
dark perfumed wood thickly incrusted with nacre, a present from
Lady Radley, his guardian's wife, a pretty professional invalid, who
had spent the preceding winter in Cairo, was lying a note from Lord
Henry, and beside it was a book bound in yellow paper,[7] the cover

7. Dorian's yellow book is one of the most famous puzzles in literature. The case for identifying it as J.-K. Huysmans's *À Rebours* (1884) is weakened by the evidence of TS
   cancellations by Stoddart of the details of "The Secret of Raoul by Catulle Sarrazin."
   Details of the book make it clear that it was largely imaginary, as Wilde reported in

slightly torn and the edges soiled. A copy of the third edition of *The St. James's Gazette*[8] had been placed on the tea-tray. It was evident that Victor had returned. He wondered if he had met the men in the hall as they were leaving the house, and had wormed out of them what they had been doing. He would be sure to miss the picture—had no doubt missed it already, while he had been laying the tea-things. The screen had not been set back, and a blank space was visible on the wall. Perhaps some night he might find him creeping upstairs and trying to force the door of the room. It was a horrible thing to have a spy in one's house. He had heard of rich men who had been blackmailed all their lives by some servant who had read a letter, or overheard a conversation, or picked up a card with an address, or found beneath a pillow a withered flower or a shred of crumpled lace.

He sighed, and, having poured himself out some tea, opened Lord Henry's note. It was simply to say that he sent him round the evening paper, and a book that might interest him, and that he would be at the club at eight-fifteen. He opened *The St. James's* languidly, and looked through it. A red pencil-mark on the fifth page caught his eye. It drew attention to the following paragraph:

> "INQUEST ON AN ACTRESS.—An inquest was held this morning at the Bell Tavern, Hoxton Road, by Mr. Danby, the District Coroner, on the body of Sibyl Vane, a young actress recently engaged at the Royal Theatre, Holborn. A verdict of death by misadventure was returned. Considerable sympathy was expressed for the mother of the deceased, who was greatly affected during the giving of her own evidence, and that of Dr. Birrell, who had made the post-mortem examination of the deceased."

He frowned, and, tearing the paper in two went across the room and flung the pieces away. How ugly it all was! And how horribly real ugliness made things! He felt a little annoyed with Lord Henry for having sent him the report. And it was certainly stupid of him to have marked it with red pencil. Victor might have read it. The man knew more than enough English for that.

Perhaps he had read it, and had begun to suspect something. And, yet, what did it matter? What had Dorian Gray to do with Sibyl Vane's death? There was nothing to fear. Dorian Gray had not killed her.

His eye fell on the yellow book that Lord Henry had sent him. What was it, he wondered. He went towards the little pearl-coloured

---

Letters (313), although partly suggested by Huysmans's novel. The imaginary "Catulle Sarrazin" seems to have been taken from the names of two contemporary French men of letters known to Wilde: Gabriel Sarrazin, a critic, and Catulle Mendes, a poet.

8. *The St. James's Gazette* was one of the London papers read by people in Wilde's set. He wrote occasional reviews and debated the art and morality issue in its columns after the appearance of the *Lippincott's* edition; see pp. 357–67.

octagonal stand, that had always looked to him like the work of some
strange Egyptian bees that wrought in silver, and taking up the volume, flung himself into an arm-chair, and began to turn over the
leaves. After a few minutes he became absorbed. It was the strangest book that he had ever read. It seemed to him that in exquisite
raiment, and to the delicate sound of flutes, the sins of the world
were passing in dumb show before him. Things that he had dimly
dreamed of were suddenly made real to him. Things of which he had
never dreamed were gradually revealed.

It was a novel without a plot, and with only one character, being,
indeed, simply a psychological study of a certain young Parisian,
who spent his life trying to realize in the nineteenth century all the
passions and modes of thought that belonged to every century except
his own, and to sum up, as it were, in himself the various moods
through which the world-spirit had ever passed, loving for their mere
artificiality those renunciations that men have unwisely called virtue, as much as those natural rebellions that wise men still call
sin. The style in which it was written was that curious jewelled
style, vivid and obscure at once, full of *argot*[9] and of archaisms, of
technical expressions and of elaborate paraphrases, that character-
izes the work of some of the finest artists of the French school of
Symbolistes.[1] There were in it metaphors as monstrous as orchids,
and as subtle in colour. The life of the senses was described in the
terms of mystical philosophy. One hardly knew at times whether
one was reading the spiritual ecstasies of some mediæval saint or the
morbid confessions of a modern sinner. It was a poisonous book.
The heavy odour of incense seemed to cling about its pages and to
trouble the brain. The mere cadence of the sentences, the subtle
monotony of their music, so full as it was of complex refrains and
movements elaborately repeated, produced in the mind of the lad,
as he passed from chapter to chapter, a form of reverie, a malady of
dreaming, that made him unconscious of the falling day and creeping shadows.

Cloudless, and pierced by one solitary star, a copper-green sky
gleamed through the windows. He read on by its wan light till he
could read no more. Then, after his valet had reminded him several
times of the lateness of the hour, he got up, and, going into the next

9. The idiom or slang of a particular group or class, especially associated with lowlifes
(French).
1. Wilde changed this from *Lippincott's* "Decadents." The Symbolistes were mainly
French poets, such as Charles Baudelaire, Arthur Rimbaud, Stéphane Mallarmé, Paul
Verlaine, and Auguste Villiers de l'Isle-Adam; they also included writers such as Huysmans and Pierre Loüys, who combined strong romanticism with contempt for realism
and middle-class values. In art, the movement led to an emphasis on elusive and subtle
states of mind and feeling, conveyed by symbols as the language expressing realities
hidden behind appearances. Arthur Symons helped to popularize the movement in
England with *The Symbolist Movement in Literature* (1899).

room, placed the book on the little Florentine table that always stood at his bedside, and began to dress for dinner.

It was almost nine o'clock before he reached the club, where he found Lord Henry sitting alone, in the morning-room, looking very much bored.

"I am so sorry, Harry," he cried, "but really it is entirely your fault. That book you sent me so fascinated me that I forgot how the time was going."

"Yes: I thought you would like it," replied his host, rising from his chair.

"I didn't say I liked it, Harry. I said it fascinated me. There is a great difference."

"Ah, you have discovered that?" murmured Lord Henry. And they passed into the dining-room.

Chapter XI[1]

For years, Dorian Gray could not free himself from the influence of this book. Or perhaps it would be more accurate to say that he never sought to free himself from it. He procured from Paris no less than nine large-paper copies of the first edition, and had them bound in different colours, so that they might suit his various moods and the changing fancies of a nature over which he seemed, at times, to have almost entirely lost control. The hero, the wonderful young Parisian, in whom the romantic and the scientific temperaments were so strangely blended,[2] became to him a kind of prefiguring type of himself. And, indeed, the whole book seemed to him to contain the story of his own life, written before he had lived it.[3]

In one point he was more fortunate than the novel's fantastic hero. He never knew—never, indeed, had any cause to know—that somewhat grotesque dread of mirrors, and polished metal surfaces, and still water, which came upon the young Parisian so early in his life, and was occasioned by the sudden decay of a beauty that had once, apparently, been so remarkable. It was with an almost cruel joy—and perhaps in nearly every joy, as certainly in every pleasure, cruelty has its place—that he used to read the latter part of the book,

1. This was chapter 9 in the *Lippincott's Magazine* edition.
2. An allusion to the chapter on Leonardo da Vinci in Walter Pater's *The Renaissance* (see pp. 318–33).
3. A prophetic phrase for Wilde. After completing the *Lippincott's* edition, he was to meet two young men, either of whom might have posed for Dorian: John Gray and Lord Alfred Douglas. The Wilde-Douglas affair (see p. 381) proved ruinous for both men, sending Wilde to prison, bankruptcy, exile, and eventually death. Douglas remained under a cloud as a result of the affair; later in life, he wrote a series of attacks on Wilde, retractions, and apologies.

with its really tragic, if somewhat overemphasized, account of the sorrow and despair of one who had himself lost what in others, and the world, he had most dearly valued.

For the wonderful beauty that had so fascinated Basil Hallward, and many others besides him, seemed never to leave him. Even those who had heard the most evil things against him, and from time to time strange rumours about his mode of life crept through London and became the chatter of the clubs, could not believe anything to his dishonour when they saw him. He had always the look of one who had kept himself unspotted from the world. Men who talked grossly became silent when Dorian Gray entered the room. There was something in the purity of his face that rebuked them. His mere presence seemed to recall to them the memory of the innocence that they had tarnished. They wondered how one so charming and grace-ful as he was could have escaped the stain of an age that was at once sordid and sensual.

Often, on returning home from one of those mysterious and pro-longed absences that gave rise to such strange conjecture among those who were his friends, or thought that they were so, he him-self would creep upstairs to the locked room, open the door with the key that never left him now, and stand, with a mirror, in front of the portrait that Basil Hallward had painted of him, looking now at the evil and aging face on the canvas, and now at the fair young face that laughed back at him from the polished glass. The very sharpness of the contrast used to quicken his sense of pleasure. He grew more and more enamoured of his own beauty, more and more interested in the corruption of his own soul. He would examine with minute care, and sometimes with a monstrous and terrible delight, the hideous lines that seared the wrinkling forehead or crawled around the heavy sensual mouth, wondering sometimes which were the more horrible, the signs of sin or the signs of age. He would place his white hands beside the coarse bloated hands of the picture, and smile. He mocked the misshapen body and the failing limbs.

There were moments, indeed, at night, when, lying sleepless in his own delicately-scented chamber, or in the sordid room of the little ill-famed tavern near the Docks,[4] which, under an assumed name, and in disguise, it was his habit to frequent, he would think of the ruin he had brought upon his soul, with a pity that was all the more poignant because it was purely selfish. But moments such as these were rare. That curiosity about life which Lord Henry had first stirred in him, as they sat together in the garden of their friend,

---

4. This is an area of London of some notoriety, where a man of Dorian's reputation should not be seen, for it can bring immediate censure or even alienation from his social circle.

seemed to increase with gratification. The more he knew, the more he desired to know. He had mad hungers that grew more ravenous as he fed them.

Yet he was not really reckless, at any rate in his relations to society. Once or twice every month during the winter, and on each Wednesday evening[5] while the season lasted, he would throw open to the world his beautiful house and have the most celebrated musicians of the day to charm his guests with the wonders of their art. His little dinners, in the settling of which Lord Henry always assisted him, were noted as much for the careful selection and placing of those invited, as for the exquisite taste shown in the decoration of the table, with its subtle symphonic arrangements of exotic flowers, and embroidered cloths, and antique plate of gold and silver. Indeed, there were many, especially among the very young men, who saw, or fancied that they saw, in Dorian Gray the true realization of a type of which they had often dreamed in Eton or Oxford days, a type that was to combine something of the real culture of the scholar with all the grace and distinction and perfect manner of a citizen of the world. To them he seemed to be of the company of those whom Dante describes as having sought to "make themselves perfect by the worship of beauty." Like Gautier, he was one for whom "the visible world existed."[6]

And, certainly, to him Life itself was the first, the greatest, of the arts, and for it all the other arts seemed to be but a preparation. Fashion, by which what is really fantastic becomes for a moment universal, and Dandyism,[7] which, in its own way, is an attempt to assert the absolute modernity of beauty, had, of course, their fascination for him. His mode of dressing, and the particular styles that from time to time he affected, had their marked influence on the young exquisites of the Mayfair balls and Pall Mall club[8] windows, who copied him in everything that he did, and tried to reproduce the accidental charm of his graceful, though to him only half-serious, fopperies.

For, while he was but too ready to accept the position that was almost immediately offered to him on his coming of age, and found, indeed, a subtle pleasure in the thought that he might really become to the London of his own day what to imperial Neronian Rome

---

5. Wednesday was Wilde's at-home day—that is, an evening when he would entertain those who would care to call. The London social season ran from May through July.
6. The phrase is from Gautier's poem "Preface to 'Albertus'" (1832).
7. A philosophy of elegant manners and dress after the fashion of Beau Brummell (1778–1840), Dandyism takes a critical if witty view of contemporary mores and, more seriously, of the human condition. Its artificiality was intended as a protest against cant and self-righteousness.
8. One of the most famous and prestigious addresses in London, the street was celebrated for its private clubs.

the author of the "Satyricon"[9] once had been, yet in his inmost heart he desired to be something more than a mere *arbiter elegantiarum,* to be consulted on the wearing of a jewel, or the knotting of a necktie, or the conduct of a cane. He sought to elaborate some new scheme of life that would have its reasoned philosophy and its ordered principles, and find in the spiritualizing of the senses its highest realization.

The worship of the senses has often, and with much justice, been decried, men feeling a natural instinct of terror about passions and sensations that seem stronger than themselves, and that they are conscious of sharing with the less highly organized forms of existence. But it appeared to Dorian Gray that the true nature of the senses had never been understood, and that they had remained savage and animal merely because the world had sought to starve them into submission or to kill them by pain, instead of aiming at making them elements of a new spirituality, of which a fine instinct for beauty was to be the dominant characteristic. As he looked back upon man moving through History, he was haunted by a feeling of loss. So much had been surrendered! and to such little purpose! There had been mad wilful rejections, monstrous forms of self-torture and self-denial, whose origin was fear, and whose result was a degradation infinitely more terrible than that fancied degradation from which, in their ignorance, they had sought to escape, Nature, in her wonderful irony, driving out the anchorite to feed with the wild animals of the desert and giving to the hermit the beasts of the field as his companions.

Yes: there was to be, as Lord Henry had prophesied, a new Hedonism[1] that was to recreate life, and to save it from that harsh, uncomely puritanism that is having, in our own day, its curious revival. It was to have its service of the intellect, certainly; yet, it was never to accept any theory or system that would involve the sacrifice of any mode of passionate experience. Its aim, indeed, was to be experience itself, and not the fruits of experience, sweet or bitter as they might be. Of the asceticism that deadens the senses, as of the vulgar profligacy that dulls them, it was to know nothing. But it was to teach man to concentrate himself upon the moments of a life that is itself but a moment.

9. Petronius, author of the *Satyricon* (first century CE), which both satirized and was an instance of the decadence of Nero's Rome, was himself an intimate of the emperor. His title, "arbiter elegantiarum," was partly descriptive of his role as director of revels for the emperor and partly a pun on his name and fashion: Gaius Petronius Arbiter.
1. If what came before was the new Dandyism of the nineteenth-century aesthete, what follows here is Wilde's variation on the philosophy put forward by Pater in the Conclusion to *The Renaissance* (see pp. 333–36) and as the "New Cyrenaicism" in his *Marius the Epicurean* 2.9.

There are few of us who have not sometimes wakened before dawn, after one of those dreamless nights that make us almost enamoured of death, or one of those nights of horror and misshapen joy, when through the chambers of the brain sweep phantoms more terrible than reality itself, and instinct with that vivid life that lurks in all grotesques, and that lends to Gothic art[2] its enduring vitality, this art being, one might fancy, especially the art of those whose minds have been troubled with the malady of reverie. Gradually white fingers creep through the curtains, and they appear to tremble. In black fantastic shapes, dumb shadows crawl into the corners of the room, and crouch there. Outside, there is the stirring of birds among the leaves, or the sound of men going forth to their work, or the sigh and sob of the wind coming down from the hills, and wandering round the silent house, as though it feared to wake the sleepers, and yet must needs call forth sleep from her purple cave. Veil after veil of thin dusky gauze is lifted, and by degrees the forms and colours of things are restored to them, and we watch the dawn remaking the world in its antique pattern. The wan mirrors get back their mimic life. The flameless tapers stand where we had left them, and beside them lies the half-cut book that we had been studying, or the wired flower that we had worn at the ball, or the letter that we had been afraid to read, or that we had read too often. Nothing seems to us changed. Out of the unreal shadows of the night comes back the real life that we had known. We have to resume it where we had left off, and there steals over us a terrible sense of the necessity for the continuance of energy in the same wearisome round of stereotyped habits, or a wild longing, it may be, that our eyelids might open some morning upon a world that had been refashioned anew in the darkness for our pleasure, a world in which things would have fresh shapes and colours, and be changed, or have other secrets, a world in which the past would have little or no place, or survive, at any rate, in no conscious form of obligation or regret, the remembrance even of joy having its bitterness, and the memories of pleasure their pain.

It was the creation of such worlds as these that seemed to Dorian Gray to be the true object, or amongst the true objects, of life; and in his search for sensations that would be at once new and delightful, and possess that element of strangeness that is so essential to romance, he would often adopt certain modes of thought that he knew to be really alien to his nature, abandon himself to their subtle influences, and then, having, as it were, caught their colour and

---

2. A style of architecture prevalent in Western Europe from the twelfth to the sixteenth century, of which the chief characteristic is the pointed arch. Applied also to buildings, architectural details, and ornamentation.

satisfied his intellectual curiosity, leave them with that curious indifference that is not incompatible with a real ardour of temperament, and that indeed, according to certain modern psychologists, is often a condition of it.[3]

It was rumoured of him once that he was about to join the Roman Catholic communion;[4] and certainly the Roman ritual had always a great attraction for him. The daily sacrifice, more awful really than all the sacrifices of the antique world, stirred him as much by its superb rejection of the evidence of the senses as by the primitive simplicity of its elements and the eternal pathos of the human tragedy that it sought to symbolize. He loved to kneel down on the cold marble pavement, and watch the priest, in his stiff flowered dalmatic, slowly and with white hands moving aside the veil of the tabernacle, or raising aloft the jewelled lantern-shaped monstrance[5] with that pallid wafer that at times, one would fain think, is indeed the "*paniscælestis*," the bread of angels, or, robed in the garments of the Passion of Christ, breaking the Host into the chalice, and smiting his breast for his sins. The fuming censers, that the grave boys, in their lace and scarlet, tossed into the air like great gilt flowers, had their subtle fascination for him. As he passed out, he used to look with wonder at the black confessionals, and long to sit in the dim shadow of one of them and listen to men and women whispering through the worn grating the true story of their lives.

But he never fell into the error of arresting his intellectual development by any formal acceptance of creed or system, or of mistaking, for a house in which to live, an inn that is but suitable for the sojourn of a night, or for a few hours of a night in which there are no stars and the moon is in travail. Mysticism,[6] with its marvellous power of making common things strange to us, and the subtle antinomianism[7] that always seems to accompany it, moved

---

3. The reference is possibly to Wilhelm Wundt (1832–1920), Herbert Spencer (1820–1903), and William James (1842–1910), German, English, and American psychologists, whose influence on the new science was definitive—although less well known than that of the Austrian psychoanalyst Sigmund Freud (1856–1939)—and whose ideas are reflected in many of the meditations of Henry, Dorian, and the narrator on the relations among psychology, physiology, and morals.
4. After flirting with conversion for nearly forty years, Wilde was received into the Catholic Church on his deathbed. Many Decadents were similarly attracted to Catholicism.
5. An ornately decorated metal display stand for the consecrated host used in Roman Catholic liturgy for benedictions, processionals, and adoration vigils. An apparent confusion between consecration of the host during Mass and benediction led Wilde to substitute a vestment appropriate to the former (dalmatic) for one proper to the later (cope). A dalmatic is an outer garment, usually embroidered, having wide sleeves, worn at Mass by a deacon, abbot, bishop, or cardinal.
6. The belief in the possibility of union with or absorption into God by means of contemplation and self-surrender; also the belief in or devotion to the spiritual apprehension of truths inaccessible to the intellect.
7. An unorthodox belief of certain Christians that they are freed from the restraints of moral law by virtue of grace. By extension, it is used to refer to those who rejected moral law and church teaching.

him for a season; and for a season he inclined to the materialistic doctrines of the *Darwinismus* movement in Germany,[8] and found a curious pleasure in tracing the thoughts and passions of men to some pearly cell in the brain, or some white nerve in the body, delighting in the conception of the absolute dependence of the spirit on certain physical conditions, morbid or healthy, normal or diseased. Yet, as has been said of him before, no theory of life seemed to him to be of any importance compared with life itself. He felt keenly conscious of how barren all intellectual speculation is when separated from action and experiment. He knew that the senses, no less than the soul, have their spiritual mysteries to reveal.

And so he would now study perfumes,[9] and the secrets of their manufacture, distilling heavily-scented oils, and burning odorous gums from the East. He saw that there was no mood of the mind that had not its counterpart in the sensuous life, and set himself to discover their true relations, wondering what there was in frankincense that made one mystical, and in ambergris that stirred one's passions, and in violets that woke the memory of dead romances, and in musk that troubled the brain, and in champak that stained the imagination; and seeking often to elaborate a real psychology of perfumes, and to estimate the several influences of sweet-smelling roots, and scented pollen-laden flowers, of aromatic balms, and of dark and fragrant woods, of spikenard that sickens, of hovenia that makes men mad, and of aloes that are said to be able to expel melancholy from the soul.

At another time he devoted himself entirely to music, and in a long latticed room, with a vermilion-and-gold ceiling and walls of olive-green lacquer, he used to give curious concerts in which mad gypsies tore wild music from little zithers, or grave yellow-shawled Tunisians plucked at the strained strings of monstrous lutes, while grinning negroes beat monotonously upon copper drums, and, crouching upon scarlet mats, slim turbaned Indians blew through long pipes of reed or brass, and charmed, or feigned to charm, great hooded snakes and horrible horned adders. The harsh intervals and shrill discords of barbaric music stirred him at times when Schubert's grace, and Chopin's beautiful sorrows, and the mighty harmonies of Beethoven himself, fell unheeded on his ear. He collected together

8. The application of Darwin's theories was especially strong in Germany, where the implications of biology, comparative anatomy, anthropology, psychology, and social theory were enthusiastically explored. Wilde thought Darwin and Renan the most influential men of the times. Ernst Renan (1823–1892) was a French social philosopher and Orientalist, most noted for his application of scientific, historical methodology to Jewish and Christian traditional belief.

9. Jean Des Esseintes, the hero of *À Rebours*, makes an even more detailed and intense study of perfumes, their psychological effects, and the associations they produce.

from all parts of the world the strangest instruments that could be found, either in the tombs of dead nations or among the few savage tribes that have survived contact with Western civilizations, and loved to touch and try them. He had the mysterious *juruparis* of the Rio Negro Indians,[1] that women are not allowed to look at, and that even youths may not see till they have been subjected to fasting and scourging, and the earthen jars of the Peruvians that have the shrill cries of birds, and flutes of human bones such as Alfonso de Ovalle[2] heard in Chile, and the sonorous green jaspers that are found near Cuzco and give forth a note of singular sweetness. He had painted gourds filled with pebbles that rattled when they were shaken; the long *clarin* of the Mexicans, into which the performer does not blow, but through which he inhales the air; the harsh *ture* of the Amazon tribes, that is sounded by the sentinels who sit all day long in high trees, and can be heard, it is said, at a distance of three leagues; the *teponaztli*, that has two vibrating tongues of wood, and is beaten with sticks that are smeared with an elastic gum obtained from the milky juice of plants; the *yotl*-bells of the Aztecs, that are hung in clusters like grapes; and a huge cylindrical drum, covered with the skins of great serpents, like the one that Bernal Diaz saw when he went with Cortes into the Mexican temple, and of whose doleful sound he has left us so vivid a description. The fantastic character of these instruments fascinated him, and he felt a curious delight in the thought that art, like Nature, has her monsters, things of bestial shape and with hideous voices. Yet, after some time, he wearied of them, and would sit in his box at the Opera, either alone or with Lord Henry, listening in rapt pleasure to "Tannhäuser," and seeing in the prelude to that great work of art a presentation of the tragedy of his own soul.[3]

---

1. Wilde took details of the bizarre musical instruments from German musicologist Carl Engel's handbook *Musical Instruments,* one of the series of South Kensington Museum Art Handbooks he consulted in writing this chapter. Many descriptions are taken directly out of Engel's text.
2. Alfonso de Ovalle (1601–1651), Chilean Jesuit historian whose *Historica relacion del reino de Chile* (1646) is a classic account of colonial Chile.
3. In the legend based on the life of this historical figure, Tannhäuser is a knight and poet who seeks forgiveness after enjoying the fleshpots of Venusberg (a fictional fairyland) for a year. When Tannhäuser journeys to Rome, he is told by the Pope that forgiveness will be granted only when the Pope's staff blossoms. The miracle occurs on the third day after Tannhäuser's departure, too late to save the knight, who had returned to Venusberg in despair. In the Richard Wagner opera (1844), Tannhäuser is forgiven at the end. Gilbert alludes to Tannhäuser in Wilde's "The Critic as Artist," and the story also inspired Swinburne's poem "Laus Veneris" (1866). Wilde seems to have been affected by the struggle of sacred with profane love in the legend, a frequent theme in his own poetry and stories, and the idea of divine forgiveness through miraculous signs. Dorian is later to search his portrait in vain for such a sign.

On one occasion he took up the study of jewels,[4] and appeared at a costume ball as Anne de Joyeuse, Admiral of France,[5] in a dress covered with five hundred and sixty pearls. This taste enthralled him for years, and, indeed, may be said never to have left him. He would often spend a whole day settling and resettling in their cases the various stones that he had collected, such as the olive-green chrysoberyl that turns red by lamplight, the cymophane with its wire-like line of silver, the pistachio-coloured peridot, rose-pink and wine-yellow topazes, carbuncles of fiery scarlet with tremulous four-rayed stars, flame-red cinnamon-stones, orange and violet spinels, and amethysts with their alternate layers of ruby and sapphire. He loved the red gold of the sunstone, and the moonstone's pearly whiteness, and the broken rainbow of the milky opal. He procured from Amsterdam three emeralds of extraordinary size and richness of colour, and had a turquoise *de la vieille roche*[6] that was the envy of all the connoisseurs.

He discovered wonderful stories, also, about jewels. In Alphonso's "Clericalis Disciplina" a serpent was mentioned with eyes of real jacinth, and in the romantic history of Alexander,[7] the Conqueror of Emathia was said to have found in the vale of Jordan snakes "with collars of real emeralds growing on their backs." There was a gem in the brain of the dragon, Philostratus[8] told us, and "by the exhibition of golden letters and a scarlet robe" the monster could be thrown into a magical sleep, and slain. According to the great alchemist, Pierre de Boniface, the diamond rendered a man invisible, and the agate of India made him eloquent. The cornelian appeased anger, and the hyacinth provoked sleep, and the amethyst drove away the fumes of wine. The garnet cast out demons, and the hydropicus deprived the moon of her colour. The selenite waxed and waned with the moon, and the meloceus, that discovers thieves, could be affected only by the blood of kids. Leonardus Camillus had seen a white stone taken from the brain of a newly killed toad, that was a

4. Des Esseintes's study of jewels was more elaborate in *À Rebours*. Many of the more exotic stones mentioned here were used in Huysmans's novel as a covering on the shell of a giant tortoise, contributing to the creature's premature demise. Huysmans is interested in his hero's use of jewels to create new sensations and new aesthetic effects in his life. Wilde emphasizes equally the anecdotes connected to the jewels to add an occult, decadent flavor to the story. He culled his information on stones from A. H. Church's *Precious Stones* (1882), another of the South Kensington Museum Art Handbooks. Many of the stories come, sometimes verbatim, out of William Jones's *History and Mystery of Precious Stones* (1880), as cited in *Dorian Gray*, Murray 246.
5. One of the favorites of Henry III (1551–1589), named a duke and admiral by the French king. Both were homosexuals and appeared in public dressed as women.
6. From an old stone (French).
7. Alexander the Great (356–323 BCE), one of the earliest Western prototypes of the idealized monarch who combined the leadership and courage of the victorious warrior with the temperance and wisdom of the scholar.
8. A Greek Sophist and biographer (170–245 CE). The story comes from *Heroicus*, a fabulous account of the heroes of the Trojan War.

certain antidote against poison. The bezoar, that was found in the heart of the Arabian deer, was a charm that could cure the plague. In the nests of Arabian birds was the aspilates, that, according to Democritus,[9] kept the wearer from any danger by fire.

The King of Ceilan[1] rode through his city with a large ruby in his hand, as the ceremony of his coronation. The gates of the palace of John the Priest[2] were "made of sardius, with the horn of the horned snake inwrought, so that no man might bring poison within." Over the gable were "two golden apples, in which were two carbuncles," so that the gold might shine by day, and the carbuncles by night. In Lodge's strange romance "A Margarite of America"[3] it was stated that in the chamber of the queen one could behold "all the chaste ladies of the world, inchased out of silver, looking through fair mirrours of chrysolites, carbuncles, sapphires, and greene emeraults." Marco Polo[4] had seen the inhabitants of Zipangu place rose-coloured pearls in the mouths of the dead. A sea-monster had been enamoured of the pearl that the diver brought to King Perozes, and had slain the thief, and mourned for seven moons over its loss. When the Huns lured the king into the great pit, he flung it away—Procopius[5] tells the story—nor was it ever found again, though the Emperor Anastasius offered five hundred-weight of gold pieces for it. The King of Malabar had shown to a certain Venetian a rosary of three hundred and four pearls, one for every god that he worshipped.

When the Duke de Valentinois, son of Alexander VI, visited Louis XII of France,[6] his horse was loaded with gold leaves, according to Brantôme, and his cap had double rows of rubies that threw out a great light. Charles of England had ridden in stirrups hung with four hundred and twenty-one diamonds. Richard II[7] had a coat, valued at thirty thousand marks, which was covered with balas rubies. Hall described Henry VIII,[8] on his way to the Tower previous to his coronation, as wearing "a jacket of raised gold, the placard embroidered

---

9. Greek philosopher of Athens (460–370 BCE).
1. Formerly Ceylon, now Sri Lanka.
2. Better known as Prester John, the legendary twelfth-century priest who ruled a utopian Christian realm in Asia or Africa.
3. Thomas Lodge's euphuistic romance (1569) was based on his second voyage to South America.
4. The famous Venetian trader and world traveler (1254–1324). His book of travels introduced the West to the culture and wonders of the Orient.
5. Sixth-century Byzantine church historian, who recorded the wars of King Perozes (457–484 CE) and his death at the hands of the Ephthalites. Malabar, on the west coast of India, was ruled by Hindu kings, but seventeenth-century Portuguese missionaries brought to Malabar a strong Christian influence.
6. In addition to sharing a theatrical sort of hedonism, those mentioned in this paragraph were considered homosexuals.
7. The last English king of the House of York (1452–1485). He died in the Battle of Bosworth Field in the War of the Roses.
8. The second Tudor king of England (1491–1557). He severed the country's ties with the Roman Catholic Church and established the Church of England.

with diamonds and other rich stones, and a great bauderike about his neck of large balasses." The favourites of James I wore ear-rings of emeralds set in gold filigrane. Edward II gave to Piers Gaveston a suit of red-gold armour studded with jacinths, a collar of gold roses set with turquoise-stones, and a skull-cap *parseme*[9] with pearls. Henry II wore jewelled gloves reaching to the elbow, and had a hawk-glove sewn with twelve rubies and fifty-two great orients. The ducal hat of Charles the Rash, the last Duke of Burgundy of his race, was hung with pear-shaped pearls, and studded with sapphires.

How exquisite life had once been! How gorgeous in its pomp and decoration! Even to read of the luxury of the dead was wonderful.

Then he turned his attention to embroideries,[1] and to the tapes-tries that performed the office of frescoes in the chill rooms of the northern nations of Europe. As he investigated the subject—and he always had an extraordinary faculty of becoming absolutely absorbed for the moment in whatever he took up—he was almost saddened by the reflection of the ruin that Time brought on beautiful and won-derful things. He, at any rate, had escaped that. Summer followed summer, and the yellow jonquils bloomed and died many times, and nights of horror repeated the story of their shame, but he was unchanged. No winter marred his face or stained his flower-like bloom. How different it was with material things! Where had they passed to? Where was the great crocus-coloured robe, on which the gods fought against the giants, that had been worked by brown girls for the pleasure of Athena?[2] Where the huge velarium that Nero had stretched across the Colosseum at Rome, that Titan sail of pur-ple on which was represented the starry sky, and Apollo driving a chariot drawn by white, gilt-reined steeds? He longed to see the curious table-napkins wrought for the Priest of the Sun, on which were displayed all the dainties and viands that could be wanted for a feast; the mortuary cloth of King Chilperic,[3] with its three hundred golden bees; the fantastic robes that excited the indignation of the Bishop of Pontus, and were figured with "lions, panthers, bears, dogs, forests, rocks, hunters—all, in fact, that a painter can copy from nature;" and the coat that Charles of Orleans[4] once wore, on the

---

9. Spangled (French).
1. Wilde copied some of the passages in this section on embroideries from a November 1888 review he did as editor of *Woman's World* of Ernest Lefébure's *Embroidery and Lace: Their Manufacture and History from the Remotest Antiquity to the Present* (1888). Wilde referred to the work as a "fascinating book." Here Wilde also borrowed selec-tively from the text of Lefébure's work.
2. Pallas Athena was the Greek goddess of war, peace, and wisdom. Her Roman equiva-lent was Minerva.
3. Sixth-century Frankish king.
4. Charles d'Orleans (1394–1465), French poet, duke of Orleans, and father of Louis XII, spent a third of his life as a royal captive in England after the Battle of Agincourt (1415) in the Hundred Years' War. Finally ransomed by his future wife, Mary of Cleves,

sleeves of which were embroidered the verses of a song beginning
"Madame, je suis tout joyeux," the musical accompaniment of the
words being wrought in gold thread, and each note, of square shape
in those days, formed with four pearls. He read of the room that was
prepared at the palace at Rheims for the use of Queen Joan of Burgundy, and was decorated with "thirteen hundred and twenty-one
parrots, made in broidery, and blazoned with the king's arms, and
five hundred and sixty-one butterflies, whose wings were similarly
ornamented with the arms of the queen, the whole worked in gold."
Catherine de Médicis[5] had a mourning-bed[6] made for her of black
velvet powdered with crescents and suns. Its curtains were of damask, with leafy wreaths and garlands, figured upon a gold and silver
ground, and fringed along the edges with broideries of pearls, and
it stood in a room hung with rows of the queen's devices in cut
black velvet upon cloth of silver. Louis XIV had gold embroidered
caryatides[7] fifteen feet high in his apartment. The state bed of
Sobieski, King of Poland,[8] was made of Smyrna gold brocade embroidered in turquoises with verses from the Koran. Its supports were
of silver gilt, beautifully chased, and profusely set with enamelled
and jewelled medallions. It had been taken from the Turkish camp
before Vienna, and the standard of Mohammed had stood beneath
the tremulous gilt of its canopy.

And so, for a whole year, he sought to accumulate the most exquisite specimens that he could find of textile and embroidered work,
getting the dainty Delhi muslins, finely wrought with gold-thread
palmates and stitched over with iridescent beetles' wings; the Dacca
gauzes, that from their transparency are known in the East as
"woven air," and "running water," and "evening dew"; strange figured
cloths from Java; elaborate yellow Chinese hangings; books bound
in tawny satins or fair blue silks, and wrought with *fleurs de lys,* birds,
and images; veils of *lacis* worked in Hungary point; Sicilian brocades,
and stiff Spanish velvets; Georgian work with its gilt coins, and Japanese *Foukousas*[9] with their green-toned golds and their marvelously-
plumaged birds.

---

he spent the last third of his life at Château de Blois, where he kept court for the most
    celebrated French writers of the time, including Villon, Chastelain, and de la Marche.
5. Daughter of Florentine statesman Lorenzo the Magnificent, became queen of France
    through marriage, bore nine children, was celebrated for her love of luxury, and was
    notorious for her plots and assassinations while regent.
6. A widow's four-poster bed entirely draped in black with neither white sheets nor pillow
    cases. The rest of the bedroom would have been draped in the same way.
7. Columns sculptured in the form of female figures.
8. Sobieski ruled Poland as John III (1674–1696). His greatest achievement was the
    heroic Polish rescue of Vienna from the Ottoman Empire in 1683.
9. Embroidered or brocaded silk square gift covers, not considered part of the gift itself
    and hence a separate art form. Alternate spelling of "fukusa." *Fleurs de lys:* Symbol of
    the French aristocracy, it is a device of heraldry rather than a real flower, resembling
    banded petals of an iris.

He had a special passion, also, for ecclesiastical vestments, as indeed he had for everything connected with the service of the Church. In the long cedar chests that lined the west gallery of his house he had stored away many rare and beautiful specimens of what is really the raiment of the Bride of Christ,[1] who must wear purple and jewels and fine linen that she may hide the pallid macerated body that is worn by the suffering that she seeks for, and wounded by self-inflicted pain. He possessed a gorgeous cope[2] of crimson silk and gold-thread damask, figured with a repeating pattern of golden pomegranates set in six-petalled formal blossoms, beyond which on either side was the pine-apple device wrought in seed-pearls. The orphreys were divided into panels representing scenes from the life of the Virgin, and the coronation of the Virgin was figured in coloured silks upon the hood. This was Italian work of the fifteenth century. Another cope was of green velvet, embroidered with heart-shaped groups of acanthus-leaves, from which spread long-stemmed white blossoms, the details of which were picked out with silver thread and coloured crystals. The morse bore a seraph's head in gold-thread raised work. The orphreys were woven in a diaper of red and gold silk, and were starred with medallions of many saints and martyrs, among whom was St. Sebastian.[3] He had chasubles, also, of amber-coloured silk, and blue silk and gold brocade, and yellow silk damask and cloth of gold, figured with representations of the Passion and Crucifixion of Christ, and embroidered with lions and peacocks and other emblems; dalmatics of white satin and pink silk damask, decorated with tulips and dolphins and *fleurs de lys*; altar frontals of crimson velvet and blue linen; and many corporals, chalice-veils, and sudaria.[4] In the mystic offices to which such things were put, there was something that quickened his imagination.

For these treasures, and everything that he collected in his lovely house, were to be to him means of forgetfulness, modes by which he could escape, for a season, from the fear that seemed to him at times to be almost too great to be borne. Upon the walls of the lonely locked room where he had spent so much of his boyhood, he had

---

1. Roman Catholic nun.
2. Decorated hood or hooded cape worn over the shoulder.
3. Third-century Roman martyr, a favorite of the emperor Diocletian, who nevertheless ordered him killed by archers for his Christian faith.
4. Ecclesiastical vestments of the Catholic Church, one of Dorian's interests, were also an interest of Des Esseintes of *À·Rebours*. The Victoria and Albert Museum contained a fine collection, which Wilde knew. Accounts in the paragraphs below may have been taken from Reverend Daniel Rock's *Textile Fabrics* (London, 1876). *Chasubles:* Long, sleeveless vestments colored and usually decorated, worn outside the alb during Mass. *Altar frontals:* Decorated altar cloths hanging down in front of the altar. *Corporal:* A linen cloth on which bread and wine are placed during the consecration. *Chance veils:* Decorated square cloth coverings for chalices used during Mass. *Sudaria:* Handkerchiefs or napkins used to dry perspiration.

hung with his own hands the terrible portrait whose changing features showed him the real degradation of his life, and in front of it
had draped the purple-and-gold pall as a curtain. For weeks he
would not go there, would forget the hideous painted thing, and get
back his light heart, his wonderful joyousness, his passionate absorption in mere existence. Then, suddenly, some night he would creep
out of the house, go down to dreadful places near Blue Gate Fields,[5]
and stay there, day after day, until he was driven away. On his return
he would sit in front of the picture, sometimes loathing it and himself, but filled, at other times, with that pride of individualism that
is half the fascination of sin, and smiling, with secret pleasure, at
the misshapen shadow that had to bear the burden that should have
been his own.

After a few years he could not endure to be long out of England,
and gave up the villa that he had shared at Trouville[6] with Lord
Henry, as well as the little white walled-in house at Algiers where
they had more than once spent the winter. He hated to be separated
from the picture that was such a part of his life, and was also afraid
that during his absence some one might gain access to the room, in
spite of the elaborate bars that he had caused to be placed upon the
door.

He was quite conscious that this would tell them nothing. It was
true that the portrait still preserved, under all the foulness and ugliness of the face, its marked likeness to himself; but what could they
learn from that? He would laugh at any one who tried to taunt him.
He had not painted it. What was it to him how vile and full of shame
it looked? Even if he told them, would they believe it?

Yet he was afraid. Sometimes when he was down at his great house
in Nottinghamshire, entertaining the fashionable young men of his
own rank who were his chief companions, and astounding the
county by the wanton luxury and gorgeous splendour of his mode of
life, he would suddenly leave his guests and rush back to town to
see that the door had not been tampered with, and that the picture
was still there. What if it should be stolen? The mere thought made
him cold with horror. Surely the world would know his secret then.
Perhaps the world already suspected it.

For, while he fascinated many, there were not a few who distrusted
him.[7] He was very nearly blackballed at a West End club of which his

---

5. In the East End near Limehouse and the London Dock, between Commercial Road
   and New Road.
6. A beach resort in France, on the English Channel. It was a favorite vacation spa for
   Wilde, as was Algiers, where foreign homosexuals lived openly.
7. Dorian has changed clubs since the *Lippincott's* edition, which had him at the Carlton,
   a famous conservative political club located in Pall Mall. There was nothing to prevent
   Dorian from belonging to more than one club, however. Wilde was in fact barred from
   membership in the Savile Club shortly before writing *Dorian Gray*.

birth and social position fully entitled him to become a member, and it was said that on one occasion, when he was brought by a friend into the smoking-room of the Churchill, the Duke of Berwick and another gentleman got up in a marked manner and went out. Curious stories became current about him after he had passed his twenty-fifth year. It was rumoured that he had been seen brawling with foreign sailors in a low den in the distant parts of Whitechapel, and that he consorted with thieves and coiners and knew the mysteries of their trade. His extraordinary absences became notorious, and, when he used to reappear again in society, men would whisper to each other in corners, or pass him with a sneer, or look at him with cold searching eyes, as though they were determined to discover his secret.

Of such insolences and attempted slights he, of course, took no notice, and in the opinion of most people his frank debonnair manner, his charming boyish smile, and the infinite grace of that wonderful youth that seemed never to leave him, were in themselves a sufficient answer to the calumnies, for so they termed them, that were circulated about him. It was remarked, however, that some of those who had been most intimate with him appeared, after a time, to shun him. Women who had wildly adored him, and for his sake had braved all social censure and set convention at defiance, were seen to grow pallid with shame or horror if Dorian Gray entered the room.

Yet these whispered scandals only increased in the eyes of many, his strange and dangerous charm. His great wealth was a certain element of security. Society, civilized society at least, is never very ready to believe anything to the detriment of those who are both rich and fascinating. It feels instinctively that manners are of more importance than morals,[8] and, in its opinion, the highest respectability is of much less value than the possession of a good *chef*. And, after all, it is a very poor consolation to be told that the man who has given one a bad dinner, or poor wine, is irreproachable in his private life. Even the cardinal virtues cannot atone for half-cold *entrées*, as Lord Henry remarked once, in a discussion on the subject; and there is possibly a good deal to be said for his view. For the canons of good society are, or should be, the same as the canons of art. Form is absolutely essential to it. It should have the dignity of a ceremony, as well as its unreality, and should combine the insincere character of a romantic play with the wit and beauty that make such plays delightful to us. Is insincerity such a terrible thing? I

8. A favorite epigram of Wilde's, which appears also in "The Critic as Artist" and once again in *Lady Windermere's Fan*.

think not.[9] It is merely a method by which we can multiply our personalities.

Such, at any rate, was Dorian Gray's opinion. He used to wonder at the shallow psychology of those who conceive the Ego in man as a thing simple, permanent, reliable, and of one essence. To him, man was a being with myriad lives and myriad sensations, a complex multiform creature that bore within itself strange legacies of thought and passion, and whose very flesh was tainted with the monstrous maladies of the dead. He loved to stroll through the gaunt cold picture-gallery of his country house and look at the various portraits of those whose blood flowed in his veins. Here was Philip Herbert,[1] described by Francis Osborne, in his "Memoires on the Reigns of Queen Elizabeth and King James," as one who was "caressed by the Court for his handsome face, which kept him not long company." Was it young Herbert's life that he sometimes led? Had some strange poisonous germ crept from body to body till it had reached his own? Was it some dim sense of that ruined grace that had made him so suddenly, and almost without cause, give utterance, in Basil Hallward's studio, to the mad prayer that had so changed his life? Here, in gold-embroidered red doublet, jewelled surcoat, and gilt-edged ruff and wrist-bands, stood Sir Anthony Sherard,[2] with his silver-and-black armour piled at his feet. What had this man's legacy been? Had the lover of Giovanna of Naples bequeathed him some inheritance of sin and shame? Were his own actions merely the dreams that the dead man had not dared to realize? Here, from the fading canvas, smiled Lady Elizabeth Devereux,[3] in her gauze hood, pearl stomacher, and pink slashed sleeves. A flower was in her right hand, and her left clasped an enamelled collar of white and damask roses. On a table by her side lay a mandolin and an apple. There were large green rosettes upon her little pointed shoes. He knew her life, and the strange stories that were told about her lovers. Had he something of her temperament in him? These oval heavy-lidded eyes seemed to look curiously at him. What of George Willoughby,[4] with his powdered hair and fantastic patches? How evil he looked! The

---

9. This is the one occasion when the narrative shifts from third person to first.
1. A favorite of King James I of England. The incident is described in Osborne's *Miscellaneous Works* 2 (London, 1722) 133 (*Dorian Gray*, Murray 246).
2. One of Wilde's practical jokes. He borrowed the name from a friend and later biographer, the naïve R. H. Sherard, who was, in temperament, not at all like the fictitious lover of Giovanna of Naples. In the magazine edition, he was described as the "companion of the Prince Regent in his wildest days." When Sherard objected because he had a living relative by that name, Wilde moved him into Dorian's ancestral gallery of rogues.
3. Fictitious, but her portrait seems inspired by allegorical Flemish portraits of the sixteenth-century. The flower, collar, mandolin, and fruit all symbolize her domestic attributes.
4. Wilde may have taken the name from a baritone of the era who sang for a time with the D'Oyly Carte Opera Company.

face was saturnine and swarthy, and the sensual lips seemed to be twisted with disdain. Delicate lace ruffles fell over the lean yellow hands that were so overladen with rings. He had been a macaroni of the eighteenth century, and the friend, in his youth, of Lord Ferrars.[5] What of the second Lord Beckenham, the companion of the Prince Regent in his wildest days, and one of the witnesses at the secret marriage with Mrs. Fitzherbert?[6] How proud and handsome he was, with his chestnut curls and insolent pose! What passions had he bequeathed? The world had looked upon him as infamous. He had led the orgies at Carlton House.[7] The star of the Garter glittered upon his breast. Beside him hung the portrait of his wife, a pallid, thin-lipped woman in black. Her blood, also, stirred within him. How curious it all seemed! And his mother with her Lady Hamilton face,[8] and her moist wine-dashed lips—he knew what he had got from her. He had got from her his beauty, and his passion for the beauty of others. She laughed at him in her loose Bacchante dress. There were vine leaves in her hair. The purple spilled from the cup she was holding. The carnations of the painting had withered, but the eyes were still wonderful in their depth and brilliancy of colour. They seemed to follow him wherever he went.

Yet one had ancestors in literature, as well as in one's own race, nearer perhaps in type and temperament, many of them, and certainly with an influence of which one was more absolutely conscious. There were times when it appeared to Dorian Gray that the whole of history was merely the record of his own life, not as he had lived it in act and circumstance, but as his imagination had created it for him, as it had been in his brain and in his passions. He felt that he had known them all, those strange terrible figures that had passed across the stage of the world and made sin so marvellous and evil so full of subtlety. It seemed to him that in some mysterious way their lives had been his own.

The hero of the wonderful novel that had so influenced his life had himself known this curious fancy. In the seventh chapter he

5. An actual peerage that became extinct sometime before 1790. *Macaroni:* Named after Italian dandies of the eighteenth century, remembered in the lyric of "Yankee Doodle."
6. The regent was George, prince of Wales, later George IV, who married Mrs. Maria FitzHerbert in 1785. The marriage thereafter was ruled invalid, although their relationship continued long after George married Caroline of Brunswick. *Lord Beckenham:* A fictitious aristocrat named after the town of Beckenham.
7. The residence of the Prince of Wales, later George IV, from the time he attained his majority in 1783.
8. Lady Emma Hamilton (1765–1815), wife of Sir William Hamilton, British envoy at Naples, was a village girl from Cheshire and one of the great beauties of the day. Her likeness was painted by Thomas Gainsborough (1727–1788), by Richard Cosway (1742–1821), and by George Romney (1734–1802) in a series of works. She is remembered for her beautiful features, her Moll Flanders-to-Roxana rise to fame, and her long love affair with Admiral Nelson.

tells how, crowned with laurel, lest lightning might strike him, he had sat, as Tiberius,[9] in a garden at Capri, reading the shameful books of Elephantis,[1] while dwarfs and peacocks strutted round him and the flute-player mocked the swinger of the censer; and, as Caligula,[2] had caroused with the green-shirted jockeys in their stables, and supped in an ivory manger with a jewel-frontleted horse; and, as Domitian, had wandered through a corridor lined with marble mirrors, looking round with haggard eyes for the reflection of the dagger that was to end his days, and sick with that ennui, that terrible *tædium vitæ*, that comes on those to whom life denies nothing; and had peered through a clear emerald at the red shambles of the Circus,[3] and then, in a litter of pearl and purple drawn by silver-shod mules, been carried through the Street of Pomegranates to a House of Gold, and heard men cry on Nero Cæsar[4] as he passed by; and, as Elagabalus,[5] had painted his face with colours, and plied the distaff among the women, and brought the Moon from Carthage, and given her in mystic marriage to the Sun.

Over and over again Dorian used to read this fantastic chapter, and the two chapters immediately following, in which, as in some curious tapestries or cunningly wrought enamels, were pictured the awful and beautiful forms of those whom Vice and Blood and Weariness had made monstrous or mad: Filippo, Duke of Milan, who slew his wife, and painted her lips with a scarlet poison that her lover might suck death from the dead thing he fondled; Pietro Barbi, the Venetian, known as Paul the Second, who sought in his vanity to assume the title of Formosus,[6] and whose tiara, valued at two

---

9. Second Roman emperor (14–37 CE), who succeeded Augustus Caesar. Wilde took the details of the Roman emperors from Tiberius to Nero from Roman historian Suetonius's *Lives of the Caesars*. The following paragraph borrows heavily from John Addington Symonds, *Renaissance in Italy*, 7 vols. (1875–86). See *Dorian Gray*, Murray 246–47.

1. A female Greek author of amatory works mentioned by Suetonius and Roman poet Martial.

2. Caligula (12–41 CE) and Domitian (56–95 CE), despotic Roman emperors who were assassinated.

3. Of the major circuses of Rome (Maximus, Flaminius, Neronis, and Maxentius), this probably refers to Circus Neronis, built by Caligula in the gardens of Agrippina. A circus was an elliptical race course.

4. Roman emperor (54–68 CE), last of the Caesar family, notorious for beginning Roman persecution of Christians and for dissolute living.

5. Also called Heliogabalus (205–222 CE) because of his office as boy-priest of the Syrian sun god, he became Roman emperor in 218 and set a new standard for profligate living. He was put to death by the Praetorian guard. He reigned under the name Marcus Aurelius Antoninus, but he should not be confused with the earlier, stoic philosopher-emperor of the same name (121–180 CE).

6. Formosus (the Latin word for beautiful or well-shaped) was pope in 891–896 during very turbulent political times. I can find no evidence of Paul II's wish to take the name Formosus. Pietro Barbo (1417–1471) reigned as Pope Paul II from 1464 to 1471. He patronized the arts, helped beautify Rome, and collected antiquities. In the line above, the phrase "that her lover . . . he fondled" had been removed from the TS by Stoddart before *Lippincott's* publication. Its reappearance here can be explained best if we assume that Wilde had either the MS with him or, more likely, the revised TS when he was preparing the expanded edition. Wilde performed several restorations of this kind in the expanded edition.

hundred thousand florins, was bought at the price of a terrible
sin; Gian Maria Visconti,[7] who used hounds to chase living men,
and whose murdered body was covered with roses by a harlot who
had loved him; the Borgia on his white horse,[8] with Fratricide riding beside him, and his mantle stained with the blood of Perotto;
Pietro Riario[9] the young Cardinal Archbishop of Florence, child and
minion of Sixtus IV,[1] whose beauty was equalled only by his
debauchery, and who received Leonora of Aragon[2] in a pavilion of
white and crimson silk, filled with nymphs and centaurs, and gilded
a boy that he might serve at the feast as Ganymede or Hylas;[3]
Ezzelin,[4] whose melancholy could be cured only by the spectacle of
death, and who had a passion for red blood, as other men have for
red wine—the son of the Fiend, as was reported, and one who had
cheated his father at dice when gambling with him for his own
soul; Giambattista Cibo,[5] who in mockery took the name of Innocent, and into whose torpid veins the blood of three lads was
infused by a Jewish doctor; Sigismondo Malatesta,[6] the lover of
Isotta, and the lord of Rimini, whose effigy was burned at Rome as
the enemy of God and man, who strangled Polyssena with a napkin, and gave poison to Ginevra d'Este[7] in a cup of emerald, and in
honour of a shameful passion built a pagan church for Christian
worship; Charles VI,[8] who had so wildly adored his brother's wife
that a leper had warned him of the insanity that was coming on
him, and who, when his brain had sickened and grown strange,
could only be soothed by Saracen cards painted with the images of
Love and Death and Madness; and, in his trimmed jerkin and
jewelled cap and acanthus-like curls, Grifonetto Baglioni,[9] who
slew Astorre with his bride, and Simonetto with his page, and

7. Giovanni Maria Visconti (1388–1412), a member of the family that ruled Milan from
   the thirteenth century to 1447. He was a dissolute and cruel ruler who ultimately was
   assassinated, with the duchy passing to his brother.
8. Cesare Borgia (1476–1507), Italian soldier-politician, was the prototype for the titular
   ruler in Niccolò Machiavelli's treatise *The Prince* (1532).
9. Pietro Rario (1445–1474) was a sexually profligate nephew of Pope Sixtus IV. He was
   elevated to cardinal by his uncle.
1. Francesco della Rovere (1414–1484) reigned as Pope Sixtus IV (1471–84).
2. Leonora of Aragon (1450–1493), Duchess of Ferrara, Reggio, and Modena and aunt of
   Isabella of Aragon.
3. One of the mythical Greek Argonauts. Because of his great beauty, he was ravished
   by nymphs in Mysia and never seen again. *Ganymede:* In Greek mythology, a beautiful young boy with whom Zeus fell in love. He became Zeus's cupbearer until a jealous Hera, Zeus's wife, forced Zeus to set him among the stars as Aquarius, the water
   bearer.
4. An Italian Ghibelline leader (1194–1259), remembered as a tyrant and for the prominent place assigned to him in hell by Dante.
5. Cibo was pope from 1484 to 1492.
6. Malatesta (1416–1468) was a despotic Italian Renaissance prince.
7. Ginevra d'Este (1419–1440), first wife of Sigismondo Malatesta, who had her poisoned
   in 1440.
8. Charles VI, known as Charles the Mad, reigned France from 1380 to 1422.
9. The Baglioni family were famous for their bloody family feuds.

whose comeliness was such that, as he lay dying in the yellow piazza of Perugia,[1] those who had hated him could not choose but weep, and Atalanta, who had cursed him, blessed him.

There was a horrible fascination in them all. He saw them at night, and they troubled his imagination in the day. The Renaissance knew of strange manners of poisoning—poisoning by a helmet and a lighted torch, by an embroidered glove and a jewelled fan, by a gilded pomander and by an amber chain. Dorian Gray had been poisoned by a book. There were moments when he looked on evil simply as a mode through which he could realize his conception of the beautiful.

Chapter XII[1]

It was on the ninth of November, the eve of his own thirty-eighth birthday,[2] as he often remembered afterwards.

He was walking home about eleven o'clock from Lord Henry's, where he had been dining, and was wrapped in heavy furs, as the night was cold and foggy. At the corner of Grosvenor Square and South Audley Street a man passed him in the mist, walking very fast, and with the collar of his grey ulster[3] turned up. He had a bag in his hand. Dorian recognized him. It was Basil Hallward. A strange sense of fear, for which he could not account, came over him. He made no sign of recognition, and went on quickly, in the direction of his own house.

But Hallward had seen him. Dorian heard him first stopping on the pavement and then hurrying after him. In a few moments his hand was on his arm.

"Dorian! What an extraordinary piece of luck! I have been waiting for you in your library ever since nine o'clock. Finally I took pity on your tired servant, and told him to go to bed, as he let me out. I am off to Paris by the midnight train, and I particularly wanted to see you before I left. I thought it was you, or rather your fur coat, as you passed me. But I wasn't quite sure. Didn't you recognize me?"

"In this fog, my dear Basil? Why, I can't even recognize Grosvenor Square. I believe my house is somewhere about here, but I don't feel at all certain about it. I am sorry you are going away, as I have not seen you for ages. But I suppose you will be back soon?"

"No: I am going to be out of England for six months. I intend to take a studio in Paris, and shut myself up till I have finished a great

1. A city in Umbria, north of Rome.
1. This was chapter 10 in the *Lippincott's Magazine* edition.
2. Changed from November 7 in the *Lippincott's* edition.
3. A loose, long overcoat made of heavy, rugged fabric and often belted.

picture I have in my head. However, it wasn't about myself I wanted to talk. Here we are at your door. Let me come in for a moment. I have something to say to you."

"I shall be charmed. But won't you miss your train?" said Dorian Gray, languidly, as he passed up the steps and opened the door with his latch-key.

The lamp-light struggled out through the fog, and Hallward looked at his watch. "I have heaps of time," he answered. "The train doesn't go till twelve-fifteen, and it is only just eleven. In fact, I was on my way to the club to look for you, when I met you. You see, I shan't have any delay about luggage, as I have sent on my heavy things. All I have with me is in this bag, and I can easily get to Victoria[4] in twenty minutes."

Dorian looked at him and smiled. "What a way for a fashionable painter to travel! A Gladstone bag,[5] and an ulster! Come in, or the fog will get into the house. And mind you don't talk about anything serious. Nothing is serious nowadays. At least nothing should be."

Hallward shook his head, as he entered, and followed Dorian into the library. There was a bright wood fire blazing in the large open hearth. The lamps were lit, and an open Dutch silver spirit-case stood, with some siphons of soda-water and large cut-glass tumblers, on a little marqueterie[6] table.

"You see your servant made me quite at home, Dorian. He gave me everything I wanted, including your best gold-tipped cigarettes. He is a most hospitable creature. I like him much better than the Frenchman you used to have. What has become of the Frenchman, by the bye?"

Dorian shrugged his shoulders. "I believe he married Lady Radley's maid, and has established her in Paris as an English dressmaker. *Anglomanie*[7] is very fashionable over there now, I hear. It seems silly of the French, doesn't it? But—do you know?—he was not at all a bad servant. I never liked him, but I had nothing to complain about. One often imagines things that are quite absurd. He was really very devoted to me, and seemed quite sorry when he went away. Have another brandy-and-soda? Or would you like hock-and-seltzer? I always take hock-and-seltzer myself.[8] There is sure to be some in the next room."

---

4. Victoria Station. Located in central London, it was the rail terminus for boat-trains to France.
5. A hinged suitcase that opened flat into two equal parts.
6. A decorative inlay design, usually of wood and ivory.
7. The love of things English (French).
8. Wilde's favorite drink. *Hock:* A generic term used by the British to mean a white Rhine wine (from the German *Hochheimer Wein*). *Seltzer:* A mineral water, naturally carbonated,

"Thanks, I won't have anything more," said the painter, taking his cap and coat off, and throwing them on the bag that he had placed in the corner. "And now, my dear fellow, I want to speak to you seriously. Don't frown like that. You make it so much more difficult for me."

"What is it all about?" cried Dorian in his petulant way, flinging himself down on the sofa. "I hope it is not about myself. I am tired of myself to-night. I should like to be somebody else."

"It is about yourself," answered Hallward, in his grave, deep voice, "and I must say it to you. I shall only keep you half an hour."

Dorian sighed, and lit a cigarette. "Half an hour!" he murmured.

"It is not much to ask of you, Dorian, and it is entirely for your own sake that I am speaking. I think it right that you should know that the most dreadful things are being said against you in London."

"I don't wish to know anything about them. I love scandals about other people, but scandals about myself don't interest me. They have not got the charm of novelty."

"They must interest you, Dorian. Every gentleman is interested in his good name. You don't want people to talk of you as something vile and degraded. Of course you have your position, and your wealth, and all that kind of thing. But position and wealth are not everything. Mind you, I don't believe these rumours at all. At least, I can't believe them when I see you. Sin is a thing that writes itself across a man's face. It cannot be concealed. People talk sometimes of secret vices. There are no such things. If a wretched man has a vice, it shows itself in the lines of his mouth, the droop of his eyelids, the moulding of his hands even. Somebody—I won't mention his name, but you know him—came to me last year to have his portrait done. I had never seen him before, and had never heard anything about him at the time, though I have heard a good deal since. He offered an extravagant price. I refused him. There was something in the shape of his fingers that I hated. I know now that I was quite right in what I fancied about him. His life is dreadful. But you, Dorian, with your pure, bright, innocent face, and your marvellous untroubled youth—I can't believe anything against you. And yet I see you very seldom, and you never come down to the studio now, and when I am away from you, and I hear all these hideous things that people are whispering about you, I don't know what to say. Why is it, Dorian, that a man like the Duke of Berwick leaves the room of a club when you enter it? Why is it that so many gentlemen in London will neither go to your house or invite you to theirs? You used to be a friend

---

from the spas of Selters, a village in Prussia. The name has since become generic for carbonated mineral water, originally with a rather salty tang.

of Lord Staveley. I met him at dinner last week. Your name happened to come up in conversation, in connection with the miniatures you have lent to the exhibition at the Dudley.[9] Staveley curled his lip, and said that you might have the most artistic tastes, but that you were a man whom no pure-minded girl should be allowed to know, and whom no chaste woman should sit in the same room with. I reminded him that I was a friend of yours, and asked him what he meant. He told me. He told me right out before everybody. It was horrible! Why is your friendship so fatal to young men? There was that wretched boy in the Guards who committed suicide. You were his great friend. There was Sir Henry Ashton, who had to leave England, with a tarnished name. You and he were inseparable. What about Adrian Singleton, and his dreadful end? What about Lord Kent's only son, and his career? I met his father yesterday in St. James's Street. He seemed broken with shame and sorrow. What about the young Duke of Perth? What sort of life has he got now? What gentleman would associate with him?"

"Stop, Basil. You are talking about things of which you know nothing," said Dorian Gray, biting his lip, and with a note of infinite contempt in his voice. "You ask me why Berwick leaves a room when I enter it. It is because I know everything about his life, not because he knows anything about mine. With such blood as he has in his veins, how could his record be clean? You ask me about Henry Ashton and young Perth. Did I teach the one his vices, and the other his debauchery? If Kent's silly son takes his wife from the streets, what is that to me? If Adrian Singleton writes his friend's name across a bill, am I his keeper? I know how people chatter in England. The middle classes air their moral prejudices over their gross dinner-tables, and whisper about what they call the profligacies of their betters in order to try and pretend that they are in smart society, and on intimate terms with the people they slander. In this country, it is enough for a man to have distinction and brains for every common tongue to wag against him. And what sort of lives do these people, who pose as being moral, lead themselves? My dear fellow, you forget that we are in the native land of the hypocrite."

"Dorian," cried Hallward, "that is not the question. England is bad enough I know, and English society is all wrong. That is the reason why I want you to be fine. You have not been fine. One has a right to judge of a man by the effect he has over his friends. Yours seem to lose all sense of honour, of goodness, of purity. You have filled them with a madness for pleasure. They have gone down into

9. A gallery named in honor of the Lord Dudley bequest, whose collection of art was placed on public display in the Egyptian Hall, Piccadilly. The Egyptian Hall, still standing when *Dorian Gray* was written, was an exhibition space whose exterior Egyptian design contrasted grotesquely with adjoining Georgian town buildings.

the depths. You led them there. Yes: you led them there, and yet you can smile, as you are smiling now. And there is worse behind. I know you and Harry are inseparable. Surely for that reason, if for none other, you should not have made his sister's name a by-word."

"Take care, Basil. You go too far."

"I must speak, and you must listen. You shall listen. When you met Lady Gwendolen, not a breath of scandal had ever touched her. Is there a single decent woman in London now who would drive with her in the park? Why, even her children are not allowed to live with her. Then there are other stories—stories that you have been seen creeping at dawn out of dreadful houses and slinking in disguise into the foulest dens in London. Are they true? Can they be true? When I first heard them, I laughed. I hear them now, and they make me shudder. What about your country house, and the life that is led there? Dorian, you don't know what is said about you. I won't tell you that I don't want to preach to you. I remember Harry saying once that every man who turned himself into an amateur curate for the moment always began by saying that, and then proceeded to break his word. I do want to preach to you. I want you to lead such a life as will make the world respect you. I want you to have a clean name and a fair record. I want you to get rid of the dreadful people you associate with. Don't shrug your shoulders like that. Don't be so indifferent. You have a wonderful influence. Let it be for good, not for evil. They say that you corrupt every one with whom you become intimate, and that it is quite sufficient for you to enter a house, for shame of some kind to follow after. I don't know whether it is so or not. How should I know? But it is said of you. I am told things that it seems impossible to doubt. Lord Gloucester was one of my greatest friends at Oxford. He showed me a letter that his wife had written to him when she was dying alone in her villa at Mentone.[1] Your name was implicated in the most terrible confession I ever read. I told him that it was absurd—that I knew you thoroughly, and that you were incapable of anything of the kind. Know you? I wonder do I know you? Before I could answer that, I should have to see your soul."

"To see my soul!" muttered Dorian Gray, starting up from the sofa and turning almost white from fear.

"Yes," answered Hallward, gravely, and with deep-toned sorrow in his voice—"to see your soul. But only God can do that."

A bitter laugh of mockery broke from the lips of the younger man. "You shall see it yourself, to-night!" he cried, seizing a lamp from the table. "Come: it is your own handiwork. Why shouldn't you look at it? You can tell the world all about it afterwards, if you choose.

---

1. A popular French resort on the Riviera.

Nobody would believe you. If they did believe you, they would like me all the better for it. I know the age better than you do, though you will prate about it so tediously. Come, I tell you. You have chattered enough about corruption. Now you shall look on it face to face."

There was the madness of pride in every word he uttered. He stamped his foot upon the ground in his boyish insolent manner. He felt a terrible joy at the thought that some one else was to share his secret, and that the man who had painted the portrait that was the origin of all his shame was to be burdened for the rest of his life with the hideous memory of what he had done.

"Yes," he continued, coming closer to him, and looking steadfastly into his stern eyes, "I shall show you my soul. You shall see the thing that you fancy only God can see."

Hallward started back. "This is blasphemy, Dorian!" he cried. "You must not say things like that. They are horrible, and they don't mean anything."

"You think so?" He laughed again.

"I know so. As for what I said to you to-night, I said it for your good. You know I have been always a stanch friend to you."

"Don't touch me. Finish what you have to say."

A twisted flash of pain shot across the painter's face. He paused for a moment, and a wild feeling of pity came over him. After all, what right had he to pry into the life of Dorian Gray? If he had done a tithe of what was rumoured about him, how much he must have suffered! Then he straightened himself up, and walked over to the fireplace, and stood there, looking at the burning logs with their frost-like ashes and their throbbing cores of flame.

"I am waiting, Basil," said the young man, in a hard, clear voice.

He turned round. "What I have to say is this," he cried. "You must give me some answer to these horrible charges that are made against you. If you tell me that they are absolutely untrue from beginning to end, I shall believe you. Deny them, Dorian, deny them! Can't you see what I am going through? My God! don't tell me that you are bad, and corrupt, and shameful."

Dorian Gray smiled. There was a curl of contempt in his lips. "Come upstairs, Basil," he said quietly. "I keep a diary of my life from day to day, and it never leaves the room in which it is written. I shall show it to you if you come with me."

"I shall come with you, Dorian, if you wish it. I see I have missed my train. That makes no matter. I can go to-morrow. But don't ask me to read anything to-night. All I want is a plain answer to my question."

"That shall be given to you upstairs. I could not give it here. You will not have to read long."

Chapter XIII[1]

He passed out of the room, and began the ascent, Basil Hallward following close behind. They walked softly, as men do instinctively at night. The lamp cast fantastic shadows on the wall and staircase. A rising wind made some of the windows rattle.

When they reached the top landing, Dorian set the lamp down on the floor, and taking out the key turned it in the lock. "You insist on knowing, Basil?" he asked, in a low voice.

"Yes."

"I am delighted," he answered, smiling. Then he added, somewhat harshly, "You are the one man in the world who is entitled to know everything about me. You have had more to do with my life than you think": and, taking up the lamp, he opened the door and went in. A cold current of air passed them, and the light shot up for a moment in a flame of murky orange. He shuddered. "Shut the door behind you," he whispered, as he placed the lamp on the table.

Hallward glanced round him, with a puzzled expression. The room looked as if it had not been lived in for years. A faded Flemish tapestry, a curtained picture, an old Italian cassone, and an almost empty bookcase—that was all that it seemed to contain, besides a chair and a table. As Dorian Gray was lighting a half-burned candle that was standing on the mantelshelf, he saw that the whole place was covered with dust, and that the carpet was in holes. A mouse ran scuffling behind the wainscoting. There was a damp odour of mildew.

"So you think that it is only God who sees the soul, Basil? Draw that curtain back, and you will see mine."

The voice that spoke was cold and cruel. "You are mad, Dorian, or playing a part," muttered Hallward, frowning.

"You won't? Then I must do it myself," said the young man; and he tore the curtain from its rod, and flung it on the ground.

An exclamation of horror broke from the painter's lips as he saw in the dim light the hideous face on the canvas grinning at him. There was something in its expression that filled him with disgust and loathing. Good heavens! it was Dorian Gray's own face that he was looking at! The horror, whatever it was, had not yet entirely spoiled that marvellous beauty. There was still some gold in the thinning hair and some scarlet on the sensual mouth. The sodden eyes had kept something of the loveliness of their blue, the noble curves had not yet completely passed away from chiselled nostrils and from plastic throat. Yes, it was Dorian himself. But who had done it? He

1. This was chapter 11 in the *Lippincott's Magazine* edition.

seemed to recognize his own brush-work, and the frame was his own design. The idea was monstrous, yet he felt afraid. He seized the lighted candle, and held it to the picture. In the left-hand corner was his own name, traced in long letters of bright vermilion.

It was some foul parody, some infamous, ignoble satire. He had never done that. Still, it was his own picture. He knew it, and he felt as if his blood had changed in a moment from fire to sluggish ice. His own picture! What did it mean? Why had it altered? He turned, and looked at Dorian Gray with the eyes of a sick man. His mouth twitched, and his parched tongue seemed unable to articulate. He passed his hand across his forehead. It was dank with clammy sweat.

The young man was leaning against the mantel-shelf, watching him with that strange expression that one sees on the faces of those who are absorbed in a play when some great artist is acting. There was neither real sorrow in it nor real joy. There was simply the passion of the spectator, with perhaps a flicker of triumph in his eyes. He had taken the flower out of his coat, and was smelling it, or pretending to do so.

"What does this mean?" cried Hallward, at last. His own voice sounded shrill and curious in his ears.

"Years ago, when I was a boy," said Dorian Gray, crushing the flower in his hand, "you met me, flattered me, and taught me to be vain of my good looks. One day you introduced me to a friend of yours, who explained to me the wonder of youth, and you finished a portrait of me that revealed to me the wonder of beauty. In a mad moment, that, even now, I don't know whether I regret or not, I made a wish, perhaps you would call it a prayer . . ."

"I remember it! Oh, how well I remember it! No! the thing is impossible. The room is damp. Mildew has got into the canvas. The paints I used had some wretched mineral poison in them. I tell you the thing is impossible."

"Ah, what is impossible?" murmured the young man, going over to the window, and leaning his forehead against the cold, mist-stained glass.

"You told me you had destroyed it."

"I was wrong. It has destroyed me."

"I don't believe it is my picture."

"Can't you see your ideal in it?" said Dorian, bitterly.

"My ideal, as you call it . . ."

"As you called it."

"There was nothing evil in it, nothing shameful. You were to me such an ideal as I shall never meet again. This is the face of a satyr."

"It is the face of my soul."

"Christ! what a thing I must have worshipped! It has the eyes of a devil."

"Each of us has Heaven and Hell in him,[2] Basil," cried Dorian, with a wild gesture of despair.

Hallward turned again to the portrait, and gazed at it. "My God! if it is true," he exclaimed, "and this is what you have done with your life, why, you must be worse even than those who talk against you fancy you to be!" He held the light up again to the canvas, and examined it. The surface seemed to be quite undisturbed, and as he had left it. It was from within, apparently, that the foulness and horror had come. Through some strange quickening of inner life the leprosies of sin were slowly eating the thing away. The rotting of a corpse in a watery grave was not so fearful.

His hand shook, and the candle fell from its socket on the floor, and lay there sputtering. He placed his foot on it and put it out. Then he flung himself into the ricketty chair that was standing by the table and buried his face in his hands.

"Good God, Dorian, what a lesson! what an awful lesson!" There was no answer, but he could hear the young man sobbing at the window. "Pray, Dorian, pray," he murmured. "What is it that one was taught to say in one's boyhood? 'Lead us not into temptation. Forgive us our sins. Wash away our iniquities.[3] Let us say that together. The prayer of your pride has been answered. The prayer of your repentance will be answered also. I worshipped you too much. I am punished for it. You worshipped yourself too much. We are both punished."

Dorian Gray turned slowly around, and looked at him with tear-dimmed eyes. "It is too late, Basil," he faltered.

"It is never too late, Dorian. Let us kneel down and try if we cannot remember a prayer. Isn't there a verse somewhere, 'Though your sins be as scarlet, yet I will make them as white as snow'?"[4]

"Those words mean nothing to me now."

"Hush! don't say that. You have done enough evil in your life. My God! don't you see that accursed thing leering at us?"

Dorian Gray glanced at the picture, and suddenly an uncontrollable feeling of hatred for Basil Hallward came over him, as though it had been suggested to him by the image on the canvas, whispered into his ear by those grinning lips. The mad passions of a hunted animal stirred within him, and he loathed the man who was seated at the table, more than in his whole life he had ever loathed anything. He glanced wildly around. Something glimmered on the top of the painted chest that faced him. His eye fell on it. He knew what it was. It was a knife that he had brought up, some days before, to

---

2. Milton, *Paradise Lost* 1.254–55.
3. Basil combines elements of the Lord's Prayer and the *Lavabo* prayer of the Mass (washing of the priest's hands prior to the act of consecration).
4. Isaiah 1:18.

cut a piece of cord, and had forgotten to take away with him. He moved slowly towards it, passing Hallward as he did so. As soon as he got behind him, he seized it, and turned round. Hallward stirred in his chair as if he was going to rise. He rushed at him, and dug the knife into the great vein that is behind the ear, crushing the man's head down on the table, and stabbing again and again.

There was a stifled groan, and the horrible sound of some one choking with blood. Three times the outstretched arms shot up convulsively, waving grotesque stiff-fingered hands in the air. He stabbed him twice more, but the man did not move. Something began to trickle on the floor. He waited for a moment, still pressing the head down. Then he threw the knife on the table, and listened.

He could hear nothing, but the drip, drip on the threadbare carpet. He opened the door and went out on the landing. The house was absolutely quiet. No one was about. For a few seconds he stood bending over the balustrade, and peering down into the black seething well of darkness. Then he took out the key and returned to the room, locking himself in as he did so.

The thing was still seated in the chair, straining over the table with bowed head, and humped back, and long fantastic arms. Had it not been for the red jagged tear in the neck, and the clotted black pool that was slowly widening on the table, one would have said that the man was simply asleep.

How quickly it had all been done! He felt strangely calm, and, walking over to the window, opened it, and stepped out on the balcony. The wind had blown the fog away, and the sky was like a monstrous peacock's tail, starred with myriads of golden eyes. He looked down, and saw the policeman going his rounds and flashing the long beam of his lantern on the doors of the silent houses. The crimson spot of a prowling hansom gleamed at the corner, and then vanished. A woman in a fluttering shawl was creeping slowly by the railings, staggering as she went. Now and then she stopped, and peered back. Once, she began to sing in a hoarse voice. The policeman strolled over and said something to her. She stumbled away, laughing. A bitter blast swept across the Square. The gas-lamps flickered, and became blue, and the leafless trees shook their black iron branches to and fro. He shivered, and went back, closing the window behind him.

Having reached the door, he turned the key, and opened it. He did not even glance at the murdered man. He felt that the secret of the whole thing was not to realize the situation. The friend who had painted the fatal portrait to which all his misery had been due, had gone out of his life. That was enough.

Then he remembered the lamp. It was a rather curious one of Moorish workmanship, made of dull silver inlaid with arabesques of burnished steel, and studded with coarse turquoises. Perhaps it might be missed by his servant, and questions would be asked. He hesitated for a moment, then he turned back and took it from the table. He could not help seeing the dead thing. How still it was! How horribly white the long hands looked! It was like a dreadful wax image.

Having locked the door behind him, he crept quietly downstairs. The woodwork creaked, and seemed to cry out as if in pain. He stopped several times, and waited. No: everything was still. It was merely the sound of his own footsteps.

When he reached the library, he saw the bag and coat in the corner. They must be hidden away somewhere. He unlocked a secret press that was in the wainscoting, a press in which he kept his own curious disguises, and put them into it. He could easily burn them afterwards. Then he pulled out his watch. It was twenty minutes to two.

He sat down, and began to think. Every year—every month, almost—men were strangled in England for what he had done. There had been a madness of murder in the air. Some red star had come too close to the earth. . . . And yet what evidence was there against him? Basil Hallward had left the house at eleven. No one had seen him come in again. Most of the servants were at Selby Royal. His valet had gone to bed. . . . Paris! Yes. It was to Paris that Basil had gone, and by the midnight train, as he had intended. With his curious reserved habits, it would be months before any suspicions would be aroused. Months! Everything could be destroyed long before then.

A sudden thought struck him. He put on his fur coat and hat, and went out into the hall. There he paused, hearing the slow heavy tread of the policeman on the pavement outside, and seeing the flash of the bull's-eye[5] reflected in the window. He waited, and held his breath.

After a few moments he drew back the latch, and slipped out, shutting the door very gently behind him. Then he began ringing the bell. In about five minutes his valet appeared, half dressed, and looking very drowsy.

"I am sorry to have had to wake you up, Francis," he said, stepping in; "but I had forgotten my latch-key. What time is it?"

"Ten minutes past two, sir," answered the man, looking at the clock and blinking.

"Ten minutes past two? How horribly late! You must wake me at nine to-morrow. I have some work to do."

"All right, sir."

"Did any one call this evening?"

---

5. Generic term for a lantern with a thick, ridged lens to magnify the light. This was probably a kerosene lamp.

"Mr. Hallward, sir. He stayed here till eleven, and then he went away to catch his train."

"Oh! I am sorry I didn't see him. Did he leave any message?"

"No, sir, except that he would write to you from Paris, if he did not find you at the club."

"That will do, Francis. Don't forget to call me at nine to-morrow."

"No, sir."

The man shambled down the passage in his slippers.

Dorian Gray threw his hat and coat upon the table, and passed into the library. For a quarter of an hour he walked up and down the room biting his lip, and thinking. Then he took down the Blue Book[6] from one of the shelves, and began to turn over the leaves. "Alan Campbell, 152, Hertford Street, Mayfair."[7] Yes; that was the man he wanted.

Chapter XIV[1]

At nine o'clock the next morning his servant came in with a cup of chocolate on a tray and opened the shutters. Dorian was sleeping quite peacefully, lying on his right side, with one hand underneath his cheek. He looked like a boy who had been tired out with play, or study.

The man had to touch him twice on the shoulder before he woke, and as he opened his eyes a faint smile passed across his lips, as though he had been lost in some delightful dream. Yet he had not dreamed at all. His night had been untroubled by any images of pleasure or of pain. But youth smiles without any reason. It is one of its chiefest charms.

He turned round, and, leaning upon his elbow, began to sip his chocolate. The mellow November sun came streaming into the room. The sky was bright, and there was a genial warmth in the air. It was almost like a morning in May.

Gradually the events of the preceding night crept with silent blood-stained feet into his brain, and reconstructed themselves there with terrible distinctness. He winced at the memory of all that he had suffered, and for a moment the same curious feeling of loathing for Basil Hallward, that had made him kill him as he sat in the chair, came back to him, and he grew cold with passion. The dead man was

---

6. A social directory.

7. About half a mile south of Dorian's residence in Grosvenor Square. The model for Alan Campbell was identified by Hesketh Pearson, in *Oscar Wilde* (New York: Harper, 1946), 318–19, as Sir Peter Chalmers Mitchell, whom, over lunch at the Café Royal, Wilde once asked to describe how to get rid of a body.

1. This was chapter 12 in the *Lippincott's Magazine* edition.

still sitting there, too, and in the sunlight now. How horrible that was! Such hideous things were for the darkness, not for the day.

He felt that if he brooded on what he had gone through he would sicken or grow mad. There were sins whose fascination was more in the memory than in the doing of them, strange triumphs that gratified the pride more than the passions, and gave to the intellect a quickened sense of joy, greater than any joy they brought, or could ever bring, to the senses. But this was not one of them. It was a thing to be driven out of the mind, to be drugged with poppies, to be strangled lest it might strangle one itself.

When the half-hour struck, he passed his hand across his forehead, and then got up hastily, and dressed himself with even more than his usual care, giving a good deal of attention to the choice of his necktie and scarf-pin, and changing his rings more than once. He spent a long time also over breakfast, tasting the various dishes, talking to his valet about some new liveries that he was thinking of getting made for the servants at Selby, and going through his correspondence. At some of the letters he smiled. Three of them bored him. One he read several times over, and then tore up with a slight look of annoyance in his face. "That awful thing, a woman's memory!" as Lord Henry had once said.

After he had drunk his cup of black coffee, he wiped his lips slowly with a napkin, motioned to his servant to wait, and going over to the table sat down and wrote two letters. One he put in his pocket, the other he handed to the valet.

"Take this round to 152, Hertford Street, Francis, and if Mr. Campbell is out of town, get his address."

As soon as he was alone, he lit a cigarette, and began sketching upon a piece of paper, drawing first flowers, and bits of architecture, and then human faces. Suddenly he remarked that every face that he drew seemed to have a fantastic likeness to Basil Hallward. He frowned, and, getting up, went over to the bookcase and took out a volume at hazard. He was determined that he would not think about what had happened until it became absolutely necessary that he should do so.

When he had stretched himself on the sofa, he looked at the title-page of the book. It was Gautier's "Émaux et Camées," Charpentier's Japanese-paper edition,[2] with the Jacquemart etching. The binding was of citron-green leather, with a design of gilt trellis-work and dotted pomegranates. It had been given to him by Adrian Singleton. As he turned over the pages his eye fell on the poem about

---

2. Wilde owned a copy of the 1881 Charpentier edition of *Émaux et Camées*. The first edition was printed in Paris in 1852 and contained eighteen poems. The sixth edition, the last prepared by Gautier (1872), contained forty-seven poems.

the hand of Lacenaire, the cold yellow hand *"du supplice encore mal lavée,"* with its downy red hairs and its *"doigts de faune."*[3] He glanced at his own white taper fingers, shuddering slightly in spite of himself, and passed on, till he came to those lovely stanzas upon Venice:—

> *"Sur une gamme chromatique,*
>   *Le sein de perles ruisselant,*
> *La Vénus de l'Adriatique*
>   *Sort de l'eau son corps rose et blanc.*
>
> *Les dômes, sur l'azur des ondes*
>   *Suivant la phrase au pur contour,*
> *S'enflent comme des gorges rondes*
>   *Que soulève un soupir d'amour.*
>
> *L'esquif aborde et me dépose,*
>   *Jetant son amarre au pilier,*
> *Devant une façade rose,*
>   *Sur le marbre d'un escalier."*[4]

How exquisite they were! As one read them, one seemed to be floating down the green water-ways of the pink and pearl city, seated in a black gondola with silver prow and trailing curtains. The mere lines looked to him like those straight lines of turquoise-blue that follow one as one pushes out to the Lido.[5] The sudden flashes of

---

3. The poem is the second of two titled "Etudes de Mains." Lacenaire was a notorious murderer executed by guillotine; his preserved hand was the subject of Gautier's morbid meditation on the consciousness of evil. The lines Wilde quotes are from stanzas two and three:

> Curiosité dépravée!
> J'ai touché, malgré mes dégoûts,
> Du supplice encore mal lavée,
> Cette chair froide au duvet roux.
> Momifiée et toute jaune
> Comme la main d'un pharoon,
> Elle allonge ses doigts de faune
> Crispés par la tentation.

[Depraved curiosity! I have touched, despite my revulsion, out of pain an evil reborn in that cold flesh with the reddish down. Mummified and completely yellowed as the hand of a pharaoh, the length of its faun-colored fingers shriveled by temptation.] Dorian's own hand in the painting drips blood, and he achieves a perverse yet detached fascination as he compares his emotion at seeing his own hand with that generated by the voice of the poet contemplating the hand of the murderer Lacenaire. It must have been something very like the emotion with which Wilde contemplated himself as a sinner and criminal. Wilde's interest in murder as an art form is expressed in his essay in *Intentions*, "Pen, Pencil and Poison" (1889).
4. The three stanzas on this page are from Gautier's "Variations sur le Carnival de Venise," part 2, titled "Sur les Lagunes." They translate: "As though in a chromatic scale, her pearly breast streaming, the Venus of the Adriatic emerges from the waters, her body red and white. The cathedral domes above the blue waters, following the perfectly contoured line, swell as the rounded throat that heaves a sigh of love. As the gondola arrived, I cast the rope around a piling and landed in front of a rose-colored façade upon a marble staircase."
5. A resort isle near Venice.

colour reminded him of the gleam of the opal-and-iris-throated birds that flutter round the tall honey-combed Campanile,[6] or stalk, with such stately grace, through the dim, dust-stained arcades. Leaning back with half-closed eyes, he kept saying over and over to himself:—

> *Devant une façade rose,*
> *Sur le marbre d'un escalier.*

The whole of Venice was in those two lines. He remembered the autumn that he had passed there, and a wonderful love that had stirred him to mad, delightful follies. There was romance in every place. But Venice, like Oxford, had kept the background for romance, and, to the true romantic, background was everything, or almost everything. Basil had been with him part of the time, and had gone wild over Tintoret.[7] Poor Basil! what a horrible way for a man to die!

He sighed, and took up the volume again, and tried to forget. He read of the swallows that fly in and out of the little café at Smyrna where the Hadjis[8] sit counting their amber beads and the turbaned merchants smoke their long tasseled pipes and talk gravely to each other; he read of the Obelisk in the Place de la Concorde[9] that weeps tears of granite in its lonely sunless exile, and longs to be back by the hot, lotus-covered Nile, where there are Sphinxes, and rose-red ibises,[1] and white vultures with gilded claws, and crocodiles, with small beryl eyes that crawl over the green steaming mud; he began to brood over those verses which, drawing music from kiss-stained marble, tell of that curious statue that Gautier compares to

6. A bell tower, probably that of Saint Mark's Church, although Venice boasts many bell towers.
7. Jacopo Robusti, called Tintoretto (1518–1594), was a master Venetian painter greatly admired by Ruskin. The associations between Basil and Ruskin here are specific and unmistakable. Ruskin was a graduate of Oxford and later taught there. For him, Venice was the great city of Gothic architecture and later baroque painting. *The Stones of Venice* (1851–53) was Ruskin's masterpiece, blending art and social criticism to trace the rise and fall of Venice as recorded in its architecture.
8. Muslims who have made the Mecca pilgrimage. The beads are prayer beads. *Smyrna:* Now called İzmir, in Turkey, on the Gulf of İzmir. Dorian read of swallows in Gautier's poem "Ce Que Disent les Hirondelles" (What the swallows told) from *Émaux et Camées*. "He read . . . each other" is a loose prose translation of stanzas 6 and 7 of that poem.
9. The reference is to Gautier's "Nostalgies d'Obelisques," and from this point to "steaming mud," Wilde gives an effective prose summary of "L'Obelisque de Paris," first of the two parts of the poem. In the preceeding pages since Dorian took up Gautier's volume of poems, Wilde has been demonstrating an Aesthetic reading of selected poems by Gautier as they reflect and intensify Dorian's pathology of mind and mood. The obelisk is a single block of red granite about seventy-five feet tall. It was placed before the great temple of Luxor by Ramses II in the thirteenth century BCE. It now stands in the center of the huge square in Paris, a gift of the viceroy of Egypt to King Louis Philippe in 1831.
1. A genus of large grallatorial birds of the family *Ibididæ*, allied to the stork and heron, comprising numerous species with long legs and long slender decurved bill, inhabiting lakes and swamps in warm climates; a bird of this genus, esp. (and originally) the Sacred Ibis of Egypt (*Ibis religiosa*), with white and black plumage, an object of veneration among the ancient Egyptians [OED].

a contralto voice, the *"monstre charmant"* that couches in the porphyry-room of the Louvre.[2] But after a time the book fell from his hand. He grew nervous, and a horrible fit of terror came over him. What if Alan Campbell should be out of England? Days would elapse before he could come back. Perhaps he might refuse to come. What could he do then? Every moment was of vital importance.

They had been great friends once, five years before—almost inseparable, indeed. Then the intimacy had come suddenly to an end. When they met in society now, it was only Dorian Gray who smiled: Alan Campbell never did.

He was an extremely clever young man, though he had no real appreciation of the visible arts, and whatever little sense of the beauty of poetry he possessed he had gained entirely from Dorian. His dominant intellectual passion was for science. At Cambridge he had spent a great deal of his time working in the Laboratory, and had taken a good class in the Natural Science Tripos of his year[3] Indeed, he was still devoted to the study of chemistry, and had a laboratory of his own, in which he used to shut himself up all day long, greatly to the annoyance of his mother, who had set her heart on his standing for Parliament and had a vague idea that a chemist[4] was a person who made up prescriptions. He was an excellent musician, however, as well, and played both the violin and the piano better than most amateurs. In fact, it was music that had first brought him and Dorian Gray together—music and that indefinable attraction that Dorian seemed to be able to exercise whenever he wished, and indeed exercised often without being conscious of it. They had met at Lady Berkshire's the night that Rubinstein[5] played there, and after that used to be always seen together at the Opera, and wherever good music was going on. For eighteen months their intimacy lasted. Campbell was always either at Selby Royal or in Grosvenor Square. To him, as to many others, Dorian Gray was the type of everything that is wonderful and fascinating in life. Whether or not a quarrel had taken place between them no one ever knew. But suddenly people remarked that they scarcely spoke when they met, and that Campbell seemed always to go away early from any party at which Dorian Gray was present. He had changed, too—was strangely melancholy at times, appeared

---

2. In Paris; one of the most famous art museums in the world. *"Monstre charmant"*: The "sweet monster" of indeterminate sex is hermaphroditic.
3. The Tripos is an examination at Cambridge for the honors BA degree. Of the two great English universities, Cambridge has traditionally excelled in the sciences, Oxford in languages and the humanities.
4. The popular English name for a pharmacist.
5. Anton Rubenstein (1830–1894), composer and piano virtuoso, whose music and style of playing were heavily Romantic.

almost to dislike hearing music, and would never himself play, giving as his excuse, when he was called upon, that he was so absorbed in science that he had no time left in which to practice. And this was certainly true. Every day he seemed to become more interested in biology, and his name appeared once or twice in some of the scientific reviews, in connection with certain curious experiments.

This was the man Dorian Gray was waiting for. Every second he kept glancing at the clock. As the minutes went by he became horribly agitated. At last he got up, and began to pace up and down the room, looking like a beautiful caged thing. He took long stealthy strides. His hands were curiously cold.

The suspense became unbearable. Time seemed to him to be crawling with feet of lead, while he by monstrous winds was being swept towards the jagged edge of some black cleft of precipice. He knew what was waiting for him there; saw it indeed, and, shuddering, crushed with dank hands his burning lids as though he would have robbed the very brain of sight, and driven the eyeballs back into their cave. It was useless. The brain had its own food on which it battened, and the imagination, made grotesque by terror, twisted and distorted as a living thing by pain, danced like some foul puppet on a stand, and grinned through moving masks. Then, suddenly, Time stopped for him. Yes: that blind, slow-breathing thing crawled no more, and horrible thoughts, Time being dead, raced nimbly on in front, and dragged a hideous future from its grave, and showed it to him. He stared at it. Its very horror made him stone.

At last the door opened, and his servant entered. He turned glazed eyes upon him.

"Mr. Campbell, sir," said the man.

A sigh of relief broke from his parched lips, and the colour came back to his cheeks.

"Ask him to come in at once, Francis." He felt that he was himself again. His mood of cowardice had passed away.

The man bowed, and retired. In a few moments Alan Campbell walked in, looking very stern and rather pale, his pallor being intensified by his coal-black hair and dark eyebrows.

"Alan! this is kind of you. I thank you for coming."

"I had intended never to enter your house again, Gray. But you said it was a matter of life and death." His voice was hard and cold. He spoke with slow deliberation. There was a look of contempt in the steady searching gaze that he turned on Dorian. He kept his hands in the pockets of his Astrakhan[6] coat, and seemed not to have noticed the gesture with which he had been greeted.

---

6. A kind of cloth used chiefly as an edging or trimming for garments. It mimics the fleece of a newborn lamb.

"Yes: it is a matter of life and death, Alan, and to more than one person. Sit down."

Campbell took a chair by the table, and Dorian sat opposite to him. The two men's eyes met. In Dorian's there was infinite pity. He knew that what he was going to do was dreadful.

After a strained moment of silence, he leaned across and said, very quietly, but watching the effect of each word upon the face of him he had sent for, "Alan, in a locked room at the top of this house, a room to which nobody but myself has access, a dead man is seated at a table. He has been dead ten hours now. Don't stir, and don't look at me like that. Who the man is, why he died, how he died, are matters that do not concern you. What you have to do is this—"

"Stop, Gray. I don't want to know anything further. Whether what you have told me is true or not true, doesn't concern me. I entirely decline to be mixed up in your life. Keep your horrible secrets to yourself. They don't interest me any more."

"Alan, they will have to interest you. This one will have to interest you. I am awfully sorry for you, Alan. But I can't help myself. You are the one man who is able to save me. I am forced to bring you into the matter. I have no option. Alan, you are scientific. You know about chemistry, and things of that kind. You have made experiments. What you have got to do is to destroy the thing that is upstairs—to destroy it so that not a vestige of it will be left. Nobody saw this person come into the house. Indeed, at the present moment he is supposed to be in Paris. He will not be missed for months. When he is missed, there must be no trace of him found here. You, Alan, you must change him, and everything that belongs to him, into a handful of ashes that I may scatter in the air."

"You are mad, Dorian."

"Ah! I was waiting for you to call me Dorian."

"You are mad, I tell you—mad to imagine that I would raise a finger to help you, mad to make this monstrous confession. I will have nothing to do with this matter, whatever it is. Do you think I am going to peril my reputation for you? What is it to me what devil's work you are up to?"

"It was suicide, Alan."

"I am glad of that. But who drove him to it? You, I should fancy."

"Do you still refuse to do this for me?"

"Of course I refuse. I will have absolutely nothing to do with it. I don't care what shame comes on you. You deserve it all. I should not be sorry to see you disgraced, publicly disgraced. How dare you ask me, of all men in the world, to mix myself up in this horror? I should have thought you knew more about people's characters. Your friend Lord Henry Wotton can't have taught you much about psychology, whatever else he has taught you. Nothing will induce me to stir a step to help you. You have come to the wrong man. Go to some of your friends. Don't come to me."

"Alan, it was murder. I killed him. You don't know what he had made me suffer. Whatever my life is, he had more to do with the making or the marring of it than poor Harry has had. He may not have intended it, the result was the same."

"Murder! Good God, Dorian, is that what you have come to? I shall not inform upon you. It is not my business. Besides, without my stirring in the matter, you are certain to be arrested. Nobody ever commits a crime without doing something stupid. But I will have nothing to do with it."

"You must have something to do with it. Wait, wait a moment; listen to me. Only listen, Alan. All I ask of you is to perform a certain scientific experiment. You go to hospitals and dead-houses, and the horrors that you do there don't affect you. If in some hideous dissecting-room or fetid laboratory you found this man lying on a leaden table with red gutters scooped out in it for the blood to flow through, you would simply look upon him as an admirable subject. You would not turn a hair. You would not believe that you were doing anything wrong. On the contrary, you would probably feel that you were benefiting the human race, or increasing the sum of knowledge in the world, or gratifying intellectual curiosity, or something of that kind. What I want you to do is merely what you have often done before. Indeed, to destroy a body must be far less horrible than what you are accustomed to work at. And, remember, it is the only piece of evidence against me. If it is discovered, I am lost; and it is sure to be discovered unless you help me."

"I have no desire to help you. You forget that. I am simply indifferent to the whole thing. It has nothing to do with me."

"Alan, I entreat you. Think of the position I am in. Just before you came I almost fainted with terror. You may know terror yourself some day. No! don't think of that. Look at the matter purely from the scientific point of view. You don't inquire where the dead things on which you experiment come from. Don't inquire now. I have told you too much as it is. But I beg of you to do this. We were friends once, Alan."

"Don't speak about those days, Dorian: they are dead."

"The dead linger sometimes. The man upstairs will not go away. He is sitting at the table with bowed head and outstretched arms. Alan! Alan! If you don't come to my assistance I am ruined. Why, they will hang me, Alan! Don't you understand? They will hang me for what I have done."

"There is no good in prolonging this scene. I absolutely refuse to do anything in the matter. It is insane of you to ask me."

"You refuse?"

"Yes."

"I entreat you, Alan."

"It is useless."

The same look of pity came into Dorian Gray's eyes. Then he stretched out his hand, took a piece of paper, and wrote something on it. He read it over twice, folded it carefully, and pushed it across the table. Having done this, he got up, and went over to the window.

Campbell looked at him in surprise, and then took up the paper, and opened it. As he read it, his face became ghastly pale, and he fell back in his chair. A horrible sense of sickness came over him. He felt as if his heart was beating itself to death in some empty hollow.

After two or three minutes of terrible silence, Dorian turned round, and came and stood behind him, putting his hand upon his shoulder.

"I am so sorry for you, Alan," he murmured, "but you leave me no alternative. I have a letter written already. Here it is. You see the address. If you don't help me, I must send it. If you don't help me, I will send it. You know what the result will be. But you are going to help me. It is impossible for you to refuse now. I tried to spare you. You will do me the justice to admit that. You were stern, harsh, offensive. You treated me as no man has ever dared to treat me—no living man, at any rate. I bore it all. Now it is for me to dictate terms."

Campbell buried his face in his hands, and a shudder passed through him.

"Yes, it is my turn to dictate terms, Alan. You know what they are. The thing is quite simple. Come, don't work yourself into this fever. The thing has to be done. Face it, and do it."

A groan broke from Campbell's lips, and he shivered all over. The ticking of the clock on the mantelpiece seemed to him to be dividing Time into separate atoms of agony, each of which was too terrible to be borne. He felt as if an iron ring was being slowly tightened round his forehead, as if the disgrace with which he was threatened had already come upon him. The hand upon his shoulder weighed like a hand of lead. It was intolerable. It seemed to crush him.

"Come, Alan, you must decide at once."

"I cannot do it," he said, mechanically, as though words could alter things.

"You must. You have no choice. Don't delay."

He hesitated a moment. "Is there a fire in the room upstairs?"

"Yes, there is a gas-fire with asbestos."

"I shall have to go home and get some things from the laboratory."

"No, Alan, you must not leave the house. Write out on a sheet of note-paper what you want, and my servant will take a cab and bring the things back to you."

Campbell scrawled a few lines, blotted them, and addressed an envelope to his assistant. Dorian took the note up and read it carefully. Then he rang the bell, and gave it to his valet, with orders to return as soon as possible, and to bring the things with him.

As the hall door shut, Campbell started nervously, and, having got up from the chair, went over to the chimney-piece. He was shivering with a kind of ague. For nearly twenty minutes, neither of the men spoke. A fly buzzed noisily about the room, and the ticking of the clock was like the beat of a hammer.

As the chime struck one, Campbell turned round, and, looking at Dorian Gray, saw that his eyes were filled with tears. There was something in the purity and refinement of that sad face that seemed to enrage him. "You are infamous, absolutely infamous!" he muttered.

"Hush, Alan: you have saved my life," said Dorian.

"Your life? Good heavens! what a life that is! You have gone from corruption to corruption, and now you have culminated in crime. In doing what I am going to do, what you force me to do, it is not of your life that I am thinking."

"Ah, Alan," murmured Dorian, with a sigh, "I wish you had a thousandth part of the pity for me that I have for you." He turned away as he spoke, and stood looking out at the garden. Campbell made no answer.

After about ten minutes a knock came to the door, and the servant entered, carrying a large mahogany chest of chemicals, with a long coil of steel and platinum wire and two rather curiously-shaped iron clamps.

"Shall I leave the things here, sir?" he asked Campbell.

"Yes," said Dorian. "And I am afraid, Francis, that I have another errand for you. What is the name of the man at Richmond who supplies Selby with orchids?"

"Harden, sir."

"Yes—Harden. You must go down to Richmond at once, see Harden personally, and tell him to send twice as many orchids as I ordered, and to have as few white ones as possible. In fact, I don't want any white ones. It is a lovely day, Francis, and Richmond is a very pretty place, otherwise I wouldn't bother you about it."

"No trouble, sir. At what time shall I be back?"

Dorian looked at Campbell. "How long will your experiment take, Alan?" he said, in a calm, indifferent voice. The presence of a third person in the room seemed to give him extraordinary courage.

Campbell frowned, and bit his lip. "It will take about five hours," he answered.

"It will be time enough, then, if you are back at half-past seven, Francis. Or stay: just leave my things out for dressing. You can have the evening to yourself. I am not dining at home, so I shall not want you."

"Thank you, sir," said the man, leaving the room.

"Now, Alan, there is not a moment to be lost. How heavy this chest is! I'll take it for you. You bring the other things." He spoke rapidly, and in an authoritative manner. Campbell felt dominated by him. They left the room together.

When they reached the top landing, Dorian took out the key and turned it in the lock. Then he stopped, and a troubled look came into his eyes. He shuddered. "I don't think I can go in, Alan," he murmured.

"It is nothing to me. I don't require you," said Campbell, coldly.

Dorian half opened the door. As he did so, he saw the face of his portrait leering in the sunlight. On the floor in front of it the torn curtain was lying. He remembered that the night before he had forgotten, for the first time in his life, to hide the fatal canvas, and was about to rush forward, when he drew back with a shudder.

What was that loathsome red dew that gleamed, wet and glistening, on one of the hands, as though the canvas had sweated blood? How horrible it was!—more horrible, it seemed to him for the moment, than the silent thing that he knew was stretched across the table, the thing whose grotesque misshapen shadow on the spotted carpet showed him that it had not stirred, but was still there, as he had left it.

He heaved a deep breath, opened the door a little wider, and with half-closed eyes and averted head walked quickly in, determined that he would not look even once upon the dead man. Then, stooping down, and taking up the gold-and-purple hanging, he flung it right over the picture.

There he stopped, feeling afraid to turn round, and his eyes fixed themselves on the intricacies of the pattern before him. He heard Campbell bringing in the heavy chest, and the irons, and the other things that he had required for his dreadful work. He began to wonder if he and Basil Hallward had ever met, and, if so, what they had thought of each other.

"Leave me now," said a stern voice behind him.

He turned and hurried out, just conscious that the dead man had been thrust back into the chair, and that Campbell was gazing into a glistening yellow face. As he was going downstairs he heard the key being turned in the lock.

It was long after seven when Campbell came back into the library. He was pale, but absolutely calm. "I have done what you asked me to do," he muttered, "And now, good-bye. Let us never see each other again."

"You have saved me from ruin, Alan. I cannot forget that," said Dorian, simply.

As soon as Campbell had left, he went upstairs. There was a horrible smell of nitric acid in the room. But the thing that had been sitting at the table was gone.

Chapter XV[1]

That evening, at eight-thirty, exquisitely dressed, and wearing a large buttonhole of Parma violets, Dorian Gray was ushered into Lady Narborough's drawing-room by bowing servants. His forehead was throbbing with maddened nerves, and he felt wildly excited, but his manner as he bent over his hostess's hand was as easy and graceful as ever. Perhaps one never seems so much at one's ease as when one has to play a part. Certainly no one looking at Dorian Gray that night could have believed that he had passed through a tragedy as horrible as any tragedy of our age. Those finely-shaped fingers could never have clutched a knife for sin, nor those smiling lips have cried out on God and goodness. He himself could not help wondering at the calm of his demeanour, and for a moment felt keenly the terrible pleasure of a double life.

It was a small party, got up rather in a hurry by Lady Narborough,[2] who was a very clever woman, with what Lord Henry used to describe as the remains of really remarkable ugliness. She had proved an excellent wife to one of our most tedious ambassadors, and having buried her husband properly in a marble mausoleum, which she had herself designed, and married off her daughters to some rich, rather elderly men, she devoted herself now to the pleasures of French fiction, French cookery, and French esprit[3] when she could get it.

Dorian was one of her especial favourites, and she always told him that she was extremely glad she had not met him in early life. "I know, my dear, I should have fallen madly in love with you," she used to say, "and thrown my bonnet right over the mills for your sake. It is most fortunate that you were not thought of at the time. As it was, our bonnets were so unbecoming, and the mills were so occupied in trying to raise the wind, that I never had even a flirtation with anybody. However, that was all Narborough's fault. He was

---

1. Wilde wrote this and the next three chapters for this edition.
2. Walter Pater singles out these scenes of comic satire as especially effective counterpoints to the mounting disorder of Dorian's emotions. Frank Harris also praised the social comedy in *The Picture of Dorian Gray*, saying that none could thereafter deny Wilde a place among the leading comic geniuses in English. It was Harris (81) who asserted that with *The Picture of Dorian Gray*, Wilde had finally justified himself as an artist.
3. Wit; in this case, witty conversation.

dreadfully short-sighted, and there is no pleasure in taking in a husband who never sees anything."

Her guests this evening were rather tedious. The fact was, as she explained to Dorian, behind a very shabby fan, one of her married daughters had come up quite suddenly to stay with her, and, to make matters worse, had actually brought her husband with her. "I think it is most unkind of her, my dear," she whispered. "Of course I go and stay with them every summer after I come from Homburg,[4] but then an old woman like me must have fresh air sometimes, and besides, I really wake them up. You don't know what an existence they lead down there. It is pure unadulterated country life. They get up early, because they have so much to do, and go to bed early because they have so little to think about. There has not been a scandal in the neighbourhood since the time of Queen Elizabeth, and consequently they all fall asleep after dinner. You shan't sit next either of them. You shall sit by me, and amuse me."

Dorian murmured a graceful compliment, and looked round the room. Yes: it was certainly a tedious party. Two of the people he had never seen before, and the others consisted of Ernest Harrowden, one of those middle-aged mediocrities so common in London clubs who have no enemies, but are thoroughly disliked by their friends; Lady Ruxton, an overdressed woman of forty-seven, with a hooked nose, who was always trying to get herself compromised, but was so peculiarly plain that to her great disappointment no one would ever believe anything against her; Mrs. Erlynne,[5] a pushing nobody, with a delightful lisp, and Venetian-red hair; Lady Alice Chapman, his hostess's daughter, a dowdy dull girl, with one of those characteristic British faces, that, once seen, are never remembered; and her husband, a red-cheeked, white-whiskered creature who, like so many of his class, was under the impression that inordinate joviality can atone for an entire lack of ideas.

He was rather sorry he had come, till Lady Narborough, looking at the great ormolu gilt clock[6] that sprawled in gaudy curves on the mauve-draped mantelshelf, exclaimed: "How horrid of Henry Wotton to be so late! I sent round to him this morning on chance, and he promised faithfully not to disappoint me."

It was some consolation that Harry was to be there, and when the door opened and he heard his slow musical voice lending charm to some insincere apology, he ceased to feel bored.

---

4. A resort near Frankfurt, famous for its mineral springs.
5. The 1891 edition variously refers to Lady Ruxton and Lady Roxton. I have regularized the name to Ruxton. Mrs. Erlynne reappears as the déclassé woman with a past in Wilde's 1892 play, *Lady Windermere's Fan*. She bears a striking resemblance in more than just appearance to a middle-aged Lillie Langtry.
6. Ormolu gilt was an alloy of copper and tin or zinc resembling gold and popular during the late Victorian period for decorating furniture, jewelry, and the like.

But at dinner he could not eat anything. Plate after plate went away untasted. Lady Narborough kept scolding him for what she called "an insult to poor Adolphe, who invented the *menu* specially for you," and now and then Lord Henry looked across at him, wondering at his silence and abstracted manner. From time to time the butler filled his glass with champagne. He drank eagerly, and his thirst seemed to increase.

"Dorian," said Lord Henry, at last, as the *chaud-froid*[7] was being handed round, "what is the matter with you to-night? You are quite out of sorts."

"I believe he is in love," cried Lady Narborough, "and that he is afraid to tell me for fear I should be jealous. He is quite right. I certainly should."

"Dear Lady Narborough," murmured Dorian, smiling, "I have not been in love for a whole week—not, in fact, since Madame de Ferrol left town."

"How you men can fall in love with that woman!" exclaimed the old lady. "I really cannot understand it."

"It is simply because she remembers you when you were a little girl, Lady Narborough," said Lord Henry. "She is the one link between us and your short frocks."

"She does not remember my short frocks at all, Lord Henry. But I remember her very well at Vienna thirty years ago, and how *décolletée*[8] she was then."

"She is still *décolletée*," he answered, taking an olive in his long fingers; "and when she is in a very smart gown she looks like an *édition de luxe*[9] of a bad French novel. She is really wonderful, and full of surprises. Her capacity for family affection is extraordinary. When her third husband died, her hair turned quite gold from grief."[1]

"How can you, Harry!" cried Dorian.

"It is a most romantic explanation," laughed the hostess. "But her third husband, Lord Henry! You don't mean to say Ferrol is the fourth?"

"Certainly, Lady Narborough."

"I don't believe a word of it."

"Well, ask Mr. Gray. He is one of her most intimate friends."

"Is it true, Mr. Gray?"

---

7. A white or brown jellied sauce used as an aspic with cold meats.
8. A low-cut or plunging neckline designed to produce a tantalizing partial exposure of the female bosom. In this context, the speakers use it as a commentary on the behavior of Madame de Ferrol.
9. A sumptuously, even extravagantly, produced book with every care given to paper, illustrations, binding, and other physical attributes.
1. Algernon Moncrieff makes the same observation about Lady Harbury in Act I of *The Importance of Being Earnest*.

"She assures me so, Lady Narborough," said Dorian. "I asked her whether, like Marguerite de Navarre,[2] she had their hearts embalmed and hung at her girdle. She told me she didn't, because none of them had had any hearts at all."

"Four husbands! Upon my word that is *trop de zèle.*"[3]

"*Trop d'audace,*[4] I tell her," said Dorian.

"Oh! she is audacious enough for anything, my dear. And what is Ferrol like? I don't know him."

"The husbands of very beautiful women belong to the criminal classes," said Lord Henry, sipping his wine.

Lady Narborough hit him with her fan. "Lord Henry, I am not at all surprised that the world says that you are extremely wicked."

"But what world says that?" asked Lord Henry, elevating his eyebrows. "It can only be the next world. This world and I are on excellent terms."

"Everybody I know says you are very wicked," cried the old lady, shaking her head.

Lord Henry looked serious for some moments. "It is perfectly monstrous," he said, at last, "the way people go about nowadays saying things against one behind one's back that are absolutely and entirely true."

"Isn't he incorrigible?" cried Dorian, leaning forward in his chair.

"I hope so," said his hostess, laughing. "But really if you all worship Madame de Ferrol in this ridiculous way, I shall have to marry again so as to be in the fashion."

"You will never marry again, Lady Narborough," broke in Lord Henry. "You were far too happy. When a woman marries again it is because she detested her first husband. When a man marries again, it is because he adored his first wife. Women try their luck; men risk theirs."

"Narborough wasn't perfect," cried the old lady.

"If he had been, you would not have loved him, my dear lady," was the rejoinder. "Women love us for our defects. If we have enough of them they will forgive us everything, even our intellects. You will never ask me to dinner again, after saying this, I am afraid, Lady Narborough; but it is quite true."

"Of course it is true, Lord Henry. If we women did not love you for your defects, where would you all be? Not one of you would ever be married. You would be a set of unfortunate bachelors. Not, however, that that would alter you much. Nowadays all the married men live like bachelors, and all the bachelors like married men."

2. The same person as Margaret of Valois (see p. 41, n. 4).
3. Too much ardor (French).
4. Too much impudence (French).

"*Fin de siècle*,"[5] murmured Lord Henry.

"*Fin du globe*,"[6] answered his hostess.

"I wish it were *fin du globe*," said Dorian, with a sigh. "Life is a great disappointment."

"Ah, my dear," cried Lady Narborough, putting on her gloves, "don't tell me that you have exhausted Life. When a man says that one knows that Life has exhausted him. Lord Henry is very wicked, and I sometimes wish that I had been; but you are made to be good— you look so good. I must find you a nice wife. Lord Henry, don't you think that Mr. Gray should get married?"

"I am always telling him so, Lady Narborough," said Lord Henry, with a bow.

"Well, we must look out for a suitable match for him. I shall go through Debrett[7] carefully to-night, and draw out a list of all the eligible young ladies."

"With their ages, Lady Narborough?" asked Dorian.

"Of course, with their ages, slightly edited. But nothing must be done in a hurry. I want it to be what *The Morning Post* calls a suitable alliance, and I want you both to be happy."

"What nonsense people talk about happy marriages!" exclaimed Lord Henry. "A man can be happy with any woman, as long as he does not love her."

"Ah! what a cynic you are!" cried the old lady, pushing back her chair, and nodding to Lady Ruxton. "You must come and dine with me soon again. You are really an admirable tonic, much better than what Sir Andrew prescribes for me. You must tell me what people you would like to meet, though. I want it to be a delightful gathering."

"I like men who have a future, and women who have a past," he answered. "Or do you think that would make it a petticoat party?"

"I fear so," she said, laughing, as she stood up. "A thousand pardons, my dear Lady Ruxton," she added, "I didn't see you hadn't finished your cigarette."

"Never mind, Lady Narborough. I smoke a great deal too much. I am going to limit myself, for the future."

"Pray don't, Lady Ruxton," said Lord Henry. "Moderation is a fatal thing. Enough is as bad as a meal. More than enough is as good as a feast."

---

5. "End of the century" referred more to a state of mind and style of life than to the 1890s. The French phrase became synonymous with that sense of exhausted energy, lost values, and discontent with the commonplace that was the sad side of the Gay Nineties.

6. End of the world (French).

7. *Debrett's Peerage* was the standard reference to British and Irish aristocracy.

Lady Ruxton glanced at him curiously. "You must come and explain that to me some afternoon, Lord Henry. It sounds a fascinating theory," she murmured, as she swept out of the room.

"Now, mind you don't stay too long over your politics and scandal," cried Lady Narborough from the door. "If you do, we are sure to squabble upstairs."

The men laughed, and Mr. Chapman got up solemnly from the foot of the table and came up to the top. Dorian Gray changed his seat, and went and sat by Lord Henry. Mr. Chapman began to talk in a loud voice about the situation in the House of Commons. He guffawed at his adversaries. The word *doctrinaire*[8]—word full of terror to the British mind—reappeared from time to time between his explosions. An alliterative prefix served as an ornament of oratory. He hoisted the Union Jack[9] on the pinnacles of Thought. The inherited stupidity of the race—sound English common sense he jovially termed it—was shown to be the proper bulwark for Society.

A smile curved Lord Henry's lips, and he turned round and looked at Dorian.

"Are you better, my dear fellow?" he asked. "You seemed rather out of sorts at dinner."

"I am quite well, Harry. I am tired. That is all."

"You were charming last night. The little Duchess is quite devoted to you. She tells me she is going down to Selby."

"She has promised to come on the twentieth."

"Is Monmouth to be there too?"

"Oh, yes, Harry."

"He bores me dreadfully, almost as much as he bores her. She is very clever, too clever for a woman. She lacks the indefinable charm of weakness. It is the feet of clay that make the gold of the image precious. Her feet are very pretty, but they are not feet of clay. White porcelain feet, if you like. They have been through the fire, and what fire does not destroy, it hardens. She has had experiences."

"How long has she been married?" asked Dorian.

"An eternity, she tells me. I believe, according to the peerage, it is ten years, but ten years with Monmouth must have been like eternity, with time thrown in. Who else is coming?"

"Oh, the Willoughbys, Lord Rugby and his wife, our hostess, Geoffrey Clouston, the usual set. I have asked Lord Grotrian."

8. Someone obstinately devoted to a theory without regard to its appropriateness or its applicability; originally, a member of the French constitutionalist party after the downfall of Napoleon.
9. The national flag of England, Scotland, and Ireland, consisting of the three crosses of each nation overlaid: the red cross of St. George, and the white crosses of St. Andrew (Scotland) and St. Patrick (Ireland) on a blue field.

"I like him," said Lord Henry. "A great many people don't, but I find him charming. He atones for being occasionally somewhat over-dressed, by being always absolutely over-educated.[1] He is a very modern type."

"I don't know if he will be able to come, Harry. He may have to go to Monte Carlo with his father."

"Ah! what a nuisance people's people are! Try and make him come. By the way, Dorian, you ran off very early last night. You left before eleven. What did you do afterwards? Did you go straight home?"

Dorian glanced at him hurriedly, and frowned. "No, Harry," he said at last, "I did not get home till nearly three."

"Did you go to the club?"

"Yes," he answered. Then he bit his lip. "No, I don't mean that. I didn't go to the club. I walked about. I forget what I did. . . . How inquisitive you are, Harry! You always want to know what one has been doing. I always want to forget what I have been doing. I came in at half-past two, if you wish to know the exact time. I had left my latch-key at home, and my servant had to let me in. If you want any corroborative evidence on the subject you can ask him."

Lord Henry shrugged his shoulders. "My dear fellow, as if I cared! Let us go up to the drawing-room. No sherry, thank you, Mr. Chapman. Something has happened to you, Dorian. Tell me what it is. You are not yourself to-night."

"Don't mind me, Harry. I am irritable, and out of temper. I shall come round and see you to-morrow, or next day. Make my excuses to Lady Narborough. I shan't go upstairs. I shall go home. I must go home."

"All right, Dorian. I dare say I shall see you to-morrow at tea-time. The Duchess is coming."

"I will try to be there, Harry," he said, leaving the room. As he drove back to his own house he was conscious that the sense of terror he thought he had strangled had come back to him. Lord Henry's casual questioning had made him lose his nerves for the moment, and he wanted his nerve still. Things that were dangerous had to be destroyed. He winced. He hated the idea of even touching them.

Yet it had to be done. He realized that, and when he had locked the door of his library, he opened the secret press into which he had thrust Basil Hallward's coat and bag. A huge fire was blazing. He piled another log on it. The smell of the singeing clothes and burn-ing leather was horrible. It took him three-quarters of an hour to consume everything. At the end he felt faint and sick, and having lit

1. Algernon Moncrieff uses a variation on this line in Act II of *The Importance of Being Earnest*.

some Algerian pastilles[2] in a pierced copper brazier, he bathed his hands and forehead with a cool musk-scented vinegar.

Suddenly he started. His eyes grew strangely bright, and he gnawed nervously at his under-lip. Between two of the windows stood a large Florentine cabinet, made out of ebony, and inlaid with ivory and blue lapis.[3] He watched it as though it were a thing that could fascinate and make afraid, as though it held something that he longed for and yet almost loathed. His breath quickened. A mad craving came over him. He lit a cigarette and then threw it away. His eyelids drooped till the long fringed lashes almost touched his cheek. But he still watched the cabinet. At last he got up from the sofa on which he had been lying, went over to it, and, having unlocked it, touched some hidden spring. A triangular drawer passed slowly out. His fingers moved instinctively towards it, dipped in, and closed on something. It was a small Chinese box of black and gold-dust lacquer, elaborately wrought, the sides patterned with curved waves, and the silken cords hung with round crystals and tasseled in plaited metal threads. He opened it. Inside was a green paste[4] waxy in lustre, the odour curiously heavy and persistent.

He hesitated for some moments, with a strangely immobile smile upon his face. Then shivering, though the atmosphere of the room was terribly hot, he drew himself up, and glanced at the clock. It was twenty minutes to twelve. He put the box back, shutting the cabinet doors as he did so, and went into his bedroom.

As midnight was striking bronze blows upon the dusky air, Dorian Gray, dressed commonly, and with a muffler wrapped round his throat, crept quietly out of his house. In Bond Street he found a hansom with a good horse. He hailed it, and in a low voice gave the driver an address.[5]

The man shook his head. "It is too far for me," he muttered.

"Here is a sovereign for you," said Dorian. "You shall have another if you drive fast."

"All right, sir," answered the man, "you will be there in an hour," and after his fare had got in he turned his horse round, and drove rapidly towards the river.

2. Aromatic tablets burned as incense.
3. An opaque gemstone of varying shades of blue, similar in other respects to jade.
4. Opium in a form to be smoked, usually in a porcelain pipe.
5. The address presumably was in London's Chinatown, near the docks, where opium dens prospered.

Chapter XVI

A cold rain began to fall, and the blurred street-lamps looked ghastly in the dripping mist. The public-houses were just closing, and dim men and women were clustering in broken groups round their doors. From some of the bars came the sound of horrible laughter. In others, drunkards brawled and screamed.

Lying back in the hansom, with his hat pulled over his forehead, Dorian Gray watched with listless eyes the sordid shame of the great city, and now and then he repeated to himself the words that Lord Henry had said to him on the first day they had met, "To cure the soul by means of the senses, and the senses by means of the soul." Yes, that was the secret. He had often tried it, and would try it again now. There were opium-dens, where one could buy oblivion, dens of horror where the memory of old sins could be destroyed by the madness of sins that were new.

The moon hung low in the sky like a yellow skull. From time to time a huge misshapen cloud stretched a long arm across and hid it. The gas-lamps grew fewer, and the streets more narrow and gloomy. Once the man lost his way, and had to drive back half a mile. A steam rose from the horse as it splashed up the puddles. The side-windows of the hansom were clogged with a grey-flannel mist.

"To cure the soul by means of the senses, and the senses by means of the soul!" How the words rang in his ears! His soul, certainly, was sick to death. Was it true that the senses could cure it? Innocent blood had been spilt. What could atone for that? Ah! for that there was no atonement; but though forgiveness was impossible, forgetfulness was possible still, and he was determined to forget, to stamp the thing out, to crush it as one would crush the adder that had stung one. Indeed, what right had Basil to have spoken to him as he had done? Who had made him a judge over others? He had said things that were dreadful, horrible, not to be endured.

On and on plodded the hansom, going slower, it seemed to him, at each step. He thrust up the trap,[1] and called to the man to drive faster. The hideous hunger for opium began to gnaw at him. His throat burned, and his delicate hands twitched nervously together. He struck at the horse madly with his stick. The driver laughed, and whipped up. He laughed in answer, and the man was silent.

The way seemed interminable, and the streets like the black web of some sprawling spider. The monotony became unbearable, and, as the mist thickened, he felt afraid.

---

1. A small door in the carriage; it opens to allow communication with the driver.

Then they passed by lonely brickfields. The fog was lighter here, and he could see the strange bottle-shaped kilns with their orange fan-like tongues of fire. A dog barked as they went by, and far away in the darkness some wandering sea-gull screamed. The horse stumbled in a rut, then swerved aside, and broke into a gallop.

After some time they left the clay road, and rattled again over rough-paven streets. Most of the windows were dark, but now and then fantastic shadows were silhouetted against some lamp-lit blind. He watched them curiously. They moved like monstrous marionettes, and made gestures like live things.[2] He hated them. A dull rage was in his heart. As they turned a corner a woman yelled something at them from an open door, and two men ran after the hansom for about a hundred yards. The driver beat at them with his whip.

It is said that passion makes one think in a circle. Certainly with hideous iteration the bitten lips of Dorian Gray shaped and reshaped those subtle words that dealt with soul and sense, till he had found in them the full expression, as it were, of his mood, and justified, by intellectual approval, passions that without such justification would still have dominated his temper. From cell to cell of his brain crept the one thought; and the wild desire to live, most terrible of all man's appetites, quickened into force each trembling nerve and fibre. Ugliness that had once been hateful to him because it made things real, became dear to him now for that very reason. Ugliness was the one reality. The coarse brawl, the loathsome den, the crude violence of disordered life, the very vileness of thief and outcast, were more vivid, in their intense actuality of impression, than all the gracious shapes of Art, the dreamy shadows of Song. They were what he needed for forgetfulness. In three days he would be free.

Suddenly the man drew up with a jerk at the top of a dark lane. Over the low roofs and jagged chimney-stacks of the houses rose the black masts of ships. Wreaths of white mist clung like ghostly sails to the yards.

"Somewhere about here, sir, ain't it?" he asked huskily through the trap.

Dorian started, and peered round. "This will do," he answered, and, having got out hastily, and given the driver the extra fare he had promised him, he walked quickly in the direction of the quay.[3] Here and there a lantern gleamed at the stern of some huge merchantman. The light shook and splintered in the puddles. A red

---

2. From "Most of the windows" to "things," Wilde paraphrases a scene in his poem "The Harlot's House" (1885), lines 22–24. This is another instance of Wilde's habit of mediating a mood, emotion, or reflection through art.
3. An artificial bank or landing place, built of stone or other solid material, lying along or projecting into a navigable water for convenience of loading and unloading ships.

glare came from an outward-bound steamer that was coaling. The slimy pavement looked like a wet mackintosh.

He hurried on towards the left, glancing back now and then to see if he was being followed. In about seven or eight minutes he reached a small shabby house, that was wedged in between two gaunt factories. In one of the top-windows stood a lamp. He stopped, and gave a peculiar knock.

After a little time he heard steps in the passage, and the chain being unhooked. The door opened quietly, and he went in without saying a word to the squat misshapen figure that flattened itself into the shadow as he passed. At the end of the hall hung a tattered green curtain that swayed and shook in the gusty wind which had followed him in from the street. He dragged it aside, and entered a long, low room which looked as if it had once been a third-rate dancing-saloon. Shrill flaring gas-jets, dulled and distorted in the fly-blown mirrors that faced them, were ranged round the walls. Greasy reflectors of ribbed tin backed them, making quivering disks of light. The floor was covered with ochre-coloured[4] sawdust, trampled here and there into mud, and stained with dark rings of spilt liquor. Some Malays were crouching by a little charcoal stove playing with bone counters, and showing their white teeth as they chattered. In one corner with his head buried in his arms, a sailor sprawled over a table, and by the tawdrily-painted bar that ran across one complete side stood two haggard women mocking an old man who was brushing the sleeves of his coat with an expression of disgust. "He thinks he's got red ants on him," laughed one of them, as Dorian passed by. The man looked at her in terror, and began to whimper.

At the end of the room there was a little staircase, leading to a darkened chamber. As Dorian hurried up its three rickety steps, the heavy odour of opium[5] met him. He heaved a deep breath, and his nostrils quivered with pleasure. When he entered, a young man with smooth yellow hair, who was bending over a lamp lighting a long thin pipe, looked up at him, and nodded in a hesitating manner.

"You here, Adrian?" muttered Dorian.

"Where else should I be?" he answered, listlessly. "None of the chaps will speak to me now."

"I thought you had left England."

"Darlington is not going to do anything. My brother paid the bill at last. George doesn't speak to me either. . . . I don't care," he added,

---

4. Of an orange-yellow color produced by certain oxides of iron.
5. Originally introduced in Britain for medicinal purposes, opium had, by the late eighteenth century, become a recreational drug. Prior to the 1868 Pharmacy Act, which restricted its sale to pharmacists, anyone could legally trade in opium products. As a result, by the middle of the nineteenth century hundreds of opium-based products were available to the general public.

with a sigh. "As long as one has this stuff, one doesn't want friends. I think I have had too many friends."

Dorian winced, and looked round at the grotesque things that lay in such fantastic postures on the ragged mattresses. The twisted limbs, the gaping mouths, the staring lusterless eyes, fascinated him. He knew in what strange heavens they were suffering, and what dull hells were teaching them the secret of some new joy. They were better off than he was. He was prisoned in thought. Memory, like a horrible malady, was eating his soul away. From time to time he seemed to see the eyes of Basil Hallward looking at him. Yet he felt he could not stay. The presence of Adrian Singleton troubled him. He wanted to be where no one would know who he was. He wanted to escape from himself.

"I am going on to the other place," he said, after a pause.

"On the wharf?"

"Yes."

"That mad-cat is sure to be there. They won't have her in this place now."

Dorian shrugged his shoulders. "I am sick of women who love one. Women who hate one are much more interesting. Besides, the stuff is better."

"Much the same."

"I like it better. Come and have something to drink. I must have something."

"I don't want anything," murmured the young man.

"Never mind."

Adrian Singleton rose up wearily, and followed Dorian to the bar. A half-caste,[6] in a ragged turban and a shabby ulster, grinned a hideous greeting as he thrust a bottle of brandy and two tumblers in front of them. The women sidled up, and began to chatter. Dorian turned his back on them, and said something in a low voice to Adrian Singleton.

A crooked smile, like a Malay crease, writhed across the face of one of the women. "We are very proud to-night," she sneered.

"For God's sake don't talk to me," cried Dorian, stamping his foot on the ground. "What do you want? Money? Here it is. Don't ever talk to me again."

Two red sparks flashed for a moment in the woman's sodden eyes, then flickered out, and left them dull and glazed. She tossed her head, and raked the coins off the counter with greedy fingers. Her companion watched her enviously.

---

6. One of a mixed race; especially, in India, one born to or descended from a European father and native mother.

"It's no use," sighed Adrian Singleton. "I don't care to go back. What does it matter? I am quite happy here."

"You will write to me if you want anything, won't you?" said Dorian, after a pause.

"Perhaps."

"Good night, then."

"Good night," answered the young man, passing up the steps and wiping his parched mouth with a handkerchief.

Dorian walked to the door with a look of pain in his face. As he drew the curtain aside a hideous laugh broke from the painted lips of the woman who had taken his money. "There goes the devil's bargain!" she hiccoughed, in a hoarse voice.

"Curse you!" he answered, "don't call me that."

She snapped her fingers. "Prince Charming is what you like to be called, ain't it?" she yelled after him.

The drowsy sailor leaped to his feet as she spoke, and looked wildly round. The sound of the shutting of the hall door fell on his ear. He rushed out as if in pursuit.

Dorian Gray hurried along the quay through the drizzling rain. His meeting with Adrian Singleton had strangely moved him, and he wondered if the ruin of that young life was really to be laid at his door, as Basil Hallward had said to him with such infamy of insult. He bit his lip, and for a few seconds his eyes grew sad. Yet, after all, what did it matter to him? One's days were too brief to take the burden of another's errors on one's shoulders. Each man lived his own life, and paid his own price for living it. The only pity was one had to pay so often for a single fault. One had to pay over and over again, indeed. In her dealings with man Destiny never closed her accounts.

There are moments, psychologists tell us, when the passion for sin, or for what the world calls sin, so dominates a nature, that every fibre of the body, as every cell of the brain, seems to be instinct with fearful impulses. Men and women at such moments lose the freedom of their will. They move to their terrible end as automatons move. Choice is taken from them, and conscience is either killed, or, if it lives at all, lives but to give rebellion its fascination, and disobedience its charm. For all sins, as theologians weary not of reminding us, are sins of disobedience. When that high spirit, that morning-star of evil, fell from heaven, it was as a rebel that he fell.

Callous, concentrated on evil, with stained mind, and soul hungry for rebellion, Dorian Gray hastened on, quickening his step as he went, but as he darted aside into a dim archway, that had served him often as a short cut to the ill-famed place where he was going, he felt himself suddenly seized from behind, and before be had time to defend himself he was thrust back against the wall, with a brutal hand round his throat.

He struggled madly for life, and by a terrible effort wrenched the tightening fingers away. In a second he heard the click of a revolver, and saw the gleam of a polished barrel pointing straight at his head, and the dusky form of a short thick-set man facing him.

"What do you want?" he gasped.

"Keep quiet," said the man. "If you stir, I shoot you."

"You are mad. What have I done to you?"

"You wrecked the life of Sibyl Vane," was the answer, "and Sibyl Vane was my sister. She killed herself. I know it. Her death is at your door. I swore I would kill you in return. For years I have sought you. I had no clue, no trace. The two people who could have described you were dead. I knew nothing of you but the pet name she used to call you. I heard it to-night by chance. Make your peace with God, for to-night you are going to die."

Dorian Gray grew sick with fear. "I never knew her," he stammered. "I never heard of her. You are mad."

"You had better confess your sin, for as sure as I am James Vane, you are going to die." There was a horrible moment. Dorian did not know what to say or do. "Down on your knees!" growled the man. "I give you one minute to make your peace—no more. I go on board to-night for India, and I must do my job first. One minute. That's all."

Dorian's arms fell to his side. Paralysed with terror, he did not know what to do. Suddenly a wild hope flashed across his brain. "Stop," he cried. "How long ago is it since your sister died? Quick, tell me!"

"Eighteen years," said the man. "Why do you ask me? What do years matter?"

"Eighteen years," laughed Dorian Gray, with a touch of triumph in his voice. "Eighteen years! Set me under the lamp and look at my face!"

James Vane hesitated for a moment, not understanding what was meant. Then he seized Dorian Gray and dragged him from the archway.

Dim and wavering as was the windblown light, yet it served to show him the hideous error, as it seemed, into which he had fallen, for the face of the man he had sought to kill had all the bloom of boyhood, all the unstained purity of youth. He seemed little more than a lad of twenty summers, hardly older, if older indeed at all, than his sister had been when they had parted so many years ago. It was obvious that this was not the man who had destroyed her life.

He loosened his hold and reeled back. "My God! my God!" he cried, "and I would have murdered you!"

Dorian Gray drew a long breath. "You have been on the brink of committing a terrible crime, my man," he said, looking at him sternly.

"Let this be a warning to you not to take vengeance into your own hands."

"Forgive me, sir," muttered James Vane. "I was deceived. A chance word I heard in that damned den set me on the wrong track."

"You had better go home, and put that pistol away, or you may get into trouble," said Dorian, turning on his heel, and going slowly down the street.

James Vane stood on the pavement in horror. He was trembling from head to foot. After a little while a black shadow that had been creeping along the dripping wall, moved out into the light and came close to him with stealthy footsteps. He felt a hand laid on his arm and looked round with a start. It was one of the women who had been drinking at the bar.

"Why didn't you kill him?" she hissed out, putting haggard face quite close to his. "I knew you were following him when you rushed out from Daly's.[7] You fool! You should have killed him. He has lots of money, and he's as bad as bad."

"He is not the man I am looking for," he answered, "and I want no man's money. I want a man's life. The man whose life I want must be nearly forty now. This one is little more than a boy. Thank God, I have not got his blood upon my hands."

The woman gave a bitter laugh. "Little more than a boy!" she sneered. "Why, man, it's nigh on eighteen years since Prince Charming made me what I am."

"You lie!" cried James Vane.

She raised her hand up to heaven. "Before God I am telling the truth," she cried.

"Before God?"

"Strike me dumb if it ain't so. He is the worst one that comes here. They say he has sold himself to the devil for a pretty face. It's nigh on eighteen years since I met him. He hasn't changed much since then. I have though," she added, with a sickly leer.

"You swear this?"

"I swear it," came in hoarse echo from her flat mouth. "But don't give me away to him," she whined; "I am afraid of him. Let me have some money for my night's lodging."

He broke from her with an oath, and rushed to the corner of the street, but Dorian Gray had disappeared. When he looked back, the woman had vanished also.

---

7. A theater on Cranbourn Street, off Leicester Square, established by the American playwright Augustin Daly in 1879; long since razed.

Chapter XVII

A week later Dorian Gray was sitting in the conservatory at Selby Royal talking to the pretty Duchess of Monmouth, who with her husband, a jaded-looking man of sixty, was amongst his guests. It was tea-time, and the mellow light of the huge lace-covered lamp that stood on the table lit up the delicate china and hammered silver of the service at which the Duchess was presiding. Her white hands were moving daintily among the cups, and her full red lips were smiling at something that Dorian had whispered to her. Lord Henry was lying back in a silk-draped wicker chair looking at them. On a peach-coloured divan sat Lady Narborough pretending to listen to the Duke's description of the last Brazilian beetle that he had added to his collection. Three young men in elaborate smoking-suits were handing tea-cakes to some of the women. The house-party consisted of twelve people, and there were more expected to arrive on the next day.

"What are you two talking about?" said Lord Henry, strolling over to the table, and putting his cup down. "I hope Dorian has told you about my plan for rechristening everything, Gladys. It is a delightful idea."

"But I don't want to be rechristened, Harry," rejoined the Duchess, looking up at him with her wonderful eyes. "I am quite satisfied with my own name, and I am sure Mr. Gray should be satisfied with his."

"My dear Gladys, I would not alter either name for the world. They are both perfect. I was thinking chiefly of flowers. Yesterday I cut an orchid, for my buttonhole. It was a marvelous spotted thing, as effective as the seven deadly sins.[1] In a thoughtless moment I asked one of the gardeners what it was called. He told me it was a fine specimen of *Robinsoniana,* or something dreadful of that kind. It is a sad truth, but we have lost the faculty of giving lovely names to things. Names are everything. I never quarrel with actions. My one quarrel is with words. That is the reason I hate vulgar realism in literature. The man who could call a spade a spade should be compelled to use one. It is the only thing he is fit for."

"Then what should we call you, Harry?" she asked.

"His name is Prince Paradox," said Dorian.

"I recognize him in a flash," exclaimed the Duchess.

"I won't hear of it," laughed Lord Henry, sinking into a chair. "From a label there is no escape! I refuse the title."

---

1. The seven deadly sins are Pride, Envy, Wrath/Anger, Sloth, Avarice/Greed, Gluttony, and Lust.

"Royalties may not abdicate," fell as a warning from pretty lips.

"You wish me to defend my throne, then?"

"Yes.

"I give the truths of to-morrow."

"I prefer the mistakes of to-day," she answered.

"You disarm me, Gladys," he cried, catching the wilfulness of her mood.

"Of your shield, Harry, not of your spear."

"I never tilt against Beauty," he said, with a wave of his hand.

"That is your error, Harry, believe me. You value beauty far too much."

"How can you say that? I admit that I think that it is better to be beautiful than to be good.[2] But on the other hand no one is more ready than I am to acknowledge that it is better to be good than to be ugly."

"Ugliness is one of the seven deadly sins, then?" cried the Duchess. "What becomes of your simile about the orchid?"

"Ugliness is one of the seven deadly virtues, Gladys. You, as a good Tory, must not underrate them. Beer, the Bible, and the seven deadly virtues have made our England what she is."

"You don't like your country, then?" she asked.

"I live in it."

"That you may censure it the better."

"Would you have me take the verdict of Europe on it?" he enquired.

"What do they say of us?"

"That Tartuffe[3] has emigrated to England and opened a shop."

"Is that yours, Harry?"

"I give it to you."

"I could not use it. It is too true."

"You need not be afraid. Our countrymen never recognize a description."

"They are practical."

"They are more cunning than practical. When they make up their ledger, they balance stupidity by wealth, and vice by hypocrisy."

"Still, we have done great things."

"Great things have been thrust on us, Gladys."[4]

"We have carried their burden."

"Only as far as the Stock Exchange."

She shook her head. "I believe in the race," she cried.

---

2. An echo of the phrase in "The Critic as Artist": "aesthetics are higher than ethics."
3. The scheming religious hypocrite who is the leading character in French playwright Molière's comedy of the same name (1664).
4. *Twelfth Night* 2.5.144–46.

"It represents the survival of the pushing."[5]

"It has development."

"Decay fascinates me more."

"What of Art?" she asked.

"It is a malady."

"Love?"

"An illusion."

"Religion?"

"The fashionable substitute for Belief."

"You are a sceptic."

"Never! Scepticism is the beginning of Faith."

"What are you?"

"To define is to limit."

"Give me a clue."

"Threads snap. You would lose your way in the labyrinth."

"You bewilder me. Let us talk of some one else."

"Our host is a delightful topic. Years ago he was christened Prince Charming."

"Ah! don't remind me of that," cried Dorian Gray.

"Our host is rather horrid this evening," answered the Duchess, colouring. "I believe he thinks that Monmouth married me on purely scientific principles as the best specimen he could find of a modern butterfly."

"Well, I hope he won't stick pins into you, Duchess," laughed Dorian.

"Oh! my maid does that already, Mr. Gray, when she is annoyed with me."

"And what does she get annoyed with you about, Duchess?"

"For the most trivial things, Mr. Gray, I assure you. Usually because I come in at ten minutes to nine and tell her that I must be dressed by half-past eight."

"How unreasonable of her! You should give her warning."

"I daren't, Mr. Gray. Why, she invents hats for me. You remember the one I wore at Lady Hilstone's garden-party? You don't, but it is nice of you to pretend that you do. Well, she made it out of nothing. All good hats are made out of nothing."

"Like all good reputations, Gladys," interrupted Lord Henry. "Every effect that one produces gives one an enemy. To be popular one must be a mediocrity."

"Not with women," said the Duchess, shaking her head; "and women rule the world. I assure you we can't bear mediocrities. We

5. Parody of Herbert Spencer's maxim "survival of the fittest," often applied by the Victorians to economic and social life and referred to as the doctrine of Social Darwinism.

women, as some one says, love with our ears, just as you men love with your eyes, if you ever love at all."

"It seems to me that we never do anything else," murmured Dorian.

"Ah! then, you never really love, Mr. Gray," answered the Duchess, with mock sadness.

"My dear Gladys!" cried Lord Henry. "How can you say that? Romance lives by repetition, and repetition converts an appetite into an art. Besides, each time that one loves is the only time one has ever loved. Difference of object does not alter singleness of passion. It merely intensifies it. We can have in life but one great experience at best, and the secret of life is to reproduce that experience as often as possible."

"Even when one has been wounded by it, Harry?" asked the Duchess, after a pause.

"Especially when one has been wounded by it," answered Lord Henry.

The Duchess turned and looked at Dorian Gray with a curious expression in her eyes. "What do you say to that, Mr. Gray?" she enquired.

Dorian hesitated for a moment. Then he threw his head back and laughed. "I always agree with Harry, Duchess."

"Even when he is wrong?"

"Harry is never wrong, Duchess."

"And does his philosophy make you happy?"

"I have never searched for happiness. Who wants happiness? I have searched for pleasure."

"And found it, Mr. Gray?"

"Often. Too often."

The Duchess sighed. "I am searching for peace," she said, "and if I don't go and dress, I shall have none this evening."

"Let me get you some orchids, Duchess," cried Dorian, starting to his feet, and walking down the conservatory.

"You are flirting disgracefully with him," said Lord Henry to his cousin. "You had better take care. He is very fascinating."

"If he were not, there would be no battle."

"Greek meets Greek, then?"

"I am on the side of the Trojans. They fought for a woman."

"They were defeated."

"There are worse things than capture," she answered.

"You gallop with a loose rein."

"Pace gives life," was the *riposte*.[6]

---

6. Retort (French). Originally, the word referred to a return thrust in fencing. The fencing here is verbal.

"I shall write it in my diary to-night."

"What?"

"That a burnt child loves the fire."

"I am not even singed. My wings are untouched."

"You use them for everything, except flight."

"Courage has passed from men to women. It is a new experience for us."

"You have a rival."

"Who?"

He laughed. "Lady Narborough," he whispered. "She perfectly adores him."

"You fill me with apprehension. The appeal to Antiquity is fatal to us who are romanticists."

"Romanticists! You have all the methods of science."

"Men have educated us."

"But not explained you."

"Describe us as a sex," was her challenge.

"Sphinxes without secrets."

She looked at him, smiling. "How long Mr. Gray is!" she said. "Let us go and help him. I have not yet told him the colour of my frock."

"Ah! you must suit your frock to his flowers, Gladys."

"That would be a premature surrender."

"Romantic Art begins with its climax."

"I must keep an opportunity for retreat."

"In the Parthian[7] manner?"

"They found safety in the desert. I could not do that."

"Women are not always allowed a choice," he answered, but hardly had he finished the sentence before from the far end of the conservatory came a stifled groan, followed by the dull sound of a heavy fall. Everybody started up. The Duchess stood motionless in horror. And with fear in his eyes Lord Henry rushed through the flapping palms, to find Dorian Gray lying face downwards on the tiled floor in a death-like swoon.

He was carried at once into the blue drawing-room, and laid upon one of the sofas. After a short time he came to himself, and looked round with a dazed expression.

"What has happened?" he asked. "Oh! I remember. Am I safe here, Harry?" He began to tremble.

"My dear Dorian," answered Lord Henry, "you merely fainted. That was all. You must have overtired yourself. You had better not come down to dinner. I will take your place."

---

7. Parthians were credited with having perfected retreat as a strategy of attack by luring the enemy close enough to fire their arrows as they moved away.

"No, I will come down," he said, struggling to his feet. "I would rather come down. I must not be alone."

He went to his room and dressed. There was a wild recklessness of gaiety in his manner as he sat at table, but now and then a thrill of terror ran through him when he remembered that, pressed against the window of the conservatory, like a white handkerchief, he had seen the face of James Vane watching him.

Chapter XVIII[1]

The next day he did not leave the house, and, indeed, spent most of the time in his own room, sick with a wild terror of dying, and yet indifferent to life itself. The consciousness of being hunted, snared, tracked down, had begun to dominate him. If the tapestry did but tremble in the wind, he shook. The dead leaves that were blown against the leaded panes seemed to him like his own wasted resolutions and wild regrets. When he closed his eyes, he saw again the sailor's face peering through the mist-stained glass, and horror seemed once more to lay its hand upon his heart.

But perhaps it had been only his fancy that had called vengeance out of the night, and set the hideous shapes of punishment before him. Actual life was chaos, but there was something terribly logical in the imagination. It was the imagination that set remorse to dog the feet of sin. It was the imagination that made each crime bear its misshapen brood. In the common world of fact the wicked were not punished, nor the good rewarded. Success was given to the strong, failure thrust upon the weak. That was all. Besides, had any stranger been prowling round the house he would have been seen by the servants or the keepers. Had any footmarks been found on the flower-beds, the gardeners would have reported it. Yes: it had been merely fancy. Sibyl Vane's brother had not come back to kill him. He had sailed away in his ship to founder in some winter sea. From him, at any rate, he was safe. Why, the man did not know who he was, could not know who he was. The mask of youth had saved him.

And yet if it had been merely an illusion, how terrible it was to think that conscience could raise such fearful phantoms, and give them visible form, and make them move before one! What sort of life would his be if, day and night, shadows of his crime were to peer at him from silent corners, to mock him from secret places, to whisper in his ear as he sat at the feast, to wake him with icy fingers as he lay asleep! As the thought crept through his brain, he grew pale with terror, and the air seemed to him to have become suddenly

---

1. Last of the new chapters that Wilde added to this edition.

colder. Oh! in what a wild hour of madness he had killed his friend! How ghastly the mere memory of the scene! He saw it all again. Each hideous detail came back to him with added horror. Out of the black cave of Time, terrible and swathed in scarlet, rose the image of his sin. When Lord Henry came in at six o'clock, he found him crying as one whose heart will break.

It was not till the third day that he ventured to go out. There was something in the clear, pine-scented air of that winter morning that seemed to bring him back his joyousness and his ardour for life. But it was not merely the physical conditions of environment that had caused the change. His own nature had revolted against the excess of anguish that had sought to maim and mar the perfection of its calm. With subtle and finely-wrought temperaments it is always so. Their strong passions must either bruise or bend. They either slay the man, or themselves die. Shallow sorrows and shallow loves live on. The loves and sorrows that are great are destroyed by their own plenitude. Besides, he had convinced himself that he had been the victim of a terror-stricken imagination, and looked back now on his fears with something of pity and not a little of contempt.

After breakfast he walked with the Duchess for an hour in the garden, and then drove across the park to join the shooting-party. The crisp frost lay like salt upon the grass. The sky was an inverted cup of blue metal. A thin film of ice bordered the flat reed-grown lake.

At the corner of the pine-wood he caught sight of Sir Geoffrey Clouston, the Duchess's brother, jerking two spent cartridges out of his gun. He jumped from the cart, and having told the groom to take the mare home, made his way towards his guest through the with- ered bracken and rough undergrowth.

"Have you had good sport, Geoffrey?" he asked.

"Not very good, Dorian. I think most of the birds have gone to the open. I dare say it will be better after lunch, when we get to new ground."

Dorian strolled along by his side. The keen aromatic air, the brown and red lights that glimmered in the wood, the hoarse cries of the beaters[2] ringing out from time to time, and the sharp snaps of the guns that followed, fascinated him, and filled him with a sense of delightful freedom. He was dominated by the carelessness of happiness, by the high indifference of joy.

Suddenly from a lumpy tussock of old grass, some twenty yards in front of them, with black-tipped ears erect, and long hinder limbs throwing it forward, started a hare. It bolted for a thicket of alders. Sir Geoffrey put his gun to his shoulder, but there was something

---

2. A man employed in rousing and driving game.

in the animal's grace of movement that strangely charmed Dorian Gray, and he cried out at once, "Don't shoot it, Geoffrey. Let it live."

"What nonsense, Dorian!" laughed his companion, and as the hare bounded into the thicket he fired. There were two cries heard, the cry of a hare in pain, which is dreadful, the cry of a man in agony, which is worse.

"Good heavens! I have hit a beater!" exclaimed Sir Geoffrey. "What an ass the man was to get in front of the guns! Stop shooting there!" he called out at the top of his voice. "A man is hurt."

The head-keeper came running up with a stick in his hand.

"Where, sir? Where is he?" he shouted. At the same time the firing ceased along the line.

"Here," answered Sir Geoffrey, angrily, hurrying towards the thicket. "Why on earth don't you keep your men back? Spoiled my shooting for the day."

Dorian watched them as they plunged into the alder-clump, brushing the lithe, swinging branches aside. In a few moments they emerged, dragging a body after them into the sunlight. He turned away in horror. It seemed to him that misfortune followed wherever he went. He heard Sir Geoffrey ask if the man was really dead, and the affirmative answer of the keeper. The wood seemed to him to have become suddenly alive with faces. There was the trampling of myriad feet, and the low buzz of voices. A great copper-breasted pheasant came beating through the boughs overhead.

After a few moments, that were to him, in his perturbed state, like endless hours of pain, he felt a hand laid on his shoulder. He started, and looked round.

"Dorian," said Lord Henry, "I had better tell them that the shooting is stopped for to-day. It would not look well to go on."

"I wish it were stopped for ever, Harry," he answered, bitterly. "The whole thing is hideous and cruel. Is the man . . . ?"

He could not finish the sentence.

"I am afraid so," rejoined Lord Henry. "He got the whole charge of shot in his chest. He must have died almost instantaneously. Come; let us go home."

They walked side by side in the direction of the avenue for nearly fifty yards without speaking. Then Dorian looked at Lord Henry, and said, with a heavy sigh, "It is a bad omen, Harry, a very bad omen."

"What is?" asked Lord Henry. "Oh! this accident, I suppose. My dear fellow, it can't be helped. It was the man's own fault. Why did he get in front of the guns? Besides, it is nothing to us. It is rather awkward for Geoffrey, of course. It does not do to pepper beaters. It makes people think that one is a wild shot. And Geoffrey is not; he shoots very straight. But there is no use talking about the matter."

Dorian shook his head. "It is a bad omen, Harry. I feel as if something horrible were going to happen to some of us. To myself, perhaps," he added, passing his hand over his eyes, with a gesture of pain.

The elder man laughed. "The only horrible thing in the world is *ennui*, Dorian. That is the one sin for which there is no forgiveness. But we are not likely to suffer from it, unless these fellows keep chattering about this thing at dinner. I must tell them that the subject is to be tabooed. As for omens, there is no such thing as an omen. Destiny does not send us heralds. She is too wise or too cruel for that. Besides, what on earth could happen to you, Dorian? You have everything in the world that a man can want. There is no one who would not be delighted to change places with you."

"There is no one with whom I would not change places, Harry. Don't laugh like that. I am telling you the truth. The wretched peasant who has just died is better off than I am. I have no terror of Death. It is the coming of death that terrifies me. Its monstrous wings seem to wheel in the leaden air around me. Good heavens! don't you see a man moving behind the trees there, watching me, waiting for me?"

Lord Henry looked in the direction in which the trembling gloved hand was pointing. "Yes," he said, smiling, "I see the gardener waiting for you. I suppose he wants to ask you what flowers you wish to have on the table to-night. How absurdly nervous you are, my dear fellow! You must come and see my doctor, when we get back to town."

Dorian heaved a sigh of relief as he saw the gardener approaching. The man touched his hat, glanced for a moment at Lord Henry in a hesitating manner, and then produced a letter, which he handed to his master. "Her Grace told me to wait for an answer," he murmured.

Dorian put the letter into his pocket. "Tell her Grace that I am coming in," he said, coldly. The man turned round, and went rapidly in the direction of the house.

"How fond women are of doing dangerous things!" laughed Lord Henry. "It is one of the qualities in them that I admire most. A woman will flirt with anybody in the world as long as other people are looking on."

"How fond you are of saying dangerous things, Harry! In the present instance you are quite astray. I like the Duchess very much, but I don't love her."

"And the Duchess loves you very much, but she likes you less, so you are excellently matched."

"You are talking scandal, Harry, and there is never any basis for scandal."

"The basis of every scandal is an immoral certainty," said Lord Henry, lighting a cigarette.

"You would sacrifice anybody, Harry, for the sake of an epigram."

"The world goes to the altar of its own accord," was the answer.

"I wish I could love," cried Dorian Gray, with a deep note of pathos in his voice. "But I seem to have lost the passion, and forgotten the desire. I am too much concentrated on myself. My own personality has become a burden to me. I want to escape, to go away, to forget. It was silly of me to come down here at all. I think I shall send a wire to Harvey to have the yacht got ready. On a yacht one is safe."

"Safe from what, Dorian? You are in some trouble. Why not tell me what it is? You know I would help you."

"I can't tell you, Harry," he answered, sadly. "And I dare say it is only a fancy of mine. This unfortunate accident has upset me. I have a horrible presentiment that something of the kind may happen to me."

"What nonsense!"

"I hope it is, but I can't help feeling it. Ah! here is the Duchess, looking like Artemis[3] in a tailor-made gown. You see we have come back, Duchess."

"I have heard all about it, Mr. Gray," she answered. "Poor Geoffrey is terribly upset. And it seems that you asked him not to shoot the hare. How curious!"

"Yes, it was very curious. I don't know what made me say it. Some whim, I suppose. It looked the loveliest of little live things. But I am sorry they told you about the man. It is a hideous subject."

"It is an annoying subject," broke in Lord Henry. "It has no psychological value at all. Now if Geoffrey had done the thing on purpose, how interesting he would be! I should like to know some one who had committed a real murder."

"How horrid of you, Harry!" cried the Duchess. "Isn't it, Mr. Gray? Harry, Mr. Gray is ill again. He is going to faint."

Dorian drew himself up with an effort, and smiled. "It is nothing, Duchess," he murmured; "my nerves are dreadfully out of order. That is all. I am afraid I walked too far this morning. I didn't hear what Harry said. Was it very bad? You must tell me some other time. I think I must go and lie down. You will excuse me, won't you?"

They had reached the great flight of steps that led from the conservatory on to the terrace. As the glass door closed behind Dorian, Lord Henry turned and looked at the Duchess with his slumberous eyes. "Are you very much in love with him?" he asked.

She did not answer for some time, but stood gazing at the landscape. "I wish I knew," she said at last.

---

3. In Greek mythology, goddess of the hunt and fertility and twin of Apollo. Artemis frequently appeared dressed in animal hides.

He shook his head. "Knowledge would be fatal. It is the uncertainty that charms one. A mist makes things wonderful."

"One may lose one's way."

"All ways end at the same point, my dear Gladys."

"What is that?"

"Disillusion."

"It was my *début* in life," she sighed.

"It came to you crowned."

"I am tired of strawberry leaves."[4]

"They become you."

"Only in public."

"You would miss them," said Lord Henry.

"I will not part with a petal."

"Monmouth has ears."

"Old age is dull of hearing."

"Has he never been jealous?"

"I wish he had been."

He glanced about as if in search of something. "What are you looking for?" she enquired.

"The button from your foil,"[5] he answered. "You have dropped it."

She laughed. "I have still the mask."

"It makes your eyes lovelier," was his reply.

She laughed again. Her teeth showed like white seeds in a scarlet fruit.

Upstairs, in his own room, Dorian Gray was lying on a sofa, with terror in every tingling fibre of his body. Life had suddenly become too hideous a burden for him to bear. The dreadful death of the unlucky beater, shot in the thicket like a wild animal, had seemed to him to pre-figure death for himself also. He had nearly swooned at what Lord Henry had said in a chance mood of cynical jesting.

At five o'clock he rang his bell for his servant, and gave him orders to pack his things for the night-express to town, and to have the brougham at the door by eight-thirty. He was determined not to sleep another night at Selby Royal. It was an ill-omened place. Death walked there in the sunlight. The grass of the forest had been spotted with blood.

Then he wrote a note to Lord Henry, telling him that he was going up to town to consult his doctor, and asking him to entertain his guests in his absence. As he was putting it into the envelope, a knock came to the door, and his valet informed him that the head-keeper

4. Since strawberry-leaf images are worked into the design of the coronet, the reference here is to Gladys's title as duchess.
5. The tip on a fencing foil was used to prevent injury during a fencing match. Dueling without the button would be a blood match.

wished to see him. He frowned, and bit his lip. "Send him in," he muttered, after some moments' hesitation.

As soon as the man entered Dorian pulled his cheque-book out of a drawer, and spread it out before him.

"I suppose you have come about the unfortunate accident of this morning, Thornton?" he said, taking up a pen.

"Yes, sir," answered the gamekeeper.

"Was the poor fellow married? Had he any people dependent on him?" asked Dorian, looking bored. "If so, I should not like them to be left in want, and will send them any sum of money you may think necessary."

"We don't know who he is, sir. That is what I took the liberty of coming to you about."

"Don't know who he is?" said Dorian, listlessly. "What do you mean? Wasn't he one of your men?"

"No, sir. Never saw him before. Seems like a sailor, sir."

The pen dropped from Dorian Gray's hand, and he felt as if his heart had suddenly stopped beating. "A sailor?" he cried out. "Did you say a sailor?"

"Yes, sir. He looks as if he had been a sort of sailor; tattooed on both arms, and that kind of thing."

"Was there anything found on him?" said Dorian, leaning forward and looking at the man with startled eyes. "Anything that would tell his name?"

"Some money, sir—not much, and a six-shooter.[6] There was no name of any kind. A decent-looking man, sir, but rough-like. A sort of sailor we think."

Dorian started to his feet. A terrible hope fluttered past him. He clutched at it madly. "Where is the body?" he exclaimed. "Quick! I must see it at once."

"It is in an empty stable in the Home Farm, sir. The folk don't like to have that sort of thing in their houses. They say a corpse brings bad luck."

"The Home Farm! Go there at once and meet me. Tell one of the grooms to bring my horse round. No. Never mind. I'll go to the stables myself. It will save time."

In less than a quarter of an hour Dorian Gray was galloping down the long avenue as hard as he could go. The trees seemed to sweep past him in spectral procession, and wild shadows to fling themselves across his path. Once the mare swerved at a white gate-post and nearly threw him. He lashed her across the neck with his crop. She cleft the dusky air like an arrow. The stones flew from her hoofs.

6. A six-chambered revolver able to fire six shots without being reloaded.

At last he reached the Home Farm. Two men were loitering in the yard. He leapt from the saddle and threw the reins to one of them. In the farthest stable a light was glimmering. Something seemed to tell him that the body was there, and he hurried to the door, and put his hand upon the latch.

There he paused for a moment, feeling that he was on the brink of a discovery that would either make or mar his life. Then he thrust the door open, and entered.

On a heap of sacking in the far corner was lying the dead body of a man dressed in a coarse shirt and a pair of blue trousers. A spotted handkerchief had been placed over the face. A coarse candle, stuck in a bottle, sputtered beside it.

Dorian Gray shuddered. He felt that his could not be the hand to take the handkerchief away, and called out to one of the farm-servants to come to him.

"Take that thing off the face. I wish to see it," he said, clutching at the doorpost for support.

When the farm-servant had done so, he stepped forward. A cry of joy broke from his lips. The man who had been shot in the thicket was James Vane.

He stood there for some minutes looking at the dead body. As he rode home, his eyes were full of tears, for he knew he was safe.

Chapter XIX[1]

"There is no use your telling me that you are going to be good," cried Lord Henry, dipping his white fingers into a red copper bowl filled with rose-water. "You are quite perfect. Pray, don't change."

Dorian Gray shook his head. "No, Harry, I have done too many dreadful things in my life. I am not going to do any more. I began my good actions yesterday."

"Where were you yesterday?"

"In the country, Harry. I was staying at a little inn by myself."

"My dear boy," said Lord Henry, smiling, "anybody can be good in the country. There are no temptations there. That is the reason why people who live out of town are so absolutely uncivilized. Civilization is not by any means an easy thing to attain to. There are only two ways by which man can reach it. One is by being cultured, the other by being corrupt. Country people have no opportunity of being either, so they stagnate."

---

1. Wilde divided the last chapter of the *Lippincott's Magazine* edition (13), made some additions and other changes, and turned it into the two last chapters of this edition.

"Culture and corruption," echoed Dorian. "I have known something of both. It seems terrible to me now that they should ever be found together. For I have a new ideal, Harry. I am going to alter. I think I have altered."

"You have not yet told me what your good action was. Or did you say you had done more than one?" asked his companion, as he spilt into his plate a little crimson pyramid of seeded strawberries, and through a perforated shell-shaped spoon snowed white sugar upon them.

"I can tell you, Harry. It is not a story I could tell to any one else. I spared somebody. It sounds vain, but you understand what I mean. She was quite beautiful, and wonderfully like Sibyl Vane. I think it was that which first attracted me to her. You remember Sibyl, don't you? How long ago that seems! Well, Hetty was not one of our own class, of course. She was simply a girl in a village. But I really loved her. I am quite sure that I loved her. All during this wonderful May that we have been having, I used to run down and see her two or three times a week. Yesterday she met me in a little orchard. The apple-blossoms kept tumbling down on her hair, and she was laughing. We were to have gone away together this morning at dawn. Suddenly I determined to leave her as flower-like as I had found her."

"I should think the novelty of the emotion must have given you a thrill of real pleasure, Dorian," interrupted Lord Henry. "But I can finish your idyll for you. You gave her good advice, and broke her heart. That was the beginning of your reformation."

"Harry, you are horrible! You mustn't say these dreadful things. Hetty's heart is not broken. Of course she cried, and all that. But there is no disgrace upon her. She can live, like Perdita,[2] in her garden of mint and marigold."

"And weep over a faithless Florizel,"[3] said Lord Henry, laughing, as he leaned back in his chair. "My dear Dorian, you have the most curiously boyish moods. Do you think this girl will ever be really contented now with any one of her own rank? I suppose she will be married some day to a rough carter or a grinning ploughman. Well, the fact of having met you, and loved you, will teach her to despise her husband, and she will be wretched. From a moral point of view, I cannot say that I think much of your great renunciation. Even as a beginning, it is poor. Besides, how do you know that Hetty isn't

---

2. Daughter of Leontes and Hermione in Shakespeare's *A Winter's Tale*, Perdita was abandoned by her parents.
3. In *A Winter's Tale*, the son of King Polixenes who falls in love with Perdita, a supposed shepherdess. Florizel, however, remains faithful, and after several misadventures, the impediments are removed and the lovers marry.

floating at the present moment in some star-lit mill-pond, with lovely water-lilies round her, like Ophelia?"[4]

"I can't bear this, Harry! You mock at everything, and then suggest the most serious tragedies. I am sorry I told you now. I don't care what you say to me. I know I was right in acting as I did. Poor Hetty! As I rode past the farm this morning, I saw her white face at the window, like a spray of jasmine. Don't let us talk about it any more, and don't try to persuade me that the first good action I have done for years, the first little bit of self-sacrifice I have ever known, is really a sort of sin. I want to be better. I am going to be better. Tell me something about yourself. What is going on in town? I have not been to the club for days."

"The people are still discussing poor Basil's disappearance."

"I should have thought they had got tired of that by this time," said Dorian, pouring himself out some wine, and frowning slightly.

"My dear boy, they have only been talking about it for six weeks, and the British public are really not equal to the mental strain of having more than one topic every three months. They have been very fortunate lately, however. They have had my own divorce-case, and Alan Campbell's suicide. Now they have got the mysterious disappearance of an artist. Scotland Yard[5] still insists that the man in the grey ulster who left for Paris by the midnight train on the ninth of November was poor Basil, and the French police declare that Basil never arrived in Paris at all. I suppose in about a fortnight we shall be told that he has been seen in San Francisco. It is an odd thing, but every one who disappears is said to be seen at San Francisco. It must be a delightful city, and possess all the attractions of the next world."[6]

"What do you think has happened to Basil?" asked Dorian, holding up his Burgundy against the light, and wondering how it was that he could discuss the matter so calmly.

"I have not the slightest idea. If Basil chooses to hide himself, it is no business of mine. If he is dead, I don't want to think about him. Death is the only thing that ever terrifies me. I hate it."

"Why?" said the younger man, wearily.

"Because," said Lord Henry, passing beneath his nostrils the gilt trellis of an open vinaigrette box,[7] "one can survive everything nowadays except that. Death and vulgarity are the only two facts in the nineteenth century that one cannot explain away. Let us have our

4. Doomed beloved of the title character in Shakespeare's *Hamlet*; died by drowning in a pond.
5. Home of London's Metropolitan police department.
6. Wilde visited San Francisco in 1883 during his American lecture tour. The reference to the attractions of the other world is likely an ironic reference to Hades or the underworld.
7. Aromatic salts.

coffee in the music-room, Dorian. You must play Chopin[8] to me. The man with whom my wife ran away played Chopin exquisitely. Poor Victoria! I was very fond of her. The house is rather lonely without her. Of course married life is merely a habit, a bad habit. But then one regrets the loss even of one's worst habits. Perhaps one regrets them the most. They are such an essential part of one's personality."

Dorian said nothing, but rose from the table, and, passing into the next room, sat down to the piano and let his fingers stray across the white and black ivory of the keys. After the coffee had been brought in, he stopped, and, looking over at Lord Henry, said, "Harry, did it ever occur to you that Basil was murdered?"

Lord Henry yawned. "Basil was very popular, and always wore a Waterbury watch.[9] Why should he have been murdered? He was not clever enough to have enemies. Of course he had a wonderful genius for painting. But a man can paint like Velasquez[1] and yet be as dull as possible. Basil was really rather dull. He only interested me once, and that was when he told me, years ago, that he had a wild adoration for you, and that you were the dominant motive of his art."

"I was very fond of Basil," said Dorian, with a note of sadness in his voice. "But don't people say that he was murdered?"

"Oh, some of the papers do. It does not seem to me to be at all probable. I know there are dreadful places in Paris, but Basil was not the sort of man to have gone to them. He had no curiosity. It was his chief defect."

"What would you say, Harry, if I told you that I had murdered Basil?" said the younger man. He watched him intently after he had spoken.

"I would say, my dear fellow, that you were posing for a character that doesn't suit you. All crime is vulgar, just as all vulgarity is crime. It is not in you, Dorian, to commit a murder. I am sorry if I hurt your vanity by saying so, but I assure you it is true. Crime belongs exclusively to the lower orders. I don't blame them in the smallest degree. I should fancy that crime was to them what art is to us, simply a method of procuring extraordinary sensations."

"A method of procuring sensations? Do you think, then, that a man who has once committed a murder could possibly do the same crime again? Don't tell me that."

"Oh! anything becomes a pleasure if one does it too often," cried Lord Henry, laughing. "That is one of the most important secrets of

---

8. Frederic Chopin (1810–1849), one of Wilde's favorite piano composers, referred to frequently in his writing from the early poetry to *De Profundis*.
9. An inexpensive pocket watch, hence of little interest to a thief.
1. Diego Rodríguez de Silva y Velázquez (1599–1660), the great Spanish painter much admired by Wilde.

life. I should fancy, however, that murder is always a mistake. One should never do anything that one cannot talk about after dinner. But let us pass from poor Basil. I wish I could believe that he had come to such a really romantic end as you suggest; but I can't. I dare say he fell into the Seine off an omnibus, and that the conductor hushed up the scandal. Yes: I should fancy that was his end. I see him lying now on his back under those dull-green waters with the heavy barges floating over him, and long weeds catching in his hair. Do you know, I don't think he would have done much more good work. During the last ten years his painting had gone off very much."

Dorian heaved a sigh, and Lord Henry strolled across the room and began to stroke the head of a curious Java parrot, a large grey-plumaged bird, with pink crest and tail, that was balancing itself upon a bamboo perch. As his pointed fingers touched it, it dropped the white scurf of crinkled lids over black glass-like eyes, and began to sway backwards and forwards.

"Yes," he continued, turning round, and taking his handkerchief out of his pocket; "his painting had quite gone off. It seemed to me to have lost something. It had lost an ideal. When you and he ceased to be great friends, he ceased to be a great artist. What was it separated you? I suppose he bored you. If so, he never forgave you. It's a habit bores have. By the way, what has become of that wonderful portrait he did of you? I don't think I have ever seen it since he finished it. Oh! I remember your telling me years ago that you had sent it down to Selby, and that it had got mislaid or stolen on the way. You never got it back? What a pity! It was really a masterpiece. I remember I wanted to buy it. I wish I had now. It belonged to Basil's best period. Since then, his work was that curious mixture of bad painting and good intentions that always entitles a man to be called a representative British artist. Did you advertise for it? You should."

"I forget," said Dorian. "I suppose I did. But I never really liked it. I am sorry I sat for it. The memory of the thing is hateful to me. Why do you talk of it? It used to remind me of those curious lines in some play—'Hamlet,' I think—how do they run?—

> "'Like the painting of a sorrow,
> A face without a heart.'[2]

Yes: that is what it was like."

Lord Henry laughed. "If a man treats life artistically, his brain is his heart," he answered, sinking into an arm-chair.

---

2. *Hamlet* 4.7.108–09. The lines spoken by King Claudius are part of a question: "Laertes, was your father dear to you? / Or are you like the painting of a sorrow, / A face without a heart?"

Dorian Gray shook his head, and struck some soft chords on the piano. "'Like the painting of a sorrow,'" he repeated, "'a face without a heart.'"

The elder man lay back and looked at him with half-closed eyes. "By the way, Dorian," he said, after a pause, "'what does it profit a man if he gain the whole world and lose—how does the quotation run?—his own soul'?"[3]

The music jarred and Dorian Gray started, and stared at his friend. "Why do you ask me that, Harry?"

"My dear fellow," said Lord Henry, elevating his eyebrows in surprise, "I asked you because I thought you might be able to give me an answer. That is all. I was going through the Park last Sunday, and close by the Marble Arch there stood a little crowd of shabby-looking people listening to some vulgar street-preacher. As I passed by, I heard the man yelling out that question to his audience. It struck me as being rather dramatic. London is very rich in curious effects of that kind. A wet Sunday, an uncouth Christian in a mackintosh,[4] a ring of sickly white faces under a broken roof of dripping umbrellas, and a wonderful phrase flung into the air by shrill, hysterical lips—it was really very good in its way, quite a suggestion. I thought of telling the prophet that Art had a soul, but that man had not. I am afraid, however, he would not have understood me."

"Don't, Harry. The soul is a terrible reality. It can be bought, and sold, and bartered away. It can be poisoned, or made perfect. There is a soul in each one of us. I know it."

"Do you feel quite sure of that, Dorian?"

"Quite sure."

"Ah! then it must be an illusion. The things one feels absolutely certain about are never true. That is the fatality of Faith, and the lesson of Romance. How grave you are! Don't be so serious. What have you or I to do with the superstitions of our age? No: we have given up our belief in the soul. Play me something. Play me a nocturne,[5] Dorian, and, as you play, tell me, in a low voice, how you have kept your youth. You must have some secret. I am only ten years older than you are, and I am wrinkled, and worn, and yellow. You are really wonderful, Dorian. You have never looked more charming than you do to-night. You remind me of the day I saw you first. You were rather cheeky, very shy, and absolutely extraordinary. You have changed, of course, but not in appearance. I wish you would tell me your secret. To get back my youth I would do anything in the world, except take exercise, get up early, or be respectable. Youth! There is

---

3. Mark 8:36.
4. Originally, a full-length coat or cloak made of waterproof rubberized material. Subsequently, a rainproof coat made of this or some other material.
5. A composition suggestive of night, usually of a quiet, meditative character [OED].

nothing like it. It's absurd to talk of the ignorance of youth. The only people to whose opinions I listen now with any respect are people much younger than myself. They seem in front of me. Life has revealed to them her latest wonder. As for the aged, I always contradict the aged. I do it on principle. If you ask them their opinion on something that happened yesterday, they solemnly give you the opinions current in 1820, when people wore high stocks,[6] believed in everything, and knew absolutely nothing. How lovely that thing you are playing is! I wonder did Chopin write it at Majorca,[7] with the sea weeping round the villa, and the salt spray dashing against the panes? It is marvellously romantic. What a blessing it is that there is one art left to us that is not imitative! Don't stop. I want music to-night. It seems to me that you are the young Apollo, and that I am Marsyas[8] listening to you. I have sorrows, Dorian, of my own, that even you know nothing of. The tragedy of old age is not that one is old, but that one is young. I am amazed sometimes at my own sincerity. Ah, Dorian, how happy you are. What an exquisite life you have had! You have drunk deeply of everything. You have crushed the grapes against your palate. Nothing has been hidden from you. And it has all been to you no more than the sound of music. It has not marred you.[9] You are still the same."

"I am not the same, Harry."

"Yes: you are the same. I wonder what the rest of your life will be. Don't spoil it by renunciations. At present you are a perfect type. Don't make yourself incomplete. You are quite flawless now. You need not shake your head: you know you are. Besides, Dorian, don't deceive yourself. Life is not governed by will or intention. Life is a question of nerves, and fibres, and slowly built-up cells in which thought hides itself and passion has its dreams.[1] You may fancy yourself safe, and think yourself strong. But a chance tone of colour in a room or a morning sky, a particular perfume that you had once loved and that brings subtle memories with it, a line from a forgotten poem that you had come across again, a cadence from a piece of music that you had ceased to play—I tell you, Dorian, that it is on things like these that our lives depend. Browning writes about that

6. Neckcloths, worn in the reign of George IV (1820–30).
7. Chopin lived there with George Sand (Amandine Dupin) during their romance and wrote some of his finest and most tempestuous music during that time.
8. A minor diety who challenged Apollo to a musical contest of skill. His punishment for presumption was to be flayed alive by the god. Marsyas was adopted by the Decadents as a sort of aesthetic Prometheus, symbolizing their own rebellious artistic practice.
9. An echo of Pater, who compares the world's thought and experiences to "the sound of lyres and flutes" that lives only in the expression of Mona Lisa's face and hands (see p. 331). In this as in so many other instances, Lord Henry reveals how little he understands his protégé.
1. Lord Henry's speech on art and life echoes Pater's "Leonardo da Vinci" (in *The Renaissance*; see pp. 318–33).

somewhere,[2] but our own senses will imagine them for us. There are moments when the odour of *lilas blanc* passes suddenly across me, and I have to live the strangest month of my life over again. I wish I could change places with you, Dorian. The world has cried out against us both, but it has always worshipped you. It always will worship you. You are the type of what the age is searching for, and what it is afraid it has found. I am so glad that you have never done anything, never carved a statue, or painted a picture, or produced anything outside of yourself! Life has been your art. You have set yourself to music. Your days are your sonnets."

Dorian rose up from the piano, and passed his hand through his hair. "Yes, life has been exquisite," he murmured, "but I am not going to have the same life, Harry. And you must not say these extravagant things to me. You don't know everything about me. I think that if you did, even you would turn from me. You laugh. Don't laugh."

"Why have you stopped playing, Dorian? Go back and give me the nocturne over again: Look at that great honey-coloured moon that hangs in the dusky air. She is waiting for you to charm her, and if you play she will come closer to the earth. You won't? Let us go to the club, then. It has been a charming evening, and we must end it charmingly. There is some one at White's who wants immensely to know you—young Lord Poole, Bournemouth's eldest son. He has already copied your neckties, and has begged me to introduce him to you. He is quite delightful, and rather reminds me of you."

"I hope not," said Dorian, with a sad look in his eyes. "But I am tired to-night, Harry. I shan't go to the club. It is nearly eleven, and I want to go to bed early."

"Do stay. You have never played so well as to-night. There was something in your touch that was wonderful. It had more expression than I had ever heard from it before."

"It is because I am going to be good," he answered, smiling. "I am a little changed already."

"You cannot change to me, Dorian," said Lord Henry. "You and I will always be friends."

"Yet you poisoned me with a book once. I should not forgive that. Harry, promise me that you will never lend that book to any one. It does harm."

"My dear boy, you are really beginning to moralize. You will soon be going about like the converted, and the revivalist, warning people against all the sins of which you have grown tired. You are much too delightful to do that. Besides, it is no use. You and I are what we are, and will be what we will be. As for being poisoned by a book,

---

2. A recurrent theme in Robert Browning's poetry, appearing in "A Toccata of Galuppi's" and more obliquely in "Bishop Blougram's Apology," lines 183–86.

there is no such thing as that. Art has no influence upon action. It annihilates the desire to act. It is superbly sterile. The books that the world calls immoral are books that show the world its own shame. That is all.[3] But we won't discuss literature. Come round to-morrow. I am going to ride at eleven. We might go together, and I will take you to lunch afterwards with Lady Branksome. She is a charming woman, and wants to consult you about some tapestries she is thinking of buying. Mind you come. Or shall we lunch with our little Duchess? She says she never sees you now. Perhaps you are tired of Gladys? I thought you would be. Her clever tongue gets on one's nerves. Well, in any case, be here at eleven."

"Must I really come, Harry?"

"Certainly. The Park is quite lovely now. I don't think there have been such lilacs since the year I met you."

"Very well. I shall be here at eleven," said Dorian. "Good-night, Harry." As he reached the door he hesitated for a moment, as if he had something more to say. Then he sighed and went out.

Chapter XX

It was a lovely night, so warm that he threw his coat over his arm, and did not even put his silk scarf round his throat. As he strolled home, smoking his cigarette, two young men in evening dress passed him. He heard one of them whisper to the other, "That is Dorian Gray." He remembered how pleased he used to be when he was pointed out, or stared at, or talked about. He was tired of hearing his own name now. Half the charm of the little village where he had been so often lately was that no one knew who he was. He had often told the girl whom he had lured to love him that he was poor, and she had believed him. He had told her once that he was wicked, and she had laughed at him, and answered that wicked people were always very old and very ugly. What a laugh she had!—just like a thrush singing. And how pretty she had been in her cotton dresses and her large hats! She knew nothing, but she had everything that he had lost.

When he reached home, he found his servant waiting up for him. He sent him to bed, and threw himself down on the sofa in the library, and began to think over some of the things that Lord Henry had said to him.

Was it really true that one could never change? He felt a wild longing for the unstained purity of his boyhood—his rose-white

3. Wilde took a similar line at his first trial in defending *Dorian Gray* against charges of its alleged pernicious influence.

boyhood, as Lord Henry had once called it. He knew that he had tarnished himself, filled his mind with corruption and given horror to his fancy; that he had been an evil influence to others, and had experienced a terrible joy in being so; and that of the lives that had crossed his own it had been the fairest and the most full of promise that he had brought to shame. But was it all irretrievable? Was there no hope for him?

Ah! in what a monstrous moment of pride and passion he had prayed that the portrait should bear the burden of his days, and he keep the unsullied splendour of eternal youth! All his failure had been due to that. Better for him that each sin of his life had brought its sure, swift penalty along with it. There was purification in punishment. Not "Forgive us our sins" but "Smite us for our iniquities" should be the prayer of man to a most just God.

The curiously-carved mirror that Lord Henry had given to him, so many years ago now, was standing on the table, and the white-limbed Cupids laughed round it as of old. He took it up, as he had done on that night of horror, when he had first noted the change in the fatal picture, and with wild tear-dimmed eyes looked into its polished shield. Once, some one who had terribly loved him, had written to him a mad letter, ending with these idolatrous words: "The world is changed because you are made of ivory and gold. The curves of your lips rewrite history." The phrases came back to his memory, and he repeated them over and over to himself. Then he loathed his own beauty, and flinging the mirror on the floor crushed it into silver splinters beneath his heel. It was his beauty that had ruined him, his beauty and the youth that he had prayed for. But for those two things, his life might have been free from stain. His beauty had been to him but a mask, his youth but a mockery. What was youth at best? A green, an unripe time, a time of shallow moods, and sickly thoughts. Why had he worn its livery? Youth had spoiled him.

It was better not to think of the past. Nothing could alter that. It was of himself, and of his own future, that he had to think. James Vane was hidden in a nameless grave in Selby churchyard. Alan Campbell had shot himself one night in his laboratory, but had not revealed the secret that he had been forced to know. The excitement, such as it was, over Basil Hallward's disappearance would soon pass away. It was already waning. He was perfectly safe there. Nor, indeed, was it the death of Basil Hallward that weighed most upon his mind. It was the living death of his own soul that troubled him. Basil had painted the portrait that had marred his life. He could not forgive him that. It was the portrait that had done everything. Basil had said things to him that were unbearable, and that he had yet borne with patience. The murder had been simply the madness of a moment.

As for Alan Campbell, his suicide had been his own act. He had chosen to do it. It was nothing to him.

A new life! That was what he wanted. That was what he was waiting for. Surely he had begun it already. He had spared one innocent thing, at any rate. He would never again tempt innocence. He would be good.

As he thought of Hetty Merton, he began to wonder if the portrait in the locked room had changed. Surely it was not still so horrible as it had been? Perhaps if his life became pure, he would be able to expel every sign of evil passion from the face. Perhaps the signs of evil had already gone away. He would go and look.

He took the lamp from the table and crept upstairs. As he unbarred the door, a smile of joy flitted across his strangely young-looking face and lingered for a moment about his lips. Yes, he would be good, and the hideous thing that he had hidden away would no longer be a terror to him. He felt as if the load had been lifted from him already.

He went in quietly, locking the door behind him, as was his custom, and dragged the purple hanging from the portrait. A cry of pain and indignation broke from him. He could see no change, save that in the eyes there was a look of cunning, and in the mouth the curved wrinkle of the hypocrite. The thing was still loathsome—more loathsome, if possible, than before—and the scarlet dew that spotted the hand seemed brighter, and more like blood newly spilt. Then he trembled. Had it been merely vanity that had made him do his one good deed? Or the desire for a new sensation, as Lord Henry had hinted, with his mocking laugh? Or that passion to act a part that sometimes makes us do things finer than we are ourselves? Or, perhaps, all these? And why was the red stain larger than it had been? It seemed to have crept like a horrible disease over the wrinkled fingers. There was blood on the painted feet, as though the thing had dripped—blood even on the hand that had not held the knife. Confess? Did it mean that he was to confess? To give himself up, and be put to death? He laughed. He felt that the idea was monstrous. Besides, even if he did confess, who would believe him? There was no trace of the murdered man anywhere. Everything belonging to him had been destroyed. He himself had burned what had been below-stairs. The world would simply say that he was mad. They would shut him up if he persisted in his story. . . . Yet it was his duty to confess, to suffer public shame, and to make public atonement. There was a God who called upon men to tell their sins to earth as well as to heaven. Nothing that he could do would cleanse him till he had told his own sin. His sin? He shrugged his shoulders. The death of Basil Hallward seemed very little to him. He was thinking of Hetty Merton. For it was an unjust mirror, this mirror of his soul that he was looking at. Vanity? Curiosity?

Hypocrisy? Had there been nothing more in his renunciation than that? There had been something more. At least he thought so. But who could tell? . . . No. There had been nothing more. Through vanity he had spared her. In hypocrisy he had worn the mask of goodness. For curiosity's sake he had tried the denial of self. He recognized that now.[1]

But this murder—was it to dog him all his life? Was he always to be burdened by his past? Was he really to confess? Never. There was only one bit of evidence left against him. The picture itself—that was evidence. He would destroy it. Why had he kept it so long? Once it had given him pleasure to watch it changing and growing old. Of late he had felt no such pleasure. It had kept him awake at night. When he had been away, he had been filled with terror lest other eyes should look upon it. It had brought melancholy across his passions. Its mere memory had marred many moments of joy. It had been like conscience to him. Yes, it had been conscience. He would destroy it.

He looked round, and saw the knife that had stabbed Basil Hallward. He had cleaned it many times, till there was no stain left upon it. It was bright, and glistened. As it had killed the painter, so it would kill the painter's work, and all that that meant. It would kill the past, and when that was dead he would be free. It would kill this monstrous soul-life, and without its hideous warnings, he would be at peace.[2] He seized the thing, and stabbed the picture with it.

There was a cry heard, and a crash. The cry was so horrible in its agony that the frightened servants woke, and crept out of their rooms. Two gentlemen, who were passing in the Square below, stopped, and looked up at the great house. They walked on till they met a policeman, and brought him back. The man rang the bell several times, but there was no answer. Except for a light in one of the top windows, the house was all dark. After a time, he went away, and stood in an adjoining portico and watched.

"Whose house is that, constable?" asked the elder of the two gentlemen.

"Mr. Dorian Gray's, sir," answered the policeman.

They looked at each other, as they walked away, and sneered. One of them was Sir Henry Ashton's uncle.

Inside, in the servants' part of the house, the half-clad domestics were talking in low whispers to each other. Old Mrs. Leaf was crying, and wringing her hands. Francis was as pale as death.

---

1. Wilde added the lines beginning "No. There had been nothing more" to the end of the paragraph in this edition.
2. Wilde added this sentence to this edition.

After about a quarter of an hour, he got the coachman and one of the footmen and crept upstairs. They knocked, but there was no reply. They called out. Everything was still. Finally, after vainly trying to force the door, they got on the roof, and dropped down on to the balcony. The windows yielded easily: their bolts were old.

When they entered, they found hanging upon the wall a splendid portrait of their master as they had last seen him, in all the wonder of his exquisite youth and beauty. Lying on the floor was a dead man, in evening dress, with a knife in his heart. He was withered, wrinkled, and loathsome of visage. It was not till they had examined the rings that they recognized who it was.

The Picture of Dorian Gray
(1890)

Chapter I

The studio was filled with the rich odor of roses, and when the light summer wind stirred amidst the trees of the garden there came through the open door the heavy scent of the lilac, or the more delicate perfume of the pink-flowering thorn.

From the corner of the divan of Persian saddle-bags on which he was lying, smoking, as usual,[1] innumerable cigarettes, Lord Henry Wotton could just catch the gleam of the honey-sweet and honey-colored blossoms of the laburnum, whose tremulous branches seemed hardly able to bear the burden of a beauty so flame-like as theirs; and now and then the fantastic shadows of birds in flight flitted across the long tussore-silk curtains that were stretched in front of the huge window, producing a kind of momentary Japanese effect, and making him think of those pallid jade-faced painters who, in an art that is necessarily immobile,[2] seek to convey the sense of swiftness and motion. The sullen murmur of the bees shouldering their way through the long unmown grass, or circling with monotonous insistence round the black-crocketed spires of the early June hollyhocks,[3] seemed to make the stillness more oppressive, and the dim roar of London was like the bourdon note of a distant organ.

In the centre of the room, clamped to an upright easel, stood the full-length portrait of a young man of extraordinary personal beauty, and in front of it, some little distance away, was sitting the artist himself, Basil Hallward, whose sudden disappearance some years ago caused, at the time, such public excitement, and gave rise to so many strange conjectures.

As he looked at the gracious and comely form he had so skilfully mirrored in his art, a smile of pleasure passed across his face, and

---

1. Changed to "as was his custom" in 1891.
2. Several refinements are made in this description in 1891.
3. "Black-crocketed . . . hollyhocks" changed to "dusty gilt horns of the straggling wood-bine" in 1891.

seemed about to linger there. But he suddenly started up, and, closing his eyes, placed his fingers upon the lids, as though he sought to
imprison within his brain some curious dream from which he
feared he might awake.

"It is your best work, Basil, the best thing you have ever done,"
said Lord Henry, languidly. "You must certainly send it next year to
the Grosvenor. The Academy is too large and too vulgar. The Grosvenor is the only place."[4]

"I don't think I will[5] send it anywhere," he answered, tossing his
head back in that odd way that used to make his friends laugh at
him at Oxford. "No: I won't send it anywhere."[6]

Lord Henry elevated his eyebrows, and looked at him in amazement through the thin blue wreaths of smoke that curled up in such
fanciful whorls from his heavy opium-tainted cigarette. "Not send
it anywhere? My dear fellow, why? Have you any reason? What odd
chaps you painters are! You do anything in the world to gain a reputation. As soon as you have one, you seem to want to throw it away.
It is silly of you, for there is only one thing in the world worse than
being talked about, and that is not being talked about. A portrait
like this would set you far above all the young men in England, and
make the old men quite jealous, if old men are ever capable of any
emotion."

"I know you will laugh at me," he replied, "but I really can't
exhibit it. I have put too much of myself into it."

Lord Henry stretched his long legs out on the divan and shook
with laughter.[7]

"Yes, I knew you would laugh; but it is quite true, all the same."

"Too much of yourself in it! Upon my word, Basil, I didn't know
you were so vain; and I really can't see any resemblance between you,
with your rugged strong face and your coal-black hair, and this young
Adonis, who looks as if he was made of ivory and rose-leaves. Why,
my dear Basil, he is a Narcissus and you—well, of course you have
an intellectual expression, and all that. But beauty, real beauty,
ends where an intellectual expression begins. Intellect is in itself an
exaggeration,[8] and destroys the harmony of any face. The moment
one sits down to think, one becomes all nose, or all forehead, or
something horrid. Look at the successful men in any of the learned
professions. How perfectly hideous they are! Except, of course, in

---

4. This last sentence omitted in 1891.
5. Wilde wrote Coulson Kernahan, editor of the revised edition for Ward, Lock & Company, asking that he "look after my 'wills' and 'shalls' in proof," explaining that his
   "usage was Celtic not English" (*Letters* 289).
6. Typescript draft of the work (TS) has "and yet, you are quite right about it. It is my best
   work."
7. This sentence slightly altered in 1891.
8. Changed to "a mode of exaggeration" in 1891.

the Church. But then in the Church they don't think. A bishop keeps on saying at the age of eighty what he was told to say when he was a boy of eighteen, and consequently[9] he always looks absolutely delightful. Your mysterious young friend, whose name you have never told me, but whose picture really fascinates me, never thinks. I feel quite sure of that. He is a brainless, beautiful thing, who should be always here in winter when we have no flowers to look at, and always here in summer when we want something to chill our intelligence. Don't flatter yourself, Basil: you are not in the least like him."

"You don't understand me, Harry. Of course I am not like him. I know that perfectly well. Indeed, I should be sorry to look like him. You shrug your shoulders? I am telling you the truth. There is a fatality about all physical and intellectual distinction, the sort of fatality that seems to dog through history the faltering steps of kings.[1] It is better not to be different from one's fellows. The ugly and the stupid have the best of it in this world. They can sit quietly and gape at the play. If they know nothing of victory, they are at least spared the knowledge of defeat. They live as we all should live, undisturbed, indifferent, and without disquiet. They neither bring ruin upon others nor ever receive it from alien hands. Your rank and wealth, Harry; my brains, such as they are,—my fame,[2] whatever it may be worth; Dorian Gray's good looks,—we will all suffer for what the gods have given us, suffer terribly."

"Dorian Gray? is that his name?" said Lord Henry, walking across the studio towards Basil Hallward.

"Yes; that is his name. I didn't intend to tell it to you."

"But why not?"

"Oh, I can't explain. When I like people immensely I never tell their names to any one. It seems like surrendering a part of them. You know how I love secrecy. It is the only thing that can make modern life wonderful or mysterious to us.[3] The commonest thing is delightful if one only hides it. When I leave town I never tell my people where I am going. If I did, I would lose all my pleasure. It is a silly habit, I dare say, but somehow it seems to bring a great deal of romance into one's life. I suppose you think me awfully foolish about it?"

"Not at all," answered Lord Henry, laying his hand upon his shoulder;[4] "not at all, my dear Basil. You seem to forget that I am married, and the one charm of marriage is that it makes a life of deception necessary for both parties. I never know where my wife is, and

---

9. Changed to "as a natural consequence" in 1891.
1. Holograph draft of the work (MS) has "to dog the steps of kings."
2. Changed to "art" in 1891.
3. Wilde made four stylistic changes in the first four lines of this paragraph in 1891.
4. "Laying . . . shoulder" deleted in 1891. This is the first of many such deletions or rewrites eliminating descriptions of physical contact suggestive of homoerotic behavior.

my wife never knows what I am doing. When we meet,—we do meet occasionally, when we dine out together, or go down to the duke's,—we tell each other the most absurd stories with the most serious faces. My wife is very good at it,—much better, in fact, than I am. She never gets confused over her dates, and I always do. But when she does find me out, she makes no row at all. I sometimes wish she would; but she merely laughs at me."

"I hate the way you talk about your married life, Harry," said Basil Hallward, shaking his hand off,[5] and strolling towards the door that led into the garden. "I believe that you are really a very good husband, but that you are thoroughly ashamed of your own virtues. You are an extraordinary fellow. You never say a moral thing, and you never do a wrong thing. Your cynicism is simply a pose."

"Being natural is simply a pose, and the most irritating pose I know," cried Lord Henry, laughing; and the two young men went out into the garden together, and for a time they did not speak.[6]

After a long pause Lord Henry pulled out his watch. "I am afraid I must be going, Basil," he murmured, "and before I go I insist on your answering a question I put to you some time ago."

"What is that?" asked Basil Hallward, keeping his eyes fixed on the ground.

"You know quite well."

"I do not, Harry."

"Well, I will tell you what it is."

"Please don't."[7]

"I must. I want you to explain to me why you won't exhibit Dorian Gray's picture. I want the real reason."

"I told you the real reason."

"No, you did not. You said it was because there was too much of yourself in it. Now, that is childish."

"Harry," said Basil Hallward, looking him straight in the face,[8] "every portrait that is painted with feeling[9] is a portrait of the artist, not of the sitter. The sitter is merely the accident, the occasion. It is not he who is revealed by the painter; it is rather the painter who, on the colored canvas, reveals himself. The reason I will not exhibit this picture is that I am afraid that I have shown with it the secret of my own soul."

Lord Harry laughed. "And what is that?" he asked.

"I will tell you," said Hallward; and an expression of perplexity came over his face.

---

5. "Shaking . . . off" deleted in 1891.
6. Wilde changed the last phrase in 1891.
7. This sentence and Henry's "I must" deleted in 1891.
8. Wilde canceled the phrase "taking hold of his hand" in MS.
9. Wilde changed the original "passion" to "feeling" in MS.

"I am all expectation, Basil," murmured his companion, looking at him.

"Oh, there is really very little to tell, Harry," answered the young painter; "and I am afraid you will hardly understand it. Perhaps you will hardly believe it."

Lord Henry smiled, and, leaning down, plucked a pink-petalled daisy from the grass, and examined it. "I am quite sure I shall understand it," he replied, gazing intently at the little golden white-feathered disk,[1] "and I can believe anything, provided that it is incredible."

The wind shook some blossoms from the trees, and the heavy lilac-blooms, with their clustering stars, moved to and fro in the languid air. A grasshopper began to chirrup in the grass, and a long thin dragon-fly floated by on its brown gauze wings.[2] Lord Henry felt as if he could hear Basil Hallward's heart beating, and he wondered what was coming.

"Well, this is incredible," repeated Hallward, rather bitterly,— "incredible to me at times. I don't know what it means.[3] The story is simply this. Two months ago I went to a crush at Lady Brandon's. You know we poor painters have to show ourselves in society from time to time, just to remind the public that we are not savages. With an evening coat and a white tie, as you told me once, anybody, even a stock-broker, can gain a reputation for being civilized. Well, after I had been in the room about ten minutes, talking to huge overdressed dowagers and tedious Academicians, I suddenly became conscious that some one was looking at me. I turned half-way round, and saw Dorian Gray for the first time. When our eyes met, I felt that I was growing pale. A curious instinct of terror came over me. I knew that I had come face to face with some one whose mere personality was so fascinating that, if I allowed it to do so, it would absorb my whole nature, my whole soul, my very art itself. I did not want any external influence in my life. You know yourself, Harry, how independent I am by nature. My father destined me for the army. I insisted on going to Oxford. Then he made me enter my name at the Middle Temple. Before I had eaten half a dozen dinners I gave up the Bar, and announced my intention of becoming a painter.[4] I have always been my own master; had at least always been so, till I met Dorian Gray. Then—But I don't know how to explain it to you. Something seemed to tell me that I was on the verge of a terrible crisis in my life. I had a strange feeling that Fate had in

---

1. Wilde deleted "that had charmed all the poets from Chaucer to Tennyson" in MS and modified the style of the epigram following in 1891. The epigram appeared written in TS.
2. Several stylistic changes made here in 1891.
3. Opening lines of this paragraph deleted in 1891.
4. "My father . . . painter" deleted in 1891. The Middle Temple is one of four legal societies of London through which one prepared for the practice of law before the English bar.

store for me exquisite joys and exquisite sorrows. I knew that if I spoke to Dorian I would become absolutely devoted to him, and that I ought not to speak to him.[5] I grew afraid, and turned to quit the room. It was not conscience that made me do so: it was cowardice. I take no credit to myself for trying to escape."

"Conscience and cowardice are really the same things, Basil. Conscience is the trade-name of the firm. That is all."

"I don't believe that, Harry. However, whatever was my motive,— and it may have been pride, for I used to be very proud,—I certainly struggled to the door. There, of course, I stumbled against Lady Brandon. 'You are not going to run away so soon, Mr. Hallward?' she screamed out. You know her shrill horrid voice?"

"Yes; she is a peacock in everything but beauty," said Lord Henry, pulling the daisy to bits with his long, nervous fingers.

"I could not get rid of her. She brought me up to Royalties, and people with Stars and Garters, and elderly ladies with gigantic tiaras and hooked noses. She spoke of me as her dearest friend. I had only met her once before, but she took it into her head to lionize me. I believe some picture of mine had made a great success at the time, at least had been chattered about in the penny newspapers, which is the nineteenth-century standard of immortality. Suddenly I found myself face to face with the young man whose personality[6] had so strangely stirred me. We were quite close, almost touching. Our eyes met again. It was made of me, but I asked Lady Brandon to introduce me to him. Perhaps it was not so mad, after all. It was simply inevitable. We would have spoken to each other without any introduction. I am sure of that. Dorian told me so afterwards. He, too, felt that we were destined to know each other."

"And how did Lady Brandon describe this wonderful young man? I know she goes in for giving a rapid *précis* of all her guests. I remember her bringing me up to a most truculent and red-faced old gentleman covered all over with orders and ribbons, and hissing into my ear, in a tragic whisper which must have been perfectly audible to everybody in the room, something like 'Sir Humpty Dumpty— you know—Afghan frontier—Russian intrigues: very successful man—wife killed by an elephant—quite inconsolable—wants to marry a beautiful American widow—everybody does nowadays— hates Mr. Gladstone—but very much interested in beetles: ask him what he thinks of Schouvaloff.'[7] I simply fled. I simply fled. I like to

5. "I knew . . . to him" changed in MS from "I would never leave him till either he or I were dead" and omitted from the 1891 text.
6. Changed in MS from "beauty had so stirred me."
7. "Something like . . . Schouvaloff" removed from 1891 text. Lady Brandon's rapid précis is cited by Sherard, Harris, and others as a parody of the speech of Lady Wilde, Oscar's mother. She was noted for her salons when the family lived in Dublin and later, more modestly, in London. William Gladstone (1809–1898), English statesman and

find out people for myself. But poor Lady Brandon treats her guests exactly as an auctioneer treats his goods. She either explains them entirely away, or tells one everything about them except what one wants to know. But what did she say about Mr. Dorian Gray?"

"Oh, she murmured, 'Charming boy—poor dear mother and I quite inseparable—engaged to be married to the same man—I mean married on the same day—how very silly of me! Quite forget what he does—afraid he—doesn't do anything—oh, yes, plays the piano—or is it the violin, dear Mr. Gray?' We could neither of us help laughing, and we became friends at once."

"Laughter is not a bad beginning for a friendship, and it is the best ending for one," said Lord Henry, plucking another daisy.

Hallward buried his face in his hands.[8] "You don't understand what friendship is, Harry," he murmured,—"or what enmity is, for that matter. You like every one; that is to say, you are indifferent to every one."

"How horribly unjust of you!" cried Lord Henry, tilting his hat back, and looking up at the little clouds that were drifting across the hollowed turquoise of the summer sky, like ravelled skeins of glossy white silk. "Yes; horribly unjust of you. I make a great difference between people. I choose my friends for their good looks, my acquaintances for their characters, and my enemies for their brains.[9] A man can't be too careful in the choice of his enemies. I have not got one who is a fool. They are all men of some intellectual power, and consequently they all appreciate me. Is that very vain of me? I think it is rather vain."

"I should think it was, Harry. But according to your category I must be merely an acquaintance."

"My dear old Basil, you are much more than an acquaintance."

"And much less than a friend. A sort of brother, I suppose?"

"Oh, brothers! I don't care for brothers. My elder brother won't die, and my younger brothers seem never to do anything else."

"Harry!"

"My dear fellow, I am not quite serious. But I can't help detesting my relations. I suppose it comes from the fact that we can't stand other people having the same faults as ourselves. I quite sympathize with the rage of the English democracy against what they call the vices of the upper classes. They feel that drunkenness, stupidity, and immorality should be their own special property, and that if any one of us makes an ass of himself he is poaching on their preserves.

four-time prime minister, was known as a social and political reformer. Count Peter Schouvaloff (1827–1889), Russian envoy to London from 1873 to 1879, helped preserve amicable relations with England during the Russo-Turkish War (1877–78).
8. Wilde made several stylistic changes in the preceding eight lines in the 1891 text.
9. Another epigram Wilde touched up a little in 1891.

When poor Southwark got into the Divorce Court, their indignation was quite magnificent. And yet I don't suppose that ten per cent of the lower orders live correctly."[1]

"I don't agree with a single word that you have said, and, what is more, Harry, I don't believe you do either."

Lord Henry stroked his pointed brown beard, and tapped the toe of his patent-leather boot with a tasselled malacca cane. "How English you are, Basil! If one puts forward an idea to a real Englishman,—always a rash thing to do,—he never dreams of considering whether the idea is right or wrong.[2] The only thing he considers of any importance is whether one believes it one's self. Now, the value of an idea has nothing whatsoever to do with the sincerity of the man who expresses it. Indeed, the probabilities are that the more insincere the man is, the more purely intellectual will the idea be, as in that case it will not be colored by either his wants, his desires, or his prejudices. However, I don't propose to discuss politics, sociology, or metaphysics with you. I like persons better than principles. Tell me more about Dorian Gray. How often do you see him?"

"Every day. I couldn't be happy if I didn't see him every day. Of course sometimes it is only for a few minutes. But a few minutes with somebody one worships mean a great deal."

"But you don't really worship him?"

"I do."

"How extraordinary! I thought you would never care for anything but your painting,—your art, I should say. Art sounds better, doesn't it?"[3]

"He is all my art to me now. I sometimes think, Harry, that there are only two eras of any importance in the history of the world. The first is the appearance of a new medium for art, and the second is the appearance of a new personality for art also. What the invention of oil-painting was to the Venetians, the face of Antinoüs was to late Greek sculpture, and the face of Dorian Gray will some day be to me. It is not merely that I paint from him, draw from him, model from him. Of course I have done all that. He has stood as Paris in dainty armor, and as Adonis with huntsman's cloak and polished boar-spear. Crowned with heavy lotus-blossoms, he has sat

1. J. M. Stoddart, *Lippincott's* editor, changed TS reading "live with their wives," removing an expression inadmissible to the American public. Wilde let these and similar changes stand even though they are clearly inferior to his original.
2. Wilde altered details here and in the preceding two paragraphs in 1891. Lord Henry originally owned a "straw-colored moustache" and a "Henry Deux" beard, but lost them both in MS. Both were features of the appearance of Lord Ronald Sutherland-Gower, a candidate for the original of Lord Henry.
3. Wilde revised the dialogue above in 1891, leaving out "worship" and muting the homoerotic overtones.

on the prow of Adrian's barge, looking into the green, turbid Nile. He has leaned over the still pool of some Greek woodland, and seen in the water's silent silver the wonder of his own beauty. But he is much more to me than that. I won't tell you that I am dissatisfied with what I have done of him, or that his beauty is such that art cannot express it. There is nothing that art cannot express, and I know that the work I have done since I met Dorian Gray is good work, is the best work of my life. But in some curious way—I wonder will you understand me?—his personality has suggested to me an entirely new manner in art, an entirely new mode of style. I see things differently, I think of them differently. I can now re-create life in a way that was hidden from me before. 'A dream of form in days of thought,'—who is it who says that? I forget; but it is what Dorian Gray has been to me. The merely visible presence of this lad,[4]—for he seems to me little more than a lad, though he is really over twenty,—his merely visible presence,—ah! I wonder can you realize all that that means? Unconsciously he defines for me the lines of a fresh school, a school that is to have in itself all the passion of the romantic spirit, all the perfection of the spirit that is Greek. The harmony of soul and body,—how much that is! We in our madness have separated the two, and have invented a realism that is bestial, an ideality that is void. Harry! Harry! if you only knew what Dorian Gray is to me! You remember that landscape of mine, for which Agnew offered me such a huge price, but which I would not part with? It is one of the best things I have ever done. And why is it so? Because, while I was painting it, Dorian Gray sat beside me."[5]

"Basil, this is quite wonderful! I must see Dorian Gray."[6]

Hallward got up from the seat, and walked up and down the garden.[7] After some time he came back. "You don't understand, Harry," he said. "Dorian Gray is merely to me a motive in art. He is never more present in my work than when no image of him is there. He is simply a suggestion, as I have said, of a new manner. I see him in

4. "Lad" substituted for "boy" here and in several other places in MS. Wilde removed "Though twenty summers have shown him roses less scarlet than his lips" in MS.
5. Wilde made several changes in this paragraph in 1891. In MS, Wilde deleted "and as he leaned across to look at it, his lips just touched my hand. The world becomes young to me when I hold his hand. . . ." In 1891, Wilde added another sentence here emphasizing Dorian's influence on Basil's art.
6. Henry's response in MS is too heavily blotted to read fully, but he protests Basil's being in Dorian's power: "to make yourself the slave of your slave. It is worse than wicked, it is silly. I hate Dorian Gray!" In one stroke, Wilde rid himself of some silly dialogue and removed a clue, perhaps, to the nature of the relationship between Dorian and Basil as a form of homoerotic bondage so fashionable among the English that the French referred to it as *le vice anglais*.
7. Wilde canceled the following at this point in MS: "A curious smile crossed his face. He seemed like a man in a dream."

the curves of certain lines, in the loveliness and the subtleties of certain colors. That is all."

"Then why won't you exhibit his portrait?"

"Because I have put into it all the extraordinary romance of which, of course, I have never dared to speak to him. He knows nothing about it. He will never know anything about it. But the world might guess it; and I will not bare my soul to their shallow, prying eyes. My heart shall never be put under their microscope. There is too much of myself in the thing, Harry,—too much of myself!"[8]

"Poets are not so scrupulous as you are. They know how useful passion is for publication. Nowadays a broken heart will run to many editions."

"I hate them for it. An artist should create beautiful things, but should put nothing of his own life into them. We live in an age when men treat art as if it were meant to be a form of autobiography. We have lost the abstract sense of beauty. If I live, I will show the world what it is; and for that reason the world shall never see my portrait of Dorian Gray."

"I think you are wrong, Basil, but I won't argue with you. It is only the intellectually lost who ever argue. Tell me, is Dorian Gray very fond of you?"

Hallward considered for a few moments. "He likes me," he answered, after a pause; "I know he likes me. Of course I flatter him dreadfully. I find a strange pleasure in saying things to him that I know I shall be sorry for having said. I give myself away.[9] As a rule, he is charming to me, and we walk home together from the club arm in arm, or sit in the studio and talk of a thousand things. Now and then, however, he is horribly thoughtless, and seems to take a real delight in giving me pain. Then I feel, Harry, that I have given away my whole soul to some one[1] who treats it as if it were a flower to put in his coat, a bit of decoration to charm his vanity, an ornament for a summer's day."

"Days in summer, Basil, are apt to linger. Perhaps you will tire sooner than he will. It is a sad thing to think of, but there is no doubt that Genius lasts longer than Beauty. That accounts for the fact that we all take such pains to over-educate ourselves. In the wild struggle

8. Wilde altered this and the preceding paragraphs in every revision. He removed from MS (after "the world might guess it") "where there is merely love, they would see something evil. Where there is spiritual passion, they would suggest something vile."
9. Wilde dropped this sentence from the 1891 text together with the phrase "walk home together from the club arm in arm" from the next sentence.
1. The following lines were canceled at this point in MS: "who seems to take a real delight in giving me pain. I seem quite adjusted to it. I can imagine myself doing it. But not to him, not to him. Once or twice we have been away together. Then I have had him all to myself. I am horribly jealous of him, of course. I never let him talk to me of the people he knows. I like to isolate him from the rest of life and to think that he absolutely belongs to me. He does not, I know. But it gives me pleasure to think he does."

for existence, we want to have something that endures, and so we fill our minds with rubbish and facts, in the silly hope of keeping our place. The thoroughly well informed man,—that is the modern ideal. And the mind of the thoroughly well informed man is a dreadful thing. It is like a bric-à-brac shop, all monsters and dust, and everything priced above its proper value. I think you will tire first, all the same. Some day you will look at Gray, and he will seem to you to be a little out of drawing, or you won't like his tone of color, or something. You will bitterly reproach him in your own heart, and seriously think that he has behaved very badly to you. The next time he calls, you will be perfectly cold and indifferent. It will be a great pity, for it will alter you. The worst of having a romance is that it leaves one so unromantic."[2]

"Harry, don't talk like that.[3] As long as I live, the personality of Dorian Gray will dominate me. You can't feel what I feel. You change too often."

"Ah, my dear Basil, that is exactly why I can feel it. Those who are faithful know only the pleasures of love: it is the faithless who know love's tragedies." And Lord Henry struck a light on a dainty silver case, and began to smoke a cigarette with a self-conscious and self-satisfied air, as if he had summed up life in a phrase. There was a rustle of chirruping sparrows in the ivy, and the blue cloud-shadows chased themselves across the grass like swallows. How pleasant it was in the garden! And how delightful other people's emotions were!—much more delightful than their ideas, it seemed to him. One's own soul, and the passions of one's friends,—those were the fascinating things in life. He thought with pleasure of the tedious luncheon that he had missed by staying so long with Basil Hallward. Had he gone to his aunt's, he would have been sure to meet Lord Goodbody there, and the whole conversation would have been about the housing of the poor, and the necessity for model lodging-houses.[4] It was charming to have escaped all that! As he thought of his aunt, an idea seemed to strike him. He turned to Hallward, and said, "My dear fellow, I have just remembered."

"Remembered what, Harry?"

"Where I heard the name of Dorian Gray."

"Where was it?" asked Hallward, with a slight frown.

---

2. In 1891, Wilde added the mitigating phrase "of any kind" after "having a romance."
3. The following lines were canceled in MS: "I am not afraid of things, but I am afraid of words. I cannot understand how it is that no prophecy has ever been fulfilled. None has I know. And yet it seems to me that to say a thing is to bring it to pass. Whatever has found expression becomes true, and what has not found expression can never happen. As for genius lasting longer than beauty, it is only the transitory that stirs me. What is permanent is monstrous and produces no effect. Our senses become dulled by what is always with us." These lines have a strong flavor of Pater about them.
4. Wilde made several alterations here in 1891, including the addition of the aphorism beginning "each class" (see p. 15).

"Don't look so angry, Basil. It was at my aunt's, Lady Agatha's. She told me she had discovered a wonderful young man, who was going to help her in the East End, and that his name was Dorian Gray. I am bound to state that she never told me he was good-looking. Women have no appreciation of good looks. At least, good women have not. She said that he was very earnest, and had a beautiful nature. I at once pictured to myself a creature with spectacles and lank hair, horridly freckled, and tramping about on huge feet. I wish I had known it was your friend."

"I am very glad you didn't, Harry."

"Why?"

"I don't want you to meet him."

"Mr. Dorian Gray is in the studio, sir," said the butler, coming into the garden.

"You must introduce me now," cried Lord Henry, laughing.

Basil Hallward turned to the servant, who stood blinking in the sunlight. "Ask Mr. Gray to wait, Parker: I will be in in a few moments." The man bowed, and went up the walk.

Then he looked at Lord Henry. "Dorian Gray is my dearest friend," he said. "He has a simple and a beautiful nature. Your aunt was quite right in what she said of him. Don't spoil him for me. Don't try to influence him. Your influence would be bad. The world is wide, and has many marvellous people in it. Don't take away from me the one person that makes life absolutely lovely to me, and that gives to my art whatever wonder or charm it possesses.[5] Mind, Harry, I trust you." He spoke very slowly, and the words seemed wrung out of him almost against his will.

"What nonsense you talk!" said Lord Henry, smiling, and, taking Hallward by the arm, he almost led him into the house.[6]

Chapter II

As they entered they saw Dorian Gray. He was seated at the piano, with his back to them, turning over the pages of a volume of Schumann's "Forest Scenes." "You must lend me these, Basil," he cried. "I want to learn them. They are perfectly charming."

"That entirely depends on how you sit to-day, Dorian."

"Oh, I am tired of sitting, and I don't want a life-sized portrait of myself," answered the lad, swinging round on the music-stool, in a wilful, petulant manner. When he caught sight of Lord Henry, a

---

5. "That makes . . . me" and "or wonder" in the next line were dropped in 1891; following "possess," Wilde added "my life as an artist depends on him."
6. The original conclusion of the chapter, canceled in MS, read "'I don't suppose I shall care for him, and I am quite sure he won't care for me,' replied Lord Henry, smiling. . . ."

faint blush colored his cheeks for a moment, and he started up. "I beg your pardon, Basil, but I didn't know you had any one with you."

"This is Lord Henry Wotton, Dorian, an old Oxford friend of mine. I have just been telling him what a capital sitter you were, and now you have spoiled everything."

"You have not spoiled my pleasure in meeting you, Mr. Gray," said Lord Henry, stepping forward and shaking him by the hand. "My aunt has often spoken to me about you. You are one of her favorites, and, I am afraid, one of her victims also."

"I am in Lady Agatha's black books at present," answered Dorian, with a funny look of penitence. "I promised to go to her club in White-chapel with her last Tuesday, and I really forgot all about it. We were to have played a duet together,—three duets, I believe. I don't know what she will say to me. I am far too frightened to call."

"Oh, I will make your peace with my aunt. She is quite devoted to you. And I don't think it really matters about your not being there. The audience probably thought it was a duet. When Aunt Agatha sits down to the piano she makes quite enough noise for two people."

"That is very horrid to her, and not very nice to me," answered Dorian, laughing.

Lord Henry looked at him. Yes, he was certainly wonderfully handsome, with his finely-curved scarlet lips, his frank blue eyes, his crisp gold hair. There was something in his face that made one trust him at once. All the candor of youth was there, as well as all youth's passionate purity. One felt that he had kept himself unspotted from the world. No wonder Basil Hallward worshipped him. He was made to be worshipped.[1]

"You are too charming to go in for philanthropy, Mr. Gray,—far too charming." And Lord Henry flung himself down on the divan, and opened his cigarette-case.

Hallward had been busy mixing his colors and getting his brushes ready. He was looking worried, and when he heard Lord Henry's last remark he glanced at him, hesitated for a moment, and then said, "Harry, I want to finish this picture to-day. Would you think it awfully rude of me if I asked you to go away?"

Lord Henry smiled, and looked at Dorian Gray. "Am I to go, Mr. Gray?" he asked.

"Oh, please don't, Lord Henry. I see that Basil is in one of his sulky moods; and I can't bear him when he sulks. Besides, I want you to tell me why I should not go in for philanthropy."

"I don't know that I shall tell you that, Mr. Gray.[2] But I certainly will not run away, now that you have asked me to stop. You don't

1. This last sentence was removed in 1891.
2. Wilde added an epigram here in 1891.

really mind, Basil, do you? You have often told me that you liked your sitters to have some one to chat to."

Hallward bit his lip. "If Dorian wishes it, of course you must stay. Dorian's whims are laws to everybody, except himself."

Lord Henry took up his hat and gloves. "You are very pressing, Basil, but I am afraid I must go. I have promised to meet a man at the Orleans.—Good-by, Mr. Gray. Come and see me some afternoon in Curzon Street. I am nearly always at home at five o'clock. Write to me when you are coming. I should be sorry to miss you."

"Basil," cried Dorian Gray, "if Lord Henry goes I shall go too. You never open your lips while you are painting, and it is horribly dull standing on a platform and trying to look pleasant. Ask him to stay. I insist upon it."

"Stay, Harry, to oblige Dorian, and to oblige me," said Hallward, gazing intently at his picture. "It is quite true, I never talk when I am working, and never listen either, and it must be dreadfully tedious for my unfortunate sitters. I beg you to stay."

"But what about my man at the Orleans?"

Hallward laughed. "I don't think there will be any difficulty about that. Sit down again, Harry.—And now, Dorian, get up on the platform, and don't move about too much, or pay any attention to what Lord Henry says. He has a very bad influence over all his friends, with the exception of myself."

Dorian stepped up on the dais, with the air of a young Greek martyr, and made a little *moue* of discontent to Lord Henry, to whom he had rather taken a fancy. He was so unlike Hallward. They made a delightful contrast. And he had such a beautiful voice.[3] After a few moments he said to him, "Have you really a very bad influence, Lord Henry? As bad as Basil says?"

"There is no such thing as a good influence, Mr. Gray. All influence is immoral,—immoral from the scientific point of view."

"Why?"

"Because to influence a person is to give him one's own soul. He does not think his natural thoughts, or burn with his natural passions. His virtues are not real to him. His sins, if there are such things as sins, are borrowed. He becomes an echo of some one else's music, an actor of a part that has not been written for him. The aim of life is self-development. To realize one's nature perfectly,—that is what each of us is here for. People are afraid of themselves, nowadays. They have forgotten the highest of all duties, the duty that one owes to one's self. Of course they are charitable. They feed the hungry, and clothe the beggar. But their own souls starve, and are naked. Courage has gone out of our race. Perhaps we never really

3. Wilde added "to whom . . . voice" in TS.

had it. The terror of society, which is the basis of morals, the terror of God, which is the secret of religion,—these are the two things that govern us. And yet—"

"Just turn your head a little more to the right, Dorian, like a good boy," said Hallward, deep in his work, and conscious only that a look had come into the lad's face that he had never seen there before.

"And yet," continued Lord Henry, in his low, musical voice, and with that graceful wave of the hand that was always so characteristic of him, and that he had even in his Eton days, "I believe that if one man were to live his life out fully and completely, were to give form to every feeling, expression to every thought, reality to every dream,—I believe that the world would gain such a fresh impulse of joy that we would forget all the maladies of mediævalism, and return to the Hellenic ideal,—to something finer, richer, than the Hellenic ideal, it may be. But the bravest man among us is afraid of himself. The mutilation of the savage has its tragic survival in the self-denial that mars our lives. We are punished for our refusals. Every impulse that we strive to strangle broods in the mind, and poisons us. The body sins once, and has done with its sin, for action is a mode of purification. Nothing remains then but the recollection of a pleasure, or the luxury of a regret. The only way to get rid of a temptation is to yield to it. Resist it, and your soul grows sick with longing for the things it has forbidden to itself, with desire for what its monstrous laws have made monstrous and unlawful. It has been said that the great events of the world take place in the brain. It is in the brain, and the brain only, that the great sins of the world take place also. You, Mr. Gray, you yourself, with your rose-red youth and your rose-white boyhood, you have had passions that have made you afraid, thoughts that have filled you with terror, day-dreams and sleeping dreams whose mere memory might stain your cheek with shame—"

"Stop!" murmured Dorian Gray, "stop! you bewilder me. I don't know what to say. There is some answer to you, but I cannot find it. Don't speak, Let me think, or, rather, let me try not to think."[4]

For nearly ten minutes he stood there motionless, with parted lips, and eyes strangely bright. He was dimly conscious that entirely fresh impulses[5] were at work within him, and they seemed to him to have come really from himself. The few words that Basil's friend had said to him—words spoken by chance, no doubt, and with wilful paradox in them—had yet touched some secret chord, that had never been touched before, but that he felt was now vibrating and throbbing to curious pulses.

---

4. Wilde added this and the following five paragraphs to TS on an inserted page and in a long marginal note ending with ". . . of the silence."
5. Wilde changed this word to "influences" in 1891.

Music had stirred him like that. Music had troubled him many times. But music was not articulate. It was not a new world, but rather a new chaos, that it created in us. Words! Mere words! How terrible they were! How clear, and vivid, and cruel! One could not escape from them. And yet what a subtle magic there was in them! They seemed to be able to give a plastic form to formless things, and to have a music of their own as sweet as that of viol or of lute. Mere words! Was there anything so real as words?

Yes; there had been things in his boyhood that he had not understood. He understood them now. Life suddenly became fiery-colored to him. It seemed to him that he had been walking in fire. Why had he not known it?

Lord Henry watched him, with his sad smile. He knew the precise psychological moment when to say nothing. He felt intensely interested. He was amazed at the sudden impression that his words had produced, and, remembering a book that he had read when he was sixteen, which had revealed to him much that he had not known before, he wondered whether Dorian Gray was passing through the same experience. He had merely shot an arrow into the air. Had it hit the mark? How fascinating the lad was!

Hallward painted away with that marvellous bold touch of his, that had the true refinement and perfect delicacy that come only from strength. He was unconscious of the silence.

"Basil, I am tired of standing," cried Dorian Gray, suddenly. "I must go out and sit in the garden. The air is stifling here."

"My dear fellow, I am so sorry. When I am painting, I can't think of anything else. But you never sat better. You were perfectly still. And I have caught the effect I wanted,—the half-parted lips, and the bright look in the eyes. I don't know what Harry has been saying to you, but he has certainly made you have the most wonderful expression. I suppose he has been paying you compliments. You mustn't believe a word that he says."

"He has certainly not been paying me compliments. Perhaps that is the reason I don't think I believe anything he has told me."

"You know you believe it all," said Lord Henry, looking at him with his dreamy, heavy-lidded eyes. "I will go out to the garden with you. It is horridly hot in the studio.—Basil, let us have something iced to drink, something with strawberries in it."

"Certainly, Harry. Just touch the bell, and when Parker comes I will tell him what you want. I have got to work up this background, so I will join you later on. Don't keep Dorian too long. I have never been in better form for painting than I am to-day. This is going to be my masterpiece. It is my masterpiece as it stands."

Lord Henry went out to the garden, and found Dorian Gray burying his face in the great cool lilac-blossoms, feverishly drinking in
their perfume as if it had been wine. He came close to him, and put
his hand upon his shoulder. "You are quite right to do that," he murmured. "Nothing can cure the soul but the senses, just as nothing
can cure the senses but the soul."

The lad started and drew back. He was bareheaded, and the leaves
had tossed his rebellious curls and tangled all their gilded threads.
There was a look of fear in his eyes, such as people have when they
are suddenly awakened. His finely-chiselled nostrils quivered, and
some hidden nerve shook the scarlet of his lips and left them
trembling.

"Yes," continued Lord Henry, "that is one of the great secrets of
life,—to cure the soul by means of the senses, and the senses by
means of the soul. You are a wonderful creature. You know more than
you think you know, just as you know less than you want to know."

Dorian Gray frowned and turned his head away, he could not help
liking the tall, graceful young man who was standing by him. His
romantic olive-colored face and worn expression interested him.
There was something in his low, languid voice that was absolutely
fascinating. His cool, white, flower-like hands, even, had a curious
charm. They moved, as he spoke, like music, and seemed to have a
language of their own. But he felt afraid of him, and ashamed of
being afraid. Why had it been left for a stranger to reveal him to himself? He had known Basil Hallward for months, but the friendship
between then had never altered him. Suddenly there had come some
one across his life who seemed to have disclosed to him life's mystery. And, yet, what was there to be afraid of? He was not a school-
boy, or a girl. It was absurd to be frightened.

"Let us go and sit in the shade," said Lord Henry. "Parker has
brought out the drinks, and if you stay any longer in this glare you
will be quite spoiled, and Basil will never paint you again. You really
must not let yourself become sunburnt. It would be very unbecoming to you."

"What does it matter?" cried Dorian, laughing, as he sat down on
the seat at the end of the garden.

"It should matter everything to you, Mr. Gray."

"Why?"

"Because you have now the most marvellous youth, and youth is
the one thing worth having."

"I don't feel that, Lord Henry."

"No, you don't feel it now. Some day, when you are old and wrinkled and ugly, when thought has seared your forehead with its lines,
and passion branded your lips with its hideous fires, you will feel

it, you will feel it terribly.[6] Now, wherever you go, you charm the world. Will it always be so?

"You have a wonderfully beautiful face, Mr. Gray. Don't frown. You have. And Beauty is a form of Genius,—is higher, indeed, than Genius, as it needs no explanation. It is one of the great facts of the world, like sunlight, or spring-time, or the reflection in dark waters of that silver shell we call the moon.[7] It cannot be questioned. It has its divine right of sovereignty. It makes princes of those who have it. You smile? Ah! when you have lost it you won't smile.

"People say sometimes that Beauty is only superficial. That may be so. But at least it is not so superficial as Thought. To me, Beauty is the wonder of wonders. It is only shallow people who do not judge by appearances. The true mystery of the world is the visible, not the invisible.

"Yes, Mr. Gray, the gods have been good to you. But what the gods give they quickly take away. You have only a few years in which really to live. When your youth goes, your beauty will go with it, and then you will suddenly discover that there are no triumphs left for you, or have to content yourself with those mean triumphs that the memory of your past will make more bitter than defeats. Every month as it wanes brings you nearer to something dreadful. Time is jealous of you, and wars against your lilies and your roses. You will become sallow, and hollow-cheeked, and dull-eyed. You will suffer horribly.

"Realize your youth while you have it. Don't squander the gold of your days, listening to the tedious, trying to improve the hopeless failure, or giving away your life to the ignorant, the common, and the vulgar, which are the aims, the false ideals, of our age. Live! Live the wonderful life that is in you! Let nothing be lost upon you. Be always searching for new sensations. Be afraid of nothing.

"A new hedonism,—that is what our century wants. You might be its visible symbol. With your personality there is nothing you could not do. The world belongs to you for a season.

"The moment I met you I saw that you were quite unconscious of what you really are, what you really might be. There was so much about you that charmed me that I felt I must tell you something about yourself. I thought how tragic it would be if you were wasted. For there is such a little time that your youth will last,—such a little time.

"The common hill-flowers wither, but they blossom again. The laburnum will be as golden next June as it is now. In a month there will be purple stars on the clematis, and year after year the green

6. Wilde canceled these lines here in TS: "If you set yourself to know life, you will look evil; if you are afraid of life you will look common."
7. The lines "Beauty is a form of genius . . . the moon" were originally spoken by Basil in the previous chapter. Wilde relocated them here in MS and transferred them to Henry.

night of its leaves will have its purple stars. But we never get back
our youth. The pulse of joy that beats in us at twenty, becomes sluggish. Our limbs fail, our senses rot. We degenerate into hideous
puppets, haunted by the memory of the passions of which we were
too much afraid, and the exquisite temptations that we did not dare
to yield to. Youth! Youth! There is absolutely nothing in the world
but youth!"

Dorian Gray listened, open-eyed and wondering. The spray of lilac
fell from his hand upon the gravel. A furry bee came and buzzed
round it for a moment. Then it began to scramble all over the fret-
ted purple of the tiny blossoms. He watched it with that strange
interest in trivial things that we try to develop when things of high
import make us afraid, or when we are stirred by some new emotion, for which we cannot find expression, or when some thought
that terrifies us lays sudden siege to the brain and calls on us to
yield.[8] After a time it flew away. He saw it creeping into the stained
trumpet of a Tyrian convolvulus. The flower seemed to quiver, and
then swayed gently to and fro.

Suddenly Hallward appeared at the door of the studio, and made
frantic signs for them to come in. They turned to each other, and
smiled.

"'I am waiting,' cried Hallward. "Do come in. The light is quite
perfect, and you can bring your drinks."

They rose up, and sauntered down the walk together. Two green-
and-white butterflies fluttered past them, and in the pear-tree at the
end of the garden a thrush began to sing.

"You are glad you have met me, Mr. Gray," said Lord Henry, looking at him.

"Yes, I am glad now. I wonder shall I always be glad?"

"Always! That is a dreadful word. It makes me shudder when I
hear it. Women are so fond of using it. They spoil every romance by
trying to make it last forever.[9] It is a meaningless word, too. The
only difference between a caprice and a life-long passion is that
the caprice lasts a little longer."

As they entered the studio, Dorian Gray put his hand upon Lord
Henry's arm. "In that case, let our friendship be a caprice," he murmured, flushing at his own boldness, then stepped upon the platform
and resumed his pose.

Lord Henry flung himself into a large wicker arm-chair, and
watched him. The sweep and dash of the brush on the canvas made
the only sound that broke the stillness, except when Hallward

---

8. Wilde added "or when we are stirred . . . to yield" in the margin of TS.
9. Wilde canceled the following at this point in MS: "Like priests, they terrify one at the
    prospect of certain eternity, attempt to terrify one, I should say."

stepped back now and then to look at his work from a distance. In the slanting beams that streamed through the open door-way the dust danced and was golden. The heavy scent of the roses seemed to brood over everything.

After about a quarter of an hour, Hallward stopped painting, looked for a long time at Dorian Gray, and then for a long time at the picture, biting the end of one of his huge brushes, and smiling. "It is quite finished," he cried, at last, and stooping down he wrote his name in thin vermilion letters on the left-hand corner of the canvas.

Lord Henry came over and examined the picture. It was certainly a wonderful work of art, and a wonderful likeness as well.[1]

"My dear fellow, I congratulate you most warmly," he said.— "Mr. Gray, come and look at yourself."

The lad started, as if awakened from some dream. "Is it really finished?" he murmured, stepping down from the platform.

"Quite finished," said Hallward. "And you have sat splendidly today. I am awfully obliged to you."

"That is entirely due to me," broke in Lord Henry. "Isn't it, Mr. Gray?"

Dorian made no answer, but passed listlessly in front of his picture and turned towards it. When he saw it he drew back, and his cheeks flushed for a moment with pleasure. A look of joy came into his eyes, as if he had recognized himself for the first time. He stood there motionless, and in wonder, dimly conscious that Hallward was speaking to him, but not catching the meaning of his words. The sense of his own beauty came on him like a revelation. He had never felt it before. Basil Hallward's compliments had seemed to him to be merely the charming exaggerations of friendship. He had listened to them, laughed at them, forgotten them. They had not influenced his nature. Then had come Lord Henry, with his strange panegyric on youth, his terrible warning of its brevity. That had stirred him at the time, and now, as he stood gazing at the shadow of his own loveliness, the full reality of the description flashed across him. Yes, there would be a day when his face would be wrinkled and wizen, his eyes dim and colorless, the grace of his figure broken and deformed. The scarlet would pass away from his lips, and the

---

1. Wilde canceled here the following passage in MS: "Most modern portrait painting comes under the head of elegant fiction or if it aims at realism, gives one something between a caricature and a photograph. But this was different. It had all the mystery of life, and all the mystery of beauty. Within the world, as men know it, there is a finer world that only artists know of—artists or those to whom the temperament of the artist has been given. Creation within creation—that is what Basil Hallward named it, that is what he had attained to."

gold steal from his hair. The life that was to make his soul would mar his body. He would become ignoble,[2] hideous, and uncouth.

As he thought of it, a sharp pang of pain struck like a knife across him, and made each delicate fibre of his nature quiver. His eyes deepened into amethyst, and a mist of tears came across them. He felt as if a hand of ice had been laid upon his heart.

"Don't you like it?" cried Hallward at last, stung a little by the lad's silence, and not understanding what it meant.

"Of course he likes it," said Lord Henry. "Who wouldn't like it? It is one of the greatest things in modern art. I will give you anything you like to ask for it. I must have it."

"It is not my property, Harry."

"Whose property is it?"

"Dorian's, of course."

"He is a very lucky fellow."

"How sad it is!" murmured Dorian Gray, with his eyes still fixed upon his own portrait. "How sad it is! I shall grow old, and horrid, and dreadful. But this picture will remain always young. It will never be older than this particular day of June. . . . If it was only the other way! If it was I who were to be always young, and the picture that were to grow old! For this—for this—I would give everything! Yes, there is nothing in the whole world I would not give!"[3]

"You would hardly care for that arrangement, Basil," cried Lord Henry, laughing. "It would be rather hard lines on you."

"I should object very strongly, Harry."

Dorian Gray turned and looked at him. "I believe you would, Basil. You like your art better than your friends. I am no more to you than a green bronze figure. Hardly as much, I dare say."

Hallward stared in amazement. It was so unlike Dorian to speak like that. What had happened? He seemed almost angry. His face was flushed and his cheeks burning.

"Yes," he continued, "I am less to you than your ivory Hermes[4] or your silver Faun. You will like them always. How long will you like me? Till I have my first wrinkle, I suppose. I know, now, that when one loses one's good looks, whatever they may be, one loses everything. Your picture has taught me that. Lord Henry is perfectly

---

2. Wilde changed this to "dreadful" in 1891.
3. Wilde altered this passage each time he revised his text. In MS, he canceled after "dreadful" the following: "Life will send its lines across my face. Passion will crease it and thought twist it from its form." In TS, Wilde added "Yes, there is nothing . . . give!" He added to it again in 1891: "I would give my soul for that."
4. Originally "Sylvanus" in MS, but changed there. Sylvanus was a Roman divinity, a variation of Pan, god of woods, fields, and grottoes, who looked young despite his antiquity.

right. Youth is the only thing worth having. When I find that I am growing old, I will kill myself."[5]

Hallward turned pale, and caught his hand. "Dorian! Dorian!" he cried, "don't talk like that. I have never had such a friend as you, and I shall never have such another. You are not jealous of material things, are you?"

"I am jealous of everything whose beauty does not die. I am jealous of the portrait you have painted of me. Why should it keep what I must lose? Every moment that passes takes something from me, and gives something to it. Oh, if it was only the other way! If the picture could change, and I could be always what I am now! Why did you paint it? It will mock me some day,—mock me horribly!"[6] The hot tears welled into his eyes; he tore his hand away, and, flinging himself on the divan, he buried his face in the cushions, as if he was praying.

"This is your doing, Harry," said Hallward, bitterly.

"My doing?"

"Yes, yours, and you know it."[7]

Lord Henry shrugged his shoulders. "It is the real Dorian Gray,— that is all," he answered.

"It is not."

"If it is not, what have I to do with it?"[8]

"You should have gone away when I asked you."

"I stayed when you asked me."

"Harry, I can't quarrel with my two best friends at once, but between you both you have made me hate the finest piece of work I have ever done, and I will destroy it. What is it but canvas and color? I will not let it come across our three lives and mar them."

Dorian Gray lifted his golden head from the pillow, and looked at him with pallid face and tear-stained eyes, as he walked over to the deal painting-table that was set beneath the large curtained window. What was he doing there? His fingers were straying about among the litter of tin tubes and dry brushes, seeking for something. Yes, it was the long palette-knife, with its thin blade of lithe steel. He had found it at last. He was going to rip up the canvas.

With a stifled sob he leaped from the couch, and, rushing over to Hallward, tore the knife out of his hand, and flung it to the end of the studio. "Don't Basil, don't!" he cried. "It would be murder!"

"I am glad you appreciate my work at last, Dorian," said Hallward, coldly, when he had recovered from his surprise. "I never thought you would."

---

5. Wilde added this sentence in TS.
6. "Oh, if it was only . . . horribly!" was added by Wilde in TS.
7. Wilde dropped Henry's question and Basil's answer in 1891.
8. Wilde wrote this into TS after removing "*comme vous voulez, mon cher.*"

"Appreciate it? I am in love with it, Basil. It is part of myself, I feel that."

"Well, as soon as you are dry, you shall be varnished, and framed, and sent home. Then you can do what you like with yourself." And he walked across the room and rang the bell for tea. "You will have tea, of course, Dorian? And so will you, Harry? Tea is the only simple pleasure left to us."

"I don't like simple pleasures," said Lord Henry. "And I don't like scenes, except on the stage. What absurd fellows you are, both of you! I wonder who it was defined man as a rational animal. It was the most premature definition ever given. Man is many things, but he is not rational. I am glad he is not, after all: though I wish you chaps would not squabble over the picture. You had much better let me have it, Basil. This silly boy doesn't really want it, and I do."

"If you let any one have it but me, Basil, I will never forgive you!" cried Dorian Gray. "And I don't allow people to call me a silly boy."

"You know the picture is yours, Dorian. I gave it to you before it existed."

"And you know you have been a little silly, Mr. Gray, and that you don't really mind being called a boy."

"I should have minded very much this morning, Lord Henry."

"Ah! this morning! You have lived since then."[9]

There came a knock to the door, and the butler entered with the tea-tray and set it down upon a small Japanese table. There was a rattle of cups and saucers and the hissing of a fluted Georgian urn. Two globe-shaped china dishes were brought in by a page. Dorian Gray went over and poured the tea out. The two men sauntered languidly to the table, and examined what was under the covers.

"Let us go to the theatre to-night," said Lord Henry. "There is sure to be something on, somewhere. I have promised to dine at White's, but it is only with an old friend, so I can send him a wire and say that I am ill, or that I am prevented from coming in consequence of a subsequent engagement. I think that would be a rather nice excuse: it would have the surprise of candor."

"It is such a bore putting on one's dress-clothes," muttered Hallward. "And, when one has them on, they are so horrid."

"Yes," answered Lord Henry, dreamily, "the costume of our day is detestable. It is so sombre, so depressing. Sin is the only color-element left in modern life."

"You really must not say things like that before Dorian, Harry."

"Before which Dorian? The one who is pouring out tea for us, or the one in the picture?"

"Before either."

9. Wilde wrote the preceding three sentences into TS.

"I should like to come to the theatre with you, Lord Henry," said the lad.

"Then you shall come; and you will come too, Basil, won't you?"

"I can't really. I would sooner not. I have a lot of work to do."

"Well, then, you and I will go alone, Mr. Gray."

"I should like that awfully."

Basil Hallward bit his lip and walked over, cup in hand, to the picture. "I will stay with the real Dorian," he said, sadly.

"Is it the real Dorian?" cried the original of the portrait, running across to him. "Am I really like that?"

"Yes; you are just like that."

"How wonderful, Basil!"[1]

"At least you are like it in appearance. But it will never alter," said Hallward. "That is something."

"What a fuss people make about fidelity!" murmured Lord Henry. "And, after all, it is purely a question for physiology. It has nothing to do with our own will. It is either an unfortunate accident, or an unpleasant result of temperament.[2] Young men want to be faithful, and are not; old men want to be faithless, and cannot: that is all one can say."

"Don't go to the theatre to-night, Dorian," said Hallward. "Stop and dine with me."

"I can't, really."

"Why?"

"Because I have promised Lord Henry to go with him."

"He won't like you better for keeping your promises. He always breaks his own. I beg you not to go."

Dorian Gray laughed and shook his head.

"I entreat you."

The lad hesitated, and looked over at Lord Henry, who was watching them from the tea-table with an amused smile.

"I must go, Basil," he answered.

"Very well," said Hallward; and he walked over and laid his cup down on the tray. "It is rather late, and, as you have to dress, you had better lose no time. Good-by, Harry; good-by, Dorian. Come and see me soon. Come to-morrow."

"Certainly."

"You won't forget?"

"No, of course not."

"And . . . Harry!"

"Yes, Basil?"

---

1. Wilde added this and the preceding two sentences to TS.
2. Wilde dropped this sentence in 1891 and made some alterations to the sentence preceding it.

"Remember what I asked you, when in the garden this morning."

"I have forgotten it."

"I trust you."

"I wish I could trust myself," said Lord Henry, laughing.—"Come, Mr. Gray, my hansom is outside, and I can drop you at your own place.—Good-by, Basil. It has been a most interesting afternoon."

As the door closed behind them, Hallward flung himself down on a sofa, and a look of pain came into his face.

Chapter III[1]

One afternoon, a month later, Dorian Gray was reclining in a luxurious arm-chair, in the little library of Lord Henry's house in Curzon Street. It was, in its way, a very charming room, with its high panelled wainscoting of olive-stained oak, its cream-colored frieze and ceiling of raised plaster-work, and its brick-dust felt carpet strewn with long-fringed silk Persian rugs. On a tiny satinwood table stood a statuette by Clodion, and beside it lay a copy of "Les Cent Nouvelles," bound for Margaret of Valois by Clovis Eve, and powdered with the gilt daisies that the queen had selected for her device. Some large blue china jars, filled with parrot-tulips, were ranged on the mantel-shelf, and through the small leaded panes of the window streamed the apricot-colored light of a summer's day in London.

Lord Henry had not come in yet. He was always late on principle, his principle being that punctuality is the thief of time. So the lad was looking rather sulky, as with listless fingers he turned over the pages of an elaborately-illustrated edition of "Manon Lescaut" that he had found in one of the bookcases. The formal monotonous ticking of the Louis Quatorze clock annoyed him. Once or twice he thought of going away.

At last he heard a light step outside, and the door opened. "How late you are, Harry!" he murmured.

"I am afraid it is not Harry, Mr. Gray," said a woman's voice.

He glanced quickly round, and rose to his feet. "I beg your pardon. I thought—"

"You thought it was my husband. It is only his wife. You must let me introduce myself. I know you quite well by your photographs. I think my husband has got twenty-seven of them."

"Not twenty-seven, Lady Henry?"

---

1. The first of the new chapters added in 1891 was inserted before the original chapter 3 here.

"Well, twenty-six, then.[2] And I saw you with him the other night at the Opera." She laughed nervously, as she spoke, and watched him with her vague forget-me-not eyes. She was a curious woman, whose dresses always looked as if they had been designed in a rage and put on in a tempest. She was always in love with somebody, and, as her passion was never returned, she had kept all her illusions. She tried to look picturesque, but only succeeded in being untidy. Her name was Victoria, and she had a perfect mania for going to church.

"That was at 'Lohengrin,' Lady Henry, I think?"

"Yes; it was at dear 'Lohengrin.' I like Wagner's music better than any other music. It is so loud that one can talk the whole time, without people hearing what one says. That is a great advantage: don't you think so, Mr. Gray?"

The same nervous staccato laugh broke from her thin lips, and her fingers began to play with a long paper-knife.

Dorian smiled, and shook his head: "I am afraid I don't think so, Lady Henry. I never talk during music,—at least during good music. If one hears bad music, it is one's duty to drown it by conversation."

"Ah! that is one of Harry's views, isn't it, Mr. Gray? But you must not think I don't like good music. I adore it, but I am afraid of it. It makes me too romantic. I have simply worshipped pianists,—two at a time, sometimes. I don't know what it is about them. Perhaps it is that they are foreigners. They all are, aren't they? Even those that are born in England become foreigners after a time, don't they? It is so clever of them, and such a compliment to art. Makes it quite cosmopolitan, doesn't it? You have never been to any of my parties, have you, Mr. Gray? You must come. I can't afford orchids, but I spare no expense in foreigners. They make one's rooms look so picturesque. But here is Harry!—Harry, I came in to look for you, to ask you something,—I forget what it was,—and I found Mr. Gray here. We have had such a pleasant chat about music. We have quite the same views. No; I think our views are quite different. But he has been most pleasant. I am so glad I've seen him."

"I am charmed, my love, quite charmed," said Lord Henry, elevating his dark crescent-shaped eyebrows and looking at them both with an amused smile.—"So sorry I am late, Dorian. I went to look after a piece of old brocade in Wardour Street, and had to bargain for hours for it. Nowadays people know the price of everything, and the value of nothing."[3]

---

2. Wilde changed the number of photographs for humorous effect in 1891.
3. This well-known epigram was added in TS. It reappeared in *Lady Windermere's Fan* and for an encore in *The Importance of Being Earnest*.

"I am afraid I must be going," exclaimed Lady Henry, after an awkward silence, with her silly sudden laugh. "I have promised to drive with the duchess.—Good-by, Mr. Gray.—Good-by, Harry. You are dining out, I suppose? So am I. Perhaps I shall see you at Lady Thornbury's."

"I dare say, my dear," said Lord Henry, shutting the door behind her, as she flitted out of the room, looking like a bird-of-paradise that had been out in the rain, and leaving a faint odor of patchouli[4] behind her. Then he shook hands with Dorian Gray, lit a cigarette, and flung himself down on the sofa.

"Never marry a woman with straw-colored hair, Dorian," he said, after a few puffs.

"Why, Harry?"

"Because they are so sentimental."

"But I like sentimental people."

"Never marry at all, Dorian. Men marry because they are tired; women, because they are curious: both are disappointed."

"I don't think I am likely to marry, Harry. I am too much in love. That is one of your aphorisms. I am putting it into practice, as I do everything you say."[5]

"Whom are you in love with?" said Lord Henry, looking at him with a curious smile.

"With an actress," said Dorian Gray, blushing.

Lord Henry shrugged his shoulders. "That is a rather commonplace *début*," he murmured.

"You would not say so if you saw her, Harry."

"Who is she?"

"Her name is Sibyl[6] Vane."

"Never heard of her."

"No one has. People will some day, however, She is a genius."

"My dear boy, no woman is a genius: women are a decorative sex. They never have anything to say, but they say it charmingly. They represent the triumph of matter over mind, just as we men represent the triumph of mind over morals. There are only two kinds of women, the plain and the colored. The plain women are very useful. If you want to gain a reputation for respectability, you have merely to take them down to supper. The other women are very charming. They commit one mistake, however. They paint in order to try to look young. Our grandmothers painted in order to try to talk brilliantly. *Rouge* and *esprit* used to go together. That has all gone out now. As

4. Wilde changed the perfume to frangipani in 1891. Patchouli was a scent identified with London prostitutes.
5. This sentence was added in TS.
6. Stoddart changed the spelling from Wilde's "Sybil" here and throughout the text of this edition, and it remained "Sibyl" in the 1891 text.

long as a woman can look ten years younger than her own daughter, she is perfectly satisfied. As for conversation, there are only five women in London worth talking to, and two of these can't be admitted into decent society. However, tell me about your genius. How long have you known her?"

"About three weeks. Not so much. About two weeks and two days."

"How did you come across her?"

"I will tell you, Harry; but you mustn't be unsympathetic about it. After all, it never would have happened if I had not met you. You filled me with a wild desire to know everything about life. For days after I met you, something seemed to throb in my veins. As I lounged in the Park, or strolled down Piccadilly, I used to look at every one who passed me, and wonder with a mad curiosity what sort of lives they led. Some of them fascinated me. Others filled me with terror. There was an exquisite poison in the air. I had a passion for sensations.

"One evening about seven o'clock I determined to go out in search of some adventure. I felt that this gray, monstrous London of ours, with its myriads of people, its splendid sinners, and its sordid sins, as you once said, must have something in store for me. I fancied a thousand things.

"The mere danger gave me a sense of delight. I remembered what you had said to me on that wonderful night when we first dined together, about the search for beauty being the poisonous secret of life. I don't know what I expected, but I went out, and wandered eastward, soon losing my way in a labyrinth of grimy streets and black, grassless squares. About half-past eight I passed by a little third-rate theatre, with great flaring gas-jets and gaudy play-bills. A hideous Jew, in the most amazing waistcoat I ever beheld in my life, was standing at the entrance, smoking a vile cigar. He had greasy ringlets, and an enormous diamond blazed in the centre of a soiled shirt. ' 'Ave a box, my lord?' he said, when he saw me, and he took off his hat with an act of gorgeous servility. There was something about him, Harry, that amused me. He was such a monster. You will laugh at me, I know, but I really went in and paid a whole guinea for the stage-box. To the present day I can't make out why I did so; and yet if I hadn't!—my dear Harry, if I hadn't, I would have missed the greatest romance of my life. I see you are laughing. It is horrid of you!"

"I am not laughing, Dorian; at least I am not laughing at you. But you should not say the greatest romance of your life. You should say the first romance of your life. You will always be loved, and you will always be in love with love.[7] There are exquisite things in store for you. This is merely the beginning."

---

7. Wilde added three more sentences here in 1891.

"Do you think my nature so shallow?" cried Dorian Gray, angrily.

"No; I think your nature so deep."

"How do you mean?"

"My dear boy, people who only love once in their lives are really shallow people. What they call their loyalty, and their fidelity, I call either the lethargy of custom or the lack of imagination. Faithlessness is to the emotional life what consistency is to the intellectual life,—simply a confession of failure.[8] But I don't want to interrupt you. Go on with your story."

"Well, I found myself seated in a horrid little private box, with a vulgar drop-scene staring me in the face. I looked out behind the curtain, and surveyed the house. It was a tawdry affair, all Cupids and cornucopias, like a third-rate wedding-cake. The gallery and pit were fairly full, but the two rows of dingy stalls were quite empty, and there was hardly a person in what I suppose they called the dress-circle. Women went about with oranges and ginger-beer, and there was a terrible consumption of nuts going on."

"It must have been just like the palmy days of the British Drama."

"Just like, I should fancy, and very horrid. I began to wonder what on earth I should do, when I caught sight of the play-bill. What do you think the play was, Harry?"

"I should think 'The Idiot Boy, or Dumb but Innocent.' Our fathers used to like that sort of piece, I believe. The longer I live, Dorian, the more keenly I feel that whatever was good enough for our fathers is not good enough for us. In art, as in politics, *les grand-pères ont toujours tort.*"

"This play was good enough for us, Harry. It was 'Romeo and Juliet.' I must admit I was rather annoyed at the idea of seeing Shakespeare done in such a wretched hole of a place. Still, I felt interested, in a sort of way. At any rate, I determined to wait for the first act. There was a dreadful orchestra, presided over by a young Jew who sat at a cracked piano, that nearly drove me away, but at last the drop-scene was drawn up, and the play began. Romeo was a stout elderly gentleman, with corked eyebrows, a husky tragedy voice, and a figure like a beer-barrel. Mercutio was almost as bad. He was played by the low-comedian, who had introduced gags of his own and was on most familiar terms with the pit. They were as grotesque as the scenery, and that looked as if it had come out of a pantomime of fifty years ago. But Juliet! Harry, imagine a girl, hardly seventeen years of age, with a little flower-like face, a small Greek head with plaited coils of dark-brown hair, eyes that were violet wells of passion, lips

---

8. Wilde added this epigram in TS and followed it up with four additional sentences in 1891.

that were like the petals of a rose. She was the loveliest thing I had
ever seen in my life. You said to me once that pathos left you
unmoved, but that beauty, mere beauty, could fill your eyes with
tears. I tell you, Harry, I could hardly see this girl for the mist of
tears that came across me. And her voice,—I never heard such a
voice. It was very low at first, with deep mellow notes, that seemed
to fall singly upon one's ear. Then it became a little louder, and
sounded like a flute or a distant hautbois. In the garden-scene it had
all the tremulous ecstasy that one hears just before dawn when
nightingales are singing. There were moments, later on, when it had
the wild passion of violins. You know how a voice can stir one. Your
voice and the voice of Sibyl Vane are two things that I shall never
forget. When I close my eyes, I hear them, and each of them says
something different. I don't know which to follow. Why should I not
love her? Harry, I do love her. She is everything to me in life. Night
after night I go to see her play. One evening she is Rosalind, and
the next evening she is Imogen. I have seen her die in the gloom of
an Italian tomb, sucking the poison from her lover's lips. I have
watched her wandering through the forest of Arden, disguised as a
pretty boy in hose and doublet and dainty cap. She has been mad,
and has come into the presence of a guilty king, and given him rue
to wear, and bitter herbs to taste of. She has been innocent, and the
black hands of jealousy have crushed her reed-like throat. I have
seen her in every age and in every costume. Ordinary women never
appeal to one's imagination. They are limited to their century. No
glamour ever transfigures them. One knows their minds as easily as
one knows their bonnets. One can always find them. There is no
mystery in one of them. They ride in the Park in the morning, and
chatter at tea-parties in the afternoon. They have their stereotyped
smile, and their fashionable manner. They are quite obvious. But an
actress! How different an actress is! Why didn't you tell me that the
only thing worth loving is an actress?"

"Because I have loved so many of them, Dorian."

"Oh, yes, horrid people with dyed hair and painted faces."

"Don't run down dyed hair and painted faces. There is an extraordinary charm in them, sometimes."

"I wish now I had not told you about Sibyl Vane."

"You could not have helped telling me, Dorian. All through your
life you will tell me everything you do."

"Yes, Harry, I believe that is true. I cannot help telling you things.
You have a curious influence over me. If I ever did a crime, I would
come and confide it to you. You would understand me."

"People like you—the wilful sunbeams of life—don't commit
crimes, Dorian. But I am much obliged for the compliment, all the

same. And now tell me,—reach me the matches, like a good boy: thanks,—tell me, what are your relations with Sibyl Vane?"[9]

Dorian Gray leaped to his feet, with flushed cheeks and burning eyes.[1] "Harry, Sibyl Vane is sacred!"

"It is only the sacred things that are worth touching, Dorian," said Lord Henry, with a strange touch of pathos in his voice. "But why should you be annoyed? I suppose she will be yours[2] some day. When one is in love, one always begins by deceiving one's self, and one always ends by deceiving others. That is what the world calls romance. You know her, at any rate, I suppose?"

"Of course I know her. On the first night I was at the theatre, the horrid old Jew came round to the box after the performance was over, and offered to bring me behind the scenes and introduce me to her. I was furious with him, and told him that Juliet had been dead for hundreds of years, and that her body was lying in a marble tomb in Verona. I think, from his blank look of amazement, that he thought I had taken too much champagne, or something."

"I am not surprised."

"I was not surprised either. Then he asked me if I wrote for any of the newspapers. I told him I never even read them. He seemed terribly disappointed at that, and confided to me that all the dramatic critics were in a conspiracy against him, and that they were all to be bought."

"I believe he was quite right there. But, on the other hand, most of them are not at all expensive."[3]

"Well, he seemed to think they were beyond his means. By this time the lights were being put out in the theatre, and I had to go. He wanted me to try some cigars which he strongly recommended. I declined. The next night, of course, I arrived at the theatre again. When he saw me he made me a low bow, and assured me that I was a patron of art. He was a most offensive brute, though he had an extraordinary passion for Shakespeare. He told me once, with an air of pride, that his three bankruptcies were entirely due to the poet, whom he insisted on calling 'The Bard.'[4] He seemed to think it a distinction."

"It was a distinction, my dear Dorian,—a great distinction. But when did you first speak to Miss Sibyl Vane?"

---

9. This is another bowdlerization by Stoddart. Wilde's version was "is Sibyl Vane your mistress?" Stoddart rewrote it in its present form, and although Wilde made an addition in 1891, he did not restore the original reading.
1. Stoddart changed TS: "How dare you suggest such a thing, Harry? It is horrible."
2. Stoddart changed this from TS: "your mistress." Wilde altered the Stoddart emendation in 1891, making it a little stronger.
3. Wilde altered this passage slightly in 1891.
4. Wilde substituted this phrase in TS for "Shakespeare." In 1891, the number of bankruptcies was increased to five.

"The third night. She had been playing Rosalind. I could not help going round. I had thrown her some flowers, and she had looked at me; at least I fancied that she had. The old Jew was persistent. He seemed determined to bring me behind, so I consented. It was curious my not wanting to know her, wasn't it?"

"No; I don't think so."

"My dear Harry, why?"

"I will tell you some other time. Now I want to know about the girl."

"Sibyl? Oh, she was so shy, and so gentle. There is something of a child about her. Her eyes opened wide in exquisite wonder when I told her what I thought of her performance, and she seemed quite unconscious of her power. I think we were both rather nervous. The old Jew stood grinning at the door-way of the dusty greenroom, making elaborate speeches about us both, while we stood looking at each other like children. He would insist on calling me 'My Lord,' so I had to assure Sibyl that I was not anything of the kind. She said quite simply to me, 'You look more like a prince.'"

"Upon my word, Dorian, Miss Sibyl knows how to pay compliments."

"You don't understand her, Harry. She regarded me merely as a person in a play. She knows nothing of life. She lives with her mother, a faded tired woman who played Lady Capulet in a sort of magenta dressing-wrapper on the first night, and who looks as if she had seen better days."

"I know that look. It always depresses me."

"The Jew wanted to tell me her history, but I said it did not interest me."

"You were quite right. There is always something infinitely mean about other people's tragedies."

"Sibyl is the only thing I care about. What is it to me where she came from? From her little head to her little feet, she is absolutely and entirely divine. I go to see her act every night of my life, and every night she is more marvellous."

"That is the reason, I suppose, that you will never dine with me now. I thought you must have some curious romance on hand. You have; but it is not quite what I expected."

"My dear Harry, we either lunch or sup together every day, and I have been to the Opera with you several times."

"You always come dreadfully late."

"Well, I can't help going to see Sibyl play, even if it is only for an act. I get hungry for her presence; and when I think of the wonderful soul that is hidden away in that little ivory body, I am filled with awe."

"You can dine with me to-night, Dorian, can't you?"

He shook his head. "To-night she is Imogen," he answered, "and to-morrow night she will be Juliet."

"When is she Sibyl Vane?"

"Never."

"I congratulate you."

"How horrid you are! She is all the great heroines of the world in one. She is more than an individual. You laugh, but I tell you she has genius. I love her, and I must make her love me. You, who know all the secrets of life, tell me how to charm Sibyl Vane to love me! I want to make Romeo jealous. I want the dead lovers of the world to hear our laughter, and grow sad. I want a breath of our passion to stir their dust into consciousness, to wake their ashes into pain. My God, Harry, how I worship her!" He was walking up and down the room as he spoke. Hectic spots of red burned on his cheeks. He was terribly excited.

Lord Henry watched him with a subtle sense of pleasure. How different he was now from the shy, frightened boy he had met in Basil Hallward's studio! His nature had developed like a flower, had borne blossoms of scarlet flame. Out of its secret hiding-place had crept his Soul, and Desire had come to meet it on the way.

"And what do you propose to do?" said Lord Henry, at last.

"I want you and Basil to come with me some night and see her act. I have not the slightest fear of the result. You won't be able to refuse to recognize her genius. Then we must get her out of the Jew's hands. She is bound to him for three years—at least for two years and eight months—from the present time. I will have to pay him something, of course. When all that is settled, I will take a West-End theatre and bring her out properly. She will make the world as mad as she has made me."

"Impossible, my dear boy!"

"Yes, she will. She has not merely art, consummate art-instinct, in her, but she has personality also; and you have often told me that it is personalities, not principles, that move the age."

"Well, what night shall we go?"

"Let me see. To-day is Tuesday. Let us fix to-morrow. She plays Juliet to-morrow."

"All right. The Bristol at eight o'clock; and I will get Basil."

"Not eight, Harry, please. Half-past six. We must be there before the curtain rises. You must see her in the first act, where she meets Romeo."

"Half-past six! What an hour! It will be like having a meat-tea. However, just as you wish. Shall you see Basil between this and then? Or shall I write to him?"

"Dear Basil! I have not laid eyes on him for a week. It is rather horrid of me, as he has sent me my portrait in the most wonderful frame, designed by himself, and, though I am a little jealous of it for being a whole month younger than I am, I must admit that I delight in it. Perhaps you had better write to him. I don't want to see him alone. He says things that annoy me."

Lord Henry smiled. "He gives you good advice, I suppose. People are very fond of giving away what they need most themselves."

"You don't mean to say that Basil has got any passion or any romance in him?"

"I don't know whether he has any passion, but he certainly has romance," said Lord Henry, with an amused look in his eyes. "Has he never let you know that?"

"Never. I must ask him about it. I am rather surprised to hear it. He is the best of fellows, but he seems to me to be just a bit of a Philistine. Since I have known you, Harry, I have discovered that."

"Basil, my dear boy, puts everything that is charming in him into his work. The consequence is that he has nothing left for life but his prejudices, his principles, and his common sense. The only artists I have ever known who are personally delightful are bad artists. Good artists give everything to their art, and consequently are perfectly uninteresting in themselves. A great poet, a really great poet, is the most unpoetical of all creatures. But inferior poets are absolutely fascinating. The worse their rhymes are, the more picturesque they look. The mere fact of having published a book of second-rate sonnets makes a man quite irresistible. He lives the poetry that he cannot write. The others write the poetry that they dare not realize."

"I wonder is that really so, Harry?" said Dorian Gray, putting some perfume on his handkerchief out of a large gold-topped bottle that stood on the table. "It must be, if you say so. And now I must be off. Imogen is waiting for me. Don't forget about to-morrow. Good-by."

As he left the room, Lord Henry's heavy eyelids drooped, and he began to think. Certainly few people had ever interested him so much as Dorian Gray, and yet the lad's mad adoration of some one else caused him not the slightest pang of annoyance or jealousy. He was pleased by it. It made him a more interesting study. He had been always enthralled by the methods of science, but the ordinary subject-matter of science had seemed to him trivial and of no import. And so he had begun by vivisecting himself, as he had ended by vivisecting others. Human life,—that appeared to him the one thing worth investigating. There was nothing else of any value, compared to it. It was true that as one watched life in its curious crucible of pain and pleasure, one could not wear over one's face a mask of glass, or keep the sulphurous fumes from troubling the brain and making the imagination turbid with monstrous fancies and misshapen dreams. There were poisons so subtle that to know their properties one had to sicken of them. There were maladies so strange that one had to pass through them if one sought to understand their nature. And, yet, what a great reward one received! How wonderful the whole world became to one! To note the curious hard logic of passion, and the emotional colored life of the intellect,—to observe where they met, and where they separated, at what point they became one, and at what point they were at discord,—there was a delight in that! What matter what the cost was? One could never pay too high a price for any sensation.

He was conscious—and the thought brought a gleam of pleasure into his brown agate eyes—that it was through certain words of his, musical words said with musical utterance, that Dorian Gray's soul had turned to this white girl and bowed in worship before her. To a large extent, the lad was his own creation. He had made him premature. That was something. Ordinary people waited till life disclosed to them its secrets, but to the few, to the elect, the mysteries of life were revealed before the veil was drawn away. Sometimes this was the effect of art, and chiefly of the art of literature, which dealt immediately with the passions and the intellect. But now and then a complex personality took the place and assumed the office of art, was indeed, in its way, a real work of art, Life having its elaborate masterpieces, just as poetry has, or sculpture, or painting.

Yes, the lad was premature. He was gathering his harvest while it was yet spring. The pulse and passion of youth were in him, but he was becoming self-conscious. It was delightful to watch him. With his beautiful face, and his beautiful soul, he was a thing to wonder at. It was no matter how it all ended, or was destined to end. He was like one of those gracious figures in a pageant or a play, whose joys seem to be remote from one, but whose sorrows stir one's sense of beauty, and whose wounds are like red roses.

Soul and body, body and soul—how mysterious they were! There was animalism in the soul, and the body had its moments of spirituality. The senses could refine, and the intellect could degrade. Who could say where the fleshly impulse ceased, or the psychical impulse began? How shallow were the arbitrary definitions of ordinary psychologists! And yet how difficult to decide between the claims of the various schools! Was the soul a shadow seated in the house of sin? Or was the body really in the soul, as Giordano Bruno thought? The separation of spirit from matter was a mystery, and the union of spirit with matter was a mystery also.

He began to wonder whether we should ever make psychology so absolute a science that each little spring of life would be revealed to us. As it was, we always misunderstood ourselves, and rarely understood others. Experience was of no ethical value. It was merely the name we gave to our mistakes. Men had, as a rule, regarded it as a mode of warning, had claimed for it a certain moral efficacy in the formation of character, had praised it as something that taught us what to follow and showed us what to avoid. But there was no motive power in experience. It was as little of an active cause as conscience itself. All that it really demonstrated was that our future would be the same as our past, and that the sin we had done once, and with loathing, we would do many times, and with joy.

It was clear to him that the experimental method was the only method by which one could arrive at any scientific analysis of the passions; and certainly Dorian Gray was a subject made to his hand, and seemed to promise rich and fruitful results. His sudden mad love for Sibyl Vane was a psychological phenomenon of no small interest. There was no doubt that curiosity had much to do with it, curiosity and the desire for new experiences; yet it was not a simple but rather a very complex passion. What there was in it of the purely sensuous instinct of boyhood had been transformed by the workings of the imagination, changed into something that seemed to the boy himself to be remote from sense, and was for that very reason all the more dangerous. It was the passions about whose origin we deceived ourselves that tyrannized most strongly over us. Our weakest motives were those of whose nature we were conscious. It often happened that when we thought we were experimenting on others we were really experimenting on ourselves.

While Lord Henry sat dreaming on these things, a knock came to the door, and his valet entered, and reminded him it was time to dress for dinner. He got up and looked out into the street. The sunset had smitten into scarlet gold the upper windows of the houses opposite. The panes glowed like plates of heated metal. The sky above was like a faded rose. He thought of Dorian Gray's young fiery-colored life, and wondered how it was all going to end.

When he arrived home, about half-past twelve o'clock, he saw a telegram lying on the hall-table. He opened it and found it was from Dorian. It was to tell him that he was engaged to be married to Sibyl Vane.

Chapter IV[1]

"I suppose you have heard the news, Basil?" said Lord Henry on the following evening, as Hallward was shown into a little private room at the Bristol where dinner had been laid for three.

"No, Harry," answered Hallward, giving his hat and coat to the bowing waiter. "What is it? Nothing about politics, I hope? They don't interest me. There is hardly a single person in the House of

---

1. Wilde added another chapter (6) here in 1891.

Commons worth painting; though many of them would be the better for a little whitewashing."

"Dorian Gray is engaged to be married," said Lord Henry, watching him as he spoke.

Hallward turned perfectly pale, and a curious look flashed for a
moment into his eyes, and then passed away, leaving them dull.[2]
"Dorian engaged to be married!" he cried. "Impossible!"

"It is perfectly true."

"To whom?"

"To some little actress or other."

"I can't believe it. Dorian is far too sensible."

"Dorian is far too wise not to do foolish things now and then, my
dear Basil."

"Marriage is hardly a thing that one can do now and then, Harry,"
said Hallward, smiling.

"Except in America.[3] But I didn't say he was married. I said he was
engaged to be married. There is a great difference. I have a distinct
remembrance of being married, but I have no recollection at all of
being engaged.[4] I am inclined to think that I never was engaged."

"But think of Dorian's birth, and position, and wealth. It would
be absurd for him to marry so much beneath him."

"If you want him to marry this girl, tell him that, Basil. He is sure
to do it then.[5] Whenever a man does a thoroughly stupid thing, it is
always from the noblest motives."

"I hope the girl is good, Harry. I don't want to see Dorian tied to
some vile creature, who might degrade his nature and ruin his
intellect."

"Oh, she is more than good—she is beautiful," murmured Lord
Henry, sipping a glass of vermouth and orange-bitters. "Dorian says
she is beautiful; and he is not often wrong about things of that
kind. Your portrait of him has quickened his appreciation of the
personal appearance of other people. It has had that excellent effect,
among others. We are to see her to-night, if that boy doesn't forget
his appointment."[6]

"But do you approve of it, Harry?" asked Hallward, walking up and
down the room, and biting his lip. "You can't approve of it, really. It is
some silly infatuation."

"I never approve, or disapprove, of anything now. It is an absurd
attitude to take towards life. We are not sent into the world to air

2. Wilde changed these lines in 1891, muting Basil's reaction.
3. Wilde added this in TS.
4. "I have a distinct . . . being engaged" was added in TS.
5. "But think of Dorian's birth . . . do it then" was added in MS margin, and the following
   sentence was added in TS.
6. Wilde added several lines here in 1891.

our moral prejudices. I never take any notice of what common people say, and I never interfere with what charming people do. If a personality fascinates me, whatever the personality chooses to do is absolutely delightful to me. Dorian Gray falls in love with a beautiful girl who acts Shakespeare, and proposes to marry her. Why not? If he wedded Messalina he would be none the less interesting. You know I am not a champion of marriage. The real drawback to marriage is that it makes one unselfish. And unselfish people are colorless. They lack individuality. Still, there are certain temperaments that marriage makes more complex. They retain their egotism, and add to it many other egos. They are forced to have more than one life. They become more highly organized. Besides, every experience is of value, and, whatever one may say against marriage, it is certainly an experience. I hope that Dorian Gray will make this girl his wife, passionately adore her for six months, and then suddenly become fascinated by some one else. He would be a wonderful study."[7]

"You don't mean all that, Harry; you know you don't. If Dorian Gray's life were spoiled, no one would be sorrier than yourself. You are much better than you pretend to be."

Lord Henry laughed. "The reason we all like to think so well of others is that we are all afraid for ourselves. The basis of optimism is sheer terror. We think that we are generous because we credit our neighbor with those virtues that are likely to benefit ourselves. We praise the banker that we may overdraw our account, and find good qualities in the highwayman in the hope that he may spare our pockets.[8] I mean everything that I have said. I have the greatest contempt for optimism.[9] And as for a spoiled life, no life is spoiled but one whose growth is arrested. If you want to mar a nature, you have merely to reform it. But here is Dorian himself. He will tell you more than I can."

"My dear Harry, my dear Basil, you must both congratulate me!" said the boy, throwing off his evening cape with its satin-lined wings, and shaking each of his friends by the hand in turn. "I have never been so happy. Of course it is sudden: all really delightful things are. And yet it seems to me to be the one thing I have been looking for all my life." He was flushed with excitement and pleasure, and looked extraordinarily handsome.

"I hope you will always be very happy, Dorian," said Hallward, "but I don't quite forgive you for not having let me know of your engagement. You let Harry know."

7. Wilde made several minor changes in this paragraph in 1891.
8. "And find good qualities . . . pockets" added in TS.
9. This sentence and the four immediately following were added in TS.

"And I don't forgive you for being late for dinner," broke in Lord Henry, putting his hand on the lad's shoulder, and smiling as he spoke. "Come, let us sit down and try what the new *chef* here is like, and then you will tell us how it all came about."

"There is really not much to tell," cried Dorian, as they took their seats at the small round table. "What happened was simply this. After I left you yesterday evening, Harry, I had some dinner at that curious little Italian restaurant in Rupert Street,[1] you introduced me to, and went down afterwards to the theatre. Sibyl was playing Rosalind. Of course the scenery was dreadful, and the Orlando absurd. But Sibyl! You should have seen her! When she came on in her boy's dress she was perfectly wonderful. She wore a moss-colored velvet jerkin with cinnamon sleeves, slim brown cross-gartered hose, a dainty little green cap with a hawk's feather caught in a jewel, and a hooded cloak lined with dull red. She had never seemed to me more exquisite. She had all the delicate grace of that Tanagra figurine that you have in your studio, Basil. Her hair clustered round her face like dark leaves round a pale rose. As for her acting—well, you will see her to-night. She is simply a born artist. I sat in the dingy box absolutely enthralled. I forgot that I was in London and in the nineteenth century. I was away with my love in a forest that no man had ever seen. After the performance was over I went behind, and spoke to her. As we were sitting together, suddenly there came a look into her eyes that I had never seen there before. My lips moved towards hers. We kissed each other. I can't describe to you what I felt at that moment. It seemed to me that all my life had been narrowed to one perfect point of rose-colored joy. She trembled all over, and shook like a white narcissus. Then she flung herself on her knees and kissed my hands. I feel that I should not tell you all this, but I can't help it. Of course our engagement is a dead secret. She has not even told her own mother. I don't know what my guardians will say. Lord Radley is sure to be furious. I don't care. I shall be of age in less than a year, and then I can do what I like. I have been right, Basil, haven't I, to take my love out of poetry, and to find my wife in Shakespeare's plays? Lips that Shakespeare taught to speak have whispered their secret in my ear. I have had the arms of Rosalind around me, and kissed Juliet on the mouth."

"Yes, Dorian, I suppose you were right," said Hallward, slowly.

"Have you seen her to-day?" asked Lord Henry.

Dorian Gray shook his head. "I left her in the forest of Arden, I shall find her in an orchard in Verona."

1. Wilde added this detail in TS.

Lord Henry sipped his champagne in a meditative manner. "At what particular point did you mention the word marriage, Dorian? and what did she say in answer? Perhaps you forgot all about it."

"My dear Harry, I did not treat it as a business transaction, and I did not make any formal proposal. I told her that I loved her, and she said she was not worthy to be my wife. Not worthy! Why, the whole world is nothing to me compared to her."

"Women are wonderfully practical," murmured Lord Henry,—"much more practical than we are. In situations of that kind we often forget to say anything about marriage, and they always remind us."

Hallward laid his hand upon his arm. "Don't, Harry. You have annoyed Dorian. He is not like other men. He would never bring misery upon any one. His nature is too fine for that."

Lord Henry looked across the table. "Dorian is never annoyed with me," he answered. "I asked the question for the best reason possible, for the only reason, indeed, that excuses one for asking any question,—simple curiosity. I have a theory that it is always the women who propose to us, and not we who propose to the women, except, of course, in middle-class life. But then the middle classes are not modern."

Dorian Gray laughed, and tossed his head. "You are quite incorrigible, Harry; but I don't mind. It is impossible to be angry with you. When you see Sibyl Vane you will feel that the man who could wrong her would be a beast without a heart. I cannot understand how any one can wish to shame what he loves. I love Sibyl Vane. I wish to place her on a pedestal of gold, and to see the world worship the woman who is mine. What is marriage? An irrevocable vow. And it is an irrevocable vow that I want to take.[2] Her trust makes me faithful, her belief makes me good. When I am with her, I regret all that you have taught me. I become different from what you have known me to be. I am changed, and the mere touch of Sibyl Vane's hand makes me forget you and all your wrong, fascinating, poisonous, delightful[3] theories."

"You will always like me, Dorian," said Lord Henry. "Will you have some coffee, you fellows?—Waiter, bring coffee, and *fine-champagne*, and some cigarettes. No: don't mind the cigarettes; I have some.—Basil, I can't allow you to smoke cigars. You must have a cigarette. A cigarette is the perfect type of a perfect pleasure. It is exquisite, and it leaves one unsatisfied. What more can you want?—Yes, Dorian, you will always be fond of me. I represent to you all the sins you have never had the courage to commit."

2. Wilde crossed out the following in MS: "Why she would loathe me if she thought I merely meant to use her till I grew weary of her and then throw her away."
3. "Delightful" added in TS. Wilde inserted almost two additional pages at this point in 1891.

"What nonsense you talk, Harry!" cried Dorian Gray, lighting his cigarette from a fire-breathing silver dragon that the waiter had placed on the table. "Let us go down to the theatre. When you see Sibyl you will have a new ideal of life. She will represent something to you that you have never known."

"I have known everything," said Lord Henry, with a sad[4] look in his eyes, "but I am always ready for a new emotion. I am afraid that there is no such thing, for me at any rate. Still, your wonderful girl may thrill me. Dorian, you will come with me.—I am so sorry, Basil, but there is only room for two in the brougham. You must follow us in a hansom."

They got up and put on their coats, sipping their coffee standing. Hallward was silent and preoccupied. There was a gloom over him. He could not bear this marriage, and yet it seemed to him to be better than many other things that might have happened. After a few moments, they all passed down-stairs. He drove off by himself, as had been arranged, and watched the flashing lights of the little brougham in front of him. A strange sense of loss came over him. He felt that Dorian Gray would never again be to him all that he had been in the past. His eyes darkened,[5] and the crowded flaring streets became blurred to him. When the cab drew up at the doors of the theatre, it seemed to him that he had grown years older.

Chapter V

For some reason or other, the house was crowded that night, and the fat Jew manager who met them at the door was beaming from ear to ear with an oily, tremulous smile. He escorted them to their box with a sort of pompous humility, waving his fat jewelled hands, and talking at the top of his voice. Dorian Gray loathed him more than ever. He felt as if he had come to look for Miranda and had been met by Caliban. Lord Henry, upon the other hand, rather liked him. At least he declared he did, and insisted on shaking him by the hand, and assured him that he was proud to meet a man who had discovered a real genius and gone bankrupt over Shakespeare. Hallward amused himself with watching the faces in the pit. The heat was terribly oppressive, and the huge sunlight flamed like a monstrous dahlia with petals of fire. The youths in the gallery had taken off their coats and waistcoats and hung them over the side. They talked to each other across the theatre, and shared their oranges with the tawdry painted girls who sat by them. Some women were

---

4. Changed to "tired" in 1891.
5. Wilde substituted "darkened" for "filled with tears" in MS.

laughing in the pit; their voices were horribly shrill and discordant. The sound of the popping of corks came from the bar.

"What a place to find one's divinity in!" said Lord Henry.

"Yes!" answered Dorian Gray. "It was here I found her, and she is divine beyond all living things. When she acts you will forget everything. These common people here, with their coarse faces and brutal gestures, become quite different when she is on the stage. They sit silently and watch her. They weep and laugh as she wills them to do. She makes them as responsive as a violin. She spiritualizes them, and one feels that they are of the same flesh and blood as one's self."

"Oh, I hope not!" murmured Lord Henry, who was scanning the occupants of the gallery through his opera-glass.

"Don't pay any attention to him, Dorian," said Hallward. "I understand what you mean, and I believe in this girl. Any one you love must be marvellous, and any girl that has the effect you describe must be fine and noble. To spiritualize one's age,—that is something worth doing. If this girl can give a soul to those who have lived without one, if she can create the sense of beauty in people whose lives have been sordid and ugly, if she can strip them of their selfishness and lend them tears for sorrows that are not their own, she is worthy of all your adoration, worthy of the adoration of the world. This marriage is quite right. I did not think so at first, but I admit it now. God[1] made Sibyl Vane for you. Without her you would have been incomplete.

"Thanks, Basil," answered Dorian Gray, pressing his hand. "I knew that you would understand me. Harry is so cynical, he terrifies me. But here is the orchestra. It is quite dreadful, but it only lasts for about five minutes. Then the curtain rises, and you will see the girl to whom I am going to give all my life, to whom I have given everything that is good in me."

A quarter of an hour afterwards, amidst an extraordinary turmoil of applause, Sibyl Vane stepped on to the stage. Yes, she was certainly lovely to look at—one of the loveliest creatures, Lord Henry thought, that he had ever seen. There was something of the fawn in her shy grace and startled eyes. A faint blush, like the shadow of a rose in a mirror of silver, came to her cheeks as she glanced at the crowded, enthusiastic house. She stepped back a few paces, and her lips seemed to tremble. Basil Hallward leaped to his feet and began to applaud. Dorian Gray sat motionless, gazing on her, like a man in a dream. Lord Henry peered through his opera-glass, murmuring, "Charming! charming!"

The scene was the hall of Capulet's house, and Romeo in his pilgrim's dress had entered with Mercutio and his friends. The band,

---

1. Changed to "the gods" in 1891.

such as it was, struck up a few bars of music, and the dance began. Through the crowd of ungainly, shabbily-dressed actors, Sibyl Vane moved like a creature from a finer world. Her body swayed, as she danced, as a plant sways in the water. The curves of her throat were like the curves of a white lily. Her hands seemed to be made of cool ivory.

Yet she was curiously listless. She showed no sign of joy when her eyes rested on Romeo. The few lines she had to speak,—

> Good pilgrim, you do wrong your hand too much,
>   Which mannerly devotion shows in this;
> For saints have hands that pilgrims' hands do touch,
>   And palm to palm is holy palmers' kiss,—

with the brief dialogue that follows, were spoken in a thoroughly artificial manner. The voice was exquisite, but from the point of view of tone it was absolutely false. It was wrong in color. It took away all the life from the verse. It made the passion unreal.

Dorian Gray grew pale as he watched her. Neither of his friends dared to say anything to him. She seemed to them to be absolutely incompetent. They were horribly disappointed.

Yet they felt that the true test of any Juliet is the balcony scene of the second act. They waited for that. If she failed there, there was nothing in her.

She looked charming as she came out in the moonlight. That could not be denied. But the staginess of her acting was unbearable, and grew worse as she went on. Her gestures became absurdly artificial. She over-emphasized everything that she had to say. The beautiful passage,—

> Thou knowest the mask of night is on my face,
> Else would a maiden blush bepaint my cheek
> For that which thou hast heard me speak to-night,—

was declaimed with the painful precision of a school-girl who has been taught to recite by some second-rate professor of elocution. When she leaned over the balcony and came to those wonderful lines,—

> Although I joy in thee,
> I have no joy of this contract to-night:
> It is too rash, too unadvised, too sudden;
> Too like the lightning, which doth cease to be
> Ere one can say, "It lightens." Sweet, good-night!
> This bud of love by summer's ripening breath
> May prove a beauteous flower when next we meet,—

she spoke the words as if they conveyed no meaning to her. It was not nervousness. Indeed, so far from being nervous, she seemed absolutely self-contained. It was simply bad art. She was a complete failure.

Even the common uneducated audience of the pit and gallery lost their interest in the play. They got restless, and began to talk loudly and to whistle. The Jew manager, who was standing at the back of the dress-circle, stamped and swore with rage. The only person unmoved was the girl herself.

When the second act was over there came a storm of hisses, and Lord Henry got up from his chair and put on his coat. "She is quite beautiful, Dorian," he said, "but she can't act. Let us go."

"I am going to see the play through," answered the lad, in a hard, bitter voice. "I am awfully sorry that I have made you waste an evening, Harry. I apologize to both of you."

"My dear Dorian, I should think Miss Vane was ill," interrupted Hallward. "We will come some other night."

"I wish she was ill," he rejoined. "But she seems to me to be simply callous and cold. She has entirely altered. Last night she was a great artist. To-night she is merely a commonplace, mediocre actress."

"Don't talk like that about any one you love, Dorian. Love is a more wonderful thing than art."

"They are both simply forms of imitation," murmured Lord Henry. "But do let us go. Dorian, you must not stay here any longer. It is not good for one's morals to see bad acting. Besides, I don't suppose you will want your wife to act. So what does it matter if she plays Juliet like a wooden doll? She is very lovely, and if she knows as little about life as she does about acting, she will be a delightful experience. There are only two kinds of people who are really fascinating,—people who know absolutely everything, and people who know absolutely nothing. Good heavens, my dear boy, don't look so tragic! The secret of remaining young is never to have an emotion that is unbecoming. Come to the club with Basil and myself. We will smoke cigarettes and drink to the beauty of Sibyl Vane. She is beautiful. What more can you want?"

"Please go away, Harry," cried the lad. "I really want to be alone.—Basil, you don't mind my asking you to go? Ah! can't you see that my heart is breaking?" The hot tears came to his eyes. His lips trembled, and, rushing to the back of the box, he leaned up against the wall, hiding his face in his hands.

"Let us go, Basil," said Lord Henry, with a strange tenderness in his voice; and the two young men passed out together.

A few moments afterwards the footlights flared up, and the curtain rose on the third act. Dorian Gray went back to his seat. He looked pale, and proud, and indifferent. The play dragged on, and seemed interminable. Half of the audience went out, tramping in heavy boots, and laughing. The whole thing was a *fiasco*. The last act was played to almost empty benches.

As soon as it was over, Dorian Gray rushed behind the scenes into the greenroom. The girl was standing alone there, with a look of triumph on her face. Her eyes were lit with an exquisite fire. There was a radiance about her. Her parted lips were smiling over some secret of their own.

When he entered, she looked at him, and an expression of infinite joy came over her. "How badly I acted to-night, Dorian!" she cried.

"Horribly!" he answered, gazing at her in amazement,—"horribly! It was dreadful. Are you ill? You have no idea what it was. You have no idea what I suffered."

The girl smiled. "Dorian," she answered, lingering over his name with long-drawn music in her voice, as though it were sweeter than honey to the red petals of her lips,—"Dorian, you should have understood. But you understand now, don't you?"

"Understand what?" he asked, angrily.

"Why I was so bad to-night. Why I shall always be bad. Why I shall never act well again."

He shrugged his shoulders. "You are ill, I suppose. When you are ill you shouldn't act. You make yourself ridiculous. My friends were bored. I was bored."

She seemed not to listen to him. She was transfigured with joy. An ecstasy of happiness dominated her.

"Dorian, Dorian," she cried, "before I knew you, acting was the one reality of my life. It was only in the theatre that I lived. I thought that it was all true. I was Rosalind one night, and Portia the other. The joy of Beatrice was my joy, and the sorrows of Cordelia were mine also.[2] I believed in everything. The common people who acted with me seemed to me to be godlike. The painted scenes were my world. I knew nothing but shadows, and I thought them real. You came,—oh, my beautiful love!—and you freed my soul from prison. You taught me what reality really is. To-night, for the first time in my life, I saw through the hollowness, the sham, the silliness, of the empty pageant in which I had always played. To-night, for the first time, I became conscious that the Romeo was hideous, and old, and painted, that the moonlight in the orchard was false, that the scenery was vulgar, and that the words I had to speak were unreal, were not my words, not what I wanted to say. You had brought me something higher, something of which all art is but a reflection. You have made me understand what love really is. My love! my love! I am sick of shadows. You are more to me than all art can ever be. What have I

---

2. Wilde rewrote this line in TS, changing it from "If I died as Desdemona, I came back as Juliet."

to do with the puppets of a play? When I came on to-night, I could not understand how it was that everything had gone from me. Suddenly it dawned on my soul what it all meant. The knowledge was exquisite to me. I heard them hissing, and I smiled. What should they know of love? Take me away, Dorian—take me away with you, where we can be quite alone. I hate the stage. I might mimic a passion that I do not feel, but I cannot mimic one that burns me like fire. Oh, Dorian, Dorian, you understand now what it all means? Even if I could do it, it would be profanation for me to play at being in love. You have made me see that."

He flung himself down on the sofa, and turned away his face. "You have killed my love," he muttered.

She looked at him in wonder, and laughed. He made no answer. She came across to him, and stroked his hair with her little fingers. She knelt down and pressed his hands to her lips. He drew them away, and a shudder ran through him.

Then he leaped up, and went to the door. "Yes," he cried, "you have killed my love. You used to stir my imagination. Now you don't even stir my curiosity. You simply produce no effect. I loved you because you were wonderful, because you had genius and intellect, because you realized the dreams of great poets and gave shape and substance to the shadows of art. You have thrown it all away. You are shallow and stupid. My God! how mad I was to love you! What a fool I have been! You are nothing to me now. I will never see you again. I will never think of you. I will never mention your name. You don't know what you were to me, once. Why, once . . . Oh, I can't bear to think of it! I wish I had never laid eyes upon you! You have spoiled the romance of my life. How little you can know of love, if you say it mars your art! What are you without your art? Nothing. I would have made you famous, splendid, magnificent. The world would have worshipped you, and you would have belonged to me. What are you now? A third-rate actress with a pretty face."

The girl grew white, and trembled. She clinched her hands together, and her voice seemed to catch in her throat. "You are not serious, Dorian?" she murmured. "You are acting."

"Acting! I leave that to you. You do it so well," he answered, bitterly.

She rose from her knees, and, with a piteous expression of pain in her face, came across the room to him. She put her hand upon his arm, and looked into his eyes. He thrust her back. "Don't touch me!" he cried.

A low moan broke from her, and she flung herself at his feet, and lay there like a trampled flower. "Dorian, Dorian, don't leave me!" she whispered. "I am so sorry I didn't act well. I was thinking of you all the time. But I will try,—indeed, I will try. It came so suddenly across me, my love for you. I think I should never have known it if

you had not kissed me,—if we had not kissed each other. Kiss me
again, my love. Don't go away from me. I couldn't bear it.[3] Can't you
forgive me for to-night? I will work so hard, and try to improve. Don't
be cruel to me because I love you better than anything in the world.
After all, it is only once that I have not pleased you. But you are quite
right, Dorian. I should have shown myself more of an artist. It was
foolish of me; and yet I couldn't help it. Oh, don't leave me, don't
leave me." A fit of passionate sobbing choked her. She crouched on
the floor like a wounded thing, and Dorian Gray, with his beautiful
eyes, looked down at her, and his chiselled lips curled in exquisite
disdain. There is always something ridiculous about the passions of
people whom one has ceased to love. Sibyl Vane seemed to him to
be absurdly melodramatic. Her tears and sobs annoyed him.

"I am going," he said at last, in his calm, clear voice. "I don't wish
to be unkind, but I can't see you again. You have disappointed me."

She wept silently, and made no answer, but crept nearer to him.
Her little hands stretched blindly out, and appeared to be seeking
for him.[4] He turned on his heel, and left the room. In a few moments
he was out of the theatre.

Where he went to, he hardly knew. He remembered wandering
through dimly-lit streets with gaunt black-shadowed archways and
evil-looking houses. Women with hoarse voices and harsh laughter
had called after him. Drunkards had reeled by cursing, and chattering to themselves like monstrous apes.[5] He had seen grotesque
children huddled upon door-steps, and had heard shrieks and oaths
from gloomy courts.

When the dawn was just breaking, he found himself at Covent
Garden. Huge carts filled with nodding lilies rumbled slowly down
the polished empty street. The air was heavy with the perfume of
the flowers, and their beauty seemed to bring him an anodyne for
his pain. He followed into the market, and watched the men unloading their wagons. A white-smocked carter offered him some cherries. He thanked him, wondered why he refused to accept any money
for them, and began to eat them listlessly. They had been plucked at
midnight, and the coldness of the moon had entered into them. A
long line of boys carrying crates of striped tulips, and of yellow and
red roses, defiled in front of him, threading their way through the
huge jade-green piles of vegetables. Under the portico, with its gray
sun-bleached pillars, loitered a troop of draggled bareheaded girls,

---

3. Wilde added foreshadowing here in 1891.
4. This sentence added in TS.
5. Wilde wrote in TS, then crossed out the following lines: "A man with curious eyes had
   suddenly peered into his face and then dogged him with stealthy footsteps, passing and
   repassing him many times." It is likely that Sibyl's avenging brother, James, added in
   1891, may have originated in these lines.

waiting for the auction to be over.[6] After some time he hailed a hansom and drove home. The sky was pure opal now, and the roofs of the houses glistened like silver against it.[7] As he was passing through the library towards the door of his bedroom, his eye fell upon the portrait Basil Hallward had painted of him. He started back in surprise,[8] and then went over to it and examined it. In the dim arrested light that struggled through the cream-colored silk blinds, the face seemed to him to be a little changed. The expression looked different. One would have said that there was a touch of cruelty in the mouth. It was certainly curious.

He turned round, and, walking to the window, drew the blinds up. The bright dawn flooded the room, and swept the fantastic shadows into dusky corners, where they lay shuddering. But the strange expression that he had noticed in the face of the portrait seemed to linger there, to be more intensified even. The quivering, ardent sunlight showed him the lines of cruelty round the mouth as clearly as if he had been looking into a mirror after he had done some dreadful thing.

He winced, and, taking up from the table an oval glass framed in ivory Cupids, that Lord Henry had given him, he glanced hurriedly into it. No line like that warped his red lips. What did it mean?

He rubbed his eyes, and came close to the picture, and examined it again. There were no signs of change when he looked into the actual painting, and yet there was no doubt that the whole expression had altered. It was not a mere fancy of his own. The thing was horribly apparent.

He threw himself into a chair, and began to think. Suddenly there flashed across his mind what he had said in Basil Hallward's studio the day the picture had been finished. Yes, he remembered it perfectly. He had uttered a mad wish that he himself might remain young, and the portrait grow old; that his own beauty might be untarnished, and the face on the canvas bear the burden of his passions and his sins; that the painted image might be seared with the lines of suffering and thought, and that he might keep all the delicate bloom and loveliness of his then just conscious boyhood. Surely his prayer had not been answered? Such things were impossible. It seemed monstrous even to think of them. And, yet, there was the picture before him, with the touch of cruelty in the mouth.

Cruelty! Had he been cruel? It was the girl's fault, not his. He had dreamed of her as a great artist, had given his love to her because

6. "A long line . . . to be over" added in TS.
7. This sentence also added in TS. Wilde expanded and revised the rest of the paragraph in 1891.
8. In MS, the following lines were canceled at this point: "then he smiled to himself and went on into his bedroom. 'It is merely an effect of light,' he murmured. 'I did not know that the dawn was so unbecoming.'"

he had thought her great. Then she had disappointed him. She had been shallow and unworthy. And, yet, a feeling of infinite regret came over him, as he thought of her lying at his feet sobbing like a little child. He remembered with what callousness he had watched her. Why had he been made like that? Why had such a soul been given to him? But he had suffered also. During the three terrible hours that the play had lasted, he had lived centuries of pain, æon upon æon of torture. His life was well worth hers. She had marred him for a moment, if he had wounded her for an age. Besides, women were better suited to bear sorrow than men. They lived on their emotions. They only thought of their emotions. When they took lovers, it was merely to have some one with whom they could have scenes. Lord Henry had told him that, and Lord Henry knew what women were. Why should he trouble about Sibyl Vane? She was nothing to him now.

But the picture? What was he to say of that?[9] It held the secret of his life, and told his story. It had taught him to love his own beauty. Would it teach him to loathe his own soul? Would he ever look at it again?

No; it was merely an illusion wrought on the troubled senses. The horrible night that he had passed had left phantoms behind it. Suddenly there had fallen upon his brain that tiny scarlet speck that makes men mad. The picture had not changed. It was folly to think so.

Yet it was watching him, with its beautiful marred face and its cruel smile. Its bright hair gleamed in the early sunlight. Its blue eyes met his own. A sense of infinite pity, not for himself, but for the painted image of himself, came over him. It had altered already, and would alter more. Its gold would wither into gray. Its red and white roses would die. For every sin that he committed, a stain would fleck and wreck its fairness. But he would not sin. The picture, changed or unchanged, would be to him the visible emblem of conscience. He would resist temptation. He would not see Lord Henry any more—would not, at any rate, listen to those subtle poisonous theories that in Basil Hallward's garden had first stirred within him the passion for impossible things. He would go back to Sibyl Vane, make her amends, marry her, try to love her again. Yes, it was his duty to do so. She must have suffered more than he had. Poor child! He had been selfish and cruel to her. The fascination that she had exercised over him would return. They would be happy together. His life with her would be beautiful and pure.

He got up from his chair, and drew a large screen right in front of the portrait, shuddering as he glanced at it. "How horrible!" he

---

9. Wilde canceled the following in TS: "Where was he to hide it? It could not be left for common eyes to gaze at."

murmured to himself, and he walked across to the window and opened it. When he stepped out on the grass, he drew a deep breath. The fresh morning air seemed to drive away all his sombre passions. He thought only of Sibyl Vane. A faint echo of his love came back to him. He repeated her name over and over again. The birds that were singing in the dew-drenched garden seemed to be telling the flowers about her.

Chapter VI

It was long past noon when he awoke. His valet had crept several times into the room on tiptoe to see if he was stirring, and had wondered what made his young master sleep so late. Finally his bell sounded, and Victor came in softly with a cup of tea, and a pile of letters, on a small tray of old Sèvres china, and drew back the olive-satin curtains, with their shimmering blue lining, that hung in front of the three tall windows.

"Monsieur has well slept this morning," he said, smiling.

"What o'clock is it, Victor?"[1] asked Dorian Gray, sleepily.

"One hour and a quarter, monsieur."

How late it was! He sat up, and, having sipped some tea, turned over his letters. One of them was from Lord Henry, and had been brought by hand that morning. He hesitated for a moment, and then put it aside. The others he opened listlessly. They contained the usual collection of cards, invitations to dinner, tickets for private views, programmes of charity concerts, and the like, that are showered on fashionable young men every morning during the season. There was a rather heavy bill, for a chased silver Louis-Quinze toilet-set, that he had not yet had the courage to send on to his guardians, who were extremely old-fashioned people and did not realize that we live in an age when only unnecessary things are absolutely necessary to us; and there were several very courteously worded communications from Jermyn Street money-lenders offering to advance any sum of money at a moment's notice and at the most reasonable rates of interest.

After about ten minutes he got up, and, throwing on an elaborate dressing-gown, passed into the onyx-paved bath-room. The cool water refreshed him after his long sleep. He seemed to have forgotten all that he had gone through. A dim sense of having taken part

---

1. In MS the valet was named Jacques. The conversation was in French, as it was whenever Dorian and Jacques spoke. Wilde changed this to English in stages: first, Dorian's speech in MS, then the name of the valet and his dialogue.

in some strange tragedy came to him once or twice, but there was the unreality of a dream about it.

As soon as he was dressed, he went into the library and sat down to a light French breakfast, that had been laid out for him on a small round table close to an open window. It was an exquisite day. The warm air seemed laden with spices. A bee flew in, and buzzed round the blue-dragon bowl, filled with sulphur-yellow roses, that stood in front of him. He felt perfectly happy.

Suddenly his eye fell on the screen that he had placed in front of the portrait, and he started.

"Too cold for Monsieur?" asked his valet, putting an omelette on the table. "I shut the window?"

Dorian shook his head. "I am not cold," he murmured.

Was it all true? Had the portrait really changed? Or had it been simply his own imagination that had made him see a look of evil where there had been a look of joy? Surely a painted canvas could not alter? The thing was absurd. It would serve as a tale to tell Basil some day. It would make him smile.

And, yet, how vivid was his recollection of the whole thing! First in the dim twilight, and then in the bright dawn, he had seen the touch of cruelty in the warped lips. He almost dreaded his valet leaving the room. He knew that when he was alone he would have to examine the portrait. He was afraid of certainty. When the coffee and cigarettes had been brought and the man turned to go, he felt a mad desire to tell him to remain. As the door closed behind him he called him back. The man stood waiting for his orders. Dorian looked at him for a moment. "I am not at home to any one, Victor," he said, with a sigh. The man bowed and retired.

He rose from the table, lit a cigarette, and flung himself down on a luxuriously-cushioned couch that stood facing the screen. The screen was an old one of gilt Spanish leather, stamped and wrought with a rather florid Louis-Quatorze pattern. He scanned it curiously, wondering if it had ever before concealed the secret of a man's life.

Should he move it aside, after all? Why not let it stay there? What was the use of knowing? If the thing was true, it was terrible. If it was not true, why trouble about it? But what if, by some fate or deadlier chance, other eyes than his spied behind, and saw the horrible change? What should he do if Basil Hallward came and asked to look at his own picture? He would be sure to do that. No; the thing had to be examined, and at once. Anything would be better than this dreadful state of doubt.

He got up, and locked both doors. At least he would be alone when he looked upon the mask of his shame. Then he drew the screen aside, and saw himself face to face. It was perfectly true. The portrait had altered.

As he often remembered afterwards, and always with no small wonder, he found himself at first gazing at the portrait with a feeling of almost scientific interest.[2] That such a change should have taken place was incredible to him. And yet it was a fact. Was there some subtle affinity between the chemical atoms, that shaped themselves into form and color on the canvas, and the soul that was within him? Could it be that what that soul thought, they realized?— that what it dreamed, they made true? Or was there some other, more terrible reason? He shuddered, and felt afraid, and, going back to the couch, lay there, gazing at the picture in sickened horror.[3]

One thing, however, he felt that it had done for him. It had made him conscious how unjust, how cruel, he had been to Sibyl Vane. It was not too late to make reparation for that. She could still be his wife. His unreal and selfish love would yield to some higher influence, would be transformed into some nobler passion, and the portrait that Basil Hallward had painted of him would be a guide to him through life, would be to him what holiness was to some, and conscience to others, and the fear of God to us all. There were opiates for remorse, drugs that could lull the moral sense to sleep. But here was a visible symbol of the degradation of sin. Here was an ever-present sign of the ruin men brought upon their souls.

Three o'clock struck, and four, and half-past four, but he did not stir. He was trying to gather up the scarlet threads of life, and to weave them into a pattern; to find his way through the sanguine labyrinth of passion through which he was wandering. He did not know what to do, or what to think.[4] Finally, he went over to the table and wrote a passionate letter to the girl he had loved, imploring her forgiveness, and accusing himself of madness. He covered page after page with wild words of sorrow, and wilder words of pain.[5] There is a luxury in self-reproach. When we blame ourselves we feel that no one else has a right to blame us. It is the confession, not the priest, that gives us absolution. When Dorian Gray had finished the letter, he felt that he had been forgiven.

Suddenly there came a knock to the door, and he heard Lord Henry's voice outside. "My dear Dorian, I must see you. Let me in at once. I can't bear your shutting yourself up like this."

He made no answer at first, but remained quite still. The knocking still continued, and grew louder. Yes, it was better to let Lord

2. Originally, the MS read "He was strangely calm at this moment."
3. Wilde added the last two sentences of this paragraph in TS.
4. Wilde added to TS the first three sentences of this paragraph.
5. This sentence added in TS.

Henry in, and to[6] explain to him the new life he was going to lead, to quarrel with him if it became necessary to quarrel, to part if parting was inevitable. He jumped up, drew the screen hastily across the picture, and unlocked the door.

"I am so sorry for it all, my dear boy," said Lord Henry, coming in. "But you must not think about it too much."

"Do you mean about Sibyl Vane?" asked Dorian.

"Yes, of course," answered Lord Henry, sinking into a chair, and slowly pulling his gloves off. "It is dreadful, from one point of view, but it was not your fault.[7] Tell me, did you go behind and see her after the play was over?"

"Yes."

"I felt sure you had. Did you make a scene with her?"

"I was brutal, Harry,—perfectly brutal. But it is all right now. I am not sorry for anything that has happened. It has taught me to know myself better."

"Ah, Dorian, I am so glad you take it in that way! I was afraid I would find you plunged in remorse, and tearing your nice hair."

"I have got through all that," said Dorian, shaking his head, and smiling. "I am perfectly happy now. I know what conscience is, to begin with. It is not what you told me it was. It is the divinest thing in us. Don't sneer at it, Harry, any more,—at least not before me. I want to be good. I can't bear the idea of my soul being hideous."

"A very charming artistic basis for ethics, Dorian! I congratulate you on it. But how are you going to begin?"

"By marrying Sibyl Vane."

"Marrying Sibyl Vane!" cried Lord Henry, standing up, and looking at him in perplexed amazement. "But, my dear Dorian—"

"Yes, Harry, I know what you are going to say. Something dreadful about marriage. Don't say it. Don't ever say things of that kind to me again. Two days ago I asked Sibyl to marry me. I am not going to break my word to her. She is to be my wife."

"Your wife! Dorian! . . . Didn't you get my letter? I wrote to you this morning, and sent the note down, by my own man."

"Your letter? Oh, yes, I remember. I have not read it yet, Harry. I was afraid there might be something in it that I wouldn't like."

Lord Henry walked across the room, and, sitting down by Dorian Gray, took both his hands in his, and held them tightly. "Dorian," he said, "my letter—don't be frightened—was to tell you that Sibyl Vane is dead."

---

6. TS originally read "to sever their friendship at once."
7. Wilde canceled in TS the following: "And besides, no one knows that you were at the theatre last night." The *Lippincott's* text misprinted "slowing pulling his gloves off."

A cry of pain rose from the lad's lips, and he leaped to his feet, tearing his hands away from Lord Henry's grasp. "Dead! Sibyl dead! It is not true! It is a horrible lie!"

"It is quite true, Dorian," said Lord Henry, gravely. "It is in all the morning papers. I wrote down to you to ask you not to see any one till I came. There will have to be an inquest, of course, and you must not be mixed up in it. Things like that make a man fashionable in Paris. But in London people are so prejudiced. Here, one should never make one's *début* with a scandal. One should reserve that to give an interest to one's old age. I don't suppose they know your name at the theatre. If they don't, it is all right. Did any one see you going round to her room? That is an important point."

Dorian did not answer for a few moments. He was dazed with horror. Finally he murmured, in a stifled voice, "Harry, did you say an inquest? What did you mean by that? Did Sibyl—? Oh, Harry, I can't bear it! But be quick. Tell me everything at once."

"I have no doubt it was not an accident, Dorian, though it must be put in that way to the public. As she was leaving the theatre with her mother, about half-past twelve or so, she said she had forgotten something up-stairs. They waited some time for her, but she did not come down again. They ultimately found her lying dead on the floor of her dressing-room. She had swallowed something by mistake, some dreadful thing they use at theatres. I don't know what it was, but it had either prussic acid or white lead in it. I should fancy it was prussic acid, as she seems to have died instantaneously. It is very tragic, of course, but you must not get yourself mixed up in it. I see by the *Standard* that she was seventeen. I should have thought she was almost younger than that. She looked such a child, and seemed to know so little about acting. Dorian, you mustn't let this thing get on your nerves. You must come and dine with me, and afterwards we will look in at the Opera. It is a Patti night, and everybody will be there. You can come to my sister's box. She has got some smart women with her."

"So I have murdered Sibyl Vane," said Dorian Gray, half to himself,—"murdered her as certainly as if I had cut her little throat with a knife. And the roses are not less lovely for all that. The birds sing just as happily in my garden. And to-night I am to dine with you, and then go on to the Opera, and sup somewhere I suppose, afterwards. How extraordinarily dramatic life is! If I had read all this in a book, Harry, I think I would have wept over it. Somehow, now that it has happened actually, and to me, it seems far too wonderful for tears. Here is the first passionate love-letter I have ever written in my life. Strange, that my first passionate love-letter should have been addressed to a dead girl. Can they feel, I wonder, those white silent people we call the dead? Sibyl! Can she feel, or know, or listen?

Oh, Harry, how I loved her once! It seems years ago to me now. She was everything to me. Then came that dreadful night—was it really only last night?—when she played so badly, and my heart almost broke. She explained it all to me. It was terribly pathetic. But I was not moved a bit. I thought her shallow. Then something happened that made me afraid. I can't tell you what it was, but it was awful. I said I would go back to her. I felt I had done wrong. And now she is dead. My God! my God! Harry, what shall I do? You don't know the danger I am in, and there is nothing to keep me straight. She would have done that for me. She had no right to kill herself. It was selfish of her."

"My dear Dorian, the only way a woman can ever reform a man is by boring him so completely that he loses all possible interest in life. If you had married this girl you would have been wretched. Of course you would have treated her kindly. One can always be kind to people about whom one cares nothing. But she would have soon found out that you were absolutely indifferent to her. And when a woman finds that out about her husband, she either becomes dreadfully dowdy, or wears very smart bonnets that some other woman's husband has to pay for. I say nothing about the social mistake, but I assure you that in any case the whole thing would have been an absolute failure."

"I suppose it would," muttered the lad, walking up and down the room, and looking horribly pale. "But I thought it was my duty. It is not my fault that this terrible tragedy has prevented my doing what was right. I remember your saying once that there is a fatality about good resolutions—that they are always made too late. Mine certainly were."

"Good resolutions are simply a useless attempt to interfere with scientific laws. Their origin is pure vanity. Their result is absolutely *nil*. They give us, now and then, some of those luxurious sterile emotions that have a certain charm for us. That is all that can be said for them."

"Harry," cried Dorian Gray, coming over and sitting down beside him, "why is it that I cannot feel this tragedy as much as I want to? I don't think I am heartless. Do you?"

"You have done too many foolish things in your life[8] to be entitled to give yourself that name, Dorian," answered Lord Henry, with his sweet, melancholy smile.

The lad frowned. "I don't like that explanation, Harry," he rejoined, "but I am glad you don't think I am heartless. I am nothing of the kind. I know I am not. And yet I must admit that this thing that has happened does not affect me as it should. It seems to me to be

8. Wilde made a change here in 1891.

simply like a wonderful ending to a wonderful play. It has all the terrible beauty of a great tragedy, in which I took part, a tragedy, but by which I have not been wounded."

"It is an interesting question," said Lord Henry, who found an exquisite pleasure in playing on the lad's unconscious egotism,—"an extremely interesting question. I fancy that the explanation is this. It often happens that the real tragedies of life occur in such an inartistic manner that they hurt us by their crude violence, their absolute incoherence, their absurd want of meaning, their entire lack of style. They affect us just as vulgarity affects us. They give us an impression of sheer brute force, and we revolt against that. Sometimes, however, a tragedy that has artistic elements of beauty crosses our lives. If these elements of beauty are real, the whole thing simply appeals to our sense of dramatic effect. Suddenly we find that we are no longer the actors but the spectators of the play. Or rather we are both. We watch ourselves, and the mere wonder of the spectacle enthralls us. In the present case, what is it that has really happened? Some one has killed herself for love of you. I wish I had ever had such an experience. It would have made me in love with love for the rest of my life. The people who have adored me—there have not been very many, but there have been some—have always insisted on living on, long after I had ceased to care for them, or they to care for me. They have become stout and tedious, and when I meet them they go in at once for reminiscences. That awful memory of woman! What a fearful thing it is! And what an utter intellectual stagnation it reveals! One should absorb the color of life, but one should never remember its details. Details are always vulgar.

"Of course, now and then things linger. I once wore nothing but violets all through one season, as mourning for a romance that would not die. Ultimately, however, it did die. I forget what killed it. I think it was her proposing to sacrifice the whole world for me. That is always a dreadful moment. It fills one with the terror of eternity. Well,—would you believe it?—a week ago, at Lady Hampshire's, I found myself seated at dinner next the lady in question, and she insisted on going over the whole thing again, and digging up the past, and raking up the future. I had buried my romance in a bed of poppies. She dragged it out again, and assured me that I had spoiled her life. I am bound to state that she ate an enormous dinner, so I did not feel any anxiety. But what a lack of taste she showed! The one charm of the past is that it is the past. But women never know when the curtain has fallen. They always want a sixth act, and as soon as the interest of the play is entirely over they propose to continue it. If they were allowed to have their way, every comedy would have a tragic ending, and every tragedy would culminate in a farce. They are charmingly artificial, but they have no

sense of art. You are more fortunate than I am. I assure you, Dorian,
that not one of the women I have known would have done for me
what Sibyl Vane did for you. Ordinary women always console themselves. Some of them do it by going in for sentimental colors. Never
trust a woman who wears mauve, whatever her age may be, or a
woman over thirty-five who is fond of pink ribbons. It always means
that they have a history. Others find a great consolation in suddenly
discovering the good qualities of their husbands. They flaunt their
conjugal felicity in one's face, as if it was the most fascinating sins.
Religion consoles some. Its mysteries have all the charm of a flirtation, a woman once told me; and I can quite understand it. Besides,
nothing makes one so vain as being told that one is a sinner. There
is really no end to the consolations that women find in modern life.
Indeed, I have not mentioned the most important one of all."

"What is that, Harry?" said Dorian Gray, listlessly.

"Oh, the obvious one. Taking some one else's admirer when one
loses one's own. In good society that always whitewashes a woman.
But really, Dorian, how different Sibyl Vane must have been from
all the women one meets! There is something to me quite beautiful
about her death. I am glad I am living in a century when such wonders happen. They make one believe in the reality of the things that
shallow, fashionable people play with, such as romance, passion, and
love."

"I was terribly cruel to her. You forget that."

"I believe that women appreciate cruelty more than anything else.
They have wonderfully primitive instincts. We have emancipated
them, but they remain slaves looking for their masters, all the
same. They love being dominated. I am sure you were splendid. I
have never seen you angry, but I can fancy how delightful you
looked. And, after all, you said something to me the day before yesterday that seemed to me at the time to be merely fanciful, but that
I see now was absolutely true, and it explains everything."

"What was that, Harry?"

"You said to me that Sibyl Vane represented to you all the heroines of romance—that she was Desdemona one night, and Ophelia
the other; that if she died as Juliet, she came to life as Imogen."

"She will never come to life again now," murmured the lad, burying his face in his hands.

"No, she will never come to life. She has played her last part. But
you must think of that lonely death in the tawdry dressing-room simply as a strange lurid fragment from some Jacobean tragedy, as a
wonderful scene from Webster, or Ford, or Cyril Tourneur. The girl
never really lived, and so she has never really died. To you at least
she was always a dream, a phantom that flitted through Shakespeare's plays and left them lovelier for its presence, a reed through

which Shakespeare's music sounded richer and more full of joy. The
moment she touched actual life, she marred it, and it marred her,
and so she passed away. Mourn for Ophelia, if you like. Put ashes
on your head because Cordelia was strangled. Cry out against
Heaven because the daughter of Brabantio died. But don't waste
your tears over Sibyl Vane. She was less real than they are."

There was a silence. The evening darkened in the room. Noiselessly, and with silver feet, the shadows crept in from the garden.
The colors faded wearily out of things.

After some time Dorian Gray looked up. "You have explained me
to myself, Harry," he murmured, with something of a sigh of relief.
"I felt all that you have said, but somehow I was afraid of it, and I
could not express it to myself. How well you know me! But we will
not talk again of what has happened. It has been a marvellous experience. That is all. I wonder if life has still in store for me anything
as marvellous."

"Life has everything in store for you, Dorian. There is nothing
that you, with your extraordinary good looks, will not be able to do."

"But suppose, Harry, I became haggard, and gray, and wrinkled?
What then?"

"Ah, then," said Lord Henry, rising to go,—"then, my dear Dorian,
you would have to fight for your victories. As it is, they are brought
to you. No, you must keep your good looks. We live in an age that
reads too much to be wise, and that thinks too much to be beautiful. We cannot spare you. And now you had better dress, and drive
down to the club. We are rather late, as it is."

"I think I shall join you at the Opera, Harry. I feel too tired to eat
anything. What is the number of your sister's box?"

"Twenty-seven, I believe. It is on the grand tier. You will see her
name on the door. But I am sorry you won't come and dine."

"I don't feel up to it," said Dorian, wearily. "But I am awfully
obliged to you for all that you have said to me. You are certainly my
best friend. No one has ever understood me as you have."

"We are only at the beginning of our friendship, Dorian," answered
Lord Henry, shaking him by the hand. "Good-by. I shall see you
before nine-thirty, I hope. Remember, Patti is singing."

As he closed the door behind him, Dorian Gray touched the bell,
and in a few minutes Victor appeared with the lamps and drew the
blinds down. He waited impatiently for him to go. The man seemed
to take an interminable time about everything.

As soon as he had left, he rushed to the screen, and drew it back.
No; there was no further change in the picture. It had received the
news of Sibyl Vane's death before he had known of it himself. It was
conscious of the events of life as they occurred. The vicious cruelty
that marred the fine lines of the mouth had, no doubt, appeared at

the very moment that the girl had drunk the poison, whatever it was. Or was it indifferent to results? Did it merely take cognizance of what passed within the soul? he wondered, and hoped that some day he would see the change taking place before his very eyes, shuddering as he hoped it.

Poor Sibyl! what a romance it had all been! She had often mimicked death on the stage, and at last Death himself had touched her, and brought her with him. How had she played that dreadful scene? Had she cursed him, as she died? No; she had died for love of him, and love would always be a sacrament to him now. She had atoned for everything, by the sacrifice she had made of her life. He would not think any more of what she had made him go through, that horrible night at the theatre. When he thought of her, it would be as a wonderful tragic figure to show Love had been a great reality. A wonderful tragic figure? Tears came to his eyes as he remembered her child-like look and winsome fanciful ways and shy tremulous grace. He wiped them away hastily, and looked again at the picture.[9]

He felt that the time had really come for making his choice. Or had his choice already been made? Yes, life had decided that for him,—life, and his own infinite curiosity about life. Eternal youth, infinite passion, pleasures subtle and secret, wild joys and wilder sins,—he was to have all these things. The portrait was to bear the burden of his shame: that was all.

A feeling of pain came over him as he thought of the desecration that was in store for the fair face on the canvas. Once, in boyish mockery of Narcissus, he had kissed, or feigned to kiss, those painted lips that now smiled so cruelly at him. Morning after morning he had sat before the portrait wondering at its beauty, almost enamoured of it, as it seemed to him at times. Was it to alter now with every mood to which he yielded? Was it to become a hideous and loathsome thing, to be hidden away in a locked room, to be shut out from the sunlight that had so often touched to brighter gold the waving wonder of the hair? The pity of it! the pity of it!

For a moment he thought of praying that the horrible sympathy that existed between him and the picture might cease. It had changed in answer to a prayer; perhaps in answer to a prayer it might remain unchanged. And, yet, who, that knew anything about Life, would surrender the chance of remaining always young, however fantastic that chance might be, or with what fateful consequences it might be fraught? Besides, was it really under his control? Had it indeed been prayer that had produced the substitution? Might there not be some curious scientific reason for it all? If thought could exercise its influence upon a living organism, might

9. This paragraph added in TS.

not thought exercise an influence upon dead and inorganic things? Nay, without thought or conscious desire, might not things external to ourselves vibrate in unison with our moods and passions, atom calling to atom, in secret love or strange affinity? But the reason was of no importance. He would never again tempt by a prayer any terrible power. If the picture was to alter, it was to alter. That was all. Why inquire too closely into it?[1]

For there would be a real pleasure in watching it. He would be able to follow his mind into its secret places. This portrait would be to him the most magical of mirrors. As it had revealed to him his own body, so it would reveal to him his own soul. And when winter came upon it, he would still be standing where spring trembles on the verge of summer. When the blood crept from its face, and left behind a pallid mask of chalk with leaden eyes, he would keep the glamour of boyhood. Not one blossom of his loveliness would ever fade. Not one pulse of his life would ever weaken. Like the gods of the Greeks, he would be strong, and fleet, and joyous. What did it matter what happened to the colored image on the canvas? He would be safe. That was everything.

He drew the screen back into its former place in front of the picture, smiling as he did so, and passed into his bedroom, where his valet was already waiting for him. An hour later he was at the Opera, and Lord Henry was leaning over his chair.

Chapter VII

As he was sitting at breakfast next morning, Basil Hallward was shown into the room.

"I am so glad I have found you, Dorian," he said, gravely. "I called last night, and they told me you were at the Opera. Of course I knew that was impossible. But I wish you had left word where you had really gone to. I passed a dreadful evening, half afraid that one tragedy might be followed by another. I think you might have telegraphed for me when you heard of it first. I read of it quite by chance in a late edition of the *Globe*, that I picked up at the club. I came here at once, and was miserable at not finding you. I can't tell you how heart-broken I am about the whole thing. I know what you must suffer. But where were you? Did you go down and see the girl's mother? For a moment I thought of following you there. They gave the address in the paper. Somewhere in the Euston Road, isn't it? But I was afraid of intruding upon a sorrow that I could not lighten.

---

1. This paragraph added in TS.

Poor woman! What a state she must be in! And her only child, too![1] What did she say about it all?"

"My dear Basil, how do I know?" murmured Dorian, sipping some pale-yellow wine from a delicate gold-beaded bubble of Venetian glass, and looking dreadfully bored. "I was at the Opera. You should have come on there. I met Lady Gwendolen, Harry's sister, for the first time. We were in her box. She is perfectly charming; and Patti sang divinely. Don't talk about horrid subjects. If one doesn't talk about a thing, it has never happened. It is simply expression, as Harry says, that gives reality to things. Tell me about yourself and what you are painting."

"You went to the Opera?" said Hallward, speaking very slowly, and with a strained touch of pain in his voice. "You went to the Opera while Sibyl Vane was lying dead in some sordid lodging? You can talk to me of other women being charming, and of Patti singing divinely, before the girl you loved has even the quiet of a grave to sleep in? Why, man, there are horrors in store for that little white body of hers!"

"Stop, Basil! I won't hear it!" cried Dorian, leaping to his feet. "You must not tell me about things. What is done is done. What is past is past."

"You call yesterday the past?"

"What has the actual lapse of time got to do with it? It is only shallow people who require years to get rid of an emotion. A man who is master of himself can end a sorrow as easily as he can invent a pleasure. I don't want to be at the mercy of my emotions. I want to use them, to enjoy them, and to dominate them."

"Dorian, this is horrible! Something has changed you completely. You look exactly the same wonderful boy who used to come down to my studio, day after day, to sit for his picture. But you were simple, natural, and affectionate then. You were the most unspoiled creature in the whole world. Now, I don't know what has come over you. You talk as if you had no heart, no pity in you. It is all Harry's influence. I see that."

The lad flushed up, and, going to the window, looked out on the green, flickering garden for a few moments. "I owe a great deal to Harry, Basil," he said, at last,—"more than I owe to you. You only taught me to be vain."

"Well, I am punished for that, Dorian,—or shall be some day."

"I don't know what you mean, Basil," he exclaimed, turning round. "I don't know what you want. What do you want?"

"I want the Dorian Gray I used to know."

---

1. Wilde let this stand in 1891, but added Dorian's reply below that Sibyl had a brother (an invention of the revised edition; see p. 90).

"Basil," said the lad, going over to him, and putting his hand on his shoulder, "you have come too late. Yesterday when I heard that Sibyl Vane had killed herself—"

"Killed herself! Good heavens! is there no doubt about that?" cried Hallward, looking up at him with an expression of horror.

"My dear Basil! Surely you don't think it was a vulgar accident? Of course she killed herself.[2] It is one of the great romantic tragedies of the age. As a rule, people who act lead the most commonplace lives. They are good husbands, or faithful wives, or something tedious. You know what I mean,—middle-class virtue, and all that kind of thing. How different Sibyl was! She lived her finest tragedy. She was always a heroine. The last night she played—the night you saw her—she acted badly because she had known the reality of love. When she knew its unreality, she died, as Juliet might have died. She passed again into the sphere of art. There is something of the martyr about her. Her death has all the pathetic uselessness of martyrdom, all its wasted beauty. But, as I was saying, you must not think I have not suffered. If you had come in yesterday at a particular moment,—about half-past five, perhaps, or a quarter to six,—you would have found me in tears. Even Harry, who was here, who brought me the news, in fact, had no idea what I was going through. I suffered immensely, then it passed away. I cannot repeat an emotion. No one can, except sentimentalists. And you are awfully unjust, Basil. You come down here to console me. That is charming of you. You find me consoled, and you are furious. How like a sympathetic person! You remind me of a story Harry told me about a certain philanthropist who spent twenty years of his life in trying to get some grievance redressed, or some unjust law altered,—I forget exactly what it was. Finally he succeeded, and nothing could exceed his disappointment. He had absolutely nothing to do, almost died of *ennui*, and became a confirmed misanthrope. And besides, my dear old Basil, if you really want to console me, teach me rather to forget what has happened, or to see it from a proper artistic point of view. Was it not Gautier who used to write about *la consolation des arts*? I remember picking up a little vellum-covered book in your studio one day and chancing on that delightful phrase. Well, I am not like that young man you told me of when we were down at Marlowe together, the young man who used to say that yellow satin could console one for all the miseries of life. I love beautiful things that one can touch and handle. Old brocades, green bronzes, lacquer-work, carved ivories, exquisite surroundings, luxury, pomp,—there is much to be got from all these. But the artistic temperament that they create, or at any rate reveal, is still more to me. To become the

---

2. Wilde added lines here in 1891.

spectator of one's own life, as Harry says, is to escape the suffering of life. I know you are surprised at my talking to you like this. You have not realized how I have developed. I was a school-boy when you knew me. I am a man now. I have new passions, new thoughts, new ideas. I am different, but you must not like me less. I am changed, but you must always be my friend. Of course I am very fond of Harry. But I know that you are better than he is. You are not stronger,—you are too much afraid of life,—but you are better. And how happy we used to be together! Don't leave me, Basil, and don't quarrel with me. I am what I am. There is nothing more to be said."

Hallward felt strangely moved. Rugged and straightforward as he was, there was something in his nature that was purely feminine in its tenderness.[3] The lad was infinitely dear to him, and his personality had been the great turning-point in his art. He could not bear the idea of reproaching him any more. After all, his indifference was probably merely a mood that would pass away. There was so much in him that was good, so much in him that was noble.

"Well, Dorian," he said, at length, with a sad smile, "I won't speak to you again about this horrible thing, after to-day. I only trust your name won't be mentioned in connection with it. The inquest is to take place this afternoon. Have they summoned you?"

Dorian shook his head, and a look of annoyance passed over his face at the mention of the word "inquest." There was something so crude and vulgar about everything of the kind. "They don't know my name," he answered.

"But surely she did?"

"Only my Christian name, and that I am quite sure she never mentioned to any one. She told me once that they were all rather curious to learn who I was, and that she invariably told them my name was Prince Charming. It was pretty of her. You must do me a drawing of her, Basil. I should like to have something more of her than the memory of a few kisses and some broken pathetic words."

"I will try and do something, Dorian, if it would please you. But you must come and sit to me yourself again. I can't get on without you."

"I will never sit to you again, Basil. It is impossible!" he exclaimed, starting back.

Hallward stared at him, "My dear boy, what nonsense!" he cried. "Do you mean to say you don't like what I did of you? Where is it? Why have you pulled the screen in front of it? Let me look at it. It is the best thing I have ever painted. Do take that screen away, Dorian. It is simply horrid of your servant hiding my work like that. I felt the room looked different as I came in."

3. This sentence deleted in 1891.

"My servant has nothing to do with it, Basil. You don't imagine I let him arrange my room for me? He settles my flowers for me sometimes,—that is all. No; I did it myself. The light was too strong on the portrait."

"Too strong! Impossible, my dear fellow! It is an admirable place for it. Let me see it." And Hallward walked towards the corner of the room.

A cry of terror broke from Dorian Gray's lips, and he rushed between Hallward and the screen. "Basil," he said, looking very pale, "you must not look at it. I don't wish you to."

"Not look at my own work! you are not serious. Why shouldn't I look at it?" exclaimed Hallward, laughing.

"If you try to look at it, Basil, on my word of honor I will never speak to you again as long as I live. I am quite serious. I don't offer any explanation, and you are not to ask for any. But, remember, if you touch this screen, everything is over between us."

Hallward was thunderstruck. He looked at Dorian Gray in absolute amazement. He had never seen him like this before. The lad was absolutely pallid with rage. His hands were clinched, and the pupils of his eyes were like disks of blue fire. He was trembling all over.

"Dorian!"

"Don't speak!"

"But what is the matter? Of course I won't look at it if you don't want me to," he said, rather coldly, turning on his heel, and going over towards the window. "But, really, it seems rather absurd that I shouldn't see my own work, especially as I am going to exhibit it in Paris in the autumn. I shall probably have to give it another coat of varnish before that, so I must see it some day, and why not to-day?"

"To exhibit it! You want to exhibit it?" exclaimed Dorian Gray, a strange sense of terror creeping over him. Was the world going to be shown his secret? Were people to gape at the mystery of his life? That was impossible. Something—he did not know what—had to be done at once.

"Yes: I don't suppose you will object to that. Georges Petit is going to collect all my best pictures for a special exhibition in the Rue de Sèze, which will open the first week in October. The portrait will only be away a month. I should think you could easily spare it for that time. In fact, you are sure to be out of town. And if you hide it always behind a screen, you can't care much about it."

Dorian Gray passed his hand over his forehead. There were beads of perspiration there. He felt that he was on the brink of a horrible danger. "You told me a month ago that you would never exhibit it," he said. "Why have you changed your mind? You people who go in for being consistent have just as many moods as others. The only

difference is that your moods are rather meaningless. You can't have
forgotten that you assured me most solemnly that nothing in the
world would induce you to send it to any exhibition. You told Harry
exactly the same thing." He stopped suddenly, and a gleam of light
came into his eyes. He remembered that Lord Henry had said to him
once, half seriously and half in jest, "If you want to have an interesting quarter of an hour, get Basil to tell you why he won't exhibit
your picture. He told me why he wouldn't, and it was a revelation to
me." Yes, perhaps Basil, too, had his secret. He would ask him and
try.

"Basil," he said, coming over quite close, and looking him straight
in the face, "we have each of us a secret. Let me know yours, and I
will tell you mine. What was your reason for refusing to exhibit my
picture?"

Hallward shuddered in spite of himself. "Dorian, if I told you, you
might like me less than you do, and you would certainly laugh at
me. I could not bear your doing either of those two things. If you
wish me never to look at your picture again, I am content. I have
always you to look at. If you wish the best work I have ever done to
be hidden from the world, I am satisfied. Your friendship is dearer
to me than any fame or reputation."

"No, Basil, you must tell me," murmured Dorian Gray. "I think I
have a right to know." His feeling of terror had passed away, and curiosity had taken its place. He was determined to find out Basil Hallward's mystery.

"Let us sit down, Dorian," said Hallward, looking pale and pained.
"Let us sit down. I will sit in the shadow, and you shall sit in the
sunlight. Our lives are like that. Just answer me one question. Have
you noticed in the picture something that you did not like?—
something that probably at first did not strike you, but that revealed
itself to you suddenly?"[4]

"Basil!" cried the lad, clutching the arms of his chair with trembling hands, and gazing at him with wild, startled eyes.

"I see you did. Don't speak. Wait till you hear what I have to say.
It is quite true that I have worshipped you with far more romance
of feeling than a man usually[5] gives to a friend. Somehow, I had
never loved a woman. I suppose I never had time. Perhaps, as Harry
says, a really *grande passion* is the privilege of those who have
nothing to do, and that is the use of the idle classes in a country.
Well, from the moment I met you, your personality had the most
extraordinary influence over me. I quite admit that I adored you

4. Wilde deleted the following in MS: "Something that filled you perhaps with a sense of
shame?" He made further alterations in 1891.
5. Stoddart changed Wilde's "should ever give" to this reading in TS.

madly, extravagantly, absurdly. I was jealous of every one to whom you spoke. I wanted to have you all to myself. I was only happy when I was with you. When I was away from you, you were still present in my art. It was all wrong and foolish. It is all wrong and foolish still. Of course I never let you know anything about this. It would have been impossible. You would not have understood it; I did not understand it myself. One day I determined to paint a wonderful portrait of you. It was to have been my masterpiece. It is my masterpiece. But, as I worked at it, every flake and film of color seemed to me to reveal my secret.[6] I grew afraid that the world would know of my idolatry. I felt, Dorian, that I had told too much. Then it was that I resolved never to allow the picture to be exhibited. You were a little annoyed; but then you did not realize all that it meant to me. Harry, to whom I talked about it, laughed at me. But I did not mind that. When the picture was finished, and I sat alone with it, I felt that I was right. Well, after a few days the portrait left my studio, and as soon as I had got rid of the intolerable fascination of its presence it seemed to me that I had been foolish in imagining that I had said anything in it, more than that you were extremely good-looking and that I could paint. Even now I cannot help feeling that it is a mistake to think that the passion one feels in creation is ever really shown in the work one creates. Art is more abstract than we fancy. From and color tell us of form and color—that is all. It often seems to me that art conceals the artist far more completely than it ever reveals him. And so when I got this offer from Paris I determined to make your portrait the principal thing in my exhibition. It never occurred to me that you would refuse. I see now that you were right. The picture must not be shown. You must not be angry with me, Dorian, for what I have told you. As I said to Harry, once, you are made to be worshipped."[7]

Dorian Gray drew a long breath. The color came back to his cheeks, and a smile played about his lips. The peril was over. He was safe for the time. Yet he could not help feeling infinite pity for the young man who had just made this strange confession to him. He wondered if he would ever be so dominated by the personality of a friend. Lord Harry had the charm of being very dangerous. But that was all.[8] He was too clever and too cynical to be really fond of. Would there ever be some one who would fill him with a strange idolatry? Was that one of the things that life had in store?

---

6. Stoddart canceled the following in TS: "There was love in every line, and in every touch there was passion."
7. Wilde made extensive revisions to this paragraph in 1891, deleting two passages.
8. Wilde canceled "He felt no romance for him" in TS.

"It is extraordinary to me, Dorian," said Hallward, "that you should have seen this in the picture.[9] Did you really see it?"

"Of course I did."

"Well, you don't mind my looking at it now?"

Dorian shook his head. "You must not ask me that, Basil. I could not possibly let you stand in front of that picture."

"You will some day, surely?"

"Never."

"Well, perhaps you are right. And now good-by, Dorian. You have been the one person in my life of whom I have been really fond.[1] I don't suppose I shall often see you again. You don't know what it cost me to tell you all that I have told you."

"My dear Basil," cried Dorian, "what have you told me? Simply that you felt that you liked me too much. That is not even a compliment."

"It was not intended as a compliment. It was a confession."

"A very disappointing one."

"Why, what did you expect, Dorian? You didn't see anything else in the picture, did you? There was nothing else to see?"

"No: there was nothing else to see. Why do you ask? But you mustn't talk about not meeting me again, or anything of that kind. You and I are friends, Basil, and we must always remain so."

"You have got Harry," said Hallward, sadly.

"Oh, Harry!" cried the lad, with a ripple of laughter. "Harry spends his days in saying what is incredible, and his evenings in doing what is improbable. Just the sort of life I would like to lead. But still I don't think I would go to Harry if I was in trouble. I would sooner go to you, Basil."

"But you won't sit to me again?"

"Impossible!"

"You spoil my life as an artist by refusing, Dorian. No man comes across two ideal things. Few come across one."

"I can't explain it to you, Basil, but I must never sit to you again. I will come and have tea with you. That will be just as pleasant."

"Pleasanter for you, I am afraid," murmured Hallward, regretfully. "And now good-by. I am sorry you won't let me look at the picture once again. But that can't be helped. I quite understand what you feel about it."

As he left the room, Dorian Gray smiled to himself. Poor Basil! how little he knew of the true reason! And how strange it was that, instead of having been forced to reveal his own secret, he had succeeded, almost by chance, in wresting a secret from his friend! How

9. A canceled passage in MS reads "Perhaps you did not see it. But you suspected it. You were conscious of something you did not like."

1. MS originally had "whom I have loved."

much that strange confession explained to him! Basil's absurd fits
of jealousy, his wild devotion, his extravagant panegyrics, his curious reticences—he understood them all now, and he felt sorry. There
was something tragic in a friendship so colored by romance.[2]

He sighed, and touched the bell. The portrait must be hidden
away at all costs. He could not run such a risk of discovery again. It
had been mad of him to have the thing remain, even for an hour, in
a room to which any of his friends had access.

Chapter VIII

When his servant entered, he looked at him steadfastly, and wondered if he had thought of peering behind the screen. The man was
quite impassive, and waited for his orders. Dorian lit a cigarette, and
walked over to the glass and glanced into it. He could see the reflection of Victor's face perfectly. It was like a placid mask of servility.
There was nothing to be afraid of, there. Yet he thought it best to be
on his guard.

Speaking very slowly, he told him to tell the housekeeper that he
wanted to see her, and then to go to the frame-maker's and ask him
to send two of his men round at once. It seemed to him that as the
man left the room he peered in the direction of the screen. Or was
that only his fancy?[1]

After a few moments, Mrs. Leaf, a dear old lady in a black silk
dress, with a photograph of the late Mr. Leaf framed in a large gold
brooch at her neck, and old-fashioned thread mittens on her wrinkled hands, bustled into the room.

"Well, Master Dorian," she said, "what can I do for you?[2] I beg
your pardon, sir,"—here came a courtesy,—"I shouldn't call you Master Dorian any more. But, Lord bless you, sir, I have known you since
you were a baby, and many's the trick you've played on poor old Leaf.
Not that you were not always a good boy, sir; but boys will be boys,
Master Dorian, and jam is a temptation to the young, isn't it, sir?"

He laughed. "You must always call me Master Dorian, Leaf. I will
be very angry with you if you don't. And I assure you I am quite as
fond of jam now as I used to be. Only when I am asked out to tea I am
never offered any. I want you to give me the key of the room at the
top of the house."

2. Stoddart changed the original reading in TS, "something infinitely tragic in a romance
   that was at once so passionate and so sterile," to this more circumspect version.
1. Wilde added this effect in TS, which originally read "the man bowed and retired."
2. Wilde's 1891 revision all but removed the comic side of Leaf's personality found here.
   Most of her dialogue and Dorian's replies were changed in both substance and tone.
   This is the lone instance when Wilde eclipsed a character or diluted a scene in his last
   revision.

"The old school-room, Master Dorian? Why, it's full of dust. I must get it arranged and put straight before you go into it. It's not fit for you to see, Master Dorian. It is not, indeed."

"I don't want it put straight, Leaf. I only want the key."

"Well, Master Dorian, you'll be covered with cobwebs if you goes into it. Why, it hasn't been opened for nearly five years—not since his lordship died."

He winced at the mention of his dead uncle's name. He had hateful memories of him. "That does not matter, Leaf," he replied. "All I want is the key."

"And here is the key, Master Dorian," said the old lady, after going over the contents of her bunch with tremulously uncertain hands. "Here is the key. I'll have it off the ring in a moment. But you don't think of living up there, Master Dorian, and you so comfortable here?"

"No, Leaf, I don't. I merely want to see the place, and perhaps store something in it,—that is all. Thank you, Leaf. I hope your rheumatism is better; and mind you send me up jam for breakfast."

Mrs. Leaf shook her head. "Them foreigners doesn't understand jam, Master Dorian. They calls it 'compot.' But I'll bring it to you myself some morning, if you lets me."

"That will be very kind of you, Leaf," he answered, looking at the key; and, having made him an elaborate courtesy, the old lady left the room, her face wreathed in smiles. She had a strong objection to the French valet. It was a poor thing, she felt, for any one to be born a foreigner.

As the door closed, Dorian put the key in his pocket, and looked round the room. His eye fell on a large purple satin coverlet heavily embroidered with gold, a splendid piece of late seventeenth-century Venetian work that his uncle had found in a convent near Bologna. Yes, that would serve to wrap the dreadful thing in. It had perhaps served often as a pall for the dead. Now it was to hide something that had a corruption of its own, worse than the corruption of death itself,—something that would breed horrors and yet would never die. What the worm was to the corpse, his sins would be to the painted image on the canvas. They would mar its beauty, and eat away its grace. They would defile it, and make it shameful. And yet the thing would still live on. It would be always alive.

He shuddered, and for a moment he regretted that he had not told Basil the true reason why he had wished to hide the picture away. Basil would have helped him to resist Lord Henry's influence, and the still more poisonous influences that came from his own temperament. The love that he bore him—for it was really love—had something noble and intellectual in it. It was not that mere physical admiration of beauty that is born of the senses, and that dies when the senses tire.

It was such love as Michael Angelo had known, and Montaigne, and Winckelmann, and Shakespeare himself. Yes, Basil could have saved him. But it was too late now. The past could always be annihilated. Regret, denial, or forgetfulness could do that. But the future was inevitable. There were passions in him that would find their terrible outlet, dreams that would make the shadow of their evil real.

He took up from the couch the great purple-and-gold texture that covered it, and, holding it in his hands, passed behind the screen. Was the face on the canvas viler than before? It seemed to him that it was unchanged; and yet his loathing of it was intensified. Gold hair, blue eyes, and rose-red lips,—they all were there. It was simply the expression that had altered. That was horrible in its cruelty. Compared to what he saw in it of censure or rebuke, how shallow Basil's reproaches about Sibyl Vane had been!—how shallow, and of what little account! His own soul was looking out at him from the canvas and calling him to judgment. A look of pain came across him, and he flung the rich pall over the picture. As he did so, a knock came to the door. He passed out as his servant entered.

"The persons are here, monsieur."[3]

He felt that the man must be got rid of at once. He must not be allowed to know where the picture was being taken to. There was something sly about him, and he had thoughtful, treacherous eyes. Sitting down at the writing-table, he scribbled a note to Lord Henry, asking him to send him round something to read, and reminding him that they were to meet at eight-fifteen that evening.

"Wait for an answer," he said, handing it to him, "and show the men in here."

In two or three minutes there was another knock, and Mr. Ashton himself, the celebrated frame-maker of South Audley Street, came in with a somewhat rough-looking young assistant. Mr. Ashton was a florid, red-whiskered little man, whose admiration for art was considerably tempered by the inveterate impecuniosity of most of the artists who dealt with him. As a rule, he never left his shop. He waited for people to come to him. But he always made an exception in favor of Dorian Gray. There was something about Dorian that charmed everybody. It was a pleasure even to see him."

"What can I do for you, Mr. Gray?" he said, rubbing his fat freckled hands. "I thought I would do myself the honor of coming round in person. I have just got a beauty of a frame, sir. Picked it up at a sale. Old Florentine. Came from Fonthill, I believe. Admirably suited for a religious picture, Mr. Gray."

---

3. Victor originally spoke in French in MS. This was followed by Dorian's directions given in French to take a letter round to Lord Henry in Curzon Street and to ask for the "French book of which he had spoken to him."

"I am so sorry you have given yourself the trouble of coming round, Mr. Ashton. I will certainly drop in and look at the frame,— though I don't go in much for religious art,—but to-day I only want a picture carried to the top of the house for me. It is rather heavy, so I thought I would ask you to lend me a couple of your men."

"No trouble at all, Mr. Gray. I am delighted to be of any service to you. Which is the work of art, sir?"

"This," replied Dorian, moving the screen back. "Can you move it, covering and all, just as it is? I don't want it to get scratched going up-stairs."

"There will be no difficulty, sir," said the genial frame-maker, beginning, with the aid of his assistant, to unhook the picture from the long brass chains by which it was suspended. "And, now, where shall we carry it to, Mr. Gray?"

"I will show you the way, Mr. Ashton, if you will kindly follow me. Or perhaps you had better go in front. I am afraid it is right at the top of the house. We will go up by the front staircase, as it is wider."

He held the door open for them, and they passed out into the hall and began the ascent. The elaborate character of the frame had made the picture extremely bulky, and now and then, in spite of the obsequious protests of Mr. Ashton, who had a true tradesman's dislike of seeing a gentleman doing anything useful, Dorian put his hand to it so as to help them.

"Something of a load to carry, sir," gasped the little man, when they reached the top landing. And he wiped his shiny forehead.

"A terrible load to carry,"[4] murmured Dorian, as he unlocked the door that opened into the room that was to keep for him the curious secret of his life and hide his soul from the eyes of men.

He had not entered the place for more than four years,—not, indeed, since he had used it first as a play-room when he was a child and then as a study when he grew somewhat older. It was a large, well-proportioned room, which had been specially built by the last Lord Sherard for the use of the little nephew whom, being himself childless, and perhaps for other reasons, he had always hated and desired to keep at a distance. It did not appear to Dorian to have much changed. There was the huge Italian *cassone*, with its fantastically-painted panels and its tarnished gilt mouldings, in which he had so often hidden himself as a boy. There was the sat-inwood book-case filled with his dog-eared school-books. On the wall behind it was hanging the same ragged Flemish tapestry where a faded king and queen were playing chess in a garden, while a

4. Wilde changed this line three times. In TS, there was another sort of pun in Dorian's reply: "There is a good deal of heaviness in modern art." In 1891, Wilde changed it again to the deliberately prosaic "I am afraid it is rather heavy," emphasizing a different mood entirely.

company of hawkers rode by, carrying hooded birds on their gauntleted wrists. How well he recalled it all! Every moment of his lonely childhood came back to him, as he looked round. He remembered the stainless purity of his boyish life, and it seemed horrible to him that it was here that the fatal portrait was to be hidden away. How little he had thought, in those dead days, of all that was in store for him!

But there was no other place in the house so secure from prying eyes as this. He had the key, and no one else could enter it. Beneath its purple pall, the face painted on the canvas could grow bestial, sodden, and unclean. What did it matter? No one could see it. He himself would not see it. Why should he watch the hideous corruption of his soul? He kept his youth,—that was enough. And, besides, might not his nature grow finer, after all? There was no reason that the future should be so full of shame. Some love might come across his life, and purify him, and shield him from those sins that seemed to be already stirring in spirit and in flesh,—those curious unpictured sins whose very mystery lent them their subtlety and their charm. Perhaps, some day, the cruel look would have passed away from the scarlet sensitive mouth, and he might show to the world Basil Hallward's masterpiece.

No; that was impossible. The thing upon the canvas was growing old, hour by hour, and week by week. Even if it escaped the hideousness of sin, the hideousness of age was in store for it. The cheeks would become hollow or flaccid. Yellow crow's-feet would creep round the fading eyes and make them horrible. The hair would lose its brightness, the mouth would gape or droop, would be foolish or gross, as the mouths of old men are. There would be the wrinkled throat, the cold blue-veined hands, the twisted body, that he remembered in the uncle who had been so stern to him in his boyhood. The picture had to be concealed. There was no help for it.

"Bring it in, Mr. Ashton, please," he said, wearily, turning round. "I am sorry I kept you so long. I was thinking of something else."

"Always glad to have a rest, Mr. Gray," answered the frame-maker, who was still gasping for breath. "Where shall we put it, sir?"

"Oh, anywhere, Here, this will do. I don't want to have it hung up. Just lean it against the wall. Thanks."

"Might one look at the work of art, sir?"

Dorian started. "It would not interest you, Mr. Ashton," he said, keeping his eye on the man. He felt ready to leap upon him and fling him to the ground if he dared to lift the gorgeous hanging that concealed the secret of his life. "I won't trouble you any more now. I am much obliged for your kindness in coming round."

"Not at all, not at all, Mr. Gray. Ever ready to do anything for you, sir." And Mr. Ashton tramped down-stairs, followed by the assistant, who glanced back at Dorian with a look of shy wonder in his rough, uncomely face. He had never seen any one so marvellous.

When the sound of their footsteps had died away, Dorian locked the door, and put the key in his pocket. He felt safe now. No one would ever look on the horrible thing. No eye but his would ever see his shame.

On reaching the library he found that it was just after five o'clock, and that the tea had been already brought up. On a little table of dark perfumed wood thickly incrusted with nacre, a present from his guardian's wife, Lady Radley, who had spent the preceding winter in Cairo, was lying a note from Lord Henry, and beside it was a book bound in yellow paper, the cover slightly torn and the edges soiled. A copy of the third edition of the *St. James's Gazette* had been placed on the tea-tray. It was evident that Victor had returned. He wondered if he had met the men in the hall as they were leaving the house and had wormed out of them what they had been doing. He would be sure to miss the picture,—had no doubt missed it already, while he had been laying the tea-things. The screen had not been replaced, and the blank space on the wall was visible. Perhaps some night he might find him creeping up-stairs and trying to force the door of the room. It was a horrible thing to have a spy in one's house. He had heard of rich men who had been blackmailed all their lives by some servant who had read a letter, or overheard a conversation, or picked up a card with an address, or found beneath a pillow a withered flower or a bit of crumpled lace.

He sighed, and, having poured himself out some tea, opened Lord Henry's note. It was simply to say that he sent him round the evening paper, and a book that might interest him, and that he would be at the club at eight-fifteen. He opened the *St. James's* languidly, and looked through it. A red pencil-mark on the fifth page caught his eye. He read the following paragraph:

> "INQUEST ON AN ACTRESS.—An inquest was held this morning at the Bell Tavern, Hoxton Road, by Mr. Danby, the District Coroner, on the body of Sibyl Vane, a young actress recently engaged at the Royal Theatre, Holborn. A verdict of death by misadventure was returned. Considerable sympathy was expressed for the mother of the deceased, who was greatly affected during the giving of her own evidence, and that of Dr. Birrell, who had made the post-mortem examination of the deceased."

He frowned slightly, and, tearing the paper in two, went across the room and flung the pieces into a gilt basket.[5] How ugly it all was! And how horribly real ugliness made things! He felt a little annoyed

5. Wilde reduced this to "flung away" in 1891.

with Lord Henry for having sent him the account. And it was certainly stupid of him to have marked it with red pencil. Victor might have read it. The man knew more than enough English for that.[6]

Perhaps he had read it, and had begun to suspect something. And, yet, what did it matter? What had Dorian Gray to do with Sibyl Vane's death? There was nothing to fear. Dorian Gray had not killed her.

His eye fell on the yellow book that Lord Henry had sent him. What was it, he wondered. He went towards the little pearl-colored octagonal stand, that had always looked to him like the work of some strange Egyptian bees who wrought in silver, and took the volume up.[7] He flung himself into an arm-chair, and began to turn over the leaves. After a few minutes, he became absorbed. It was the strangest book he had ever read. It seemed to him that in exquisite raiment, and to the delicate sound of flutes, the sins of the world were passing in dumb show before him. Things that he had dimly dreamed of were suddenly made real to him. Things of which he had never dreamed were gradually revealed.

It was a novel without a plot, and with only one character, being, indeed, simply a psychological study of a certain young Parisian, who spent his life trying to realize in the nineteenth century all the passions and modes of thought that belonged to every century except his own, and to sum up, as it were, in himself the various moods through which the world-spirit had ever passed, loving for their mere artificiality those renunciations that men have unwisely called virtue, as much as those natural rebellions that wise men still call sin. The style in which it was written was that curious jewelled style, vivid and obscure at once, full of *argot* and of archaisms, of technical expressions and of elaborate paraphrases, that characterizes the work of some of the finest artists of the French school of *Décadents*.[8] There were in it metaphors as monstrous as orchids, and as evil in color. The life of the senses was described in the terms of mystical philosophy. One hardly knew at times whether one

---

6. A vestige of Jacques, the French valet, in MS.
7. Stoddart canceled the following here: "*Le Secret de Raoul* par Catulle Sarrazin. What a curious title." All subsequent references to the title of the notorious yellow book were also removed by Stoddart. The author and title are fictitious, although Wilde knew a Gabriel Sarrazin, a French writer who reviewed for Wilde's *Woman's World* magazine. The title may have suggested to Stoddart the scandalous French novel by Rachilde (Marguerite Vallette), *Monsieur Venus* (1889), in which there is a character M. Raoule de Vénérande. The fictitious title may have had its origin in a letter Wilde sent to Robert Ross in July 1889, following publication of "The Portrait of Mr. W. H." in *Blackwood's*: "Now that Willie Hughes has been revealed to the world, we must have another secret" (*Letters* 247). That is the kind of inside joke Wilde enjoyed playing in his fiction for the benefit of friends. Willie Hughes is the hypothetical original of the "Mr. W. H." to whom Shakespeare dedicated his sonnets.
8. Wilde added "full of *argot* . . . elaborate paraphrases" and "the work . . . artists of" in TS. *Décadents* was changed to *Symbolistes* in 1891.

was reading the spiritual ecstasies of some mediæval saint or the morbid confessions of a modern sinner. It was a poisonous book. The heavy odor of incense seemed to cling about its pages and to trouble the brain. The mere cadence of the sentences, the subtle monotony of their music, so full as it was of complex refrains and movements elaborately repeated, produced in the mind of the lad, as he passed from chapter to chapter, a form of revery, a malady of dreaming, that made him unconscious of the falling day and the creeping shadows.

Cloudless, and pierced by one solitary star, a copper-green sky gleamed through the windows. He read on by its wan light till he could read no more. Then, after his valet had reminded him several times of the lateness of the hour, he got up, and, going into the next room, placed the book on the little Florentine table that always stood at his bedside, and began to dress for dinner.

It was almost nine o'clock before he reached the club, where he found Lord Henry sitting alone, in the morning-room, looking very bored.

"I am so sorry, Harry," he cried, "but really it is entirely your fault. That book you sent me so fascinated me that I forgot what the time was."

"I thought you would like it," replied his host, rising from his chair.

"I didn't say I liked it, Harry. I said it fascinated me. There is a great difference."

"Ah, if you have discovered that, you have discovered a great deal," murmured Lord Henry, with his curious smile. "Come, let us go in to dinner. It is dreadfully late, and I am afraid the champagne will be too much iced."[9]

Chapter IX

For years, Dorian Gray could not free himself from the memory of this book. Or perhaps it would be more accurate to say that he never sought to free himself from it. He procured from Paris no less than five large-paper copies of the first edition, and had them bound in different colors, so that they might suit his various moods and the changing fancies of a nature over which he seemed, at times, to have almost entirely lost control. The hero, the wonderful young Parisian, in whom the romantic temperament and the scientific temperament were so strangely blended, became to him a kind of prefiguring type of himself. And, indeed, the whole book seemed to him to contain the story of his own life, written before he had lived it.

9. Wilde shortened and simplified the last paragraph in 1891, changing its focus.

In one point he was more fortunate than the book's[1] fantastic hero. He never knew—never, indeed, had any cause to know—that some-what grotesque dread of mirrors, and polished metal surfaces, and still water, which came upon the young Parisian[2] so early in his life, and was occasioned by the sudden decay of a beauty that had once, apparently, been so remarkable. It was with an almost cruel joy—and perhaps in nearly every joy, as certainly in every pleasure, cruelty has its place—that he used to read the latter part[3] of the book, with its really tragic, if somewhat over-emphasized, account of the sorrow and despair of one who had himself lost what in others, and in the world, he had most valued.

He, at any rate, had no cause to fear that. The boyish beauty that had so fascinated Basil Hallward, and many others besides him, seemed never to leave him. Even those who had heard the most evil things against him (and from time to time strange rumors about his mode of life crept through London and became the chatter of the clubs) could not believe anything to his dishonor when they saw him. He had always the look of one who had kept himself unspotted from the world. Men who talked grossly became silent when Dorian Gray entered the room. There was something in the purity of his face that rebuked them. His mere presence seemed to recall to them the innocence that they had tarnished. They wondered how one so charming and graceful as he was could have escaped the stain of an age that was at once sordid and sensuous.

He himself, on returning home from one of those mysterious and prolonged absences that gave rise to such strange conjecture among those who were his friends, or thought that they were so, would creep up-stairs to the locked room, open the door with the key that never left him, and stand, with a mirror, in front of the portrait that Basil Hallward had painted of him, looking now at the evil and aging face on the canvas, and now at the fair young face that laughed back at him from the polished glass. The very sharpness of the contrast used to quicken his sense of pleasure. He grew more and more enamoured of his own beauty, more and more interested in the corruption of his own soul. He would examine with minute care, and often with a monstrous and terrible delight, the hideous lines that seared the wrinkling forehead or crawled around the heavy sensual mouth, wondering sometimes which were the more horrible, the signs of sin or the signs of age. He would place his white hands beside the

---

1. Stoddart changed from "Catulle Sarrazin's."
2. Stoddart's substitute for Wilde's "Raoul."
3. Canceled in MS: "twelfth and thirteenth chapters." No parallels seem to exist in these and other allusions between the contents of the yellow book and either *À Rebours* or *Monsieur Venus* except for similarities in tone, general subject matter, and angle of treatment.

coarse bloated hands of the picture, and smile. He mocked the misshapen body and the failing limbs.

There were moments, indeed, at night, when, lying sleepless in his own delicately-scented chamber, or in the sordid room of the little ill-famed tavern near the Docks, which, under an assumed name, and in disguise, it was his habit to frequent, he would think of the ruin he had brought upon his soul, with a pity that was all the more poignant because it was purely selfish. But moments such as these were rare. That curiosity about life that, many years before, Lord Henry had first stirred in him, as they sat together in the garden of their friend, seemed to increase with gratification. The more he knew, the more he desired to know. He had mad hungers that grew more ravenous as he fed them.

Yet he was not really reckless, at any rate in his relations to society. Once or twice every month during the winter, and on each Wednesday evening while the season lasted, he would throw open to the world his beautiful house and have the most celebrated musicians of the day to charm his guests with the wonders of their art. His little dinners, in the settling of which Lord Henry always assisted him, were noted as much for the careful selection and placing of those invited, as for the exquisite taste shown in the decoration of the table, with its subtle symphonic arrangements of exotic flowers, and embroidered cloths, and antique plate of gold and silver. Indeed, there were many, especially among the very young men, who saw, or fancied that they saw, in Dorian Gray the true realization of a type of which they had often dreamed in Eton or Oxford days, a type that was to combine something of the real culture of the scholar with all the grace and distinction and perfect manner of a citizen of the world. To them he seemed to belong to those whom Dante describes as having sought to "make themselves perfect by the worship of beauty." Like Gautier, he was one for whom "the visible world existed."

And, certainly, to him life itself was the first, the greatest, of the arts, and for it all the other arts seemed to be but a preparation. Fashion, by which what is really fantastic becomes for a moment universal, and Dandyism, which, in its own way, is an attempt to assert the absolute modernity of beauty, had, of course, their fascination for him. His mode of dressing, and the particular styles that he affected from time to time, had their marked influence on the young exquisites of the Mayfair balls and Pall Mall club windows, who copied him in everything that he did, and tried to reproduce the accidental charm of his graceful, though to him only half-serious, fopperies.

For, while he was but too ready to accept the position that was almost immediately offered to him on his coming of age, and found, indeed, a subtle pleasure in the thought that he might really become to the London of his own day what to imperial Neronian Rome the author of the "Satyricon" had once been, yet in his inmost heart he desired to be something more than a mere *arbiter elegantiarum*, to be consulted on the wearing of a jewel, or the knotting of a necktie, or the conduct of a cane. He sought to elaborate some new scheme of life that would have its reasoned philosophy and its ordered principles and find in the spiritualizing of the senses its highest realization.

The worship of the senses has often, and with much justice, been decried, men feeling a natural instinct of terror about passions and sensations that seem stronger than ourselves, and that we are conscious of sharing with the less highly organized forms of existence. But it appeared to Dorian Gray that the true nature of the senses had never been understood, and that they had remained savage and animal merely because the world had sought to starve them into submission or to kill them by pain, instead of aiming at making them elements of a new spirituality, of which a fine instinct for beauty was to be the dominant characteristic. As he looked back upon man moving through History, he was haunted by a feeling of loss. So much had been surrendered! and to such little purpose! There had been mad wilful rejections, monstrous forms of self-torture and self-denial, whose origin was fear, and whose result was a degradation infinitely more terrible than that fancied degradation from which, in their ignorance, they had sought to escape, Nature in her wonderful irony driving the anchorite out to herd with the wild animals of the desert and giving to the hermit the beasts of the field as his companions.

Yes, there was to be, as Lord Henry had prophesied, a new hedonism that was to re-create life, and to save it from that harsh, uncomely puritanism that is having, in our own day, its curious revival. It was to have its service of the intellect, certainly; yet it was never to accept any theory or system that would involve the sacrifice of any mode of passionate experience. Its aim, indeed, was to be experience itself, and not the fruits of experience, sweet or bitter as they might be. Of the asceticism that deadens the senses, as of the vulgar profligacy that dulls them, it was to know nothing. But it was to teach man to concentrate himself upon the moments of a life that is itself but a moment.

There are few of us who have not sometimes wakened before dawn, either after one of those dreamless nights that make one almost enamoured of death, or one of those nights of horror and misshapen joy, when through the chambers of the brain sweep phantoms more terrible than reality itself, and instinct with that vivid life that lurks in all grotesques, and that lends to Gothic art its enduring vitality, this art being, one might fancy, especially the art of those whose minds have been troubled with the malady of revery. Gradually white fingers creep through the curtains, and they appear to tremble. Black fantastic shadows crawl into the corners of the room, and crouch there. Outside, there is the stirring of birds among the leaves, or the sound of men going forth to their work, or the sigh and sob of the wind coming down from the hills, and wandering round the silent house, as though it feared to wake the sleepers. Veil after veil of thin dusky gauze is lifted, and by degrees the forms and colors of things are restored to them, and we watch the dawn remaking the world in its antique pattern. The wan mirrors get back their mimic life. The flameless tapers stand where we have left them, and beside them lies the half-read book that we had been studying, or the wired flower that we had worn at the ball, or the letter that we had been afraid to read, or that we had read too often. Nothing seems to us changed. Out of the unreal shadows of the night comes back the real life that we had known. We have to resume it where we had left off, and there steals over us a terrible sense of the necessity for the continuance of energy in the same wearisome round of stereotyped habits, or a wild longing, it may be, that our eyelids might open some morning upon a world that had been re-fashioned anew for our pleasure in the darkness, a world in which things would have fresh shapes and colors, and be changed, or have other secrets, a world in which the past would have little or no place, or survive, at any rate, in no conscious form of obligation or regret, the remembrance even of joy having its bitterness, and the memories of pleasure their pain.

It was the creation of such worlds as these that seemed to Dorian Gray to be the true object, or among the true objects, of life; and in his search for sensations that would be at once new and delightful, and possess that element of strangeness that is so essential to romance, he would often adopt certain modes of thought that he knew to be really alien to his nature, abandon himself to their subtle influences, and then, having, as it were, caught their color and satisfied his intellectual curiosity, leave them with that curious indifference that is not incompatible with a real ardor of temperament, and that indeed, according to certain modern psychologists, is often a condition of it.

It was rumored of him once that he was about to join the Roman Catholic communion; and certainly the Roman ritual had always a great attraction for him. The daily sacrifice, more awful really than all the sacrifices of the antique world, stirred him as much by its superb rejection of the evidence of the senses as by the primitive simplicity of its elements and the eternal pathos of the human tragedy that it sought to symbolize. He loved to kneel down on the cold marble pavement, and with the priest, in his stiff flowered cope,[4] slowly and with white hands moving aside the veil of the tabernacle, and raising aloft the jewelled lantern-shaped monstrance with that pallid wafer that at times, one would fain think, is indeed the "panis cælestis," the bread of angels, or, robed in the garments of the Passion of Christ, breaking the Host into the chalice, and smiting his breast for his sins. The fuming censers, that the grave boys, in their lace and scarlet, tossed into the air like great gilt flowers, had their subtle fascination for him. As he passed out, he used to look with wonder at the black confessionals, and long to sit in the dim shadow of one of them and listen to men and women whispering through the tarnished grating the true story of their lives.

But he never fell into the error of arresting his intellectual development by any formal acceptance of creed or system, or of mistaking, for a house in which to live, an inn that is but suitable for the sojourn of a night, or for a few hours of a night in which there are no stars and the moon is in travail. Mysticism, with its marvellous power of making common things strange to us, and the subtle antinomianism that always seems to accompany it, moved him for a season; and for a season he inclined to the materialistic doctrines of the *Darwinismus* movement in Germany, and found a curious pleasure in tracing the thoughts and passions of men to some pearly cell in the brain, or some white nerve in the body,[5] delighting in the conception of the absolute dependence of the spirit on certain physical conditions, morbid or healthy, normal or diseased. Yet, as has been said of him before, no theory of life seemed to him to be of any importance compared with life itself. He felt keenly conscious of how barren all all intellectual speculation is when separated from action and experiment. He knew that the senses, no less than the soul, have their mysteries to reveal.

And so he would now study perfumes, and the secrets of their manufacture, distilling heavily-scented oils, and burning odorous gums from the East. He saw that there was no mood of the mind that had not its counterpart in the sensuous life, and set himself to discover their true relations, wondering what there was in frankincense that made one mystical, and in ambergris that stirred one's passions, and in violets that woke the memory of dead romances, and in musk that troubled the brain, and in champak that stained the imagination; and seeking often to elaborate a real psychology of perfumes, and to estimate the several influences of sweet-smelling

---

4. Changed to "dalmatic" in 1891.
5. Stoddart or another editor at *Lippincott's* knew anatomy better than Wilde and revised the TS from Wilde's "ivory cell . . . or scarlet nerve."

roots, and scented pollen-laden flowers, of aromatic balms, and of dark and fragrant woods, of spikenard that sickens, of hovenia that makes men mad, and of aloes that are said to be able to expel melancholy from the soul.

At another time he devoted himself entirely to music, and in a long latticed room, with a vermilion-and-gold ceiling and walls of olive-green lacquer, he used to give curious concerts in which mad gypsies tore wild music from little zithers, or grave yellow-shawled Tunisians plucked at the strained strings of monstrous lutes, while grinning negroes beat monotonously upon copper drums, or turbaned Indians, crouching upon scarlet mats, blew through long pipes of reed or brass, and charmed, or feigned to charm, great hooded snakes and horrible horned adders. The harsh intervals and shrill discords of barbaric music stirred him at times when Schubert's grace, and Chopin's beautiful sorrows, and the mighty harmonies of Beethoven himself, fell unheeded on his ear. He collected together from all parts of the world the strangest instruments that could be found, either in the tombs of dead nations or among the few savage tribes that have survived contact with Western civilizations, and loved to touch and try them. He had the mysterious *juruparis* of the Rio Negro Indians, that women are not allowed to look at, and that even youths may not see till they have been subjected to fasting and scourging, and the earthen jars of the Peruvians that have the shrill cries of birds, and flutes of human bones such as Alfonso de Ovalle heard in Chili, and the sonorous green stones that are found near Cuzco and give forth a note of singular sweetness. He had painted gourds filled with pebbles that rattled when they were shaken; the long *clarin* of the Mexicans, into which the performer does not blow, but through which he inhales the air; the harsh *turé* of the Amazon tribes, that is sounded by the sentinels who sit all day long in trees, and that can be heard, it is said, at a distance of three leagues; the *teponaztli,* that has two vibrating tongues of wood, and is beaten with sticks that are smeared with an elastic gum obtained from the milky juice of plants; the *yotl*-bells of the Aztecs, that are hung in clusters like grapes; and a huge cylindrical drum, covered with the skins of great serpents, like the one that Bernal Diaz saw when he went with Cortes into the Mexican temple, and of whose doleful sound he has left us so vivid a description. The fantastic character of these instruments fascinated him, and he felt a curious delight in the thought that Art, like Nature, has her monsters, things of bestial shape and with hideous voices. Yet, after some time, he wearied of them, and would sit in his box at the Opera, either alone or with Lord Henry, listening in rapt pleasure to "Tannhäuser," and seeing in that great work of art a presentation of the tragedy of his own soul.

On another occasion he took up the study of jewels, and appeared at a costume ball as Anne de Joyeuse, Admiral of France, in a dress covered with five hundred and sixty pearls. He would often spend a whole day settling and resettling in their cases the various stones that he had collected, such as the olive-green chrysoberyl that turns red by lamplight, the cymophane with its wire-like line of silver, the pistachio-colored peridot, rose-pink and wine-yellow topazes, carbuncles of fiery scarlet with tremulous four-rayed stars, flame-red cinnamon-stones, orange and violet spinels, and amethysts with their alternate layers of ruby and sapphire. He loved the red gold of the sunstone, and the moonstone's pearly whiteness, and the broken rainbow of the milky opal. He procured from Amsterdam three emeralds of extraordinary size and richness of color, and had a turquoise *de la vieille roche* that was the envy of all the connoisseurs.

He discovered wonderful stories, also, about jewels.[6] In Alphonso's "Clericalis Disciplina" a serpent was mentioned with eyes of real jacinth, and in the romantic history of Alexander he was said to have found snakes in the vale of Jordan "with collars of real emeralds growing on their backs." There was a gem in the brain of the dragon, Philostratus told us, and "by the exhibition of golden letters and a scarlet robe" the monster could be thrown into a magical sleep, and slain. According to the great alchemist Pierre de Boniface, the diamond rendered a man invisible, and the agate of India made him eloquent. The cornelian appeased anger, and the hyacinth provoked sleep, and the amethyst drove away the fumes of wine. The garnet cast out demons, and the hydropicus deprived the moon of her color. The selenite waxed and waned with the moon, and the meloceus, that discovers thieves, could be affected only by the blood of kids. Leonardus Camillus had seen a white stone taken from the brain of a newly-killed toad, that was a certain antidote against poison. The bezoar, that was found in the heart of the Arabian deer, was a charm that could cure the plague. In the nests of Arabian birds was the aspilates, that, according to Democritus, kept the wearer from any danger by fire.

The King of Ceilan rode through his city with a large ruby in his hand, as the ceremony of his coronation. The gates of the palace of John the Priest were "made of sardius, with the horn of the horned snake inwrought, so that no man might bring poison within." Over

6. Wilde added four paragraphs here in three long MS pages to TS beginning "He discovered wonderful stories . . ." and ending "luxury of the dead was wonderful" on the next page. The following lines of the insert never appeared in print. Since there were no instructions from Stoddart or other editorial marks, the omission may have been a typesetting error or a deliberate omission to avoid an ambiguity of reference or syntax: "It was a pearl that Julius Caesar had given to Servilia when he loved her. Their child had been Brutus. [New paragraph] The young priest of the Sun, who while yet a boy had been slain for his sins, used to walk in jewelled shoes on dust of gold and silver."

the gable were "two golden apples, in which were two carbuncles," so that the gold might shine by day, and the carbuncles by night. In Lodge's strange romance "A Margarite of America" it was stated that in the chamber of Margarite were seen "all the chaste ladies of the world, inchased out of silver, looking through fair mirrours of chrysolites, carbuncles, sapphires, and greene emeraults." Marco Polo had watched the inhabitants of Zipangu place a rose-colored pearl in the mouth of the dead. A sea-monster had been enamoured of the pearl that the diver brought to King Perozes, and had slain the thief, and mourned for seven moons over his loss. When the Huns lured the king into the great pit, he flung it away,—Procopius tells the story,—nor was it ever found again, though the Emperor Anastasius offered five hundred-weight of gold pieces for it. The King of Malabar had shown a Venetian a rosary of one hundred and four pearls, one for every god that he worshipped.[7]

When the Duke de Valentinois, son of Alexander VI., visited Louis XII. of France, his horse was loaded with gold leaves, according to Brantôme, and his cap had double rows of rubies that threw out a great light. Charles of England had ridden in stirrups hung with three hundred and twenty-one diamonds. Richard II. had a coat, valued at thirty thousand marks, which was covered with balas rubies. Hall described Henry VIII., on his way to the Tower previous to his coronation, as wearing "a jacket of raised gold, the placard embroidered with diamonds and other rich stones, and a great bauderike about his neck of large balasses." The favourites of James I. wore ear-rings of emeralds set in gold filigrane. Edward II. gave to Piers Gaveston a suit of red-gold armor studded with jacinths, and a collar of gold roses set with turquoise-stones, and a skull-cap *parsemé* with pearls. Henry II. wore jewelled gloves reaching to the elbow, and had a hawk-glove set with twelve rubies and fifty-two great pearls. The ducal hat of Charles the Rash, the last Duke of Burgundy of his race, was studded with sapphires and hung with pear-shaped pearls.

How exquisite life had once been! How gorgeous in its pomp and decoration! Even to read of the luxury of the dead was wonderful.

Then he turned his attention to embroideries, and to the tapestries that performed the office of frescos in the chill rooms of the Northern nations of Europe. As he investigated the subject,—and he always had an extraordinary faculty of becoming absolutely absorbed for the moment in whatever he took up,—he was almost saddened by the reflection of the ruin that time brought on beautiful and wonderful things. He, at any rate, had escaped that. Summer followed summer, and the yellow jonquils bloomed and died

---

7. Wilde changed this to "three hundred and four pearls" in 1891.

many times, and nights of horror repeated the story of their shame, but he was unchanged. No winter marred his face or stained his flower-like bloom. How different it was with material things! Where had they gone to? Where was the great crocus-colored robe, on which the gods fought against the giants, that had been worked for Athena? Where the huge velarium that Nero had stretched across the Colosseum at Rome, on which were represented the starry sky, and Apollo driving a chariot drawn by white gilt-reined steeds? He longed to see the curious table-napkins wrought for Elagabalus,[8] on which were displayed all the dainties and viands that could be wanted for a feast; the mortuary cloth of King Chilperic, with its three hundred golden bees; the fantastic robes that excited the indignation of the Bishop of Pontus, and were figured with "lions, panthers, bears, dogs, forests, rocks, hunters,—all, in fact, that a painter can copy from nature;" and the coat that Charles of Orleans once wore, on the sleeves of which were embroidered the verses of a song beginning *"Madame, je suis tout joyeux,"* the musical accompaniment of the words being wrought in gold thread, and each note, a square shape in those days, formed with four pearls. He read of the room that was prepared at the palace at Rheims for the use of Queen Joan of Burgundy, and was decorated with "thirteen hundred and twenty-one parrots, made in broidery, and blazoned with the king's arms, and five hundred and sixty-one butterflies, whose wings were similarly ornamented with the arms of the queen, the whole worked in gold." Catherine de Médicis had a mourning-bed made for her of black velvet powdered with crescents and suns. Its curtains were of damask, with leafy wreaths and garlands, figured upon a gold and silver ground, and fringed along the edges with broideries of pearls, and it stood in a room hung with rows of the queen's devices in cut black velvet upon cloth of silver. Louis XIV. had gold-embroidered caryatides fifteen feet high in his apartment. The state bed of Sobieski, King of Poland, was made of Smyrna gold brocade embroidered in turquoises with verses from the Koran. Its supports were of silver gilt, beautifully chased, and profusely set with enamelled and jewelled medallions. It had been taken from the Turkish camp before Vienna, and the standard of Mohammed had stood under it.

And so, for a whole year, he sought to accumulate the most exquisite specimens that he could find of textile and embroidered work, getting the dainty Delhi muslins, finely wrought, with gold-thread palmates, and stitched over with irridescent beetles' wings; the Dacca gauzes, that from their transparency are known in the East as "woven

8. Wilde changed this to "Priest of the Sun" in 1891. Elagabalus was priest of the sun god at Emesa (now Homs, in present-day Syria) and later Roman emperor under the name Marcus Aurelius Antoninus.

air," and "running water," and "evening dew;" strange figured cloths from Java; elaborate yellow Chinese hangings; books bound in tawny satins or fair blue silks and wrought with *fleurs de lys,* birds, and images; veils of *lacis* worked in Hungary point; Sicilian brocades, and stiff Spanish velvets; Georgian work with its gilt coins, and Japanese *Foukousas* with their green-toned golds and their marvellously-plumaged birds.

He had a special passion, also, for ecclesiastical vestments, as indeed he had for everything connected with the service of the Church. In the long cedar chests that lined the west gallery of his house he had stored away many rare and beautiful specimens of what is really the raiment of the Bride of Christ, who must wear purple and jewels and fine linen that she may hide the pallid macerated body that is worn by the suffering that she seeks for, and wounded by self-inflicted pain. He had a gorgeous cope of crimson silk and gold-thread damask, figured with a repeating pattern of golden pomegranates set in six-petalled formal blossoms, beyond which on either side was the pine-apple device wrought in seed-pearls. The orphreys were divided into panels representing scenes from the life of the Virgin, and the coronation of the Virgin was figured in colored silks upon the hood. This was Italian work of the fifteenth century. Another cope was of green velvet, embroidered with heart-shaped groups of acanthus-leaves, from which spread long-stemmed white blossoms, the details of which were picked out with silver thread and colored crystals. The morse bore a seraph's head in gold-thread raised work. The orphreys were woven in a diaper of red and gold silk, and were starred with medallions of many saints and martyrs, among whom was St. Sebastian. He had chasubles, also, of amber-colored silk, and blue silk and gold brocade, and yellow silk damask and cloth of gold, figured with representations of the Passion and Crucifixion of Christ, and embroidered with lions and peacocks and other emblems; dalmatics of white satin and pink silk damask, decorated with tulips and dolphins and *fleurs de lys;* altar frontals of crimson velvet and blue linen; and many corporals, chalice-veils, and sudaria. In the mystic offices to which these things were put there was something that quickened his imagination.[9]

For these things, and everything that he collected in his lovely house, were to be to him means of forgetfulness, modes by which he could escape, for a season, from the fear that seemed to him at times to be almost too great to be borne. Upon the walls of the lonely locked room where he had spent so much of his boyhood, he had hung with his own hands the terrible portrait whose changing features showed him the real degradation of his life, and had draped

9. Wilde added this paragraph on two handwritten pages inserted into TS.

the purple-and-gold pall in front of it as a curtain. For weeks he would not go there, would forget the hideous painted thing, and get back his light heart, his wonderful joyousness, his passionate pleasure in mere existence. Then, suddenly, some night he would creep out of the house, go down to dreadful places near Blue Gate Fields,[1] and stay there, day after day, until he was driven away.[2] On his return he would sit in front of the picture, sometimes loathing it and himself, but filled, at other times, with that pride of rebellion that is half the fascination of sin, and smiling, with secret pleasure, at the misshapen shadow that had to bear the burden that should have been his own.

After a few years he could not endure to be long out of England, and gave up the villa that he had shared at Trouville with Lord Henry, as well as the little white walled-in house at Algiers where he had more than once spent his winter. He hated to be separated from the picture that was such a part of his life, and he was also afraid that during his absence some one might gain access to the room, in spite of the elaborate bolts and bars that he had caused to be placed upon the door.

He was quite conscious that this would tell them nothing. It was true that the portrait still preserved, under all the foulness and ugliness of the face, its marked likeness to himself; but what could they learn from that? He would laugh at any one who tried to taunt him. He had not painted it. What was it to him how vile and full of shame it looked? Even if he told them, would they believe it?

Yet he was afraid. Sometimes when he was down at his great house in Nottinghamshire, entertaining the fashionable young men of his own rank who were his chief companions, and astounding the county by the wanton luxury and gorgeous splendor of his mode of life, he would suddenly leave his guests and rush back to town to see that the door had not been tampered with and that the picture was still there. What if it should be stolen? The mere thought made him cold with horror. Surely the world would know his secret then. Perhaps the world already suspected it.

For, while he fascinated many, there were not a few who distrusted him. He was blackballed at a West End club of which his birth and social position fully entitled him to become a member, and on one occasion, when he was brought by a friend into the smoking-room of the Carlton,[3] the Duke of Berwick and another gentleman got up in a marked manner and went out. Curious stories became current

1. Wilde originally wrote "the Docks."
2. The last phrase is Stoddart's. The original read "till they almost drove him out in horror and had to be appeased with monstrous bribes."
3. Changed in 1891. The Carlton was a famous conservative political club located in Pall Mall.

about him after he had passed his twenty-fifth year. It was said that
he had been seen brawling with foreign sailors in a low den in the
distant parts of Whitechapel, and that he consorted with thieves
and coiners and knew the mysteries of their trade. His extraordinary
absences became notorious, and, when he used to reappear again
in society, men[4] would whisper to each other in corners, or pass him
with a sneer, or look at him with cold searching eyes, as if they were
determined to discover his secret.

Of such insolences and attempted slights he, of course, took no
notice, and in the opinion of most people his frank debonair manner, his charming boyish smile, and the infinite grace of that wonderful youth that seemed never to leave him, were in themselves a
sufficient answer to the calumnies (for so they called them) that
were circulated about him. It was remarked, however, that those who
had been most intimate with him appeared, after a time, to shun
him. Of all his friends, or so-called friends, Lord Henry Wotton was
the only one who remained loyal to him.[5] Women who had wildly
adored him, and for his sake had braved all social censure and set
convention at defiance, were seen to grow pallid with shame or horror if Dorian Gray entered the room.[6]

Yet these whispered scandals only lent him, in the eyes of many,
his strange and dangerous charm. His great wealth was a certain
element of security. Society, civilized society at least, is never very
ready to believe anything to the detriment of those who are both rich
and charming. It feels instinctively that manners are of more importance than morals, and the highest respectability is of less value
in its opinion that the possession of a good *chef*. And, after all, it is
a very poor consolation to be told that the man who has given one a
bad dinner, or poor wine, is irreproachable in his private life. Even
the cardinal virtues cannot atone for cold *entrées*, as Lord Henry
remarked once, in a discussion on the subject; and there is possibly a good deal to be said for his view. For the canons of good society are, or should be, the same as the canons of art. Form is
absolutely essential to it. It should have the dignity of a ceremony, as
well as its unreality, and should combine the insincere character of
a romantic play with the wit and beauty that make such plays

4. Stoddart canceled the following here: "who were jealous of the strange love he inspired
   in women."
5. Stoddart also canceled a marginal insert that ended the sentence "and in the eyes of
   some it was a question whether that was an honor or a disgrace."
6. The conclusion of this paragraph, crossed out by Stoddart in TS, was as follows: "It
   was said that even the sinful creatures who prowl the streets at night had cursed him
   as he passed by, seeing in him a corruption greater than their own and knowing but
   too well the horror of his real life." An additional passage in the same spirit, which
   Wilde blotted out in MS, described Dorian's appeal in terms of his "strange and dangerous charm."

charming. Is insincerity such a terrible thing? I think not. It is merely a method by which we can multiply our personalities.

Such, at any rate, was Dorian Gray's opinion. He used to wonder at the shallow psychology of those who conceive the Ego in man as a thing simple, permanent, reliable, and of one essence. To him, man was a being with myriad lives and myriad sensations, a complex multi-form creature that bore within itself strange legacies of thought and passion, and whose very flesh was tainted with the monstrous maladies of the dead. He loved to stroll through the gaunt cold picture-gallery of his country-house and look at the various portraits of those whose blood flowed in his veins. Here was Philip Herbert, described by Francis Osborne, in his "Memories on the Reigns of Queen Elizabeth and King James," as one who was "caressed by the court for his handsome face, which kept him not long company." Was it young Herbert's life that he sometimes led? Had some strange poisonous germ crept from body to body till it had reached his own? Was it some dim sense of that ruined grace that had made him so suddenly, and almost without cause, give utterance, in Basil Hallward's studio, to that mad prayer that had so changed his life? Here, in gold-embroidered red doublet, jewelled surcoat, and gilt-edged ruff and wrist-bands, stood Sir Anthony Sherard, with his silver-and-black armor piled at his feet. What had this man's legacy been? Had the lover of Giovanna of Naples bequeathed him some inheritance of sin and shame? Were his own actions merely the dreams that the dead man had not dared to realize? Here, from the fading canvas, smiled Lady Elizabeth Devereux, in her gauze hood, pearl stomacher, and pink slashed sleeves. A flower was in her right hand, and her left clasped an enameled collar of white and damask roses. On a table by her side lay a mandolin and an apple. There were large green rosettes upon her little pointed shoes. He knew her life, and the strange stories that were told about her lovers.[7] Had he something of her temperament in him? Those oval heavy-lidded eyes seemed to look curiously at him. What of George Willoughby, with his powdered hair and fantastic patches? How evil he looked! The face was saturnine and swarthy, and the sensual lips seemed to be twisted with disdain. Delicate lace ruffles fell over the lean yellow hands that were so overladen with rings. He had been a macaroni of the eighteenth century, and the friend, in his youth, of Lord Ferrars. What of the second Lord Sherard, the companion of the Prince Regent in his wildest days, and one of the witnesses at the secret marriage with Mrs. Fitzherbert? How proud

---

7. Wilde added and Stoddart canceled the following, thus reinstating the original reading: "the deaths of those whom she had granted her favors."

and handsome he was, with his chestnut curls and insolent pose! What passions had he bequeathed? The world had looked upon him as infamous. He had led the orgies at Carlton House. The star of the Garter glittered upon his breast. Beside him hung the portrait of his wife, a pallid, thin-lipped woman in black. Her blood, also, stirred within him. How curious it all seemed!

Yet one had ancestors in literature, as well as in one's own race, nearer perhaps in type and temperament, many of them, and certainly with an influence of which one was more absolutely conscious. There were times when it seemed to Dorian Gray that the whole of history was merely the record of his own life, not as he had lived it in act and circumstance, but as his imagination had created it for him, as it had been in his brain and in his passions. He felt that he had known them all, those strange terrible figures that had passed across the stage of the world and made sin so marvellous and evil so full of wonder. It seemed to him that in some mysterious way their lives had been his own.

The hero[8] of the dangerous novel that had so influenced his life had himself had this curious fancy. In a chapter[9] of the book he tells how, crowned with a laurel, lest lightning might strike him, he had sat, as Tiberius, in a garden at Capri, reading the shameful books of Elephantis, while dwarfs and peacocks strutted round him and the flute-player mocked the swinger of the censer; and, as Caligula,[1] had caroused with the green-shirted jockeys in their stables, and supped in an ivory manger with a jewel-frontleted horse; and, as Domitian, had wandered through a corridor lined with marble mirrors, looking round with haggard eyes for the reflection of the dagger that was to end his days, and sick with that ennui, that *tædium vitæ* that comes on those to whom life denies nothing; and had peered through a clear emerald at the red shambles of the Circus, and then, in a litter of pearl and purple drawn by silver-shod mules, been carried through the Street of Pomegranates to a House of Gold, and heard men cry on Nero Cæsar as he passed by; and, as Elagabalus, had painted his face with colors, and plied the distaff among the women, and brought the Moon from Carthage, and given her in mystic marriage to the Sun.

Over and over again Dorian used to read this fantastic chapter,[2] and the chapter immediately following, in which the hero describes

---

8. Originally, "Raoul" in TS. In 1891, Wilde changed "dangerous" to "wonderful."
9. "Fourth" is canceled in TS. Wilde changed it to "seventh" in 1891.
1. Stoddart deleted "had drank the live philter of Caesonia, and wore the habit of Venus by night, and by day a false gilded beard."
2. Changed by Wilde from "passage" in TS. In the next line, Stoddart substituted "the hero" for "Raoul."

the curious tapestries that he had had woven for him from Gustave Moreau's[3] designs, and on which were pictured the awful and beautiful forms of those whom Vice and Blood and Weariness had made monstrous or mad.[4] Filippo, Duke of Milan, who slew his wife, and painted her lips with a scarlet poison; Pietro Barbi, the Venetian, known as Paul the Second, who sought in his vanity to assume the title of Formosus, and whose tiara, valued at two hundred thousand florins, was bought at the price of a terrible sin; Gian Maria Visconti, who used hounds to chase living men, and whose murdered body was covered with roses by a harlot who had loved him; the Borgia on his white horse, with Fratricide[5] riding beside him, and his mantle stained with the blood of Perotto; Pietro Riario, the young Cardinal Archbishop of Florence, child and minion of Sixtus IV., whose beauty was equalled only by his debauchery, and who received Leonora of Aragon in a pavilion of white and crimson silk, filled with nymphs and centaurs, and gilded a boy that he might serve her at the feast as Ganymede or Hylas; Ezzelin, whose melancholy could be cured only by the spectacle of death, and who had a passion for red blood, as other men have for red wine,—the son of the Fiend, as was reported, and one who had cheated his father at dice when gambling with him for his own soul; Giambattista Cibo, who in mockery took the name of Innocent, and into whose torpid veins the blood of three lads was infused by a Jewish doctor; Sigismondo Malatesta, the lover of Isotta, and the lord of Rimini, whose effigy was burned at Rome as the enemy of God and man, who strangled Polyssena with a napkin, and gave poison to Ginerva d'Este in a cup of emerald, and in honor of a shameful passion built a pagan church for Christian worship; Charles VI., who had so wildly adored his brother's wife that a leper had warned him of the insanity that was coming on him, and who could only be soothed by Saracen cards painted with the images of Love and Death and Madness; and, in his trimmed jerkin and jewelled cap and acanthus-like curls, Grifonetto Baglioni, who slew Astorre with his bride, and Simonetto with his page, and whose comeliness was such that, as he lay dying in the yellow piazza of Perugia, those who had hated him could not choose but weep, and Atalanta, who had cursed him, blessed him.

There was a horrible fascination in them all. He saw them at night, and they troubled his imagination in the day. The Renaissance knew

---

3. A famous painter (1826–1898) of Decadent themes and subjects, whose style became synonymous with the movement. Wilde added his name in TS and removed it in 1891.
4. Stoddart changed the original "Lust" to "Vice" in the line above, deleted "here was Manfred, King of Apulia who dressed always in green, and consorted only with cortezans and buffoons," and in the line below, after "scarlet poison," canceled "that her guilty lover might suck swift death from the dead thing he had fondled."
5. Stoddart removed "Incest and" here in TS. Wilde restored "harlot" to the line above after Stoddart had changed it to "one."

of strange manners of poisoning,—poisoning by a helmet and a lighted torch, by an embroidered glove and a jewelled fan, by a gilded pomander and by an amber chain. Dorian Gray had been poisoned by a book.[6] There were moments when he looked on evil simply as a mode through which he could realize his conception of the beautiful.

Chapter X

It was on the 7th[1] of November, the eve of his own thirty-second birthday, as he often remembered afterwards.

He was walking home about eleven o'clock from Lord Henry's, where he had been dining, and was wrapped in heavy furs, as the night was cold and foggy. At the corner of Grosvenor Square and South Audley Street a man passed him in the mist, walking very fast, and with the collar of his gray ulster turned up. He had a bag in his hand. He recognized him. It was Basil Hallward. A strange sense of fear, for which he could not account, came over him. He made no sign of recognition, and went on slowly, in the direction of his own house.

But Hallward had seen him. Dorian heard him first stopping, and then hurrying after him. In a few moments his hand was on his arm.

"Dorian! What an extraordinary piece of luck! I have been waiting for you ever since nine o'clock in your library. Finally I took pity on your tired servant, and told him to go to bed, as he let me out. I am off to Paris by the midnight train, and I wanted particularly to see you before I left. I thought it was you, or rather your fur coat, as you passed me. But I wasn't quite sure. Didn't you recognize me?"

"In this fog, my dear Basil? Why, I can't even recognize Grosvenor Square. I believe my house is somewhere about here, but I don't feel at all certain about it. I am sorry you are going away, as I have not seen you for ages. But I suppose you will be back soon?"

"No: I am going to be out of England for six months. I intend to take a studio in Paris, and shut myself up till I have finished a great picture I have in my head. However, it wasn't about myself I wanted to talk. Here we are at your door. Let me come in for a moment. I have something to say to you."

"I shall be charmed. But won't you miss your train?" said Dorian Gray, languidly, as he passed up the steps and opened the door with his latch-key.

---

6. The original ending of the chapter read "Lord Henry had given him one, and Basil Hallward had painted the other." Wilde then moved the lines beginning "The Renaissance" to their present location on the page.
1. Changed to "9th" in 1891 and the birthday from the "thirty-second" to "thirty-eighth."

The lamp-light struggled out through the fog, and Hallward looked at his watch. "I have heaps of time," he answered. "The train doesn't go till twelve-fifteen, and it is only just eleven. In fact, I was on my way to the club to look for you, when I met you. You see, I shan't have any delay about luggage, as I have sent on my heavy things. All I have with me is in this bag, and I can easily get to Victoria in twenty minutes."

Dorian looked at him and smiled. "What a way for a fashionable painter to travel! A Gladstone bag, and an ulster! Come in, or the fog will get into the house. And mind you don't talk about anything serious. Nothing is serious nowadays. At least nothing should be."

Hallward shook his head, as he entered, and followed Dorian into the library. There was a bright wood fire blazing in the large open hearth. The lamps were lit, and an open Dutch silver spirit-case stood, with some siphons of soda-water and large cut-glass tumblers, on a little table.

"You see your servant made me quite at home, Dorian. He gave me everything I wanted, including your best cigarettes. He is a most hospitable creature. I like him much better than the Frenchman you used to have. What has become of the Frenchman, by the bye?"

Dorian shrugged his shoulders. "I believe he married Lady Ashton's maid, and has established her in Paris as an English dressmaker. *Anglomanie* is very fashionable over there now, I hear. It seems silly of the French, doesn't it? But—do you know?—he was not at all a bad servant. I never liked him, but I had nothing to complain about. One often imagines things that are quite absurd. He was really very devoted to me, and seemed quite sorry when he went away. Have another brandy-and-soda? Or would you like hock-and-seltzer? I always take hock-and-seltzer myself. There is sure to be some in the next room."

"Thanks, I won't have anything more," said Hallward, taking his cap and coat off, and throwing them on the bag that he had placed in the corner. "And now, my dear fellow, I want to speak to you seriously. Don't frown like that. You make it so much more difficult for me."

"What is it all about?" cried Dorian, in his petulant way, flinging himself down on the sofa. "I hope it is not about myself. I am tired of myself to-night. I should like to be somebody else."

"It is about yourself," answered Hallward, in his grave, deep voice, "and I must say it to you. I shall only keep you half an hour."

Dorian sighed, and lit a cigarette. "Half an hour!" he murmured.

"It is not much to ask of you, Dorian, and it is entirely for your own sake that I am speaking. I think it right that you should know

that the most dreadful things are being said about you in London,—
things that I could hardly repeat to you."[2]

"I don't wish to know anything about them. I love scandals about
other people, but scandals about myself don't interest me. They have
not got the charm of novelty."

"They must interest you, Dorian. Every gentleman is interested
in his good name. You don't want people to talk of you as something
vile and degraded. Of course you have your position, and your wealth,
and all that kind of thing. But position and wealth are not everything. Mind you, I don't believe these rumors at all. At least, I can't
believe them when I see you. Sin is a thing that writes itself across
a man's face. It cannot be concealed. People talk of secret vices.
There are no such things as secret vices. If a wretched man has a
vice, it shows itself in the lines of his mouth, the droop of his eyelids, the moulding of his hands, even. Somebody—I won't mention
his name, but you know him—came to me last year to have his portrait done. I had never seen him before, and had never heard
anything about him at the time, though I have heard a good deal
since. He offered an extravagant price. I refused him. There was
something in the shape of his fingers that I hated. I know now that
I was quite right in what I fancied about him. His life is dreadful.
But you, Dorian, with your pure, bright, innocent face, and your
marvellous untroubled youth,—I can't believe anything against
you. And yet I see you very seldom, and you never come down to the
studio now, and when I am away from you, and I hear all these hideous things that people are whispering about you, I don't know what
to say. Why is it, Dorian, that a man like the Duke of Berwick leaves
the room of a club when you enter it? Why is it that so many gentlemen in London will neither go to your house nor invite you to theirs?
You used to be a friend of Lord Cawdor. I met him at dinner last
week. Your name happened to come up in conversation, in connection with the miniatures you have lent to the exhibition at the Dudley. Cawdor curled his lip, and said that you might have the most
artistic tastes, but that you were a man whom no pure-minded girl
should be allowed to know, and whom no chaste woman should sit
in the same room with. I reminded him that I was a friend of yours,
and asked him what he meant. He told me. He told me right out
before everybody. It was horrible! Why is your friendship so fateful
to young men?[3] There was that wretched boy in the Guards who
committed suicide. You were his great friend. There was Sir Henry

2. This line was dropped in 1891.
3. Stoddart substituted the rest of the sentence after "why is" for the original reading:
"why is it that every young man that you take up seems to come to grief, to go to the bad
at once?"

Ashton, who had to leave England, with a tarnished name. You and
he were inseparable. What about Adrian Singleton, and his dreadful end? What about Lord Kent's only son, and his career? I met his
father yesterday in St. James Street. He seemed broken with
shame and sorrow. What about the young Duke of Perth? What sort
of life has he got now? What gentleman would associate with him?[4]
Dorian, Dorian, your reputation is infamous. I know you and Harry
are great friends. I say nothing about that now, but surely you need
not have made his sister's name a by-word. When you met Lady
Gwendolen, not a breath of scandal had ever touched her. Is there
a single decent woman in London now who would drive with her in
the Park? Why, even her children are not allowed to live with her.
Then there are other stories,—stories that you have been seen
creeping at dawn out of dreadful houses and slinking in disguise into
the foulest dens in London. Are they true? Can they be true? When
I first heard them, I laughed. I hear them now, and they make me
shudder. What about your country-house, and the life that is led
there? Dorian, you don't know what is said about you.[5] I won't tell
you that I don't want to preach to you. I remember Harry saying
once that every man who turned himself into an amateur curate
for the moment always said that, and then broke his word. I do
want to preach to you. I want you to lead such a life as will make
the world respect you. I want you to have a clean name and a fair
record. I want you to get rid of the dreadful people you associate
with. Don't shrug your shoulders like that. Don't be so indifferent.
You have a wonderful influence. Let it be for good, not evil. They
say that you corrupt every one whom you become intimate with,
and that it is quite sufficient for you to enter a house, for shame of
some kind to follow after you. I don't know whether it is so or not.
How should I know? But it is said of you. I am told things that it
seems impossible to doubt. Lord Gloucester was one of my greatest
friends at Oxford. He showed me a letter that his wife had written
to him when she was dying alone in her villa at Mentone. Your
name was implicated in[6] the most terrible confession I ever read. I
told him that it was absurd,—that I knew you thoroughly, and that
you were incapable of anything of the kind. Know you? I wonder do
I know you? Before I could answer that, I should have to see your
soul."

"To see my soul!" muttered Dorian Gray, starting up from the sofa
and turning almost white from fear.

---

4. Wilde added a new paragraph here in 1891.
5. Stoddart canceled the following in TS: "It is quite sufficient to say of a young man that
   he goes to stay at Selby Royal, for people to sneer and titter."
6. Stoddart changed this from "It was" and then canceled the next sentence: "He said that
   he suspected you."

"Yes," answered Hallward, gravely, and with infinite sorrow in his voice,—"to see your soul. But only God can do that."

A bitter laugh of mockery broke from the lips of the younger man. "You shall see it yourself, to-night!" he cried, seizing a lamp from the table. "Come: it is your own handiwork. Why shouldn't you look at it? You can tell the world all about it afterwards, if you choose. Nobody would believe you. If they did believe you, they'd like me all the better for it. I know the age better than you do, though you will prate about it so tediously. Come, I tell you. You have chattered enough about corruption. Now you shall look on it face to face."[7]

There was the madness of pride in every word he uttered. He stamped his foot upon the ground in his boyish insolent manner. He felt a terrible joy at the thought that some one else was to share his secret, and that the man who had painted the portrait that was the origin of all his shame was to be burdened for the rest of his life with the hideous memory of what he had done.

"Yes," he continued, coming closer to him, and looking steadfastly into his stern eyes, "I will show you my soul. You shall see the thing that you fancy only God can see."

Hallward started back. "This is blasphemy, Dorian!" he cried. "You must not say things like that. They are horrible, and they don't mean anything."

"You think so?" He laughed again.

"I know so. As for what I said to you to-night, I said it for your good. You know I have been always devoted[8] to you."

"Don't touch me. Finish what you have to say."

A twisted flash of pain shot across Hallward's face. He paused for a moment, and a wild feeling of pity came over him. After all, what right had he to pry into the life of Dorian Gray? If he had done a tithe of what was rumored about him, how much he must have suffered! Then he straightened himself up, and walked over to the fireplace, and stood there, looking at the burning logs with their frost-like ashes and their throbbing cores of flame.

"I am waiting, Basil," said the young man, in a hard, clear voice.

He turned round. "What I have to say is this," he cried. "You must give me some answer to these horrible charges that are made against you. If you tell me that they are absolutely untrue from beginning to end, I will believe you. Deny them, Dorian, deny them! Can't you see what I am going through? My God! don't tell me that you are infamous![9]

7. Wilde canceled these lines in MS: "Now, I will show you my soul. You shall see the thing you fancy only God can see."
8. Changed to "a staunch friend" in 1891.
9. Wilde made a change here in 1891.

Dorian Gray smiled. There was a curl of contempt in his lips. "Come up-stairs, Basil," he said, quietly. "I keep a diary of my life from day to day, and it never leaves the room in which it is written. I will show it to you if you come with me."

"I will come with you, Dorian, if you wish it. I see I have missed my train. That makes no matter. I can go to-morrow. But don't ask me to read anything to-night. All I want is a plain answer to my question."

"That will be given to you up-stairs. I could not give it here. You won't have to read long. Don't keep me waiting."

Chapter XI

He passed out of the room, and began the ascent, Basil Hallward following close behind. They walked softly, as men instinctively do at night. The lamp cast fantastic shadows on the wall and staircase. A rising wind made some of the windows rattle.

When they reached the top landing, Dorian set the lamp down on the floor, and taking out the key turned it in the lock. "You insist on knowing, Basil?" he asked, in a low voice.

"Yes."

"I am delighted," he murmured, smiling. Then he added, somewhat bitterly, "You are the one man in the world who is entitled to know everything about me. You have had more to do with my life than you think." And, taking up the lamp, he opened the door and went in. A cold current of air passed them, and the light shot up for a moment in a flame of murky orange. He shuddered. "Shut the door behind you," he said, as he placed the lamp on the table.

Hallward glanced round him, with a puzzled expression. The room looked as if it had not been lived in for years. A faded Flemish tapestry, a curtained picture, an old Italian *cassone,* and an almost empty bookcase,—that was all that it seemed to contain, besides a chair and a table. As Dorian Gray was lighting a half-burned candle that was standing on the mantel-shelf, he saw that the whole place was covered with dust, and that the carpet was in holes. A mouse ran scuffling behind the wainscoting. There was a damp odor of mildew.

"So you think that it is only God who sees the soul, Basil? Draw that curtain back, and you will see mine."

The voice that spoke was cold and cruel. "You are mad, Dorian, or playing a part," muttered Hallward, frowning.

"You won't? Then I must do it myself," said the young man; and he tore the curtain from its rod, and flung it on the ground.

An exclamation of horror broke from Hallward's lips as he saw in the dim light the hideous thing on the canvas leering at him.[1] There was something in its expression that filled him with disgust and loathing. Good heavens! It was Dorian Gray's own face that he was looking at! The horror, whatever it was, had not yet entirely marred that marvelous beauty. There was still some gold in the thinning hair and some scarlet on the sensual lips. The sodden eyes had kept something of the loveliness of their blue, the noble curves had not yet passed entirely away from chiseled nostrils and from plastic throat. Yes, it was Dorian himself. But who had done it? He seemed to recognize his own brush-work, and the frame was his own design. The idea was monstrous, yet he felt afraid. He seized the lighted candle, and held it to the picture. In the left-hand corner was his own name, traced in long letters of bright vermilion.

It was some foul parody, some infamous, ignoble satire. He had never done that. Still, it was his own picture. He knew it, and he felt as if his blood had changed from fire to sluggish ice in a moment. His own picture! What did it mean? Why had it altered? He turned, and looked at Dorian Gray with the eyes of a sick man. His mouth twitched, and his parched tongue seemed unable to articulate. He passed his hand across his forehead. It was dank with clammy sweat.

The young man was leaning against the mantel-shelf, watching him with that strange expression that is on the faces of those who are absorbed in a play when a great artist is acting. There was neither real sorrow in it nor real joy. There was simply the passion of the spectator, with perhaps a flicker of triumph in the eyes. He had taken the flower out of his coat, and was smelling it, or pretending to do so.

"What does this mean?" cried Hallward, at last. His own voice sounded shrill and curious in his ears.

"Years ago, when I was a boy," said Dorian Gray, "you met me, devoted yourself to me, flattered me, and taught me to be vain of my good looks. One day you introduced me to a friend of yours, who explained to me the wonder of youth, and you finished a portrait of me that revealed to me the wonder of beauty. In a mad moment, that I don't know, even now, whether I regret or not, I made a wish. Perhaps you would call it a prayer. . . ."

"I remember it! Oh, how well I remember it! No! the thing is impossible. The room is damp. The mildew has got into the canvas.

---

1. To compare this and the following paragraphs with the revised, 1891 text (see p. 130) is to appreciate how many little improvements Wilde made in revising the first printed version. The evidence of the texts therefore contradicts the myth that Wilde tossed off his work hastily and carelessly.

The paints I used had some wretched mineral poison in them. I tell you the thing is impossible."[2]

"Ah, what is impossible?" murmured the young man, going over to the window, and leaning his forehead against the cold, mist-stained glass.

"You told me you had destroyed it."

"I was wrong. It has destroyed me."

"I don't believe it is my picture."

"Can't you see your romance in it?" said Dorian, bitterly.[3]

"My romance, as you call it . . ."

"As you called it."

"There was nothing evil in it, nothing shameful. This is the face of a satyr."

"It is the face of my soul."

"God![4] what a thing I must have worshipped! This has the eyes of a devil."

"Each of us has Heaven and Hell in him, Basil," cried Dorian, with a wild gesture of despair.

Hallward turned again to the portrait, and gazed at it. "My God! If it is true," he exclaimed, "and this is what you have done with your life, why, you must be worse even than those who talk against you fancy you to be!" He held the light up again to the canvas, and examined it. The surface seemed to be quite undisturbed, and as he had left it. It was from within, apparently, that the foulness and horror had come. Through some strange quickening of inner life the leprosies of sin were slowly eating the thing away. The rotting of a corpse in a watery grave was not so fearful.

His hand shook, and the candle fell from its socket on the floor, and lay there sputtering. He placed his foot on it and put it out. Then he flung himself into the rickety chair that was standing by the table and buried his face in his hands.

"Good God, Dorian, what a lesson! what an awful lesson!" There was no answer, but he could hear the young man sobbing at the window.

"Pray, Dorian, pray," he murmured. "What is it that one was taught to say in one's boyhood? 'Lead us not into temptation. Forgive us our sins. Wash away our iniquities.' Let us say that together. The prayer of your pride has been answered. The prayer of your repentance will be answered also. I worshipped you too much. I am punished for it. You worshipped yourself too much. We are both punished."

---

2. Wilde added in TS margin, "The room is damp . . . impossible."
3. Wilde changed "romance" to "ideal" in 1891 and added another line further down (see p. 131).
4. Stoddart changed the original "Christ!" here, but Wilde put it back into the 1891 text.

Dorian Gray turned slowly around, and looked at him with tear-dimmed eyes. "It is too late, Basil," he murmured.

"It is never too late, Dorian. Let us kneel down and try if we can remember a prayer. Isn't there a verse somewhere, 'Though your sins be as scarlet, yet I will make them white as snow'?"

"Those words mean nothing to me now."

"Hush! don't say that. You have done enough evil in your life. My God! Don't you see that accursed thing leering at us?"

Dorian Gray glanced at the picture, and suddenly an uncontrollable feeling of hatred for Basil Hallward came over him.[5] The mad passions of a hunted animal stirred within him, and he loathed the man who was seated at the table, more than he had ever loathed anything in his whole life. He glanced wildly around. Something glimmered on the top of the painted chest that faced him. His eye fell on it. He knew what it was. It was a knife that he had brought up, some days before, to cut a piece of cord, and had forgotten to take away with him. He moved slowly towards it, passing Hallward as he did so. As soon as he got behind him, he seized it, and turned round. Hallward moved in his chair as if he was going to rise. He rushed at him, and dug the knife into the great vein that is behind the ear, crushing the man's head down on the table, and stabbing again and again.

There was a stifled groan, and the horrible sound of some one choking with blood. The outstretched arms shot up convulsively three times, waving grotesque stiff-fingered hands in the air. He stabbed him once more, but the man did not move. Something began to trickle on the floor. He waited for a moment, still pressing the head down. Then he threw the knife on the table, and listened.

He could hear nothing, but the drip, drip on the threadbare carpet. He opened the door, and went out on the landing. The house was quite quiet. No one was stirring.

He took out the key, and returned to the room, locking himself in as he did so.

The thing was still seated in the chair, straining over the table with bowed head, and humped back, and long fantastic arms. Had it not been for the red jagged tear in the neck, and the clotted black pool that slowly widened on the table, one would have said that the man was simply asleep.

How quickly it had all been done! He felt strangely calm, and, walking over to the window, opened it, and stepped out on the balcony. The wind had blown the fog away, and the sky was like a monstrous peacock's tail, starred with myriads of golden eyes. He looked down, and saw the policeman going his rounds and flashing

5. Wilde added "as though . . . grinning lips" in 1891.

a bull's-eye lantern on the doors of the silent houses. The crimson spot of a prowling hansom gleamed at the corner, and then vanished. A woman in a ragged shawl was creeping round by the railings, staggering as she went. Now and then she stopped, and peered back. Once, she began to sing in a hoarse voice. The policeman strolled over and said something to her. She stumbled away, laughing. A bitter blast swept across the Square. The gas-lamps flickered, and became blue, and the leafless trees shook their black iron branches as if in pain.[6] He shivered, and went back, closing the window behind him.

He passed to the door, turned the key, and opened it. He did not even glance at the murdered man. He felt that the secret of the whole thing was not to realize the situation. The friend who had painted the fatal portrait, the portrait to which all his misery had been due, had gone out of his life. That was enough.

Then he remembered the lamp. It was a rather curious one of Moorish workmanship, made of dull silver inlaid with arabesques of burnished steel. Perhaps it might be missed by his servant, and questions would be asked. He turned back, and took it from the table. How still the man was! How horribly white the long hands looked! He was like a dreadful wax image.

He locked the door behind him, and crept quietly down-stairs. The wood-work creaked, and seemed to cry out as if in pain. He stopped several times, and waited. No: everything was still. It was merely the sound of his own footsteps.

When he reached the library, he saw the bag and coat in the corner. They must be hidden away somewhere. He unlocked a secret press that was in the wainscoting, and put them into it. He could easily burn them afterwards. Then he pulled out his watch. It was twenty minutes to two.

He sat down, and began to think. Every year—every month, almost—men were strangled in England for what he had done. There had been a madness of murder in the air. Some red star had come too close to the earth.

Evidence? What evidence was there against him? Basil Hallward had left the house at eleven. No one had seen him come in again. Most of the servants were at Selby Royal. His valet had gone to bed.

Paris! Yes. It was to Paris that Basil had gone, by the midnight train, as he had intended. With his curious reserved habits, it would be months before any suspicions would be aroused. Months? Everything could be destroyed long before then.

6. Wilde changed this from "in the uncertain gloom" in TS and made another alteration in the effect in 1891.

A sudden thought struck him. He put on his fur coat and hat, and went out into the hall. There he paused, hearing the slow heavy tread of the policeman outside on the pavement, and seeing the flash of the lantern reflected in the window. He waited, holding his breath.

After a few moments he opened the front door, and slipped out, shutting it very gently behind him. Then he began ringing the bell. In about ten minutes his valet appeared, half dressed, and looking very drowsy.

"I am sorry to have had to wake you up, Francis," he said, stepping in, "but I had forgotten my latch-key. What time is it?"

"Five minutes past two, sir," answered the man, looking at the clock and yawning.

"Five minutes past two? How horribly late! You must wake me at nine to-morrow. I have some work to do."

"All right, sir."

"Did any one call this evening?"

"Mr. Hallward, sir. He stayed here till eleven, and then he went away to catch his train."

"Oh! I am sorry I didn't see him. Did he leave any message?"

"No, sir, except that he would write to you."[7]

"That will do, Francis. Don't forget to call me at nine tomorrow."

"No, sir."

The man shambled down the passage in his slippers.

Dorian Gray threw his hat and coat upon the yellow marble table, and passed into the library. He walked up and down the room for a quarter of an hour, biting his lip, and thinking.[8] Then he took the Blue Book down from one of the shelves, and began to turn over the leaves. "Alan Campbell, 152, Hertford Street, Mayfair." Yes; that was the man he wanted.

Chapter XII

At nine o'clock the next morning his servant came in with a cup of chocolate on a tray, and opened the shutters. Dorian was sleeping quite peacefully, lying on his right side, with one hand underneath his cheek. He looked like a boy who had been tired out with play, or study.

The man had to touch him twice on the shoulder before he woke, and as he opened his eyes a faint smile passed across his lips, as though he had been having some delightful dream, yet he had not dreamed at all. His night had been untroubled by any images of

7. Wilde added "except . . . you" in **TS**.
8. Wilde added this sentence in TS.

pleasure or of pain. But youth smiles without any reason. It is one of its chiefest charms.[1]

He turned round, and, leaning on his elbow, began to drink his chocolate. The mellow November sun was streaming into the room. The sky was bright blue, and there was a genial warmth in the air. It was almost like a morning in May.

Gradually the events of the preceding night crept with silent blood-stained feet into his brain, and reconstructed themselves there with terrible distinctness. He winced at the memory of all that he had suffered, and for a moment the same curious feeling of loathing for Basil Hallward, that had made him kill him as he sat in the chair, came back to him, and he grew cold with passion. The dead man was still sitting there, too, and in the sunlight now. How horrible that was! Such hideous things were for the darkness, not for the day.

He felt that if he brooded on what he had gone through he would sicken or grow mad. There were sins whose fascination was more in the memory than in the doing of them, strange triumphs that grati-fied the pride more than the passions, and gave to the intellect a quickened sense of joy, greater than any joy they brought, or could ever bring, to the senses. But this was not one of them. It was a thing to be driven out of the mind, to be drugged with poppies, to be stran-gled lest it might strangle one itself.

He passed his hand across his forehead, and then got up hastily,[2] and dressed himself with even more than his usual attention, giv-ing a good deal of care to the selection of his necktie and scarf-pin, and changing his rings more than once.

He spent a long time over breakfast, tasting the various dishes, talking to his valet about some new liveries that he was thinking of getting made for the servants at Selby, and going through his cor-respondence. Over some of the letters he smiled. Three of them bored him. One he read several times over, and then tore up with a slight look of annoyance in his face. "That awful thing, a woman's memory!" as Lord Henry had once said.

When he had drunk his coffee, he sat down at the table, and wrote two letters. One he put in his pocket, the other he handed to the valet.

"Take this round to 152, Hertford Street, Francis, and if Mr. Camp-bell is out of town, get his address."

As soon as he was alone, he lit a cigarette, and began sketching upon a piece of paper, drawing flowers, and bits of architecture, first, and then faces. Suddenly he remarked that every face that he drew seemed to have an extraordinary likeness to Basil Hallward. He

---

1. Wilde added the last two sentences in TS.
2. Here Wilde canceled the following in TS: "and having thrown on his heavy white dress-ing gown, passed into the bathroom. When he came out again, he felt calmer."

frowned, and, getting up, went over to the bookcase and took out a volume at hazard. He was determined that he would not think about what had happened, till it became absolutely necessary to do so.

When he had stretched himself on the sofa, he looked at the title-page of the book. It was Gautier's "Émaux et Camées,"[3] Charpentier's Japanese-paper edition, with the Jacquemart etching. The binding was of citron-green leather with a design of gilt trellis-work and dotted pomegranates. It had been given to him by Adrian Singleton.[4] As he turned over the pages his eye fell on the poem about the hand of Lacenaire, the cold yellow hand *"du supplice encore mal lavée,"* with its downy red hairs and its *"doigts de faune."* He glanced at his own white taper fingers, and passed on, till he came to those lovely verses upon Venice:

> Sur une gamme chromatique,
>   Le sein de perles ruisselant,
> La Vénus de l'Adriatique
>   Sort de l'eau son corps rose et blanc.
>
> Les dômes, sur l'azur des ondes
>   Suivant la phrase au pur contour,
> S'enflent comme des gorges rondes
>   Que soulève un soupir d'amour.
>
> L'esquif aborde et me dépose,
>   Jetant son amarre au pilier,
> Devant une façade rose,
>   Sur le marbre d'un escalier.

How exquisite they were! As one read them, one seemed to be floating down the green water-ways of the pink and pearl city, lying in a black gondola with silver prow and trailing curtains. The mere lines looked to him like those straight lines of turquoise-blue that follow one as one pushes out to the Lido. The sudden flashes of color reminded him of the gleam of the opal-and-iris-throated birds that flutter round the tall honey-combed Campanile, or stalk, with such stately grace, through the dim arcades. Leaning back with half-closed eyes, he kept saying over and over to himself,—

> Devant une façade rose,
>   Sur le marbre d'un escalier.

The whole of Venice was in those two lines. He remembered the autumn that he had passed there, and a wonderful love that had

---

3. Wilde's original choice in MS was a volume of "sonnets by Verlaine."
4. Wilde added "the binding . . . Singleton" in MS.

stirred him to delightful fantastic follies. There was romance in every place. But Venice, like Oxford, had kept the background for romance, and background was everything, or almost everything. Basil had been with him part of the time, and had gone wild over Tintoret. Poor Basil! What a horrible way for a man to die!

He sighed, and took up the book again, and tried to forget. He read of the swallows that fly in and out of the little café at Smyrna where the Hadjis sit counting their amber beads and the turbaned merchants smoke their long tasselled pipes and talk gravely to each other; of the Obelisk in the Place de la Concorde that weeps tears of granite in its lonely sunless exile, and longs to be back by the hot lotus-covered Nile, where there are Sphinxes, and rose-red ibises, and white vultures with gilded claws, and crocodiles, with small beryl eyes, that crawl over the green steaming mud; and of that curious statue that Gautier compares to a contralto voice, the *"monstre charmant"* that couches in the porphyry-room of the Louvre. But after a time the book fell from his hand. He grew nervous, and a horrible fit of terror came over him. What if Alan Campbell should be out of England? Days would elapse before he could come back. Perhaps he might refuse to come. What could he do then? Every moment was of vital importance.

They had been great friends once, five years before,—almost inseparable, indeed. Then the intimacy had come suddenly to an end. When they met in society now, it was only Dorian Gray who smiled: Alan Campbell never did.

He was an extremely clever young man, though he had no real appreciation of the visible arts, and whatever little sense of the beauty of poetry he possessed he had gained entirely from Dorian. His dominant intellectual passion was for science. At Cambridge he had spent a great deal of his time working in the Laboratory, and had taken a good class in the Natural Science tripos of his year. Indeed, he was still devoted to the study of chemistry, and had a laboratory of his own, in which he used to shut himself up all day long, greatly to the annoyance of his mother, who had set her heart on his standing for Parliament and had a vague idea that a chemist was a person who made up prescriptions. He was an excellent musician, however, as well, and played both the violin and the piano better than most amateurs. In fact, it was music that had first brought him and Dorian Gray together,—music and that indefinable attraction that Dorian seemed to be able to exercise whenever he wished, and indeed exercised often without being conscious of it. They had met at Lady Berkshire's the night that Rubinstein played there, and after that used to be always seen together at the Opera, and wherever good music was going on. For eighteen months their intimacy lasted. Campbell was always either at Selby Royal or in

Grosvenor Square. To him, as to many others, Dorian Gray was the type of everything that is wonderful and fascinating in life. Whether or not a quarrel had taken place between them no one ever knew. But suddenly people remarked that they scarcely spoke when they met, and that Campbell seemed always to go away early from any party at which Dorian Gray was present. He had changed, too,—was strangely melancholy at times, appeared almost to dislike hearing music of any passionate character, and would never himself play, giving as his excuse, when he was called upon, that he was so absorbed in science that he had no time left in which to practise. And this was certainly true. Every day he seemed to become more interested in biology, and his name appeared once or twice in some of the scientific reviews, in connection with certain curious experiments.

This was the man that Dorian Gray was waiting for, pacing up and down the room, glancing every moment at the clock, and becoming horribly agitated as the minutes went by. At last the door opened, and his servant entered.[5]

"Mr. Alan Campbell, sir."

A sigh of relief broke from his parched lips, and the color came back to his cheeks.

"Ask him to come in at once, Francis."

The man bowed, and retired. In a few moments, Alan Campbell walked in, looking very stern and rather pale, his pallor being intensified by his coal-black hair and dark eyebrows.

"Alan! this is kind of you. I thank you for coming."

"I had intended never to enter your house again, Gray. But you said it was a matter of life and death." His voice was hard and cold. He spoke with slow deliberation. There was a look of contempt in the steady searching gaze that he turned on Dorian. He kept his hands in the pockets of his Astrakhan coat, and appeared not to have noticed the gesture with which he had been greeted.

"It is a matter of life and death, Alan, and to more than one person. Sit down."

Campbell took a chair by the table, and Dorian sat opposite to him. The two men's eyes met. In Dorian's there was infinite pity. He knew that what he was going to do was dreadful.

After a strained moment of silence, he leaned across and said, very quietly, but watching the effect of each word upon the face of the man he had sent for,[6] "Alan, in a locked room at the top of this house, a room to which nobody but myself has access, a dead man is seated at a table. He has been dead ten hours now. Don't stir, and

5. Wilde made alterations and additions here in 1891.
6. Wilde added "very quietly . . . sent for" in TS.

don't look at me like that. Who the man is, why he died, how he died, are matters that do not concern you. What you have to do is this—"

"Stop, Gray. I don't want to know anything further. Whether what you have told me is true or not true, doesn't concern me. I entirely decline to be mixed up in your life. Keep your horrible secrets to yourself. They don't interest me any more."

"Alan, they will have to interest you. This one will have to interest you. I am awfully sorry for you, Alan. But I can't help myself. You are the one man who is able to save me. I am forced to bring you into the matter. I have no option. Alan, you are a scientist. You know about chemistry, and things of that kind. You have made experiments. What you have got to do is to destroy the thing that is up-stairs,—to destroy it so that not a vestige will be left of it. Nobody saw this person come into the house. Indeed, at the present moment he is supposed to be in Paris. He will not be missed for months. When he is missed, there must be no trace of him found here. You, Alan, you must change him, and everything that belongs to him, into a handful of ashes that I may scatter in the air."

"You are mad, Dorian."

"Ah! I was waiting for you to call me Dorian."

"You are mad, I tell you,—mad to imagine that I would raise a finger to help you, mad to make this monstrous confession. I will have nothing to do with this matter, whatever it is. Do you think I am going to peril my reputation for you? What is it to me what devil's work you are up to?"

"It was a suicide, Alan."

"I am glad of that. But who drove him to it? You, I should fancy."

"Do you still refuse to do this, for me?"

"Of course I refuse. I will have absolutely nothing to do with it. I don't care what shame comes on you. You deserve it all. I should not be sorry to see you disgraced, publicly disgraced. How dare you ask me, of all men in the world, to mix myself up in this horror? I should have thought you knew more about people's characters. Your friend Lord Henry Wotton can't have taught you much about psychology, whatever else he has taught you. Nothing will induce me to stir a step to help you. You have come to the wrong man. Go to some of your friends. Don't come to me."

"Alan, it was murder. I killed him. You don't know what he had made me suffer. Whatever my life is, he had more to do with the making or the marring of it than poor Harry has had. He may not have intended it, the result was the same."

"Murder! Good God, Dorian, is that what you have come to? I shall not inform upon you. It is not my business. Besides, you are certain to be arrested, without my stirring in the matter. Nobody ever commits a murder without doing something stupid. But I will have nothing to do with it."

"All I ask of you is to perform a certain scientific experiment. You go to hospitals and dead-houses, and the horrors that you do there don't affect you. If in some hideous dissecting-room or fetid laboratory you found this man lying on a leaden table with red gutters scooped out in it, you would simply look upon him as an admirable subject. You would not turn a hair. You would not believe that you were doing anything wrong. On the contrary, you would probably feel that you were benefiting the human race, or increasing the sum of knowledge in the world, or gratifying intellectual curiosity, or something of that kind. What I want you to do is simply what you have often done before. Indeed, to destroy a body must be less horrible than what you are accustomed to work at. And, remember, it is the only piece of evidence against me. If it is discovered, I am lost; and it is sure to be discovered unless you help me."

"I have no desire to help you. You forget that.[7] I am simply indifferent to the whole thing. It has nothing to do with me."

"Alan, I entreat you. Think of the position I am in. Just before you came I almost fainted with terror. No! don't think of that. Look at the matter purely from the scientific point of view. You don't inquire where the dead things on which you experiment come from. Don't inquire now. I have told you too much as it is. But I beg of you to do this. We were friends once, Alan."

"Don't speak about those days, Dorian: they are dead."

"The dead linger sometimes. The man up-stairs will not go away. He is sitting at the table with bowed head and outstretched arms. Alan! Alan! if you don't come to my assistance I am ruined. Why, they will hang me, Alan! Don't you understand? They will hang me for what I have done."[8]

"There is no good in prolonging this scene. I refuse absolutely to do anything in the matter. It is insane of you to ask me."

"You refuse absolutely?"

"Yes."

The same look of pity came into Dorian's eyes, then he stretched out his hand, took a piece of paper, and wrote something on it. He read it over twice, folded it carefully, and pushed it across the table. Having done this, he got up, and went over to the window.

Campbell looked at him in surprise, and then took up the paper, and opened it. As he read it, his face became ghastly pale, and he fell back in his chair. A horrible sense of sickness came over him.

7. Wilde canceled "Had this happened three years ago, I might have consented to be your accomplice" in MS.
8. Wilde added "Why, they . . . have done" in TS.

He felt as if his heart was beating itself to death in some empty hollow.[9]

After two or three minutes of terrible silence, Dorian turned round, and came and stood behind him, putting his hand upon his shoulder.

"I am so sorry, Alan," he murmured, "but you leave me no alternative. I have a letter written already. Here it is. You see the address. If you don't help me, I must send it. You know what the result will be. But you are going to help me. It is impossible for you to refuse now. I tried to spare you. You will do me the justice to admit that. You were stern, harsh, offensive. You treated me as no man has ever dared to treat me,—no living man, at any rate. I bore it all. Now it is for me to dictate terms."

Campbell buried his face in his hands, and a shudder passed through him.

"Yes, it is my turn to dictate terms, Alan. You know what they are. The thing is quite simple. Come, don't work yourself into this fever. The thing has to be done. Face it, and do it."

A groan broke from Campbell's lips, and he shivered all over. The ticking of the clock on the mantel-piece seemed to him to be dividing time into separate atoms of agony, each of which was too terrible to be borne. He felt as if an iron ring was being slowly tightened round his forehead, and as if the disgrace with which he was threatened had already come upon him. The hand upon his shoulder weighed like a hand of lead. It was intolerable. It seemed to crush him.

"Come, Alan, you must decide at once."

He hesitated a moment. "Is there a fire in the room up-stairs?" he murmured.

"Yes, there is a gas-fire with asbestos."

"I will have to go home and get some things from the laboratory."

"No, Alan, you will not leave the house. Write on a sheet of note-paper what you want, and my servant will take a cab and bring the things back to you."

Campbell wrote a few lines, blotted them, and addressed an envelope to his assistant. Dorian took the note up and read it carefully. Then he rang the bell, and gave it to his valet, with orders to return as soon as possible, and to bring the things with him.

When the hall door shut, Campbell started, and, having got up from the chair, went over to the chimney-piece.[1] He was shivering with a sort of ague. For nearly twenty minutes, neither of the men spoke. A fly buzzed noisily about the room, and the ticking of the clock was like the beat of a hammer.

---

9. Wilde canceled "He tried to speak, but his tongue seemed to be paralyzed" in TS.
1. Wilde canceled "The pain in his forehead was less than it had been but" in TS.

As the chime struck one, Campbell turned around, and, looking at Dorian Gray, saw that his eyes were filled with tears. There was something in the purity and the refinement of that sad face that seemed to enrage him. "You are infamous, absolutely infamous!" he muttered.

"Hush, Alan: you have saved my life," said Dorian.

"*Your* life? Good heavens! what a life that is! You have gone from corruption to corruption, and now you have culminated in crime. In doing what I am going to do, what you force me to do, it is not of *your* life that I am thinking."

"Ah, Alan," murmured Dorian, with a sigh, "I wish you had a thousandth part of the pity for me that I have for you." He turned away, as he spoke, and stood looking out at the garden. Campbell made no answer.

After about ten minutes a knock came to the door, and the servant entered, carrying a mahogany chest of chemicals, with a small electric battery set on top of it. He placed it on the table, and went out again, returning with a long coil of steel and platinum wire and two rather curiously-shaped iron clamps.

"Shall I leave the things here, sir?" he asked Campbell.

"Yes," said Dorian. "And I am afraid, Francis, that I have another errand for you. What is the name of the man at Richmond who supplies Selby with orchids?"

"Harden, sir?"

"Yes,—Harden. You must go down to Richmond at once, see Harden personally, and tell him to send twice as many orchids as I ordered, and to have as few white ones as possible. In fact, I don't want any white ones. It is a lovely day, Francis, and Richmond is a very pretty place, otherwise I wouldn't bother you about it."

"No trouble, sir. At what time shall I be back?"

Dorian looked at Campbell. "How long will your experiment take, Alan?" he said, in a calm, indifferent voice. The presence of a third person in the room seemed to give him extraordinary courage.

Campbell frowned, and bit his lip. "It will take about five hours," he answered.

"It will be time enough, then, if you are back at half-past seven, Francis. Or stay: just leave my things out for dressing. You can have the evening to yourself. I am not dining at home, so I shall not want you."

"Thank you, sir," said the man, leaving the room.

"Now, Alan, there is not a moment to be lost. How heavy this chest is! I'll take it for you. You bring the other things." He spoke rapidly, and in an authoritative manner. Campbell felt dominated by him. They left the room together.

When they reached the top landing, Dorian took out the key and turned it in the lock. Then he stopped, and a troubled look came into his eyes. He shuddered. "I don't think I can go in, Alan," he murmured.

"It is nothing to me. I don't require you," said Campbell, coldly.

Dorian half opened the door. As he did so, he saw the face of the portrait grinning in the sunlight. On the floor in front of it the torn curtain was lying. He remembered that the night before, for the first time in his life, he had forgotten to hide it, when he crept out of the room.[2]

But what was that loathsome red dew that gleamed, wet and glistening, on one of the hands, as though the canvas had sweated blood? How horrible it was!—more horrible, it seemed to him for the moment, than the silent thing that he knew was stretched across the table, the thing whose grotesque misshapen shadow on the spotted carpet showed him that it had not stirred, but was still there, as he had left it.

He opened the door a little wider, and walked quickly in, with half-closed eyes and averted head, determined that he would not look even once upon the dead man. Then, stooping down, and taking up the gold-and-purple hanging, he flung it over the picture.

He stopped, feeling afraid to turn round, and his eyes fixed themselves on the intricacies of the pattern before him. He heard Campbell bringing in the heavy chest, and the irons, and the other things that he had required for his dreadful work. He began to wonder if he and Basil Hallward had ever met, and, if so, what they had thought of each other.

"Leave me now," said Campbell.

He turned and hurried out, just conscious that the dead man had been thrust back into the chair and was sitting up in it, with Campbell gazing into the glistening yellow face. As he was going downstairs he heard the key being turned in the lock.

It was long after seven o'clock when Campbell came back into the library. He was pale, but absolutely calm. "I have done what you asked me to do," he muttered. "And now, good-by. Let us never see each other again."

"You have saved me from ruin, Alan. I cannot forget that," said Dorian, simply.

As soon as Campbell had left, he went up-stairs. There was a horrible smell of chemicals in the room. But the thing that had been sitting at the table was gone.

---

2. Wilde made some changes here in 1891.

Chapter XIII[1]

"There is no good telling me you are going to be good, Dorian," cried Lord Henry, dipping his white fingers into a red copper bowl filled with rose-water. "You are quite perfect. Pray don't change."

Dorian shook his head. "No, Harry, I have done too many dreadful things in my life. I am not going to do any more. I began my good actions yesterday."

"Where were you yesterday?"

"In the country, Harry. I was staying at a little inn by myself."

"My dear boy," said Lord Henry smiling, "anybody can be good in the country. There are no temptations there. That is the reason why people who live out of town are so uncivilized. There are only two ways, as you know, of becoming civilized. One is by being cultured, the other is by being corrupt. Country-people have no opportunity of being either, so they stagnate."

"Culture and corruption," murmured Dorian. "I have known something of both. It seems to me curious now that they should ever be found together. For I have a new ideal, Harry. I am going to alter. I think I have altered."

"You have not told me yet what your good action was. Or did you say you had done more than one?"

"I can tell you, Harry. It is not a story I could tell to any one else. I spared somebody. It sounds vain, but you understand what I mean. She was quite beautiful, and wonderfully like Sibyl Vane. I think it was that which first attracted me to her. You remember Sibyl, don't you? How long ago that seems! Well, Hetty[2] was not one of our own class, of course. She was simply a girl in a village. But I really loved her. I am quite sure that I loved her. All during this wonderful May that we have been having, I used to run down and see her two or three times a week.[3] Yesterday she met me in a little orchard. The apple-blossoms kept tumbling down on her hair, and she was laughing. We were to have gone away together this morning at dawn. Suddenly[4] I determined to leave her as flower-like as I had found her."

"I should think the novelty of the emotion must have given you a thrill of real pleasure, Dorian," interrupted Lord Henry. "But I can

1. Wilde added chapters 15–18 here in 1891. *Lippincott's* chapter 13 was then divided into 19 and 20 (1891).
2. Wilde reconstructed the first part of this paragraph in TS, adding "to her. . . . Well, Hetty" in TS.
3. Stoddart canceled "Finally, she promised to come with me to town. I had taken a house for her, and arranged everything." Wilde canceled Stoddart's emendation: "She would have come away with me."
4. Stoddart canceled "said to myself, 'I won't ruin this girl. I won't bring her to shame. And I . . .'" in TS.

finish your idyl for you. You gave her good advice, and broke her heart. That was the beginning of your reformation."

"Harry, you are horrible! You mustn't say these dreadful things. Hetty's heart is not broken. Of course she cried, and all that. But[5] there is no disgrace upon her. She can live, like Perdita, in her garden."

"And weep over a faithless Florizel," said Lord Henry, laughing. "My dear Dorian, you have the most curious boyish moods. Do you think this girl will ever be really contented now with any one of her own rank? I suppose she will be married some day to a rough carter or a grinning ploughman. Well, having met you, and loved you, will teach her to despise her husband, and she will be wretched.[6] From a moral point of view I really don't think much of your great renunciation. Even as a beginning, it is poor. Besides, how do you know that Hetty isn't floating at the present moment in some mill-pond, with water-lilies round her, like Ophelia?"

"I can't bear this, Harry! You mock at everything, and then suggest the most serious tragedies. I am sorry I told you now. I don't care what you say to me, I know I was right in acting as I did. Poor Hetty! As I rode past the farm this morning, I saw her white face at the window, like a spray of jasmine. Don't let me talk about it any more, and don't try to persuade me that the first good action I have done for years, the first little bit of self-sacrifice I have ever known, is really a sort of sin. I want to be better. I am going to be better. Tell me something about yourself. What is going on in town? I have not been to the club for days."

"The people are still discussing poor Basil's disappearance."

"I should have thought they had got tired of that by this time," said Dorian, pouring himself out some wine, and frowning slightly.

"My dear boy, they have only been talking about it for six weeks, and the public are really not equal to the mental strain of having more than one topic every three months. They have been very fortunate lately, however. They have had my own divorce-case, and Alan Campbell's suicide. Now they have got the mysterious disappearance of an artist. Scotland Yard still insists that the man in the gray ulster who left Victoria by the midnight train on the 7th of November was poor Basil, and the French police declare that Basil never arrived in Paris at all. I suppose in about a fortnight we will be told that he has been seen in San Francisco. It is an odd thing,

---

5. Stoddart canceled "her life is not spoiled" here in TS.
6. Stoddart again canceled a passage, this one a marginal addition by Wilde: "Upon the other hand, had she become your mistress, she would have lived in the society of charming and cultivated men. You would have educated her, taught her how to dress, how to talk, how to move. You would have made her perfect, and she would have been extremely happy. After a time, no doubt, you would have grown tired of her. She would have made a scene. You would have made a settlement. Then a new career would have begun for her."

but every one who disappears is said to be seen at San Francisco. It must be a delightful city, and possess all the attractions of the next world."

"What do you think has happened to Basil?" asked Dorian, holding up his Burgundy against the light, and wondering how it was that he could discuss the matter so calmly.

"I have not the slightest idea. If Basil chooses to hide himself, it is no business of mine. If he is dead, I don't want to think about him. Death is the only thing that ever terrifies me. I hate it. One can survive everything nowadays except that. Death and vulgarity are the only two facts in the nineteenth century that one cannot explain away. Let us have our coffee in the music-room, Dorian. You must play Chopin to me. The man with whom my wife ran away played Chopin exquisitely. Poor Victoria![7] I was very fond of her. The house is rather lonely without her."

Dorian said nothing, but rose from the table, and, passing into the next room, sat down to the piano and let his fingers stray across the keys. After the coffee had been brought in, he stopped, and, looking over at Lord Henry, said, "Harry, did it ever occur to you that Basil was murdered?"

Lord Henry yawned. "Basil had no enemies, and always wore a Waterbury watch. Why should he be murdered?[8] He was not clever enough to have enemies. Of course he had a wonderful genius for painting. But a man can paint like Velasquez and yet be as dull as possible. Basil was really rather dull. He only interested me once, and that was when he told me, years ago, that he had a wild adoration for you."

"I was very fond of Basil," said Dorian, with a sad look in his eyes. "But don't people say that he was murdered?"

"Oh, some of the papers do. It does not seem to be probable. I know there are dreadful places in Paris, but Basil was not the sort of man to have gone to them. He had no curiosity. It was his chief defect.[9] Play me a nocturne, Dorian, and, as you play, tell me, in a low voice, how you have kept your youth. You must have some secret. I am only ten years older than you are, and I am wrinkled, and bald, and yellow. You are really wonderful, Dorian. You have never looked more charming than you do to-night. You remind me of the day I saw you first. You were rather cheeky, very shy, and absolutely

---

7. Stoddart canceled the following: "She was desperately in love with you at one time, Dorian. It used to amuse me to watch her paying you compliments. You were so charmingly indifferent. Do you know I really miss her? She never bored me. She was so delightfully improbable in everything that she did." Wilde added several lines here in 1891.
8. Wilde added "and always . . . murdered?" in TS.
9. Wilde added about four new pages here in 1891, beginning "What would you say, Harry" and ending with "given up our belief in the soul" (see pp. 176–78).

extraordinary. You have changed, of course, but not in appearance. I wish you would tell me your secret. To get back my youth I would do anything in the world, except take exercise, get up early, or be respectable. Youth! There is nothing like it. It's absurd to talk of the ignorance of youth. The only people whose opinions I listen to now with any respect are people much younger than myself. They seem in front of me. Life has revealed to them her last wonder. As for the aged, I always contradict the aged. I do it on principle. If you ask them their opinion on something that happened yesterday, they solemnly give you the opinions current in 1820, when people wore high stocks and knew absolutely nothing. How lovely that thing you are playing is! I wonder did Chopin write it at Majorca, with the sea weeping round the villa, and the salt spray dashing against the panes? It is marvelously romantic. What a blessing it is that there is one art left to us that is not imitative! Don't stop. I want music to-night. It seems to me that you are the young Apollo, and that I am Marsyas listening to you. I have sorrows, Dorian, of my own, that even you know nothing of.[1] The tragedy of old age is not that one is old, but that one is young.[2] I am amazed sometimes at my own sincerity. Ah, Dorian, how happy you are! What an exquisite life you have had.[3] You have drunk deeply of everything. You have crushed the grapes against your palate. Nothing has been hidden from you. But it has all been to you no more than the sound of music. It has not marred you. You are still the same.

"I wonder what the rest of your life will be. Don't spoil it by renunciations. At present you are a perfect type. Don't make yourself incomplete. You are quite flawless now. You need not shake your head: you know you are. Besides, Dorian, don't deceive yourself. Life is not governed by will or intention. Life is a question of nerves, and fibres, and slowly-built-up cells in which thought hides itself and passion has its dreams. You may fancy yourself safe, and think yourself strong. But a chance tone of color in a room or a morning sky, a particular perfume that you had once loved and that brings strange memories with it, a line from a forgotten poem that you had come across again, a cadence from a piece of music that you had ceased to play,—I tell you, Dorian, that it is on things like these that our lives depend. Browning writes about that somewhere; but our own senses will imagine them for us. There are moments when the odor of heliotrope passes suddenly across me, and I have to live the strangest year of my life over again.[4]

---

1. Wilde canceled in MS "moments of anguish and regret" here.
2. Wilde added this epigram in TS.
3. Wilde canceled the following in TS: "I have always been too much of a critic. I have been afraid of things wounding me, and have looked on."
4. Wilde made alterations here in 1891 (see p. 179).

"I wish I could change places with you, Dorian. The world has cried out against us both, but it has always worshipped you. It always will worship you. You are the type of what the age is searching for, and what it is afraid it has found. I am so glad that you have never done anything, never carved a statue, or painted a picture, or produced anything outside of yourself! Life has been your art. You have set yourself to music. Your days have been your sonnets."

Dorian rose up from the piano, and passed his hand through his hair. "Yes, life has been exquisite," he murmured, "but I am not going to have the same life, Harry. And you must not say these extravagant things to me. You don't know everything about me. I think that if you did, even you would turn from me. You laugh. Don't laugh."

"Why have you stopped playing, Dorian? Go back and play the nocturne over again. Look at that great honey-colored moon that hangs in the dusky air. She is waiting for you to charm her, and if you play she will come closer to the earth. You won't? Let us go to the club, then. It has been a charming evening, and we must end it charmingly. There is some one at the club who wants immensely to know you,—young Lord Poole, Bournmouth's eldest son. He has already copied your neckties, and has begged me to introduce him to you. He is quite delightful, and rather reminds me of you."

"I hope not," said Dorian, with a touch of pathos in his voice. "But I am tired to-night, Harry. I won't go to the club. It is nearly eleven, and I want to go to bed early."

"Do stay. You have never played so well as to-night. There was something in your touch that was wonderful. It had more expression than I had ever heard from it before."

"It is because I am going to be good," he answered, smiling. "I am a little changed already."

"Don't change, Dorian; at any rate, don't change to me. We must always be friends."

"Yet you poisoned me with a book once. I should not forgive that. Harry, promise me that you will never lend that book to any one. It does harm."

"My dear boy, you are really beginning to moralize. You will soon be going about warning people against all the sins of which you have grown tired. You are much too delightful to do that. Besides, it is no use. You and I are what we are, and will be what we will be.[5] Come round to-morrow. I am going to ride at eleven, and we might go together. The Park is quite lovely now. I don't think there have been such lilacs since the year I met you."

---

5. A dozen lines or so were added here in 1891, nearly half of which argue against art influencing human action.

"Very well. I will be here at eleven," said Dorian. "Good-night, Harry." As he reached the door he hesitated for a moment, as if he had something more to say. Then he sighed and went out.[6]

It was a lovely night, so warm that he threw his coat over his arm, and did not even put his silk scarf round his throat. As he strolled home, smoking his cigarette, two young men in evening dress passed him. He heard one of them whisper to the other, "That is Dorian Gray." He remembered how pleased he used to be when he was pointed out, or stared at, or talked about. He was tired of hearing his own name now. Half the charm of the little village where he had been so often lately was that no one knew who he was. He had told the girl whom he had made love him that he was poor, and she had believed him. He had told her once that he was wicked, and she had laughed at him, and told him that wicked people were always very old and very ugly. What a laugh she had!—just like a thrush singing. And how pretty she had been in her cotton dresses and her large hats! She knew nothing, but she had everything that he had lost.

When he reached home, he found his servant waiting up for him. He sent him to bed, and threw himself down on the sofa in the library, and began to think over some of the things that Lord Henry had said to him.

Was it really true that one could never change? He felt a wild longing for the unstained purity of his boyhood,—his rose-white boyhood, as Lord Henry had once called it. He knew that he had tarnished himself, filled his mind with corruption, and given horror to his fancy; that he had been an evil influence to others, and had experienced a terrible joy in being so; and that of the lives that had crossed his own it had been the fairest and the most full of promise that he had brought to shame. But was it all irretrievable? Was there no hope for him?[7]

It was better not to think of the past. Nothing could alter that. It was of himself, and of his own future, that he had to think,[8] Alan Campbell had shot himself one night in his laboratory, but had not revealed the secret that he had been forced to know. The excitement, such as it was, over Basil Hallward's disappearance would soon pass away. It was already waning. He was perfectly safe there. Nor, indeed, was it the death of Basil Hallward that weighed most upon his mind. It was the living death of his own soul that troubled him. Basil had painted the portrait that had marred his life. He could not forgive him that. It was the portrait that had done everything. Basil had said

---

6. Chapter 19 (1891) ends here.
7. Wilde added two paragraphs here in 1891.
8. Wilde added a reference to Sibyl's brother here in 1891.

things to him that were unbearable, and that he had yet borne with patience. The murder had been simply the madness of a moment. As for Alan Campbell, his suicide had been his own act. He had chosen to do it. It was nothing to him.

A new life! That was what he wanted. That was what he was waiting for. Surely he had begun it already. He had spared one innocent thing, at any rate. He would never again tempt innocence. He would be good.

As he thought of Hetty Merton, he began to wonder if the portrait in the locked room had changed. Surely it was not still so horrible as it had been? Perhaps if his life became pure, he would be able to expel every sign of evil passion from the face. Perhaps the signs of evil had already gone away. He would go and look.

He took the lamp from the table and crept up-stairs. As he unlocked the door, a smile of joy flitted across his young face and lingered for a moment about his lips. Yes, he would be good, and the hideous thing that he had hidden away would no longer be a terror to him. He felt as if the load had been lifted from him already.

He went in quietly, locking the door behind him, as was his custom, and dragged the purple hanging from the portrait. A cry of pain and indignation broke from him. He could see no change, unless that in the eyes there was a look of cunning, and in the mouth the curved wrinkle of the hypocrite. The thing was still loathsome,— more loathsome, if possible, than before,—and the scarlet dew that spotted the hand seemed brighter, and more like blood newly spilt.

Had it been merely vanity that had made him do his one good deed? Or the desire of a new sensation, as Lord Henry had hinted, with his mocking laugh? Or that passion to act a part that sometimes makes us do things finer than we are ourselves? Or, perhaps, all these?

Why was the red stain larger than it had been? It seemed to have crept like a horrible disease over the wrinkled fingers. There was blood on the painted feet, as though the thing had dripped,—blood even on the hand that had not held the knife.

Confess? Did it mean that he was to confess? To give himself up, and be put to death? He laughed. He felt that the idea was monstrous. Besides, who would believe him, even if he did confess? There was no trace of the murdered man anywhere. Everything belonging to him had been destroyed. He himself had burned what had been below-stairs. The world would simply say he was mad. They would shut him up if he persisted in his story.

Yet it was his duty to confess, to suffer public shame, and to make public atonement. There was a God who called upon men to tell their sins to earth as well as to heaven. Nothing that he could do would cleanse him till he had told his own sin. His sin? He shrugged his shoulders. The death of Basil Hallward seemed very little to him. He was thinking of Hetty Merton.

It was an unjust mirror, this mirror of his soul that he was looking at. Vanity? Curiosity? Hypocrisy? Had there been nothing more in his renunciation than that? There had been something more. At least he thought so. But who could tell?[9]

And this murder,—was it to dog him all his life? Was he never to get rid of the past? Was he really to confess? No. There was only one bit of evidence left against him. The picture itself,—that was evidence.

He would destroy it. Why had he kept it so long? It had given him pleasure once to watch it changing and growing old. Of late he had felt no such pleasure. It had kept him awake at night. When he had been away, he had been filled with terror lest other eyes should look upon it. It had brought melancholy across his passions. Its mere memory had marred many moments of joy. It had been like conscience to him. Yes, it had been conscience. He would destroy it.

He looked round, and saw the knife that had stabbed Basil Hallward. He had cleaned it many times, till there was no stain left upon it. It was bright, and glistened.[1] As it had killed the painter, so it would kill the painter's work, and all that that meant. It would kill the past, and when that was dead he would be free.[2] He seized it, and stabbed the canvas with it, ripping the thing right up from top to bottom.[3]

There was a cry heard, and a crash. The cry was so horrible in its agony that the frightened servants woke, and crept out of their rooms. Two gentlemen, who were passing in the Square below, stopped, and looked up at the great house. They walked on till they met a policeman, and brought him back. The man rang the bell several times, but there was no answer. The house was all dark, except for a light in one of the top windows. After a time, he went away, and stood in the portico of the next house and watched.

"Whose house is that, constable?" asked the elder of the two gentlemen.

"Mr. Dorian Gray's, sir," answered the policeman.

They looked at each other, as they walked away, and sneered. One of them was Sir Henry Ashton's uncle.

Inside, in the servants' part of the house, the half-clad domestics were talking in low whispers to each other. Old Mrs. Leaf was crying, and wringing her hands.[4] Francis was as pale as death.

---

9. Wilde added five lines here in 1891.
1. Wilde canceled in MS "He took it up and darted it into the canvas."
2. Wilde added this sentence in TS and another in 1891.
3. Wilde deleted "ripping . . . bottom," after changing "canvas" to "picture."
4. Wilde changed TS from "One of the maids was crying."

After about a quarter of an hour, he got the coachman and one of the footmen and crept up-stairs. They knocked, but there was no reply. They called out. Everything was still. Finally, after vainly trying to force the door, they got on the roof, and dropped down on to the balcony. The windows yielded easily: the bolts were old.

When they entered, they found hanging upon the wall a splendid portrait of their master as they had last seen him, in all the wonder of his exquisite youth and beauty. Lying on the floor was a dead man in evening dress, with a knife in his heart. He was withered, wrinkled and loathsome of visage. It was not till they had examined the rings that they recognized who it was.[5]

---

5. In TS, Wilde altered the original ending: "When they entered, they found on the wall the portrait of a young man of extraordinary personal beauty, their master as they had last seen him. Lying on the floor was a dead body, withered, wrinkled, and loathsome of visage with a knife in its heart."

BACKGROUNDS

A Note on "Backgrounds"

"I am large, I contain multitudes."
—Walt Whitman, "Song of Myself"

Throughout his creative life, Oscar Wilde proved to be a marvelous fabricator. He could form beautiful and effective prose with workman-like efficiency, and he also had the deft ability to distill defining features of literary antecedents into original and imaginatively engaging works. *The Picture of Dorian Gray* in many ways embodies Wilde's fine sense of literary tradition, highlights the major influences of his literary apprenticeship, and introduces the mature style that characterized his writings in the 1890s.

In presenting backgrounds to Wilde's writing, this Norton Critical Edition attempts a delicate balance. No writers of any merit produce their works absent the influence of powerful imaginations that preceded them. Particular influences will vary from author to author, but the consistent feature of awareness of a literary tradition remains a constant. Wilde, trained as a classicist and deeply aware of contemporary literature and aesthetic theory, doubtless had a range of forces shaping his creative efforts. Limitations of space, however, have forced the editor to offer a selective sampling of both influential writers and Wilde's early creative efforts derived from that engagement.

The following collection of backgrounds to *The Picture of Dorian Gray* attempts to illustrate some specific influences as they appear in the work of other writers and then as they are interpreted in Wilde's own work. Although the expunged details of the "yellow book" in the manuscript and typescript reveal that Joris-Karl Huysmans's *À Rebours* (*Against the Grain*) was less definitively influential on the writing of *The Picture of Dorian Gray* than critics had once supposed, there is no denying that its influence was both important and direct. That is why a representative chapter is included here in translation. As Wilde admitted in a letter of April 15, 1892: "The book in *Dorian Gray* is one of the many books I have never written, but it is partly suggested by Huysmans's *À Rebours*, which you will get at any French booksellers" (*Letters* 313). The chief parallels between *À Rebours* and *The Picture of Dorian Gray* may be summarized briefly: Each develops an interest in curious and even arcane history; each emphasizes the aesthetic and even sensuous dimensions of church ritual and pageantry; each reflects a love of Renaissance demonology and the baroque temper in art and in mores; each shows devotion to the exotic, to sensation, and to decadent taste; each offers the reader extensive if not tedious inventories of jewels, perfumes, and other luxuries of art; and each hints at a spectrum of forbidden practices, especially homoeroticism. But for all these similarities, we should recall that unlike Des Esseintes, the hero of À Rebours, Dorian does not cultivate mere vicarious pleasures, even though he certainly does indulge in sensations artificially produced. The approaches to life of the two self-destructive protagonists are quite distinct. Each fails for different reasons in his quest to create a life that is an extension of art, and the fatal miscalculation in both cases was the willful confusion of art with life.

The selections from Walter Pater's The Renaissance reveal two kinds of influence. The direct borrowings, paraphrasings, and echoes of The Renaissance in Dorian Gray are many, but perhaps no single chapter served as a more obvious source for some of the most telling effects than "Leonardo da Vinci," as the notes testify. Almost the entire chapter is reprinted here to give the reader the sense of the whole out of which Wilde selected some of the most famous and also most appropriate passages to express his own intentions. The famous Conclusion of The Renaissance was for Wilde what John Ruskin's chapter "On the Nature of Gothic" was for designer William Morris. It contained the outline of a philosophy of art that was quickly taken by Pater's disciples as a philosophy of life. While it may be argued that Morris understood and followed Ruskin more faithfully than Wilde interpreted Pater, the Conclusion was a document that interpreted past culture from a perspective whose assumptions and very language were conspicuously modern. It seemed in a few pages to synthesize classic tenets of hedonism, Renaissance cultural enlightenment, modern science, and liberalism. It was in its way a foreshadowing of modern existentialism, only with art at the center of life rather than ethical idealism. Pater was well enough aware of the possible seductiveness of the philosophy espoused in the Conclusion and so removed what was perhaps the book's most famous chapter from its second edition. It was reinstated by Pater in the third and subsequent editions. Wilde's application of Pater's speculations in the practical sphere is evident enough in the two fictional lives he was creating at the time: Dorian's and his own.

The selections from Wilde's own essays included in this edition offer the reader an opportunity to assess the extent to which the ideas and themes of The Picture of Dorian Gray occupied Wilde's mind and imagination during the years from 1889 to 1891. The portions of his essays reprinted here emphasize the thematic unity, aesthetic consistency, and stylistic echoings of his poems, short stories, essays, novel, and even plays. Particular comparisons between essays and novel will reveal the ways Wilde expressed and developed his ideas in these different genres.

JORIS-KARL HUYSMANS

From Against the Grain[†]

* * *

He sank into an easy chair and meditated.

He had long been skilled in the science of smell. He believed that this sense could give one delights equal to those of hearing and sight; each sense being susceptible, if naturally keen and if properly cultivated, to new impressions, which it could intensify, coordinate and compose into that unity which constitutes a creative work. And it was not more abnormal and unnatural that an art should be called into existence by disengaging odors than that another art should be evoked by detaching sound waves or by striking the eye with diversely colored rays. But if no person could discern, without intuition developed by study, a painting by a master from a daub, a melody of Beethoven from one by Clapisson, no more could any one at first, without preliminary initiation, help confusing a bouquet invented by a sincere artist with a pot pourri made by some manufacturer to be sold in groceries and bazaars.

In this art, the branch devoted to achieving certain effects by artificial methods particularly delighted him.

Perfumes, in fact, rarely come from the flowers whose names they bear. The artist who dared to borrow nature's elements would only produce a bastard work which would have neither authenticity nor style, inasmuch as the essence obtained by the distillation of flowers would bear but a distant and vulgar relation to the odor of the living flower, wafting its fragrance into the air.

Thus, with the exception of the inimitable jasmine which it is impossible to counterfeit, all flowers are perfectly represented by the blend of aromatic spirits, stealing the very personality of the model, and to it adding that nuance the more, that heady scent, that rare touch which entitled a thing to be called a work of art.

To resume, in the science of perfumery, the artist develops the natural odor of the flowers, working over his subject like a jeweler refining the lustre of a gem and making it precious.

Little by little, the arcana of this art, most neglected of all, was revealed to Des Esseintes who could now read this language, as diversified and insinuating as that of literature, this style with its unexpected concision under its vague flowing appearance.

To achieve this end he had first been compelled to master the grammar and understand the syntax of odors, learning the secret of

[†] From *À Rebours* (*Against the Grain*), trans. John Howard (New York: Lieber & Lewis, 1922), pp. 168–85.

the rules that regulate them, and, once familiarized with the dialect, he compared the works of the masters, of the Atkinsons and Lubins, the Chardins and Violets, the Legrands and Piesses; then he separated the construction of their phrases, weighed the value of their words and the arrangement of their periods.

Later on, in this idiom of fluids, experience was able to support theories too often incomplete and banal.

Classic perfumery, in fact, was scarcely diversified, almost colorless and uniformly issuing from the mold cast by the ancient chemists. It was in its dotage, confined to its old alambics, when the romantic period was born and had modified the old style, rejuvenating it, making it more supple and malleable.

Step by step, its history followed that of our language. The perfumed Louis XIII style, composed of elements highly prized at that time, of iris powder, musk, chive and myrtle water already designated under the name of "water of the angels," was hardly sufficient to express the cavalier graces, the rather crude tones of the period which certain sonnets of Saint-Amand have preserved for us. Later, with myrrh and olibanum, the mystic odors, austere and powerful, the pompous gesture of the great period, the redundant artifices of oratorial art, the full, sustained harmonious style of Bossuet and the masters of the pulpit were almost possible. Still later, the sophisticated, rather bored graces of French society under Louis XV, more easily found their interpretation in the almond which in a manner summed up this epoch; then, after the ennui and jadedness of the first empire, which misused Eau de Cologne and rosemary, perfumery rushed, in the wake of Victor Hugo and Gautier, towards the Levant. It created oriental combinations, vivid Eastern nosegays, discovered new intonations, antitheses which until then had been unattempted, selected and made use of antique nuances which it complicated, refined and assorted. It resolutely rejected that voluntary decrepitude to which it had been reduced by the Malesherbes, the Boileaus, the Andrieuxes and the Baour-Lormians, wretched distillers of their own poems.

But this language had not remained stationery since the period of 1830. It had continued to evolve and, patterning itself on the progress of the century, had advanced parallel with the other arts. It, too, had yielded to the desires of amateurs and artists, receiving its inspiration from the Chinese and Japanese, conceiving fragrant albums, imitating the *Takeoka* bouquets of flowers, obtaining the odor of *Rondeletia* from the blend of lavender and clove; the peculiar aroma of Chinese ink from the marriage of patchouli and camphor; the emanation of Japanese *Hovenia* by compounds of citron, clove and neroli.

Des Esseintes studied and analyzed the essences of these fluids, experimenting to corroborate their texts. He took pleasure in playing the rôle of a psychologist for his personal satisfaction, in taking apart and re-assembling the machinery of a work, in separating the pieces forming the structure of a compound exhalation, and his sense of smell had thereby attained a sureness that was all but perfect.

Just as a wine merchant has only to smell a drop of wine to recognize the grape, as a hop dealer determines the exact value of hops by sniffing a bag, as a Chinese trader can immediately tell the origin of the teas he smells, knowing in what farms of what mountains, in what Buddhistic convents it was cultivated, the very time when its leaves were gathered, the state and the degree of torrefaction, the effect upon it of its proximity to the plum-tree and other flowers, to all those perfumes which change its essence, adding to it an unexpected touch and introducing into its dryish flavor a hint of distant fresh flowers; just so could Des Esseintes, by inhaling a dash of perfume, instantly explain its mixture and the psychology of its blend, and could almost give the name of the artist who had composed and given it the personal mark of his individual style.

Naturally he had a collection of all the products used by perfumers. He even had the real Mecca balm, that rare balm cultivated only in certain parts of Arabia Petraea and under the monopoly of the ruler.

Now, seated in his dressing room in front of his table, he thought of creating a new bouquet; and he was overcome by that moment of wavering confidence familiar to writers when, after months of inaction, they prepare for a new work.

Like Balzac who was wont to scribble on many sheets of paper so as to put himself in a mood for work, Des Esseintes felt the necessity of steadying his hand by several initial and unimportant experiments. Desiring to create heliotrope, he took down bottles of vanilla and almond, then changed his idea and decided to experiment with sweet peas.

He groped for a long time, unable to effect the proper combinations, for orange is dominant in the fragrance of this flower. He attempted several combinations and ended in achieving the exact blend by joining tuberose and rose to orange, the whole united by a drop of vanilla.

His hesitation disappeared. He felt alert and ready for work; now he made some tea by blending cassie with iris, then, sure of his technique, he decided to proceed with a fulminating phrase whose thunderous roar would annihilate the insidious odor of almond still hovering over his room.

He worked with amber and with Tonkin musk, marvelously powerful; with patchouli, the most poignant of vegetable perfumes whose flower, in its habitat, wafts an odor of mildew. Try what he would, the eighteenth century obsessed him; the panier robes and furbelows appeared before his eyes; memories of Boucher's *Venus* haunted him; recollections of Themidor's romance, of the exquisite Rosette pursued him. Furious, he rose and to rid himself of the obsession, with all his strength he inhaled that pure essence of spikenard, so dear to Orientals and so repulsive to Europeans because of its pronounced odor of valerian. He was stunned by the violence of the shock. As though pounded by hammer strokes, the filigranes of the delicate odor disappeared; he profited by the period of respite to escape the dead centuries, the antiquated fumes, and to enter, as he formerly had done, less limited or more recent works.

He had of old loved to lull himself with perfumes. He used effects analogous to those of the poets, and employed the admirable order of certain pieces of Baudelaire, such as *Irreparable* and *le Balcon,* where the last of the five lines composing the strophe is the echo of the first verse and returns, like a refrain, to steep the soul in infinite depths of melancholy and languor.

He strayed into reveries evoked by those aromatic stanzas, suddenly brought to his point of departure, to the motive of his meditation, by the return of the initial theme, reappearing, at stated intervals, in the fragrant orchestration of the poem.

He actually wished to saunter through an astonishing, diversified landscape, and he began with a sonorous, ample phrase that suddenly opened a long vista of fields for him.

With his vaporizers, he injected an essence formed of ambrosia, lavender and sweet peas into this room; this formed an essence which, when distilled by an artist, deserves the name by which it is known: "extract of wild grass"; into this he introduced an exact blend of tuberose, orange flower and almond, and forthwith artificial lilacs sprang into being, while the linden-trees rustled, their thin emanations, imitated by extract of London tilia, drooping earthward.

This *décor,* arranged with a few broad lines, receding as far as the eye could reach, under his closed lids, he introduced a light rain of human and half feline essences, possessing the aroma of petticoats, breathing of the powdered, painted woman, the stephanotis, ayapana, opopanax, champala, sarcanthus and cypress wine, to which he added a dash of syringa, in order to give to the artificial life of paints which they exhaled, a suggestion of natural dewy laughter and pleasures enjoyed in the open air.

Then, through a ventilator, he permitted these fragrant waves to escape, only preserving the field which he renewed, compelling it to return in his strophes like a ritornello.

The women had gradually disappeared. Now the plain had grown solitary. Suddenly, on the enchanted horizon, factories appeared whose tall chimneys flared like bowls of punch.

The odor of factories and of chemical products now passed with the breeze which was simulated by means of fans; nature exhaled its sweet effluvia amid this putrescence.

Des Esseintes warmed a pellet of storax, and a singular odor, at once repugnant and exquisite, pervaded the room. It partook of the delicious fragrance of jonquil and of the stench of gutta percha and coal oil. He disinfected his hands, inserted his resin in a hermetically sealed box, and the factories disappeared.

Then, among the revived vapors of the lindens and meadow grass, he threw several drops of new mown hay, and, amid this magic site for the moment despoiled of its lilacs, sheaves of hay were piled up, introducing a new season and scattering their fine effluence into these summer odors.

At last, when he had sufficiently enjoyed this sight, he suddenly scattered the exotic perfumes, emptied his vaporizers, threw in his concentrated spirits, poured his balms, and, in the exasperated and stifling heat of the room there rose a crazy sublimated nature, a paradoxical nature which was neither genuine nor charming, reuniting the tropical spices and the peppery breath of Chinese sandal wood and Jamaica hediosmia with the French odors of jasmine, hawthorn and verbena. Regardless of seasons and climates he forced trees of diverse essences into life, and flowers with conflicting fragrances and colors. By the clash of these tones he created a general, nondescript, unexpected, strange perfume in which reappeared, like an obstinate refrain, the decorative phrase of the beginning, the odor of the meadows fanned by the lilacs and lindens.

Suddenly a poignant pain seized him; he felt as though wimbles were drilling into his temples. Opening his eyes he found himself in his dressing room, seated in front of his table. Stupefied, he painfully walked across the room to the window which he half opened. A puff of wind dispelled the stifling atmosphere which was enveloping him. To exercise his limbs, he walked up and down gazing at the ceiling where crabs and sea-wrack stood out in relief against a background as light in color as the sands of the seashore. A similar *décor* covered the plinths and bordered the partitions which were covered with Japanese sea-green crêpe, slightly wrinkled, imitating a river rippled by the wind. In this light current swam a rose petal, around which circled a school of tiny fish painted with two strokes of the brush.

But his eyelids remained heavy. He ceased to pace about the short space between the baptistery and the bath; he leaned against the window. His dizziness ended. He carefully stopped up the vials, and used the occasion to arrange his cosmetics. Since his arrival at Fontenay he had not touched them; and now was quite astonished to behold once more this collection formerly visited by so many women. The flasks and jars were lying heaped up against each other. Here, a porcelain box contained a marvelous white cream which, when applied on the cheeks, turns to a tender rose color, under the action of the air—to such a true flesh-color that it procures the very illusion of a skin touched with blood; there, lacquer objects incrusted with mother of pearl enclosed Japanese gold and Athenian green, the color of the cantharis wing, gold and green which change to deep purple when wetted; there were jars filled with filbert paste, the serkis of the harem, emulsions of lilies, lotions of strawberry water and elders for the complexion, and tiny bottles filled with solutions of Chinese ink and rose water for the eyes. There were tweezers, scissors, rouge and powder-puffs, files and beauty patches.

He handled this collection, formerly bought to please a mistress who swooned under the influence of certain aromatics and balms,— a nervous, unbalanced woman who loved to steep the nipples of her breasts in perfumes, but who never really experienced a delicious and overwhelming ecstacy save when her head was scraped with a comb or when she could inhale, amid caresses, the odor of perspiration, or the plaster of unfinished houses on rainy days, or of dust splashed by huge drops of rain during summer storms.

He mused over these memories, and one afternoon spent at Pantin through idleness and curiosity, in company with this woman at the home of one of her sisters, returned to him, stirring in him a forgotten world of old ideas and perfumes; while the two women prattled and displayed their gowns, he had drawn near the window and had seen, through the dusty panes, the muddy street sprawling before him, and had heard the repeated sounds of galoches over the puddles of the pavement.

This scene, already far removed, came to him suddenly, strangely and vividly. Pantin was there before him, animated and throbbing in this greenish and dull mirror into which his unseeing eyes plunged. A hallucination transported him far from Fontenay. Beside reflecting the street, the mirror brought back thoughts it had once been instrumental in evoking, and plunged in revery, he repeated to himself this ingenious, sad and comforting composition he had formerly written upon returning to Paris:

"Yes, the season of downpours is come. Now behold water-spouts vomiting as they rush over the pavements, and rubbish marinates in puddles that fill the holes scooped out of the macadam.

"Under a lowering sky, in the damp air, the walls of houses have black perspiration and their air-holes are fetid; the loathsomeness of existence increases and melancholy overwhelms one; the seeds of vileness which each person harbors in his soul, sprout. The craving for vile debaucheries seizes austere people and base desires grow rampant in the brains of respectable men.

"And yet I warm myself, here before a cheerful fire. From a basket of blossoming flowers comes the aroma of balsamic benzoin, geranium and the whorl-flowered bent-grass which permeates the room. In the very month of November, at Pantin, in the rue de Paris, springtime persists. Here in my solitude I laugh at the fears of families which, to shun the approaching cold weather, escape on every steamer to Cannes and to other winter resorts.

"Inclement nature does nothing to contribute to this extraordinary phenomenon. It must be said that this artificial season at Pantin is the result of man's ingenuity.

"In fact, these flowers are made of taffeta and are mounted on wire. The springtime odor filters through the window joints, exhaled from the neighboring factories, from the perfumeries of Pinaud and Saint James.

"For the workmen exhausted by the hard labors of the plants, for the young employes who too often are fathers, the illusion of a little healthy air is possible, thanks to these manufacturers.

"So, from this fabulous subterfuge of a country can an intelligent cure arise. The consumptive men about town who are sent to the South die, their end due to the change in their habits and to the nostalgia for the Parisian excesses which destroyed them. Here, under an artificial climate, libertine memories will reappear, the languishing feminine emanations evaporated by the factories. Instead of the deadly ennui of provincial life, the doctor can thus platonically substitute for his patient the atmosphere of the Parisian women and of boudoirs. Most often, all that is necessary to effect the cure is for the subject to have a somewhat fertile imagination.

"Since, nowadays, nothing genuine exists, since the wine one drinks and the liberty one boldly proclaims are laughable and a sham, since it really needs a healthy dose of good will to believe that the governing classes are respectable and that the lower classes are worthy of being assisted or pitied, it seems to me," concluded Des Esseintes, "to be neither ridiculous nor senseless, to ask of my fellow men a quantity of illusion barely equivalent to what they spend daily in idiotic ends, so as to be able to convince themselves that the town of Pantin is an artificial Nice or a Menton.

"But all this does not prevent me from seeing," he said, forced by weakness from his meditations, "that I must be careful to mistrust these delicious and abominable practices which may ruin my constitution." He sighed. "Well, well, more pleasures to moderate, more precautions to be taken."

And he passed into his study, hoping the more easily to escape the spell of these perfumes.

He opened the window wide, glad to be able to breath the air. But it suddenly seemed to him that the breeze brought in a vague tide of bergamot with which jasmine and rose water were blent. Agitated, he asked himself whether he was not really under the yoke of one of those possessions exercised in the Middle Ages. The odor changed and was transformed, but it persisted. A faint scent of tincture of tolu,

of balm of Peru and of saffron, united by several drams of amber
and musk, now issued from the sleeping village and suddenly, the
metamorphosis was effected, those scattered elements were blent,
and once more the frangipane spread from the valley of Fontenay
as far as the fort, assailing his exhausted nostrils, once more shat-
tering his helpless nerves and throwing him into such a prostration
that he fell unconscious on the window sill.

WALTER PATER

From Leonardo da Vinci[†]

* * *

* * * But it is still by a certain mystery in his work, and something
enigmatical beyond the usual measure of great men, that he fascinates, or perhaps half repels. His life is one of sudden revolts, with
intervals in which he works not at all, or apart from the main scope
of his work. By a strange fortune the works on which his more popular fame rested disappeared early from the world, as the *Battle of
the Standard;* or are mixed obscurely with the work of meaner hands,
as the *Last Supper.* His type of beauty is so exotic that it fascinates
a larger number than it delights, and seems more than that of any
other artist to reflect ideas and views and some scheme of the world
within; so that he seemed to his contemporaries to be the possessor
of some unsanctified and secret wisdom; as, to Michelet and others,
to have anticipated modern ideas. He trifles with his genius, and
crowds all his chief work into a few tormented years of later life; yet
he is so possessed by his genius that he passes unmoved through
the most tragic events, overwhelming his country and friends, like
one who comes across them by change on some secret errand.

His *legend,* as the French say, with the anecdotes which everyone
knows, is one of the most brilliant in Vasari. Later writers merely
copied it, until, in 1804, Carlo Amoretti applied to it a criticism
which left hardly a date fixed, and not one of those anecdotes
untouched. The various questions thus raised have since that time
become, one after another, subjects of special study, and mere antiquarianism has in this direction little more to do. For others remain
the editing of the thirteen books of his manuscripts, and the separation by technical criticism of what in his reputed works is really
his, from what is only half his, or the work of his pupils. But a lover

† From *The Renaissance: Studies in Art and Poetry* (London and New York: Macmillan
   & Company, 1888). Unless otherwise indicated, notes are Pater's. Of the ten chap-
   ters in the 1888 edition, this is the sixth, famous for its description of Leonardo's
   Mona Lisa (c. 1503–19). It is followed here by the Conclusion.

of strange souls may still analyze for himself the impression made on him by those works, and try to reach through it a definition of the chief elements of Leonardo's genius. The *legend,* corrected and enlarged by its critics, may now and then intervene to support the results of this analysis.

His life has three divisions—thirty years at Florence, nearly twenty years at Milan, then nineteen years of wandering, till he sinks to rest under the protection of Francis the First at the Château de Cloux. The dishonor of illegitimacy hangs over his birth. Piero Antonio, his father, was of a noble Florentine house, of Vinci in the Val d'Arno, and Leonardo, brought up delicately among the true children of that house, was the love child of his youth, with the keen, puissant nature such children often have. We see him in his youth fascinating all men by his beauty, improvising music and songs, buying the caged birds and setting them free, as he walked the streets of Florence, fond of odd bright dresses and spirited horses.

From his earliest years he designed many objects, and constructed models in relief, of which Vasari mentions some of women smiling. His father, pondering over this promise in the child, took him to the workshop of Andrea del Verrocchio, then the most famous artist in Florence. Beautiful objects lay about there—reliquaries, pyxes, silver images for the pope's chapel at Rome, strange fancywork of the Middle Ages, keeping odd company with fragments of antiquity, then but lately discovered. Another student Leonardo may have seen there—a boy into whose soul the level light and aerial illusions of Italian sunsets had passed, in after days famous as Perugino, Verrocchio was an artist of the earlier Florentine type, carver, painter, and worker in metals, in one; designer, not of pictures only, but of all things for sacred or household use, drinking vessels, ambries, instruments of music, making them all fair to look upon, filling the common ways of life with the reflection of some far-off brightness; and years of patience had refined his hand till his work was now sought after from distant places.

It happened that Verrocchio was employed by the brethren of Vallombrosa to paint the Baptism of Christ, and Leonardo was allowed to finish the angel in the left-hand corner. It was one of those moments in which the progress of a great thing—here, that of the art of Italy—presses hard and sharp on the happiness of an individual, through whose discouragement and decrease, humanity, in more fortunate persons, comes a step nearer to its final success.

For beneath the cheerful exterior of the mere well-paid craftsman, chasing brooches for the copes of Santa Maria Novella, or twisting metal screens for the tombs of the Medici, lay the ambitious desire of expanding the destiny of Italian art by a larger

knowledge and insight into things, a purpose in art not unlike
Leonardo's still unconscious purpose; and often, in the modeling
of drapery, or of a lifted arm, or of hair cast back from the face
there came to him something of the freer manner and richer
humanity of a later age. But in this *Baptism* the pupil had surpassed
the master; and Verrocchio turned away as one stunned, and as if
his sweet earlier work must thereafter be distasteful to him, from
the bright animated angel of Leonardo's hand.

The angel may still be seen in Florence, a space of sunlight in the
cold, labored old picture; but the legend is true only in sentiment,
for painting had always been the art by which Verrocchio set least
store. And as in a sense he anticipates Leonardo, so to the last Leonardo recalls the studio of Verrocchio, in the love of beautiful toys,
such as the vessel of water for a mirror, and lovely needlework about
the implicated hands in the *Modesty and Vanity,* and of reliefs, like
those cameos which in the *Virgin of the Balances* hang all round the
girdle of Saint Michael, and of bright variegated stones, such as the
agates in the *Saint Anne,* and in a hieratic preciseness and grace, as
of a sanctuary swept and garnished. Amid all the cunning and intri-
cacy of his Lombard manner this never left him. Much of it there
must have been in that lost picture of *Paradise,* which he prepared as
a cartoon for tapestry, to be woven in the looms of Flanders. It was
the perfection of the older Florentine style of miniature painting,
with patient putting of each leaf upon the trees and each flower in
the grass, where the first man and woman were standing.

And because it was the perfection of that style, it awoke in Leonardo some seed of discontent which lay in the secret places of his
nature. For the way to perfection is through a series of disgusts; and
this picture—all that he had done so far in his life at Florence—was
after all in the old slight manner. His art, if it was to be something
in the world, must be weighted with more of the meaning of nature
and purpose of humanity. Nature was "the true mistress of higher
intelligences." So he plunged into the study of nature. And in doing
this he followed the manner of the older students; he brooded over
the hidden virtues of plants and crystals, the lines traced by the stars
as they moved in the sky, over the correspondences which exist
between the different orders of living things, through which, to eyes
opened, they interpret each other; and for years he seemed to those
about him as one listening to a voice, silent for other men.

He learned here the art of going deep, of tracking the sources of
expression to their subtlest retreats, the power of an intimate presence in the things he handled. He did not at once or entirely desert
his art; only he was no longer the cheerful, objective painter, through
whose soul, as through clear glass, the bright figures of Florentine
life, only made a little mellower and more pensive by the transit,

passed onto the white wall. He wasted many days in curious tricks of design, seeming to lose himself in the spinning of intricate devices of lines and colors. He was smitten with a love of the impossible—the perforation of mountains, changing the course of rivers, raising great buildings, such as the church of San Giovanni, in the air; all those feats for the performance of which natural magic professes to have the key. Later writers, indeed, see in these efforts an anticipation of modern mechanics; in him they were rather dreams, thrown off by the overwrought and laboring brain. Two ideas were especially fixed in him, as reflexes of things that had touched his brain in childhood beyond the measure of other impressions—the smiling of women and the motion of great waters.

And in such studies some interfusion of the extremes of beauty and terror shaped itself, as an image that might be seen and touched, in the mind of this gracious youth, so fixed that for the rest of his life it never left him; and as catching glimpses of it in the strange eyes or hair of chance people, he would follow such about the streets of Florence till the sun went down, of whom many sketches of his remain. Some of these are full of a curious beauty, that remote beauty apprehended only by those who have sought it carefully; who, starting with acknowledged types of beauty, have refined as far upon these, as these refine upon the world of common forms. But mingled inextricably with this there is an element of mockery also; so that, whether in sorrow of scorn, he caricatures Dante even. Legions of grotesques sweep under his hand; for has not nature too her grotesques—the rent rock, the distorting light of evening on lonely roads, the unveiled structure of man in the embryo, or the skeleton?

All these swarming fancies unite in the *Medusa* of the Uffizi. Vasari's story of an earlier Medusa, painted on a wooden shield, is perhaps an invention; and yet, properly told, has more of the air of truth about it than anything else in the whole legend. For its real subject is not the serious work of a man, but the experiment of a child. The lizards and glowworms and other strange small creatures which haunt an Italian vineyard bring before one the whole picture of a child's life in a Tuscan dwelling, half castle, half farm; and are as a true to nature as the pretended astonishment of the father for whom the boy has prepared a surprise. It was not in play that he painted that other Medusa, the one great picture which he left behind him in Florence. The subject has been treated in various ways; Leonardo alone cuts to its center; he alone realizes it as the head of a corpse, exercising its power through all the circumstances of death. What may be called the fascination of corruption penetrates in every touch its exquisitely finished beauty. About the dainty lines of the cheek the bat flits unheeded. The delicate snakes seem literally strangling each other in terrified struggle to escape from the Medusa brain. The hue which violent death always brings with it is in the features: features singularly massive and grand, as we catch them inverted, in a dexterous foreshortening, sloping upward, almost sliding down upon us, crown foremost, like a great calm stone against which the wave of serpents breaks. But it is a subject that may well be left to the beautiful verses of Shelley.

The science of that age was all divination, clairvoyance, unsubjected to our exact modern formulas, seeking in an instant of vision to concentrate a thousand experiences. Later writers, thinking only of the well-ordered treatise on painting which a Frenchman, Raffaelle du Fresne, a hundred years afterwards, compiled from Leonardo's bewildered manuscripts, written strangely, as his manner was, from right to left, have imagined a rigid order in his inquiries. But this rigid order was little in accordance with the restlessness of his character; and if we think of him as the mere reasoner who subjects design to anatomy, and composition to mathematical rules, we shall hardly have of him that impression which those about him received from him. Poring over his crucibles, making experiments with color, trying by a strange variation of the alchemist's dream to discover the secret, not of an elixir to make man's natural life immortal, but rather of giving immortality to the subtlest and most delicate effects of painting, he seemed to them rather the sorcerer or the magician, possessed of curious secrets and a hidden knowledge, living in a world of which he alone possessed the key. What his philosophy seems to have been most like is that of Paracelsus or Cardan; and much the spirit of the older alchemy still hangs about it, with its confidence in short cuts and odd byways to knowledge. To him philosophy was to be something giving strange swiftness and double sight, divining the sources of springs beneath the earth or of expression beneath the human countenance, clairvoyant of occult gifts in common or uncommon things, in the reed at the brookside, or the star which draws near to us but once in a century. How, in this way, the clear purpose was overclouded, the fine chaser's hand perplexed, we but dimly see; the mystery which at no point quite lifts from Leonardo's life is deepest here. But it is certain that at one period of his life he had almost ceased to be an artist.

The year 1483—the year of the birth of Raphael and the thirty-first of Leonardo's life—is fixed as the date of his visit to Milan by the letter in which he recommends himself to Lodovico Sforza, and offers to tell him, for a price, strange secrets in the air of war. It was that Sforza who murdered his young nephew by slow poison, yet was so susceptible of religious impressions that he blended mere earthly passions with a sort of religious sentimentalism, and who took for his device the mulberry tree—symbol, in its long delay and sudden yielding of flowers and fruit together, of a wisdom which economizes all forces for an opportunity of sudden and sure effect. The fame of Leonardo had gone before him, and he was to model a colossal statue of Francesco, the first duke of Milan. As for Leonardo himself, he came not as an artist at all, or careful of the fame of one; but as a player on the harp, a strange harp of silver of his own construction, shaped in some curious likeness to a horse's skull. The capricious spirit of Lodovico was susceptible also of the charm of music, and Leonardo's nature had a kind of spell in it. Fascination is always the word descriptive of him. No portrait of his youth remains; but all tends to make us believe that up to this time some charms of voice and aspect, strong enough to balance the disadvantage of his birth, had played about him. His physical strength was great; it was said that he could bend a horseshoe like a coil of lead.

The Duomo, the work of artists from beyond the Alps, so fantastic to the eye of a Florentine, used to the mellow, unbroken surfaces of Giotto and Arnolfo, was then in all its freshness; and below, in the streets of Milan, moved a people as fantastic, changeful, and dreamlike. To Leonardo least of all men could there be anything poisonous in the exotic flowers of sentiment which grew there. It was a life of brilliant sins and exquisite amusements—Leonardo became a celebrated designer of pageants—and it suited the quality of his genius, composed in almost equal parts of curiosity and the desire of beauty, to take things as they came.

Curiosity and the desire of beauty—these are the two elementary forces in Leonardo's genius; curiosity often in conflict with the desire of beauty, but generating, in union with it, a type of subtle and curious grace.

The movement of the fifteenth century was twofold; partly the Renaissance, partly also the coming of what is called the "modern spirit," with its realism, its appeal to experience, it comprehended a return to antiquity, and a return to nature. Raphael represents the return to antiquity, and Leonardo the return to nature. In this return to nature, he was seeking to satisfy a boundless curiosity by her perpetual surprises, a microscopic sense of finish by her finesse, or delicacy of operation, that *subtilitas naturae* which Bacon notices. So we find him often in intimate relations with men of science, with Fra Luca Paccioli the mathematician, and the anatomist Marc Antonio della Torre. His observations and experiments fill thirteen volumes of manuscript; and those who can judge describe him as anticipating long before, by rapid intuition, the later ideas of science. He explained the obscure light of the unilluminated part of the moon, knew that the sea had once covered the mountains which contain shells, and the gathering of the equatorial waters above the polar.

He who thus penetrated into the most secret parts of nature preferred always the more to the less remote, what, seeming exceptional, was an instance of law more refined, the construction about things of a peculiar atmosphere and mixed lights. He paints flowers with such curious felicity that different writers have attributed to him a fondness for particular flowers, as Clement the cyclamen, and Rio the jasmine; while, at Venice, there is a stray leaf from his portfolio dotted all over with studies of violets and the wild rose. In him first, appears the taste for what is bizarre or *recherché* in landscape; hollow places full of the green shadow of bituminous rocks, ridged reefs of trap-rock which cut the water into quaint sheets of light— their exact antitype is in our own western seas; all the solemn effects of moving water; you may follow it springing from its distant source among the rocks on the heath of the *Madonna of the Balances,* passing as a little fall into the treacherous calm of the *Madonna of the Lake,* next, as a goodly river, below the cliffs of the *Madonna of the Rocks,* washing the white walls of its distant villages, stealing out in a network of divided streams in *La Gioconda* to the seashore of the *Saint Anne*—that delicate place, where the wind passes like the hand of some fine etcher over the surface, and the untorn shells are lying thick upon the sand, and the tops of the rocks, to which the waves never rise, are green with grass, grown as fine as hair. It is the landscape, not of dreams or of fancy, but of places far withdrawn, and hours selected from a thousand with a miracle of finesse. Through Leonardo's strange veil of sight things reach him so; in no ordinary night or day, but as in faint light of eclipse, or in some brief interval of falling rain at daybreak, or through deep water.

And not into nature only; but he plunged also into human personality, and became above all a painter of portraits; faces of a modeling more skillful than has been seen before or since, embodied with a reality which almost amounts to illusion, on dark air. To take a character as it was, and delicately sound its stops, suited one so curious in observation, curious in invention. So he painted the portraits of Lodovico's mistresses, Lucretia Crivelli and Cecilia Galerani the poetess, of Lodovico himself, and the Duchess Beatrice. The portrait of Cecilia Galerani is lost, but that of Lucretia Crivelli has been identified with *La Belle Feronière* of the Louvre, and Lodovico's pale, anxious face still remains in the Ambrosian Library. Opposite is the portrait of Beatrice d'Este, in whom Leonardo seems to have caught some presentiment of early death, painting her precise and grave, full of the refinement of the dead, in sad earth-colored raiment, set with pale stones.

Sometimes this curiosity came in conflict with the desire of beauty; it tended to make him go too far below that outside of things in which art begins and ends. This struggle between the reason and its ideas, and the senses, the desire of beauty, is the key to Leonardo's life at Milan—his restlessness, his endless retouchings, his odd experiments with color. How much must he leave unfinished, how much recommence! His problem was the transmutation of ideas into images. What he had attained so far had been the mastery of that earlier Florentine style, with its naive and limited sensuousness. Now he was to entertain in this narrow medium those divinations of a humanity too wide for it, that larger vision of the opening world, which is only not too much for the great, irregular art of Shakespeare; and everywhere the effort is visible in the work of his hands. This agitation, this perpetual delay, give him an air of weariness and ennui. To others he seems to be aiming at an impossible effect, to do something that art, that painting, can never do. Often the expression of physical beauty at this or that point seems strained and marred in the effort, as in those heavy German foreheads—too heavy and German for perfect beauty.

For there was a touch of Germany in that genius which, as Goethe said, had *müde sich gedacht* ("thought itself weary"). What an anticipation of modern Germany, for instance, in that debate on the question whether sculpture or painting is the nobler art.[1] But there is this difference between him and the German, that, with all that curious science, the German would have thought nothing more was needed; and the name of Goethe himself reminds one how great for the artist may be the danger of overmuch science; how Goethe, who, in the *Elective Affinities* and the first part of *Faust,* does transmute ideas into images, who wrought many such transmutations, did not invariably find the spell-word, and in the second part of *Faust* presents us with a mass of science which has almost no artistic characters at all. But Leonardo will never work till the happy moment comes—that moment of *bien-être,* which to imaginative men is a moment of invention. On this moment he waits; other moments are but a preparation, or aftertaste of it. Few men distinguish between them as jealously as he did. Hence, so many flaws even in the choicest work. But for Leonardo the distinction is absolute, and in the moment of *bien-être,* the alchemy complete; the idea is stricken into colour and imagery; a cloudy mysticism is refined to a subdued and graceful mystery, and painting pleases the eye while it satisfies the soul.

This curious beauty is seen above all in his drawings, and in these chiefly in the abstract grace of the bounding lines. Let us take some

---

1. How princely, how characteristic of Leonardo, the answer: *Quanto più, un' arte porta seco fatica di corpo, tanto più è vile!* [To the degree an art bears the strain of the body, the lower it is—*Editor*].

of these drawings, and pause over them awhile; and, first, one of those at Florence—the heads of a woman and a little child, set side by side, but each in its own separate frame. First of all, there is much pathos in the reappearance in the fuller curves of the face of the child, of the sharper, more chastened lines of the worn and older face, which leaves no doubt that the heads are those of a little child and its mother. A feeling for maternity is indeed always characteristic of Leonardo; and this feeling is further indicated here by the half-humorous pathos of the diminutive, rounded shoulders of the child. You may note a like pathetic power in drawings of a young man, seated in a stooping posture, his face in his hands, as in sorrow; of a slave sitting in an uneasy inclined posture, in some brief interval of rest; of a small Madonna and Child, peeping sideways in half-reassured terror, as a mighty griffin with batlike wings, one of Leonardo's finest *inventions,* descends suddenly from the air to snatch up a lion wandering near them. But note in these, as that which especially belongs to art, the contour of the young man's hair, the poise of the slave's arm above his head, and the curves of the head of the child, following the little skull within, thin and fine as some seashell worn by the wind.

Take again another head, still more full of sentiment, but of a different kind, a little drawing in red chalk which everyone remembers who has examined at all carefully the drawings by old masters at the Louvre. It is a face of doubtful sex, set in the shadow of its own hair, the cheekline in high light against it, with something voluptuous and full in the eyelids and the lips. Another drawing might pass for the same face in childhood, with parched and feverish lips, but with much sweetness in the loose, short-waisted childish dress, with necklace and *bulla,* and in the daintily bound hair. We might take the threat of suggestion which these two drawings offer, when thus set side by side, following it through the drawings at Florence, Venice, and Milan, construct a sort of series, illustrating better than anything else Leonardo's type of womanly beauty. Daughters of Herodias, with their fantastic headdresses knotted and folded so strangely, to leave the dainty oval of the face disengaged, they are not of the Christian family, or of Raphael's. They are the clairvoyants, through whom, as through delicate instruments, one becomes aware of the subtler forces of nature, and the modes of their action, all that is magnetic in it, all those finer conditions wherein material things rise to that subtlety of operation which constitutes them spiritual, where only the finer nerve and the keener touch can follow; it is as if in certain revealing instances we actually saw them at their work on human flesh. Nervous, electric, faint always with some inexplicable faintness, they seem to be subject to exceptional conditions, to feel powers at work in the common air unfelt by others, to become, as it were, receptables of them, and pass them on to us in a chain of secret influences.

But among the more youthful heads there is one at Florence, which Love chooses for its own—the head of a young man, which may well be the likeness of Andrea Salaino, beloved of Leonardo for his curled and waving hair—*belli capelli ricci e inanellati*—and afterward his favorite pupil and servant. Of all the interests in living men and women which may have filled his life at Milan, this attachment alone is recorded; and in return, Salaino identified himself so entirely with Leonardo, that the picture of *Saint Anne,* in the Louvre, has been attributed to him. It illustrates Leonardo's usual choice of pupils, men of some natural charm of person or intercourse like Salaino, or men of birth, and princely habits of life like Francesco Melzi—men with just enough genius to be capable of initiation into his secret, for the sake of which they were ready to efface their own individuality. Among them, retiring often to the villa of the Melzi at Canonica al Vaprio, he worked at his fugitive manuscripts and sketches, working for the present hour, and for a few only, perhaps chiefly for himself. Other artists have been as careless of present or future applause, in self-forgetfulness, or because they set moral or political ends above the ends of the art; but in him this solitary culture of beauty seems to have hung upon a kind of self-love, and a carelessness in the work of art of all but art itself. Out of the secret places of a unique temperament he brought strange blossoms and fruits hitherto unknown; and for him, the novel impression conveyed, the exquisite effect woven, counted as an end in itself—a perfect end.

And these pupils of his acquired his manner so thoroughly, that though the number of Leonardo's authentic works is very small indeed, there is a multitude of other men's pictures, through which we undoubtedly see him, and come very near to his genius. Sometimes, as in the little picture of the *Madonna of the Balances,* in which, from the bosom of his mother, Christ is weighing the pebbles of the brook against the sins of men, we have a hand, rough enough by contrast, working upon some fine hint or sketch of his. Sometimes, as in the subjects of the *Daughter of Herodias* and the *Head of John the Baptist,* the lost originals have been re-echoed and varied upon again and again by Luini and others. At other times the original remains, but has been a mere theme or motive, a type of which the accessories might be modified or changed; and these variations have but brought out the more the purpose, or expression of the original. It is so with the so-called *Saint John the Baptist* of the Louvre—one of the few naked figures Leonardo painted—whose delicate brown flesh and woman's hair no one would go out into the wilderness to seek, and whose treacherous smile would have us understand something far beyond the outward gesture, or circumstance. But the long, reedlike cross in the hand, which suggests Saint John the Baptist, becomes faint in a copy of the Ambrosian Library, and disappears altogether in another, in the Palazzo Rosso at Genoa. Returning from the last to the original, we are no longer surprised by Saint John's strange likeness to the *Bacchus* which hangs near it, which set Théophile Gautier thinking of Heine's notion of decayed gods, who, to maintain themselves, after the fall of paganism, took employment in the new religion. We recognize one of those symbolical inventions in which the ostensible subject is used, not as matter for definite pictorial realization, but as the starting point of a train of sentiment, as subtle and vague as a piece of music. No one ever ruled over his subject more entirely than Leonardo, or bent it more dexterously to purely artistic ends. And so it comes to pass that though he handles sacred subjects continually, he is the most profane of painters; the given person or subject, Saint John in the Desert, or the Virgin on the knees of Saint Anne, is often merely the pretext for a kind of work which carries one quite out of the range of its conventional associations.

About the *Last Supper,* its decay and restorations, a whole literature has risen up, Goethe's pensive sketch of its sad fortunes being far the best. The death in childbirth of the Duchess Beatrice was followed in Lodovico by one of those paroxysms of religious feeling which in him were constitutional. The low, gloomy Dominican church of Saint Mary of the Graces had been the favorite shrine of Beatrice. She had spent her last days there, full of sinister presentiments; at last it had been almost necessary to remove her from it by force; and now it was here that mass was said a hundred times a day for her repose. On the damp wall of the refectory, oozing with mineral salts, Leonardo painted the *Last Supper.* A hundred anecdotes were told about it, his retouchings and delays. They show him refusing to work except at the moment of invention, scornful of whoever thought that art was a work of mere industry and rule, often coming the whole length of Milan to give a single touch. He painted it, not in fresco, where all must be impromptu, but in oils, the new method which he had been one of the first to welcome, because it allowed of so many afterthoughts, so refined a working out of perfection. It turned out that on a plastered wall no process could have been less durable. Within fifty years it had fallen into decay. And now we have to turn back to Leonardo's own studies, above all, to one drawing of the central head at the Brera, which in a union of tenderness and severity in the face lines, reminds one of the monumental work of Mino da Fiesole, to trace it as it was.

It was another effort to set a given subject out of the range of its conventional associations. Strange, after all the misrepresentations of the Middle Ages, was the effort to see it, not as the pale host of the altar, but as one taking leave of his friends. Five years afterwards, the young Raphael, at Florence, painted it with sweet and solemn effect in the refectory of Saint Onofrio; but still with all the mystical unreality of the school of Perugino. Vasari pretends that the central head was never finished; but finished or unfinished, or owing part of its effect to a mellowing decay, this central head does but consummate the sentiment of the whole company; ghosts through which you see the wall, faint as the shadows of the leaves upon the wall on autumn afternoons—this figure is but the faintest, most spectral of them all. It is the image of what the history it symbolizes has been more and more ever since, paler and paler as it recedes from us. Criticism came with its appeal from mystical unrealities to originals, and restored no lifelike reality but these transparent shadows, spirits which have not flesh and bones.

The *Last Supper* was finished in 1497; in 1498 the French entered Milan, and whether or not the Gascon bowman used it as a mark for their arrows, the model of Francesco Sforza certainly did not survive. What, in that age, such work was capable of being, of what nobility, amid what racy truthfulness to fact, we may judge from the bronze statue of Bartolomeo Colleoni on horseback, modeled by Leonardo's master, Verrocchio—he died of grief, it was said, because, the mold accidentally failing, he was unable himself to complete it— still standing in the piazza of Saint John and Saint Paul at Venice. Some traces of the thing may remain in certain of Leonardo's drawings, and also, perhaps, by a singular circumstance, in a faroff town of France. For Lodovico became a prisoner, and ended his days at Loches in Touraine; allowed, it is said, at last to breathe fresher air for awhile in one of the rooms of a high tower there, after many years of captivity in the dungeons below, where all seems sick with barbarous feudal memories, and where his prison is still shown, its walls covered with strange painted arabesques, ascribed by tradition to his hand, amused a little thus through the tedious years—vast helmets and faces and pieces of armor, among which in great letters the motto *Infelix Sum*, is woven in and out, and in which perhaps it is not too fanciful to see the fruit of a wistful afterdreaming over all those experiments with Leonardo on the armed figure of the great duke, which had occupied the two so often, during the days of his fortune at Milan.

The remaining years of Leonardo's life are more or less years of wandering. From his brilliant life at court he had saved nothing, and he returned to Florence a poor man. Perhaps necessity kept his spirit excited: the next four years are one prolonged rapture or ecstasy of invention. He painted the pictures of the Louvre, his most authentic works, which came there straight from the cabinet of Francis the

First, at Fontainebleau. One picture of his, the *Saint Anne*—not the
Saint Anne of the Louvre, but a mere cartoon, now in London—
revived for a moment a sort of appreciation more common in an
earlier time, when good pictures had still seemed miraculous; and
for two days a crowd of people of all qualities passed in naïve excitement through the chamber where it hung, and gave Leonardo a taste
of Cimabue's triumph. But his work was less with the saints than
with the living women of Florence; for he lived still in the polished
society that he loved, and in the houses of Florence, left perhaps a
little subject to light thoughts by the death of Savonarola, (the latest
gossip is of an undraped Mona Lisa, found in some out-of-the-way
corner of the late Orléans collection) he saw Ginevra di Benci, and
Lisa, the young third wife of Francesco del Giocondo. As we have
seen him using incidents of the sacred legend, not for their own sake,
or as mere subjects for pictorial realization, but as a symbolical
language for fancies all his own, so now he found a vent for his
thoughts in taking one of these languid women, and raising her, as
Leda or Pomona, Modesty or Vanity, to the seventh heaven of symbolical expression.

La Gioconda is, in the truest sense, Leonardo's masterpiece, the
revealing instance of his mode of thought and work. In suggestive-
ness, only the *Melancholia* of Dúrer is comparable to it; and no crude
symbolism disturbs the effect of its subdued and graceful mystery.
We all know the face and hands of the figure, set in its marble chair,
in that cirque of fantastic rocks, as in some faint light under sea.
Perhaps of all ancient pictures time has chilled it least.[2] As often
happens with works in which invention seems to reach its limit,
there is an element in it given to, not invented by, the master. In that
inestimable folio of drawings, once in the possession of Vasari, were
certain designs by Verrocchio, faces of such impressive beauty that
Leonardo in his boyhood copied them many times. It is hard not to
connect with these designs of the elder, by-passed master, as with
its germinal principle, the unfathomable smile, always with a touch
of something sinister in it, which plays over all Leonardo's work.
Besides, the picture is a portrait. From childhood we see this image
defining itself on the fabric of his dreams; and but for express historical testimony, we might fancy that this was but his ideal lady,
embodied and beheld at last. What was the relationship of a living
Florentine to this creature of his thought? By means of what strange
affinities had the person and the dream grown up thus apart, and
yet so closely together? Present from the first, incorporeal in Leonardo's thought, dimly traced in the designs of Verrocchio, she is
found present at last in Il Giocondo's house. That there is much of

2. Yet for Vasari there was some further magic of crimson in the lips and cheeks, lost for us.

mere portraiture in the picture is attested by the legend that by artificial means, the presence of mimes and flute players, that subtle
expression was protracted on the face. Again, was it in four years,
and by renewed labor never really completed, or in four months, and
as by stroke of magic, that the image was projected?

The presence that thus rose so strangely beside the waters, is
expressive of what in the ways of a thousand years man had come to
desire. Hers is the head upon which all "the ends of the world are
come," and the eyelids are a little weary. It is a beauty wrought out
from within upon the flesh, the deposit, little cell by cell, of strange
thoughts and fantastic reveries and exquisite passions. Set it for a
moment beside one of those white Greek goddesses or beautiful
women of antiquity, and how would they be troubled by this beauty,
into which the soul with all its maladies has passed? All the
thoughts and experience of the world have etched and molded there,
in that which they have the power to refine and make expressive the
outward form, the animalism of Greece, the lust of Rome, the reverie of the Middle Ages with its spiritual ambition and imaginative
loves, the return of the pagan world, the sins of the Borgias. She is
older than the rocks among which she sits; like the vampire, she has
been dead many times, and learned the secrets of the grave; and has
been a diver in deep seas, and keeps their fallen day about her; and
trafficked for strange webs with Eastern merchants; and, as Leda,
was the mother of Helen of Troy, and, as Saint Anne, the mother of
Mary; and all this has been to her but as the sound of lyres and
flutes, and lives only in the delicacy with which it has molded the
changing lineaments, and tinged the eyelids and the hands. The
fancy of a perpetual life, sweeping together ten thousand experiences, is an old one; and modern thought has conceived the idea of
humanity as wrought upon by, and summing up in itself, all modes
of thought and life. Certainly Lady Lisa might stand as the embodiment of the old fancy, the symbol of the modern idea.

During these years at Florence, Leonardo's history is the history
of his art; he himself is lost in the bright cloud of it. The outward
history begins again in 1502, with a wild journey through central
Italy, which he makes as the chief engineer of Cesare Borgia. The
biographer, putting together the stray jottings of his manuscripts,
may follow him through every day of it, up the strange tower of Siena,
which looks toward Rome, elastic like a bent bow, down to the
seashore at Piombino, each place appearing as fitfully as in a fever
dream.

One other great work was left for him to do, a work all trace of
which soon vanished, *The Battle of the Standard*, in which he had
Michelangelo for his rival. The citizens of Florence, desiring to dec-
orate the walls of the great council chamber, had offered the work

for competition, and any subject might be chosen from the Florentine wars of the fifteenth century. Michelangelo chose for his cartoon an incident of the war with Pisa, in which the Florentine
soldiers, bathing in the Arno, are surprised by the sound of trumpets, and run to arms. His design has reached us only in an old
engraving, which perhaps helps us less than what we remember of
the background of his *Holy Family* in the Uffizi to imagine in what
superhuman form, such as might have beguiled the heart of an
earlier world, those figures may have risen from the water. Leonardo
chose an incident from the battle of Anghiari, in which two parties
of soldiers fight for a standard. Like Michelangelo's, his cartoon is
lost, and has come to us only in sketches, and in a fragment of
Rubens. Through the accounts given we may discern some lust of
terrible things in it, so that even the horses tore each other with their
teeth; and yet one fragment of it, in a drawing of his at Florence, is far
different—a waving field of lovely armor, the chased edgings running
like lines of sunlight from side to side. Michelangelo was twenty-
seven years old; Leonardo more than fifty; and Raphael, then nineteen years old, visiting Florence for the first time, came and watched
them as they worked.

We catch a glimpse of him again, at Rome in 1514, surrounded
by his mirrors and vials and furnaces, making strange toys that
seemed alive of wax and quicksilver. The hesitation which had
haunted him all through life, and made him like one under a spell,
was upon him now with double force. No one had ever carried political indifferentism farther; it had always been his philosophy to "fly
before the storm"; he is for the Sforzas, or against them, as the tide
of their fortune turns. Yet now in the political society of Rome, he
came to be suspected of concealed French sympathies. It paralyzed
him to find himself among enemies; and he turned wholly to France,
which had long courted him.

France was about to become an Italy more Italian than Italy itself.
Francis the First, like Lewis the Twelfth before him, was attracted
by the finesse of Leonardo's work; *La Gioconda* was already in his
cabinet, and he offered Leonardo the little Château de Cloux, with
its vineyards and meadows, in the pleasant valley of the Masse, just
outside the walls of the town of Amboise, where, especially in the
hunting season, the court then frequently resided. *A Monsieur Lyo-
nard, peintre du Roy pour Amboyse*—so the letter of Francis the
First is headed. It opens a prospect, one of the most attractive in
the history of art, where, under a strange mixture of lights, Italian
art dies away as a French exotic.

Two questions remain, after much busy antiquarianism, concerning Leonardo's death—the question of the form of his religion, and
the question whether Francis the First was present at the time. They

are of about equally little importance in the estimate of Leonardo's genius. The directions in his will about the thirty masses and the great candles for the church of Saint Florentin are things of course, their real purpose being immediate and practical; and on no theory of religion could these hurried offices be of much consequence. We forget them in speculating how one who had been always so desirous of beauty, but desired it always in such definite and precise forms, as hands or flowers or hair, looked forward now into the vague land, and experienced the last curiosity.

Conclusion [to *The Renaissance*][1]

Αέγει που Ἡράκλειτος ὅτι ἄντα χωρεί καί οὖδέν μένει[2]

To regard all things and principles of things as inconstant modes or fashions has more and more become the tendency of modern thought. Let us begin with that which is without—our physical life. Fix upon it in one of its more exquisite intervals, the moment, for instance, of delicious recoil from the flood of water in summer heat. What is the whole physical life in that moment but a combination of natural elements to which science gives their names? But those elements, phosphorus and lime and delicate fibres, are present not in the human body alone: we detect them in places most remote from it. Our physical life is a perpetual motion of them—the passage of the blood, the waste and repairing of the lenses of the eye, the modification of the tissues of the brain under every ray of light and sound—processes which science reduces to simpler and more elementary forces. Like the elements of which we are composed, the action of these forces extends beyond us: it rusts iron and ripens corn. Far out on every side of us those elements are broadcast, driven in many currents; and birth and gesture and death and the springing of violets from the grave are but a few out of ten thousand resultant combinations. That clear, perpetual outline of face and limb is but an image of ours, under which we group them—a design in a web, the actual threads of which pass out beyond it. This at least of flame-like our life has, that it is but the concurrence, renewed from moment to moment, of forces parting sooner or later on their ways.

Or if we begin with the inward world of thought and feeling, the whirlpool is still more rapid, the flame more eager and devouring.

---

1. This brief "Conclusion" was omitted in the second edition of this book, as I conceived it might possibly mislead some of those young men into whose hands it might fall. On the whole, I have thought it best to reprint it here, with some slight changes which bring it closer to my original meaning. I have dealt more fully in *Marius the Epicurean* with the thoughts suggested by it.
2. Heraclitus says, "All things give way; nothing remains" (Greek)—*Editor*.

There it is no longer the gradual darkening of the eye, the gradual fading of colour from the wall—movements of the shore-side, where the water flows down indeed, though in apparent rest—but the race of the mid-stream, a drift of momentary acts of sight and passion and thought. At first sight experience seems to bury us under a flood of external objects, pressing upon us with a sharp and importunate, reality, calling us out of ourselves in a thousand forms of action. But when reflexion begins to play upon those objects they are dissipated under its influence; the cohesive force seems suspended like some trick of magic; each object is loosed into a group of impressions— colour, odour, texture—in the mind of the observer. And if we continue to dwell in thought on this world, not of objects in the solidity with which language invests them, but of impressions, unstable, flickering, inconsistent, which burn and are extinguished with our consciousness of them, it contracts still further: the whole scope of observation is dwarfed into the narrow chamber of the individual mind. Experience, already reduced to a group of impressions, is ringed round for each one of us by that thick wall of personality through which no real voice has ever pierced on its way to us, or from us to that which we can only conjecture to be without. Every one of those impressions is the impression of the individual in his isolation, each mind keeping as a solitary prisoner its own dream of a world. Analysis goes a step farther still, and assures us that those impressions of the individual mind to which, for each one of us, experience dwindles down, are in perpetual flight; that each of them is limited by time, and that as time is infinitely divisible, each of them is infinitely divisible also; all that is actual in it being a single moment, gone while we try to apprehend it, of which it may ever be more truly said that it has ceased to be than that it is. To such a tremulous wisp constantly re-forming itself on the stream, to a single sharp impression, with a sense in it, a relic more or less fleeting, of such moments gone by, what is real in our life fines itself down. It is with this movement, with the passage and dissolution of impressions, images, sensations, that analysis leaves off—that continual vanishing away, that strange, perpetual weaving and unweaving of ourselves.

Philosophiren, says Novalis, *ist dephlegmatisiren vivificiren.*[3] The service of philosophy, of speculative culture, towards the human spirit, is to rouse, to startle it to a life of constant and eager observation. Every moment some form grows perfect in hand or face; some tone on the hills or the sea is choicer than the rest; some mood of passion or insight or intellectual excitement is irresistibly real and attractive to us,—for that moment only. Not the fruit of experience,

---

3. To philosophize is to cast off inertia, to vitalize (German)—*Editor.*

but experience itself, is the end. A counted number of pulses only is given to us of a variegated, dramatic life. How may we see in them all that is to be seen in them by the finest senses? How shall we pass most swiftly from point to point, and be present always at the focus where the greater number of vital forces unite in their purest energy?

To burn always with this hard, gemlike flame, to maintain this ecstasy, is success in life. In a sense it might even be said that our failure is to form habits: for, after all, habit is relative to a stereotyped world, and meantime it is only the roughness of the eye that makes any two persons, things, situations, seem alike. While all melts under our feet, we may well grasp at any exquisite passion, or any contribution to knowledge that seems by a lifted horizon to set the spirit free for a moment, or any stirring of the senses, strange dyes, strange colours, and curious odours, or work of the artist's hands, or the face of one's friend. Not to discriminate every moment some passionate attitude in those about us, and in the very brilliancy of their gifts some tragic dividing of forces on their ways, is, on this short day of frost and sun, to sleep before evening. With this sense of the splendour of our experience and of its awful brevity, gathering all we are into one desperate effort to see and touch, we shall hardly have time to make theories about the things we see and touch. What we have to do is to be for ever curiously testing new opinions and courting new impressions, never acquiescing in a facile orthodoxy of Comte, or of Hegel, or of our own. Philosophical theories or ideas, as points of view, instruments of criticism, may help us to gather up what might otherwise pass unregarded by us. "Philosophy is the microscope of thought." The theory or idea or system which requires of us the sacrifice of any part of this experience, in consideration of some interest into which we cannot enter, or some abstract theory we have not identified with ourselves, or of what is only conventional, has no real claim upon us.

One of the most beautiful passages of Rousseau is that in the sixth book of the *Confessions,* where he describes the awakening in him of the literary sense. An undefinable taint of death had clung always about him, and now in early manhood he believed himself smitten by mortal disease. He asked himself how he might make as much as possible of the interval that remained; and he was not biassed by anything in his previous life when he decided that it must be by intellectual excitement, which he found just then in the clear, fresh writings of Voltaire. Well! we are all *condamnés,* as Victor Hugo says: we are all under sentence of death but with a sort of indefinite reprieve—*les hommes sont tous condamnés à mort avec des sursis indéfinis.*[4] we have an interval, and then our place knows us no more.

---

4. Men are all condemned to death with indefinite reprieves (French)—*Editor.*

Some spend this interval in listlessness, some in high passions, the wisest, at least among "the children of this world,"[5] in art and song. For our one chance lies in expanding that interval, in getting as many pulsations as possible into the given time. Great passions may give us this quickened sense of life, ecstasy and sorrow of love, the various forms of enthusiastic activity, disinterested or otherwise, which come naturally to many of us. Only be sure it is passion—that it does yield you this fruit of a quickened, multiplied consciousness. Of such wisdom, the poetic passion, the desire of beauty, the love of art for its own sake, has most. For art comes to you proposing frankly to give nothing but the highest quality to your moments as they pass, and simply for those moments' sake.

OSCAR WILDE

From The Critic as Artist[†]

Part Two

* * *

GILBERT. Yes: the critic will be an interpreter, if he chooses. He can pass from his synthetic impression of the work of art as a whole, to an analysis or exposition of the work itself, and in this lower sphere, as I hold it to be, there are many delightful things to be said and done. Yet his object will not always be to explain the work of art. He may seek rather to deepen its mystery, to raise round it, and round its maker, that mist of wonder which is dear to both gods and worshippers alike. Ordinary people are "terribly at ease in Zion." They propose to walk arm in arm with the poets, and have a glib ignorant way of saying "Why should we read what is written about Shakespeare and Milton? We can read the plays and the poems. That is enough." But an appreciation of Milton is, as the late Rector of Lincoln remarked once, the reward of consummate scholarship. And he who desires to understand Shakespeare truly must understand the relations in which Shakespeare stood to the Renaissance and the Reformation, to the age of Elizabeth and the age of James; he must be familiar with the history of the struggle for supremacy between the old classical forms and the new spirit of romance, between the school of Sidney, and Daniel, and Jonson, and the school of Marlowe and Marlowe's greater son; he must know the materials that were at Shakespeare's disposal, and the method in which he used them,

---

5. Luke 16:8—*Editor.*
† From *Intentions* (Leipzig: Heinemann and Balestier, 1891), pp. 125–42.

and the conditions of theatric presentation in the sixteenth and seventeenth centuries, their limitations and their opportunities for freedom, and the literary criticism of Shakespeare's day, its aims and modes and canons; he must study the English language in its progress, and blank or rhymed verse in its various developments; he must study the Greek drama, and the connection between the art of the creator of the Agamemnon and the art of the creator of Macbeth; in a word, he must be able to bind Elizabethan London to the Athens of Pericles, and to learn Shakespeare's true position in the history of European drama and the drama of the world. The critic will certainly be an interpreter, but he will not treat Art as a riddling Sphinx, whose shallow secret may be guessed and revealed by one whose feet are wounded and who knows not his name. Rather, he will look upon Art as a goddess whose mystery it is his province to intensify, and whose majesty his privilege to make more marvellous in the eyes of men.

And here, Ernest, this strange thing happens. The critic will indeed be an interpreter, but he will not be an interpreter in the sense of one who simply repeats in another form a message that has been put into his lips to say. For, just as it is only by contact with the art of foreign nations that the art of a country gains that individual and separate life that we call nationality, so, by curious inversion, it is only by intensifying his own personality that the critic can interpret the personality and work of others, and the more strongly this personality enters into the interpretation, the more real the interpretation becomes, the more satisfying, the more convincing, and the more true.

ERNEST. I would have said that personality would have been a disturbing element.

GILBERT. No; it is an element of revelation. If you wish to understand others you must intensify your own individualism.

ERNEST. What, then, is the result?

GILBERT. I will tell you, and perhaps I can tell you best by definite example. It seems to me that, while the literary critic stands of course first, as having the wider range, and larger vision, and nobler material, each of the arts has a critic, as it were, assigned to it. The actor is a critic of the drama. He shows the poet's work under new conditions, and by a method special to himself. He takes the written word, and action, gesture, and voice become the media of revelation. The singer, or the player on lute and viol, is the critic of music. The etcher of a picture robs the painting of its fair colours, but shows us by the use of a new material its true colour-quality, its tones and values, and the relations of its masses, and so is, in his way, a critic of it, for the critic is he who exhibits to us a work of art in a form different from that of the work itself, and the employment of a new material is a critical as well as a creative element. Sculpture, too, has its critic, who may be either the carver of a gem, as he was in Greek days, or some painter like Mantegna, who sought to reproduce on canvas the beauty of plastic line and the symphonic dignity of processional bas-relief. And in the case of all these creative critics of art it is evident that personality is an absolute essential for any real interpretation. When Rubinstein plays to us the *Sonata Appassionata* of Beethoven, he gives us not merely Beethoven, but also himself, and so gives us Beethoven absolutely—Beethoven reinterpreted through a rich artistic nature, and made vivid and wonderful to us by a new and intense personality. When a greater actor plays Shakespeare we have the same experience. His own individuality becomes a vital part of the interpretation. People sometimes say that actors give us their own Hamlets, and not Shakespeare's; and this fallacy—for it is a fallacy—is, I regret to say, repeated by that charming and graceful writer who has lately deserted the turmoil of literature for the peace of the House of Commons, I mean the author of *Obiter Dicta*. In point of fact, there is no such thing as Shakespeare's Hamlet. If Hamlet has something of the definiteness of a work of art, he has also all the obscurity that belongs to life. There are as many Hamlets as there are melancholies.

ERNEST. As many Hamlets as there are melancholies?

GILBERT. Yes: and as art springs from personality, so it is only to personality that it can be revealed, and from the meeting of the two comes right interpretative criticism.

ERNEST. The critic, then, considered as the interpreter, will give no less than he receives, and lend as much as he borrows?

GILBERT. He will be always showing us the work of art in some new relation to our age. He will always be reminding us that great works of art are living things—are, in fact, the only things that live. So much, indeed, will he feel this, that I am certain that, as civilisation progresses and we become more highly organised, the elect spirits of each age, the critical and cultured spirits, will grow less and less interested in actual life, and *will seek to gain their impressions almost entirely from what Art has touched*. For life is terribly deficient in form. Its catastrophes happen in the wrong way and to the wrong people. There is a grotesque horror about its comedies, and its tragedies seem to culminate in farce. One is always wounded when one approaches it. Things last either too long, or not long enough.

ERNEST. Poor life! Poor human life! Are you not even touched by the tears that the Roman poet tells us are part of its essence?

GILBERT. Too quickly touched by them, I fear. For, when one looks back upon the life that was so vivid in its emotional intensity, and filled with such fervent moments of ecstasy or of joy, it all seems to be a dream and an illusion. What are the unreal things, but the passions that once burned one like fire? What are the incredible things, but the things that one has faithfully believed? What are the improbable things? The things that one has done oneself. No, Ernest; life cheats us with shadows, like a puppet-master. We ask it for pleasure. It gives it to us, with bitterness and disappointment in its train. We come across some noble grief that we think will lend the purple dignity of tragedy to our days, but it passes away from us, and things less noble take its place, and on some grey windy dawn, or odorous eve of silence and of silver, we find ourselves looking with callous wonder, or dull heart of stone at the trees of gold-flecked hair that we had once so wildly worshipped and so madly kissed.

ERNEST. Life then is a failure?

GILBERT. From the artistic point of view, certainly. And the chief things that makes life a failure from this artistic point of view is the thing that lends to life its sordid security, the fact that one can never repeat exactly the same emotion. How different it is in the world of Art! * * *

It is a strange thing, this transference of emotion. We sicken with the same maladies as the poets, and the singer lends us his pain. Dead lips have their message for us, and hearts that have fallen to dust can communicate their joy. We run to kiss the bleeding mouth of Fantine, and we follow Manon Lescaut over the whole world. Ours is the love-madness of the Tyrian, and the terror of Orestes is ours also. There is no passion that we cannot feel, no pleasure that we may not gratify, and we can choose the time of our initiation and the time of our freedom also. Life! Life! Don't let us go to life for our fulfillment or our experience. It is a thing narrowed by circumstances, incoherent in its utterance, and without that fine correspondence of form and spirit which is the only thing that can satisfy the artistic and critical temperament. It makes us pay too high a price for its wares, and we purchase the meanest of its secret at a cost that is monstrous and infinite.

ERNEST. Must we go, then, to Art for everything?

GILBERT. For everything. Because Art does not hurt us. The tears that we shed at a play are a type of the exquisite sterile emotions that it is the function of Art to awaken. We weep, but we are not wounded. We grieve, but our grief is not bitter. In the actual life of man, sorrow, as Spinoza says somewhere, is a passage to a lesser perfection. But the sorrow with which Art fills us both purifies and initiates, if I may quote once more from the great art critic of the Greeks. It is through Art, and through Art only, that we can realise our perfection; through Art, and through Art only, that we can shield ourselves from the sordid perils of actual existence. This results not merely from the fact that nothing that one can imagine is worth doing, and that one can imagine everything, but from the subtle law that emotional forces, like the forces of the physical sphere, are limited in extent and energy. One can feel so much, and no more. And how can it matter with what pleasure life tries to tempt one, or with what pain it seeks to maim and mar one's soul, if in the spectacle of the lives of those who have never existed one has found the true secret of joy, and wept away one's tears over their deaths who, like Cordelia and the daughter of Brabantio, can never die?

ERNEST. Stop a moment. It seems to me that in everything that you have said there is something radically immoral.

GILBERT. All art is immoral.

ERNEST. All art?

GILBERT. Yes. For emotion for the sake of emotion is the aim of art, and emotion for the sake of action is the aim of life, and of that practical organisation of life that we call society. Society, which is the beginning and basis of morals, exists simply for the concentration of human energy, and in order to ensure its own continuance and healthy stability it demands, and no doubt rightly demands, of each of its citizens that he should contribute some form of productive labour to the common weal, and toil and travail that the day's work may be done. Society often forgives the criminal; it never forgives the dreamer. The beautiful sterile emotions that art excites in us are hateful in its eyes, and so completely are people dominated by the tyranny of this dreadful social ideal that they are always coming shamelessly up to one at Private Views and other places that are open to the general public, and saying in a loud stentorian voice, "What are you doing?" whereas "What are you thinking?" is the only question that any single civilised being should ever be allowed to whisper to another. They mean well, no doubt, these honest beaming folk. Perhaps that is the reason why they are so excessively tedious. But some one should teach them that while, in the opinion of society, Contemplation is the gravest sin of which any citizen can be guilty, in the opinion of the highest culture it is the proper occupation of man.

ERNEST. Contemplation?

GILBERT. Contemplation. I said to you some time ago that it was far more difficult to talk about a thing than to do it. Let me say to you now that to do nothing at all is the most difficult thing in the world, the most difficult and the most intellectual. To Plato, with his passion for wisdom, this was the noblest form of energy. To Aristotle, with his passion for knowledge, this was the noblest form of energy also. It was to this that the passion for holiness led the saint and the mystic of mediæval days.

ERNEST. We exist, then, to do nothing?

GILBERT. It is to do nothing that the elect exist. Action is limited and relative. Unlimited and absolute is the vision of him who sits at ease and watches, who walks in loneliness and dreams. But we who are born at the close of this wonderful age, are at once too cultured and too critical, too intellectually subtle and too curious of exquisite pleasures, to accept any speculations about life in exchange for life itself. To us the *città divina*[1] is colourless, and the *fruitio Dei*[2] without meaning. Metaphysics do not satisfy our temperaments, and religious ecstasy is out of date. The world through which the Academic philosopher becomes "the spectator of all time and of all existence" is not really an ideal world, but simply a world of abstract ideas. When we enter it, we starve amidst the chill mathematics of thought. The courts of the city of God are not open to us now. Its gates are guarded by Ignorance, and to pass them we have to surrender all that in our nature is most divine. It is enough that our fathers believed. They have exhausted the faith-faculty of the species. Their legacy to us is the scepticism of which they were afraid. Had they put it into words, it might not live within us as thought. No, Ernest, no. We cannot go back to the saint. There is far more to be learned from the sinner. We cannot go back to the philosopher, and the mystic leads us astray. Who, as Mr. Pater suggests somewhere, would exchange the curve of a single rose-leaf for that formless intangible Being which Plato rates so high? What to us is the Illumination of Philo, the Abyss of Eckhart, the vision of Böhme, the monstrous Heaven itself that was revealed to Swedenborg's blinded eyes? Such things are less than the yellow trumpet of one daffodil of the field, far less than the meanest of the visible arts; for, just as Nature is matter struggling into mind, so Art is mind expressing itself under the conditions of matter, and thus, even in the lowliest of her manifestations, she speaks to both sense and soul alike. To the æsthetic temperament the vague is always repellent. The Greeks were a nation of artists, because they were spared the sense of the infinite. Like Aristotle, like Goethe after he had read Kant, we desire the concrete, and nothing but the concrete can satisfy us.

ERNEST. What then do you propose?

GILBERT. It seems to me that with the development of the critical spirit we shall be able to realise, not merely our own lives, but the collective life of the race, and so to make ourselves absolutely modern, in the true meaning of the word modernity. For he to whom the present is the only thing that is present, knows nothing of the age in which he lives. To realise the nineteenth century, one must realise every century that has preceded it and that has contributed to its making. To know anything about oneself, one must know all

1. Heavenly city (Italian).
2. Enjoyment of God (Latin).

about others. There must be no mood with which one cannot sym-
pathise, no dead mode of life that one cannot make alive. Is this
impossible? I think not. By revealing to us the absolute mechanism
of all action, and so freeing us from the self-imposed and trammel-
ling burden of moral responsibility, the scientific principle of Heredity has become, as it were, the warrant for the contemplative life. It
has shown us that we are never less free than when we try to act.
It has hemmed us round with the nets of the hunter, and written
upon the wall the prophecy of our doom. We may not watch it, for
it is within us. We may not see it, save in a mirror that mirrors the
soul. It is Nemesis without her mask. It is the last of the Fates, and
the most terrible. It is the only one of the Gods whose real name
we know.

And yet, while in the sphere of practical and external life it has
robbed energy of its freedom and activity of its choice, in the subjective sphere, where the soul is at work, it comes to us, this terrible
shadow, with many gifts in its hands, gifts of strange temperaments
and subtle susceptibilities, gifts of wild ardours and chill moods of
indifference, complex multiform gifts of thoughts that are at variance with each other, and passions that war against themselves. And
so, it is not our own life that we live, but the lives of the dead, and
the soul that dwells within us is no single spiritual entity, making
us personal and individual, created for our service, and entering into
us for our joy. It is something that has dwelt in fearful places, and
in ancient sepulchres has made its abode. It is sick with many maladies, and has memories of curious sins. It is wiser than we are, and
its wisdom is bitter. It fills us with impossible desires, and makes us
follow what we know we cannot gain. One thing, however, Ernest,
it can do for us. It can lead us away from surroundings whose beauty
is dimmed to us by the mist of familiarity, or whose ignoble ugliness
and sordid claims are marring the perfection of our development. It
can help us to leave the age in which we were born, and to pass into
other ages, and find ourselves not exiled from their air. It can teach
us how to escape from our experience, and to realise the experiences
of those who are greater than we are. The pain of Leopardi crying
out against life becomes our pain. Theocritus blows on his pipe, and
we laugh with the lips of nymph and shepherd. In the wolfskin of
Pierre Vidal we flee before the hounds, and in the armour of Lancelot we ride from the bower of the Queen. We have whispered the
secret of our love beneath the cowl of Abelard, and in the stained
raiment of Villon have put our shame into song. We can see the
dawn through Shelley's eyes, and when we wander with Endymion
the Moon grows amorous of our youth. Ours is the anguish of Atys,
and ours the weak rage and noble sorrows of the Dane. Do you think
that it is the imagination that enables us to live these countless lives?

Yes: it is the imagination; and the imagination is the result of heredity. It is simply concentrated race-experience.

ERNEST. But where in this is the function of the critical spirit?

GILBERT. The culture that this transmission of racial experiences makes possible can be made perfect by the critical spirit alone, and indeed may be said to be one with it. For who is the true critic but he who bears within himself the dreams, and ideas, and feelings of myriad generations, and to whom no form of thought is alien, no emotional impulse obscure? And who the true man of culture, if not he who by fine scholarship and fastidious rejection has made instinct self-conscious and intelligent, and can separate the work that has distinction from the work that has it not, and so by contact and comparison makes himself master of the secrets of style and school, and understands their meanings, and listens to their voices, and develops that spirit of disinterested curiosity which is the real root, as it is the real flower, of the intellectual life, and thus attains to intellectual clarity, and, having learned "the best that is known and thought in the world," lives—it is not fanciful to say so—with those who are the Immortals.

*　*　*

From The Decay of Lying[†]

*　*　*

VIVIAN. * * * Personal experience is a most vicious and limited circle. All that I desire to point out is the general principle that Life imitates Art far more than Art imitates Life, and I feel sure that if you think seriously about it you will find that it is true. Life holds the mirror up to Art, and either reproduces some strange type imagined by painter or sculptor, or realises in fact what has been dreamed in fiction. Scientifically speaking, the basis of life—the energy of life, as Aristotle would call it—is simply the desire for expression, and Art is always presenting various forms through which the expression can be attained. Life seizes on them and uses them, even if they be to her own hurt. Young men have committed suicide because Rolla did so, have died by their own hand because by his own hand Werther died. Think of what we owe to the imitation of Christ, of what we owe to the imitation of Cæsar.

CYRIL. The theory is certainly a very curious one, but to make it complete you must show that Nature, no less than Life, is an imitation of Art. Are you prepared to prove that?

† From *Intentions* (Leipzig: Heinemann and Balestier, 1891), pp. 32–45.

VIVIAN. My dear fellow, I am prepared to prove anything.

CYRIL. Nature follows the landscape painter then, and takes her effects from him?

VIVIAN. Certainly. Where, if not from the Impressionists, do we get those wonderful brown fogs that come creeping down our streets, blurring the gas-lamps and changing the houses into monstrous shadows? To whom, if not to them and their master, do we owe the lovely silver mists that brood over our river, and turn to faint forms of fading grace curved bridge and swaying barge? The extraordinary change that has taken place in the climate of London during the last ten years is entirely due to a particular school of Art. You smile. Consider the matter from a scientific or a metaphysical point of view, and you will find that I am right. For what is Nature? Nature is no great mother who has borne us. She is our creation. It is in our brain that she quickens to life. Things are because we see them, and what we see, and how we see it, depends on the Arts that have influenced us. To look at a thing is very different from seeing a thing. One does not see anything until one sees its beauty. Then, and then only, does it come into existence. At present, people see fogs, not because there are fogs, but because poets and painters have taught them the mysterious loveliness of such effects. There may have been fogs for centuries in London. I dare say there were. But no one saw them, and so we do not know anything about them. They did not exist till Art had invented them. Now, it must be admitted, fogs are carried to excess. They have become the mere mannerism of a clique, and the exaggerated realism of their method gives dull people bronchitis. Where the cultured catch an effect, the uncultured catch cold. And so, let us be humane, and invite Art to turn her wonderful eyes elsewhere. She has done so already, indeed. That white quivering sunlight that one sees now in France, with its strange blotches of mauve, and its restless violet shadows, is her latest fancy, and, on the whole, Nature reproduces it quite admirably. Where she used to give us Corots and Daubignys, she gives us now exquisite Monets and entrancing Pissaros. Indeed there are moments, rare, it is true, but still to be observed from time to time, when Nature becomes absolutely modern. Of course she is not always to be relied upon. The fact is that she is in this unfortunate position. Art creates an incomparable and unique effect, and, having done so, passes on to other things. Nature, upon the other hand, forgetting that imitation can be made the sincerest form of insult, keeps on repeating this effect until we all become absolutely wearied of it. Nobody of any real culture, for instance, ever talks nowadays about the beauty of a sunset. Sunsets are quite old-fashioned. They belong to the time when Turner was the last note in art. To admire them is a distinct sign of provincialism of temperament. Upon the other hand, they go on.

Yesterday evening Mrs. Arundel insisted on my going to the window, and looking at the glorious sky, as she called it. Of course, I had to look at it. She is one of those absurdly pretty Philistines, to whom one can deny nothing. And what was it? It was simply a very second-rate Turner, a Turner of a bad period, with all the painter's worst faults exaggerated and over-emphasised. Of course, I am quite ready to admit that Life very often commits the same error. She produces her false Renés and her sham Vautrins, just as Nature gives us, on one day a doubtful Cuyp, and on another a more than questionable Rousseau. Still, Nature irritates one more when she does things of that kind. It seems so stupid, so obvious, so unnecessary. A false Vautrin might be delightful. A doubtful Cuyp is unbearable. However, I don't want to be too hard on Nature. I wish the Channel, especially at Hastings, did not look quite so often like a Henry Moore, grey pearl with yellow lights, but then, when Art is more varied, Nature will, no doubt, be more varied also. That she imitates Art, I don't think even her worst enemy would deny now. It is the one thing that keeps her in touch with civilised man. But have I proved my theory to your satisfaction?

CYRIL. You have proved it to my dissatisfaction, which is better. But even admitting this strange imitative instinct in Life and Nature, surely you would acknowledge that Art expresses the temper of its age, the spirit of its time, the moral and social conditions that surround it, and under whose influence it is produced.

VIVIAN. Certainly not! Art never expresses anything but itself. This is the principle of my new æsthetics; and it is this, more than that vital connection between form and substance, on which Mr. Pater dwells, that makes basic the type of all the arts. Of course, nations and individuals, with that healthy natural vanity which is the secret of existence, are always under the impression that it is of them that the Muses are talking, always trying to find in the calm dignity of imaginative art some mirror of their own turbid passions, always forgetting that the singer of life is not Apollo, but Marsyas. Remote from reality, and with her eyes turned away from the shadows of the cave, Art reveals her own perfection, and the wondering crowd that watches the opening of the marvellous, many-petalled rose fancies that it is its own history that is being told to it, its own spirit that is finding expression in a new form. But it is not so. The highest art rejects the burden of the human spirit, and gains more from a new medium or a fresh material than she does from any enthusiasm for art, or from any lofty passion, or from any great awakening of the human consciousness. She develops purely on her own lines. She is not symbolic of any age. It is the ages that are her symbols.

Even those who hold that Art is representative of time and place and people, cannot help admitting that the more imitative an art is, the less it represents to us the spirit of its age. The evil faces of the Roman emperors look out at us from the foul porphyry and spotted jasper in which the realistic artists of the day delighted to work, and we fancy that in those cruel lips and heavy sensual jaws we can find the secret of the ruin of the Empire. But it was not so. The vices of Tiberius could not destroy that supreme civilisation, any more than the virtues of the Antonines could save it. It fell for other, for less interesting reasons. The sibyls and prophets of the Sistine may indeed serve to interpret for some that new birth of the emancipated spirit that we call the Renaissance; but what do the drunken boors and bawling peasants of Dutch art tell us about the great soul of Holland? The more abstract, the more ideal an art is, the more it reveals to us the temper of its age. If we wish to understand a nation by means of its art, let us look at its architecture or its music.

CYRIL. I quite agree with you there. The spirit of an age may be best expressed in the abstract ideal arts, for the spirit itself is abstract and ideal. Upon the other hand, for the visible aspect of an age, for its look, as the phrase goes, we must of course go to the arts of imitation.

VIVIAN. I don't think so. After all, what the imitative arts really give us are merely the various styles of particular artists, or of certain schools of artists. Surely you don't imagine that the people of the Middle Ages bore any resemblance at all to the figures on mediæval stained glass, or in mediæval stone and wood carving, or on mediæval metal-work, or tapestries, or illuminated MSS. They were probably very ordinary-looking people, with nothing grotesque, or remarkable, or fantastic in their appearance. The Middle Ages, as we know them in art, are simply a definite form of style, and there is no reason at all why an artist with this style should not be produced in the nineteenth century. No great artist ever sees things as they really are. If he did, he would cease to be an artist. Take an example from our own day. I know that you are fond of Japanese things. Now, do you really imagine that the Japanese people; as they are presented to us in art, have any existence? If you do, you have never understood Japanese art at all. The Japanese people are the deliberate self-conscious creation of certain individual artists. If you set a picture by Hokusai, or Hokkei, or any of the great native painters, beside a real Japanese gentleman or lady, you will see that there is not the slightest resemblance between them. The actual people who live in Japan are not unlike the general run of English people; that is to say, they are extremely commonplace, and have nothing curious or extraordinary about them. In fact, the whole of Japan is a pure invention. There is no such country, there are no such people. One of our most charming painters went recently to the Land of the

Chrysanthemum in the foolish hope of seeing the Japanese. All he saw, all he had the chance of painting, were a few lanterns and some fans. He was quite unable to discover the inhabitants, as his delightful exhibition at Messrs. Dowdeswell's Gallery showed only too well. He did not know that the Japanese people are, as I have said, simply a mode of style, an exquisite fancy of art. And so, if you desire to see a Japanese effect, you will not behave like a tourist and go to Tokio. On the contrary, you will stay at home, and steep yourself in the work of certain Japanese artists, and then, when you have absorbed the spirit of their style, and caught their imaginative manner of vision, you will go some afternoon and sit in the Park, or stroll down Piccadilly, and if you cannot see an absolutely Japanese effect there, you will not see it anywhere. Or, to return again to the past, take as another instance the ancient Greeks. Do you think that Greek art ever tells us what the Greek people were like? Do you believe that the Athenian women were like the stately dignified figures of the Parthenon frieze, or like those marvellous goddesses who sat in the triangular pediments of the same building? If you judge from the art, they certainly were so. But read an authority, like Aristophanes for instance. You will find that the Athenian ladies laced tightly, wore high-heeled shoes, dyed their hair yellow, painted and rouged their faces, and were exactly like any silly fashionable or fallen creature of our own day. The fact is that we look back on the ages entirely through the medium of Art, and Art, very fortunately, has never once told us the truth.

CYRIL. But modern portraits by English painters, what of them? Surely they are like the people they pretend to represent?

VIVIAN. Quite so. They are so like them that a hundred years from now no one will believe in them. The only portraits in which one believes are portraits where there is very little of the sitter and a very great deal of the artist. Holbein's drawings of the men and women of his time impress us with a sense of their absolute reality. But this is simply because Holbein compelled life to accept his conditions, to restrain itself within his limitations, to reproduce his type, and to appear as he wished it to appear. It is style that makes us believe in a thing—nothing but style. Most of our modern portrait painters are doomed to absolute oblivion. They never paint what they see. They paint what the public sees, and the public never sees anything.

CRYIL. Well, after that I think I should like to hear the end of your article.

VIVIAN. With pleasure. Whether it will do any good I really cannot say. Ours is certainly the dullest and most prosaic century possible. Why, even Sleep has played us false, and has closed up the gates of ivory, and opened the gates of horn. The dreams of the great middle classes of this country, as recorded in Mr Myers's two bulky

volumes on the subject and in the Transactions of the Psychical
Society, are the most depressing things I have ever read. There is
not even a fine nightmare among them. They are commonplace, sordid, and tedious. As for the Church, I cannot conceive anything
better for the culture of a country than the presence in it of a body
of men whose duty it is to believe in the supernatural, to perform
daily miracles, and to keep alive that mythopœic faculty which is so
essential for the imagination. But in the English Church a man succeeds, not through his capacity for belief, but through his capacity
for disbelief. Ours is the only Church where the sceptic stands at
the altar, and where St Thomas is regarded as the ideal apostle.
Many a worthy clergyman, who passes his life in admirable works
of kindly charity, lives and dies unnoticed and unknown; but it is
sufficient for some shallow uneducated passman out of either University to get up in his pulpit and express his doubts about Noah's
ark, or Balaam's ass, or Jonah and the whale, for half of London to
flock to hear him, and to sit open-mouthed in rapt admiration at his
superb intellect. The growth of common sense in the English Church
is a thing very much to be regretted. It is really a degrading conces-
sion to a low form of realism. It is silly, too. It springs from an entire
ignorance of psychology. Man can believe the impossible, but man
can never believe the improbable. However, I must read the end of
my article:—

"What we have to do, what at any rate it is our duty to do, is revive
this old art of Lying. Much of course may be done, in the way of
educating the public, by amateurs in the domestic circle, at literary
lunches, and at afternoon teas. But this is merely the light and graceful side of lying, such as was probably heard at Cretan dinner parties. There are many other forms. Lying for the sake of gaining some
immediate personal advantage, for instance—lying with a moral
purpose, as it is usually called—though of late it has been rather
looked down upon, was extremely popular with the antique world.
Athena laughs when Odysseus tells her 'his words of sly devising,'
as Mr William Morris phrases it, and the glory of mendacity illu-
mines the pale brow of the stainless hero of Euripidean tragedy, and
sets among the noble women of the past the young bride of one of
Horace's most exquisite odes. Later on, what at first had been
merely a natural instinct was elevated into a self-conscious science.
Elaborate rules were laid down for the guidance of mankind, and
an important school of literature grew up round the subject. Indeed,
when one remembers the excellent philosophical treatise of Sanchez
on the whole question, one cannot help regretting that no one has
ever thought of publishing a cheap and condensed edition of the
works of that great casuist. A short primer, 'When to Lie and How,'
if brought out in an attractive and not too expensive a form, would

no doubt command a large sale, and would prove of real practical service to many earnest and deep-thinking people. Lying for the sake of the improvement of the young, which is the basis of home education, still lingers amongst us, and its advantages are so admirably set forth in the early books of Plato's *Republic* that it is unnecessary to dwell upon them here. It is a mode of lying for which all good mothers have peculiar capabilities, but it is capable of still further development, and has been sadly overlooked by the School Board. Lying for the sake of a monthly salary is, of course, well known in Fleet Street, and the profession of a political leader-writer is not without its advantages. But it is said to be a somewhat dull occupation, and it certainly does not lead to much beyond a kind of ostentatious obscurity. The only form of lying that is absolutely beyond reproach is Lying for its own sake, and the highest development of this is, as we have already pointed out, Lying in Art. Just as those who do not love Plato more than Truth cannot pass beyond the threshold of the Academe, so those who do not love Beauty more than Truth never know the inmost shrine of Art. The solid stolid British intellect lies in the desert sands like the Sphinx in Flaubert's marvellous tale, and fantasy, *La Chimère*, dances round it, and calls to it with her false, flute-toned voice. It may not hear her now, but surely some day, when we are all bored to death with the commonplace character of modern fiction, it will hearken to her and try to borrow her wings.

"And when that day dawns, or sunset reddens, how joyous we shall be! Facts will be regarded as discreditable, Truth will be found mourning over her fetters, and Romance, with her temper of wonder, will return to the land. The very aspect of the world will change to our startled eyes. Out of the sea will rise Behemoth and Leviathan, and sail round the high-pooped galleys, as they do on the delightful maps of those ages when books on geography were actually readable. Dragons will wander about the waste places, and the phoenix will soar from her nest of fire into the air. We shall lay our hands upon the basilisk, and see the jewel in the toad's head. Champing his gilded oats, the Hippogriff will stand in our stalls, and over our heads will float the Blue Bird singing of beautiful and impossible things, of things that are lovely and that never happen, of things that are not and that should be. But before this comes to pass we must cultivate the lost art of Lying."

CYRIL. Then we must entirely cultivate it at once. But in order to avoid making any error, I want you to tell me briefly the doctrines of the new æsthetics.

VIVIAN. Briefly, then, they are these. Art never expresses anything but itself. It has an independent life, just as Thought has, and develops purely on its own lines. It is not necessarily realistic in an age of realism, nor spiritual in an age of faith. So far from being the creation of its time, it is usually in direct opposition to it, and the only history that it preserves for us is the history of its own progress. Sometimes it returns upon its footsteps, and revives some antique form, as happened in the archaistic movement of late Greek Art, and in the pre-Raphaelite movement of our own day. At other times it entirely anticipates its age, and produces in one century work that it takes another century to understand, to appreciate, and to enjoy. In no case does it reproduce its age. To pass from the art of a time to the time itself is the great mistake that all historians commit.

The second doctrine is this. All bad art comes from returning to Life and Nature, and elevating them into ideals. Life and Nature may sometimes be used as part of Art's rough material, but before they are of any real service to Art they must be translated into artistic conventions. The moment Art surrenders its imaginative medium it surrenders everything. As a method Realism is a complete failure, and the two things that every artist should avoid are modernity of form and modernity of subject-matter. To us, who live in the nineteenth century, any century is a suitable subject for art except our own. The only beautiful things are the things that do not concern us. It is, to have the pleasure of quoting myself, exactly because Hecuba is nothing to us that her sorrows are so suitable a motive for a tragedy. Besides, it is only the modern that ever becomes old-fashioned. M Zola sits down to give us a picture of the Second Empire. Who cares for the Second Empire now? It is out of date. Life goes faster than Realism, but Romanticism is always in front of Life.

The third doctrine is that Life imitates Art far more than Art imitates Life. This results not merely from Life's imitative instinct, but from the fact that the self-conscious aim of Life is to find expression, and that Art offers it certain beautiful forms through which it may realise that energy. It is a theory that has never been put forward before, but it is extremely fruitful, and throws an entirely new light upon the history of Art.

It follows, as a corollary from this, that external Nature also imitates Art. The only effects that she can show us are effects that we have already seen through poetry, or in paintings. This is the secret of Nature's charm, as well as the explanation of Nature's weakness.

The final revelation is that Lying, the telling of beautiful untrue things, is the proper aim of Art. But of this I think I have spoken at sufficient length. And now let us go out on the terrace, where "droops the milk-white peacock like a ghost," while the evening star "washes the dusk with silver." At twilight nature becomes a wonderfully suggestive effect, and is not without loveliness, though perhaps its chief use is to illustrate quotations from the poets. Come! We have talked long enough.

REVIEWS AND
REACTIONS

A Note on "Reviews and Reactions"

The Picture of Dorian Gray occupies an important place in the social and legal history of literature. The reviews, responses, and testimony collected in this section are the very raw materials of a chapter in that history, one that seems to possess a dramatic form of its own rarely found in life outside art. It was Wilde who insisted in one of his most celebrated paradoxes from "The Decay of Lying" that "life imitates art," but then in the record of controversy that followed in the wake of *Dorian Gray*, life had more than a little assistance from the artist. Seldom has a work of art reflected its times in more ways than *Dorian Gray*. It is a benchmark of Decadence in English, a key to the psychic and creative life of its author, and a mirror of the prejudices of an era that used it against its author in a court of law as evidence of his moral corruption.

We might well wish to use *Dorian Gray* to measure important cultural and social changes over the intervening years. It is necessary to remind ourselves that the novel was considered scandalous in its day by many. Wilde, eager to press the point with one eye on sales and the other on culture, insisted that his book was "poisonous but perfect," thus inflaming his critics the more. Today's sympathies are almost entirely with the author and against his critics, at least on the matter of art and morality, as chronicled briefly in the following pages.

Readers who have looked into the text of the *Lippincott's Magazine* edition of the novel above will be more aware of what the fuss was all about than those who have read only the revised edition, through which the novel has been known since its publication by Ward, Lock & Company. However, even to the alerted reader, the issues and consequences of the controversy will seem disproportionate to the apparent cause unless some of the emotional and cultural feeling of those years can be recaptured. Even American readers of *Lippincott's* gave *Dorian Gray* a far more friendly response than the London critics. In the Sunday *New York Times* for June 29, 1890, the London correspondent filed the following report on the *Dorian Gray* eruption:

> Up to the appearance of "In Darkest Africa" [explorer Henry Morton Stanley's book], Oscar Wilde's novel in *Lippincott's* had monopolized the attention of Londoners who talk about books. It must have excited vastly more interest here than in America simply because since last year's exposure of what are euphemistically styled the West End scandals, Englishmen have been abnormally sensitive to the faintest suggestion of pruriency in the direction of friendships. Very likely this bestial suspicion did not cross the mind of one

American reader out of ten thousand, but here the whole town leaped at it with avidity, and one moral journal called for the intervention of the Public Prosecutor. So much has been said about this phase of the book that Wilde is writing long letters to the press, not denying the imputation that his work is a study in puppydom, but insisting that such beings are more picturesque than good people.[1]

The "West End scandals" mentioned in the report received some attention in the New York press, chiefly the *Herald,* but had little to interest American readers except for the suggestion that a member of the English royal family had been mentioned in connection with "loathsome and disgusting practices" (one of the dysphemisms of the times for homosexuality). In the English press, however, the scandals, also referred to as the "Cleveland Street affair," nearly grew to the proportions of a Victorian Watergate, involving cover-up charges against the prime minister, Lord Salisbury, and his government; several sensational trials of telegraph boys procured for a gay brothel at 19 Cleveland Street that catered to dandies and aristocrats; the scandalous involvement of Lord Arthur Somerset, a member of the Prince of Wales's household; and the rumored involvement of Prince Albert Victor ("Eddy"), eldest son of the Prince of Wales and second in line to the English throne.[2]

The most publicized of the trials arising out of the affair was a libel suit brought by Henry James Fitzroy, earl of Euston, against Ernest Parke, editor of the *North London Press.* It was tried at the Old Bailey criminal court on January 15, 1890. The guilty verdict of "libel without justification" sent Parke to prison for a year and effectively ended press coverage of the Cleveland Street affair until Labouchere's dramatic parliamentary accusations of official cover-up. On the whole, the affair had provided the press with stories of scandals in high places and degradations in low ones for about five months, carrying into March 1890, sixty days before the *Lippincott's Dorian Gray* appeared on the newsstands.

Several months before the Cleveland Street affair broke in the press, Wilde published "The Portrait of Mr. W. H." in *Blackwell's Magazine,* which contributed as much as the notoriety of the Cleveland Street affair to prejudice press critics against Wilde's aesthetic puppets. The story offers an elegant and deliberately transparent defense of an old theory that Shakespeare's sonnets were dedicated to and written for a young actor, Willie Hughes, whose existence has never been proven. "The Portrait of Mr. W. H." demonstrates the thesis of "The Critic as Artist" that true criticism should be creative enough to move beyond the limits of its materials to the region of artistic invention. Wilde's story both creates and disposes of the fiction of Willie Hughes as the "Mr. W. H." to whom Shakespeare made his dedication. The Hughes theory almost perfectly explains the problem of the dedication; it is

1. *New York Times* (Sunday, June 29, 1890), p. 1.
2. The scandal is fully discussed in H. Montgomery Hyde, *Their Good Names* (London: Hamilton, 1970); by the same author in *The Cleveland Street Scandal* (New York: Coward, 1976); and in Colin Simpson, et al., *The Cleveland Street Affair* (Boston: Little, Brown, 1976).

flawed only by the total absence of any evidence that Willie Hughes ever existed. "The Portrait of Mr. W. H." demonstrates in a manner deliberately paradoxical the superiority of art (in this case criticism) to life. But it was not the perverse cleverness of Wilde's argument that put his critics on notice as much as it was Wilde's espousal of a view that implied that England's greatest poet was gay and, what was worse, had plenty of company among the world's geniuses.

The critics had little to say publicly on the matter of their suspicions, perhaps because Shakespeare was beyond the reach of cavil or because of the tone and manner of Wilde's witty, fictionalized scholarship. However, given the provocation of "The Portrait of Mr. W. H." and the intervening Cleveland Street scandal, it is little wonder that *Dorian Gray* produced the nearly hysterical reaction in the press that it did, especially in the *Pall Mall Gazette,* whose editor, William Stead, found muckraking and personal exposé good for circulation. To what extent Wilde expected or even counted on this reaction it is impossible to say, but he proved more than a match for his adversaries. The exchanges in the press, especially in the *St. James's Gazette,* brought out the best of Wilde's polemical talents, as the letters in this section attest.

The criticism leveled at *Dorian Gray* stresses several points. The foremost is, of course, the morality issue, and the objection was that Wilde had published an account of male friendship that stressed inadmissible homosexual attitudes. We may openly wonder at the apparent naïveté of the Victorians and at the emotional impact Wilde's story had on so many press critics. To some extent, at least, the naïveté was an effect of the prevailing code that the way to deal with unpleasant things was to suppress any mention of them. Wilde broke that code at a time when people in the press were especially sensitive on the issue and seems to have compelled some to recognize the existence of behavior with which many of Wilde's press critics were well acquainted through practice but to which they would and could not publicly admit. To be sure, we should give the Victorian establishment its due. Wilde knew that to raise the spectre of homosexualism, however indirectly, would cause a sensation; and he said as much.

Other related charges against the morality of the story mentioned Wilde's treatment of vice and crime, the poisonous atmosphere of sin and corruption that Wilde builds up so suggestively. His defense was that this was necessary for working out Dorian's fate. Again we see in the criticism the suggestion that an author should avoid aspects of life that the Victorian middle class simply did not wish to acknowledge or think about.

The complaint that the characters are mere puppets who strike poses and converse was a criticism that Wilde himself made of the novel, along with an admission that *Dorian Gray* contained too many melodramatic incidents.[3] While he does have more changes of scene in the revised novel, the focus of the action remains London, with a brief excursion to the country estate of Selby Royal.

3. The term "puppyism," a variation of which was used by a reviewer for the *St. James's Gazette* and by Wilde in a response, meant "affectation or excessive art in costume or posture," according to Eric Partridge, *A Dictionary of Slang and Unconventional English,* 5th ed. (New York: Macmillan, 1961), p. 669.

Two happy and important exceptions to the otherwise predictable and dreary insistence upon critical moralizing from contemporaries are included here, partly as a contrast to the art and morality debate and partly because each marks an important critical statement about the novel. The Hawthorne essay, a review of the *Lippincott's* version published in the following number, raises important issues about the novel's properties as fantasy and romance, issues that have not received the attention they deserve from subsequent critics. The Pater essay was a review of the revised bound novel of 1891 and gives valuable insights into Wilde's intentions and practice in making his last revision of the novel. Pater was especially qualified to do this by virtue of his position as Wilde's mentor and confidant during the writing of *Dorian Gray* and by virtue of his own powers of criticism and analysis. Although more thorough and complete studies of the novel have been produced in the intervening century, Pater's review remains the best analysis of the novel.

The effect of the "art and morality" debate, as it subsequently came to be known, on Wilde's writing and life has yet to be studied in sufficient depth. However, one or two conclusions relevant to this collection may be outlined here. Certainly the debate produced the rejoinders Wilde published separately as "The Preface" to *Dorian Gray,* and its influence is at work both in the revised versions of the essays collected in 1891 under the title *Intentions* and in parts of "The Soul of Man under Socialism," which appeared in the *Fortnightly Review* (February 1891), the number immediately preceding that of "The Preface." The effect on Wilde's life is more difficult to assess, but his victories in the press seem to have encouraged him to live more boldly and more dangerously than he had in the past. To the extent that there is linkage, the art and morality debate and the famous defense of *Dorian Gray* at Wilde's first trial may seem to be engagements in the long war over free speech and censorship still being vigorously discussed at all levels of society.

A brief account of events surrounding the trials will be useful for the contemporary reader unfamiliar with one of the juicier late Victorian scandals. The trial at which *Dorian Gray* made up the "literary part of the case" was the first of three prosecutions involving Oscar Wilde in the spring of 1895. The first trial was an action for libel brought by Wilde against the Marquess of Queensberry, who had left his card at Wilde's club with the words "For Oscar Wilde posing as a somdomite [*sic*]" scrawled upon it. Not only was the critical word misspelled but also the card itself had been put in an envelope by the porter and seen by no one. No action need have been taken, except that Wilde was convinced by Alfred Douglas, Queensberry's estranged son, that this was an opportunity to send his father to prison. Douglas had made a spectacle of himself both posing as and being Wilde's "boy," and Queensberry had grown more and more publicly outraged by this behavior and had threatened to make a scandal. When Wilde brought his ill-conceived charges, Queensberry pleaded justification. Although Wilde stoutly maintained the pose of one entirely innocent of the alleged libel, he was in fact guilty of a great deal more than Queensberry asserted.

Wilde had to face Edward Carson, an able criminal barrister and a former Trinity College, Dublin, classmate. Perhaps a renewal of their youthful rivalry added even more spirit to a courtroom clash that has become one of the classic duels in trial history. Although the literary phase was by no means the strong point of Carson's case, he pursued a line of questioning that raised once again the art and morality issue. Carson was determined to prove that Wilde was a corrupt person and had exercised a morally bad influence over Alfred Douglas. However, the art and morality issue was one on which Wilde was well schooled, and he clearly got the better of the exchanges. Had the rest of the trial gone as well as Wilde's celebrated defense of his novel, he would have walked off in triumph. As it was, however, on the second day of the trial, Carson scored heavily in questioning Wilde about a series of associations with newsboys, telegraph boys, and young men identified by the police as homosexual prostitutes. When Carson produced and began questioning these witnesses about their relations with Wilde, the jig was up. Wilde's counsel, Sir Edward Clarke, conceded justification for the libel, thereby hoping to avoid criminal prosecution against his client. That action was not long in coming. However, a decent interval was allowed for Wilde to follow the example of Lord Arthur Somerset of Cleveland Street fame and leave the country. Everyone held his breath; but instead of "levant-ing," as it was called, Wilde stayed in a room at the Cadogen Hotel and awaited martyrdom in a nearly paralyzed state of indecision and appre-hension. Two trials followed, the first ending in a hung jury, the second in conviction, which sent Wilde away for two years at hard labor.

The cost of the Queensberry trial ruined Wilde financially, and the conviction and imprisonment destroyed him socially and as a writer. Wilde's genius flourished in society but withered in prison and died dur-ing his continental exile, plagued as he was by poverty and ill health and haunted by the specter of his ruined life. And yet a sympathetic observer cannot help but conclude that Wilde had blindly reached toward a stage of self-development that would raise him above the sordidness of his own life, and he found it in suffering. He died in Paris as the nineteenth century ended and the twentieth began, in November 1900.

ST. JAMES'S GAZETTE

A Study in Puppydom[†]

(June 24, 1890)

Time was (it was in the '70's) when we talked about Mr Oscar Wilde; time came (it came in the '80's) when he tried to write poetry and, more adventurous, we tried to read it;[1] time is when we had forgot-ten him, or only remember him as the late editor of *The Woman's*

[†] From *St. James's Gazette* (June 24, 1890), rpt. in *Oscar Wilde: Art and Morality*, ed. Stuart Mason (1912; rpt. in New York: Haskell House, 1971), pp. 27–34. All notes are Mason's. Stuart Mason (1872–1927) wrote under the pseudonym Christopher Sclater Millard.

1. His *Poems*, published by David Bogue in 1881 at 10s. 6d., went through two editions and five printings within a year.

World[2]—a part for which he was singularly unfitted, if we are to judge him by the work which he has been allowed to publish in *Lippincott's Magazine* and which Messrs Ward, Lock & Co. have not been ashamed to circulate in Great Britain. Not being curious in ordure, and not wishing to offend the nostrils of decent persons, we do not propose to analyse "The Picture of Dorian Gray": that would be to advertise the developments of an esoteric prurience. Whether the Treasury or the Vigilance Society will think it worth while to prosecute Mr Oscar Wilde or Messrs Ward, Lock & Co., we do not know; but on the whole we hope they will not.

The puzzle is that a young man of decent parts, who enjoyed (when he was at Oxford)[3] the opportunity of associating with gentlemen, should put his name (such as it is) to so stupid and vulgar a piece of work. Let nobody read it in the hope of finding witty paradox or racy wickedness. The writer airs his cheap research among the garbage of the French *Décadents* like any drivelling pedant, and he bores you unmercifully with his prosy rigmaroles about the beauty of the Body and the corruption of the Soul. The grammar is better than Ouida's; the erudition equal; but in every other respect we prefer the talented lady who broke off with "pious aposiopesis" when she touched upon "the horrors which are described in the pages of Suetonius and Livy"—not to mention the yet worse infamies believed by many scholars to be accurately portrayed in the lost works of Plutarch, Venus, and Nicodemus, especially Nicodemus.

Let us take one peep at the young men in Mr Oscar Wilde's story. Puppy No. 1 is the painter of the picture of Dorian Gray; Puppy No. 2 is the critic (a courtesy lord, skilled in all the knowledge of the Egyptians and aweary of all the sins and pleasures of London); Puppy No. 3 is the original, cultivated by Puppy No. 1 with a "romantic friendship." The Puppies fall a-talking: Puppy No. 1 about his Art, Puppy No. 2 about his sins and pleasures and the pleasures of sin, and Puppy No. 3 about himself—always about himself, and generally about his face, which is "brainless and beautiful." The Puppies appear to fill up the intervals of talk by plucking daisies and playing with them, and sometimes by drinking "something with strawberry in it." The youngest Puppy is told that he is charming; but he mustn't sit in the sun for fear of spoiling his complexion. When he is rebuked for being a naughty, wilful boy, he makes a pretty *moue*—this man of twenty! This is how he is addressed by the Blasé Puppy at their first meeting:

"Yes, Mr. Gray, the gods have been good to you. But what the gods give they quickly take away. . . . When your youth goes, your beauty

---

2. Wilde edited this publication for Messrs. Cassell from 1887 to 1889.
3. Wilde was a demy (a foundation scholar) of Magdalen College, 1874–78. The term came from the amount of a demy's allowance, which was half that of a fellow.

will go with it, and then you will suddenly discover that there are no triumphs left for you. . . . Time is jealous of you, and wars against your lilies and roses. You will become sallow, and hollow-cheeked, and dull-eyed. You will suffer horribly."

Why, bless our souls! haven't we read something of this kind somewhere in the classics? Yes, of course we have! But in what recondite author? Ah—yes—no—yes, it *was* in Horace! What an advantage it is to have received a classical education! And how it will astonish the Yankees! But we must not forget our Puppies, who have probably occupied their time in lapping "something with strawberry in it." Puppy No. 1 (the Art Puppy) has been telling Puppy No. 3 (the Doll Puppy) how much he admires him. What is the answer? "I am less to you than your ivory Hermes or your silver Faun. You will like them always. How long will you like me? Till I have my first wrinkle, I suppose. I know now that when one loses one's good looks, whatever they may be, one loses everything. . . . I am jealous of the portrait you have painted of me. Why should it keep what I must lose? . . . Oh, if it was only the other way! If the picture could only change, and I could be always what I am now!"

No sooner said than done! The picture *does* change: the original doesn't. Here's a situation for you! Théophile Gautier could have made it romantic, entrancing, beautiful. Mr Stevenson could have made it convincing, humorous, pathetic. Mr Anstey could have made it screamingly funny. It has been reserved for Mr Oscar Wilde to make it dull and nasty. The promising youth plunges into every kind of mean depravity, and ends in being "cut" by fast women and vicious men. He finishes with murder: the New Voluptuousness always leads up to blood-shedding—that is part of the cant. The gore and gashes wherein Mr Rider Haggard takes a chaste delight are the natural diet for a cultivated palate which is tired of mere licentiousness. And every wickedness or filthiness committed by Dorian Gray is faithfully registered upon his face in the picture; but his living features are undisturbed and unmarred by his inward vileness. This is the story which Mr Oscar Wilde has tried to tell; a very lame story it is, and very lamely it is told.

Why has he told it? There are two explanations; and, so far as we can see, not more than two. Not to give pleasure to his readers: the thing is too clumsy, too tedious, and—alas! that we should say it—too stupid. Perhaps it was to shock his readers, in order that they might cry Fie! upon him and talk about him, much as Mr Grant Allen recently tried in *The Universal Review* to arouse, by a licentious theory of the sexual relations, an attention which is refused to his popular chatter about other men's science. Are we then to suppose that Mr Oscar Wilde has yielded to the craving for a notoriety which he once earned by talking fiddle-faddle about other men's art, and sees

his only chance of recalling it by making himself obvious at the cost
of being obnoxious, and by attracting the notice which the olfactory
sense cannot refuse to the presence of certain self-asserting organ-
isms? That is an uncharitable hypothesis, and we would gladly abandon it. It may be suggested (but is it more charitable?) that he derives
pleasure from treating a subject merely because it is disgusting. The
phenomenon is not unknown in recent literature; and it takes two
forms, in appearance widely separate—in fact, two branches from the
same root, a root which draws its life from malodorous putrefaction.
One development is found in the Puritan prurience which produced
Tolstoy's "Kreutzer Sonata" and Mr Stead's famous outbursts.[4] That is
odious enough and mischievous enough, and it is rightly execrated,
because it is tainted with an hypocrisy not the less culpable because
charitable persons may believe it to be unconscious. But is it more
odious or more mischievous than the "frank Paganism" (that is the
word, is it not?) which delights in dirtiness and confesses its delight?
Still they are both chips from the same block—"The Maiden Tribute
of Modern Babylon"[5] and "The Picture of Dorian Gray"—and both of
them ought to be chucked into the fire. Not so much because they are
dangerous and corrupt (they are corrupt but not dangerous) as
because they are incurably silly, written by simpleton *poseurs* (whether
they call themselves Puritan or Pagan) who know nothing about the
life which they affect to have explored, and because they are mere
catchpenny revelations of the non-existent, which, if they reveal anything at all, are revelations only of the singularly unpleasant minds
from which they emerge.

OSCAR WILDE

To the Editor of the *St. James's Gazette*[†]

25 June [*1890*]   *16 Tite Street*

Sir, I have read your criticism of my story, *The Picture of Dorian Gray*,
and I need hardly say that I do not propose to discuss its merits or

4. In the *Pall Mall Gazette*.
5. *Pall Mall Gazette*, July 6–10, 1885.
† From *St. James's Gazette* (June 26, 1890); rpt. in *The Letters of Oscar Wilde*, ed. Rupert
    Hart-Davis (London: Hart-Davis; rpt. in New York: Harcourt, 1962), p. 257. Sidney
    James Mark Low (1857–1932, knighted 1918) was editor of the *St. James's Gazette* 1888–
    97. Wilde's only novel, *The Picture of Dorian Gray*, was first published on June 20, 1890,
    in the July number of *Lippincott's Monthly Magazine*, where it occupied pp. 3–100. It
    was extensively reviewed. The *St. James's Gazette* printed a scurrilous notice on June 24,
    under the heading "A Study in Puppydom." Its anonymous author was Samuel Henry
    Jeyes (1857–1911). The full text of all the important reviews of, and letters about,
    Dorian Gray is given in Stuart Mason's *Art and Morality* (1912). This letter of Wilde's
    was published on June 26, under the heading MR OSCAR WILDE'S "BAD CASE."

demerits, its personalities or its lack of personality. England is a free country, and ordinary English criticism is perfectly free and easy. Besides, I must admit that, either from temperament or from taste, or from both, I am quite incapable of understanding how any work of art can be criticised from a moral standpoint. The sphere of art and the sphere of ethics are absolutely distinct and separate; and it is to the confusion between the two that we owe the appearance of Mrs Grundy, that amusing old lady who represents the only original form of humour that the middle classes of this country have been able to produce. What I do object to most strongly is that you should have placarded the town with posters on which was printed in large letters: MR OSCAR WILDE'S LATEST ADVERTISEMENT; A BAD CASE.

Whether the expression "A Bad Case" refers to my book or to the present position of the Government, I cannot tell. What was silly and unnecessary was the use of the term "advertisement."

I think I may say without vanity—though I do not wish to appear to run vanity down—that of all men in England I am the one who requires least advertisement. I am tired to death of being advertised. I feel no thrill when I see my name in a paper. The chronicler does not interest me any more. I wrote this book entirely for my own pleasure, and it gave me very great pleasure to write it. Whether it becomes popular or not is a matter of absolute indifference to me. I am afraid, sir, that the real advertisement is your cleverly written article. The English public, as a mass, takes no interest in a work of art until it is told that the work in question is immoral, and your *réclame* will, I have no doubt, largely increase the sale of the magazine; in which sale, I may mention with some regret, I have no pecuniary interest.

I remain, sir, your obedient servant OSCAR WILDE

ST. JAMES'S GAZETTE

Editorial Note[†]

(June 25, 1890)

In the preceding column will be found the best reply which Mr Oscar Wilde can make to our recent criticism of his mawkish and nauseous story, "The Picture of Dorian Gray." Mr Wilde tells us that he is constitutionally unable to understand how any work of art can be criticised from a moral standpoint. We were quite aware that ethics and æsthetics are different matters, and that is why the greater part

† From *St. James's Gazette* (June 25, 1890); rpt. in *Oscar Wilde: Art and Morality*, ed. Stuart Mason (1912; rpt. in New York: Haskell House, 1971), pp. 37–38.

of our criticism was devoted not so much to the nastiness of "The Picture of Dorian Gray," but to its dulness and stupidity. Mr Wilde pretends that we have advertised it. So we have, if any readers are attracted to a book which, we have warned them, will bore them insufferably.

That the story is corrupt cannot be denied; but we added, and assuredly believe, that it is not dangerous, because, as we said, it is tedious and stupid.

Mr Wilde tells us that he wrote the story for his own pleasure, and found great pleasure in writing it. We congratulate him; there is no triumph more precious to your "æsthete" than the discovery of a delight which outsiders cannot share or even understand. The author of "The Picture of Dorian Gray" is the only person likely to find pleasure in it.

OSCAR WILDE

To the Editor of the *St. James's Gazette*†

26 June [1890]   *16 Tite Street*

In your issue of today you state that my brief letter published in your columns is the "best reply" I can make to your article upon *Dorian Gray*. This is not so. I do not propose to fully discuss the matter here, but I feel bound to say that your article contains the most unjustifiable attack that has been made upon any man of letters for many years. The writer of it, who is quite incapable of concealing his personal malice, and so in some measure destroys the effect he wishes to produce, seems not to have the slightest idea of the temper in which a work of art should be approached. To say that such a book as mine should be "chucked into the fire" is silly. That is what one does with newspapers.

Of the value of pseudo-ethical criticism in dealing with artistic work I have spoken already. But as your writer has ventured into the perilous grounds of literary criticism I ask you to allow me, in fairness not merely to myself but to all men to whom literature is a fine art, to say a few words about his critical method.

He begins by assailing me with much ridiculous virulence because the chief personages in my story are "puppies." They *are* puppies.

---

† From *St. James's Gazette* (June 27, 1890); rpt. in *The Letters of Oscar Wilde*, ed. Rupert Hart-Davis (London: Hart-Davis; rpt. in New York: Harcourt, 1962), pp. 258–59. The editorial note which accompanied Wilde's letter of the 25th was so offensive that it called forth this further letter, which appeared on the 27th, under the heading MR OSCAR WILDE AGAIN.

Does he think that literature went to the dogs when Thackeray wrote about puppydom? I think that puppies are extremely interesting from an artistic as well as from a psychological point of view. They seem to me to be certainly far more interesting than prigs; and I am of opinion that Lord Henry Wotton is an excellent corrective of the tedious ideal shadowed forth in the semi-theological novels of our age.

He then makes vague and fearful insinuations about my grammar and my erudition. Now, as regards grammar, I hold that, in prose at any rate, correctness should always be subordinate to artistic effect and musical cadence; and any pecularities of syntax that may occur in *Dorian Gray* are deliberately intended, and are introduced to show the value of the artistic theory in question. Your writer gives no instance of any such peculiarity. This I regret, because I do not think that any such instances occur.

As regards erudition, it is always difficult, even for the most modest of us, to remember that other people do not know quite as much as one does oneself. I myself frankly admit I cannot imagine how a casual reference to Suetonius and Petronius Arbiter can be construed into evidence of a desire to impress an unoffending and ill-educated public by an assumption of superior knowledge. I should fancy that the most ordinary of scholars is perfectly well acquainted with the *Lives of the Caesars* and with the *Satyricon*. The *Lives of the Caesars*, at any rate, forms part of the curriculum at Oxford for those who take the Honour School of *Literæ Humaniores*; and as for the *Satyricon*, it is popular even among passmen, though I suppose they are obliged to read it in translations.

The writer of the article then suggests that I, in common with that great noble artist Count Tolstoi, take pleasure in a subject because it is dangerous. About such a suggestion there is this to be said. Romantic art deals with the exception and with the individual. Good people, belonging as they do to the normal, and so, commonplace, type, are artistically uninteresting. Bad people are, from the point of view of art, fascinating studies. They represent colour, variety and strangeness. Good people exasperate one's reason; bad people stir one's imagination. Your critic, if I must give him so honourable a title, states that the people in my story have no counterpart in life; that they are, to use his vigorous if somewhat vulgar phrase, "mere catchpenny revelations of the non-existent." Quite so. If they existed they would not be worth writing about. The function of the artist is to invent, not to chronicle. There are no such people. If there were I would not write about them. Life by its realism is always spoiling the subject-matter of art. The supreme pleasure in literature is to realise the non-existent.

And finally, let me say this. You have reproduced, in a journalistic form, the comedy of *Much Ado about Nothing*, and have, of course, spoilt it in your reproduction. The poor public, hearing, from an authority so high as your own, that this is a wicked book that should be coerced and suppressed by a Tory Government, will, no doubt, rush to it and read it. But, alas! they will find that it is a story with a moral. And the moral is this: All excess, as well as all renunciation, brings its own punishment. The painter, Basil Hallward, worshipping physical beauty far too much, as most painters do, dies by the hand of one in whose soul he has created a monstrous and absurd vanity. Dorian Gray, having led a life of mere sensation and pleasure, tries to kill conscience, and at that moment kills himself. Lord Henry Wotton seeks to be merely the spectator of life. He finds that those who reject the battle are more deeply wounded than those who take part in it. Yes; there is a terrible moral in *Dorian Gray*—a moral which the prurient will not be able to find in it, but which will be revealed to all whose minds are healthy. Is this an artistic error? I fear it is. It is the only error in the book. OSCAR WILDE

ST. JAMES'S GAZETTE

Editorial Note[†]

(June 26, 1890)

Mr Oscar Wilde may perhaps be excused for being angry at the remarks which we allowed ourselves to make concerning his "moral tale" of the Three Puppies and the Magic Picture; but he should not misrepresent us. He says we suggested that his novel was a "wicked book which should be coerced and suppressed by a Tory Government." We did nothing of the kind. The authors of books of much less questionable character have been proceeded against by the Treasury or the Vigilance Society; but we expressly said that we hope Mr Wilde's masterpiece would be left alone.

Then, Mr Wilde (like any young lady who has published her first novel "at the request of numerous friends") falls back on the theory of the critic's "personal malice." This is unworthy of so experienced a literary gentleman. We can assure Mr Wilde that the writer of that article had, and has, no "personal malice" or personal feeling towards him. We can surely censure a work which we believe to be silly, and know to be offensive, without the imputation of malice—especially when that book is written by one who is so clearly capable of better things.

† From *St. James's Gazette* (June 26, 1890); rpt. in *Oscar Wilde: Art and Morality*, ed. Stuart Mason (1912; rpt. in New York: Haskell House, 1971), pp. 44–46.

As for the critical question, Mr Wilde is beating the air when he defends idealism and "romantic art" in literature. In the words of Mrs Harris to Mrs Gamp, "Who's a-deniging of it?"

Heaven forbid that we should refuse to an author the "supreme pleasure of realising the nonexistent"; or that we should judge the "æsthetic" from the purely "ethical" standpoint.

No; our criticism starts from lower ground. Mr Wilde says that his story is a moral tale, because the wicked persons in it come to a bad end. We will not be so rude as to quote a certain remark about morality which one Mr Charles Surface made to Mr Joseph Surface. We simply say that every critic has the right to point out that a work of art or literature is dull and incompetent in its treatment— as "The Picture of Dorian Gray" is; and that its dulness and incompetence are not redeemed because it constantly hints, not obscurely, at disgusting sins and abominable crimes—as "The Picture of Dorian Gray" does.

OSCAR WILDE

To the Editor of the *St. James's Gazette*[†]

27 June [1890]   *16 Tite Street*

Sir, As you still keep up, though in a somewhat milder form than before, your attacks on me and my book, you not merely confer on me the right but you impose upon me the duty, of reply.

You state, in your issue of today, that I misrepresented you when I said that you suggested that a book so wicked as mine should be "suppressed and coerced by a Tory Government." Now you did not propose this, but you did suggest it. When you declare that you do not know whether or not the Government will take action about my book, and remark that the authors of books much less wicked have been proceeded against in law, the suggestion is quite obvious. In your complaint of misrepresentation you seem to me, sir, to have been not quite candid. However, as far as I am concerned, the suggestion is of no importance. What is of importance is that the editor of a paper like yours should appear to countenance the monstrous theory that the Government of a country should exercise a censorship over imaginative literature. This is a theory against which I, and all men of letters of my acquaintance, protest most strongly; and any

---

† From *St. James's Gazette* (June 28, 1890); rpt. in *The Letters of Oscar Wilde*, ed. Rupert Hart-Davis (London: Hart-Davis; rpt. in New York: Harcourt, 1962), pp. 259–61. Once again the editor of the *St. James's Gazette* had added an abusive note to Wilde's previous letter. This one appeared on June 28, under the heading MR OSCAR WILDE'S DEFENCE.

critic who admits the reasonableness of such a theory shows at once
that he is quite incapable of understanding what literature is, and
what are the rights that literature possess[es]. A Government might
just as well try to teach painters how to paint, or sculptors how to
model, as attempt to interfere with the style, treatment and subject-
matter of the literary artist; and no writer, however eminent or
obscure, should ever give his sanction to a theory that would degrade
literature far more than any didactic or so-called immoral book
could possibly do.

You then express your surprise that "so experienced a literary gentleman" as myself should imagine that your critic was animated
by any feeling of personal malice towards him. The phrase "literary gentleman" is a vile phrase; but let that pass. I accept quite readily your assurance that your critic was simply criticising a work of
art in the best way that he could; but I feel that I was fully justified
in forming the opinion of him that I did. He opened his article by a
gross personal attack on myself. This, I need hardly say, was an absolutely unpardonable error of critical taste. There is no excuse for it,
except personal malice; and you, sir, should not have sanctioned it.
A critic should be taught to criticise a work of art without making
any reference to the personality of the author. This, in fact, is the
beginning of criticism. However, it was not merely his personal
attack on me that made me imagine that he was actuated by malice. What really confirmed me in my first impression was his reiter-
ated assertion that my book was tedious and dull. Now, if I were
criticising my book, which I have some thoughts of doing, I think I
would consider it my duty to point out that it is far too crowded with
sensational incident, and far too paradoxical in style, as far, at any
rate, as the dialogue goes. I feel that from a standpoint of art these
are two defects in the book. But tedious and dull the book is not.
Your critic has cleared himself of the charge of personal malice, his
denial and yours being quite sufficient in the manner; but he has
only done so by a tacit admission that he has really no critical
instinct about literature and literary work, which, in one who writes
about literature, is, I need hardly say, a much graver fault than malice of any kind.

Finally, sir, allow me to say this. Such an article as you have published really makes one despair of the possibility of any general culture in England. Were I a French author, and my book brought out
in Paris, there is not a single literary critic in France, on any paper
of higher standing, who would think for a moment of criticising it
from an ethical standpoint. If he did so, he would stultify himself,
not merely in the eyes of all men of letters, but in the eyes of the
majority of the public. You have yourself often spoken against
Puritanism. Believe me, sir, Puritanism is never so offensive and

destructive as when it deals with art matters. It is there that its influence is radically wrong. It is this Puritanism, to which your critic has given expression, that is always marring the artistic instinct of the English. So far from encouraging it, you should set yourself against it, and should try to teach your critics to recognise the essential difference between art and life. The gentleman who criticised my book is in a perfectly hopeless confusion about it, and your attempt to help him out by proposing that the subject-matter of art should be limited does not mend matters. It is proper that limitations should be placed on action. It is not proper that limitations should be placed on art. To art belong all things that are and all things that are not, and even the editor of a London paper has no right to restrain the freedom of art in the selection of subject-matter.

I now trust, sir, that these attacks on me and on my book will cease. There are forms of advertisement that are unwarranted and unwarrantable.

I am, sir, your obedient servant. OSCAR WILDE

ST. JAMES'S GAZETTE

Editorial Note[†]

(September 24, 1890)

Mr Oscar Wilde has explained. We know now how "Dorian Gray" came to be written. In 1887, about the genial season of Christmas, a Canadian lady artist[1] yearned to transfer to the glowing canvas the classic features of Mr Oscar Wilde. Mr Wilde gave her a sitting. When the sitting was over and Mr Wilde had looked at the portrait, it occurred to him that a thing of beauty, when it takes the form of a middle-aged gentleman, is unhappily not a joy for ever. "What a tragic thing it is," he exclaimed. "This portrait will never grow older, and I shall. If," he added, "if it was only the other way." Then the passion of his soul sought refuge in prose composition, and the result was "Dorian Gray." No wonder Mr Wilde didn't like it when we hinted that this great work was a study of puppydom, and its hero himself a puppy of an unpleasant kind.

---

† From St. James's Gazette (September 24, 1890); rpt. in Oscar Wilde: Art and Morality, ed. Stuart Mason (1912; rpt. in New York: Haskell House, 1971), p. 63.
1. Frances Richards, a pupil of French portrait painter Carolus-Durand.

DAILY CHRONICLE

Review[†]

(June 30, 1890)

Dulness and dirt are the chief features of *Lippincott's* this month. The element in it that is unclean, though undeniably amusing, is furnished by Mr Oscar Wilde's story of "The Picture of Dorian Gray." It is a tale spawned from the leprous literature of the French *Décadents*—a poisonous book, the atmosphere of which is heavy with the mephitic odours of moral and spiritual putrefaction—a gloating study of the mental and physical corruption of a fresh, fair and golden youth, which might be horrible and fascinating but for its effeminate frivolity, its studied insincerity, its theatrical cynicism, its tawdry mysticism, its flippant philosophisings, and the contaminating trail of garish vulgarity which is over all Mr Wilde's elaborate Wardour Street æstheticism and obtrusively cheap scholarship.

Mr Wilde says his book has "a moral." The "moral," so far as we can collect it, is that man's chief end is to develop his nature to the fullest by "always searching for new sensations," that when the soul gets sick the way to cure it is to deny the senses nothing, for "nothing," says one of Mr Wilde's characters, Lord Henry Wotton, "can cure the soul but the senses, just as nothing can cure the senses but the soul." Man is half angel and half ape, and Mr Wilde's book has no real use if it be not to inculcate the "moral" that when you feel yourself becoming too angelic you cannot do better than to rush out and make a beast of yourself. There is not a single good and holy impulse of human nature, scarcely a fine feeling or instinct that civilisation, art, and religion have developed throughout the ages as part of the barriers between Humanity and Animalism that is not held up to ridicule and contempt in "Dorian Gray," if, indeed, such strong words can be fitly applied to the actual effect of Mr Wilde's airy levity and fluent impudence. His desperate effort to vamp up a "moral" for the book at the end is, artistically speaking, coarse and crude, because the whole incident of Dorian Gray's death is, as they say on the stage, "out of the picture." Dorian's only regret is that unbridled indulgence in every form of secret and unspeakable vice, every resource of luxury and art, and sometimes still more piquant to the jaded young man of fashion, whose lives "Dorian Gray" pretends to sketch, by every abomination of vulgarity and squalor is—what? Why, that it will leave traces of premature age and loathsome

† From *Daily Chronicle* (June 30, 1890); rpt. in *Oscar Wilde: Art and Morality,* ed. Stuart Mason (1912; rpt. in New York: Haskell House, 1971), pp. 65–69.

sensualness on his pretty face, rosy with the loveliness that endeared youth of his odious type to the paralytic patricians of the Lower Empire.

Dorian Gray prays that a portrait of himself which an artist, who raves about him as young men do about the women they love not wisely but too well, has painted may grow old instead of the original. This is what happens by some supernatural agency, the introduction of which seems purely farcical, so that Dorian goes on enjoying unfading youth year after year, and might go on for ever using his senses with impunity "to cure his soul," defiling English society with the moral pestilence which is incarnate in him, but for one thing. That is his sudden impulse not merely to murder the painter—which might be artistically defended on the plea that it is only a fresh development of his scheme for realising every phase of life-experience—but to rip up the canvas in a rage, merely because, though he had permitted himself to do one good action, it had not made his portrait less hideous. But all this is inconsistent with Dorian Gray's cool, calculating, conscienceless character, evolved logically enough by Mr Wilde's "New Hedonism."

Then Mr Wilde finishes his story by saying that on hearing a heavy fall Dorian Gray's servants rushed in, found the portrait on the wall as youthful looking as ever, its senile ugliness being transferred to the foul profligate himself, who is lying on the floor stabbed to the heart. This is a sham moral, as indeed everything in the book is a sham, except the one element in the book which will taint every young mind that comes in contact with it. That element is shockingly real, and it is the plausibly insinuated defence of the creed that appeals to the senses "to cure the soul" whenever the spiritual nature of man suffers from too much purity and self-denial.

The rest of this number of *Lippincott* consists of articles of harmless padding.

OSCAR WILDE

To the Editor of the *Daily Chronicle*[†]

30 June [1890]   *16 Tite Street*

Sir, Will you allow me to correct some errors into which your critic has fallen in his review of my story, *The Picture of Dorian Gray*, published in today's issue of your paper?

† From *Daily Chronicle* (July 2, 1890); rpt. in *The Letters of Oscar Wilde*, ed. Rupert Hart-Davis (London: Hart-Davis; rpt. in New York: Harcourt, 1962), pp. 265–67.

Your critic states, to begin with, that I make desperate attempts to "vamp up" a moral in my story. Now, I must candidly confess that I do not know what "vamping" is. I see, from time to time, mysterious advertisements in the newspapers about "How to Vamp," but what vamping really means remains a mystery to me—a mystery that, like all other mysteries, I hope some day to explore.

However, I do not propose to discuss the absurd terms used by modern journalism. What I want to say is that, so far from wishing to emphasise any moral in my story, the real trouble I experienced in writing the story was that of keeping the extremely obvious moral subordinate to the artistic and dramatic effect.

When I first conceived the idea of a young man selling his soul in exchange for eternal youth—an idea that is old in the history of literature, but to which I have given new form—I felt that, from an aesthetic point of view, it would be difficult to keep the moral in its proper secondary place; and even now I do not feel quite sure that I have been able to do so. I think the moral too apparent. When the book is published in a volume I hope to correct this defect.

As for what the moral is, your critic states that it is this—that when a man feels himself becoming "too angelic" he should rush out and make a "beast of himself!" I cannot say that I consider this a moral. The real moral of the story is that all excess, as well as all renunciation, brings its punishment, and this moral is so far artistically and deliberately suppressed that it does not enunciate its law as a general principle, but realises itself purely in the lives of individuals, and so becomes simply a dramatic element in a work of art, and not the object of the work of art itself.

Your critic also falls into error when he says that Dorian Gray, having a "cool, calculating, conscienceless character," was inconsistent when he destroyed the picture of his own soul, on the ground that the picture did not become less hideous after he had done what, in his vanity, he had considered his first good action. Dorian Gray has not got a cool, calculating, conscienceless character at all. On the contrary, he is extremely impulsive, absurdly romantic, and is haunted all through his life by an exaggerated sense of conscience which mars his pleasures for him and warns him that youth and enjoyment are not everything in the world. It is finally to get rid of the conscience that had dogged his steps from year to year that he destroys the picture; and thus in his attempt to kill conscience Dorian Gray kills himself.

Your critic then talks about "obtrusively cheap scholarship." Now, whatever a scholar writes is sure to display scholarship in the distinction of style and the fine use of language; but my story contains no learned or pseudo-learned discussions, and the only literary books that it alludes to are books that any fairly educated reader may be supposed to be acquainted with, such as the *Satyricon* of Petronius Arbiter, or Gautier's *Émaux et Camées*. Such books as Alphonso's *Clericalis Disciplina* belong not to culture, but to curiosity. Anybody may be excused for not knowing them.

Finally, let me say this—the aesthetic movement produced certain colours, subtle in their loveliness and fascinating in their almost mystical tone. They were, and are, our reaction against the crude primaries of a doubtless more respectable but certainly less cultivated age. My story is an essay on decorative art. It reacts against the crude brutality of plain realism. It is poisonous if you like, but you cannot deny that it is also perfect, and perfection is what we artists aim at.

I remain, sir, your obedient servant OSCAR WILDE

SCOTS OBSERVER

From Reviews and Magazines[†]

(July 5, 1890)

Why go grubbing in muck heaps? The world is fair, and the proportion of healthy-minded men and honest women to those that are foul, fallen, or unnatural is great. Mr Oscar Wilde has again been writing stuff that were better unwritten; and while "The Picture of Dorian Gray," which he contributes to *Lippincott's*, is ingenious, interesting, full of cleverness, and plainly the work of a man of letters, it is false art—for its interest is medico-legal; it is false to human nature—for its hero is a devil; it is false to morality—for it is not made sufficiently clear that the writer does not prefer a course of unnatural iniquity to a life of cleanliness, health, and sanity. The story—which deals with matters only fitted for the Criminal Investigation Department or a hearing in camera—is discreditable alike to author and editor. Mr Wilde has brains, and art, and style; but if he can write for none but outlawed noblemen and perverted telegraph-boys, the sooner he takes to tailoring (or some other decent trade) the better for his own reputation and the public morals.

---

† From *Scots Observer* (July 5, 1890); rpt. in *Oscar Wilde: Art and Morality*, ed. Stuart Mason (1912; rpt. in New York: Haskell House, 1971), pp. 75–76.

OSCAR WILDE

To the Editor of the *Scots Observer*[†]

9 July 1890   *16 Tite Street, Chelsea*

Sir, You have published a review of my story, *The Picture of Dorian Gray*. As this review is grossly unjust to me as an artist, I ask you to allow me to exercise in your columns my right of reply.

* * *

Your reviewer, sir, while admitting that the story in question is "plainly the work of a man of letters," the work of one who has "brains, and art, and style," yet suggests, and apparently in all seriousness, that I have written it in order that it should be read by the most depraved members of the criminal and illiterate classes. Now, sir, I do not suppose that the criminal and illiterate classes ever read anything except newspapers. They are certainly not likely to be able to understand anything of mine. So let them pass, and on the broad question of why a man of letters writes at all let me say this. The pleasure that one has in creating a work of art is a purely personal pleasure, and it is for the sake of this pleasure that one creates. The artist works with his eye on the object. Nothing else interests him. What people are likely to say does not even occur to him. He is fascinated by what he has in hand. He is indifferent to others. I write because it gives me the greatest possible artistic pleasure to write. If my work pleases the few, I am gratified. If it does not, it causes me no pain. As for the mob, I have no desire to be a popular novelist. It is far too easy.

Your critic then, sir, commits the absolutely unpardonable crime of trying to confuse the artist with his subject-matter. For this, sir, there is no excuse at all. Of one who is the greatest figure in the world's literature since Greek days Keats remarked that he had as much pleasure in conceiving the evil as he had in conceiving the good.[1] Let your reviewer, sir, consider the bearings of Keats's fine

---

† From *Scots Observer* (July 12, 1890); rpt. in *The Letters of Oscar Wilde*, ed. Rupert Hart-Davis (London: Hart-Davis; rpt. in New York: Harcourt, 1962), pp. 265–67. The *Scots Observer's* anonymous notice of *Dorian Gray* on July 5 was for long thought to have been written by W. E. Henley, the paper's editor; the author was in fact his henchman Charles Whibley (1860–1930). The outlawed nobleman and perverted telegraph-boys refer to Lord Arthur Somerset and the Cleveland Street scandal of 1889. This letter of Wilde's appeared on July 12, under the heading MR WILDE'S REJOINDER. It was reprinted in *Miscellanies*.

1. "The poetical character . . . has as much delight in conceiving an Iago as an Imogen. What shocks the virtuous philosopher delights the cameleon poet." John Keats to scholar and friend Richard Woodhouse, October 27, 1818.

criticism, for it is under these conditions that every artist works. One stands remote from one's subject-matter. One creates it, and one contemplates it. The further away the subject-matter is, the more freely can the artist work. Your reviewer suggests that I do not make it sufficiently clear whether I prefer virtue to wickedness or wickedness to virtue. An artist, sir, has no ethical sympathies at all. Virtue and wickedness are to him simply what the colours on his palette are to the painter. They are no more, and they are no less. He sees that by their means a certain artistic effect can be produced, and he produces it. Iago may be morally horrible and Imogen stainlessly pure. Shakespeare, as Keats said, had as much delight in creating the one as he had in creating the other.

It was necessary, sir, for the dramatic development of this story to surround Dorian Gray with an atmosphere of moral corruption. Otherwise the story would have had no meaning and the plot no issue. To keep this atmosphere vague and indeterminate and wonderful was the aim of the artist who wrote the story. I claim, sir, that he has succeeded. Each man sees his own sin in Dorian Gray. What Dorian Gray's sins are no one knows. He who finds them has brought them.

In conclusion, sir, let me say how really deeply I regret that you should have permitted such a notice as the one I feel constrained to write on to have appeared in your paper. That the editor of the *St James's Gazette* should have employed Caliban as his art-critic was possibly natural. The editor of the *Scots Observer* should not have allowed Thersites to make mows in his review. It is unworthy of so distinguished a man of letters. I am, etc. OSCAR WILDE

JULIAN HAWTHORNE

The Romance of the Impossible†

Fiction, which flies at all game, has latterly taken to the Impossible as its quarry. The pursuit is interesting and edifying, if one goes properly equipped, and with adequate skill. But if due care is not exercised, the Impossible turns upon the hunter and grinds him to powder. It is a very dangerous and treacherous kind of wild-fowl. The conditions of its existence—if existence can be predicted of that which does not exist—are so peculiar and abstruse that only genius is really capable of taming it and leading it captive. But the capture,

† From *Lippincott's Monthly Magazine* (September 1890); rpt. in *Oscar Wilde: Art and Morality*, ed. Stuart Mason (1912; rpt. in New York: Haskell House, 1971), pp. 175–85. Julian Hawthorne (1846–1934) was the son of the American novelist Nathaniel Hawthorne.

when it is made, is so delightful and fascinating that every tyro would like to try. One is reminded of the princess of the fairy tale, who was to be won on certain preposterous terms, and if the terms were not met, the discomfited suitor lost his head. Many misguided or over-weening youths perished; at last the One succeeded. Failure in a romance of the Impossible is apt to be a disastrous failure; on the other hand, success carries great rewards.

Of course, the idea is not a new one. The writings of the alchemists are stories of the Impossible. The fashion has never been entirely extinct. Balzac wrote the "Peau de Chagrin," and probably this tale is as good a one as was ever written of that kind. The possessor of the Skin may have everything he wishes for; but each wish causes the Skin to shrink, and when it is all gone the wisher is annihilated with it. By the art of the writer this impossible thing is made to appear quite feasible; by touching the chords of coincidence and fatality, the reader's common sense is soothed to sleep. We feel that all this might be, and yet no natural law be violated; and yet we know that such a thing never was and never will be. But the vitality of the story, as of all good stories of the sort, is due to the fact that it is the symbol of a spiritual verity: the life of indulgence, the selfish life, destroys the soul. This psychic truth is so deeply felt that its sensible embodiment is rendered plausible. In the case of another famous romance—"Frankenstein"—the technical art is entirely wanting: a worse story, from the literary point of view, has seldom been written. But the soul of it, so to speak, is so potent and obvious that, although no one actually reads the book nowadays, everybody knows the gist of the idea. "Frankenstein" has entered into the language, for it utters a perpetual truth of human nature.

At the present moment, the most conspicuous success in the line we are considering is Stevenson's "Dr Jekyll and Mr Hyde." The author's literary skill, in that awful little parable, is at its best, and makes the most of every point. To my thinking, it is an artistic mistake to describe Hyde's transformation as actually taking place in plain sight of the audience; the sense of spiritual mystery is thereby lost, and a mere brute miracle takes its place. But the tale is strong enough to carry this imperfection, and the moral significance of it is so catholic—it so comes home to every soul that considers it—that it has already made an ineffaceable impression on the public mind. Every man is his own Jekyll and Hyde, only without the magic powder. On the bookshelf of the Impossible, Mr Stevenson's book may take its place beside Balzac's.

Mr Oscar Wilde, the apostle of beauty, has in the July number of *Lippincott's Magazine* a novel or romance (it partakes of the qualities of both), which everybody will want to read. It is a story strange in conception, strong in interest, and fitted with a tragic and ghastly climax. Like many stories of its class, it is open to more than one interpretation; and there are, doubtless, critics who will deny that it has any meaning at all. It is, at all events, a salutary departure from the ordinary English novel, with the hero and heroine of different social stations, the predatory black sheep, the curate, the settlements, and Society. Mr Wilde, as we all know, is a gentleman of an original and audacious turn of mind, and the commonplace is scarcely possible to him. Besides, his advocacy of novel ideas in life, art, dress, and demeanour had led us to expect surprising things from him; and in this literary age it is agreed that a man may best show the best there is in him by writing a book. Those who read Mr Wilde's story in the hope of finding in it some compact and final statement of his theories of life and manners will be satisfied in some respects, and dissatisfied in others; but not many will deny that the book is a remarkable one, and would attract attention even had it appeared without the author's name on the title page.

"The Picture of Dorian Gray" begins to show its quality in the opening pages. Mr Wilde's writing has what is called "colour"—the quality that forms the mainstay of many of Ouida's works,—and it appears in the sensuous descriptions of nature and of the decorations and environments of the artistic life. The general aspect of the characters and the tenor of their conversation remind one a little of "Vivian Gray" and a little of "Pelham," but the resemblance does not go far: Mr Wilde's objects and philosophy are different from those of either Disraeli or Bulwer. Meanwhile his talent for aphorisms and epigrams may fairly be compared with theirs: some of his clever sayings are more than clever,—they show real insight and a comprehensive grasp. Their wit is generally cynical; but they are put into the mouth of one of the characters, Lord Harry, and Mr Wilde himself refrains from definitely committing himself to them; though one cannot help suspecting that Mr Wilde regards Lord Harry as being an uncommonly able fellow. Be that as it may, Lord Harry plays the part of Old Harry in the story, and lives to witness the destruction of every other person in it. He may be taken as an imaginative type of all that is most evil and most refined in modern civilisation,—a charming, gentle, witty, euphemistic Mephistopheles, who depreciates the vulgarity of goodness, and muses aloud about "those renunciations that men have unwisely called virtue, and those natural rebellions that wise men still call sin." Upon the whole, Lord Harry is the most ably portrayed character in the book, though not the most original in conception. Dorian Gray himself is as nearly a new idea in fiction as one has nowadays a right to expect. If he had been adequately realised and worked out, Mr Wilde's first novel would have been remembered after more meritorious ones were forgotten. But, even as "nemo repente fuit turpissimus," so no one, or hardly any one, creates a thoroughly original figure at a first essay. Dorian never quite solidifies. In fact, his portrait is rather the more real thing of the two. But this needs explanation.

The story consists of a strong and marvelous central idea, illustrated by three characters, all men. There are a few women in the background, but they are only mentioned: they never appear to speak for themselves. There is, too, a valet who brings in his master's breakfasts, and a chemist who, by some scientific miracle, disposes of a human body: but, substantially, the book is taken up with the artist who paints the portrait, with his friend Lord Harry aforesaid, and with Dorian Gray, who might, so far as the story goes, stand alone. He and his portrait are one, and their union points to the moral of the tale.

The situation is as follows: Dorian Gray is a youth of extraordinary physical beauty and grace, and pure and innocent of soul. An artist sees him and falls æsthetically in love with him, and finds in him a new inspiration in his art, both direct and general. In the lines of his form and features, and in his colouring and movement, are revealed fresh and profound laws: he paints him in all guises and combinations, and it is seen and admitted on all sides that he has never before painted so well. At length he concentrates all his knowledge and power in a final portrait, which has the vividness and grace of life itself, and, considering how much both of the sitter and of the painter is embodied in it, might almost be said to live. The portrait is declared by Lord Harry to be the greatest work of modern art; and the painter himself thinks so well of it that he resolves never to exhibit it, even as he would shrink from exposing to public gaze the privacies of his own nature.

On the day of the last sitting a singular incident occurs. Lord Harry, meeting on that occasion for the first time with Dorian, is no less impressed than was Hallward, the artist, with the youth's radiant beauty and freshness. But whereas Hallward would keep Dorian unspotted from the world, and would have him resist evil temptations and all the allurements of corruption, Lord Harry, on the contrary, with a truly Satanic ingenuity, discourses to the young man on the matchless delights and privileges of youth. Youth is the golden period of life: youth comes never again: in youth only are the senses endowed with divine potency; only then are joys exquisite and pleasures unalloyed. Let it therefore be indulged without stint. Let no harsh and cowardly restraints be placed upon its glorious impulses. Men are virtuous through fear and selfishness. They are too dull or too timid to take advantage of the godlike gifts that are showered upon them in the morning of existence; and before they can realise the folly of their self-denial, the morning has passed, and weary day is upon them, and the shadows of night are near. But let Dorian, who is matchless in the vigour and resources of his beauty, rise above the base shrinking from life that calls itself goodness. Let him accept and welcome every natural impulse of his nature. The tragedy of old age is not that one is old, but that one is young: let him so live that when old age comes he shall at least have the satisfaction of knowing that no opportunity of pleasure and indulgence has escaped untasted.

This seductive sermon profoundly affects the innocent Dorian, and he looks at life and himself with new eyes. He realises the value as well as the transitoriness of that youth and beauty which hitherto he had accepted as a matter of course and as a permanent possession. Gazing on his portrait, he laments that it possesses the immortality of liveliness and comeliness that is denied to him; and, in a sort of imaginative despair, he utters a wild prayer that to the portrait, and not to himself, may come the feebleness and hideousness of old age; that whatever sins he may commit, to whatever indulgences he may surrender himself, not upon him but upon the portrait may the penalties and disfigurements fall. Such is Dorian's prayer; and, though at first he suspects it not, his prayer is granted. From that hour the evil of his life is registered upon the face and form of his pictured presentment, while he himself goes unscathed. Day by day, each fresh sin that he commits stamps its mark of degradation upon the painted image. Cruelty, sensuality, treachery, all nameless crimes, corrupt and render hideous the effigy on the canvas; he sees in it the gradual pollution and ruin of his soul, while his own fleshy features preserve unstained all the freshness and virginity of his sinless youth. The contrast at first alarms and horrifies him; but at length he becomes accustomed to it, and finds a sinister delight in watching the progress of the awful change. He locks up the portrait in a secret chamber, and constantly retires thither to ponder over the ghastly miracle. No one but he knows or suspects the incredible truth; and he guards like a murder-secret this visible revelation of the difference between what he is and what he seems. This is a powerful situation; and the reader may be left to discover for himself how Mr Wilde works it out.

WALTER PATER

A Novel by Mr. Oscar Wilde[†]

There is always something of an excellent talker about the writing of Mr Oscar Wilde; and in his hands, as happens so rarely with those who practise it, the form of dialogue is justified by its being really

† From *The Book-man* (November 1891); rpt. in *Oscar Wilde: Art and Morality*, ed. Stuart Mason (1912; rpt. in New York: Haskell House, 1971), pp. 188–95.

alive. His genial, laughter-loving sense of life and its enjoyable intercourse, goes far to obviate any crudity there may be in the paradox,
with which, as with the bright and shining truth which often underlies it, Mr Wilde, startling his "countrymen," carries on, more perhaps
than any other writer, the brilliant critical work of Matthew Arnold.
"The Decay of Lying,"[1] for instance, is all but unique in its half-
humorous, yet wholly convinced, presentment of certain valuable
truths of criticism. Conversational ease, the fluidity of life, felicitous
expression, are qualities which have a natural alliance to the successful writing of fiction; and side by side with Mr Wilde's "Intentions" (so he entitles his critical efforts) comes a novel, certainly
original, and affording the reader a fair opportunity of comparing
his practice as a creative artist with many a precept he has enounced
as critic concerning it.

A wholesome dislike of the commonplace, rightly or wrongly identified by him with the *bourgeois,* with our middle-class—its habits
and tastes—leads him to protest emphatically against so-called
"realism" in art; life, as he argues, with much plausibility, as a
matter of fact, when it is really awake, following art—the fashion
an effective artist sets; while art, on the other hand, influential and
effective art, has never taken its cue from actual life. In "Dorian
Gray" he is true certainly, on the whole, to the æsthetic philosophy
of his "Intentions"; yet not infallibly, even on this point: there is a
certain amount of the intrusion of real life and its sordid aspects—
the low theatre, the pleasures and griefs, the faces of some very
unrefined people, managed, of course, cleverly enough. The inter-
lude of Jim Vane, his half-sullen but wholly faithful care for his
sister's honour, is as good as perhaps anything of the kind, marked
by a homely but real pathos, sufficiently proving a versatility in the
writer's talent, which should make his books popular. Clever always,
this book, however, seems intended to set forth anything but a
homely philosophy of life for the middle-class—a kind of dainty
Epicurean theory, rather—yet fails, to some degree, in this; and one
can see why. A true Epicureanism aims at a complete though harmonious development of man's entire organism. To lose the moral
sense therefore, for instance, the sense of sin and righteousness,
as Mr Wilde's hero—his heroes are bent on doing as speedily, as
completely as they can, is to lose, or lower, organisation, to become
less complex, to pass from a higher to a lower degree of development. As a story, however, a partly supernatural story, it is first-rate
in artistic management; those Epicurean niceties only adding to the
decorative colour of its central figure, like so many exotic flowers,

1. Appeared first in *The Nineteenth Century,* January 1889, and was afterward included
in "Intentions" [*Mason's note*].

like the charming scenery and the perpetual, epigrammatic, surprising, yet so natural, conversations, like an atmosphere all about
it. All that pleasant accessory detail, taken straight from the culture,
the intellectual and social interests, the conventionalities, of the
moment, have, in fact, after all, the effect of the better sort of realism, throwing into relief the adroitly-devised supernatural element
after the manner of Poe, but with a grace he never reached, which
supersedes that earlier didactic purpose, and makes the quite suf-
ficing interest of an excellent story.

We like the hero, and, spite of his, somewhat unsociable, devotion to his art, Hallward, better than Lord Henry Wotton. He has
too much of a not very really refined world in and about him, and
his somewhat cynic opinions, which seem sometimes to be those of
the writer, who may, however, have intended Lord Henry as a satiric
sketch. Mr Wilde can hardly have intended him, with his cynic
amity of mind and temper, any more than the miserable end of
Dorian himself, to figure the motive and tendency of a true Cyre-
naic or Epicurean doctrine of life. In contrast with Hallward, the
artist, whose sensibilities idealise the world around him, the personality of Dorian Gray, above all, into something magnificent and
strange, we might say that Lord Henry, and even more the, from the
first, suicidal hero, loses too much in life to be a true Epicurean—
loses so much in the way of impressions, of pleasant memories, and
subsequent hopes, which Hallward, by a really Epicurean economy,
manages to secure. It should be said, however, in fairness, that the
writer is impersonal: seems not to have identified himself entirely
with any one of his characters: and Wotton's cynicism, or whatever
it be, at least makes a very clever story possible. He becomes the
spoiler of the fair young man, whose bodily form remains un-aged;
while his picture, the *chef d'œuvre* of the artist Hallward, changes
miraculously with the gradual corruption of his soul. How true, what
a light on the artistic nature, is the following on actual personalities and their revealing influence in art. We quote it as an example
of Mr Wilde's more serious style.

> I sometimes think that there are only two eras of any importance
> in the world's history. The first is the appearance of a new
> medium for art, and the second is the appearance of a new per-
> sonality for art also. What the invention of oil-painting was to the
> Venetians, the face of Antinoüs was to late Greek sculpture, and
> the face of Dorian Gray will some day be to me. It is not merely
> that I paint from him, draw from him, sketch from him. Of
> course I have done all that. But he is much more to me than a
> model or a sitter. I won't tell you that I am dissatisfied with what
> I have done of him, or that his beauty is such that Art cannot
> express it. There is nothing that Art cannot express, and I know

that the work I have done, since I met Dorian Gray, is good work, is the best work of my life. But in some curious way . . . his personality has suggested to me an entirely new manner in art, an entirely new mode of style. I see things differently, I think of them differently. I can now recreate life in a way that was hidden from me before.

Dorian himself, though certainly a quite unsuccessful experiment in Epicureanism, in life as a fine art, is (till his inward spoiling takes visible effect suddenly, and in a moment, at the end of his story) a beautiful creation. But his story is also a vivid, though carefully considered, exposure of the corruption of a soul, with a very plain moral pushed home, to the effect that vice and crime make people coarse and ugly. General readers nevertheless, will probably care less for this moral, less for the fine, varied, largely appreciative culture of the writer, in evidence from page to page, than for the story itself, with its adroitly managed supernatural incidents, its almost equally wonderful applications of natural science; impossible, surely, in fact, but plausible enough in fiction. Its interest turns on that very old theme, old because based on some inherent experience or fancy of the human brain, of a double life: of Doppelgänger—not of two *persons*, in this case, but of the man and his portrait; the latter of which, as we hinted above, changes, decays, is spoiled, while the former, through a long course of corruption, remains, to the outward eye, unchanged, still in all the beauty of a seemingly immaculate youth—"the devil's bargain." But it would be a pity to spoil the reader's enjoyment by further detail. We need only emphasise once more, the skill, the real subtlety of art, the ease and fluidity withal of one telling a story by word of mouth, with which the consciousness of the supernatural is introduced into, and maintained amid, the elaborately conventional, sophisticated, disabused world Mr Wilde depicts so cleverly, so mercilessly. The special fascination of the piece is, of course, just there—at that point of contrast. Mr Wilde's work may fairly claim to go with that of Edgar Poe, and with some good French work of the same kind, done, probably, in more or less conscious imitation of it.

Art Versus Morality:
Dorian Gray on Trial

The first trial was an action for libel brought by Wilde at the instigation of Lord Alfred Douglas against the latter's father, John Sholto Douglas, eighth Marquess of Queensberry. The purpose of the suit was to punish and silence "The Scarlet Marquess," who had threatened both Wilde and his own son Alfred with scandal. Indeed, he had threatened in a letter to his son to shoot Wilde on sight if rumors of Wilde's homosexual activities should be proved publicly. To that end, perhaps, Queensberry left the now famous calling card with the words "For Oscar Wilde posing as a somdomite [*sic*]." Those were the fighting words that provoked Wilde to sue for criminal libel. During the trial, Queensberry's defense attorney, Edward Carson, confronted Wilde with *Dorian Gray* as evidence of his corrupting influence on Alfred Douglas.

From Edward Carson's Cross-Examination of Wilde (First Trial)[†]

*   *   *

After the criticisms that were passed on *Dorian Gray,* was it modified a good deal?—No. Additions were made. In one case it was pointed out to me—not in a newspaper or anything of that sort, but by the only critic of the century whose opinion I set high, Mr. Walter Pater—that a certain passage was liable to misconstruction, and I made an addition.

This is in your introduction to *Dorian Gray:* "There is no such thing as a moral or an immoral book. Books are well written, or badly written." That expresses your view?—My view on art, yes.

Then, I take it, that no matter how immoral a book may be, if it is well written, it is, in your opinion, a good book?—Yes, if it were well written so as to produce a sense of beauty, which is the highest

†   From *The Three Trials of Oscar Wilde*, ed. H. Montgomery Hyde (New York: University Books, 1956), pp. 124–33. Originally published as *Notable British Trials Series*, Vol. 70: *Trials of Oscar Wilde* (London: William Hodge & Company, 1948). Reprinted by permission of Curtis Brown Group, Ltd, London, on behalf of The Estate of H. Montgomery Hyde. Copyright © H. Montgomery Hyde, 1948. Notes are Hyde's.

sense of which a human being can be capable. If it were badly written, it would produce a sense of disgust.

Then a well-written book putting forward perverted moral views may be a good book?—No work of art ever puts forward views. Views belong to people who are not artists.

A perverted novel might be a good book?—I don't know what you mean by a "perverted" novel.

Then I will suggest *Dorian Gray* as open to the interpretation of being such a novel?—That could only be to brutes and illiterates. The views of Philistines on art are incalculably stupid.

An illiterate person reading *Dorian Gray* might consider it such a novel?—The views of illiterates on art are unaccountable. I am concerned only with my view of art. I don't care twopence what other people think of it.

The majority of persons would come under your definition of Philistines and illiterates?—I have found wonderful exceptions.

Do you think that the majority of people live up to the position you are giving us?—I am afraid they are not cultivated enough.

Not cultivated enough to draw the distinction between a good book and a bad book?—Certainly not.

The affection and love of the artist of *Dorian Gray* might lead an ordinary individual to believe that it might have a certain tendency?—I have no knowledge of the views of ordinary individuals.

You did not prevent the ordinary individual from buying your book?—I have never discouraged him.

[MR. CARSON then read the following extracts from *The Picture of Dorian Gray,* in which the painter Basil Hallward tells Lord Henry Wooton of his first meetings with Dorian Gray. The quotations were from the original version of the work as it appeared in *Lippincott's Monthly Magazine* for July, 1890.]

> . . . The story is simply this. Two months ago I went to a crush at Lady Brandon's. You know we poor painters have to show ourselves in society from time to time, just to remind the public that we are not savages. With an evening coat and a white tie, as you told me once, anybody, even a stockbroker, can gain a reputation for being civilized. Well, after I had been in the room about ten minutes, talking to huge over-dressed dowagers and tedious Academicians, I suddenly became conscious that some one was looking at me. I turned half-way round, and saw Dorian Gray for the first time. When our eyes met, I felt that I was growing pale. A curious instinct of terror came over me. I knew that I had come face to face with some one whose mere personality was so fascinating that, if I allowed it to do so, it would absorb my whole nature, my whole soul, my very art itself. I did not want any external influence in my life. You know yourself,

Harry, how independent I am by nature. My father destined me for the army. I insisted on going to Oxford. Then he made me enter my name at the Middle Temple. Before I had eaten half a dozen dinners I gave up the Bar, and announced my intention of becoming a painter. I have always been my own master; had at least always been so, till I met Dorian Gray. Then—but I don't know how to explain it to you. Something seemed to tell me that I was on the verge of a terrible crisis in my life. I had a strange feeling that Fate had in store for me exquisite joys and exquisite sorrows. I knew that if I spoke to Dorian I would become absolutely devoted to him, and that I ought not to speak to him. I grew afraid, and turned to quit the room. It was not conscience that made me do so: it was cowardice. I take no credit to myself for trying to escape.

* * *

Cross-examination continued—Now I ask you, Mr. Wilde, do you consider that that description of the feeling of one man towards a youth just grown up was a proper or an improper feeling?—I think it is the most perfect description of what an artist would feel on meeting a beautiful personality that was in some way necessary to his art and life.

You think that is a feeling a young man should have towards another?—Yes, as an artist.

[Counsel began to read another extract from the book. Witness asked for a copy and was given one of the original version]

MR. CARSON (in calling witness's attention to the place—*Lippincott's Monthly Magazine*, Vol. XLVI, at p. 56)—I believe it was left out in the purged edition.

WITNESS—I do not call it purged.

MR. CARSON—Yes, I know that; but we will see.

"Let us sit down, Dorian," said Hallward, looking pale and pained. "Let us sit down. I will sit in the shadow, and you shall sit in the sunlight. Our lives are like that. Just answer me one question. Have you noticed in the picture something that you did not like?—something that probably at first did not strike you, but that revealed itself to you suddenly?"

"Basil!" cried the lad, clutching the arms of his chair with trembling hands, and gazing at him with wild, startled eyes.

"I see you did. Don't speak. Wait till you hear what I have to say. It is quite true that I have worshipped you with far more romance of feeling than a man usually gives to a friend. Somehow, I have never loved a woman. I suppose I never had time. Perhaps, as Harry says, a really 'grande passion' is the privilege of those who have nothing to do, and that is the use of the idle classes in a country. Well, from the moment I met you, your personality had the most extraordinary influence over me. I quite admit that I adored you madly, extravagantly, absurdly. I was jealous of every one to whom you spoke. I wanted to have you all to myself. I was only happy when I was with you. When I was away from you, you were still present in my art. It was all wrong and foolish. It is all wrong and foolish still. Of course I never let you know anything about this. It would have been impossible. You would not have understood it; I did not understand it myself. One day I determined to paint a wonderful portrait of you. It was to have been my masterpiece. It is my masterpiece. But, as I worked at it, every flake and film of colour seemed to me to reveal my secret. I grew afraid that the world would know of my idolatry. I felt, Dorian, that I had told too much. Then, it was that I resolved never to allow the picture to be exhibited. You were a little annoyed; but then you did not realize all that it meant to me. Harry, to whom I talked about it, laughed at me. But I did not mind that. When the picture was finished and I sat alone with it, I felt that I was right. Well, after a few days the portrait left my studio, and as soon as I had got rid of the intolerable fascination of its presence it seemed to me that I had been foolish in imagining that I had said anything in it, more than that you were extremely good-looking and that I could paint. Even now I cannot help feeling that it is a mistake to think that the passion one feels in creation is ever really shown in the work one creates. Art is more abstract than we fancy. Form and colour tell us of form and colour—that is all. It often seems to me that art conceals the artist far more completely than it ever reveals him. And so when I got this offer from Paris I determined to make your portrait the principal thing in my exhibition. It never occurred to me that you would refuse. I see now that you were right. The picture must not be shown. You must not be angry with me, Dorian, for what I have told you. As I said to Harry, once, you are made to be worshipped."

Cross-examination continued—Do you mean to say that that passage describes the natural feeling of one man towards another?—It would be the influence produced by a beautiful personality.

A beautiful person?—I said a "beautiful personality." You can describe it as you like. Dorian Gray's was a most remarkable personality.

May I take it that you, as an artist, have never known the feeling described here?—I have never allowed any personality to dominate my art.

Then you have never known the feeling you described?—No. It is a work of fiction.

So far as you are concerned you have no experience as to its being a natural feeling?—I think it is perfectly natural for any artist to admire intensely and love a young man. It is an incident in the life of almost every artist.

But let us go over it phrase by phrase. "I quite admit that I adored you madly." What do you say to that? Have you ever adored a young man madly?—No, not madly; I prefer love—that is a higher form.

Never mind about that. Let us keep down to the level we are at now?—I have never given adoration to anybody except myself. (Loud laughter.)

I suppose you think that a very smart thing?—Not at all.

Then you have never had that feeling?—No. The whole idea was borrowed from Shakespeare, I regret to say—yes, from Shakespeare's sonnets.

I believe you have written an article to show that Shakespeare's sonnets were suggestive of unnatural vice?—On the contrary I have written an article to show that they are not.[1] I objected to such a perversion being put upon Shakespeare.

"I have adored you extravagantly"?—Do you mean financially?

Oh, yes, financially! Do you think we are talking about finance?—I don't know what you are talking about.

Don't you? Well, I hope I shall make myself very plain before I have done. "I was jealous of every one to whom you spoke." Have you ever been jealous of a young man?—Never in my life.

"I wanted to have you all to myself." Did you ever have that feeling?—No; I should consider it an intense nuisance, an intense bore.

"I grew afraid that the world would know of my idolatry." Why should he grow afraid that the world should know of it?—Because there are people in the world who cannot understand the intense devotion, affection, and admiration that an artist can feel for a wonderful and beautiful personality. These are the conditions under which we live. I regret them.

These unfortunate people, that have not the high understanding that you have, might put it down to something wrong?—Undoubtedly; to any point they chose. I am not concerned with the ignorance of others.

---

1. "The Portrait of Mr. W. H.," which appeared in *Blackwood's Edinburgh Magazine*, Vol. cxlvi, No. 885 (July, 1889). A revised and enlarged version of this essay was later announced by Wilde's publishers, but the manuscript which had been returned to Wilde by the publishers on the day of his arrest, mysteriously disappeared, no doubt stolen during the sale of Wilde's effects in his bankruptcy. It turned up many years afterward in New York, where the complete text was published in a limited edition in 1921 by Mr. Mitchell Kennerley, the collector who had acquired the manuscript.

In another passage Dorian Gray receives a book. Was the book to which you refer a moral book?—Not well written, but it gave me an idea.

Was not the book you have in mind of a certain tendency?—I decline to be cross-examined upon the work of another artist. It is an impertinence and a vulgarity.

[Witness admitted that the book in question was a French work, *À Rebours,* by J.-K. Huysmans. MR. CARSON persisted in his desire to elicit the witness's view as to the morality of this book, with the result that SIR EDWARD CLARKE appealed to MR. JUSTICE COLLINS, who ruled against any further reference to it.[2]

MR. CARSON then read a further extract from *The Picture of Dorian Gray,* quoting the following conversation between the painter and Dorian Gray.]

> ". . . I think it right that you should know that the most dreadful things are being said about you in London—things that I could hardly repeat to you."
>
> "I don't wish to know anything about them. I love scandals about other people, but scandals about myself don't interest me. They have not got the charm of novelty."
>
> "They must interest you, Dorian. Every gentleman is interested in his good name. You don't want people to talk of you as something vile and degraded. Of course you have your position, and your wealth, and all that kind of thing. But position and wealth are not everything. Mind you, I don't believe these rumours at all. At least, I can't believe them when I see you. Sin is a thing that writes itself across a man's face. It cannot be concealed. People talk of secret vices. There are no such things as secret vices. If a wretched man has a vice, it shows itself in the lines of his mouth, the droop of his eyelids, the moulding of his hands even. Somebody—I won't mention his name, but you know him—came to me last year to have his portrait done. I had never seen him before, and had never heard anything about him at the time, though I have heard a good deal since. He offered an extravagant price. I refused him. There was something in the shape of his fingers that I hated. I know now that I was quite right in what I fancied about him. His life is dreadful. But you, Dorian, with your pure, bright, innocent face, and your marvellous untroubled youth—I can't believe anything

2. *À Rebours* was first published in 1884. "It was a novel without a plot," wrote Wilde in the passage alluded to by Carson in *The Picture of Dorian Gray,* "and with only one character, being, indeed, simply a psychological study of a certain young Parisian, who spent his life trying to realize in the nineteenth century all the passions and modes of thought that belonged to every century except his own, and to sum up, as it were, in himself the various modes through which the world-spirit had ever passed, loving for their mere artificiality those renunciations that men have unwisely called virtue, as much as those natural rebellions that wise men still call sin."

against you. And yet I see you very seldom, and you never come down to the studio now, and when I am away from you, and I hear all these hideous things that people are whispering about you, I don't know what to say. Why is it, Dorian, that a man like the Duke of Berwick leaves the room of a club when you enter it? Why is it that so many gentlemen in London will neither go to your house nor invite you to theirs? You used to be a friend of Lord Cawdor. I met him at dinner last week. Your name happened to come up in conversation, in connexion with the miniatures you have lent to the exhibition at the Dudley. Cawdor curled his lip, and said that you might have the most artistic tastes, but that you were a man whom no pure-minded girl should be allowed to know, and whom no chaste woman should sit in the same room with. I reminded him that I was a friend of yours, and asked him what he meant. He told me. He told me right out before everybody. It was horrible! Why is your friendship so fateful to young men? There was that wretched boy in the Guards who committed suicide. You were his great friend. There was Sir Henry Ashton, who had to leave England with a tarnished name. You and he were inseparable. What about Adrian Singleton, and his dreadful end? What about Lord Kent's only son, and his career? I met his father yesterday in St. James Street. He seemed broken with shame and sorrow. What about the young Duke of Perth? What sort of life has he got now? What gentleman would associate with him? Dorian, Dorian, your reputation is infamous. . . ."

Cross-examination continued—Does not this passage suggest a charge of unnatural vice?—It describes Dorian Gray as a man of very corrupt influence, though there is no statement as to the nature of the influence. But as a matter of fact I do not think that one person influences another, nor do I think there is any bad influence in the world.

A man never corrupts a youth?—I think not.

Nothing could corrupt him?—If you are talking of separate ages.

No, sir, I am talking common sense?—I do not think one person influences another.

You don't think that flattering a young man, making love to him, in fact, would be likely to corrupt him?—No.

Where was Lord Alfred Douglas staying when you wrote that letter to him?—At the Savoy; and I was at Babbacombe, near Torquay.

It was a letter in answer to something he had sent you?—Yes, a poem.

Why should a man of your age address a boy nearly twenty years younger as "My own boy"?—I was fond of him. I have always been fond of him.

Do you adore him?—No, but I have always liked him. I think it is
a beautiful letter. It is a poem. I was not writing an ordinary letter.
You might as well cross-examine me as to whether *King Lear* or a
sonnet of Shakespeare was proper.

Apart from art, Mr. Wilde?—I cannot answer apart from art.

Suppose a man who was not an artist had written this letter, would
you say it was a proper letter?—A man who was not an artist could
not have written that letter.

Why?—Because nobody but an artist could write it. He certainly
could not write the language unless he were a man of letters.

I can suggest, for the sake of your reputation, that there is nothing very wonderful in this "red rose-leaf lips of yours"?—A great deal
depends on the way it is read.

"Your slim gilt soul walks between passion and poetry." Is that a
beautiful phrase?—Not as you read it, Mr. Carson. You read it very
badly.

I do not profess to be an artist; and when I hear you give evidence, I am glad I am not—

* * *

From Edward Carson's Opening Speech for the Defense (First Trial)[†]

* * *

Let us contrast the position which Mr. Wilde took up in cross-
examination as to his books, which are for the select and not for
the ordinary individual, with the position he assumed as to the
young men to whom he was introduced and those he picked up for
himself. His books were written by an artist for artists; his words
were not for Philistines or illiterates. Contrast that with the way in
which Mr. Wilde chose his companions! He took up with Charles
Parker, a gentleman's servant, whose brother was a gentleman's servant; with young Alphonse Conway, who sold papers on the pier at
Worthing; and with Scarfe, also a gentlemen's servant. Then his
excuse was no longer that he was dwelling in regions of art but that
he had such a noble, such a democratic soul (Laughter.), that he
drew no social distinctions, and that it was quite as much pleasure

† From *The Three Trials of Oscar Wilde*, ed. H. Montgomery Hyde (New York: University
Books, 1956), pp. 166–67. Originally published as *Notable British Trials Series*, Vol. 70:
Trials of Oscar Wilde (London: William Hodge & Company, 1948). Reprinted by permission of Curtis Brown Group, Ltd, London, on behalf of The Estate of H. Montgomery Hyde. Copyright © H. Montgomery Hyde, 1948.

to have the sweeping boy from the streets to lunch or dine with him as the greatest *littérateur* or artist.

In my judgment, if the case had rested on Mr. Wilde's literature alone, Lord Queensberry would have been absolutely justified in the course he has taken. Lord Queensberry has undertaken to prove that Mr. Wilde has been "posing" as guilty of certain vices. Mr. Wilde never complained of the immorality of the story "The Priest and the Acolyte" which appeared in *The Chameleon*. He knows no distinction, in fact, between a moral and an immoral book. Nor does he care whether the article is in its very terms blasphemous. All that Mr. Wilde says is that he did not approve of the story from a literary point of view. What is that story? It is a story of the love of a priest for the acolyte who attended him at Mass. Exactly the same idea that runs through the two letters to Lord Alfred Douglas runs through that story, and also through *The Picture of Dorian Gray*. When the boy was discovered in the priest's bed, the priest made exactly the same defence as Mr. Wilde has made—that the world does not understand the beauty of this love. The same idea runs through these two letters which Mr. Wilde has called beautiful, but which I call an abominable piece of disgusting immorality.

Moreover, there is in this same *Chameleon* a poem which shows some justification for the frightful anticipations which Lord Queensberry entertained for his son. The poem was written by Lord Alfred Douglas and was seen by Mr. Wilde before its publication. Is it not a terrible thing that a young man on the threshold of life, who has for several years been dominated by Oscar Wilde and has been "adored and loved" by Oscar Wilde, as the two letters prove, should thus show the tendency of his mind upon this frightful subject? What would be the horror of any man whose son wrote such a poem?

Passing now to *The Picture of Dorian Gray,* it is the tale of a beautiful young man who, by the conversation of one who has great literary power and ability to speak in epigrams—just as Mr. Wilde has—and who, by reading of exactly the same kind as that in "Phrases and Philosophies for the Use of the Young," has his eyes opened to what they are pleased to call the "delights of the world." If *Dorian Gray* is a book which it can be conclusively proved advocates the vice imputed to Mr. Wilde, what answer, then, is there to Lord Queensberry's plea of justification?

✳   ✳   ✳

CRITICISM

JOSEPH CARROLL

Aestheticism, Homoeroticism, and Christian Guilt in *The Picture of Dorian Gray*[†]

Since the advent of the poststructuralist revolution some thirty years ago, interpretive literary criticism has suppressed two concepts that had informed virtually all previous literary thinking: (1) the idea of the author as an individual person and an originating source for literary meaning, and (2) the idea of "human nature" as the represented subject and common frame of reference for literary depictions. Under the tutelage of Barthes, Derrida, and Foucault, literary critics learned to speak of authors, characters, settings, and plots not as individuals situated in a natural world but as discursive formations constituted by the circulation of linguistic, cultural, and ideological energies. In the three decades during which poststructuralism has dominated academic literary study, a different kind of revolution—evolutionary, Darwinian, and naturalistic—has been transforming the social sciences. Sociobiology, evolutionary psychology, Darwinian anthropology, behavioral ecology, cognitive archaeology, and behavioral genetics do not all agree with one another in every respect, but they are all nonetheless aspects or phases of a common research program. The central working hypothesis in this program is that the human species, like all other species, has evolved in an adaptive relation to its environment and that as a consequence it has a distinct, genetically transmitted, species-typical set of characteristics—anatomical, physiological, hormonal, neurological, and behavioral. That set of characteristics is what in common language is meant by "human nature." Literature has always given us subjectively evocative depictions of human nature, and Darwinian social science is now giving us a more comprehensive and scientifically precise account of it. The sense of individual agency is one crucial aspect of human nature, and that aspect is now being explored in complementary ways by personality psychology and by cognitive neuroscience.[1]

Over the past decade or so, a scattered handful of literary scholars has broken away from the dominant poststructuralist paradigm

[†] From *Philosophy and Literature* 29.2 (October 2005): 286–304. Notes have been renumbered and edited to cite this Third Norton Critical Edition. © 2005 Johns Hopkins University Press. Reprinted with permission of Johns Hopkins UP.

1. See David Buss, "Social Adaptation and Five Major Factors of Personality," in *The Five-Factor Model of Personality: Theoretical Perspectives*, ed. Jerry S. Wiggins (New York: Guilford Press, 1996), pp. 180–207; Ralph Adolphs, "Cognitive Neuroscience of Human Social Behavior," *Nature Reviews Neuroscience* 4 (2003): 165–78.

and has sought to make use of the new scientific information on human nature.[2] The simplest and most obvious way to use this information is to examine the behavior depicted in literary texts and to correlate that behavior with "human universals," that is, with forms of behavior that appear in every known culture and that thus appear to be embedded in the nature of the species. Seeking depictions of universals has produced valuable results for literary study, but this first move in Darwinian criticism does not exhaust the range of possibility in the analysis of literary meaning. Human nature is complex and sometimes divided against itself; individuals vary, and some variations depart from species-typical patterns, even in the most adaptively crucial aspects of survival and reproduction. Moreover, literary meaning involves more than the represented subject matter. Authors imbue texts with meanings and affects peculiar to themselves; authors engage in communicative transactions with audiences; and texts have formal and aesthetic properties that are not reducible to represented subject matter. All of these aspects of the total literary situation are part of literary meaning, and all of them can and should fall within the range of analysis available to Darwinian literary study.[3]

Oscar Wilde's *The Picture of Dorian Gray* offers two special challenges to Darwinian criticism. First, the novel is saturated with homoerotic sexual feeling, and it thus defies any simple reading in terms of behavior oriented to reproductive success. Second, the central conflicts in the novel involve two competing visions of human nature, and in their conceptual structure neither of those visions corresponds very closely to the quasi-Darwinian conceptual structure implicit in most realist and naturalist fiction. One vision derives from the aestheticist doctrines of Walter Pater, and the other from a traditional Christian conception of the soul. Pater's ideas about human motives and the human moral character are at variance both with Christianity and with Darwinism. Christianity and Darwinism share certain concepts of the human moral and social character, but they couch those concepts in different idioms, and they would invoke wholly different causal explanations for how human nature came to be the way it is. Wilde does not develop his themes in Darwinian terms, but the novel can still be read and understood from a Darwinian perspective. If Darwinian psychology gives a true account of human nature, including its homoerotic variations and the affective

2. See Harold Fromm, "The New Darwinism in the Humanities: From Plato to Pinker," *Hudson Review* 56 (2003): 89–99; "The New Darwinism in the Humanities: Back to Nature, Again," *Hudson Review* 56 (2003): 315–27.
3. See Joseph Carroll, "Human Nature and Literary Meaning: A Theoretical Model Illustrated with a Critique of *Pride and Prejudice*," in *Literary Darwinism: Evolution, Human Nature, and Literature* (New York: Routledge, 2004), pp. 187–216.

and ethical dimensions of religious beliefs, it can explain the meaning structure of *Dorian Gray*.

In weighing the effects of Wilde's homosexuality on the meaning of the novel, I shall use the incisive Darwinian analysis of homosexual behavior provided by Donald Symons in *The Evolution of Human Sexuality*. I shall not concern myself with the still controverted—and for my purposes irrelevant—question as to whether homosexuality is or is not an adaptive form of behavior. I shall instead compare the psychological character of homosexual and heterosexual relationships. In analysing the conflict between homoeroticism and the Christian ethos, as Wilde conceives it, I shall invoke a Darwinian conception of species-typical evolved sex differences, and I shall correlate homoeroticism with male sexual psychology and the Christian ethos with the maternal female character. I shall argue that Wilde associates aestheticism with homoeroticism and that he sets both in opposition to the idea of lasting affectional bonds and self-sacrificing love. As an aesthete devoted solely to sensual pleasures, Wilde's protagonist repudiates the idea of affectional bonds, and it is that repudiation which produces the mood of guilt and horror in which the novel culminates. Wilde partially identifies with his own protagonist, and he is himself riven by the conflict between homoerotic aestheticism and Christian pathos. The unresolved conflicts in the plot of the novel reflect deep divisions in his own personal identity.

In recent years a number of studies have discussed the specifically homosexual character of *Dorian Gray*, and by making this issue into an explicit theme these studies have taken a crucial new step toward a true understanding of the deep symbolic structure in Wilde's novel. But most of these studies have been written from a liberationist standpoint; most have been written from within a Foucauldian framework of sexual theory, treating of homosexuality as a discursive construct or a literary trope; and none has made use of evolutionary psychology.[4] Both liberationist commitments and poststructuralist ideas lead critics away from the central artistic purposes and the basic structures of meaning in Wilde's novel. A commitment to

4. See Ed Cohen, "Writing Gone Wilde: Homoerotic Desire in the Closet of Representation," *PMLA* 102 (1987): 801–13; Eve Kosofsky Sedgwick, *Epistemology of the Closet* (Berkeley: U of California P, 1990), chapter 3; Jeff Nunokawa, "Homosexual Desire and the Effacement of the Self in *The Picture of Dorian Gray*," *American Imago: Studies in Psychoanalysis and Culture* 49 (1992): 311–21; Liang-ya Liou, "The Politics of a Transgressive Desire: Oscar Wilde's *The Picture of Dorian Gray*," *Studies in Language and Literature* 6 (1994): 101–25; Joseph Bristow, "'A Complex Multiform Creature:' Wilde's Sexual Identities," in *The Cambridge Companion to Oscar Wilde*, ed. Peter Raby (Cambridge: Cambridge UP, 1997), pp. 195–218; Edward S. Brinkley, "Homosexuality as (Anti)Illness: Oscar Wilde's *The Picture of Dorian Gray* and Gabriele d'Annunzio's *Il Piacere*," *Studies in Twentieth-Century Literature* 22 (1998): 61–82; Ian Small, *Oscar Wilde: Recent Research, a Supplement to "Oscar Wilde Revalued"* (Greensboro, NC: ELT Press, 2000), chapter 3.

a liberationist standpoint typically involves a determination to envision all homosexual experience in a positive light. As a result, most of the recent gender criticism of Wilde's novel has avoided registering the elements of guilt and self-loathing in Wilde's self-image, and those elements are central to the meaning of the story—to its characterization, plot, theme, style, and tone. (Three studies of *Dorian Gray* have acknowledged negative elements in Wilde's depiction of homosexual experience.)[5] Poststructuralism repudiates, in Jonathan Dollimore's phrase, "the model of deep human subjectivity."[6] If the fundamental artistic motive in the novel is to articulate the conflicts in the depths of Wilde's own identity, the poststructuralist affiliations of current gender theory would necessarily join with its liberationist commitments in casting a veil over the meaning of his novel. In order to gain a true understanding of the deep symbolic structure of Wilde's novel, we must combine a recognition of deep human subjectivity with a recognition of Wilde's own conflicted feelings about his homosexuality. If we deploy this combination, we are in a position, for the first time, fully to grasp Wilde's meaning.

A Darwinian critique of *Dorian Gray* would acknowledge the way in which all its symbolic figurations—sexual, religious, and philosophical—are culturally and historically conditioned, but it would also identify the way in which those culturally conditioned figurations organize the elemental, biologically grounded dispositions of human nature. The symbolic figurations in Wilde's story cannot be limited to the socially encoded values and conventional literary meanings available within a specific cultural context. Wilde, like all artists, assimilates the cultural configurations available to him, but he penetrates to their elemental sources in human nature, and he uses these configurations as a medium through which to articulate his own individual identity—his own sexual, social, moral, and intellectual character.

Dorian Gray is a wealthy young man of exceptional beauty. His friend Basil Hallward paints a portrait of him that captures that beauty. While he is posing for the painting, Basil's friend Lord Henry Wotton tells Dorian that youth and beauty are the only things worth having in life and admonishes him to live fully, since his own youth must soon fade. Dorian exclaims that he wishes he could change places with the painting so that the painting would grow old but that he would remain young. His wish is granted, though he does not

5. Jeffrey Meyers, *Homosexuality and Literature 1890–1930* (Montreal: McGill-Queens UP, 1977), chapter 2; Philip Cohen, *The Moral Vision of Oscar Wilde* (Cranbury, NJ: Associated UP, 1978), chapter 4; Claude J. Summers, *Gay Fictions: Wilde to Stonewall: Studies in a Male Homosexual Literary Tradition* (New York: Frederick Ungar, 1990), chapter 2.
6. Jonathan Dollimore, *Sexual Dissidence: Augustine to Wilde, Freud to Foucault* (Oxford: Oxford UP, 1991), p. 64.

realize it until some time later. He becomes engaged to a young actress, Sybil Vane, whose talent as an actress he admires. When she falls in love with him, her acting deteriorates, he rejects her, and she kills herself in despair. Under Lord Henry's tutelage, Dorian finds that he can regard her death coldly, as an aesthetic event, and he then notices that the painting has changed; it has acquired a look of cruelty about the mouth. Dorian hides the painting in his old school room, and as he ages, pursuing a life divided between aesthetic cultivation and debauchery, he never changes in appearance. He remains young and beautiful, while the portrait grows steadily older and more hideously ugly, manifesting in its deformity the moral corruption of Dorian's "soul." Years later, Basil hears rumors that Dorian is secretly leading a depraved life and asks Dorian to tell him the truth about his behavior. In response, Dorian shows him the painting. Basil is horrified and calls on Dorian to repent and reform. Instead, Dorian stabs Basil and kills him, and the hand in the painting becomes stained with blood. Some time after, in a thematically irrelevant episode that bulks out a slender narrative, Sybil Vane's brother discovers Dorian's identity. He blames Dorian for Sybil's death and plans to murder him but is himself killed in a hunting accident. Having escaped destruction, Dorian makes an effort to behave generously to a girl by not seducing her. He hopes his generosity will be reflected in the painting, but the face in the painting only takes on a new expression of cunning hypocrisy. In loathing and revulsion, Dorian stabs the painting in the heart. The knife stroke kills Dorian himself, and he and the painting once again change places. The image in the painting becomes young and beautiful; and Dorian Gray, as a corpse, is old and loathsome.

The three chief male figures in the novel all embody aspects of Wilde's own identity, and that identity is fundamentally divided against itself. The novel is thus a "psychodrama." Writing in a period before poststructuralism had cordoned off "deep human subjectivity," Barbara Charlesworth gives a succinct formulation to this view of the novel. "Wilde, even more consciously than most writers, split himself into various characters and saw in all of them some portion of his actual or potential self . . . his was a nature of contradictions from which he could find no escape . . . With the intelligence to understand all the conflicts of his age, yet without the ability or the will to resolve them, Wilde was finally broken by them."[7] In a letter to a friend, Wilde himself suggests an autobiographical dimension for the characters in the novel, but his own commentary tacitly smoothes over both the sinister aspects of the three characters and

7. Barbara Charlesworth, *Dark Passages: The Decadent Consciousness in Victorian Literature* (Madison: U of Wisconsin P, 1965), pp. 54, 79.

the conflicts among them. He says that *Dorian Gray* "contains much of me in it. Basil Hallward is what I think I am: Lord Henry, what the world thinks me: Dorian what I would like to be—in other ages perhaps."[8] What he does not say in his letter is that Dorian is beautiful but selfish, sensual, and cruel; Lord Henry is a worldly cynic incapable of registering the moral horror that leads Dorian to murder and suicide; and that Basil is enthralled by Dorian's beauty but appalled at the moral quality of his life. The conflicts emerging out of these values and dispositions constitute the central structures of meaning in the story. The idea that the characters embody aspects of Wilde's own conflicted identity stands in sharp contrast with the poststructuralist idea that the characters embody various aporias, gaps, and paradoxes inherent in "textuality."[9]

For Wilde, identity consists of two main elements, sensual pleasure and moral pathos, and in his moral universe these two elements are usually set in opposition to one another. Sensual pleasure associates itself with egoism, worldly vanity, and cruelty. Moral pathos is sometimes associated with devoted love, but it manifests itself primarily as pity for the poor and as tenderness toward children. Erotic passion allies itself with sensual pleasure. The morally negative side of Wilde's identity is distinctly male and predatory, and the positive side distinctly female and maternal. In Wilde, the moral sense couches itself explicitly and imaginatively in Christian terms—in terms of self-sacrificing love, sin, remorse, redemption, and the soul.

The most overt and explicit manifestations of Wilde's polar thematic structure appear in his fairy tales—stories that have medieval characters and settings and that are saturated with the spirit and mood of medieval religious experience. In the fairy tales, Christian pathos usually triumphs over egoistic cruelty and sensual pleasure. The Happy Prince and the swallow that serve as his messenger sacrifice themselves for love and pity, and God sanctifies their sacrifice. The Selfish Giant repents of his selfishness, embraces the Christ Child, and is taken to heaven. The Young King renounces wealth and pomp that feeds off the suffering of the poor, and when his subjects revolt, God himself intervenes and crowns him with glory. The Star Child is arrogant and cruel, but he is sore afflicted, repents, humbles himself in self-sacrificing penance, and as a reward

8. Oscar Wilde, *The Letters of Oscar Wilde,* ed. Rupert Hart-Davis (New York: Harcourt, Brace, 1962), p. 352; hereafter cited as *Letters.*
9. Poststructuralist readings include Elana Gomel, "Oscar Wilde, *The Picture of Dorian Gray,* and the (Un)Death of the Author," *Narrative* 12 (2001): 74–92; Michael Patrick Gillespie, "Picturing Dorian Gray: Resistant Readings in Wilde's Novel," *English Literature in Transition 1880–1920* 35 (1992): 7–25; and Nils Clausson, "Culture and Corruption: Paterian Self-Development *versus* Gothic Degeneration in Oscar Wilde's *The Picture of Dorian Gray,*" *Papers on Language and Literature* 39 (2003): 339–64.

is crowned king. The Nightingale impales her heart on a thorn, sacrificing her life for love. The young man and woman for whom she makes the sacrifice are not worthy of it, but Wilde's own sublime lyricism implicitly affirms its intrinsic beauty: "So the nightingale pressed closer against the thorn, and the thorn touched her heart, and a fierce pang of pain shot through her. Bitter, bitter was the pain, and wilder and wilder grew her song, for she sang of the Love that is perfected by Death, of the Love that dies not in the tomb."[1] When Basil invokes the spectre of guilt at living solely for selfish pleasure, Lord Henry tells him that "'mediaeval art is charming, but mediaeval emotions are out of date.'"[2] Clearly Lord Henry has not been reading Wilde's fairy stories, and his flippant dismissal of guilt underscores his inadequacy as an interpreter of Dorian's experience. It is nonetheless the case that in *Dorian Gray* the Christian ethos manifests itself only negatively, as guilt and anguish. There is no moment of transfiguring redemption at the end. It is not a fairy tale but a horror story, and in that respect, it is perhaps more true to Wilde's own life than the stories that depict redemptive transfigurations.

Dorian is not all of Wilde, but he is part of him, and the qualities exemplified in Dorian's career have two main sources in Wilde's own experience, one an intellectual source, and the other a personal, sexual source. The chief intellectual source is the philosophy of aestheticism propounded by Walter Pater. The personal, sexual source is the homoerotic sensibility that places a maximal value on youth, beauty, and transient sensual pleasure. Pater was himself homosexual, though possibly celibate, and in Wilde's own mind aestheticism and homoeroticism converge into a distinct complex of feeling and value. Dorian's life turns out to be something like an experimental test case for the validity of Pater's aestheticist philosophy, and the experiment falsifies the philosophy. Dorian lives badly and ends badly, but the retributional structure does not simply eliminate the Paterian component from Wilde's sensibility. That component is inextricably linked with Wilde's temperament and his sexual identity. (Several of the scholars who have commented on Wilde's use of Pater in *Dorian Gray* have recognized Wilde's ambivalence toward Pater but have emphasized the negative, satiric aspects of Wilde's treatment.)[3]

1. Oscar Wilde, *Complete Shorter Fiction,* ed. Isobel Murray (Oxford: Oxford U Press, 1979), p. 108.
2. Oscar Wilde, *The Picture of Dorian Gray,* ed. Michael Patrick Gillespie (New York: W. W. Norton, 2019) p. 68; hereafter abbreviated as *DG.*
3. Instances include Richard Ellman, "Overtures to Salome," in *Oscar Wilde: A Collection of Critical Essays,* ed. Richard Ellman (Englewood Cliffs, NJ: Prentice-Hall, 1969), pp. 87–91; Robert K. Martin, "Parody and Homage: The Presence of Pater in *Dorian Gray,*" *The Victorian Newsletter* 69 (Spring 1983): 15–18; Julia Prewitt Brown, *Cosmopolitan Criticism:*

The key tenets of Pater's philosophy are divulged in one highly condensed and vastly influential passage in the "Conclusion" to *Studies in the Renaissance*. Pater treats of humans as egoistic isolates for whom reality consists only of transient sensory impressions:

> Every one of those impressions is the impression of an individual in his isolation, each mind keeping as a solitary prisoner its own dream of a world. . . . To such a tremulous wisp constantly re-forming itself on the stream, to a single sharp impression, with a sense in it, a relic more or less fleeting, of such moments gone by, what is real in our life fines itself down. It is with this movement, with the passage and dissolution of impressions, images, sensations, that analysis leaves off—that continual vanishing away, that strange, perpetual, weaving and unweaving of ourselves.[4]

Throughout *Dorian Gray*, Wilde echoes the explicit ethical doctrines of this brief essay. Pater declares that "not the fruit of experience, but experience itself is the end" (*Renaissance*, p. 188). And Lord Henry inducts Dorian into the philosophy of a "new Hedonism" the aim of which "was to be experience itself, and not the fruits of experience, sweet or bitter as they might be. . . . It was to teach man to concentrate himself upon the moments of a life that is itself but a moment" (*DG*, p. 108). In answer to Pater's evocation of the amorphous and unstable character of the individual ego, Dorian "used to wonder at the shallow psychology of those who conceive the Ego in man as a thing simple, permanent, reliable, and of one essence. To him, man was a being with myriad lives and myriad sensations, a complex, multiform creature" (*DG*, p. 120). Pater suggests that, "our failure is to form habits" (*Renaissance*, p. 189). And Lord Henry proclaims, "'The people who love only once in their lives are really the shallow people. What they call their loyalty, and their fidelity, I call either the lethargy of custom or their lack of imagination. Faithfulness is to the emotional life what consistency is to the life of the intellect—imply a confession of failure'" (*DG*, p. 45).

By emphasizing the single moment of sensation and the isolated but amorphous ego, Pater eliminates the two central components of moral life—the bonds we have with other lives, and the continuity of identity through time. Following Pater, Lord Henry tells Dorian that "'the aim of life is self-development. To realize one's nature perfectly—that is what each of us is here to do'" (*DG*, p. 19). What

---

Oscar Wilde's Philosophy of Art (Charlottesville: UP of Virginia, 1997); John Paul Riquelme, "Oscar Wilde's Aesthetic Gothic: Walter Pater, Dark Enlightenment, and *The Picture of Dorian Gray*," *Modern Fiction Studies* 46 (2000): 609–31.
    4. Walter Pater, *The Renaissance: Studies in Art and Poetry*, ed. Donald Hall (Berkeley: U of California P, 1980), pp. 187–88; hereafter cited as *Renaissance*.

Pater and Lord Henry fail to understand, is that the "self" cannot be cultivated or "developed" in isolation from its relations with others. Nor can it be developed with an emphasis on isolated moments of sensation; it bears within it the burden of all its past acts. As Darwin understood, those two forms of extension—of the self in relation to others, and of the self extending over time—are the very basis and substance of moral life:

> A moral being is one who is capable of comparing his past and future actions or motives, and of approving or disapproving of them . . . Man, from the activity of his mental faculties, cannot avoid reflection: past impressions and images are incessantly passing through his mind with distinctness. Now with those animals which live permanently in a body, the social instincts are ever present and persistent. . . . They feel at all times, without the stimulus of any special passion or desire, some degree of love and sympathy. . . . A man who possessed no trace of such feeling would be an unnatural monster. . . . Conscience looks backwards and judges past actions, inducing that kind of dissatisfaction, which if weak we call regret, and if severe remorse.[5]

Darwin's analysis refers to "man" in general, that is, to human nature. Generalizing from his own temperament as an isolated, introverted aesthete, Pater developed a philosophy of the goals and purposes of life that are not congruent with human nature and that are thus not functional and adequate for most people. Wilde partially accepted Pater's vision; Dorian Gray embodies Wilde's own disposition to live in absorbed and egoistic delight at pure aesthetic sensation. But in Wilde's personality that disposition is set in active and even violent tension with the sense of social bonding and the continuity of the individual identity.

In Wilde's own imagination, the egoistic sensualism of Pater's decadent aestheticism correlates with the emphasis on promiscuous and impersonal sex that is a distinguishing feature of a homoerotic sensibility, and Wilde's intuition in this regard gains confirmation in the research of Donald Symons. In *The Evolution of Human Sexuality,* Symons collates and analyzes multiple studies of homosexual behavior. On the basis of these studies, he concludes that male homosexual behavior is characterized by promiscuous, impersonal sex. He explains this pattern of behavior by invoking the Darwinian logic of differences in the reproductive interests of males and females, and the corresponding differences in male and female sexual psychology. Males and females have co-evolved, but their sexual

---

5. Charles Darwin, *The Descent of Man, and Selection in Relation to Sex,* ed. John Tyler Bonner and Robert M. May (Princeton: Princeton UP, 1981), pp. 88–91.

character is partially complementary and partially conflicting. Males can benefit reproductively by promiscuous sexual encounters, and male sexual psychology is more prone to casual sex. Females benefit most by enlisting the sustained support of a male who possesses material resources and is willing to invest them in the woman and in her offspring. Men tend toward promiscuous desire; women seek lasting relationships. Men are on average adapted preferentially to value youth and beauty in a mate, and women are on average adapted preferentially to value status and resources in a mate. Because men and women have co-evolved in adaptive interdependency, men are adapted to seek the status and resources women value, and women are adapted to be attentive to those aspects of beauty that motivate men. In strongly hierarchical, polygynous societies, men of high rank and wealth have multiple wives or concubines (and the lowest ranking males are consequently excluded from sexual relations altogether). In monogamous societies, males partially suppress their desire for multiple sexual partners, though pornography, prostitution, adultery, and "serial monogamy" still cater to evolved male proclivities for diffuse sexual experience. In homosexual communities, Symons explains, the male desire for promiscuous sexual encounters is not constrained to compromise with female dispositions toward long-term pair bonding. The result is that male homosexual communities produce a culture of promiscuous sexual encounters. (Lesbians, in contrast, maximize female proclivities for stable, long-term pair bonds.)[6]

Dorian Gray has an overt heterosexual plot, and there is no explicit homosexuality in the story—it could hardly have been published had there been—but the putatively heterosexual liaison with Sybil is of a purely aesthetic character, and the atmosphere of the story is saturated with homoerotic feeling and style. That feeling and style make themselves felt from the opening lines of the novel, and the first several scenes establish its sexual orientation by interweaving four chief elements: images of luxuriant sensuality, an overriding preoccupation with male beauty, the depiction of effeminate mannerisms among the characters, and a perpetual patter of snide remarks that are hostile to women, to marriage, and to sexual fidelity. None of these four elements would by itself decisively signal a homoerotic orientation, but in the combination Wilde produces, the effect is unmistakable and strongly evocative. Luxuriant sensuality is not exclusively homoerotic, but when it is closely associated with a fixation on male beauty, it invests that fixation with an erotic charge. Antagonism to heterosexual bonding is not in itself an

6. Donald Symons, *The Evolution of Human Sexuality* (Oxford: Oxford UP, 1979), chapter nine, "Test Cases: Hormones and Homosexuals."

unequivocal marker of homoeroticism. Heterosexual males can also express dislike for being tied down, but when coupled with homo-erotic sensuality and with effeminacy of manners, antagonism to female desires for "fidelity" assumes a specifically homoerotic char-acter. Recent historians of gender roles have argued that until Wilde's trials for homosexual practices, in 1895, effeminacy of manners was not unequivocally associated in the public mind with a specifically homosexual persona; they argue also that Wilde's own persona and the public response to his trials were pivotal in fixing the modern public image of the homosexual.[7] But even before Wilde's trials, effeminacy would by definition already have signalled a disrup-tion or crossing of gender boundaries, and that disruption, since it is associated with an erotically charged fixation on male beauty, gives a sufficiently distinct signal of the sexual orientation that animates Wilde's characters. Among heterosexuals, feminine characteristics act as a stimulus or trigger for male sexual desire. One chief reason effeminacy can be so easily integrated with a homoerotic persona is that effeminacy indirectly suggests that the effeminate male could himself be an object of male sexual desire. (The original serialized version of *Dorian Gray* contains a few more overtly homoerotic ges-tures and expressions than the book version.)

Evoking a homoerotic atmosphere is central to Wilde's artistic purposes. From the very first lines of the novel, he uses all the resources of his style to orient the reader to his own distinctively homoerotic sensibility, and he makes a point of locating that sensi-bility in relation to the themes of Pater's aesthetic philosophy:

> The studio was filled with the rich odour of roses, and when the light summer wind stirred amidst the trees of the garden there came through the open door the heavy scent of the lilac, or the more delicate perfume of the pink-flowering thorn.
>
> From the corner of the divan of Persian saddle-bags on which he was lying, smoking, as was his custom, innumerable ciga-rettes, Lord Henry Wotton could just catch the gleam of the honey-sweet and honey-coloured blossoms of the laburnum, whose tremulous branches seemed hardly able to bear the bur-den of a beauty so flame-like as theirs; and now and then the fantastic shadows of birds in flight flitted across the long tussore-silk curtains that were stretched in front of the huge window, producing a kind of momentary Japanese effect . . . (*DG*, p. 5)

7. See Ed Cohen, *Talk on the Wilde Side: Toward a Genealogy of a Discourse on Male Sexualities* (New York: Routledge, 1993); Alan Sinfield, *The Wilde Century: Effemi-nacy, Oscar Wilde and the Queer Movement* (London: Cassell, 1994); Joseph Bristow, *Effeminate England: Homoerotic Writing after 1885* (New York: Columbia UP, 1995); Thais Morgan, "Victorian Effeminacies," in *Victorian Sexual Dissidence,* ed. Richard Dellamora (Chicago: U of Chicago P, 1999), pp. 109–25.

Pater had proclaimed that "this, at least of flame-like our life has, that it is but the concurrence, renewed from moment to moment, of forces parting sooner or later on their ways," and he had character- ized the ultimate constituent of experience, the impression, as "a tremulous wisp" (*Renaissance*, pp. 187, 188). By importing Pater's distinctive idiom ("flame-like," "tremulous") into Basil's studio, Wilde gives Pater's abstract doctrines not just a concrete habitation and a name but also a sexual orientation. In its delicate and luxuri- ous sensuality and its emphasis on art-like effects, the evocation of this scene strikes a new note in English fiction. It registers a distinct sensibility, and one defining aspect of that sensibility is an over- whelming preoccupation with male beauty. Dorian is first intro- duced, through his portrait, as "a young man of extraordinary personal beauty" (*DG*, p. 6). Lord Henry expands expressively on this flat denotation—"this young Adonis, who looks as if he was made out of ivory and rose-leaves. Why, my dear Basil, he is a Narcissus'" (*DG*, p. 7). When he meets Dorian in person, Lord Henry reflects, "'Yes, he was certainly handsome, with his finely-curved scarlet lips, his frank blue eyes, his crisp gold hair'" (*DG*, p. 17). Basil does not merely register Dorian's youthful beauty; he identifies it as the central value in his own ethos: "'You have the most marvellous youth, and youth is the one thing worth having'" (*DG*, p. 22). After Lord Henry has told Dorian that youth and beauty are the only things worth having, Dorian cries out that he is jealous of the por- trait whose beauty will not die, while he will only get older and uglier. "'Oh, if it were only the other way! If the picture could change, and I could be always what I am now! Why did you paint it? It will mock me some day—mock me horribly!' The hot tears welled into his eyes; he tore his hand away, and, flinging himself on the divan, he buried his face in the cushions" (*DG*, p. 26). Scenes of women lying prone and weeping are common enough in Victorian fiction; scenes depicting males in that posture are vanishingly rare. By flinging himself on a divan, weeping over the prospect of his own lost beauty, Dorian crosses a gender boundary in two distinct ways: he displays a passionate preoccupation with his own personal appear- ance, and he indulges in histrionic emotional expressiveness.

In these opening scenes, delicate and luxurious sensualism, a pre- occupation with male beauty, and effeminate manners combine to produce a distinctly homoerotic atmosphere. As a polemical accom- paniment to this atmosphere, Lord Henry keeps up a drumbeat of denigrating comments against heterosexual bonding. "'You seem to forget that I am married,'" he tells Basil, "'and the one charm of mar- riage is that it makes a life of deception absolutely necessary for both parties'" (*DG*, p. 8). In response to Basil's confession that for so long as he lives "'the personality of Dorian Gray will dominate me,'" Lord Henry responds, "'Those who are faithful know only the trivial side of love; it is the faithless who know love's tragedies'" (*DG*, p. 15). Faithfulness is, as Lord Henry says in a passage already quoted, "'simply a confession of failure.'" Commitment or bonded attachment is a "trivial" form of personal interaction; promiscuous and opportunistic liaisons animated by transient appetites are the "serious" and substantial forms of interpersonal relation. These contentions are not abstract, universal, and gender neutral. Lord Henry is quite clear about the sexual orientations implicit in the conflict of values he propounds. "'Always! That is a dreadful word. It makes me shudder when I hear it. Women are so fond of using it. They spoil every romance by trying to make it last forever'" (*DG*, p. 24). (Elaine Showalter comments on the misogyny in the novel but does not register the antagonism to long-term bonding as the focal point of Lord Henry's polemic.)[8] The folly of fidelity is one of Lord Henry's favorite themes—a complement to his themes of sensual indulgence and self-cultivation as the ultimate aims in life. "'What a fuss people make about fidelity!' exclaimed Lord Henry. 'Why, even in love it is purely a question for physiology. It has nothing to do with our own will. Young men want to be faithful, and are not; old men want to be faithless, and cannot'" (*DG*, p. 28). These are universalizing claims about the nature of human intimacy, but what they universalize is not human nature in its heterosexual form; it is a specifically homosexual ethos produced by isolating and totalising male dispositions toward promiscuity.

Lord Henry's assault on normative heterosexuality is subversive and revolutionary on a grand scale. "'The longer I live, Dorian, the more keenly I feel that whatever was good enough for our fathers is not good enough for us. In art, as in politics, *les grandpères ont toujours tort*'" (*DG*, p. 45). This claim could not be more boldly sweeping. In art and politics, *the grandfathers are always wrong.* Not wrong on this or that principle or point of taste or value—wrong generally, wrong fundamentally, wrong simply by virtue of being who and what they are, wrong precisely because, as heterosexuals, they became grandfathers.

Wilde invests part of his identity in each of the three characters, and the relations among them reveal the divisions within that identity. Lord Henry is what the world thinks Wilde is because in his own essayistic writings Wilde actually says many of the same things that Lord Henry says. Lord Henry often sounds like Wilde, but unlike Wilde, Lord Henry is not himself an artist. His creativity limits itself to the formulation of epigrams. Basil is a moralist, not a

---

8. Elaine Showalter, *Sexual Anarchy: Gender and Culture at the Fin de Siècle* (New York: Penguin, 1990), pp. 175–78.

wit, but he is also a true artist. For Wilde, the central enigma of personal identity is that the creative spirit, as it is embodied in Basil, is fundamentally divided against itself. Basil is devoted to Dorian as the embodiment of purely sensual beauty, but he also believes in the "soul"; he believes, that is, in the continuity of moral identity—in the bonds we have with others that form part of our own inner selves. He argues that one would have to pay "'a terrible price'" for "'living merely for one's self,'" a price in "'remorse, in suffering, in . . . well, in the consciousness of degradation'" (*DG*, p. 68). The plot tacitly affirms these suppositions, and Dorian himself thinks of the painting in the same terms Basil uses to explain the logic of moral consequences. The painting becomes "the visible symbol of the degradation of sin," an "ever-present sign of the ruin men brought upon their souls." As such, it would "be a guide to him through life, would be what holiness is to some and conscience to others, and the fear of God to us all" (*DG*, p. 81).

Basil acknowledges the reality of conscience, but as an artist he is also hopelessly dependent on Dorian. Basil works most success-fully as an artist when he is most fully under the sway of Dorian's "personality," and when Dorian distances himself from Basil, Basil's art goes into decline (*DG*, p. 177). In his early days, Basil's con-science is blind and his art successful. In his final encounter with Dorian, his conscience awakes to the moral horror of a purely aes-theticist orientation, and he calls on Dorian to repent and reform. As Dorian unveils the portrait and Basil sees it for the first time in two decades, "An exclamation of horror broke from the painter's lips as he saw in the dim light the hideous face on the canvas grinning at him. There was something in its expression that filled him with disgust and loathing . . . It was some foul parody, some infamous, ignoble satire. He had never done that. Still, it was his own picture. He knew it, and he felt as if his blood had changed in a moment from fire to sluggish ice. His own picture! What did it mean?"

> "Can't you see your ideal in it?" Said Dorian, bitterly . . ."
> "There was nothing evil in it, nothing shameful . . ."
> "It is the face of my soul."
>   "Christ! What a thing I must have worshipped! It has the eyes of a devil." (*DG*, p. 131)

Lord Henry's discourse dominates the earlier portions of the story. For the final portions, Lord Henry reveals himself as wholly inade-quate to interpret the meaning of the events in which he has participated. As Marlow says of Kurtz's fiancée in *Heart of Dark-ness*, Lord Henry is "'out of it.'"[9] He does not know that Dorian has

---

9. Joseph Conrad, *Heart of Darkness*, ed. Robert Hampson (London: Penguin, 1995), p. 80.

murdered Basil, and he does not know that Dorian's portrait—his inner self—bears the marks of corruption and degradation. Despite the appearance of his rhetorical dominance in the exchanges with Basil and Dorian, Lord Henry is less capable of registering the full meaning of the story than either of them. Dorian most fully lives out the doctrine of egoistic hedonism, but he also feels the countervailing force of conscience. Basil feels the horror of moral corruption, but he also feels the haunting pull of beauty. Both of these characters are divided against themselves, but they do at least have depths of personal identity. Lord Henry is simple and whole, but he is also flat, two-dimensional. He professes a philosophy of surfaces, and his observations on the course of Dorian's career remain wholly on the surface. He mockingly quotes a street preacher's question—what does it profit a man if he gain the whole world and lose his soul? In response, Dorian assures him, with unwonted fervor and sincerity, that "'the soul is a terrible reality. It can be bought, and sold, and bartered away. It can be poisoned or made perfect'" (*DG,* p. 178). Lord Henry disclaims the very existence of the soul, and Dorian's soul thus remains a closed book to him.

The plot of *Dorian Gray* is retributional, but the meaning of the novel is not exhausted by any simple moral message. Defending himself against critics who accused the novel of promoting immoral behavior, Wilde asserts that "the real moral of the story is that all excess, as well as all renunciation, brings its punishment, and this moral is so far artistically and deliberately suppressed that it does not enunciate its laws as a general principle, but realises itself purely in the lives of individuals, and so becomes simply a dramatic element in a work of art, and not the object of the work of art itself" (*Letters,* p. 263). This is a rather trite and bland account of the didactic message conveyed by Dorian's disastrous career. Dorian's problem is not merely that he indulges in "excess." His problem is that he fails to create or sustain affectional bonds. He betrays all the people who are closest to him; he destroys them or leads them to ruin. But a more important point, in qualification of this appeal to didactic structure, is that didacticism is a form of resolution; it is an affirmation of an assured set of normative values, and the novel affirms no such set of normative values. There is no resolution of conflict in the story itself, and Wilde as narrator occupies no position above and apart from the story. There is at no point in the novel a single dominant perspective, standing apart from all three characters and encompassing them, that provides a normative, authoritative vision of the whole. The vision of the whole is nothing more, or less, than the enactment of the conflicted, unresolved relations among the three chief characters.

The most likely candidate for the role of internal moral guide would be Basil, but Basil is fundamentally compromised by his subjection to Dorian's "personality." He is himself guilty of an unconscious complicity with the values that animate Dorian's behavior. That complicity is revealed in the crucial episode during which the supernatural transformation in the painting takes place. While Basil is finishing the painting, Dorian is listening to Lord Henry propound the doctrine of hedonistic aestheticism. Lord Henry's talk is enchanting to Dorian, and it is the immediate prelude to the supernatural interchange that takes place between himself and the painting. At the end of the sitting, Basil apologizes for fatiguing Dorian. "'When I am painting, I can't think of anything else. But you never sat better. You were perfectly still. And I have caught the effect I wanted—the half-parted lips, and the bright look in the eyes. I don't know what Harry has been saying to you, but he has certainly made you have the most wonderful expression'" (*DG*, p. 21). Basil has explicitly warned Dorian not to listen to Lord Henry and has told him that Lord Henry "'has a very bad influence over all his friends'" (*DG*, p. 18). He would not himself like what Lord Henry says to Dorian, but he very much likes the effect Lord Henry's words have on Dorian, and capturing that effect brings him to the highest point of his own artistic achievement.

In his devotion to Dorian, Basil tacitly associates himself with the aestheticist ethos, but aestheticism is not the whole of art for either Basil or Wide. In speaking of Sybil's artistic purpose as an actress, Basil articulates a moral conception of art like that which informs Wilde's fairy tales. "'To spiritualize one's age—that is something worth doing. If this girl can give a soul to those who have lived without one, if she can create the sense of beauty in people whose lives have been sordid and ugly, if she can strip them of their selfishness and lend them tears for sorrows that are not their own, she is worthy of all your adoration, worthy of all the adoration in the world'" (*DG*, p. 70). In this conception, the chief function of the artist is not that of celebrating sensuous beauty but that of creating empathy—of suppressing selfishness and making people feel for the sorrows of others. It is this conception of art that dominates the fairy tales, but within *Dorian Gray* it can neither achieve dominance nor be wholly suppressed.

In his conversation with Dorian about Sybil's suicide, Basil attempts to assert his own moral perspective but fails to sway Dorian and ultimately yields to him, thus tacitly acknowledging his own dependence on Dorian's identity. In speaking of Sybil's death, Dorian's speech has been more coldly and heartlessly selfish than at any previous time; it has all of Lord Henry's cynicism with none of his whimsical humor. He describes her death as "'one of the great romantic tragedies of the age'" and contrasts it with the "'tedious'" "'middle-class virtues'" of "'commonplace lives'" (*DG*, p. 91). He dispenses with sorrow and seeks to see the whole episode only "from a proper artistic point of view'" (*DG*, p. 92). Given Basil's temperament and values, one would anticipate that he would be profoundly shocked and alienated by this speech, but Dorian appeals to his friendship, and "the painter felt strangely moved. The lad was infinitely dear to him, and his personality had been the great turning point in his art. He could not bear the idea of reproaching him any more. After all, his indifference was probably a mood that would pass away. There was so much in him that was good, so much that was noble" (*DG*, p. 92). Basil's fascination with Dorian compromises his moral judgment. He cannot distinguish between the charm of Dorian's "personality" and his own sense of the "good" and "noble." His language, recorded in free indirect discourse, is that of someone rationalizing the bad behavior of a friend or lover, and there is no evidence from the text, no verbal clues, that at this point the narrator has any ironic detachment from Basil's perspective. His confusion about Dorian's value as a person seems to reflect Wilde's own perplexity, and that perplexity is at the very heart of the story.

Darwin tells us that humans have an evolved moral sense that consists in empathic human bonds extending over time and generating a sense of personal responsibility. When that sense of human connection is violated, he explains, we feel guilt and remorse. Basil confirms these contentions, and the plot of the story gives them symbolic form. Wilde does not invoke Darwin's psychological theory. He speaks instead of "'the soul'" and the "'sense of degradation,'" but the moral and psychological content of Wilde's Christian imagery is interchangeable with Darwin's naturalistic analysis. Wilde is intoxicated by Pater's aestheticism, but his own intuitions tell him that Pater's concept of human nature is profoundly false. It is adequate to sustain a two-dimensional character like Lord Henry, who scarcely seems to exist outside the medium of his epigrams. It is not adequate to sustain either Basil or Dorian. Like Kurtz in *Heart of Darkness*, Dorian has a glimpse, before his death, of the horror of his own soul. Unlike Conrad's Marlow, though, Wilde does not try to invest that moment of vision with redemptive power. Dorian loathes himself, but, except by killing himself, he never stops being himself. Suicide is not a form of resolution. It is a capitulation to ultimate failure.

Wilde's conception of an unresolvable conflict between the aesthetic and moral sides of his own identity is not a criterion of artistic success or artistic failure. It is merely the subject and animating spirit of his novel. One central measure of the novel's success as a work of art is the degree to which its figurative structure, its stylistic

devices, and its tonal qualities are adequate to articulate that subject. The sustained psychodramatic interactions of the characters
and the virtuoso interplay of cynical wit, voluptuous aestheticism,
and morbid horror fulfill Wilde's artistic purposes. The novel is in
many ways painful and unpleasant, but it is nonetheless a small masterpiece. In order to appreciate Wilde's artistic achievement in this
novel, we have to recognize that despite all its sensuous luxuriance
and provocative wittiness, its culminating dramatic moment depicts
a loathsome self-image stabbed to the heart. The central artistic purpose in *Dorian Gray* is to articulate the anguish in the depths of
Wilde's own identity.

NILS CLAUSSON

"Culture and Corruption": Paterian Self-Development *versus* Gothic Degeneration in Oscar Wilde's *The Picture of Dorian Gray*†

> "Culture and corruption," murmured Dorian, "I have known some-
> thing of both."
> —Oscar Wilde, *The Picture of Dorian Gray*

> I hold that no work of art can be tried otherwise than by laws
> deduced from itself: whether or not it be consistent with itself is
> the question.
> —Thomas Wainewright, quoted by Wilde
> in "Pen, Pencil, and Poison"

Recent genre theory reminds us of just how often our disagreements
about the meaning or interpretation of a text are actually debates
about *how* the text should be read, or, more precisely, what *kind* of
text it should be read *as*. If we are persuaded that a text is indeed an
urban eclogue, a *Bildungsroman,* a Horatian ode, a parody of pastoral, or an example of postmodern female Gothic, we are more likely
also to be persuaded of the critic's interpretation of that text's meaning. Thus a critic who interprets *Who's Afraid of Virginia Woolf?* as
a modern secular morality play is not so much claiming to have
found the meaning of the text as he or she is trying to persuade us
to read the text as a particular kind of play. *What* a text means is
inseparable from *how* it is read, and since we must always read a
text *as something,* genre often asserts itself as a set of instructions,

---

† From *Papers on Language and Literature* 39.4 (Fall 2003): 339–64. Notes have been
renumbered. Copyright © The Board of Trustees, Southern Illinois University Edwards-
ville. Reprinted by permission.

implicit or explicit, on how to read a text. The debate over the genre, and thereby the meaning, of Oscar Wilde's novel *The Picture of Dorian Gray* exemplifies this protocol of reading.

Dorian Gray[1] has always provoked contradictory interpretations, but underlying the disagreements about the work's meaning there has persisted a more fundamental debate about what *kind* of novel it should be read *as*. This debate is discernible in the early reviews, though somewhat obscured by the hysteria over the novel's alleged immorality. Reading the novel as an English imitation of a decadent French text, for example, the reviewer for the *Daily Chronicle* denounced it as "a tale spawned from the leprous literature of the French *Décadents,* a poisonous book, the atmosphere of which is heavy with mephitic odours of moral and spiritual putrefaction" (*NCE* 368). The *St. James Gazette* repeated this attack: "The writer airs his cheap research among the garbage of the French *Décadents* like any drivelling pedant" (*NCE* 358). But while the popular secular press was denouncing Wilde's novel for its "spiritual putrefaction," Christian publications, such as the *Christian Leader,* the *Christian World,* and *Light,* which interpreted it as an ethical parable or moral fable, praised it as "a work of high moral import" (qtd. in Pearce 169). In America, Julian Hawthorne (son of Nathaniel Hawthorne) was undecided whether *Dorian Gray* was "a novel or romance (it partakes of both)." But he finally settled on "parable" and pronounced the novel "a salutary departure from the ordinary English novel" (*NCE* 375). Clearly, the judgment of early reviewers depended, at least to some extent, on the genre in which they placed the novel.

Modern critics are as divided about the novel's meaning as the original reviewers were obsessed with its morality. But what has not changed is the role the perceived genre of the novel plays in interpretation.[2] While some critics read the novel as belonging to a single

---

1. *The Picture of Dorian Gray* was first published in the July 1890 issue of *Lippincott's Monthly Magazine.* That edition has been reprinted in the [First] Norton Critical Edition of *Dorian Gray,* edited by Donald L. Lawler and also in an edition introduced by Jeremy Reed. In response to the hostile reviews of the *Lippincott's* edition, Wilde revised and expanded the novel. The revised edition, published in 1891, is the one that is usually reprinted and on which most critical discussions of the novel are based. Although Lawler acknowledges that the 1890 edition "has its own character and integrity" ([First] *NCE* xii), I disagree with his judgment that the revised edition is artistically superior: the six chapters that Wilde added weaken the novel's artistic unity, and the cuts he made to remove the explicitly homosexual language of the first version seriously compromise the meaning of the original. Quotations in this essay are from the 1890 *Lippincott's* edition in the [Third] Norton Critical Edition and will be abbreviated as *DG* 90; the Norton Critical Edition of the revised and expanded novel will be abbreviated as *DG* 91. Quotations from contemporary reviews are also taken from the [Third] Norton Critical Edition and will be abbreviated as *NCE.*
2. For a thorough survey of [late-twentieth-century] criticism of the novel, see Valentina Di Pietro's "An Annotated Secondary Bibliography on *The Picture of Dorian Gray* (1980–1999)" (*The Victorian Newsletter* 98 [Autumn 2000]: 5–10).

genre and assume that the conventions of that genre provide the key
to unlock the text's meaning, others see it as a kind of heteroglossia
combining two or more genres. In "*The Picture of Dorian Gray:* Wilde's
Parable of the Fall," for example, Joyce Carol Oates finds the novel to
be "a curious hybrid. Certainly it possesses a 'supernatural' dimension,
and its central image is Gothic; yet in other respects it is Restoration
comedy" (427). For her, the novel's generic anomalies make its message at once transparently clear and enigmatically opaque:

> While in one sense *The Picture of Dorian Gray* is as transpar-
> ent as a medieval allegory, and its structure as workman-like
> as Marlowe's *Dr. Faustus,* to which it bears an obvious family
> resemblance, in another sense it remains a puzzle: knotted, con-
> voluted, brilliantly enigmatic. (Oates 422–23)

But, as her title indicates, Oates ultimately sees the primary, governing genre as parable. Even those critics who find multiple genres
in *Dorian Gray* tend to privilege one. The two most favored candi-
dates for the novel's controlling genre have remained fable and parable. Joseph Pearce has recently joined this chorus: "The plot of the
novel," he says, "unfurls like a parable, illuminating the grave spiritual dangers involved in a life of immoral action and experiment"
(164), language that echoes that of the Christian reviewers in 1890.
In a dissenting voice, Shelton Waldrep argues for *Dorian Gray* as a
realist novel: "Wilde had to work within the confines of some specific variation on the theme of realism" (103). Kerry Powell has
uncovered Wilde's indebtedness to a popular, late-Victorian sub-
genre that he designates as "'magic' picture fiction" (148). In "Fiction
and Allegory," Edouard Roditi classifies *Dorian Gray* as an "*Erzie-
hungsroman* of dandyism" ([First] *NCE* 371) in the tradition of Robert Plumer Ward's *Tremaine* (1825), Disraeli's *Vivian Gray* (1826),
and Bulwer Lytton's *Pelham* (1828). Confronted with the novel's
generic diversity, Rachel Bowlby concludes that "*Dorian Gray* does
not in fact fall straightforwardly into any generic category" and finds
it to be an amalgam of "innumerable different forms and styles . . .
alternating and overlapping in no particular order and with no . . .
appearance of either a conventional linear narrative in the mode of
realism, or a consistent symbolic line in the mode of allegory" (190).
As if parodically anticipating later critics, Wilde, in a letter to the
editor of the *Daily Chronicle,* called *Dorian Gray* "an essay on decorative art" (qtd. in Ellmann 321).

   Mindful of Jerusha McCormack's warning that "it is hard to say
anything original about *The Picture of Dorian Gray,* largely because
there is so little that is original in it" (110), I have no desire to ref-
eree this debate or to offer my own candidate for the true genre of
Dorian Gray. Nevertheless, I hope to shed some new light on the

conflicting readings of the novel's generic affiliations, as well as on its meaning and artistic success, by arguing that *The Picture of Dorian Gray* is neither governed by a single unifying genre nor dispersed intertextually (and unoriginally) among multiple heterogeneous ones, but rather is disjunctively situated between two conflicting genres, each of which is related to one of the two antithetical literary and cultural discourses that the novel engages but cannot successfully integrate: namely, self-development (including what we would today call "sexual liberation") and Gothic degeneration. The degeneration theme links the novel generically to such other *fin-de-siècle* Gothic stories as Robert Louis Stevenson's *Strange Case of Dr. Jekyll and Mr. Hyde* (1886) and Arthur Machen's *The Great God Pan* (1894), while the self-development theme relates it to the novel of self-development, of which Walter Pater's *Marius the Epicurian* (1885) and the unfinished *Gaston de Latour* (1888) are perhaps the most obvious generic models, given Pater's acknowledged influence on Wilde.

The novel's indebtedness to Pater's *Marius the Epicurian* and to the Gothic tradition is well established. In her introduction to the Oxford English Novels edition of *Dorian Gray* (1974), Isobel Murray argues that Wilde is "combining two fairly well known traditions, the 'Gothick' one of, for example, Maturin's *Melmoth the Wanderer* and Poe's 'The Oval Portrait', and the 'decadent' one of Gautier's *Mademoiselle de Maupin,* Huysmans' *À Rebours* and Pater's *Marius the Epicurian*" (xx). I agree that the intertexts Murray identifies are present in *Dorian Gray,* but, in my view, the Gothic texts most relevant to Wilde's novel are not the earlier ones of Maturin (to whom Wilde was distantly related) and Poe, but the contemporary *fin-de-siècle* Gothic tales of Stevenson, Machen, Wells, and Stoker, among which David Punter places it in his study *The Literature of Terror* (1980). "One thing can be said at the outset which underlies the meaning of decadence in connexion with these texts," says Punter about the Gothic revival, "and that is that they are all concerned in one way or another with the problem of degeneration" (239). Decadence and degeneration in *Dorian Gray* are thus related primarily to *fin-de-siècle* Gothic rather than to the Paterian novel of self-development. As I hope to show, however, the Gothic plot of *Dorian Gray* is ultimately inconsistent with the Paterian plot of self-development, for the twin themes of self-development and degeneration are antithetical, if not contradictory, suggesting as they do positive and negative movements, respectively. These double genres—the literary and the popular—create generic dissonances as the Gothic plot of degeneration takes over and eventually supersedes the incompatible Paterian plot of self-development and individual liberation. The "Gothic" Wilde thus finds himself committed to the implications of a narrative of degeneration that undercuts the Paterian ideal of self-development posited by Lord Henry in the early chapters. In particular, the goal of (homo) sexual liberation promised by the self-development plot is subverted by the necessity, within the conventions of the *fin-de-siècle* Gothic tale of degeneration, of seeing Dorian's emerging homosexuality, along with his other crimes and sins, as further evidence of his degeneration. Jeremy Reed, in his introduction to a recent edition of *Dorian Gray,* places the novel in a tradition of subversive fiction: "One could justifiably argue for Oscar Wilde's *The Picture of Dorian Gray* comprising a blueprint for the subversive genre of fiction which in the 20th century has counted amongst its numbers the works of Jean Genet, William Burroughs, and J. G. Ballard" (5). But much as I would like to see Wilde as fathering such a tradition—and there can be little doubt that *Dorian Gray* is a subversive work—I believe that the potentially subversive homosexual plot of the novel is itself seriously, even fatally, subverted by the association between homosexuality and degeneration required by the Gothic plot.

The early chapters of *Dorian Gray* are dominated by the Paterian self-development plot, so much so that Isobel Murray classifies the novel as the story of "the growth, education and development of an exceptional youth, who through personalities, a book, a picture, is moulded or moulds himself, discovering himself what he believes in" (viii). The first half of the novel is certainly indebted to the *Bildungsroman.* Wilde's preoccupation with the idea of self-development is clearly evident from the works he published as he wrote and then revised *Dorian Gray.* Four months before the novel appeared in *Lippincott's Monthly Magazine,* Wilde reviewed a translation of the writings of the Chinese philosopher Chuang Tsu. In "A Chinese Sage" (published in *The Speaker,* February 8, 1890), Wilde wrote,

> It may be true that the ideal of self-culture and self-development, which is the aim of his scheme of life, and the basis of his scheme of philosophy, is an ideal somewhat needed by an age like ours, in which most people are so anxious to educate their neighbours that they have actually no time left in which to educate themselves. (*Soul of Man* 294–95)

But it is in "The Soul of Man Under Socialism," his most important and ambitious essay on culture and politics, that Wilde most fully explores the issue of self-development, or what he calls "Individualism." In that essay, which appeared in *The Fortnightly Review* in February 1891 while he was revising *Dorian Gray,* Wilde explores the political conditions of self-development. As Jonathan Dollimore points out, individualism for Wilde "is both desire for a radical personal freedom and a desire for society itself to be radically different, the first being inseparable from the second" (41). Sounding like a socialist Lord Henry, Wilde expresses his regret "that society should be constructed on such a basis that man has been forced into a groove in which he cannot freely develop what is wonderful, and fascinating, and delightful in him—in which, in fact, he misses the true pleasure and joy of living" (*Soul of Man* 255).

In keeping with Wilde's project of self-development, the opening chapters of *Dorian Gray* focus on the innocent Dorian's awakening, under the twin influences of Basil's homoerotic painting and Lord Henry's subversive philosophy, into "the true pleasure and joy of living":

> He [Dorian] was dimly conscious that entirely fresh impulses were at work within him, and they seemed to him to have come really from himself. The few words that Basil's friend had said to him—words spoken by chance, no doubt, and with willful paradox in them—had yet touched some secret chord, that had never been touched before, but that he felt was now vibrating and throbbing to curious pulses. (*DG* 90: 201)

Moreover, words such as "vibrating," "throbbing," "secret chord," "curious pulses" (and "impulses," changed to *influences* in *DG* 91) all suggest that, as recent critics have argued, a central element of that development is Dorian's discovery of his own homosexuality.[3] "By projecting the revelation, growth, and demise of Dorian's 'personality' onto an aesthetic consideration of artistic creation," says Ed Cohen, "Wilde demonstrates how the psychosexual development of an individual gives rise to the 'double consciousness' of a marginalized group" (166–67). It was precisely the explicitness of the homosexual theme, we must not forget, that outraged many early reviewers.

Just how explicitly homoerotic the 1890 version is became readily evident in 1988, when the Norton Critical Edition printed both the 1890 *Lippincott's* version and the revised (expanded and expurgated) 1891 edition. It is clear, for example, that the reason Hallward does not want to exhibit Dorian's painting is that it discloses Hallward's

---

3. I am, of course, aware of the ongoing debate about the social constructionist theory of gay identity and that some recent Wilde scholars have argued, provocatively if not always convincingly, that modern, post-Stonewall conceptions of gay identity are anachronistic when applied to Wilde and to other homosexuals of the 1890s. For a survey of this important debate, see "Gay, Queer, and Gender Criticism," Chapter 3 of Melissa Knox's *Oscar Wilde in the 1990s* (Rochester, NY: Camden House, 2001), as well as "New Paradigms in Literary & Cultural History," Chapter 3 of Ian Small's *Oscar Wilde: Recent Research* (Greensboro: ELT Press, 2000). Two important books are Ed Cohen's *Talk on the Wilde Side: Toward a Genealogy of a Discourse on Male Sexualities* (New York: Routledge, 1993) and Alan Sinfield's *The Wilde Century: Effeminacy, Oscar Wilde, and the Queer Moment* (New York: Columbia UP, 1994). See also Joseph Bristow's "'A Complex Multiform Creature': Wilde's Sexual Identities" (*The Cambridge Companion to Oscar Wilde*. Ed. Peter Raby. Cambridge: Cambridge UP, 1997. 195–218).

obvious homosexual attraction to Dorian (just as Wilde's novel revealed the sexual inclination of its author). Basil's final declaration of his true feelings for Dorian is unmistakably homoerotic:

> "It is quite true that I have worshipped you with far more romance of feeling than a man usually gives to a friend. Somehow, I had never loved a woman. . . . Well, from the moment I met you, your personality had the most extraordinary influence over me. I quite admit that I adored you madly, extravagantly, absurdly. I was jealous of every one to whom you spoke. I wanted to have you all to myself. I was only happy when I was with you. When I was away from you, you were still present in my art. It was all wrong and foolish. It is all wrong and foolish still. Of course I never let you know anything about this. It would have been impossible. You would not have understood it; I did not understand it myself." (*DG* 90: 251–52)

In contrast to Hallward's repression of his sexual attraction to Dorian (sublimated through art), Lord Henry's philosophy of unfettered self-development can be read as an implicit recommendation to homosexuals to realize their true being, despite the misguided restraints of society and religion. "The aim of life is self-development," he tells Dorian:

> "To realize one's nature perfectly,—that is what each of us is here for. People are afraid of themselves nowadays. They have forgotten the highest of all duties, the duty that one owes to one's self. . . . The terror of society, which is the basis of morals, the terror of God, which is the secret of religion—these are the two things that govern us." (*DG* 90: 200–01)

Furthermore, Lord Henry explicitly links the quest for self-development, "the duty that one owes to one's self," to an attack on restrictive *laws,* and, in the homosexual context of the scene, it would be hard not to see his words—especially "monstrous laws"—as alluding to the Labouchère Amendment to *The Criminal Law Amendment Act* (1885), which criminalized private consensual sexual acts between adult males:

> "I believe that if one man were to live his life out fully and completely, were to give form to every feeling, expression to every thought, reality to every dream,—I believe that the world would gain such a fresh impulse of joy that we would forget all the maladies of mediævalism, and return to the Hellenic ideal,—to something finer, richer, than the Hellenic ideal, it may be. But the bravest man among us is afraid of himself. The mutilation of the savage has its tragic survival in the self-denial that mars our lives. We are punished for our refusals. Every impulse

that we strive to strangle broods in the mind, and poisons us. . . . The only way to get rid of a temptation is to yield to it. Resist it, and your soul grows sick with longing for the things it has forbidden to itself, with desire for what its monstrous laws have made monstrous and unlawful." (*DG* 90: 201)

It is hard to imagine that a sophisticated homosexual man reading Lord Henry's subversive words in 1890 would not see their immediate and obvious relevance to his own life, regardless of what other meanings could legitimately be attributed to them. Society's "monstrous laws" have made male-to-male sex "monstrous and unlawful," and the "self-denial that mars our lives" includes the denial of those sexual impulses that are not monstrous in themselves, but made monstrous only by monstrous laws. Moreover, Lord Henry's opposition between mediævalism and "the Hellenic ideal" echoes the terms in which contemporary apologies for homosexuality were argued.[4] Even more importantly, Lord Henry articulates here an early theory of the evils of repression. For it is the *repression* of same-sex sexuality, and not the sexual acts themselves, that poisons and mutilates the mind and the soul. Consequently, liberation from that repression is seen as necessary for the full development of the individual personality. John Addington Symonds expressed a similar view in *A Problem in Modern Ethics,* his apologia for homosexuality published in 1891: "It is this forcible suppression of an instinct so deeply rooted in our nature," he argued, "which first originates the morbid symptoms, that may often be observed in Urnings [sexual inverts]" (70).

Lord Henry's liberationist project, when applied to Dorian's sexual development, however, encounters a major obstacle: in Victorian society, especially after the Labouchère Amendment, it could be carried out only in secrecy. As Symonds points out,

> [T]he comrades [in a homosexual relationship] are continually forced to hide their *liaison;* their anxiety on this point is incessant; anything like an excessive intimacy, which could arouse suspicion (especially when they are not of the same age, or do

4. In *Hellenism and Homosexuality in Victorian Oxford,* Linda Dowling argues that modern male homosexual identity is partly an unintended consequence of the efforts of such Oxford Hellenists as Benjamin Jowett to establish a new Hellenism as "a ground of transcendent value alternative to Christianity." These reformers enabled Pater, Wilde, and others to formulate "a homosexual counterdiscourse able to justify male love in ideal or transcendental terms: the 'spiritual procreancy' associated specifically with Plato's *Symposium* and more generally with ancient Greece itself" (xii). In *Cultures of Darkness,* Bryan D. Palmer says "A textual, often artistic, sensibility—an enlightening idealization of masculine desire—wrote and sculpted itself across the standards of beauty in ways that legitimated homoeroticism by equating it with classicalism" (286). In "The Critic as Artist," Wilde wrote, "Whatever, in fact, is modern in our life, we owe to the Greeks. Whatever is an anachronism is due to mediævalism" (*Soul of Man* 118).

not belong to the same class in society), has to be concealed from the external world. In this way, the very commencement of the relation sets a whole chain of exciting incidents in motion; and the dread lest the secret should be betrayed or divined, prevents the unfortunate lover[s] from ever arriving at a simple happiness. (*Problem* 72)

Now the self-development novel does not generically require that its protagonist lead a double life: Pater's heroes—Marius and Gaston—do not. But the homosexual theme of Wilde's novel does require that Dorian live a double life. The theme of the double had, of course, long been associated with the Gothic novel, and just four years before *Dorian Gray* was published there appeared the classic novel of the double life, Robert Louis Stevenson's *Strange Case of Dr. Jekyll and Mr. Hyde* (1886). Early reviewers of *Dorian Gray* noted the obvious parallels with *Jekyll and Hyde,* and later critics have pointed to Stevenson's Gothic "shilling shocker" as a likely source.[5] Stevenson's sensational tale of the double self would certainly have resonated particularly strongly with Wilde and other members of the homosexual subculture that was emerging in London at the end of the nineteenth century. Lord Alfred Douglas's infatuation with the novel—he read it, on different estimates, nine or fourteen times *before* he met Wilde—certainly attests to its immediate appeal to homosexuals (D. Murray 32). By the 1880s, as such scholars as Jeffrey Weeks, Richard Dellamora, and Elaine Showalter have documented,

> the Victorian homosexual world had evolved into a secret but active subculture, with its own language, styles, practices, and meeting places. For most middle-class inhabitants of this world, homosexuality represented a double life, in which a respectable daytime world often involving marriage and family, existed alongside a night world of homoeroticism. (Showalter 10)

Dr. Jekyll's account of his youth, in particular, is described in a way that must have struck a responsive chord in contemporary homosexual readers struggling against what conventional morality—and more

---

5. Early filmmakers also saw a link between *Jekyll and Hyde* and *Dorian Gray*. In 1920 Famous Players-Lasky brought out a version starring John Barrymore and directed by John S. Robertson from a screenplay by Clara S. Beranger. Beranger borrowed the Sybil Vane sub-plot from Wilde's novel and grafted it seamlessly into Stevenson's story. As Mr. Hyde, Dr. Jekyll seduces and kills a young actress. The fatal seduction of a dance-hall girl became a standard convention of nearly all later *Jekyll and Hyde* movies. When *Dorian Gray* was finally filmed by MGM in 1945, the character of Sybil Vane was reduced from a Shakespearean actress to a music-hall Cockney, as if to bring the story more in line with the conventions established by the film adaptations of *Jekyll and Hyde*.

recently the law—regarded as "irregularities" and "degradation," and who were forced, as a result of their dual nature, to "conceal" their "pleasures":

> And indeed the worst of my faults was a certain impatient gaiety of disposition, such as . . . I found it hard to reconcile with my imperious desire to carry my head high, and wear a more than commonly grave countenance before the public. Hence it came about that I concealed my pleasures; and that when I reached years of reflection . . . I stood already committed to a profound duplicity of life.

He goes on to refer to "such irregularities as [he] was guilty of," adding that he

> regarded and hid them with an almost morbid sense of shame. . . . I was driven to reflect deeply and inveterately on that hard law of life, which lies at the root of religion and is one of the most plentiful springs of distress. Though so profound a double-dealer, I was in no sense a hypocrite; both sides of me were in dead earnest; I was no more myself when I laid aside the restraint and plunged in shame, than when I laboured, in the eye of day, at the furtherance of knowledge or the relief of sorrow and suffering. (Stevenson 75–76)

Jekyll's language here—"concealed my pleasures," "profound duplicity of life," "so profound a double-dealer," "laid aside the restraint and plunged in shame"—would certainly not be out of place in *Dorian Gray,* and a "profound duplicity of life" combined with a "morbid sense of shame" perfectly describes the lives of many gay men at the time. Later in his "statement of the case," Jekyll describes the feeling of liberation that accompanies his transformation:

> Men have before hired bravos to transact their crimes, while their own person and reputation sat under shelter. I was the first that ever did so for his pleasures. I was the first that could plod in the public eye with a load of genial respectability, and in a moment, like a schoolboy, strip off these lendings, and spring headlong into the sea of liberty. (80–81)

What Jekyll has accomplished through science is what many contemporary homosexual men desired: the ability to safely lead a double life. They, too, longed to "plod in the public eye with a load of genial respectability" and then be able to "strip off" their conventional respectability and "spring headlong into the sea of liberty." Indeed, that is precisely what Wilde and Lord Alfred Douglas did—with ever increasing recklessness.

As Elaine Showalter has pointed out, the homosexual nature of Hyde's pleasures is even more strongly hinted at in the manuscript of the novel:

> In his original draft of the manuscript, Stevenson was more explicit about the sexual practices that had driven Jekyll to a double life. Jekyll has become "from an early age . . . the slave of certain appetites," vices which are "at once criminal in the sight of the law and abhorrent in themselves. They cut me off from the sympathy of those whom I otherwise respected." (112)

Whatever Stevenson's own sexuality,[6] Showalter is surely right when she says "Stevenson was the *fin-de-siècle* laureate of the double life" (106). The description of Jekyll's appetites as "criminal in the sight of the law" is especially revealing when we realize that the novel was published in the same month as *The Criminal Law Amendment Act* went into effect. Many homosexual readers of the novel in early 1886 must have linked it to the public debate on criminalizing private male-to-male sexual acts and to their own double lives. Even if a modern "gay" sexual identity was still embryonic, it is hard to believe that members of this subculture could have read *Jekyll and Hyde* without seeing the relevance of Jekyll's double life to their own lives. So when Wilde came to write *Dorian Gray*—the story of a man who "felt keenly the terrible pleasure of a double life" (*DG* 91: 146)— he would have found in *Jekyll and Hyde* a recent model for using Gothic fiction to explore the double lives of closeted homosexuals in late-Victorian England.

In addition to the obvious Gothic theme of the double, Wilde adapts—and modifies—several other conventions of earlier Gothic fiction. In *Art of Darkness: A Poetics of Gothic,* Anne Williams identifies several conventions "familiar in gothic narratives from Walpole to the present: a vulnerable and curious heroine; a wealthy, arbitrary, and enigmatic hero/villain; and a grand, mysterious dwelling concealing the violent, implicitly sexual secrets of this *homme fatal*" (38). Wilde transforms the innocent heroine into the (initially) innocent Dorian; the wealthy and enigmatic hero/villain into the wealthy, aesthetic, and epigrammatic Lord Henry (who, Satan-like, tempts Dorian in Basil's garden); and the mysterious dwelling concealing violent, implicitly *sexual* secrets into Dorian's townhouse with the locked attic that hides his not so implicitly sexual secret. (The word

---

6. Wayne Koestenbaum says that "Stevenson served as a lightning rod for the fantasies of other male writers, some of whom were self-identified homosexuals" (33). John Addington Symonds placed Stevenson among those men whom he believed "have been, all of them, more or less sealed of the tribe of W[alt] W[hitman]" (Letter from Symonds to Herbert Harlakenden Gilchrist, 14 September 1885. *Letters* 77).

secret occurs 37 times in the novel.) Wilde also appropriates a convention common to *Frankenstein, Jekyll and Hyde,* and *The Great God Pan:* the scientific experiment with unexpectedly horrific consequences. In *Jekyll and Hyde* an experiment transforms Jekyll's personality. Wilde's novel is also the story of an experiment: Dorian's development is explicitly characterized as the result of an experiment that Lord Henry, the Gothic scientist in the role of decadent aesthete, performs on the young Dorian. Lord Henry

> had been always enthralled by the methods of science, but the ordinary subject-matter of science had seemed to him trivial and of no import. And so he had begun by vivisecting himself, as he had ended by vivisecting others. Human life,—that appeared to him the one thing worth investigating. (*DG* 90: 220)

And so Dorian becomes the subject of his unusual experiment:

> To a large extent the lad was his [Wotton's] own creation. He had made him premature. That was something . . . Yes, the lad was premature. He was gathering harvest while it was yet spring. The pulse and passion of youth were in him, but he was becoming self-conscious. It was delightful to watch him. (*DG* 90: 221)

The last line in particular suggests the empirical pose of the disinterested scientist. A few lines later, the narrator adds, "It was clear to him [Lord Henry] that *the experimental method* was the only method by which one could arrive at any *scientific analysis* of the passions; and certainly Dorian Gray was a subject made to hand, and seemed to promise rich and fruitful results" (*DG* 90: 222; italics added). Later Lord Henry says that "[Dorian] would be a wonderful study" (*DG* 90: 224). Lord Henry's effort "to project [his] soul into" Dorian's "gracious form" is described (in the 1891 edition) through a metaphor of chemical infusion: "to convey one's temperament into another as though it were a subtle fluid" (*DG* 91: 34)—just like the draught that changes Jekyll into Hyde. In *Jekyll and Hyde,* of course, the experimenter and the subject of the experiment are the same person; Wilde separates them into two characters. He also changes the mode of the transformation from science to art, and the location from the laboratory to the artist's studio. Art replaces science, hence the dominant role that works of art and books play in Wilde's novel, especially the "poisonous" book that acts like Jekyll's mysterious chemical agent.

Even more important than either these borrowings or the theme of the double is yet another convention of Gothic fiction that Wilde would have found particularly suitable to his project in *Dorian Gray:* the perennial Gothic theme of transgression. Since Lord Henry's theory of liberation from repression leading to self-realization requires transgression of existing social, moral, religious, and especially legal codes, Wilde needed a plot that could combine self-development with transgression, the later being a necessary precondition of the former. Since its beginnings in Walpole, Gothic fiction has always been a transgressive genre; as Kelly Hurley reminds us, "Gothic provided a space wherein to explore phenomena at the borders of human identity and culture—insanity, criminality, barbarity, sexual perversion" (6). This transgressiveness coincides with Wilde's own anti-authoritarian ideas expressed in his essays at this time. "Disobedience, in the eyes of anyone who has read history," he says in "The Soul of Man Under Socialism," "is man's original virtue. It is through disobedience that progress has been made, through disobedience and through rebellion" (*Soul of Man* 231). In "The Critic as Artist," the first part of which appeared in *The Nineteenth Century* in the same month that *Dorian Gray* appeared in *Lippincott's,* Gilbert, Wilde's spokesman, says,

> What is termed Sin is an essential element of progress. Without it the world would stagnate, or grow old, or become colourless. By its curiosity Sin increases the experience of the race. Through its intensified assertion of individualism it saves us from monotony of type. In its rejection of the current notions about morality, it is one with the higher ethics. . . . Self-denial is simply a method by which man arrests his progress, and self-sacrifice a survival of the mutilation of the savage, part of that old worship of pain which is so terrible a factor in the history of the world. (*Soul of Man* 125–126)

The first half of this passage could easily be Lord Henry's project for Dorian's self-realization, and the last lines actually echo Lord Henry's own words: "The mutilation of the savage has its tragic survival in the self-denial that mars our lives" (*DG* 90: 201). In Wilde's view, says Richard Ellmann, "Sin is more useful to society than martyrdom, since it is self-expressive not self-repressive. The goal is the liberation of the personality" (310). "One can fancy an intense personality being created out of sin," Wilde wrote in "Pen, Pencil, and Poison" (*Soul of Man* 103). Since "Wilde's notion of individualism," as Jonathan Dollimore explains, "is inseparable from transgressive desire and a transgressive aesthetic" (40), and since the Gothic portrays sin as self-expressive, not self-repressive, it is hardly surprising that Wilde would have found the Gothic aesthetically appealing. The problem is that *fin-de-siècle* Gothic texts like *Jekyll and Hyde* and *The Great God Pan* include not just the traditional Gothic theme of transgression but also the *fin-de-siècle* theme of degeneration, and the discourse of degeneration on which these texts draw is, quite simply, incompatible with the Paterian goal of self-development.

"Degenerationism," says Kelly Hurley in *The Gothic Body: Sexuality, Materialism, and Degeneration at the* Fin de Siècle, "is a 'gothic' discourse, and as such is a crucial imaginative and narrative source for the *fin-de-siècle* Gothic" (65). When viewed from the perspective of such *fin-de-siècle* Gothic texts as *Jekyll and Hyde* and Arthur Machen's *The Great God Pan*, the corruption mirrored in Dorian's picture is not so much "a visible symbol of the degradation of sin" (*DG* 90: 238) as it is a sign of his degeneration.[7] *The Great God Pan* was published as a novella in 1894 by John Lane, who also published Wilde's *Salomé*, but an extract from it had appeared in December 1890 in a short-lived magazine called *Whirlwind*. In Machen's Gothic tale of degeneration, a doctor performs an experiment designed to open a young girl's "inner eye" to the continuing presence of the Great God Pan. Although the girl dies, the experiment succeeds and she gives birth to a child, Helen, the result of her mother's coupling with the primordial Pan. Helen, who then becomes the focus of the story, reveals to a series of admiring men the horror that lies beneath the surface of their conventional lives, driving them to madness and death. When Helen dies, she degenerates, passing through all the stages of evolution as she reverts to the primordial slime. "The paradox of *The Great God Pan*," says Punter, "is that the visitation which liberates the human being from the repression of false assumptions also destroys the barriers which retain human individuation: the liberation of desire returns man to his primal associations with the beast and destroys the soul" (264).

A similar paradox of sexual liberation leading to destruction and degeneration takes place in *Dorian Gray*. Like Dorian, Helen—that both have Greek names cannot be accidental—seduces her male victims and then reveals to them something so horrible that they go mad and commit suicide. (Helen Vaughan's victims commit suicide when they learn her unspeakable secret; Dr. Lanyon dies of shock when he learns Dr. Jekyll's secret; and Alan Campbell commits suicide after he disposes of Basil Hallward's body by decomposing it in acid.) Dorian exercises a fatal sexual power over young men, especially young aristocrats. In his final, fatal confrontation with Dorian, Hallward asks,

7. For alternative readings of the Gothic in *Dorian Gray*, see Donald Lawler's "The Gothic Wilde" (*Rediscovering Oscar Wilde*. Ed. C. George Sandulescu. Gerrards Cross: Colin Smythe, 1994. 249–68), and Kenneth Womack's "'Withered, Wrinkled, and Loathsome of Visage': Reading the Ethics of the Soul and the Late-Victorian Gothic in *The Picture of Dorian Gray*" (*Victorian Gothic: Literary and Cultural Manifestations in the Nineteenth Century*. Ed. Ruth Robbins and Julian Wolfreys. New York: Palgrave, 2000. 168–81).

"Why is your friendship so fateful to young men? There was that wretched boy in the Guards who committed suicide. You were his great friend. There was Sir Henry Ashton, who had to leave England, with a tarnished name. You and he were inseparable. What about Adrian Singleton, and his dreadful end? What about Lord Kent's only son, and his career? . . . What about the young Duke of Perth? What sort of life has he got now? What gentleman would associate with him? Dorian, Dorian, your reputation is infamous. . . . They say that you corrupt everyone whom you become intimate with." (*DG* 90: 279–80)

Although Helen's power is unspecified in the text, it is, like Dorian's, obviously sexual. "I knew I had looked into the eyes of a lost soul," says a witness to Helen's power; "the man's outward form remained, but all hell was within it. Furious lust, and hate that was like fire, and the loss of all hope and horror that seemed to shriek aloud in the night, though his teeth were shut; and the utter blackness of despair" (Machen 97). Dorian's "outward form" (his youthful beauty) also remains, but his "lost soul," mirrored in the picture, shrieks its black despair to Hallward, who recoils in horror:

An exclamation of horror broke from Hallward's lips as he saw in the dim light the hideous thing on the canvas leering at him. There was something in its expression that filled him with disgust and loathing. Good heavens! It was Dorian Gray's own face that he was looking at! The horror, whatever it was, had not yet entirely marred that marvellous beauty. (*DG* 90: 283)

The paradox of beauty and repulsiveness in Dorian is also present in Helen Vaughan: "Every one who saw her at the police court said she was at once *the most beautiful woman and the most repulsive* they had ever set eyes on. I have spoken to a man who saw her, and I assure you he positively shuddered as he tried to describe the woman, but he couldn't tell why" (Machen 64; italics added).

The Gothic plot in *Dorian Gray,* then, is the typical plot of *fin-de-siècle* Gothic—degeneration from a higher to a lower state, from the well-formed, respectable, upper-class Dr. Jekyll to the bestial, murderous, lower-class Hyde. As Stephen Arata has observed, "*Jekyll and Hyde* articulates in Gothic fiction's exaggerated tones late-Victorian anxieties concerning degeneration, devolution, and 'criminal man'" (233). When Dr. Jekyll metamorphoses into Mr. Hyde, he degenerates to a lower, more primitive form of existence, a degeneration signaled in the novel by the repeated comparisons of him to an ape. Dorian similarly degenerates to a lower, bestial level of existence. He hides the portrait in the attic, where "the face painted on the canvas could grow *bestial,* sodden, and unclean" (*DG* 90: 258; italics added). Dorian's descent into the Victorian underworld of criminality, drugs, and sexual depravity is portrayed in language similar to that describing Hyde's parallel excursions into the same nether regions:

> He [Dorian] remembered wandering through dimly-lit streets with gaunt black-shadowed archways and evil-looking houses. Women with hoarse voices and harsh laughter had called after him. Drunkards had reeled by cursing, and chattering to themselves *like monstrous apes*. He had seen grotesque children huddled upon doorsteps, and had heard shrieks and oaths from gloomy courts. (*DG* 90: 233; italics added)

The lower classes are described as ape-like, and by his increasing association with them, Dorian becomes bestial and ape-like, too. (Not insignificantly, the word *monstrous* occurs over twenty times in the novel.) As Joseph Bristow has perceptively remarked, Dorian's personality, like that of Jekyll/Hyde, is divided between upper and lower classes as much as between good and evil: "Dorian wears a fine aristocratic face but possesses what may be referred to as a working-class (debased, gross, indecent) body, as he moves across and between different echelons of society" (60). (Wilde's own sexual encounters, it is worth recalling, were primarily with lower-class youths.)

In addition to its affinities with the degenerationist themes of contemporary Gothic fiction, *Dorian Gray* also shows unmistakable traces of contemporary non-fictional degenerationist writings, especially Richard von Krafft-Ebing's theory of the etiology of sexual perversion, specifically homosexuality. Krafft-Ebing's *Psychopathia Sexualis, with Especial Reference to Contrary Sexual Instinct: A Clinical Forensic Study*, first published in German in 1886 and translated into English in 1892, offered an exhaustive catalogue—238 cases by the twelfth edition—of sexual variations. It established the new discipline of *Sexualwissenschaft* and created the paradigm, namely the case study, for sexological research for the rest of the century. As Sam Binkley points out, Krafft-Ebing's theory of sexual deviancy was part of the larger cultural discourse of degeneration:

> Krafft-Ebing's thesis on degeneracy attributed the nebulous causes of [cultural] decline to the sexual behavior and condition of a morbid type, an invert, whose moral character was depleted by the same corrosive social forces and technological changes that had eroded and shaken the moral authority of the West. (88)

Krafft-Ebing believed that most homosexuals—a term he popularized—had a mental disease caused by hereditary degeneration, although environmental factors could influence this inborn neuropathic disposition, or "taint" as he repeatedly called it:

Since, in nearly all such cases, the individual tainted with antipathic sexual instinct displays a neuropathic predisposition in several directions, and the neuropathic predisposition may be related to hereditary degenerate conditions, this anomaly of psychosexual feeling may be clinically called a functional sign of degeneration. This inverted sexuality appears spontaneously, without external cause, with the development of sexual life as an individual manifestation of an abnormal form of sexual life, and has the force of a *congenital* phenomenon; or it develops upon a sexuality which in the beginning was normal, as a result of definite injurious influences, and thus appears as an *acquired* anomaly. Upon what conditions this enigmatic phenomenon of acquired homosexual instinct depends still remains unexplained, and is a mere hypothetical matter. Careful examination of the so-called acquired cases make it probable that predisposition—also present here—consists of a latent homosexuality, or, at least, bisexuality, which, for it to become manifest, requires the influence of accidental stimulating causes to rouse it from its dormant state. (Krafft-Ebing 239)

This model of a hereditary degenerative predisposition combined with "injurious influences" is certainly consistent with Wilde's representation of Dorian and his degeneration, which appears to be the result both of malign influence (Lord Henry's theories, the "poisonous book") and of "tainted" heredity. Read in the context of Krafft-Ebing's theories of a congenital neuropatic predisposition to degeneracy, Dorian's speculation that his "very flesh was *tainted* with the monstrous maladies of the dead" (*DG* 90: 274; italics added) is not only a *fin-de-siècle* version of what Richard Davenport-Hines calls "[G]othic's obsession with family secrets and hereditary doom" (11) but also evidence of the extent to which degenerationist discourse has penetrated Wilde's text. Significantly, the words "taint" and "tainted" are Krafft-Ebing's favorite ones for attributing hereditary causes to all types of sexual deviancy: "heavily tainted by heredity" (363); "hereditary taint" (571); "mother deeply tainted" (472); "heavily tainted by heredity" (468); "tainted by heredity" (465); "from a tainted family" (387); "probably from a tainted family" (273); "from a badly tainted family" (618); "hereditarily tainted" (60). In *The Pathology of Mind* (1895), Henry Maudsley claimed that "beneath every face are the latent faces of ancestors, beneath every character their characters" (48). When viewed from these perspectives, Dorian's speculations about his ancestors' influences on him are further evidence of degenerationist discourse in the novel:

He loved to . . . look at the various portraits of those whose blood flowed in his veins. Here was Philip Herbert, described by Francis Osborne, in his "Memoires of the Reigns of Queen Elizabeth and King James," as one who was "caressed by the court for his handsome face, which kept him not long company." Was it young Herbert's life that he sometimes led? Had some *strange poisonous germ* crept from body to body till it had reached his own? (*DG* 90: 274; italics added)

(Osborne's original text, revealingly, reads "caressed by KING JAMES for his handsome face" [I. Murray 246], clearly an allusion to James's homosexuality.) Of his ancestor Sir Anthony Sherard, Dorian wonders, "What had this man's legacy been? Had the lover of Giovanna of Naples bequeathed him some inheritance of sin and shame? Were his [Dorian's] own actions merely the dreams that the dead man had not dared to realize?" (*DG* 90: 274). And what of Lady Elizabeth Devereux? "He knew her life, and the strange stories that were told about her lovers. Had he something of her temperament in him?" (*DG* 90: 274). In particular, the use of *poisonous* here, paralleling Dorian's later application of it to the book Lord Henry gives him, implies that his degeneration is both intrinsic and acquired.

But it was not just degenerationists who attributed sexual deviation to hereditary "taint" or predisposition. Even John Addington Symonds, who in *A Problem in Modern Ethics* explicitly challenged Krafft-Ebing's theories, held that some forms of sexual inversion are inheritable:

> That sexual inversion may be and actually is transmitted, like any other quality, appears to be proved by the history of well-known families both in England and in Germany. That it is not unfrequently exhibited by persons who have a bad ancestral record, may be taken for demonstrated. (49)

Clearly, this degenerationist discourse has seeped into *Dorian Gray*.

The problem with representing Dorian's career through the language of contemporary degenerationist discourse is that doing so undermines the liberationist programme articulated by Lord Henry early in the novel. In Chapter 2, Lord Henry sees degeneration as the consequence of repressing our desires: "The pulse of joy that beats in us at twenty," he tells Dorian, "becomes sluggish. Our limbs fail, our senses rot. We *degenerate* into hideous puppets, haunted by the memory of the passions of which we were too much afraid, and the exquisite temptations that we did not dare to yield to" (*DG* 90: 205; italics added). For Lord Henry, the price of *not* rebelling against repression is degeneration, and so he recommends the Paterian ideal of self-realization. As his other writings show, Wilde certainly believed in this ideal. But he also believed that transgression and disobedience are necessary to achieve it. Wilde's theory of self-development (individualism) requires the transgressiveness of crime: "Like Jean Genet after him," says Richard Ellmann, "[Wilde] proposed an analogy between the criminal and the artist. . . . Rebelliousness and extravagance are needed if society's moulds are to be broken, as broken they must be. Art is by nature dissident" (330). "It is well for our vanity that we slay the criminal," Wilde writes in "The Critic as Artist," "for if we suffered him to live he might show us what we had gained by his crime" (*Soul of Man* 126). But the plot in which Wilde finds it necessary to embody that rebellion, a plot common to the novels of the recent Gothic revival, is one that could represent Hyde-like degeneration as the *only* alternative to a Jekyll-like life of conformity and repression. And so *all* forms of transgression, including homosexuality, become, within the conventions of that plot, signs of degeneration. "In the loosening of moral, aesthetic and sexual codes associated with *fin-de-siècle* decadence," writes Fred Botting, "the spectre of homosexuality as narcissistic, sensually indulgent and unnaturally perverse, constituted a form of deviance that signalled the irruption of regressive patterns of behaviour" (138). Transgression, what Wilde calls sin and disobedience, is first posited as necessary for self-development to take place, but is then, in compliance with the Gothic plot, shown to lead inevitably to degeneration. And while the Paterian plot of *Dorian Gray* condemns the laws that criminalize transgressive sexual acts, the Gothic degenerationist plot requires that homosexual acts be a sin and a crime from which nothing can be gained. Thus *Dorian Gray*, like most *fin-de-siècle* Gothic fictions, is pessimistic that crime can lead to gain. According to Punter, the "underlying pessimism" of *Jekyll and Hyde* "results from Stevenson's difficulty in seeing any alternative structure for the psyche: once the beast is loose, it can resolve itself only in death" (244). Similarly, in *Dorian Gray* Wilde cannot imagine any alternative to repression other than degeneration—and finally death. "Gothic," pronounces Richard Davenport-Hines, "is nothing if not hostile to progressive hopes" (4). The Gothic plot in *Dorian Gray* is ultimately hostile to the progressive hopes held out by the Paterian plot of self-actualization.

"Any attempt to extend the subject matter of art," wrote Wilde in "The Soul of Man Under Socialism," "is extremely distasteful to the public, and yet the vitality and progress of art depend in large measure on the continual extension of subject matter" (*Soul of Man* 249). *The Picture of Dorian Gray* is a provocative and important work, and in it Wilde indisputably extended the subject matter of the English novel. After June 20, 1890, the date the July issue of *Lippincott's Monthly Magazine* appeared, "Victorian literature had a different look" (Ellmann 314). But *Dorian Gray* is also a flawed work, riven by generic dissonances. The incompatibility of the novel's double genre undermines Wilde's attempt to tell a subsversive story of dissidence and transgression leading to self-development and liberation.

WORKS CITED

Arata, Stephen D. "The Sedulous Ape: Atavism, Professionalism, and Stevenson's *Jekyll and Hyde.*" *Criticism* 37.2 (Spring 1995): 233–59.

Binkley, Sam. "The Romantic Sexology of John Addington Symonds." *Journal of Homosexuality* 40.1 (2000): 79–104.

Botting, Fred. *Gothic.* London: Routledge, 1996.

Bowlby, Rachel. "Promoting Dorian Gray." Freedman 178–92.

Bristow, Joseph. "Wilde, *Dorian Gray,* and Gross Indecency." *Sexual Sameness: Textual Differences in Lesbian and Gay Writing.* Ed. Joseph Bristow. London: Routledge, 1992.

Cohen, Ed. "Writing Gone Wilde: Homoerotic Desire in the Closet of Representation." Freedman 158–77.

Davenport-Hines, Richard. *Gothic: Four Hundred Years of Excess, Horror, Evil and Ruin.* New York: North Point Press/Farrar, Straus and Giroux: 1998.

Dollimore, Jonathan. "Different Desires: Subjectivity and Transgression in Wilde and Gide." Freedman 36–54.

Dowling, Linda. *Hellenism and Homosexuality in Victorian Oxford.* Ithaca: Cornell UP, 1994.

Ellmann, Richard. *Oscar Wilde.* New York: Penguin, 1987.

Freedman, Jonathan, ed. *Oscar Wilde: A Collection of Critical Essays.* Upper Saddle River, NJ: Prentice Hall, 1996.

Hurley, Kelly. *The Gothic Body: Sexuality, Materialism, and Degeneration at the Fin de Siècle.* Cambridge: Cambridge UP, 1996.

Koestenbaum, Wayne. "The Shadow on the Bed: Dr. Jekyll, Mr. Hyde, and the Labouchère Amendment." *Critical Matrix* 1 (Spring 1988): 31–55.

Krafft-Ebing, Richard von. *Psychopathia Sexualis, with Especial Reference to Contrary Sexual Instinct: A Clinical Forensic Study.* Trans. and intro. Brian King. Burbank: Bloat, 1999.

Machen, Arthur. *The Great God Pan.* London: Creation Books, 1993.

Maudsley, Henry. *The Pathology of Mind: A Study of its Distempers, Deformities and Disorders.* London: Macmillan, 1895.

McCormack. Jerusha. "Wilde's Fiction(s)." *The Cambridge Companion to Oscar Wilde.* Ed. Peter Raby. Cambridge: Cambridge UP, 1997. 96–117.

Murray, Douglas. *Bosie: A Biography of Lord Alfred Douglas.* New York: Hyperion, 2000.

Murray, Isobel. Introduction. *The Picture of Dorian Gray*. Oxford English Novels. Oxford: Oxford UP, 1974. vii–xvi.

Oates, Joyce Carol. "*The Picture of Dorian Gray*: Wilde's Parable of the Fall." *The Picture of Dorian Gray*. Ed. Donald L. Lawler. New York: W. W. Norton & Company, 1988. 422–31.

Palmer, Bryan D. *Cultures of Darkness*. New York: Monthly Review Press, 2000.

Pearce, Joseph. *The Unmasking of Oscar Wilde*. London: HarperCollins, 2001.

Powell, Kerry. "Tom Dick and Dorian Gray: Magic Picture Mania in Late-Victorian Fiction." *Philological Quarterly* 63.2 (Spring 1983): 147–69.

Punter David. *The Literature of Terror: A History of Gothic Fictions from 1765 to the Present Day*. London: Longman, 1980.

Reed, Jeremy. Introduction. *The Picture of Dorian Gray*. [London]: Creation Books, 2000. 5–14.

Showalter, Elaine. *Sexual Anarchy: Gender and Culture at the Fin de Siècle*. New York: Penguin Books, 1990.

Stevenson, Robert Louis. *The Strange Case of Dr. Jekyll and Mr. Hyde*. Ed. Martin A. Danahay. Peterborough, Ontario: Broadview Press, 1999.

Symonds, John Addington. *The Letters of John Addington Symonds*. Ed. Herbert M. Schueller and Robert L. Peters. Vol. 3. Detroit: Wayne State UP, 1969. 3 vols. 1967–1969.

———. *A Problem in Modern Ethics: Being an Inquiry into the Phenomenon of Sexual Inversion, Addressed Especially to Medical Psychologists and Jurists*. New York: B. Blom, 1971.

Waldrep, Shelton. "The Aesthetic Realism of Oscar Wilde's *Dorian Gray*." *Studies in the Literary Imagination* 29.1 (Spring 1996): 103–12. [Rev. ed. Michael Patrick Gillespie, 2007, 2019.]

Wilde, Oscar. *The Picture of Dorian Gray*. Norton Critical Edition. Ed. Donald L. Lawler. New York: W. W. Norton & Company, 1988.

———. *The Soul of Man Under Socialism and Other Essays*. Intro. Philip Rieff. New York: Harper & Row, 1970.

Williams, Anne. *Art of Darkness: A Poetics of Gothic*. Chicago: U of Chicago P, 1995.

EMILY EELLS

More Than a Coincidence? The Pre-Raphaelites and the Sibyl Vane Subplot of *The Picture of Dorian Gray*[†]

Wilde's youthful enthusiasm for the art of the Pre-Raphaelites is well documented by his biographers who record that Walter Pater commended their aesthetics to him while he was a student at Oxford University.[1] In Wilde's first lecture, given in 1882, he hailed the Pre-Raphaelite movement as a leading force of what he called the 'English Renaissance' and praised its 'passion for physical beauty, its exclusive attention to form, its seeking for new subjects for poetry, new forms of art, new intellectual and imaginative enjoyments'.[2] Although Wilde later lost interest with the Pre-Raphaelites, the formative role their aesthetics played at the beginning of his literary career is evident in the composition of *The Picture of Dorian Gray*. He made his fictitious character Basil Hallward into the mouthpiece of Pre-Raphaelite aesthetics and had Hallward echo his lecture on the 'English Renaissance' when he explains that Dorian Gray represents 'an entirely new manner in art, an entirely new mode of style' (14) [13] and claims that 'there is nothing Art cannot express' (14) [13].[3] Basil's portrait of Dorian can be identified as a work belonging to the Pre-Raphaelite school, thanks to the photographic precision with which it 'skilfully mirrored' the subject (6). The 'most wonderful frame, specially designed' by Basil for Dorian's portrait is another indication that he followed the practice of Pre-Raphaelite artists (63). If Basil's technique can be likened to the hard-edged paintings characterizing the first wave of Pre-Raphaelitism, his veneration of Dorian's physical appearance is suggestive of the aestheticism of the second wave of Pre-Raphaelite painters, although it transposes their love of female beauty into the homosexual sphere.

[†] From *Anglo Saxonica* 2.26 (2008): 257–78. Notes have been renumbered. Page numbers in square brackets are to this Norton Critical Edition. This article is a version of a paper presented at the international seminar *A Palavra e a Imagem* (*Word and Image*) organised by the Modern Difference Programme (University of Lisbon Centre for English Studies, ULICES), Faculty of Letters, Lisbon, December 2005. Reprinted by permission of the publisher, the University of Lisbon Centre for English Studies.
1. See especially Richard Ellmann, *Oscar Wilde* 1987. (Harmondsworth: Penguin Books, 1988), pp. 31–33. On this particular point, see p. 47.
2. *The Collected Works of Oscar Wilde*. Ed. Robert Ross, 15 vols. 1908. (reprinted by Routledge/Thoemmes Press 1993). Vol. 14, p. 243.
3. Oscar Wilde. *The Picture of Dorian Gray* 1891. (Harmondsworth: Penguin Books, 1985). References to this edition by Peter Ackroyd are made in the body of the text (as page numbers indicated in parentheses).

There is critical consensus that Basil Hallward belongs to the Pre-Raphaelite school,[4] but it has hitherto passed unnoticed that the main incidents of the Sibyl Vane subplot are all coincident with (in the sense of consonant with) various paintings by the Pre-Raphaelites. The object of this paper is to consider whether it is more than a mere coincidence that there is concordance between some Pre-Raphaelite works and the elements structuring the Sibyl Vane subplot—such as the Shakespeare plays in which she performs, Dorian's worshipful love of her beauty, her recognition that he has shown her what reality really is, and her death. That concordance suggests that the Pre-Raphaelite paintings form a pictorial intertext underlying the aesthetics at work in the Sibyl Vane subplot which in turn illuminates the aesthetics at work in the novel as a whole.

Wilde frames Dorian's romance with Sibyl with allusions to the aesthetic theories of Walter Pater, a leading exponent of Pre-Raphaelitism. Lord Henry Wotton's thoughts on learning that Dorian had fallen in love with an actress outline the Paterian and pictorial intertexts informing the Sibyl Vane episode:

> He was conscious [. . .] that it was through certain words of his, musical words said with musical utterance, that Dorian Gray's soul had turned to this white girl and bowed in worship before her. (65) [51]

Wotton's musical words' echo back to the influential speech he had addressed to Dorian when they first met, based on Walter Pater's *Studies in the History of the Renaissance* and advocating a life devoted to aestheticism and hedonism. Lord Henry's incitement to 'be always searching for new sensations' (28) [23] clearly paraphrases Pater's precept in the 'Conclusion': 'What we have to do is to be for ever curiously testing new opinions and courting new impressions'.[5] Pater thus advocates aestheticism in the etymological sense of the word, meaning what is perceptible by the senses, which character-izes the sensuality of 'soft-edged' Pre-Raphaelite painting. Dorian practises the Paterian 'sermon' preached by Lord Henry,[6] when he indulges his 'passion for sensations' (55) [44] in his love for the actress Sibyl Vane. The Shakespearean intertext and the Pre-Raphaelite backdrop of the romance intertwine eroticism and the arts in what reads like an epilogue to Pater's essays on *The Renaissance*, with a double focus on Elizabethan drama and the Victorian paintings belonging to what Wilde called the 'English Renaissance'.

---

4. Christopher Nassaar. *Into the Demon Universe: A Literary Exploration of Oscar Wilde* (New Haven: Yale UP, 1974), p. 62.
5. Walter Pater. *The Renaissance: Studies in Art and Poetry* [*Studies in the History of the Renaissance*, 1873]. (London: Macmillan, 1902), p. 237.
6. This is the term Christopher Nassaar uses to qualify Lord Henry's sermon first as 'poi-sonous' and then as 'invidious'. See *Into the Demon Universe*, pp. 40 and 41.

Lord Henry hints that by 'bow[ing] in worship before [Sibyl]', Dorian partakes in the Pre-Raphaelites' cult of idealized love. Like the Pre-Raphaelites who view their lovers as works of art, Dorian falls in love with an actress who performs art and not a woman who lives life. Sibyl is portrayed as a Pre-Raphaelite 'stunner', as she embodies both art and beauty. Dorian marks his idealization of her by using the superlative form in his initial praise of her as 'the love-liest thing' (57) [46]. Her appearance is a combination of the classical ideal of perfection—denoted by her 'Greek head with plaited coils of dark-brown hair'—and the romantic ideal, as her face is 'flower-like' with its lips resembling the 'petals of a rose' and its eyes the 'violet wells of passion' (57) [46]. Sibyl is as unreachable and intangible as a woman depicted in a Pre-Raphaelite painting, whom she even resembles physically: 'The curves of her throat were the curves of a white lily. Her hands seemed to be made of ivory' (93) [71]. Dorian's appreciation of those parts of her body could be applied to numerous works by the Pre-Raphaelites who excelled in painting tapered fingers and sensuous necks. In 'The Decay of Lying', Wilde enumerates the characteristics of the Pre-Raphaelite beauty type, some of which coincide explicitly with those possessed by Sibyl Vane, 'the mystic eyes of Rossetti's dream, the long ivory throat [. . .], the blossom-like mouth and weary loveliness of the 'Laus Amoris', the passion-pale face of Andromeda, the thin hands and lithe beauty of the Vivian in 'Merlin's Dream.'[7]

Like many of Rossetti's works, his *Veronica Veronese* (1872) evokes music not only because the lady is plucking the strings of a violin, but also because the curves in her silhouette suggest musical notation in the way they seem to trace the treble clef. The frequent association between Pre-Raphaelite women and music might have inspired Wilde to endow the timbre of Sibyl Vane's voice with musical qualities that captivate Dorian:

> And her voice—I never heard such a voice. It was very low at first, with deep mellow notes that seemed to fall singly upon one's ear. Then it became a little louder, and sounded like a flute or a distant hautboy. [. . .] There were moments later on, when it had the wild passion of violins. (57–8) [46]

At the time of her death, Lord Henry refers to her as an instrument on which to play Shakespeare's music: 'she was [. . .] a reed through which Shakespeare's music sounded richer and more full of joy (115) [87]. That metaphor suggests that when Sibyl recites her lines she is not so much voicing a semantic message as creating a

---

7. *Collected Works of Oscar Wilde*, vol. 8, p. 33. The last three paintings Wilde alludes to here are by Sir Edward Coley Burne-Jones.

mood or a tonality. She transforms Shakespeare's text into a musical score, thus performing the aesthetic ideal which Walter Pater
formulated in his essay on 'The School of Giorgione' in *The Renaissance:* '[. . .] all art aspires constantly towards the condition of
music.'[8]

Lord Henry makes another muted reference to the pictorial intertext underpinning the Sibyl Vane subplot when he refers to her as
the 'white girl'. Dante Gabriel Rossetti claimed that *Ecce Ancilla
Domini* (1849–50), namely his version of 'The Annunciation' depicting Mary and the angel Gabriel both clad in white shifts, inaugurated a series of white paintings: 'In point of time it is the ancestor
of all the *white* pictures which have since become so numerous—
but here there was an ideal motive for the whiteness.'[9] Wilde's specific reference to a 'white girl' has been identified as a possible allusion
to Whistler's *Symphony in White, no. 2: The Little White Girl*
(1864),[1] thus extending the pictorial framework of the subplot to
span from Pre-Raphaelitism to the aestheticism of the 'art for art's
sake' movement.

Dorian adopts the Pre-Raphaelites' practice of making the women
they love into works of art by confusing Sibyl Vane's identity with
that of the Shakespearean characters she enacts. Like Wilde, the
Pre-Raphaelites looked back to Shakespeare as the epitome of the
English Renaissance, awarding him three stars as a 'Great' in their
'List of Immortals' (putting him second in line to the four-starred
Jesus Christ) and using his work as source for the emotion and moral
messages they sought to convey while establishing a distinctively
British art movement. Wilde uses the Shakespearean intertext to
construct the Sibyl Vane subplot of his novel, introducing her as
Miranda from *The Tempest* (91) [69], employed by a 'hideous Jew'
(55) [44] cast in the role of Caliban, but who could be nicknamed
the Merchant of London. Dorian falls in love with Sibyl when she is
performing the role of Juliet, hence his reaction when the theatre
manager proposes to introduce him to the real Sibyl Vane:

> On the first night I was at the theatre, the horrid old Jew came
> round to the box after the performance was over and offered to
> take me behind the scenes and introduce me to her. I was furi-
> ous with him, and told him that Juliet had been dead for hun-
> dreds of years and that her body was lying in a marble tomb in

8. Pater. *The Renaissance,* p. 135.
9. Letter from Rossetti to F. G. Stephens, dated 25 April 1874. Cited in Virginia Surtees.
   The Paintings and Drawings of Dante Gabriel Rossetti (1828–1882). A Catalogue Raisonné
   2 vols. (Oxford: The Clarendon Press, 1971). Catalogue number 44.
1. See *The Picture of Dorian Gray,* ed. Donald L. Lawler (New York: W. W. Norton & Company, 1988), p. 49, note 6 [51, note 9]: 'A reference to Whistler's picture of that name, on
   which Swinburne based his poem "Before the Mirror" in *Poems and Ballads* (1866)'.

Verona. I think, from his blank look of amazement, that he was under the impression that I had taken too much champagne, or something. (59) [47]

Dorian makes his love for Sibyl into a romance, constructed from literary sources. He proposes to 'take my love out of poetry and to find my wife in Shakespeare's plays' (86) [66].

Sibyl's identity is subsumed by the Shakespearean character she plays, as can be seen when Dorian refers to her as Cymbeline's daughter: 'Imogen is waiting for me' (64) [51]. Similarly, he makes a double reference to *As You Like It* and *Romeo and Juliet* when he comments that he has not yet seen Sibyl that day: 'I left her in the forest of Arden; I shall find her in an orchard in Verona (86) [66]. Dorian cites the same two plays in reference to their love-making: 'I have had the arms of Rosalind around me, and kissed Juliet on the mouth' (86) [66]. Dorian's love for Sibyl transports the couple into an unreal world, where they assume the role of fictitious characters. Sibyl is never herself: she acts constantly, as Dorian indicates in this response to Harry's question: 'When is she Sibyl Vane?'—'Never' (62) [49]. In a complementary way, Dorian playacts with Sibyl, who never knows his true identity, as he explains: 'She regarded me merely as a person in a play. She knows nothing of life' (61) [48]. She ceases to act when she experiences genuine love and can no longer mimic the emotion on stage. Her life—and her livelihood—are dependent on her art, and she is only alive when she is acting.

Just as the Pre-Raphaelites used the same model to represent a wide range of female figures from the Bible, mythology and literature, so Wilde portrays Sibyl as a protean figure who incarnates a series of Shakespearean characters. The fact that she possesses multiple identities in Dorian's eyes prompts his boast that he has seen her 'in every age and in every costume' (58) [46]. A similar statement could be made of a Pre-Raphaelite model like Jane Burden, who was represented in various guises ranging from her future husband William Morris's depiction of her as Queen Guinevere from Arthurian legend (1858)[2] to her lover Dante Gabriel Rossetti's portrait of her as Proserpine (1877). The Pre-Raphaelites' use of the women in their intimate world as models in their art adds an autobiographical dimension to their work which blurs the distinction between art and reality. Morris's depiction of his wife as the unfaithful Queen Guinevere, in the bedroom where she has committed adultery with Launcelot ominously foreshadows Jane Burden's love affair with Morris's friend Rossetti. Similarly, Rossetti's portrayal of Jane as the

---

2. The title of the painting is *La Belle Iseult* but its inspiration was Thomas Malory's 'Morte d'Arthur', in which one of the central themes is Guinevere's adulterous love for Sir Lancelot.

queen of the underworld, where she was bound to a husband who only occasionally granted her the freedom to enjoy the light of the world above, reflects his view of her marriage to Morris.

There is suggestive shadow-play between art and reality in John Everett Millais's *Ophelia* (1851–2), which depicts her suicide by drowning, triggered by Hamlet's rejection of her. The painting is an eerie foreshadowing of Elizabeth Siddal's own death caused by the laudanum she took in the wake of Rossetti's forsaking her. The intertextual link between Ophelia's fate and Sibyl Vane's suicide following rejection by Dorian Gray contains a pictorial twist to it. Millais's painting of a woman committing suicide after she has been forsaken by her lover superimposes the image of Elizabeth Siddal as Rossetti's lover onto the portrait of Ophelia. Although the Pre-Raphaelites had the metaphoric equivalent of stereoscopic vision and viewed the model both as the woman they knew in everyday life and a Shakespearean character, Sibyl's tragedy is that Dorian has eyes only for the aesthetic trappings she wears on stage, and does not see the woman behind the theatrical mask.

Walter Deverell's *Twelfth Night* (1849–1850) exemplifies the overlapping between Pre-Raphaelitism and the subplot of Wilde's novel, making the painting relevant to the argument presented here, even if neither the Shakespeare play it illustrates nor the name of the artist is cited in *The Picture of Dorian Gray*. Deverell contributed to the Pre-Raphaelite movement by introducing Elizabeth Siddal to the brotherhood when he first used her as a model in *Twelfth Night*. Beyond its biographical interest, Deverell's work deserves critical attention for its artistic merits, as it illustrates the aesthetic manifesto of the Pre-Raphaelite movement which pays tribute to early Italian Renaissance painting. The composition of *Twelfth Night*— in particular the way the architectural structures are used to construct space—replicates the composition of Benozzo Gozzoli's frescoes in the Campo Santo in Pisa which had inspired the founding of the Pre-Raphaelite brotherhood. The Pre-Raphaelites considered the engravings of Gozzoli's work as a model of early Renaissance art pre-dating Raphael. Just as Renaissance Italian artists used recognizable members of contemporary society in their depictions of Biblical scenes—notably prominent members of the Medici family who take the lead in the Procession of the Magi which Benozzo Gozzoli painted on the walls of the chapel in the Palazzo Medici Ricardi in Florence (1459–60)—so Deverell uses his contemporaries as models for his Shakespearean characters: he paints his self-portrait in the figure of Duke Orsino, casts Rossetti as the jester Feste and Elizabeth Siddal in the role of Viola disguised here as the page Cesario. The scene Deverell chose to depict (*Twelfth Night* II. iv) prefigures his own pre-mature death at the age of 27,[3] as it represents Feste singing a mournful verse from an 'old and antique song':

> Come away, come away, death,
> And in sad cypress let me be laid.
> Fly away, fly away, breath,
> I am slain by a fair cruel maid.

In an analogous way, the lines Sibyl Vane recites when she is acting Juliet or Ophelia have a performative value and foretell her own death.

Deverell's *Twelfth Night* constructs a complex artistic representation in which the pictorial composition frames the theatrical performance. The stone arched canopy delineates the space, functioning like the curtain in the theatre, and the very strong shadows in the painting evoke the presence of hidden footlights. Deverell creates another self-referential artistic representation in his depiction of a scene from *As You Like It*. Significantly, Wilde cites the same play to corroborate the point that Dorian considered Sibyl solely as an actress, who appeared more real to him when she was acting on stage than in her actions off stage. Dorian's view of Sibyl as 'a wonderful tragic figure sent on to the world's stage to show the supreme reality of love' (116–7) [88] echoes the trope in Jaques's speech:

> All the world's a stage,
> And all the men and women merely players;
> They have their exits and their entrances;
> And one man in his time plays many parts,
> His acts being seven ages. (*As You Like It* II vii.)

Dorian considers Sibyl as an actress who creates emotion through her performance, thus fulfilling the aesthetic precept formulated in the 'Preface' to Wilde's novel: 'From the point of view of feeling, the actor's craft is the type'. At the same time, by loving Sibyl the actress rather than Sibyl the woman, Dorian is enacting the paradox of Lord Henry's epigram: 'I love acting. It is so much more real than life' (89) [69]. Even Sibyl's death is considered in terms of performance, as Lord Henry compares it to that of such Shakespearean heroines as Ophelia, Juliet and Desdemona (114–5) [86]. Ironically, Sibyl's death results from her final performance as Juliet in which she let her real emotions get the better of her art. Her acting is condemned as 'simply bad art' marked by its 'absurdly artificial' gestures, her 'absolutely false' voice and the way she 'overemphasized everything that she had to say' (93–94) [71]. Sibyl's theatricality is consonant

---

3. Walter Howell Deverell was born in 1827 and died in 1854.

with the histrionic pose of the couple in Ford Maddox Brown's portrayal of *Romeo and Juliet* (1868–71). The hyperbolic representation of Romeo and Juliet's emotions in Brown's painting can be
seen as the visual equivalent of Sibyl's second-rate acting in another
instance of the coincidence between the subplot of Wilde's novel
and Pre-Raphaelite painting.

A comparison of some of the Pre-Raphaelites' illustrations of
Shakespeare and Wilde's construction of the Sibyl Vane subplot thus
reveals a common use of the meta-artistic.[4] Wilde also uses the
Shakespearean intertext not only to make a statement about artistic representation but also in his portrayal of homosexuality in the
novel's subtext. Wilde links Shakespeare's name with same-sex
love in a passage pointing to the works of Walter Pater which, as we
have already seen, cast a shadow over the Sibyl Vane episode. In a
passage referring unambiguously to homosexuality, Wilde alludes
not only to the chapters in *The Renaissance* on 'The Sonnets of
Michelangelo' and the art criticism of Wincklemann, but also to
Pater's partially published novel *Gaston de Latour,* which names
Montaigne and Ronsard in its depiction of male friendship. The
passage suggestively confuses Dorian's love for Lord Henry with
the painter Basil Hallward's love for him:

> The love that he bore him—for it was really love—had nothing
> in it that was not noble and intellectual. It was not that mere
> physical admiration of beauty that is born of the senses, and
> that dies when the senses tire. It was such a love as Michael
> Angelo had known, and Montaigne, and Wincklemann, and
> Shakespeare himself. (132) [99]

Wilde's claim that 'the whole idea [of his novel] was borrowed
from Shakespeare [. . .] from Shakespeare's sonnets'[5] was tanta-
mount to admitting that *The Picture of Dorian Gray* was a covert
representation of homosexuality. Indeed, Wilde had clearly laid the
groundwork for his novel's homosexual subtext in his short story
'The Portrait of Mr. W. H.' In that text, published a year before
Dorian Gray, Wilde read Shakespeare's sonnets as an ode to homosexual love and had one of the characters defend the thesis that
Shakespeare was in love with a male actor named Willie Hughes for
whom he wrote not only the cross-dressed role of Rosalind in *As You
Like It* but also the role of Juliet. By casting Sibyl Vane as a Shakespearean actress, Wilde associates her with the homosexual connotations of his work. He thus uses the Shakespearean intertext as an
indirect language allowing him to portray what his lover the poet

4. I am proposing this term to designate the pictorial equivalent of Gérard Genette's definition of the metadiegetic in *Figures III* (Paris: Seuil, 1972), pp. 241–3.
5. Cited by Ellmann, p. 422.

Lord Alfred Douglas called 'the love that dare not say its name.'[6] As a complement to Horst Breuer's enlightening article on the function of Shakespeare's sonnets in *The Picture of Dorian Gray*,[7] my focus here will be on how Wilde negotiated Victorian propriety in the construction of the novel's subplot by sheltering behind the respectability of Shakespearean texts—in particular *Romeo and Juliet* and *As You Like It*—which, coincidentally, were also illustrated by the Pre-Raphaelites.

Wilde's narrative of Dorian's love for Sibyl uses *Romeo and Juliet* as a structuring intertext, with Sibyl playing the lead female role both the first and the last times Dorian saw her on stage. Wilde subtly adds homosexual significance to Juliet's part in the significant choice of lines he cites in his text. They are extracted from a passage of the play which is composed as a sonnet, hence in a literary form which Wilde had explicitly associated with homosexual love in 'The Portrait of Mr. W. H.' Wilde has Sibyl recite Juliet's four line rejoinder to Romeo, who has placed his hand on hers, sanctifying it by calling it a 'holy shrine'. Romeo explains that the end he has in sight (his 'fine') befits a gentleman (reflected in the choice of the adjective 'gentle') as he proposes to kiss it:

> ROMEO   [*To Juliet*] If I profane with my unworthiest hand
> This holy shrine, the gentle fine is this:
> My lips, two blushing pilgrims, ready stand
> To smooth that rough touch with a tender kiss.
> JULIET   Good pilgrim, you do wrong your hand too much,
> Which mannerly devotion shows in this;
> For saints have hands that pilgrims' hands do touch,
> And palm to palm is holy palmers' kiss.
> ROMEO   Have not saints lips, and holy palmers too?
> JULIET   Ay, pilgrim, lips that they must use in prayer.
> ROMEO   O, then, dear saint, let lips do what hands do;
> They pray, grant thou, lest faith turn to despair.
> JULIET   Saints do not move, though grant for prayers' sake.
> ROMEO   Then move not, while my prayer's effect I take.[8]

The last line quoted in Wilde's text—'And palm to palm is holy palmers' kiss'—plays on the polysemy of the word 'palm', meaning both the inside of the hand and the tree whose branches were carried by pilgrims, hence their name of 'palmer'. The sonnet concludes with another pun, this time on the word 'move': Juliet uses it to mean 'saints do not initiate action', whereas Romeo uses it as an injunction

---

6. See his two poems 'In Praise of Shame' and 'Two Loves' in *The Chameleon*, no. 1, 1894.
7. Horst Breuer. 'Oscar Wilde's Dorian Gray and Shakespeare's Sonnets'. *English Language Notes (ELN)* vol. 42 no. 2 (December 2004), 59–68.
8. *Romeo and Juliet* I v. 91–104. Juliet's lines 95–8 are cited in Wilde's novel.

in the literal sense of 'stay still'. Wilde's citation from a text playing on the double meaning of its individual words points to the possible double meaning of the text as a whole. This sonnet operates on one level as a declaration of heterosexual love, but in the light of Wilde's theory that the Shakespearean sonnet is a coded form to refer to homosexuality, it can also be read as part of the homosexual subtext of the novel.

Wilde strengthens the link between the Sibyl Vane subplot and the homosexual subtext of his novel by playing on the sexual ambiguity related to the practice of cross-dressing on the Elizabethan stage. As the roles of both Romeo and Juliet were performed by male actors in the original performance, Wilde uses the play as a subterfuge for representing homosexual love in the ostensibly heterosexual subplot of *The Picture of Dorian Gray*. The narrative of that subplot focuses on scenes when Sibyl Vane is performing in a play whose plot involves cross-dressing, so that she appears on stage looking like an ephebic young male. The corresponding descriptions of her resonate with echoes back to the Pre-Raphaelite depictions of the same or similar scenes, for example in Deverell's *Twelfth Night,* where Viola is portrayed as an androgynous figure, with a woman's face but masquerading in men's clothing. Like the Victorian depictions of Shakespeare which use a woman as model for the female character dressed as a man, Sibyl Vane's cross-dressing involves only one layer of disguise, whereas the Elizabethan performances requiring that the female part be played by a male actor resulted in double cross-dressing. The Pre-Raphaelites made scenes of Shakespearean cross-dressing into a recurrent motif exemplified not only in Deverell's works, but also in William Holman Hunt's *Valentine Rescuing Sylvia from Proteus* (1850–51) illustrating a passage from *Two Gentlemen of Verona* in which Julia is dressed as a page. However, in these paintings, cross-dressing is used simply as a means of emphasizing role-playing, in keeping with the Pre-Raphaelite aesthetic of a self-consciously constructed art work. They are a complex representation of performance, illustrating a kind of play within the play or theatrical *mise en abyme*. In Wilde's novel, on the other hand, the references to crossing-dressing in Shakespeare are not only associated with self-reflexive art, they are also encoded with homosexual meaning.

The themes of play-acting and cross-dressing are inextricably intertwined in *As You Like It*. Rosalind and Celia flee from court to the Forest of Arden, under assumed identities: Celia adopts the name of 'Aliena' and wears the clothes of a woman of modest means, whereas Rosalind dresses up as a page and takes on the name of Ganymede, which in the Elizabethan period had acknowledged homosexual associations. Wilde used the sexually ambiguous connotations of *As*

You Like It as a strategy for investing the Sibyl-Dorian love affair with homosexual meaning. Dorian accounts for his love of Sibyl, explaining that he was especially attracted to her in the scenes where Rosalind is cross-dressed as Ganymede: 'I have watched her wandering through the forest of Arden, disguised as a pretty boy in hose and doublet and dainty cap' (58) [46]. He returns to that androgynous image of her when he informs Basil of his love for Sibyl:

> You should have seen her! When she came on in her boy's clothes, she was perfectly wonderful. She wore a moss-coloured velvet jerkin with cinnamon sleeves, slim, brown, cross-gartered hose, a dainty little green cap with a hawk's feather caught in a jewel, and a hooded cloak lined with dull red. She had never seemed to me more exquisite. She had all the delicate grace of that Tanagra figurine that you have in your studio, Basil. Her hair clustered round her face like dark leaves round a pale rose. As for her acting—well, you shall see her to-night. She is simply a born artist. I sat in the dingy box absolutely enthralled. I forgot that I was in London and in the nineteenth century. I was away with my love in a forest that no man had ever seen. (85) [65–66]

As You Like It has a key function in the economy of the novel's homosexual subtext as it is Sibyl's appearance on stage, cross-dressed as a young man, which prompts Dorian to declare his love to her (60) [48].

Coincidentally, Walter Deverell's *As You Like It* (1853) suggestively combines both performance and sexual ambiguity. Other titles for the painting are 'Rosalind Tutoring Orlando in the Ceremony of Marriage' and 'The Mock Marriage of Orlando and Rosalind', specifying that it depicts a marriage ceremony, although it looks like a wedding between two men because Rosalind, dressed as Ganymede, exchanges vows with Orlando. Celia officiates as substitute priest and expresses her reluctance to pronounce the lines corresponding to this transgressive marriage. She is prompted by Rosalind in the following rehearsal:

ROSALIND	Come, sister, you shall be the priest, and marry us. Give me your hand, Orlando. What do you say, sister?
ORLANDO	Pray thee, marry us.
CELIA	I cannot say the words.
ROSALIND	You must begin 'Will you, Orlando'—
CELIA	Go to. Will you, Orlando, have to wife this Rosalind?
ORLANDO	I will.
ROSALIND	Ay, but when?
ORLANDO	Why, now; as fast as she can marry us.
ROSALIND	Then you must say 'I take thee, Rosalind, for wife.'
ORLANDO	I take thee, Rosalind, for wife. (*As You Like It* IV i.)

The epilogue of *As You Like It* confounds the blurred gender divide dramatized in Rosalind's part with an undefined boundary between the world represented on stage and reality.[9] It is unclear whether the lines are spoken by the character in the play (Rosalind) or by the actor or actress playing the part. The speech confuses the issue because Rosalind—at this point wearing women's clothing—introduces the hypothesis 'If I were a woman', which reveals that the woman's part is in fact being played by a male actor (as was the case in the Elizabethan period). That revelation is immediately contradicted by the actor's gesture, because he takes leave by performing a feminine curtsy, thus stepping back into the world of the theatre:

> It is not the fashion to see the lady the epilogue. [. . .] If I were a woman, I would kiss as many of you as had beards that pleas'd me, complexions that lik'd me, and breaths that I defied not; and, I am sure, as many as have good beards, or good faces, or sweet breaths, will, for my kind offer, when I make curtsy, bid me farewell. (*As You Like It* Epilogue)

Wilde's use of *As You Like It* as a key intertext in his novel tightens the entangled threads of reality and art, masculinity and femininity and ties them to late nineteenth century aestheticism. The play had served as a centripetal force in Théophile Gautier's *Mademoiselle de Maupin* (1835), a novel which Wilde ranked alongside Pater's *The Renaissance,* qualifying them in turn as 'the golden book of spirit and sense, the holy writ of beauty'".[1] This French text is clearly an important intertext in *The Picture of Dorian Gray,* not only because Gautier's lenghty preface became the rallying manifesto of the 'art for art's sake' movement, but also because the narrative itself broaches the question of 'the love that dare not say its name'. In it, the eponymous heroine is a transvestite posing as a young gentleman named Théodore. The plot revolves around the rehearsals for an amateur production of *As You Like It* in which 'Théodore' plays the role of Rosalind and betrays 'his' true identity in the scenes when 'he' puts on Rosalind's costume. In Gautier's novel, the cross-dressing thus results in several layers because a woman (Mademoiselle de Maupin) dressed as a man (Théodore) plays the part of a woman (Rosalind) who has to disguise herself as a man (Ganymede).

The suggestive sexual ambiguity of *As You Like It* was given a peculiar twist in Lord and Lady Archibald Campbell's 1884–5

---

9. The analysis on the epilogue here is endebted to Jean-Jacques Chardin's 'Androgyny, Anamorphosis and Double Vision: *Fin de Siècle* revisiting of the Shakespearean Canon'. *Recherches Anglaises et Nord-Américaines*, vol. 35 (2002), 107–17.
1. *Collected Works of Oscar Wilde*, vol. 13, p. 539 for Pater; vol. 13 p. 32 for Gautier. Wilde is citing Swinburne's lines written in praise of Gautier's *Mademoiselle de Maupin*.

open-air production of the play, performed in the woods near their
home at Coombe. This production cast Lady Archibald Campbell
in role of Orlando, thus producing a complex criss-crossing of gender culminating in the mock wedding scene. At that point, a woman
acting a man's part (Lady Campbell as Orlando) exchanges wedding vows with an actress disguised as a young man. Wilde reviewed
the performance in 1885, praising in particular the masculine sug-
gestiveness of Lady Campbell's voice. His use of the terms 'strange',
'wonderful' and 'fascination' are resonant with homosexual overtones, as in his novel he makes them into code words denoting
Dorian's seductive beauty:

> Lady Archibald Campbell's Orlando was a really remarkable
> performance. Too melancholy some seemed to think it. Yet is
> not Orlando lovesick? Too dreamy, I heard it said. Yet Orlando
> is a poet. [. . .] in the low music of Lady Archibald Campbell's
> voice, and in the strange beauty of her movements and gestures,
> there was a wonderful fascination.[2]

Wilde praised the outdoor setting of the performance, which used
the real woods near Coombe Hill Farm as backdrop. The production
was unusual in the way it brought together the artistic space of the
theatre and the natural space of the world around, set as it was on
the indefinable interface between reality and art. James Abbott
McNeill Whistler's *Note in Green and Brown: Orlando at Coombe*,
a tiny oil painting (measuring only 5 7/8 by 3½ inches) now in the
Hunterian Art Gallery in Glasgow, provides a visual record of
the production.[3] It depicts the layers of transvestism introduced in
the performance, as it represents a slim figure in doublet and hose,
with a gentle lady's face. Given the web of associations surrounding
late Victorian artistic representations of *As You Like It*, we can conclude that it is more than just a coincidence that Wilde used it as an
intertext encoded with sexual ambiguity.

If Dorian relates his love for Sibyl to Shakespearean plays mediated through Pre-Raphaelite illustrations, Sibyl for her part formulates her feelings by citing a poem which gave rise to another series
of Pre-Raphaelite paintings: Tennyson's 'The Lady of Shalott' (1832).
The poem recounts the legend of a woman whose sole knowledge of
the real world is what she sees reflected in a mirror positioned opposite a window opening out onto it. Her only interaction with that
reflected reality is the art work she weaves as a representation of it,

2. Wilde's article was published in the *Dramatic Review* on June 6, 1885. Cited here from
   Collected Works of Oscar Wilde, vol. XIII. pp. 34–5.
3. Whistler's painting is dated July 1884, in other words the year before Wilde's review, suggesting that the production ran for two summers. See Andrew McClaren Young, Margaret MacDonald, Robin Spencer, Hamish Miles. *The Paintings of James McNeill Whistler*
   2 vols. (New Haven: Yale UP, 1980), Catalogue entry 317.

thus indicating that hers is a life of pure aesthetics. When she commits the fatal transgression of looking out of the window onto reality, the mirror cracks and her world of aestheticism is shattered. The
legend thus outlines Sibyl Vane's own fate, as she breaks the spell
of Dorian's love for her when she moves away from the 'magic' of
the theatre in order to confront reality. Sibyl's references to the
Shakespearean framework modulate to an allusion to Tennyson's
poem in her long speech explaining that Dorian has helped her to
see the artificiality of the theatrical world:

> I knew nothing but shadows, and I thought them real. You
> came—oh, my beautiful love!—and you freed my soul from
> prison. You taught me what reality really is. To-night, for the
> first time in my life, I saw through the hollowness, the sham,
> the silliness of the empty pageant in which I had always played.
> To-night, for the first time, I became conscious that the Romeo
> was hideous, and old, and painted, that the moonlight in the
> orchard was false, that the scenery was vulgar, and that the
> words I had to speak were unreal, were not my words, were not
> what I wanted to say. You had brought me something higher,
> something of which all art is but a reflection. You had made me
> understand what love really is. My love! My love! Prince Charm-
> ing! Prince of life! I have grown sick of shadows. (96–7) [74]

Her concluding statement and the preceding suggestion that Dorian
had helped her to dissipate the shadows of art are an allusion to 'The
Lady of Shalott''s complaint in Tennyson's poem:

> But in her web she still delights
> To weave the mirror's magic sights,
> For often thro' the silent nights
> A funeral, with plumes and lights
>   And music, went to Camelot:
> Or when the moon was overhead,
> Came two young lovers lately wed;
> 'I am half sick of shadows,' said
>   The Lady of Shalott.

Sibyl borrows the Lady of Shalott's use of the word 'shadows' to
mean art, which Dorian will echo on the following page when he
retaliates that he had loved her precisely because she gave 'shape
and substance to the shadows of art' (98) [74]. Sibyl reverses his
values by placing reality higher than art which she dismisses as 'an
empty pageant'. Dorian wants to preserve their romance in the realm
of art, whereas Sibyl attempts to transpose their romance into the
sphere of reality and thus transforms Dorian's nickname from Prince
Charming into 'Prince of life' (97) [74]. The irony of that epithet

becomes tragic, as Dorian's rejection of her as a living woman prompts her to take her life.

'The Lady of Shalott' was a recurrent theme in Pre-Raphaelite painting because it dramatized the breaking point between art and reality which paralleled the artists' own preoccupations with the relationship between artistic representation and the real world. William Holman Hunt's first version of the subject dating from 1850 was followed by his celebrated canvas of the same scene completed in 1886–1905 (and now in the Wadsworth Atheneum in Hartford, Connecticut). John Williams Waterhouse's illustrations of the poem include a canvas post-dating the publication of Wilde's novel whose title is the same line of the poem cited by Sibyl: 'I'm half sick of shadows' (1915). Elizabeth Siddal, who was not only a model but became an artist in her own right, sketched a pencil drawing of the scene which is particularly relevant to this discussion of Sibyl's citation of Tennyson's poem. In both Siddal's drawing (1853) and Wilde's text, the poem functions as an instrument allowing the woman to make her voice heard. In Siddal's drawing, the Lady of Shalott is depicted as a repressed recluse, isolated in a world of asceticism devoted to the aesthetics of weaving. Sibyl Vane invokes the poem to imply that she has been constrained by the lines she has had to learn and smothered by the stale air of theatrical art. In this way, Sibyl uses Tennyson's poem to make a statement about her status as a woman and her desire for freedom, which thus coincides with the message of Siddal's drawing of the same scene.[4]

The aesthetics underwriting Wilde's novel and Pre-Raphaelite illustrations extend beyond the framework of the Sibyl Vane chapters, so that the dialectics of reality and artistic construction, identity and playacting function as a common axis for both the subplot and the bulk of the narrative. Like Sibyl, Dorian leads a 'double life' (192) [146] and becomes a skilled actor, prompting the paradoxical statement: 'Perhaps one never seems so much at one's case as when one has to play a part' (192) [146]. Dorian constructs an aesthetic disguise to mask his true self, linking him not only to Sibyl the actress but also to Wilde himself, who famously proclaimed: 'My life is like a work of art.'[5] Wilde transposes that statement into the present perfect tense when he has Lord Henry pen Dorian's portrait in words: 'Life has been your art. You have set yourself to music. Your days are your sonnets' (238) [180]. Here Lord Henry formulates the idea that Dorian is an aesthete embodying the theory of 'art for art's sake' drawing on

4. In the conclusion to her article on 'Holman Hunt's Sage Reading of *The Lady of Shalott*', Maria Teresa de Ataíde Malafaia formulates what these women are saying. See *Anglo-Saxónica*, Series 2, no. 16/17 (2002), 295.
5. Ellmann, p. 508.

both Pater's conception of music as the purest form of art and Wilde's own appropriation of the sonnet as a coded language for homo-sexuality. Dorian is thus made of the same stuff as Sibyl, and both are artificial creations who cannot survive in the real world.

The impetus of Wilde's narrative—how Dorian preserves his good looks while his portrait becomes the reflection of his tainted soul—introduces a temporal dimension to that pictorial representation which can be related to two paintings associated with the novel's subplot. Returning to Wilde's allusion to Whistler's *Symphony in White, no. 2: The Little White Girl* (1864), we can notice that the painting's musical title harmonizes with the novelist's aestheticism and coincides with the main plot of his work, in the sense that both are self-conscious aesthetic compositions. The painting represents a woman standing in front of a mirror, surrounded by Japanese deco-rations such as a painted fan, blue porcelain pots and an azalea. The artist has created the 'Japanese effect' which Wilde defines in 'The Decay of Lying' as a pure aesthetic construction, even going so far as to argue that 'the whole of Japan is a pure invention'[6] and that 'The Japanese people are the deliberate self-conscious creation of certain individual artists.'[7] The aesthetic construction of this painting can be related to the opening scene of Wilde's novel, where 'a kind of momentary Japanese effect' (5) [5] is created by the shad-ows of the birds in flight behind the curtain stretched across the window of Basil's studio. Whistler's painting has further resonance with the novel's main plot, as the figure standing in front of an ana-morphic mirror can be likened to Dorian's relationship with his painted image. As Jonathan Miller has so perceptively pointed out, the mirror in Whistler's painting does not reflect the 'little white girl' realistically, but gives a negative image of her as ill, aged or marked by a life of dissolution.[8] In an analogous way, the progres-sive corruption of Dorian's portrait functions like an anamorphic mirror reflecting his sinister second self.

The second work which provides a pictorial intertext for the por-trait Wilde creates in his novel is a small drawing in pen and ink sketched by Walter Deverell at the time he painted his canvas enti-tled *Twelfth Night*. It depicts a scene from the same play in which a cross-dressed Viola delivers the duke's message of love to Olivia, though Viola's deceptive appearance as a youth arouses Olivia's love for her. Using Elizabeth Siddal as a model, Deverell makes this go-between a sexual in-between, as she wears the costume of a page but has the face of a young woman. The scene Deverell chose to

6. *Collected Works of Oscar Wilde*, vol. 8, p. 47.
7. *Collected Works of Oscar Wilde*, vol. 8, p. 48.
8. Jonathan Miller. *On Reflection* (London: National Gallery Publications, 1998), p. 202.

illustrate compounds the issue of sexual ambiguity with the meta-theatrical, as Olivia recognizes that the page has had to learn lines in order to perform the part and that the request to see her face is unscripted:

> OLIVIA   Have you any commission from your lord to negotiate with my face? You are now out of your text: but we will draw the curtain and show you the picture. Look you, sir, such a one I was this present: is't not well done? [*Unveiling*] (*Twelfth Night* I v.)

Olivia's speech here is built on a trope comparing her face to a portrait. Her words capture the temporal confusion characteristic of Dorian's portrait when she uses the past tense to refer to herself in the present: 'such a one I was this present'. The phrase 'this present' was a common way of dating letters in the Elizabethan period, and is used here to suggest the date juxtaposed beside the artist's signature. The sense of compound time illustrated by this Pre-Raphaelite drawing of a text which superimposes the act of artistic creation in the past and the moment the art work is viewed in the present is echoed in Wilde's novel, where it becomes the defining characteristic of Dorian's portrait.

The reflection in Whistler's mirror and the Shakespearean scene representing a criss-crossing of indirect declarations of love (the Duke's for Olivia and Olivia's for a woman posing as a man) are resonant with the aesthetics at work in *The Picture of Dorian Gray*. The concordance between word and image pinpoints the common aesthetics which provided the stuff for the Pre-Raphaelites's works and the novel by Wilde. To use the terms of the novel's subplot, we can conclude that the Pre-Raphaelites' illustrations from Shakespeare provide the background scenery to the Sibyl/Dorian romance. Considering the novel as a whole, it would be more appropriate to transpose the conclusion into musical terms, as the art works compose a kind of incidental music coincident with Wilde's own aesthetics.

WORKS CITED

Horst Breuer. 'Oscar Wilde's Dorian Gray and Shakespeare's Sonnets'. *English Language Notes (ELN)* vol. 42 no. 2 (December 2004), 59–68.

Jean-Jacques Chardin. 'Androgyny, Anamorphosis and Double Vision: *Fin de Siècle* revisiting of the Shakespearean Canon'. *Recherches Anglaises et Nord-Américaines (RANNAM)*, vol. 35 (2002), 107–17.

Richard Ellmann. *Oscar Wilde* (1987). Harmondsworth: Penguin Books, 1988.

Gérard Genette. *Figures III*. Paris: Seuil, 1972.

Maria Teresa de Ataíde Malafaia. 'Holman Hunt's Sage Reading of *The Lady of Shalott'*. *Anglo-Saxónica*, Series 2, no. 16/17 (2002), 289–96.

Andrew McClaren Young, Margaret MacDonald, Robin Spencer, Hamish Miles. *The Paintings of James McNeill Whistler* 2 vols. New Haven: Yale UP, 1980.

Jonathan Miller. *On Reflection*. London: National Gallery Publication, 1998.

Christopher Nassaar. *Into the Demon Universe: A Literary Exploration of Oscar Wilde*. New Haven: Yale UP, 1974.

Walter Pater. *The Renaissance: Studies in Art and Poetry* [*Studies in the History of the Renaissance*, 1873]. London: Macmillan, 1902.

Virginia Surtees. *The Paintings and Drawings of Dante Gabriel Rossetti (1828–1882). A Catalogue Raisonné*. 2 vols. Oxford: The Clarendon Press, 1971.

Oscar Wilde. *The Picture of Dorian Gray* (1891).
    ed. Peter Ackroyd. Harmondsworth: Penguin Books, 1985.
    ed. Donald L. Lawler. New York: Norton, 1988.
    ed. Michael Patrick Gillespie. Third ed. New York: Norton, 2020.
The Collected Works of Oscar Wilde. ed. Robert Ross, 15 vols. 1908. (reprinted by Routledge/Thoemmes Press 1993).

MICHAEL PATRICK GILLESPIE

The Picture of Dorian Gray as a Post-Modern Work[†]

Early in Oscar Wilde's novel, *The Picture of Dorian Gray,* Lord Henry Wotton presents a concise assessment of the principles he feels should govern human behavior, aptly labeled New Hedonism. His disquisition seems, at first glance, to be little more than the flippant advocacy of a shallow, self-indulgent lifestyle. In fact, he is anticipating the post-Modern vision that would emerge a half-century later. Post-Modern is a term that enjoys broad usage and multiple denotations. Let me offer my very specific sense of it. When I use that term in this essay, I am referencing the concept of an arbitrary world conceived on a purely material basis. The moral precepts that serve as the foundations for social institutions—like family, church, nation—can have no impact on our lives because the values upon which they rest and which they purport to exemplify in fact do not exist in a world without metaphysics.

[†] From *Études anglaises* (*English Studies*) 68 (January–March 2015): 19–31. Page references are to this Norton Critical Edition. Reprinted by permission of Les Belles Lettres, Paris.

(Other critics who have looked at post-Modernism in Wilde's works have focused on his essays. See, for example, Daniel T. O'Hara's "Prophetic Criticism: Oscar Wilde and His Postmodern Heirs," Andres Hoefle's "Oscar Wilde, or the prehistory of postmodern parody," and Jonathan Kemp's "The Importance of Being Postmodern: Oscar Wilde and the Untimely." However, I have not seen extended discussions of aspects of post-Modernism in his novel.)

In the opening pages of Wilde's novel, Lord Henry, speaking to Basil Hallward, sums up a view that guides him and that will evoke familiar concepts for the contemporary reader: "I like persons with no principles better than anything else in the world" (12). Shortly thereafter the seemingly supremely Victorian Basil enters the discussion. Speaking of Dorian Gray, he echoes what one could call Harry's post-Structural perspective, by saying "He is never more present in my work than when no image of him is there" (14).

Lord Henry develops the concept of materialism, going beyond aphorisms to offer a hardnosed outline of his sense of reality. In an extended disquisition, whose frivolous tone masks its far-reaching skepticism, Harry constructs an alternative world view. It demolishes the values of the Victorian society that surrounds him, and indicts those who adhere to them as fools. Selections abstracted from his presentation show the ruthlessness of his philosophy.

He begins by pointing out the distorting effect produced on an individual by the influence of conventional values:

> He does not think his natural thoughts, or burn with his natural passions. His virtues are not real to him. His sins, if there are such things as sins, are borrowed. He becomes an echo of some one else's music, an actor of a part that has not been written for him.

Lord Henry then moves to express his contempt for those inadequately committed to solipsism:

> People are afraid of themselves, nowadays. They have forgotten the highest of all duties, the duty that one owes to one's self.

And he ends with the dismissal of those afraid to face nihilism:

> The terror of society, which is the basis of morals, the terror of God, which is the secret of religion—these are the two things that govern us. . . . [T]he bravest man among us is afraid of himself. The mutilation of the savage has its tragic survival in the self-denial that mars our lives. We are punished for our refusals. Every impulse that we strive to strangle broods in the mind, and poisons us. The body sins once, and has done with its sin, for action is a mode of purification. Nothing remains then but the recollection of a pleasure, or the luxury of a regret.

The only way to get rid of a temptation is to yield to it. (Oscar Wilde. *The Picture of Dorian Gray,* pp. 19–20)

Harry's suave language masks his devastatingly harsh and arrestingly amoral conclusions. However, this is not reflexive cynicism. A close reading shows his sentiments, and those which will define the ethos of the novel, coinciding perfectly with those of a post-Modernist society. He celebrates sensuality as the only valid principle of behavior in a world without values materialism, and he expresses contempt for anyone too timid or too stupid to acknowledge that the scope of human life does not extend beyond its materiality.

Like the views expressed by characters in the works of another Irish exile, Samuel Beckett, at the core of Lord Henry's exposition stands his perception of an arbitrary world that offers nothing beyond physical actions and reactions to explain the way events unfold. Much as Beckett does in *Waiting for Godot,* in *The Picture of Dorian Gray* Wilde argues for our powerlessness to comprehend or to influence the environment that surrounds us in anything other than a transient, material fashion. Of course, Beckett's characters tend to lament living in a world without some system of values that would give their actions metaphysical significance. In contrast, Lord Henry urges one to glory in the freedom derived from the absence of moral restrictions. (Wilde does this again in his play, *The Importance of Being Earnest,* though the frivolity that runs through the dialogue makes its darker vision even more difficult to discern.[1])

For many who have encountered the novel, Harry's nihilism has been hard to detect, much less to accept. As readers, we are like Dorian, reluctant to embrace the full implications of a solely material world. Instead, we bring alternative value systems into our interpretations to explain the anomalies of the environment of the novel.[2] Because these traditional approaches are so different from the one I advocate here and because I challenge any value-based reading of the work, I think it necessary to begin my argument by explaining

1. For a more detailed examination, see chapter seven of my book, *The Aesthetics of Chaos: Nonlinear Thinking and Contemporary Literary Criticism* (Gainesville: UP of Florida, 2003), pp. 94–108.
2. See, for example, the reviews of the novella version of *The Picture of Dorian Gray* collected in the 2007 Norton Critical Edition, pp. 345–84. For examples of the reactions of more recent critics, see San Juan Epifano, Jr., *The Art of Oscar Wilde* (Princeton: Princeton UP, 1967); Christopher Nassaar, *Into the Demon Universe: a Literary Exploration of Oscar Wilde* (New Haven: Yale UP, 1974); Philip K. Cohen, *The Moral Vision of Oscar Wilde* (Rutherford, NJ: Fairleigh Dickinson UP, 1978); Reginia Gagnier, *Idyls of the Marketplace: Oscar Wilde and the Victorian Public* (Stanford: Stanford UP, 1986); Norbert Kohl, *Oscar Wilde: the Works of a Conformist Rebel* (Cambridge: Cambridge UP, 1989); Ed Cohen, *Talk on the Wilde Side: Toward a Genealogy of a Discourse on Male Sexualities,* (New York: Routledge, 1993); Alan Sinfield, *The Wilde Century: Effeminacy, Oscar Wilde and the Queer Moment* (New York: Columbia UP, 1994); Jerusha McCormack, *The Man Who Was Dorian Gray* (New York: St. Martin's Press, 2000).

how English reviewers first introduced morally centered approaches to reading *The Picture of Dorian Gray,* how Wilde struggled to dissuade readers from pursuing any value-based interpretation of his work, and how the persistent tendency to read the novel from one metaphysical perspective or another consequently distorted understandings of the work.

"The Picture of Dorian Gray" first appeared as a novella, published simultaneously in America and Great Britain in June of 1890 in *Lippincott's Magazine.* The American debut produced no untoward responses. However, a number of English reviewers unhesitatingly condemned the work as filth, unsuitable for reproduction in a mass circulation magazine. One critique in particular, printed in the *St. James's Gazette* on June 24, epitomizes the harsh tones adopted by Wilde's most acerbic English critics, and it stands as a paradigm of the indictments against the work echoed by numerous others. Entitled "A Study in Puppydom," its opening paragraph neatly encapsulates the reviewer's animosity:

> Time was (it was in the '70's) when we talked about Mr Oscar Wilde; time came (it came in the '80's) when he tried to write poetry and, more adventurous, we tried to read it; time is when we had forgotten him, or only remember him as the late editor of *The Woman's World*—a part for which he was singularly unfitted, if we are to judge him by the work which he has been allowed to publish in *Lippincott's Magazine* and which Messrs Ward, Lock & Co. have not been ashamed to circulate in Great Britain. Not being curious in ordure, and not wishing to offend the nostrils of decent persons, we do not propose to analyse "The Picture of Dorian Gray": that would be to advertise the developments of an esoteric prurience. Whether the Treasury or the Vigilance Society will think it worthwhile to prosecute Mr Oscar Wilde or Messrs Ward, Lock & Co., we do not know; but on the whole we hope they will not. . . . ("A Study in Puppydom," *St. James's Gazette,* 24 June 1890 [*DG*, 357–58])

Looking at this piece nearly one hundred and twenty-five years after it first appeared, contemporary readers instinctively see it as a hysterical reaction, blinded by prejudice and fear. Such may well have been the factors motivating the reviewer, but too much attention to tone misses the central issues of the narrative, particularly in light of Wilde's attempts at clarification.

In letters to the *St. James's Gazette* and to other journals that had published equally harsh reviews, Wilde provided ample evidence that he held very different assumptions about the purpose of a work of art. Specifically, he made a vigorous defense against criticisms derived from offended moral sensibilities. A 26 June 1890 letter highlights

Wilde's frustration with the *ad hominem* attacks that had passed as responses to his novel:

> I do not propose to fully discuss the matter here, but I feel bound to say that your article contains the most unjustifiable attack that has been made upon any man of letters for many years. The writer of it, who is quite incapable of concealing his personal malice, and so in some measure destroys the effects he wishes to produce, seems not to have the slightest idea of the temper in which of a work of art should be approached. (*DG*, 362)

Wilde goes on to assert there and in subsequent correspondence that the charges that he seeks to undermine public morality simply miss the point of his artistic aims.

Such criticism, nonetheless, persisted, and over the course of an epistolary debate lasting several months, moral posturing came to subsume all other considerations. Wilde initially tried to dismiss the distorted perspective promoted by such a discussion. However, the intensity of the debate pushed him ultimately to respond to his detractors on their own terms, debating the morality of his prose.

Nonetheless, Wilde never lost sight of the distortions that morally driven readings would produce on putative interpretations of his novel, and, to refocus critical thinking, he wrote a broad declaration of the aesthetic values that he espoused. It was first published independently in the *Fortnightly Review* in the early spring of 1891 and then as a Preface to the novel-length version of *The Picture of Dorian Gray*. While its epigrammatic style precludes reading it as a unified manifesto, several statements jump out as clear rebuttals of the critics who attacked the novel version:

> Those who find ugly meanings in beautiful things are corrupt without being charming.
>
> There is no such thing as a moral or an immoral book. Books are well written, or badly written. That is all.
>
> No artist desires to prove anything. Even things that are true can be proved.
>
> No artist has ethical sympathies. An ethical sympathy in an artist is an unpardonable mannerism of style.
>
> All art is quite useless. (*DG*, 3–4)

Like much of Wilde's writing, paradoxes and even contradictions run through the Preface. Nonetheless, by placing it immediately before the beginning of his narrative, Wilde makes an extremely important point about the novel's interpretive possibilities: No moral position informs the composition of *The Picture of Dorian Gray,* and reading one into the narrative distorts its meaning.

That is a much more radical perspective than the majority of Wilde's readers have been willing to adopt. Most have condemned responses that clashed with their own views, but they also have not hesitated to forward personal ideological agendas. Such interpretations of Wilde's novel regularize it according to the same linear patterns of thinking that Wilde's early detractors followed. In fact, Wilde's text takes a decidedly nonlinear tack. It posits an arbitrary existence with absolutely no values to anchor it.

Understanding this position is easier if we keep in mind the ideas that he outlines in his preface. Wilde has no interest in creating a philosophical tract: "No artist has ethical sympathies. An ethical sympathy in an artist is an unpardonable mannerism of style." Wilde does not see art as a means to an end but rather is seeking a purely aesthetic creation. "The artist is the creator of beautiful things." He strives toward an impractical valueless experience rather than a utilitarian one that leads us to some truth or insight. "All art is quite useless." Wilde speaks of creating a work outside the boundaries of ethical behavior, outside the advocacy of particular political, social, or spiritual beliefs. In this fashion, his art employs the same existential assumptions as Beckett's would, though admittedly in a much more optimistic tone.

At the same time, Wilde's writing is shaped by the literary tradition from which he emerged. He was adept as both a reader and a writer. He understood how the two processes informed understanding of any piece of literature. In *The Picture of Dorian Gray* Wilde blends many of the features of familiar genres, truncating, redirecting or otherwise distorting the expected patterns to suit his creative aims.

This gesture may not be immediately apparent to many who see Wilde's novel as a conventionally structured narrative typical of a great deal of nineteenth century English fiction. Certainly, similarities abound between *The Picture of Dorian Gray* and more conventional works. Wilde's novel focuses on a central character learning how to make his way in society, and it explores the results of the choices made in the process. With an awareness of the strong literary tradition linking moral consequences to human behavior, most readers are inclined to see in the narrative an ethically based assessment of Dorian's degeneration. Our experiences with other works that seem analogous lead us to believe that his evolution into an increasingly debased sensualist produces disfigurement in the painting because it reacts to his behaving as no decent man should.

However, from the opening pages, the mutability of the narrative of *The Picture of Dorian Gray* raises problems with such recourse to interpretive referentiality that find no easy resolution: It seemingly begins as a homoerotic love story, or at least a tale of obsession for beauty. It appears to move to a bildungsroman with Lord Henry's efforts to enlighten Dorian through New Hedonism. It suggests a psychological thriller as Dorian pushes the limits of his behavior through the transformation of his portrait. And it apparently ends as a morality tale when Dorian, after trying to reform, seemingly cannot bear the weight of his own conscience. Because inconsistencies in each of these categories disrupt the application of whatever conventions that readers might wish to invoke to understand this discourse, none of these classifications provides a clear direction for interpretation. This in turn raises questions regarding how we are to understand the work, and I now believe that the most comprehensive approach follows the stark perspectives of post-Modern thinking.

This nihilistic view can be difficult to accept. It challenges the basis of many received readings, but this is because our interpretations, and I include my own in this categorization, have come out of elements we impose rather than from elements in the work. By looking at a pivotal scene in the novel, Dorian's deep resentment coming out of first view of his picture, one can see both how easy it is to read familiar archetypes into the narrative and how important it is to see the text's subtle resistance to such conventional expectations:

> How sad it is! I shall grow old, and horrible, and dreadful. But this picture will remain always young. It will never be older than this particular day of June. . . . If it were only the other way! If it were I who was to be always young, and the picture that was to grow old! For that—for that—I would give everything! Yes, there is nothing in the whole world I would not give! I would give my soul for that! (*DG*, 25–26)

The moment—particularly Dorian's offer of his soul—seems to portray the prototypical desire to overcome human limitations by trading earthly success for eternal damnation. However, it is important to keep in mind all of the elements that define such a compact. It is not enough to make an offer. Someone must accept the proposal. Eve had the serpent; Faust had Mephistopheles. Numerous other figures seeking similar bargains all have a respondent. In the silent universe of post-Modernism, no one replies to Dorian.

What seems at first to be a rational consistency, identifying the events of the novel as transgressions within a broadly accepted moral universe, quickly breaks down under closer scrutiny. The painting does progressively deteriorate, seemingly at the same pace as Dorian's growing proclivity for depravities. It is also a fact that, until the very end, Dorian remains unscathed by the physical consequences normally attendant upon such a life. Nonetheless, beyond Dorian's supposition, nothing supports the idea that his portrait changes as a judgment or reflection of his moral condition. Taking that unsubstantiated judgment as an unquestionable affirmation of a causal link distorts what the text actually presents. Dorian's recognition of the start of the picture's deterioration, coming immediately after his rejection of Sybil Vane, demonstrates my point:

> [Dorian] went over to the picture, and examined it. In the dim arrested light that struggled through the cream-coloured silk blinds, the face appeared to him to be a little changed. The expression looked different. One would have said that there was a touch of cruelty in the mouth. It was certainly strange. (*DG*, 77)

The narrative makes crystal clear what Dorian thinks he sees—"the face appeared to him to be a little changed"—but what stands out here, and what remains a constant for the rest of the novel, is the subjective tone—"appeared to him—and the vague referentiality of the subsequent observation "One would have said there was a touch of cruelty in the mouth." Nonetheless, this represents a leap that goes unsubstantiated in the narrative. The physical degeneration that shifts from Dorian to the painting is represented as a *fait accompli*, but the narrative gives no explanation for it.

Nonetheless, individuals in the novel are disposed to impose a grand metaphysical meaning on the world, and early on Dorian offers the prime example of this inclination. Almost as soon as Basil Hallward completes the picture, Dorian's world becomes governed by his obsession with the painting and its transformations. The narrative goes into great detail describing his sense of connection to it and his fascination with its changes. Indeed, as noted above, in short order Dorian sees the metamorphosis of his portrait as a harsh commentary on his degenerate behavior.

Most readers are quick to adopt a similar view. However, there is no concrete evidence in the narrative that the portrait's mutation comes about as consequences of violating some moral system, no matter what Dorian believes. The painting does not make Dorian a selfish, self-centered individual. He was that when he first met Basil Hallward. In fact, the painting does not change Dorian's character in the least. It simply shields him from general public awareness of his dissolution by absorbing the physical evidence of his excess. In short, it gives him license to indulge his appetites without the immediate external confirmation of his behavior.

The narrative, in fact, discourages belief in value systems, particularly through the eloquence of Lord Henry. By proselytizing New Hedonism from the early pages of the novel, Harry continually challenges the moralistic tendencies ingrained in all of the characters. He freely proclaims his devotion to self-indulgence, encourages others to see the world from the same perspective, and refuses to accept any responsibility for the consequences his views might have on others.

At a luncheon at the home of his Aunt Agatha, Harry transfixes the other guests with his account of New Hedonism. When challenged by Mr. Erskine over the possible impact of those views on the Duchess of Harley, Lord Henry blithely dismisses any thought of responsibility for what he has said:

> "And now, my dear young friend [says Mr. Erskine], if you will allow me to call you so, may I ask if you really meant all that you said to us at lunch?"
>
> "I quite forget what I said," smiled Lord Henry. "Was it very bad?"
>
> "Very bad indeed. In fact I consider you extremely dangerous, and if anything happens to our good Duchess we shall all look on you as being primarily responsible." (*DG*, 40)

Harry's natural flippancy makes his expression of forgetfulness difficult to read. However, whether his words are actually so inconsequential that he does not remember them or whether he simply rejects the connection between his ideas and any sort of moral consequences, the conclusion is the same. Harry affirms his belief in a world that is material, transient, episodic, and arbitrary.

Throughout the novel, Lord Henry remains steadfast in this disbelief, showing no intention of succumbing to any form of morality, conventional or otherwise. Admittedly, he remains essentially a passive adherent to New Hedonism, a voyeur more interested in observation than in action. Nonetheless, he is inflexibly tied to the materialist system that his New Hedonism embodies. This becomes quite evident, late in the narrative, when Dorian stands on the brink of confiding to him an instance of the consequences of completely unrestrained behavior. Lord Henry refuses to entertain the possibility of assigning an ethical status—signaled by his rejection of the term "murder"—to the act to which Dorian alludes:

> "What would you say, Harry, if I told you that I had murdered Basil?" said the younger man. He watched him intently after he had spoken.
>
> "I would say, my dear fellow, that you were posing for a character that doesn't suit you. All crime is vulgar, just as all vulgarity is crime. It is not in you, Dorian, to commit a murder. I am

sorry if I hurt your vanity by saying so, but I assure you it is true. Crime belongs exclusively to the lower orders. I don't blame them in the smallest degree. I should fancy that crime was to them what art is to us, simply a method of procuring extraordinary sensations" (*DG*, 76)

Just as he did when confronted with Mr. Erskine's accusation of culpability, Harry deflects his friend's confessional impulse with a rhetorical flourish that barely acknowledges the other's assertions. Nonetheless, his point stands quite clear. Harry has no interest in hearing conventional acquiescence to the morality that his New Hedonism has so readily dismissed.

Dorian has a more conflicted view of the world, inflected by a metaphysical value structure from which he has never completely divested himself. The picture, demonstrably a facilitator of New Hedonism, takes on an additional role in many of the novel's interpretations because of the significance that Dorian gives it. He believes that it reflects the moral consequences of his behavior.

Dorian's view of morality has a paradoxical leaning somewhere between Harry's denial and Basil Hallward's naïve piety. As seen in this interchange with Basil, taking place just before the latter's murder, Dorian maintains a scornful dismissal of overt invocation of religious belief, but his demeanor is that of one who believes that he is beyond salvation not that of someone denying that salvation exists:

> Dorian Gray turned slowly around, and looked at him with tear-dimmed eyes. "It is too late, Basil," he faltered.
>
> "It is never too late, Dorian. Let us kneel down and try if we cannot remember a prayer. Isn't there a verse somewhere, 'Though your sins be as scarlet, yet I will make them as white as snow'?"
>
> "Those words mean nothing to me now." (*DG*, 132)

Dorian is not indifferent to belief, although Basil's socializing efforts through its application enrage him. Dorian sets his own standards for behavior, and he will not conform to anyone else's. Basil expresses hope in the efficacy of the supernatural, a sense of divine intervention as a means of restoration, moments before his death. The invitation to engage in public confession not only meets with Dorian's disdain, but also provokes in him the murderous frenzy that leads to his fatal attack on Basil in much the way a wild animal will resist the curbs of cage, leash, or muzzle.

In fact, Dorian clearly demonstrates that he does believe in salvation, though only through his own actions. When he resists the temptation to seduce Hetty Merton—"Suddenly I determined to leave her as flower-like as I had found her" (*DG*, 174)—he trumpets the act as a gesture of reform. Lord Henry recasts the experience

in material terms, seeing it as simply an extension of the fundamental tenet of New Hedonism that bases life solely on sensation:
"I should think the novelty of the emotion must have given you a
thrill of real pleasure" (*DG,* 174).

Despite Harry's dismissal, Dorian persists in the idea that a good
deed will not only reform his character but also reverse the signs of
its degeneration on the picture. A few pages after the exchange
above, the narrative articulates Dorian's expectations and his disappointment, and it prepares us for the violent reaction that these
misperceptions will provoke:

> As he thought of Hetty Merton, he began to wonder if the por-
> trait in the locked room had changed. . . . He went in quietly . . .
> and dragged the purple hanging from the portrait. A cry of pain
> and indignation broke from him. He could see no change,
> save that in the eyes there was a look of cunning, and in the
> mouth the curved wrinkle of the hypocrite. (*DG,* 183)

What Dorian considers to be a good act does not reverse the picture's degeneration. Instead, another mark of corrosion appears, and
Dorian sees this as a rebuke from the painting, a reflection of puri-
tanical displeasure over his enjoyment of eschewing the seduction
of Hetty. However, that position strains credulity. Even within a system of behavior informed by moral protocols, a great many acts,
labeled as good deeds, are initiated because they bring pleasure to
the agent. That motivation by no reasonable measure invalidates the
impact of the gesture, any more than what the same system would
call an evil act would cease to be so if the person performing it did
not enjoy doing so.

Ultimately, as Dorian will discover to his dismay, his attempts to use
links to traditional morality to understand the painting's metamorphosis prove to be no more effective than the conventional metaphysical
images that others impose on the world of the novel. If anything,
the picture stands as a testament to the amorality of actions in
Dorian's world. Physical conditions provide the narrative's only
explanation for the painting's material transformations. Dorian is a
sensualist committed to living that life fully. Such patterns of
behavior take a marked physical toll. That toll, generally reflected
on the body of the sensualist, in Wilde's story appears in Dorian's
representation on canvas.

Much like Vladimir's musings on the Good Thief in *Waiting for
Godot,* Dorian yearns nostalgically for a conventional system of values that would allow one to dismiss the emptiness consequent of the
solely material world, but the narrative provides no evidence that
such a system exists. There is no mind/body dichotomy. In the world
of the novel, I do not exist because I think, Cogito ergo sum. Rather,

like any other animal, I think as a consequence of my existence, Sum ergo cogito.

This material explanation provides a logical explanation for the action of the narrative, although it leads to a more chilling conclusion. The picture is a yardstick of material life. It registers physical changes as exertions wear out the body, but that degeneration is common to all:

> "[T]ell me, in a low voice, how you have kept your youth. You must have some secret. I am ten years older than you are, and I am wrinkled, and worn, and yellow. You are really wonderful, Dorian. You have never looked more charming than you do to-night." (DG, 78)

Of course, there is a much closer physical similarity than Henry realizes. The vigorous hedonism of Dorian places great physical demands on the body and leads to an accelerated degeneration in the portrait. Lord Henry, who is less actively committed to New Hedonism, follows a slower pace. The paradox is that Dorian's decay, though greater, remains invisible. Lord Henry's lassitude has led to slower physical erosion, but his mere ugliness is on display for all.

The painting provides the means to escape the consequences of living a purely material life in an environment that remains nostalgically committed to metaphysics. It registers the consequences of Dorian's sybaritic life without offering judgment. Dorian fails to understand this, even when Harry bluntly describes the solely material world that surrounds them.

> "The things one feels absolutely certain about are never true. That is the fatality of Faith, and the lesson of Romance. How grave you are! Don't be so serious. What have you or I to do with the superstitions of our age? No: we have given up our belief in the soul." (DG, 178)

Although it might seem anachronistic to employ the term, Dorian acts as a post-Modern man. After his initial shock over the death of Sybil Vane, in which his impulse to act according to what he sees as society's expectations is easily quashed by Lord Henry, he behaves as an animal, satisfying physical urges without qualm. Everything he experiences over the course of his life suggests that materiality is all there is to the world.

The apparent clash in the novel that many critics have seen between conventional and radically reconfigured moral systems is in fact a false dichotomy. New Hedonism is not an ethical system but rather the systematic rejection of such a possibility. It embraces the arbitrariness of the world through its privileging of experience.

It proclaims that sensation is everything, leaving unsaid the fact that sensation is the only thing.

Problems arise late in the narrative because Dorian shows nostalgia for the old moral condition. This produces psychological contradictions that he cannot overcome. In the end, he appears to be destroyed not by New Hedonism but by his rebellion against the system that shapes it or more precisely by the void that surrounds it.

At first glance this assertion runs contrary to the novel's conclusion. Dorian's decision to attack the painting, because of its failure to respond to his efforts at moral reformation and the fatal consequences he endures because of that act, seems to refocus narrative perspective on a highly conventional view of morality. In fact, the events at the end of the narrative do the opposite. They make no endorsement of any metaphysical convictions. The picture has taken on the physical consequences of Dorian's dissipation. When he attacks it, he attacks the object that has sustained his visible condition. The picture relinquishes its role and returns to its original form with the whole episode simply affirming the arbitrariness of human existence. In this it remains consistent to the narrative direction from the opening pages.

What does this mean in terms of one's reading? Our judgment of the novel's characters must change in light of an absence of morality. Readings that emphasize a particular philosophical disposition—from the moral universe to queer theory—have significance only to the extent that they are subservient to New Hedonism. The simple fact of my argument is that *The Picture of Dorian Gray* extends ideas that began with the Book of Job and stand out most overtly in the works of Samuel Beckett. We can find a great many things in the book's narrative, but by its conclusion we have evidence that all of those ideas, at least in the world of the novel, have no significance whatsoever.

WORKS CITED

Hoefle, Andres. "Oscar Wilde, or the Prehistory of Postmodern Parody." *European Journal of English Studies.* 3 (1999): 138–66.

Kemp, Jonathan. "The Importance of Being Postmodern: Oscar Wilde and the Untimely." *The Rupkatha Journal of Interdisciplinary Studies in Humanities.* Vol. 6 http://rupkatha.com/the-importance-of-being-postmodern-oscar-wilde-and-the-untimely/. Last consulted December 8, 2018.

O'Hara, Daniel T. "Prophetic Criticism: Oscar Wilde and His Postmodern Heirs." *Contemporary Literature.* 25.2 (Summer 1984): 250–59.

Wilde, Oscar. *The Picture of Dorian Gray*. A Norton Critical Edition. 2nd [3rd] edition. Ed. Michael Patrick Gillespie. New York: Norton, 2007 [2020].

RICHARD HASLAM

The Hermeneutic Hazards of Hibernicizing Oscar Wilde's *The Picture of Dorian Gray*†

CHASUBLE: . . . My sermon on the meaning of the manna in the wilderness can be adapted to almost any occasion, joyful, or, as in the present case, distressing. . . . I have preached it at harvest celebrations, christenings, confirmations, on days of humiliation and festal days. The last time I delivered it was in the Cathedral, as a charity sermon on behalf of the Society for the Prevention of Discontent among the Upper Orders. The Bishop, who was present, was much struck by some of the analogies I drew.[1]

In 1954, during Dublin's centenary celebrations of Oscar Wilde's birth, playwright Lennox Robinson stated that he "wanted to stress Wilde's Irishness" and "emphatically claim Wilde as a great Irish writer."[2] Despite Robinson's aspiration, the critical mass for successfully repatriating Wilde "as a great Irish writer" took over three decades to gather, with the process quickening during the late 1980s and early-to-mid 1990s, as scholars and advocates examined Wilde's Irish ancestry, his upbringing, and those occasions (usually in letters and conversations, but sometimes in lectures, essays, and book reviews) when he explicitly commented upon Ireland and identified himself as an Irishman or Celt. For example, Davis Coakley and Owen Dudley Edwards skillfully evoked the social and intellectual environment in which Wilde grew up and highlighted almost every reference he made to Ireland.[3] Nevertheless, by the end of the

---

† From *English Literature in Transition, 1880–1920* 57.1 (2014): 37–58. Notes have been renumbered. Page numbers in square brackets are to this Norton Critical Edition. Reprinted by permission of the publisher, ELT Press.
1. Oscar Wilde, *The Importance of Being Earnest*, Act Two, *Complete Works of Oscar Wilde*, 3rd ed. (Glasgow: Harper Collins, 1994), 381.
2. Cited in Noreen Doody, "Performance and Place: Oscar Wilde and the Irish National Interest," *The Reception of Oscar Wilde in Europe*, Stefano Evangelista, ed. (London: Continuum, 2010), 62.
3. Those who assisted the growth rate of this critical mass include Davis Coakley, *Oscar Wilde: The Importance of Being Irish* (Dublin: Town House, 1994); Terry Eagleton, *Saint Oscar* (Derry: Field Day, 1989), vii–xii; Terry Eagleton, *Heathcliff and the Great Hunger: Studies in Irish Culture* (London: Verso, 1995), 320–41; Owen Dudley Edwards, "Introduction," *The Fireworks of Oscar Wilde* (London: Barrie and Jenkins, 1989), 11–38; Owen Dudley Edwards, "The Soul of Man Under Hibernicism," *Irish Studies Review*, 11 (1995), 7–13; Owen Dudley Edwards, "Impressions of an Irish Sphinx," *Wilde the Irishman*, Jerusha McCormack, ed. (New Haven: Yale UP, 1998), 47–70; Ian Christopher Fletcher, "The Soul of Man Under Imperialism: Oscar Wilde, Race, and Empire," *Journal of Victorian Culture*, 5.2 (2000), 334–41; Richard Haslam, "Oscar Wilde and the

1990s, some scholars began to question the methodologies used to Hibernicize Wilde's literary writings as opposed to his life. Ian Small argued that several essays in Jerusha McCormack's edited collection *Wilde the Irishman* were "highly speculative and seem to strain to make connections," so that "the 'Irish dimension' (for the want of a better term) seems rather gratuitously tacked on."[4]

Imagination of the Celt," *Irish Studies Review*, 11 (1995), 2–5; Declan Kiberd, "The London Exiles: Wilde and Shaw," *The Field Day Anthology of Irish Writing*, Seamus Deane, ed. (Derry: Field Day, 1991), II: 372–515; Declan Kiberd, *Inventing Ireland: The Literature of the Modern Nation* (Cambridge: Harvard UP, 1995), 33–50; Fintan O'Toole, "Venus in Blue Jeans: Oscar Wilde, Jesse James, Crime and Fame," *Wilde the Irishman*, 71–81; Tom Paulin, "The Aesthetic Fenian: Oscar Wilde," *Ireland and the English Crisis* (Newcastle-upon-Tyne: Bloodaxe, 1984), 194–201; Richard Pine, *The Thief of Reason: Oscar Wilde and Modern Ireland* (Dublin: Gill and Macmillan, 1995); Neil Sammells, "Oscar Wilde: Quite Another Thing," *Irish Writing: Exile and Subversion*, Paul Hyland and Neil Sammells, eds. (New York: St. Martin's Press, 1991), 116–25; Neil Sammells, "Rediscovering the Irish Wilde," *Rediscovering Oscar Wilde*, Constantin-George Sandulescu, ed. (Gerrards Cross: Colin Smythe, 1994), 362–70; Deirdre Toomey, "The Story-Teller at Fault: Oscar Wilde and Irish Orality," *Wilde the Irishman*, 24–35; and David A. Upchurch, *Wilde's Use of Irish Celtic Elements in 'The Picture of Dorian Gray'* (New York: Peter Lang, 1992).

For overviews of the growing interest in the Irish Wilde during the 1990s, see Noreen Doody, "Oscar Wilde: Nation and Empire," *Palgrave Advances in Oscar Wilde Studies*, Frederick S. Roden, ed. (New York: Palgrave Macmillan, 2004), 246–66; Josephine Guy and Ian Small, *Oscar Wilde's Profession: Writing and the Culture Industry in the Late Nineteenth Century* (Oxford: Oxford UP, 2000), 5–7; Melissa Knox, *Oscar Wilde in the 1990s: The Critic as Creator* (Rochester: Camden House, 2001), 143–64; Máire Ní Fhlathúin, "The Irish Oscar Wilde: Appropriations of the Artist," *Irish Studies Review*, 7.3 (1999), 337–46; Neil Sammells, *Wilde Style: The Plays and Prose of Oscar Wilde* (Harlow: Longman, 2000), 6–22; Neil Sammells, "The Irish Wilde," *Approaches to Teaching the Works of Oscar Wilde*, Philip E. Smith II, ed. (New York: Modern Language Association, 2008), 35–41; and Ian Small, *Oscar Wilde: Recent Research. A Supplement to 'Oscar Wilde Revalued'* (Greensboro: ELT Press, 2000), 51–69.

Later contributions to the scholarly category of the Irish Wilde include Anya Clayworth, "Revising a Recalcitrant Patriot: Oscar Wilde's Irish Reviews Reconsidered," *Forum for Modern Language Studies*, 38.3 (2002), 252–60; Doody, "Performance and Place"; Declan Kiberd, *Irish Classics* (Cambridge: Harvard UP, 2001), 325–39; Jarlath Killeen, *The Faiths of Oscar Wilde: Catholicism, Folklore and Ireland* (Houndsmills: Palgrave Macmillan, 2005); Jarlath Killeen, *The Fairy Tales of Oscar Wilde* (Aldershot: Ashgate, 2007); Eiléan Ní Chuilleanáin, ed., *The Wilde Legacy* (Dublin: Four Courts Press, 2003); and Éibhear Walshe, *Oscar's Shadow: Wilde, Homosexuality and Modern Ireland* (Cork: Cork UP, 2011).

4. Small, *Oscar Wilde: Recent Research. A Supplement to 'Oscar Wilde Revalued'*, 67. Small also notes one "glaring omission" in many of the Hibernicizing studies of Wilde—"the lack of attention given to the early poems, many of which were published in Irish periodicals" (67). As several scholars have shown, the multiple revisions and publication sites of Wilde's poems (from 1875 to 1898) are highly significant for any understanding of his shifting self-presentations of national allegiance. See Nicholas Frankel, *Oscar Wilde's Decorated Books* (Ann Arbor: The U of Michigan P, 2000), 25–46; Isobel Murray, "Introduction," Oscar Wilde, *Complete Poetry* (Oxford: Oxford UP, 1997), ix–xvi; and Robin Skelton, *Celtic Contraries* (Syracuse: Syracuse UP, 1990), 1–18. The same is true for the publishing and performance history of most of Wilde's works. See Frankel, *Decorated Books*; Josephine Guy and Ian Small, *Studying Oscar Wilde: History, Criticism, and Myth* (Greensboro: ELT Press, 2006); and Guy and Small, *Oscar Wilde's Profession*. Jarlath Killeen does examine one early poem— "Requiescat"—in detail in *The Faiths of Oscar Wilde* (27–34). In addition, Curtis Marez explores how several of Wilde's early poems reveal "his devotion to a uniquely British heritage encapsulated in a canon of beauty" at the same time that he "was in some sense an Irish nationalist." See "The Other Addict: Reflections on Colonialism and Oscar Wilde's Opium Smoke Screen," *ELH* 64 (1997), 262. (On the early poems, see 262–64.) With respect to the Irish resonances of Wilde's early plays, Davis Coakley

This article builds upon Small's analysis, identifying methodological problems in early and recent attempts to Hibernicize Wilde's
works, especially *The Picture of Dorian Gray*. The goal is to contribute to what Small describes as a "useful project for future studies of
Wilde"—"to reconcile the insights generated by critical theory with
the attention to secure evidence associated with traditional empiri-
cist historiography."[5] The methodology here is also indebted to Steven Mailloux's concept of rhetorical hermeneutics, which argues
that "the hermeneutic problem of how text and reader interact" is
"ultimately inseparable" from "the *rhetorical* problem of how interpreters interact with other interpreters in trying to argue for or
against different meanings."[6]

Surveying Strategies of Similitude

Owen Dudley Edwards and others have explored how Wilde may
have transmuted within his own literary writings Irish folk material
originally assimilated from his parents.[7] However, David Upchurch

---

makes one of the more plausible cases, finding convincing correspondences in the speeches
of the eponymous heroine of *Vera, or The Nihilists* (1880) to the "revolutionary rhetoric"
of Wilde's mother during her Speranza and Young Ireland phase (*Oscar Wilde*, 182).

5. Small, *Oscar Wilde: Recent Research. A Supplement to 'Oscar Wilde Revalued'*, 13.
6. Steven Mailloux, *Reception Histories: Rhetoric, Pragmatism, and American Cultural
Politics* (Ithaca: Cornell UP, 1998), 50. As Mailloux notes, in "some ways, rhetoric and
interpretation are practical forms of the same extended human activity":

> Rhetoric is based on interpretation; interpretation is communicated through rhe-
> toric. Furthermore, as reflections on practice, hermeneutics and rhetorical theory
> are mutually defining fields: hermeneutics is the rhetoric of establishing meaning,
> and rhetoric the hermeneutics of problematic linguistic situations. When we ask
> about the meaning of a text, we receive an interpretive argument; when we seek the
> means of persuasion, we interpret the situation. As theoretical practices, herme-
> neutics involves placing a text in a meaningful context, while rhetoric requires the
> contextualization of a text's effects. (4)

7. See Edwards, "Impressions of an Irish Sphinx," *Wilde the Irishman*, 57–60; Angela
Bourke, "Hunting Out the Fairies: E. F. Benson, Oscar Wilde and the Burning of
Bridget Cleary," *Wilde the Irishman*, 39, 42–43; Jerusha McCormack, "Wilde's
Fiction(s)," *The Cambridge Companion to Oscar Wilde*, Peter Raby, ed. (Cambridge:
Cambridge UP, 1997), 117; Pine, *Thief of Reason*, 23, 31, 180, 183–84, 326; and Deirdre Toomey, "The Story-Teller at Fault: Oscar Wilde and Irish Orality," *Wilde the Irish-
man*, 24–35. For critiques of McCormack's and Pine's "lack of familiarity with folklore
scholarship," see Anne Markey, *Oscar Wilde's Fairy Tales: Origins and Contexts* (Dublin: Irish Academic Press, 2011), 6, 55–56, 154, 183. For explorations of how Lady
Wilde's version of an Irish folktale called "The Priest's Soul" may have influenced her
son's prose poem "The House of Judgment," his fantasy story "The Fisherman and His
Soul," and *The Picture of Dorian Gray*, see Philip Cohen, *The Moral Vision of Oscar
Wilde* (Rutherford: Fairleigh Dickinson UP, 1978), 70, 73–75; Edwards, "Impressions
of an Irish Sphinx," *Wilde the Irishman*, 59; Markey, *Oscar Wilde's Fairy Tales*, 173–74;
and Pine, *Thief of Reason*, 38. Wilde included "The Priest's Soul" in his post-prison
performance repertoire. See Toomey, "The Story-Teller at Fault: Oscar Wilde and Irish
Orality," *Wilde the Irishman*, 34. This tale was one of three that Wilde had
especially praised in his review of W. B. Yeats's anthology *Fairy and Folk Tales of the
Irish Peasantry*; the other two were "The Horned Women," also by his mother, and
"Teig O'Kane and the Corpse," by Douglas Hyde. See Oscar Wilde, *Reviews* (London:
Dawsons of Pall Mall, 1969), 406–11. Nonetheless, Neil Sammells finds Toomey's
readings indicative of "the dangers inherent in applying notions of authenticity to our

illustrates the challenges of such genetic criticism when he identifies the mysterious power that permits Dorian Gray to remain youthful while his portrait ages. First, he speculates that "the pink-flowering thorn" (mentioned in the novel's first sentence) growing in the garden of Basil Hallward's studio is a hawthorn.[8] Next, he notes Lady Wilde's claim that Irish peasants believed the hawthorn's branches housed "the good people" or fairies.[9] Then, he concludes that it is "the Irish fairies" who answer Dorian's prayer: "They are the most logical supernatural force because they are interested in youth and beauty, and they travel on the winds" to London, where they dwell in the branches of "their sacred tree," outside the studio.[1] This intriguing hypothesis highlights the major challenge facing Hibernicizers of Wilde's writings: his fictional works contain no explicitly Irish characters or settings. In fact, one of the few references to his compatriots in Wilde's drama or fiction is Mrs. Chevely's remark (in *An Ideal Husband*) that if "one could only teach the English how to talk, and the Irish how to listen, society here [in London] would be quite civilised."[2] One response to this absence might be to insist (by adapting Basil Hallward's words about Dorian) that Ireland "is never more present in [Wilde's] work than when no image of [it] is there."[3] There may be truth in this, but the trick is to find compelling proof.

Pursuing such proof, some critics resort to psychoanalysis—that exquisitely malleable matrix. Declan Kiberd contends that nineteenth-century Ireland functioned as "England's Unconscious" and that the English, through a series of "drastic self-repressions,"

understanding of Wilde's life and work—particularly notions of cultural, national and sexual authenticity" (*Wilde Style*, 14–15).

8. Oscar Wilde, *The Complete Works of Oscar Wilde. III. The Picture of Dorian Gray*, Joseph Bristow, ed. (Oxford: Oxford UP, 2005), 167 [5]; Upchurch, *Wilde's Use of Irish Celtic Elements in 'The Picture of Dorian Gray'*, 25.

9. Lady Wilde, *Ancient Legends, Mystic Charms, and Superstitions of Ireland. With Sketches of the Irish Past* (Boston: Ticknor and Co., 1887), I: 10–11; Upchurch, *Wilde's Use of Irish Celtic Elements in 'The Picture of Dorian Gray'*, 25.

1. Upchurch, *Wilde's Use of Irish Celtic Elements in 'The Picture of Dorian Gray'*, 25–26. Upchurch locates the germ of his thesis in the following source: Joyce Carol Oates, "The Picture of Dorian Gray: Wilde's Parable of the Fall," *Critical Inquiry*, 7 (1980), 419–28; Upchurch (24–25). For Edwards, Upchurch's thesis "gives as good an explanation as any for the forces who grant Dorian Gray's wish for eternal youth in exchange for the ageing of the picture" ("Impressions of an Irish Sphinx," *Wilde the Irishman*, 59). In addition, other critics have suggested (without providing cogent evidence) that the folklore of *Tír na nÓg* (in particular, the story of Oisin's transformation into an old man when he returns to Ireland) furnishes a relevant provenance for *The Picture of Dorian Gray*: see Bourke, "Hunting Out the Fairies," *Wilde the Irishman*, 39, 42–43; Coakley, *Oscar Wilde*, 204–205; Edwards, "Impressions of an Irish Sphinx," *Wilde the Irishman*, 58–59; McCormack, "Wilde's Fiction(s)," 111; Maureen O'Connor, "The Picture of Dorian Gray as Irish National Tale," *Writing Irishness in Nineteenth-Century British Culture*, Neil McCaw, ed. (Aldershot: Ashgate, 2004), 203; and Pine, *Thief of Reason*, 163.

2. Wilde, *An Ideal Husband, Complete Works*, 564.

3. Wilde, *The Picture of Dorian Gray*, 177 [14].

stereotyped the Irish as women or children in order to back their claim that "the Irishman was incapable of self-government." This misrepresentation occurred because the English understanding of the Anglo-Irish relationship was "nothing other than a neurosis." Drawing upon Otto Rank's Freudian concept of "the Double," Kiberd portrays Wilde's *The Importance of Being Earnest* as "a parable of Anglo-Irish relations and a pointer to their resolution."[4] Nonetheless, the word "parable" discloses Kiberd's recourse to allegoresis, or "allegorical interpretation," the hermeneutic maneuver of "explaining a work, or a figure in myth, or any created entity, as if there were another sense to which it referred, that is, presuming the work or figure to be encoded with meaning intended by the author or a higher spiritual authority."[5] This technique encourages Kiberd to homogenize Wilde's biography and his works. Thus, he tells us that "Wilde's *entire literary career* constituted an ironic comment on the tendency of Victorian Englishmen to attribute to the Irish those emotions which they had repressed within themselves" and that Wilde engaged "in a *lifelong* performance of 'Englishness' which was really a parody of the very notion."[6] Yet as Máire Ní Fhlathúin points out, such assertions disregard the contingencies and inconsistencies pervading Wilde's artistic and personal life.[7] Those who fail to consider (or choose to ignore) the power of what Russell Jackson and Small have termed "external and contingent forces" upon Wilde's life and work, and who instead detect (or construct) consistently developed and applied aesthetic and nationalist programs may be taking too literally Wilde's arch claim that "[o]nly mediocrities progress,"

4. Kiberd, *Inventing Ireland*, 29–30; 30; 43. Otto Rank, *The Double: A Psychoanalytic Study*, Harry Tucker, trans and ed. (1914; Chapel Hill: The U of North Carolina P, 1971).
5. Rita Copeland and Peter Struck, "Introduction," *The Cambridge Companion to Allegory* (Cambridge: Cambridge UP, 2010), 2. For genealogies of allegoresis, see Copeland and Struck, "Introduction," 1–11; Jean Grondin, *Introduction to Philosophical Hermeneutics*, Joel Weinsheimer, trans. (1991; New Haven: Yale UP, 1994), 1–44; and Peter Szondi, *Introduction to Literary Hermeneutics*, Martha Woodmansee, trans. (Cambridge: Cambridge UP, 1995), 1–13.
6. Kiberd, *Inventing Ireland*, 35, 36; my emphasis.
7. Ní Fhlathúin, "The Irish Oscar Wilde: Appropriations of the Artist," 341–42. Compare the following observation: "One of the reasons why critics have found it so difficult to explain Wilde's *oeuvre* in terms of any single and coherent set of ambitions is precisely because his works were produced under a wide variety of quite distinct social and commercial pressures and were addressed to very different sorts of audiences" (Small, *Oscar Wilde: Recent Research. A Supplement to 'Oscar Wilde Revalued'*, 145). Isobel Murray uses the early poems to challenge a previous version of Kiberd's argument advanced in the essays *Anglo-Irish Attitudes* (Derry: Field Day Publications, 1984) and "The London Exiles." Murray suggests that the "'Englishnesses' of [Wilde's] early poems," rather than being "part of a masterful and premeditated plan," are instead "[a] stumbling towards self-discovery—or self-creation" (Murray, "Introduction," *Complete Poetry*, xv). Kiberd elsewhere mentions briefly that the "future master of paradox was already wavering between national extremes, emulating his mother's Irish patriotism in one poem, only to salute Keats as 'poet-painter of our English land' in the next," but he ignores the implications of this wavering (*Inventing Ireland*, 34). In a later work, Kiberd makes little use of psychoanalytical critical approaches but still represents Wilde's writings as a coherent, consistently developed, and unified project (*Irish Classics*, 325–39).

whereas "[a]n artist revolves in a cycle of masterpieces, the first of which is no less perfect than the last."[8]

Kiberd's allegorizing extraction of Irish historical contexts from Wilde's literary texts relies on a strategy of similitude. For example, one of Lady Bracknell's complaints ("This shilly-shallying with the question is absurd") strikes Kiberd as "suspiciously like English claims that the Irish kept on changing their question." In addition, the phrase "even as" performs a lot of rhetorical work: "The denied double thus ends up setting the agenda of its creator, who, being unaware of it, becomes its unconscious slave. The women in the play set the agenda for men, Bunbury for Algy, butlers for masters, and so on, even as the Irish Parnellites were setting the agenda for England, repeatedly paralyzing politics at Westminister."[9] Terry Eagleton also engages in psychoanalytically historicizing allegoresis in which Ireland in the 1800s "figured as Britain's unconscious": "Just as we indulge in the world of the id in actions which the ego would find intolerable, so nineteenth-century Ireland became the place where the British were forced to betray their own principles, in a kind of negation or inversion of their conscious beliefs." Here, Eagleton's "Just as . . . so" rhetorical construction duplicates Kiberd's "even as." After stating that "Ireland represented a rebarbative world which threatened to unmask Britain's own civility," Eagleton remarks: "[N]o doubt some excessively ingenious critic could uncover an allegory for this in *The Picture of Dorian Gray*."[1] But the phrase "excessively ingenious" inadvertently reveals that such a critic would be more likely to construct an allegoresis than "uncover" an actual allegory.[2]

8. Russell Jackson and Ian Small, "Oscar Wilde: A 'Writerly' Life," *Modern Drama*, 37.1 (1994), 5; Oscar Wilde, *The Complete Letters of Oscar Wilde*, Merlin Holland and Rupert Hart-Davis, eds. (New York: Henry Holt and Company, 2000), 615.
9. Wilde, *The Importance of Being Earnest, Complete Works*, 364. Kiberd, *Inventing Ireland*, 42, 43. Other phrases that perform the same function include "just as," "as," "like," and "In a somewhat similar fashion": ibid., 35, 42, 43. Kiberd also uses the words "perhaps" and "and" to evoke similarities between Anglo-Irish relationships and *The Importance of Being Earnest*'s dialogue and characterization (42, 43). In addition, he accidentally misattributes quotations on two occasions: it is her first-born, Willie, not Oscar, that Lady Wilde imagines as "a Hero perhaps and President of the future Irish Republic." See Kiberd, *Inventing Ireland*, 46, and compare Richard Ellmann, *Oscar Wilde* (London: Hamish Hamilton, 1987), 20. Second, Kiberd presents as Wilde's what are actually Yeats's comments on certain nineteenth-century Irish novelists (49). The comments are quoted by Wilde in a review of Yeats's *Fairy and Folk Tales*. See Wilde, *Reviews*, 406.
1. Eagleton, *Heathcliff and the Great Hunger*, 9.
2. Despite declining the challenge on this page, Eagleton nonetheless later allegorizes Wilde's life and *The Importance of Being Earnest* into commentaries on the declining Anglo-Irish (*Heathcliff and the Great Hunger*, 326); he also allegorizes what he terms "Protestant Gothic" by Charles Maturin, Joseph Sheridan Le Fanu and Bram Stoker (187–99, 215–16). Four years earlier, introducing a selection of Wilde's writings, Eagleton had allegorized *The Picture of Dorian Gray* and other works by Wilde into illustrations and prophecies of Wilde's careering career and veering states of mind about being an Irishman in England. See Terry Eagleton, "Introduction," Oscar Wilde,

The critic prophesied by Eagleton turned out to be Richard Pine, whose decipherings of Irish dimensions in Wilde's works also rely on a strategy of similitude. Pine links *The Importance of Being Earnest* to Maria Edgeworth's *The Absentee* (1812) thus: "In danger of being lost even when at home, Lord Colambre is berated for wanting to go to Ireland 'merely because it's your native country'—the pre-echo of Wilde's Algernon needing to be in London to miss an appointment because the appointment is in London . . . is ominous. He knows his native country by being in another place; when he is in his native country, he no longer knows it."[3] Like Kiberd, Pine resorts to speculative psychologizing and parabolizing, finding it "distinctly possible to suppose that subconsciously Wilde, who had an acute perception of the nature of history, wrote *The Picture of Dorian Gray* not as a parable simply of 'Everyman' but more specifically as a commentary on the Irish race experience and on what had been lost in that experience."[4]

In his 2002 survey of Wilde studies, Bruce Bashford astutely dissects Pine's methodology, citing first a passage from *The Picture of Dorian Gray* and then Pine's explication:

> To him [Dorian], man was a being with myriad lives and myriad sensations, a complex multiform creature that bore within itself strange legacies of thought and passion, and whose very flesh was tainted with the monstrous maladies of the dead.

> Pushed to the edge of the landmass and to the edge of endurance, the Celt was reasserting the primacy of imagination, of mythopoeism, against the despotism of fact.[5]

For Bashford, the "lack of fit here between comment and text seems due to Pine's larger mode of reasoning," which first establishes "an analogy between an Irish view of the actual and the possible and Wilde's view of the same expressed in works not explicitly about Irishness" and "then employs the Irish side of the analogy as though it were an explanatory cause."[6] Yet, as Bashford notes, "analogies

Plays, Prose Writings and Poems (London: David Campbell Publishers [Everyman's Library], 1991), x–xi.
3. Pine, *Thief of Reason*, 58.
4. Ibid., 197–98. Reviewing Pine's book, Kevin Barry notes its allegorizing tendency, and Small takes issue with Pine's "basic assumption that there is an automatic congruence between national difference, sexual difference and artistic difference." See Kevin Barry, "Oscar and the Irish [review of Richard Pine's *The Thief of Reason*]," *The Irish Times*, 30 December 1995, Weekend 13; Small, *Oscar Wilde: Recent Research. A Supplement to 'Oscar Wilde Revalued'*, 54.
5. Wilde, *The Picture of Dorian Gray*, 288 [120]; Pine, *Thief of Reason*, 199; cited in Bruce Bashford, "When Critics Disagree: Recent Approaches to Oscar Wilde," *Victorian Literature and Culture*, 30.2 (2002), 616.
6. Bashford, "When Critics Disagree," 616. Prior to the passages Bashford cites, Pine quotes Dorian's reflection "upon man moving through History" and his impression "that the whole of history was merely the record of his own life": Wilde, *The Picture of*

often fail to meet the test of a causal explanation, namely that it is
necessary to draw the proposed analogy for the effect to be intelli-
gible"; whereas with Pine's analysis, "even if Dorian's belief in the
'myriad' possibilities we contain is somehow like a Celtic sense of
imaginative possibilities, that resemblance does not seem necessary
to understand Dorian's belief." Bashford also finds Kiberd's interpretations of *The Importance of Being Earnest* "strained." It is true, he
notes, that Kiberd, unlike Pine, "brings what he compares more
clearly under a general concept: the need to know about the self
through the other." Nevertheless, "while the concept may apply to
each instance separately—the English/Irish pair and the Algy/
Bunbury pair—the instances do not illuminate each other," and
"[i]t is hard to see how *The Importance of Being Earnest* calls to
mind Kiberd's political parable."[7]

Bashford's analysis of the methodological problems of Pine's and
Kiberd's "reasoning by analogy" remains highly relevant to subsequent efforts to Hibernicize *The Picture of Dorian Gray.*[8] For example, noting that the opium den Dorian visits is called "Daly's" and
that its hall contains "a tattered green curtain," Mary King claims
that Wilde is depicting a "shebeen," "an Irish low-life simulacrum
of high society," as part of a project to interrogate "imperialist-
nationalist narratives, and the collusive racism, which underwrites
them."[9] For support she uses the hermeneutic tactic of transposing
Orientalism into Celticism and Dorian's property "the Home Farm"
into "Gladstone's favorite rural retreat . . . 'Oak Farm,'" so that "Selby
Royal" somehow stands for "a displaced Ireland."[1] In a variation on
this type of allegoresis, Curtis Marez contends "that Wilde *refracts*
his own racialization through his character, Dorian," so that
"Dorian's forgetfulness [about his "disreputable" ancestors] *recalls*
Wilde's own experiences at Oxford, where he says he 'forgot' his Irish

---

Dorian Gray, 278, 289 [264, 275]; cited in Pine, *Thief of Reason,* 198–99. Pine then
observes, "As in 'De Profundis' he would identify Christ with the sins of the world, and
himself with Christ, so here Wilde makes Dorian into the conscience of downtrodden
generations whose great famine and great injustice had marginalised and degraded his
imagination" (*Thief of Reason,* 199; my emphasis). This clarifies his simile but does not
undermine Bashford's point about the absence of correspondence and causality
("When Critics Disagree," 616).

7. Bashford, "When Critics Disagree," 617. When Pine refrains from allegoresis, he does
contribute valuable examinations of Wilde's Irish background. For example, he goes into
greater detail than Davis Coakley about the intellectual and political quandaries of
nineteenth-century Ireland, usefully highlighting the paradoxical relevance of Sir William Wilde's description of the country as "a truly regal republic" (*Thief of Reason,* 95).

8. Bashford, "When Critics Disagree," 617.

9. Wilde, *The Picture of Dorian Gray,* 326 [160, 156]; Mary King, "Typing *Dorian Gray:*
Wilde and the Interpellated Text," *Irish Studies Review,* 9.1 (2001), 22. As Joseph Bristow notes, the name "Daly's" is probably "a private joke of some kind," alluding to "the
theatrical productions organized in the West End by the American playwright, director,
and manager John Augustin Daly (1838–99). . . ." See Bristow's endnote in the edition
of *The Picture of Dorian Gray* (452).

1. Wilde, *The Picture of Dorian Gray,* 344 [172]; Mary King, "Typing *Dorian Gray,*" 16, 24.

accent"; thus, "Dorian's origins . . . *represent* a transposition of Wilde's own trajectory," and Wilde's (presumably unconscious) motive in bringing "Dorian to the opium den" is to allow his character to confront, in the form of "the toothsome Malay sailors," "the 'colonial' identity Wilde had tried to erase." According to Marez's ingenious (albeit unconvincing) conclusion, the opium den somehow "*represents* the rage of Caliban [Wilde] who, when gazing into the mirror of Empire, cannot avoid seeing an Irish face."[2]

In an allegoresis that challenges aspects of Marez's reading, Julia Wright maintains that "Wilde's representation of the East End as the 'sordid shame of the great city' and suggestive deployment of whiteness and global collection turn the novel's narrative of personal immorality into a *fable* of imperial predation."[3] Whereas Kiberd's and Pine's allegorizing term of art is "parable," for Wright it is "fable." In her interpretation, "those in the East End, and the working classes in general, are aligned with whiteness," which "emerges, in marked distinction to the discourses of racism which underpin recent whiteness studies, as a sign for those on the margins, on the outside looking in or approaching death." Wright acknowledges that the motif of whiteness is associated just as much with the novel's upper classes but argues that the negative East End "associations trouble the conventional Victorian resonances of Wilde's references to the white hands of the aristocrats," so that in *The Picture of Dorian Gray,* "as in vampire fiction, whiteness marks both predator and prey."[4] Nevertheless, the neutral or positive tone that the narrator adopts in depicting, among other things, the whiteness of daisies, roses, orchids, ties, clouds, youth, boyhood, nerves, Philosophy's feet, dust, fire, moonstones, horses, satin, snow, sugar, piano keys, a parrot's eyelids, and various aristocratic teeth, hands, eyebrows, and beards suggests that the color may be less symbolically freighted than Wright maintains.

In her attempt to Hibernicize Wilde's novel allegorically, Maureen O'Connor also employs "reasoning by analogy," seeking to re-taxonomize *The Picture of Dorian Gray* as an Irish "national tale" by likening it to Sydney Owenson's *The Wild Irish Girl* (1806) and Charles Maturin's *The Wild Irish Boy* (1808).[5] Variations on the "just as" formula permeate the argument, which treats Morgan's and Maturin's lives and novels (in Bashford's phrase) "as though [they] were an explanatory cause" for *The Picture of Dorian Gray* and

2. Curtis Marez, "The Other Addict," 282; my emphases.
3. Wilde, *The Picture of Dorian Gray,* 324 [154]; Julia Wright, *Ireland, India, and Nationalism in Nineteenth-Century Literature* (Cambridge: Cambridge UP, 2007), 194; my emphasis.
4. Wright, *Ireland, India, and Nationalism in Nineteenth-Century Literature,* 190, 190, 192.
5. Bashford, "When Critics Disagree," 617; O'Connor, "*The Picture of Dorian Gray* as Irish National Tale," 195.

Wilde.[6] Nevertheless, O'Connor provides no evidence that Wilde regarded the earlier novels as intertexts for his own, and she ignores the multiplicity of ways—structurally, topically, thematically, tonally—in which *The Picture of Dorian Gray* is not like Morgan's and Maturin's novels.[7] As Small observes, "[I]f one is selective in one's choice of textual examples, then coherence and unity are easily contrived."[8] The same caveat applies to causally analogizing readings.

"Frightened Forest Things"

The critics surveyed above often exhibit great skill in analyzing both the intricacies of Wilde's literary works and the socio-historical contexts in which those works were written. Yet their constructions of cause-and-effect relationships (with context the cause and text the effect) between these two domains are less persuasive. In fact, the 500 pages of E. H. Mikhail's anthology of Wildean interviews and recollections, the 1,200 pages of Wilde's *Letters*, and the thousands of pages of Wilde's own works contain no cogent evidence to justify the typological patterns and *post hoc, ergo propter hoc* fallacies that some Hibernicizing critics generate.[9] These allegorizing methodologies also inform Jarlath Killeen's *The Fairy Tales of Oscar Wilde* and *The Faiths of Oscar Wilde*. Given that these two volumes represent the most substantial recent attempts to Hibernicize Wilde's literary

6. Bashford, "When Critics Disagree," 616. "*Like* the hero of the national tale, Wilde . . ."; ". . . *just as* Terry Eagleton suggests that the formal 'dishevelment of Lady Morgan's national tales' . . . Wilde emphasizes . . ."; "Morgan's *The Wild Irish Girl* was *also* liable to charges of frivolity . . ."; "*[a]s with* Wilde, Morgan was accused . . ."; "*[j]ust as* Morgan's 'theatricality . . . ,' *so did* Wilde's outrageously campy self-parody . . ."; "*[l]ikewise*"; "*[b]oth* authors"; "*recalling that* of Glorvina"; "a *similar* question"; "*[s]imilarly*"; "in *both* Morgan and Wilde"; "*similarly*"; "*recalling*"; "*also* appears"; "[Orientalism] *also* serves as an iteration of nineteenth-century British attitudes towards Ireland and the Irish"; "*[b]oth* Wilde and Morgan"; "*just as*"; "*similar* recourse"; "*like* the salutary wounds"; "*as* antihistorical *as*"; "Orientalization (*i.e.* Hibernicization)"; "*just as*": see O'Connor, "*The Picture of Dorian Gray* as Irish National Tale," 195, 195, 195, 196, 196, 196, 196, 197, 198,198, 199, 200, 200, 201, 201, 201, 202, 202, 203, 203, 205, 205; my emphasis throughout. Like King, O'Connor makes much of Daly's and the curtain (202).
7. Maturin's *Melmoth the Wanderer* (1820) did influence *The Picture of Dorian Gray*, but more through its Gothic than its Irish features. See Richard Haslam, "Melmoth (OW): Gothic Modes in *The Picture of Dorian Gray*," *Irish Studies Review*, 12.3 (December 2004), 303–14; Alison Milbank, "Sacrificial Exchange and the Gothic Double in *Melmoth the Wanderer* and *The Picture of Dorian Gray*," *Shaping Belief: Culture, Politics, and Religion in Nineteenth-Century Writing*, Victoria Morgan and Clare Williams, eds. (Liverpool: Liverpool UP, 2008), 113–28.
8. Small, *Oscar Wilde: Recent Research. A Supplement to 'Oscar Wilde Revalued'*, 145. Compare Small's observation that "it is as if the 'stories' which critics and historians want to tell about Wilde are so compelling that they dictate in advance what is to count as evidence for them" (11).
9. Wilde, *The Complete Letters of Oscar Wilde*; E. H. Mikhail, ed. *Oscar Wilde: Interviews and Recollections* (London: Macmillan, 1979), 2 vols. For an effort to establish a more empirically grounded Irish presence within *Dorian Gray*, see Richard Haslam, "Revisiting the 'Irish Dimension' in Oscar Wilde's *The Picture of Dorian Gray*," forthcoming in *Victorian Literature and Culture*.

works, their arguments and methods warrant sustained scrutiny. In
the opening pages of *The Faiths of Oscar Wilde*, Killeen acknowledges the paucity of information on Wilde's Irish upbringing and
states "that we need to develop a new hermeneutic to probe behind
the manifest content of Wilde's writings to *excavate* the Irish elements."[1] With respect to such a methodology, Neil Sammells's 1994
caveat to Hibernicizers of Wilde's life and works seems both relevant and prescient: "Rediscovering the Irish Wilde is not a matter
of *excavation,* of scraping away the accretions of Englishness to
reveal a Celtic core: it is, rather, a matter of recognizing alternative
identities simultaneously maintained."[2] Reiterating the point in a
later essay, Sammells argues that seeking "to scrape away a supposedly English surface to [Wilde's] work in order to expose an Irish or
Celtic core . . . is potentially both reductionist with respect to the
texts and essentialist with respect to race and nationality: a distinctly
un-Wildean approach to Wilde."[3] For Sammells, "To teach Wilde's
Irishness is to confront the shifting complexities that define his work
and to get students to examine not just the ways they read but the
ways in which they conceive of nationality and nation: pedagogy
through paradox, constructing Wildean ways of reading Wilde."[4]

But what would "Wildean ways of reading" Wilde's works entail?
Should we model our methods on Lord Henry Wotton's lunch-table
improvisations? "The praise of folly, as he went on, soared into a philosophy, and Philosophy herself became young, and catching the
mad music of Pleasure, wearing, one might fancy, her wine-stained
robe and wreath of ivy, danced like a Bacchante over the hills of life,
and mocked the slow Silenus for being sober. Facts fled before her
like frightened forest things."[5] This may not be the best model for
scholars who wish to maintain a fidelity to fact, an engagement with
the empirical. On the other hand, Wilde's works do contain hermeneutic caveats that could help us learn what not to do. Vivian
observes in "The Decay of Lying" that "Wordsworth went to the
lakes, but he was never a lake poet. He found in stones the sermons

---

1. Killeen, *The Faiths of Oscar Wilde,* 11; my emphasis.
2. Sammells, "Rediscovering the Irish Wilde," 369; my emphasis.
3. Sammells, "The Irish Wilde," 35.
4. Ibid., 41. However, this postmodernist analysis, like Kiberd's postcolonial one, occasionally runs afoul of Wilde's aesthetic inconstancy, on which, see also notes 4 and 7 [on pp.
   462–63 and 465] above. Sammells claims that "the determined deconstruction of essen-
   tialisms of all kinds" in Wilde's works is "one of the elements of a *consistent* political and
   aesthetic strategy," but Wilde the proto-postmodernist is less visible in works produced
   before "The Decay of Lying" and after *The Importance of Being Earnest* ("The Irish
   Wilde," 36; my emphasis). Elsewhere, Sammells sidesteps this problem by excluding
   from his examination Wilde's poetry, "which seems to me much less integrated with his
   innovative aesthetic theories, and is curiously inert as a consequence" (Sammells, *Wilde
   Style,* 3). According to Sammells, "In his poetry convention and genre deploy Wilde; in
   the prose and plays he deploys and transforms them" (*Wilde Style,* 5).
5. Wilde, *The Picture of Dorian Gray,* 204–205 [38–39].

he had already hidden there."[6] So too, "The Portrait of Mr. W. H." alerts us to the dangers of "working purely by internal evidence" and relying "not so much on demonstrable proof or formal evidence, but on a kind of spiritual and artistic sense, by which alone . . . could the true meaning of the poems be discerned."[7]

In *The Fairy Tales of Oscar Wilde,* Killeen ignores such warnings and exhumes elaborate political messages about "Irish history" and "folk-Catholic elements" from *The Happy Prince* and *A House of Pomegranates,* finding in these stories "the sermons he [Killeen] had already hidden there."[8] He justifies the allegoresis by claiming that "Wilde himself appears to have been committed to a theory of Gnosticism whereby knowledge is transmitted from the initiated to acolytes through codes and symbols and he also believed that such codes and symbols often operated in some mysterious and magical fashion on the human mind."[9] Unfortunately, Killeen provides no solid evidence that Wilde utilized in the stories any such "theory of Gnosticism," thereby raising the suspicion that this hermetic hermeneutic is itself a type of fairy tale, one originating with Killeen, not Wilde. Indeed, this possibility is raised by one of his reviewers:

> Granted that this is the case, two questions follow: how does the general reader (then or now) gain access to this esoteric knowledge; and how can such self-referential systems of interpretation be refuted? . . . We might ask: how is it that a century or so of readers have managed to make sense of and enjoy "The Selfish Giant" without connecting it to the Irish Land League? Here Killeen's earlier reference to Wilde's Gnosticism comes back to haunt him: for what he represents as the Irishness of the tales can, in the absence of any such reader-response evidence, all too easily appear as a Causabon-type "key to all mythologies," and the persuasiveness of his thesis thus becomes a matter of faith.[1]

6. Wilde, "The Decay of Lying," *The Complete Works of Oscar Wilde. IV. Criticism: Historical Criticism, Intentions, The Soul of Man,* Josephine M. Guy, ed. (Oxford: Oxford UP, 2007), 83.
7. Wilde, "The Portrait of Mr. W. H.," *Complete Works,* 308.
8. Killeen, *The Fairy Tales of Oscar Wilde,* 17.
9. Ibid., 10–11. Contrast this with Sammells: "So when approaching Wilde's Irishness, we need to find ways of helping students read his work that do not involve the cracking of a code. Wilde is not an Irish writer underneath" ("The Irish Wilde," 40).
1. Josephine Guy, "Wilde's Fairy Tales [review of Jarlath Killeen's *The Fairy Tales of Oscar Wilde*]," *ELT,* 52.1 (2009), 87, 92. In her review of *Fairy Tales,* Mimosa Stephenson is more sympathetic to Killeen's allegorizing methodology than is Guy, but she acknowledges that the stories "do not give us clear references to the near-eradication of folk-Catholicism in the Ireland of Wilde's day" and that "[a] leap of faith is required to accept Killeen's interpretation as warranted, interesting and well-developed though it may be." See Mimosa Stephenson, "[Review of Jarlath Killeen's *The Fairy Tales of Oscar Wilde*]," *Christianity and Literature,* 58.2 (2009), 329. See also Anne Markey: "To view Wilde's putative nationalism as the *key* to understanding his fairy tales would do scant justice to their polyvalent nature or to the multiple interpretations they invite" (*Oscar Wilde's Fairy Tales,* 197; my emphasis). She concludes that "Wilde's recourse to

In his earlier book-length project to Hibernicize Wilde's works, Killeen claims to possess precisely such a Gnostic, Causabonic "key": "Wilde's nationality can then be seen as an interpretive key unlocking all aspects of his work." He insists that Wilde's work "can fruitfully be analysed as expressive of an Irish Catholic heritage," comprising both "folk-Catholicism" and the "institutional Catholic Church."[2] Noting Small's concerns about the "tacked on" aspect of "the Irish dimension," Killeen undertakes to avoid applying any "amorphous allegorical thematic."[3] Nonetheless, Killeen's interpretation of *Salome* discloses the challenges involved in this undertaking. He asserts that *Salome* "critiques the muscular Protestant assault on Irish culture by Evangelical zealots, a mission that became associated with the 'Souperism' controversy of the 1840s" and that "[t]his reading is not an attempt to reduce the play to an allegorical treatment of religious relations in nineteenth-century Ireland." His approach avoids such reduction, Killeen argues, because "Wilde's emergence from an Evangelical, Famine-stricken environment is crucial to his construction of the play, and this organic relationship with his environment prevents this reading from being merely a crude allegory." Nonetheless, three factors appear to undermine these assertions. First, "crude allegory"—or, more precisely, allegoresis—shows up fairly soon: "Salome, the pagan princess who worships the moon, is an allegorical Ireland, and her position in the Roman court is analogous to that of Ireland within the Empire."[4] Second, Killeen supplies no persuasive evidence to establish that Wilde intended *Salome* to function as an allegory about Ireland. Third, his claim that "Wilde's emergence from an Evangelical, Famine-stricken environment is crucial to" creating *Salome* exemplifies the kind of "lucidly circular argument" bemoaned by one of his reviewers.[5] It is true that Wilde's half brother, Henry Wilson, was a

the Irish folk tradition" in *The Happy Prince* and *A House of Pomegranates* "is selective and far less influential than some recent commentators have suggested" (198).

2. Killeen, *The Faiths of Oscar Wilde*, 11, 1, 18, 19. For overviews of Catholicizing interpretations of Wilde, see Patrick O'Malley, *Catholicism, Sexual Deviance, and Victorian Gothic Culture* (Cambridge: Cambridge UP, 2006), 165–92; and Patrick O'Malley, "Religion," *Palgrave Advances in Oscar Wilde Studies*, 167–88.

3. Small, *Oscar Wilde: Recent Research. A Supplement to 'Oscar Wilde Revalued'*, 67; Killeen, *The Fairy Tales of Oscar Wilde*, 21.

4. Killeen, *The Faiths of Oscar Wilde*, 65, 73.

5. See D. C. Rose, "To Each His or Her Own Wilde [review of Jarlath Killeen's *The Faiths of Oscar Wilde*]," *Irish Literary Supplement*, Fall 2006, 26. In his review of *The Faiths of Oscar Wilde*, John Peters comments that Killeen's yoking of an Irish "context" to Wilde's writings "result[s] in significant jumps in reasoning" and "questionable conclusions" and Killeen's persistent portrayals of "Wilde's works as advocating Catholicism and criticizing colonialism of Ireland . . . rarely provid[e] . . . sufficient evidence for such conclusions." See John Peters, "Wilde's 'Faiths' [review of Jarlath Killeen's *The Faiths of Oscar Wilde*]," *ELT*, 50.2 (2007), 226. Nevertheless, it must be noted that other reviewers do find the methodology and the evidence plausible. See Graham Price, "[Review of Jarlath Killeen's *The Faiths of Oscar Wilde*]," *Irish University Review*, 36.1 (2006), 244–48; Dennis Taylor, "The Old Faith, 'The Old Sod,' and the New Critical

bigot and that Wilde's father told him "marvellous tales" about the Famine, but this does not mean he came in any concrete way from "an Evangelical, Famine-stricken environment." How, therefore, can this mythical background be "crucial" to our understanding of a play written in vastly different geographical, emotional, and intellectual circumstances, fifteen years after his father died?[6]

Thus, Máire Ní Fhlathúin's critique of Upchurch applies equally to Killeen: "Wilde shared a country, a landscape, a body of folklore with the 'servants in his house in town and the peasants in the country where his father owned a fishing lodge,' but [h]e did not share a mindset with them."[7] Nevertheless, Killeen strives to make it seem as though he did. For example, after the antisuperstition Thirteen Club invited Wilde to attend a dinner, he replied that he "love[s] superstitions," believing them to be "the colour element of thought and imagination" and "the opponents of common sense," that "enemy of romance."[8] Killeen frames this quotation as follows: "He [Wilde] spoke of *the superstitions of the people of Mayo* as 'the colour element of thought and imagination. They are the opponents of common sense. Common sense is the enemy of romance,' a sentiment echoing that of his mother who believed that 'the very tendency to superstition, so marked in Irish nature, arises from an instinctive dislike to the narrow limitations of common sense.'"[9] By bookending Wilde's words with the phrase "the people of Mayo" and a Lady Wilde quotation, Killeen implies—inaccurately—that Wilde refers specifically to the superstitions of the Irish poor.[1]

Wilde's mother did publish Irish folklore collections, and Wilde in his fiction, poetry, and some of his drama was more attracted to romance than realism, but these facts do not legitimize the extravagant extrapolation that "Irish folk-Catholicism was Wilde's way of interpreting the world," something that "seduced and compelled his life-long attention."[2] Furthermore, Killeen offers no cogent evidence from Wilde for the claim that "Irish folk-Catholicism" constituted his *weltanschauung,* a claim inapplicable even to Yeats and Lady Gregory, who—unlike Wilde—explicitly used Irish folklore as raw

---

Openness [review of Jarlath Killeen's *The Faiths of Oscar Wilde*]," *Religion and the Arts,* 14 (2010), 459–66.
6. Wilde, *The Complete Letters of Oscar Wilde,* 54, 316.
7. Upchurch, *Wilde's Use of Irish Celtic Elements in 'The Picture of Dorian Gray',* 1; Ní Fhlathúin, "The Irish Oscar Wilde," 340.
8. Wilde, *The Complete Letters of Oscar Wilde,* 581.
9. Killeen, *The Faiths of Oscar Wilde,* 34; Lady Wilde, *Ancient Legends, Mystic Charms, and Superstitions of Ireland,* I: 280; my emphasis.
1. The same misframing occurs in Killeen, *The Fairy Tales of Oscar Wilde,* 147. Later an introductory essay gives the quotation a more accurate context. See Jarlath Killeen, "Introduction: Wilde's Aphoristic Imagination," *Oscar Wilde,* Jarlath Killeen, ed. (Dublin: Irish Academic Press, 2011), 5.
2. Killeen, *The Faiths of Oscar Wilde,* 188. The latter passage recalls the phrases "lifelong performance" and "entire literary career" in Kiberd, *Inventing Ireland,* 36, 35.

material for their works.[3] It is true that Wilde occasionally enjoyed reading Irish folklore, as his laudatory review of Yeats's *Fairy and Folk Tales of the Irish Peasantry* (1888) indicates, although Yeats's flattering references to Lady Wilde may have inflated Wilde's praise.[4] Killeen is also correct in claiming that "in his many book reviews, Wilde was not enthusiastic about realism as a mode of writing," and he astutely identifies a relevant quotation from the same review in which Wilde praises Yeats: "This is the supreme advantage that fiction possesses over fact. It can make things artistically probable; can call for imaginative and realistic credence; can, by force of mere style, compel us to believe. The ordinary novelists, by keeping close to the ordinary incidents of commonplace life, seem to me to abdicate half their power."[5] Nonetheless, we should note that Wilde is commenting here not on Yeats's anthology but on "the marvels of occultism and hypnotism" in English author Violet Fane's novel *The Story of Helen Davenant* (1889). According to Wilde, "Romance . . . welcomes what is wonderful; the temper of wonder is part of her own secret; she loves what is strange and curious."[6] However, as *The Picture of Dorian Gray* and his other stories show, he did not find such romance in Irish idioms, settings, or subject matter. That should make us cautious about inferring that "Irish folk-Catholicism" shapes his worldview.

We can better understand Wilde's eschewal of Irish elements, ornaments, and subtexts by considering his ambivalent attitude to the use of "Scotch and Border dialect" in contemporary ballads: he playfully accepts that "dialect is dramatic . . . a vivid method of recreating a past that never existed [and] something between 'A Return to Nature' and 'A Return to the Glossary.'" In addition, despite acknowledging the impulse to treat "dialect as expressing simply the pathos of provincialisms," he concedes that "there is more in it than mere mispronunciations."[7] Nevertheless, reviewing in the same month (June 1889) a volume of Swinburne's poetry, he is less condoning: "The amount of pleasure one gets out of dialect is a matter entirely of temperament. To say 'mither' instead of 'mother' seems to many the acme of romance. There are others who are not quite so ready to believe in the pathos of provincialisms. There is,

3. Compare the following: "Oscar Wilde, by contrast [to Yeats and Lady Wilde], regarded folklore as a primitive but inferior form of literature," which "was valuable, not for its embodiment of spiritual truth or national identity, but for its contribution to the development of higher art forms." See Markey, *Oscar Wilde's Fairy Tales*, 51.
4. Wilde, *Reviews*, 406–407.
5. Wilde, *Reviews*, 413; cited in Killeen, *The Faiths of Oscar Wilde*, 83. Along with several punctuation errors, Killeen's transcription substitutes "holds" for "possesses" and omits the phrase "can call for imaginative and realistic credence." See also Killeen, "Introduction: Wilde's Aphoristic Imagination," 5.
6. Wilde, *Reviews*, 413.
7. Ibid., 506–507, 507.

however, no doubt of Mr. Swinburne's mastery over the form, whether the form be quite legitimate or not."[8] So even though his letter to George Bernard Shaw described Shaw and himself as members "of the Great Celtic School," Wilde's reviews reveal that he was wary of "the pathos of provincialisms" and that he located "the acme of romance" elsewhere than in Irish idioms and subject material.[9]

As we have seen, this poses a problem for critics who wish to dig down to an "Irish dimension" concealed beneath the surface of his works.[1] Those who seek in "Wilde's nationality" the "interpretive key" for "unlocking all aspects of his work" may end up imitating another hermeneutic locksmith, Esdras Barnivelt.[2] Barnivelt, the narrator of Alexander Pope's *A Key to the Lock*, declares that "the most demonstrative Sciences [allow] some *Postulata* . . . to be granted, upon which the rest is naturally founded." He modestly requests the reader to accept "that by the *Lock* [in Pope's *The Rape of the Lock*] is meant The Barrier Treaty," after which—of course—his allegorizing extravaganza can begin.[3] For Killeen, the equivalent *postulatum* (with an equivalent absence of external evidence) is that "Wilde saw folk-Catholicism as the best means of interrogating reality."[4]

When he turns to decoding (or encoding) *The Picture of Dorian Gray*, Killeen performs other Barniveltian moves. The apothecary

8. Wilde, *Reviews*, 522.
9. Wilde, *The Complete Letters of Oscar Wilde*, 563; Wilde, *Reviews*, 522. Occasionally, Wilde's prose exhibits national—or provincial—residuua, heteronomous birthmarks on the surface of autonomous masks. For example, in his fairy tale "The Star-Child," the pseudo-biblical diction is momentarily interrupted by the introduction of the Irish word "haggard" to describe a hay-barn (Wilde, *Complete Works*, 263). The story also refers to the Irish folklore about finding "a crock of gold"—although it is at the place where a star falls, rather than at the base of a rainbow (261).
1. Nevertheless, as Ní Fhlathúin notes, Kiberd audaciously converts this negative into a positive: "Wilde refused to write realist accounts of that degraded Ireland which he only partly knew, and he took instead Utopia for theme, knowing that this would provide not only an image of revolutionary possibility for Ireland but also a rebuke to contemporary Britain." Kiberd, *Inventing Ireland*, 50; cited in Ní Fhlathúin, "The Irish Oscar Wilde," 341.
2. Killeen, *The Faiths of Oscar Wilde*, 11. Lest I also be accused of what Bashford terms "reasoning by analogy," I should note that my juxtaposing of Killeen's methodology to Barnivelt's differs significantly from Killeen's analogies between Wilde's creative works and events in nineteenth-century Irish history: I am not asserting a causal connection between one half of the analogy and the other, but merely making a clarifying comparison.
3. Alexander Pope, *The Prose Works of Alexander Pope* (Oxford: Basil Blackwell, 1936), I: 185.
4. Killeen, *The Faiths of Oscar Wilde*, 25. Compare this claim: "Given my thesis, that Wilde was an Irish Catholic writer, and thus broadly supportive of 'supernaturalist' modes of thought" (82). As one reviewer commented, "A lot is carried by that 'Given': *given* that the moon is made of green cheese, moon rocks need to be kept away from mice [yet] hypotheses are not given, they are argued, and all too often Killeen allows his assertions to outstrip his proofs." See Rose, "To Each His or Her Own Wilde [review of Jarlath Killeen's *The Faiths of Oscar Wilde*]," 26.

interprets Pope's Belinda to "represent . . . GREAT BRITAIN, or (which is the same thing) her late MAJESTY," based on the line *"On her white Breast a sparkling Cross she bore."* According to Barnivelt, *"white"* indicates *"Albion"* and "the *Cross* . . . is the Ensign of England." However, in a move designed to satirize what he saw as the arbitrariness and inconsistency of the interpretations that *The Rape of the Lock* had endured, Pope contrives an exegetical *volte-face* for Barnivelt, who now claims that Belinda stands for "the Popish Religion, or the Whore of *Babylon*" and that the "Cross on her Breast" indicates "the Ensign of Popery."[5] This anticipates Killeen's reading of *The Picture of Dorian Gray,* in which Lord Henry first represents the seductive voice of "Catholic convert Cardinal Henry Newman" yet later becomes "Wilde's means of indicting Victorianism, not as its critic but as its best representative: inert, exploitative, rhetorical, hypocritical, evangelical, soulless, dying."[6] Later still, Lord Henry becomes "like an ethnographer diagnosing the state of innocence, only to absorb him [Dorian] in vampiric desperation for rejuvenation," his "seduction of Dorian" being "a desperate attempt to domesticate the energies of 'natural' races like the Irish, and so feed on these energies for his own needs." Dorian, too, switches from one whose "consumption of the Oriental is Wilde's method of referring to the colonising practices of England in Ireland" to one "who represents the folklore of Ireland."[7]

Such arbitrary allegoresis ushers in other inaccuracies: we learn that "[o]ne factor which links Lord Henry and Cardinal Newman is the importance which Wilde attached to both their voices."[8] After citing Lord Henry's "fascinating" voice, Killeen states: "Newman too had a 'fascinating' and seductive voice. Wilde wanted and yet feared an interview with him because, *after listening to his voice,* 'I could hardly resist [him] I am afraid."[9] However, Wilde's letter nowhere mentions Newman's voice. Killeen also discovers "irony" in the way "that Dorian, the only character who has truly managed to banish the soul as Lord Henry insists all should wants it back, and dies in the attempt to get it back."[1] Yet Dorian wishes to annihilate the painting not in order to reclaim his soul but because it is incriminating "evidence"; he wishes to "destroy" his "conscience"; and he wishes to "kill this monstrous soul-life," so that "without its hideous

---

5. Pope, *The Prose Works of Alexander Pope,* I: 185–86, 200.
6. Killeen, *The Faiths of Oscar Wilde,* 89, 96, 105.
7. Ibid., 106, 108.
8. Ibid., 89.
9. Wilde, *The Picture of Dorian Gray,* 185 [22]; Killeen, *The Faiths of Oscar Wilde,* 89; Wilde, *The Complete Letters of Oscar Wilde,* 41; my emphasis.
1. Killeen, *The Faiths of Oscar Wilde,* 95.

warnings, he would be at peace."[2] In addition, Killeen compares
Dorian's portrait to "the Catholic doctrine of Transubstantiation
[which holds] that, at the moment of consecration, the materials of
bread and wine change in substance to become the body and blood
of Christ, although they retain the 'accidental' appearances such as
taste and shape." For Killeen, Dorian's portrait also "changes substantially without any clear external cause."[3] The portrait may or
may not change "substantially," but its drastic "accidental" changes
disqualify it as a compelling transubstantial analogy, unless we
wish to believe that Wilde is alluding to Raphael's painting *The
Mass at Bolsena* (1512).

One last error epitomizes the hermeneutic hazards of "reasoning
by analogy." Killeen draws on an essay by Christopher Nassaar that
locates an apparent discrepancy between the placing of Dorian's portrait against a wall and the discovery at the novel's close of "the
picture *hanging* on the wall." Nassaar initially wonders whether "this
[is] a technical fault that Wilde did not catch"; he decides it is not,
"since the novel displays great attention to detail and was written
twice."[4] Thus, he concludes, "[i]t is logical to argue that the crash"
heard at the end "was not only the fall of Dorian's body but also the
transference of all his sins onto him from the portrait"; the misdeeds
"come crashing down, destroying him in an instant, while the weight
of the supernatural portrait is lightened dramatically, enabling it at
last to rise up and hang itself on the wall in an assertion of its
renewed innocence."[5] Via simile, Killeen then translates Nassaar's
rather ingenious hypothesis into the Catholicizing idiom of his own
argument: "the portrait—which has been placed on the ground in
the nursery for most of the text—rises and hangs again like a triumphant and glorified Christ ascending to the Father after the
degenerate attempts to destroy the soul have been defeated."[6] To
answer Josephine Guy's previously cited question, there are occasions when "such self-referential systems of interpretation" can
indeed "be refuted." In this case, we can do so empirically, by turning to a sentence (tucked away in the text) that is overlooked by both
Nassaar and Killeen: "Upon the walls of the lonely locked room
where he had spent so much of his boyhood, he had hung with his
own hands the terrible portrait whose changing features showed him

2. Wilde, *The Picture of Dorian Gray*, 356–57 [184]. Compare Wilde's letter to the *Daily
   Chronicle* (30 June 1890): "It is finally to get rid of his conscience that had dogged his
   steps from year to year that he destroys the picture; and thus in his attempt to kill conscience Dorian Gray kills himself" (Wilde, *The Complete Letters of Oscar Wilde*, 436).
3. Killeen, *The Faiths of Oscar Wilde*, 97.
4. Christopher S. Nassaar, "Wilde's *The Picture of Dorian Gray*," *The Explicator*, 57.4
   (1999), 217; cited in Killeen, *The Faiths of Oscar Wilde*, 203.
5. Nassaar, "Wilde's *The Picture of Dorian Gray*," 217.
6. Killeen, *The Faiths of Oscar Wilde*, 99–100.

the real degradation of his life."[7] Such an oversight illustrates just
how far the *ignis fatuus* of allegoresis can lead one astray.[8]

Mirrors & Scotomas

In his recent exploration of Wilde's Irish identity, *Oscar's Shadow:
Wilde, Homosexuality and Modern Ireland*, Éibhear Walshe engages
with the arguments of Kiberd, Pine, and Killeen and in the process
raises some methodological issues that provide a suitable conclusion
to this essay. Drawing on archival research, Walshe persuasively
advances the thesis that "despite some moments of homophobia,
Irish sources accommodate the 'sinner' Wilde within some aspects
of nationalist discourse," so that "[a]t the historical moment in European culture when the idea of the homosexual as a dangerous type
was evolving, Irish nationalist discourses were deployed in some
areas of cultural life to rescue or absolve Wilde from this aberrant
sexual identity."[9] Surveying this 115-year-long process, Walshe
praises Kiberd for foregrounding Wilde as "a figure of postmodern
self-invention for contemporary Ireland," but he finds Kiberd's treatment of Wilde's sexuality sometimes "strangely reductionist, particularly in his account of Speranza's influence on her second son," and
also in the way Kiberd "relegate[s] Wilde's homosexuality to the
margins, seeing it as an expression of a kind of intellectual dissent
rather than a central physical and sexual identity." For Walshe,
Kiberd also exhibits (in the latter's contribution to Jerusha McCormack's anthology *Wilde the Irishman*) "a slightly reductive habit . . .
of interpreting the formation of sexual identity as driven by intellectual choice rather than hormonal inclination." Such reservations
reemerge in Walshe's response to Pine: on the one hand, he praises

---

7. Guy, "Wilde's Fairy Tales [review of Jarlath Killeen's *The Fairy Tales of Oscar Wilde*],"
87; Wilde, *The Picture of Dorian Gray*, 286 [117–18]. On Nassaar's misreading, see Richard Haslam, "Wilde's *The Picture of Dorian Gray*," *The Explicator*, 61.2 (2003), 96–98.
8. Unsurprisingly, Killeen cites Upchurch's theories on the Irish fairies in Hallward's
garden and King's theories on the supposedly allegorical significance of Basil Hallward's "Gladstone bag" and "ulster": Upchurch, *Wilde's Use of Irish Celtic Elements in
"The Picture of Dorian Gray"*, 25–26; Killeen, *The Faiths of Oscar Wilde*, 105; Wilde,
The Picture of Dorian Gray, 292; King, "Typing *Dorian Gray*," 16; Killeen, *The Faiths of
Oscar Wilde*, 107. (Killeen, however, believes that an ulster is a hat rather than a coat.)
Of the "ulster" reading, a reviewer comments that "one might as well say that this is
true of Sherlock Holmes because he wore an ulster, or that Agatha Christie implicated
Hercule Poirot in the Congo atrocities by making him a Belgian police officer, or that
Sergeant Troy's marriage to Bathsheba Everdene refers to Hittite imperialism in Pales-
tine": Rose, "To Each His or Her Own Wilde," 26. In addition, like Kiberd and O'Connor,
Killeen employs the *abracadabra* of similitude. Within his *Dorian* chapter alone, we find:
"*Like* Lord Henry, Newman was *also*"; "*Echoing* Newman, Lord Henry"; "For *both* Newman and Lord Henry"; "Both men"; "This *shared* need"; "*just as*"; "*in much the same way
that*"; "*like* a consecrated Host"; "*like* a priest"; "*like* a triumphant and glorified Christ";
"*recalls*"; "*just as . . . so*"; "*Just as*"; "*Just as*"; "a *similar* role": Killeen, *The Faiths of Oscar
Wilde*, 90, 92, 92, 92, 92, 92, 92, 98, 98, 98, 99, 102, 104, 106, 107, 108; my emphasis
throughout.
9. Walshe, *Oscar's Shadow*, 2.

Pine's "precise delineation of Wilde's Irish background, the influence
of a nineteenth-century Irish Protestant tradition of dissent, and also
his influence on his Irish successors"; on the other hand, he finds
"reductive" Pine's "tendency . . . to see Wilde's homosexuality as a
pose, a colonial strategy, rather than as a core identity driven by
desire and by increasing sexual self-confidence."[1]

Walshe's critique of Kiberd and Pine foreshadows his concluding
observation that Wilde is now less a "shadow" than "a mirror in
which he is made to reflect the identity, class, gender and politics of
each of his 'interpreters' in Ireland, those writers and critics who
engage with his work."[2] Thus, Kiberd and Pine view Wilde through
a postcolonial lens, which, for Walshe, methodologically distorts
their perception of Wilde's sexuality. Walshe, looking at Wilde
through a gay studies lens, can see Kiberd's and Pine's distortions
but ignores other distortions, as we can see when he discusses
Killeen's studies of Wilde. For example, overlooking the kind of
methodological shortcomings highlighted in this article, Walshe
instead states that Killeen's "reading [in *The Faiths of Oscar Wilde*]
of the Wildean texts as *closet* Irish Catholic tales" results in a "study"
that is "remarkable . . . , fluently argued and original." Walshe also
finds no fault with Killeen's Gnostic techniques in *Fairy Tales*, perhaps because Walshe admits to finding the kind of methodological
"parallel" that Killeen employs "useful."[3] Here is the passage from
Killeen that Walshe cites: "As queer theorists are looking for the
signs of Wilde's sexuality in quasi-heterosexual texts like *The Importance of Being Earnest,* we have to realise that another culture saturated in the concept of the secret symbol in the nineteenth century
was Catholicism."[4]

Of course, to focus on some motifs at the expense of others we
find less absorbing is a common human failing, and the present argument too undoubtedly includes its own scotomas. As Laurence
Sterne's Tristram Shandy observes, "It is in the nature of an hypothesis, when once a man has conceived it, that it assimilates everything to itself, as proper nourishment; and, from the first moment
of your begetting it, it generally grows the stronger by everything you

---

1. Walshe, *Oscar's Shadow,* 82, 83, 86, 84–85.
2. Ibid., 120. Walshe's (noncausal) "mirror" analogy endorses Wilde's famous claim in "The
   Preface" to *The Picture of Dorian Gray* that "[i]t is the spectator, and not life, that art
   really mirrors" (168). In addition, the anonymous reader for this essay makes a useful
   (and, again, non-causal) analogy with "the protagonists of *Salome* projecting their own
   obsessions and desires onto both the moon and the princess."
3. Walshe, *Oscar's Shadow,* 107–108; my emphasis. Ibid., 108–109.
4. Killeen, *The Fairy Tales of Oscar Wilde,* 171; cited in Walshe, *Oscar's Shadow,* 109. Just to
   be clear, I am not denying that Wilde alluded to his sexual orientation in his literary
   writings—that much is obvious, although the scope of these allusions can obviously be
   debated. However, the fact that Wilde alludes to his sexual desires does not guarantee
   that he alludes in the same way to a secret affiliation with "Irish folk-Catholicism." Some
   analogies can lead us astray.

see, hear, read, or understand. This is of great use."[5] But how do we prevent confirmation bias (and all the other cognitive biases) from generating "great [ab]use"? One recourse is the kind of "disciplinary ethos" that requires us to expose our arguments to peer critique. In this way, you can discover your own blind spots and thereby aim to situate your interpretation more securely on solid evidence and modest inferences.[6] If, as Walshe argues, Wilde has become "a mirror in which he is made to reflect the identity, class, gender and politics of each of his 'interpreters' in Ireland, those writers and critics who engage with his work," then we "interpreters" are obliged all the more to identify, reflect upon, and minimize the distortions introduced into our scholarly projects by our own "identity, class, gender, and politics," which includes our choice of theoretical frameworks.[7] Peer critiques will eventually strengthen our arguments by helping us to see the blind spots of which we are presently unaware. For this reason, I welcome a vigorous and rigorous critique of this essay's arguments and evidence—not least because such a debate might also amuse the ghost of Wilde, who observed that "[w]hen critics disagree the artist is in accord with himself."[8]

DONALD L. LAWLER

Oscar Wilde's First Manuscript of *The Picture of Dorian Gray*[†]

There have been omens in the past two decades that the long suzerainty of biography, anecdote, and memoir in Oscar Wilde studies may be threatened by a new emphasis upon textual scholarship,

5. Laurence Sterne, *The Life and Opinions of Tristram Shandy, Gentleman* (1760–7) (Oxford: Oxford UP, 1983), 120. A modern take on the human tendency to ignore our blind spots terms the phenomenon "theory-induced blindness"—"a weakness of the scholarly mind," as a result of which, "once you have accepted a theory and used it as a tool in your thinking, it is extraordinarily difficult to notice its flaws." See Daniel Kahneman, *Thinking, Fast and Slow* (New York: Farrar, Straus and Giroux, 2011), 277.
6. On "disciplinary ethos," see Frederick Crews, *Follies of the Wise: Dissenting Essays* (Emeryville: Shoemaker Hoard, 2006), 306. Crews distinguishes between "two kinds of discourse . . . the *disciplinary* and the *self-ratifying*": an "essential feature" of the former "is the give-and-take, largely conducted in journals, between proponents of new hypotheses and possessors of knowledge that may or may not have been successfully accounted for in those hypotheses" (305). For Crews, "the disciplinary spirit" requires "members of a given intellectual community [to] read one another's work discriminatingly and try to show, through pointed reference to available facts, that certain apprehensions of those facts are more plausible than others" (305). It is in the spirit of such disciplinary solidarity that this essay's critical disagreements are presented.
7. Walshe, *Oscar's Shadow*, 120.
8. Wilde, *The Picture of Dorian Gray*, 168 [4]; cited in Bashford, "When Critics Disagree," 613.
† From *Studies in Bibliography: Papers of the Bibliographical Society of the University of Virginia* 25 (1972): 125–35. Reprinted by permission of *Studies in Bibliography*.

critical bibliography, and analytic literary criticism. These new directions should be seen, perhaps, as a sign of the rehabilitation of Oscar Wilde as an important literary figure. Wilde has certainly become respectable as a writer of prose if not of verse and has emerged as one of the major authors of the 1880's and 1890's. It is to be hoped that in the wake of the present revaluation of Wilde's work, there will follow a better and a more balanced assessment of his writing. If this is to be the case, there must be even more attention given to primary scholarship of a bibliographical and textual nature. Such research can offer the literary critic the necessary facts and the accurate texts with which to work. One well-known instance of such a contribution came in 1964 when the Rupert Hart-Davis edition of the Oscar Wilde *Letters* gave us, at last, an accurate text of "De Profundis."[1] The original four-act version of *The Importance of Being Earnest* did not come to light in English until Vyvyan Holland edited a composite text in 1957. Sarah Augusta Dickson's two-volume, 1956 edition of the original four-act play manuscript was valuable for reprinting the surviving drafts. The revised and enlarged *Portrait of Mr. W. H.* was not generally available until 1958, and the original, sometimes called the short version of *The Picture of Dorian Gray* was practically inaccessible outside the rare book rooms until Wilfred Edener used it as the basis for a critical edition of the novel in 1964.

The Edener edition was only the first step in providing the literary critic with adequate materials for reinterpretation and revaluation of Oscar Wilde's novel. The limited scope of the Edener edition restricted the study to recording variant readings for the two published versions of the novel. The revisions in the manuscripts have never been printed, and as yet, the problems relating to Wilde's intentions and the effects of the revisions remain to be published.[2] In the case of *Dorian Gray* and indeed many other major works by Wilde, collectors happily have preserved manuscripts and typescripts so that comparative studies of the different states of the text may be

1. Oscar Wilde, *The Letters of Oscar Wilde,* ed. Rupert Hart-Davis (1962). Other examples of textual scholarship cited above may be mentioned here: Oscar Wilde, *The Importance of Being Earnest,* ed. Sarah Augusta Dickson, 2 vols (1956); Oscar Wilde, *The Importance of Being Earnest,* Original four-act version, ed. Vyvyan Holland (1957); Oscar Wilde, *The Portrait of Mr. W. H.* Enlarged Edition, ed. Vyvyan Holland (1958); Oscar Wilde, *The Picture of Dorian Gray,* ed. Wilfried Edener (1964). Other works of interest to Wildean scholarship include Abraham Horodisch, *Oscar Wilde's "Ballad of Reading Gaol." A Bibliocritical Study* (New Preston, Connecticut, 1954); Aatos Ojala, *Aestheticism and Oscar Wilde,* 2 vols. (Helsinki, 1954–55); Stuart Mason [Christopher Sclater Millard], *Bibliography of Oscar Wilde* (1914, 1967); E. San Juan, Jr., *The Art of Oscar Wilde* (1967); L. A. Beaurline, "The Director, The Script, and Author's Revisions: A Critical Problem," *Papers in Dramatic Theory and Criticism,* ed. David M. Knauf (1969), pp. 78–91.
2. The revisions and the author's intentions and their effects on the final form of the novel are studied in my own unpublished doctoral dissertation for the University of Chicago, "An Enquiry into Oscar Wilde's Revisions of *The Picture of Dorian Gray,*" 1969.

made. Such studies may reveal more than memoirs, biographies, and letters about the composition of the work and the realized intentions of the author. With this in mind, I offer the following paper as a preliminary study in textual bibliography to a more ambitious inquiry into the significance of the *Dorian Gray* manuscripts.

The text of *The Picture of Dorian Gray* exists in two published states. The novel first appeared as the featured work of fiction in the July, 1890 number of *Lippincott's Monthly Magazine*. There are extant two manuscripts for the *Lippincott's Dorian Gray*. The holograph manuscript is at the Pierpont Morgan Library and the corrected typescript is now at the William Andrews Clark Library. In June of 1891, Wilde published *Dorian Gray*, in an expanded version. The manuscript of the book version of *Dorian Gray*, published by Ward, Lock & Company, has not been found, if indeed a full manuscript ever existed. Chapters added to the original *Lippincott's Dorian Gray* have turned up here and there over the years: Chapter III and one leaf from Chapter V are in the William Andrews Clark Library. Chapter XV is in the Berg Collection of the New York Public Library. Chapters XIV and XVI, sold at auction in the twenties, are, presumably, still in the hands of private collectors.

As far as anyone knows, *The Picture of Dorian Gray* was begun sometime in 1889. The first allusion to the novel appears in the fragment of a letter Wilde sent to J. M. Stoddart, the editor of *Lippincott's Magazine*, after Stoddart had found one of Wilde's adult fairy tales unsuitable: "I have invented a new story which is better than 'The Fisherman and his Soul,' and I am quite ready to set to work at once on it."[3] The letter is dated 17 December 1889. Subsequent references in later correspondence make it clear that Wilde was referring to *Dorian Gray* in the letter cited above. It is possible, even likely, that Wilde had begun working on the novel earlier than December of 1889. Indeed, there is some evidence to suggest that Wilde had begun work on *Dorian Gray* before October of 1889.[4] At this point, the manuscripts themselves provide the best evidence of the novel's development. The holograph manuscript, thought to be the original of the novel, was revised extensively by Wilde. These revisions affect characterization, setting, action and theme as well as commonplace minor changes in spelling, syntax, and idiom. After

3. Oscar Wilde, *The Letters of Oscar Wilde,* ed. Rupert Hart-Davis (1962), p. 251.
4. Horace Wyndham, "Edited by Oscar Wilde," *Twentieth Century,* 163 (May, 1958), p. 400. Wyndham reports that when the decision to drop Wilde as editor of *Woman's World* was made, Wilde remarked, "I shall be able to finish a novel, 'The Picture of Dorian Gray,' I have in the stocks."
   Wilde was replaced as editor of *Woman's World* in October of 1889. The fact that he contributed nothing further of his own after June of 1889 is an indication that he was given notice before that date. If this inference is correct, and if we may rely on the substantial if not the literal truth of Wyndham's anecdote, we may assume that Wilde had been at work on *Dorian Gray* before June of 1889.

the revisions in the holograph were completed, Wilde had the manuscript typed and then made further changes. The revisions in the typescript are as extensive and as significant as those made in the manuscript. It was from this corrected copy of the typescript that *The Picture of Dorian Gray* was set up in type and printed by *Lippincott's*. There is an interval of eleven months between the appearance of *Dorian Gray* in *Lippincott's* and the publication of *Dorian Gray* as a book by Ward, Lock & Co. During that period, Wilde made his final revisions of the novel, and they are the most extensive of all. He added five new chapters, introducing many new characters and continuing with the alterations he had made earlier in atmosphere, theme, and action. The new chapters Wilde added were first written out in longhand. It is not known what procedures Wilde followed for the changes he made in the already published sections of his book. He did not use the original typescript from which the *Lippincott's The Picture of Dorian Gray* was set. If Wilde followed his customary method of revising, he would have worked from a fresh typescript. However, there is no evidence that, in fact, he did so. The novel, published by Ward, Lock & Co. in June of 1891, represents the final state of the text and, therefore, expresses the author's final intention for his work. Wilde never again made any changes in the text.

In the course of examining the manuscript of *Dorian Gray,* I discovered a number of irregularities in the holograph which indicate the existence of a manuscript version of the novel prior to the earliest one now known. The evidence is, I believe, strong enough to suggest that Wilde, in fact, revised his novel not two but at least three times before its original publication by *Lippincott's*. The evidence I have to present is wholly textual, based on Wilde's handwritten corrections in the manuscript. In classifying the various corrections made by Wilde in the holograph manuscript, I discovered a significant number of cases which could not be explained as arising from simple error, stylistic alteration, or those more substantial changes involving characterization, theme, and action. The corrections I shall investigate fall under the general category of errors emended in the course of writing the manuscript or possibly, in some cases, improvements made during the writing of the holograph. This fact is easily established by the character of the text. Each of the corrections to be discussed is part of the original writing, not added above the line or in the margin during a proofreading. The kind of error and revision to be discussed in this paper has led me to the conclusion that in order to account for them, one is forced to postulate the existence of a still earlier original manuscript for the novel from which Wilde was working more or less closely. In some cases, words, parts of words, or phrases are repeated in a manner suggesting that an error had been made in copying rather than in composition. In other cases there are passages which had been deleted by Wilde from an earlier part of the holograph and moved to a later page or recopied further down on the same page. There is only one instance in which Wilde moved a passage from a later page in the manuscript to an earlier one, an exception which, in this case, does not violate the rule.

It helps us immeasurably to have an example of a text which Wilde is known to have copied so that we may see whether or not errors of the kind found in the holograph manuscript of *Dorian Gray* appear there. We have such a specimen in the very manuscript under discussion. There is one part of *The Picture of Dorian Gray* which is known to have been copied by Wilde from one of his own earlier reviews, written while he was editor of *Woman's World* from June, 1887, until October, 1889. In November of 1888, about six months before the first reports that Wilde was working on a novel, he wrote a review of Earnest Lefebure's book, *Embroidery and Lace: Their Manufacture and History from the Remotest Antiquity to the Present Day*.[5] A significant part of the review reproduces or paraphrases Lefebure's text. More important for our purposes, when Wilde was scavenging for material to include in Dorian Gray's decadent pleasure house, he transcribed a number of paragraphs into the text of *Dorian Gray* from his old review of Lefebure's book. The self-plagiarism amounts to almost three pages of the holograph manuscript.[6] The leaves in question were copied verbatim from the text of the review, as a simple comparison reveals. In these copied leaves of the novel, there are four or five cases in which Wilde later made stylistic changes in the borrowed passages. However, there is one passage with an error of copying which has a relevance for this study.

> He longed to see the curious table napkins wrought for Heliogabalus on which were displayed all the dainties and viands that could be wanted for a feast: the mortuary cloth of King Chilperic with its three hundred golden bees; the fantastic robes that excited the indignation of *King Chilperic* the Bishop of Pontus, and were embroidered. . . .[7]

The repetition of the words "King Chilperic" above (in my italics) is obviously in error. The original passage in the review read, "robes that excited the indignation of the bishop of Pontus."[8] Normally, a

5. Oscar Wilde, *The Complete Works of Oscar Wilde,* ed. Padraic Colum, XII (1923), pp. 1–21.
6. Morgan Library Manuscript, 11. 186–188. I wish to thank the Pierpont Morgan Library for permission to examine this manuscript and special thanks go to Herbert Cahoon, curator of the manuscript collection, for his generous assistance.
7. Morgan Manuscript, 1. 186. Wilde crossed out the repeated phrase in the manuscript.
8. Wilde, *Complete Works,* p. 11.

slip such as the one above would not be notable or likely to excite curiosity. Indeed, such an error would not be significant at all were it not for the fact that the mistake occurs in a passage known to have been copied by Wilde from his own review published in *Woman's World*, November, 1888.

Instances of similarly repeated phrases or expressions dramatically out of place in the narrative may be cited as evidence that the holograph manuscript is probably a copy of an earlier draft. Such errors, while not frequent, occur throughout the holograph manuscript, indicating that any prior ur-manuscript must have been a nearly complete draft of the novel.[9]

> He turned to Hallward, and said, "My dear fellow, I have just remembered."
> —"Remembered what, Harry?"
> —"Where I heard the name of Dorian Gray."
> —"Where I *heard the name of* was it" asked Hallward, with a slight frown.
>
> (1. 26.)

> I don't know what my guardians will say. Lord Radley is sure to be furious. I don't care. I shall be of age in less than a year, and then I can do what I like I *don't k* have been right, Basil, haven't I. . . ."
>
> (1. 86.)

9. In the quotations given above and below, each line is reproduced as it appears in the manuscript except that I have italicized the repeated elements. The additional examples of copying error given below will show the reader how these passages are distributed throughout the manuscript.

   A. Within the world, as men know it, there was a finer world that only artists know of,—*artists of* artists, or those to whom the temperament of the artist has been given. Creation within—that is what Basil Hallward had named it, that is what he had attained to. (1. 43.)

   B. —"Then you shall come. And you will come, too, Basil, won't you?"
   —"*Then you and I will*
   —"I can't really, I would sooner not. I have a lot of work to do."
   —"Well, then, you and I will go alone, Mr. Gray." (1. 51.)

   C. The elaborate character of the frame made the picture extremely heavy, and now and then *he put his hand to it so as to help them* in spite of Mr. Ashton who had a true tradesman's dislike of seeing a gentleman doing anything useful he put his hand to it so as to help them. (1. 160.)

   D. "Though your sins be as scarlet, yet I will make them white as snow!"
   Suddenly a wild
   —"Those words mean nothing to me, now."
   —"Hush! Don't say that. You have done enough evil in your life, My God! don't you see that damned thing leering at us?" Dorian Gray glanced at the picture, and suddenly a wild feeling of hatred for Basil Hallward came over him. (1. 219.)

In passage C above, it appears from the ink tones in the holograph manuscript that Wilde did not line through the expression "he put his hand to it" until later, probably in proofreading. I conclude from the evidence of the lighter color of the ink in the deleted passages and in the contiguous script as compared to the much darker cancel line that the repetition is a result of an anticipation of the phrase rather than merely an improvement in style.

"Nothing is serious now-a-days, at *Hallward* least, nothing should be."

Hallward shook his head as he entered. . . .

(1. 205).

In each of the cases cited above, the color tones of the ink in the manuscript indicate that Wilde recognized his mistake at once and lined through the offending words. Wilde wrote the holograph manuscript on blue lined folio paper with a steel tipped pen and an India-type ink. Close examination of the manuscript will often reveal the intervals at which the pen was dipped into the ink. In each of the passages above we have an example of one kind of error Wilde is known to have made in copying from his own book review originally written for *Woman's World*.

There are other anomalies in the manuscript which also suggest that they are errors of transcription rather than of composition. I refer to words left incomplete by Wilde and then lined through. Once again, the color tones of the ink reveal that Wilde must have crossed out the incomplete words before going on. I have chosen three representative examples of words left unfinished from different areas of the manuscript.[1]

There was something in his face that made one trust him at once. All YOU the candour of *youth* was there.

(1. 30.)

Yes: Basil could have saved him. But it was too late now. REGR The past could always be annihilated. *Regret,* denial of forgetfulness could do that.

(1. 156.)

The harsh intervals and shrill discords of barbaric music stirred him at times when Schubert's grace, and Chopin's MI beautiful sorrows, and the *mighty* harmonies of Beethoven himself fell unheeded on his ear.

(1. 183.)

Slips of the kind listed above are significant only as evidence which supports the hypothesis that some of the errors made by Wilde in the holograph manuscript were the result of a copying lapse made in the course of working from an earlier manuscript. It seems to me that the features of the manuscript cited above are of a kind that one might expect when one text is copied from another.

There is further evidence I should like to consider before concluding my case in support of the claim that there existed a manuscript

---

1. In order to demonstrate the relevance of the incomplete word, it has been necessary to abstract a significant part of the text. I have used upper case letters to indicate the unfinished word and italics to identify the word when it reappears in the text.

anterior to the holograph manuscript now in the Morgan Library. In the course of writing the holograph, Wilde transposed a number of passages forward in the text from an earlier leaf to a later one. Some passages were recopied further down on the same page. One passage was removed from a later to an earlier page, but that exception is revealing because of a change in pagination. These transposed passages are unlike any of the other cases in which Wilde moved phrases, expressions, or more complex elements around from one place to another because they were not written above the line or in the margin but are integrated in the script. This means that such passages were moved either in the course of copying or of composition. The first lines to be transposed by Wilde were spoken originally by Basil Hallward, the painter of Dorian's portrait, to Lord Henry Wotton, the man who tempts Dorian Gray with his gospel of new Hedonism. Wilde removed the passage from the dialogue of Basil Hallward and replaced it in a meditation by Lord Henry on beauty.

> I tell him that beauty like his is genius, is higher than genius, as it needs no explanation and is one of the great facts of the world, like sunlight or springtime, or the reflection in dark waters of that thin silver shell we call the moon.

Wilde transferred these lines verbatim from leaf 22 of the holograph manuscript to leaf 38. The reason for the change is that the lines are really more appropriate to Lord Henry. Also they represent an early step in reducing the importance of Basil Hallward's role in the novel. This process was continued in the revisions Wilde later made on the completed holograph and carried on in the further revisions through which the novel was put before publication in its final form in 1891. I believe that this particular incidence of transferal may be taken as evidence of a pre-existing manuscript. Had Wilde been composing as he went along, it is doubtful that such a change in the importance and in the role of a character would have been conceived before the first chapter was completed and then forgotten in subsequent chapters, whereas the changes made in later proofreading revisions of the novel reveal a consistent program to expand the characterization of Lord Henry and to reduce the influence of Basil Hallward in the story.

There are three other instances in which Wilde moved material from an earlier to a later position in the manuscript. As was the case above, no alterations were made in the passage and the lines were copied into the text without interruption. In the first of these passages, Dorian is speaking to Basil. It is the scene in which Dorian insists that Basil come with him into his abandoned nursery to see the portrait which Basil had painted many years before. The lines appeared first on manuscript leaf 212, lines 6–9. They were crossed out by Wilde and rewritten as lines 23–25 on the same leaf:

> I will show you my soul. You shall see the thing that you fancy only God can see.

The second repeated passage is a phrase which appeared in the narrator's commentary on leaf 231 of the manuscript, was cancelled by Wilde, and rewritten on the following leaf.

> . . . during the eighteen months that their friendship had lasted.

In the manuscript leaf 233, lines 30–31, the following passage is deleted, reappearing again on leaf 234 as lines 8–9. The words are those of Dorian Gray addressed to Alan Campbell, the scientist whose alchemy is enlisted to remove all traces of Basil Hallward's corpse from the upstairs nursery of Dorian's house:

> So it is, and to more than one person, Alan.

It is obvious from the character of the manuscript that Wilde transposed the passages in question as he was writing. The question is whether the manuscript in which the passages are rearranged was copied or composed. I think that at this point, we may rely, in part, on the weight of the evidence already presented in favor of the hypothesis that the manuscript is a copy rather than a first draft. Further to support this interpretation of the transposed passages in question, I should like to call the reader's attention to Wilde's own habits of composition. After each revision of a text, Wilde liked to have a clear copy. In the beginning he would make a fair copy of his rough draft himself. Later he would have a typescript made and work from that. I submit that it would have been unusual and uncharacteristic of Wilde to have made the kind of changes shown in the removal of the passages cited above while he was composing. Further, the physical evidence of the ink tones supports the view that the passages were recopied rather than moved during the course of composition. As I have mentioned earlier, since Wilde wrote in India ink with a steel tipped pen, it is often easy to tell at which points the pen was returned to the ink well. The ink in the script becomes lighter just before he refreshed the nib. Now in the instances of the transposed lines, the ink tones indicate that the cancel lines were drawn directly after the lines had been written. What is more, there is no detectable alteration in the ink tones as the passages reappear later in the text. Something of the sort should be expected, unless Wilde's memory were so retentive that he could recall as many as eight lines over sixteen pages of newly composed fiction. Otherwise, there should be some indication that Wilde had paused to relocate his original words in the manuscript.

One final passage deserves consideration. The lines below appear in the manuscript on leaf 27b. Wilde removed one passage from its original position at the top of leaf 28, made some additions and used it as the conclusion for Chapter One. Basil Hallward is speaking to Lord Henry Wotton. He begins by saying, "Don't take away the one person who makes life

> absolutely lovely to me, and that gives my art whatever wonder or charm it possesses. Mind, Harry, I trust you." He spoke very slowly, and the words seemed wrung out of him almost against his will.
> "What nonsense you talk," said Lord Henry smiling, and taking Hallward by the arm, he almost led him into the house.

This passage is the only instance I have found in which Wilde moved lines back to an earlier page. It is possible that Wilde made the change in proofreading, having forgotten to designate the beginning of Chapter Two as he composed; or he may have divided up a chapter which proved to be too long. If so, he had to have made the changes before he reached Chapter Four, which is numbered correctly. Once again, the evidence of the ink tones is helpful. There is a close match between the color tone of the ink in the first cancelled lines and the writing at the end of the chapter. Likewise there is a match up between the color tone of the ink in the last lines stricken and the first words recopied on 27b. This seems to indicate that Wilde cancelled the lines on the top of leaf 28 as soon as they were written, that he recopied them with an additional phrase or two on leaf 27b immediately afterward, and that, therefore, he was probably using another text from which he could safely copy his lines.

Of course we have been dealing here with inferences drawn from the corrections made by Wilde in the holograph manuscript of *Dorian Gray*. The evidence leads, I believe, to but one conclusion: that Wilde copied his holograph text now at the Morgan Library from a pre-existing draft. No other hypothesis accounts for the kind of mistake made by Wilde in the holograph and examined in this paper. We must assume that such errors were made in the course of transcription and that the original draft from which the holograph was copied must have covered the entire story since the transcription errors are to be found throughout the manuscript from leaf 22 to leaf 219. Therefore, the original draft was more than merely a working outline. The fact that the errors occur in passages of trivial significance suggests not only that Wilde was more likely to be distracted in copying such material but it implies that the earlier text was more or less a complete draft of the novel as it appears now in the Morgan Library holograph. Finally, we may assume that the original manuscript was probably foul papers, heavily corrected and reworked by the author. That would account for the trouble Wilde took to make a fair copy of the original. That fair copy, in turn, was extensively altered and rewritten by Wilde.

The significance of all this for Wildean criticism and for textual bibliography is easily seen. At the very least, it means that any future editor of a critical or a scholarly edition of *The Picture of Dorian Gray* should not treat the Morgan Library holograph as the original manuscript. Although it is an invaluable text in its own right, it cannot be taken to reveal all those things about Wilde's original inspiration and shaping of the novel which a first draft would expose. We must also revise upward from two to three the number of times Wilde rewrote his novel before its first publication in *Lippincott's* Magazine. Four full revisions of *Dorian Gray* before the novel took its final form suggest that the stereotyped view of Wilde as a careless and hasty writer may need reassessment. Perhaps a more thorough knowledge of Wilde's work habits would dispel some of the myths, partly self-created, about Wilde's insouciance toward his craft as a writer.

The chances of the original draft of *Dorian Gray* turning up at this late hour do not appear to be good. It is now eighty-two years since Wilde began work on the novel. Not a trace of foul papers or a working manuscript has appeared in the auction room catalogues or in lists describing the holdings of libraries or private collectors. No mention of the original draft appears in the letters or in any of the biographies and reminiscences. It is likely that Wilde himself disposed of the original manuscript. It is also possible that it was lost or destroyed at the time of the infamous auction of Wilde's property from his house at 16 Tite Street, Chelsea, in April of 1895 when the house was thrown open to curiosity seekers and souvenir hunters. At that time, it is said that many manuscripts were taken, and to this day, some have not been recovered. Another, more optimistic view is that the true original manuscript may be in the hands of a private collector or even may be languishing in someone's attic. In any case, the possible existence of another *Dorian Gray* manuscript has a potential value not only for the collector but also for the textual scholar and the literary critic.

ELLEN SCHEIBLE

Imperialism, Aesthetics, and Gothic Confrontation in *The Picture of Dorian Gray*†

In *The Picture of Dorian Gray* (1891) Oscar Wilde offers his readers a glimpse of what the downfall of British imperialism might look like if art were entirely to fall victim to excess and degeneracy. Wilde suggests that the nineteenth-century quests for both empire and hedonism could intermingle to brew a dangerous aesthetic—one with the potential to prey on the vulnerable aspects of British sensibility and culture, and to collapse even the most conventional of Victorian ideals. England's colonial enterprises in both Ireland and India haunt *Dorian Gray* as repressed subplots that surface sporadically within Wilde's more overt illustration of aesthetic and imperial insatiability. His use of colonial references, particularly those involving Ireland, work as codified tools of cultural subversion.

To underscore the subversive narrative, perhaps ironically, Wilde engages the strategies of gothic fiction, establishing a series of doubles that consists of characters, objects, and concepts. In "Oscar Wilde: The Artist as Irishman," Declan Kiberd points out that "Wilde's entire literary career constituted an ironic comment on the tendency of Victorian Englishmen to attribute to the Irish those emotions which they had repressed in themselves."[1] Many of those pairs meet in climactic moments of confrontation that threaten the necessary distance maintained by the trope of the gothic binary.[2] John Paul Riquelme has emphasized the importance of gothic tropes to Wilde's novel, particularly narrative doubling, arguing that *Dorian Gray* "proceeds against the background of Walter Pater's aesthetic writings, but also against Pater in a stronger sense. It provides in narrative form a dark, revealing double for Pater's aestheticism that emerges from a potential for dark doubling and reversal within aestheticism itself."[3] Wilde is writing "against" Paterian aesthetics in many ways, yet Riquelme's assertion—that the gothic trope of doubling is the medium through which Wilde exposes the dangers of aestheticism—highlights the importance of the gothic style in *Dorian*

---

† From *New Hibernia Review* 18.4 (Winter 2014): 131–50. Notes have been renumbered. Page numbers in square brackets are to this Norton Critical Edition. Reprinted by permission of *New Hibernia Review*, a publication of the University of St. Thomas (Minnesota).

1. Declan Kiberd, "Oscar Wilde: The Artist as Irishman," in *Wilde the Irishman,* ed. Jerusha McCormack (New Haven: Yale UP, 1998), p. 11.
2. For an in-depth analysis of gothic tropes and doubling, see Eve Kosofsky Sedgwick, *The Coherence of Gothic Conventions* (New York: Routledge, Kegan, and Paul, 1986).
3. John Paul Riquelme, "Oscar Wilde's Aesthetic Gothic: Walter Pater, Dark Enlightenment, and *The Picture of Dorian Gray,*" *Modern Fiction Studies*, 46, 3 (Fall 2000), 609.

Gray. Through the gothic convention, according to Jim Hansen, Wilde "converts the political unconscious of a popular aesthetic form . . . into an aestheticized political consciousness."[4] The novel's confrontations between art and artist; reality and art; and spectator and art each mirror the imperial confrontation between the classic positions of the colonizer and the colonized Other.

In this framework, Wilde's Irishness becomes another force that illustrates the degenerate aspects of British imperialism, including the Famine of the 1840s. In "Impressions of an Irish Sphinx," Owen Dudley Edwards argues "the Great Famine and its revelation of human responsibility for human suffering were probably the greatest individual legacies in creative response which Wilde inherited from his parents."[5] Following his parents' legacy, Wilde suggests that humanity shares responsibility for the suffering of its own members through the gothic doubling in the novel, where Dorian must confront those characters who he has forced to suffer in order for his own suffering, and ultimately his self-destruction, to ensue. Just as Victor Frankenstein cannot survive the struggle he faces with the monstrous Other he creates in Mary Shelley's *Frankenstein*, the confrontation between Wilde's depiction of a dominant self and a marginal Other ultimately results in both the death of the title character and the end of the novel's ability to sustain its narrative.

In her 1831 introduction to *Frankenstein*, Shelley recounts a dreamlike vision that ultimately led to the construction of her novel. She describes the uncanny feeling evoked when the accepted limits of humanity's creative powers are stretched beyond human control to a supernatural level. In Shelley's words, "the successive images that arose in [her] mind" carried "a vividness far beyond the usual bounds of reverie." Her memory of the "acute mental vision" she used to conjure the story of *Frankenstein* emphasizes the fear and horror that ensue when any human creator, through the uncanny aspects of his or her creation, seemingly mirrors the omniscient powers of an almighty being: "Frightful must it be; for supremely frightful would be the effect of any human endeavor to mock the stupendous mechanism of the Creator of the world. His success would terrify the artist . . . and he might sleep in the belief that the silence of the grave would quench for ever the transient existence of the hideous corpse which he had looked upon as the cradle of life."[6]

4. Jim Hansen, *Terror and Irish Modernism: The Gothic Tradition from Burke to Beckett* (Albany: SUNY P, 2009), p. 74.
5. Owen Dudley Edwards, "Impressions of an Irish Sphinx" in McCormack, *Wilde the Irishman*, p. 55.
6. Mary Shelley, *Frankenstein*, ed. Johanna M. Smith (1818; New York: Bedford/St. Martin's, 2000), p. 24.

Shelley provocatively illustrates not only the fear of the reanimation of the dead that Sigmund Freud attributes to the intellectual
uncertainty of uncanny experiences, but also the fear that an artistic creation might come to life and then confront the artist.[7] Shelley
wrote a half-century before Walter Pater coined the phrase "art for
its own sake," and her story of the origins of *Frankenstein*—of the
reanimation of humanity at the hands of an irreverent artist—
stresses that the creator of art must be held accountable for what
he or she produces; art for its own sake would be not only irresponsible but also dangerous to the artist. Further, Shelley suggests that
an artistic production maintains power—one that mirrors the power
of a colonized Other—in its ability to confront both the spectator
and the artist.

Frankenstein underscores the late eighteenth- and early nineteenth-
century Romantic engagement with an emerging conception of ideal
British autonomy that was later housed in the artistic genre of
gothic fiction and surfaced in moments of confrontation. Joseph
Valente describes British manliness during the late nineteenth
century as a "hinge" that held together "the dual effects of a char-
acteristically Irish failure to meet the magnanimous summons to
normative, liberal, which is to say British, subjectivity." In Valente's
model, British subjectivity is defined by exactly what it claims *not*
to be: inferior, weak, barbaric, and Irish. Although this concept of
subjectivity was only an ideal, not an attainable reality, it perpetu-
ated Englishness as the autonomous whole to which "modes of otherness" were opposed. For Valente, this is an ideologically constructed
category of subjectivity: "England's ethnic advantages in claiming
manliness cast the Irish inability to do so as an ethical demerit; conversely, Irish ethnic impediments to attaining manly status under-
wrote English success as an ethical achievement."[8] The cultural
attempt to construct permanent categories of Otherness—gendered,
colonial, or national—in order to stabilize the definition of British
subjectivity eventually provokes a gothic discomfort with the still-
evolving image of a capitalistic subject. This image later becomes a
formal trope—one that culminates in late-Victorian novels like Bram
Stoker's *Dracula* (1897). This is particularly true in *Dorian Gray*
where, as Riquelme points out, "Wilde has merged the aesthetic with
issues that regularly arise in Gothic writing, issues that are anthro-
pological, aesthetic, and scientific: the creation of the new and the

---

7. In *The Uncanny*, Freud cites Jentsch's definition of "intellectual uncertainty" as a starting point for his review of the uncanny: "E. Jentsch singles out, as an excellent case,
   'doubt as to whether an apparently animate object really is alive and, conversely, whether
   a lifeless object might not perhaps be animate.'" Sigmund Freud, *The Uncanny*, transl.
   David McLintock (1919; New York: Penguin, 2003), p. 135.
8. Joseph Valente, *The Myth of Manliness in Irish National Culture, 1880–1922* (Cham-
   paign: U of Illinois P, 2011), p. 14.

character of the human."[9] Unlike Wilde's project in *Dorian Gray*, Shelley's fear of the rebirth of a monstrous being in her recapitulation of the inspiration for *Frankenstein* does not directly engage the relationship between nineteenth-century aesthetics and British imperialism. However, Shelley does double the scientific discourse of the novel with the imperial quest of Robert Walton, who desires glory and fame from his expedition to the North Pole.[1] Shelley's parallel of the scientist first with the artist (in her introduction to *Frankenstein*) and then with the explorer (as the framing narrative of the novel) suggests that many acts of creation in the early nineteenth-century, whether scientific or artistic, were threatened by the same irresponsibility that would later be associated with British imperialism: the unwillingness to acknowledge the futility of colonization and the destructive economic effects of empire.

Late nineteenth-century gothic fiction often portrays the way in which excess, as the defining element of an emerging modern identity, corrupts and destroys the self that it seeks to mold. The novel, especially the gothic novel, comes dangerously close to becoming what Edward W. Said famously referred to as a "cultural artifact of bourgeois society." Of all the major literary forms, Said points out, "the novel is the most recent, its emergence the most datable, its occurrence the most Western, its normative pattern of social authority the most structured; imperialism and the novel fortified each other to such a degree that it is impossible . . . to read one without in some way dealing with the other." Said goes on to argue that the novel "and imperialism are unthinkable without each other." Said's remarks also emphasize the way in which British autonomy grounded in empire became problematized by both the growth of imperialism and by the "undisputed dominance of the British novel."[2]

Wilde's novel exhibits the parallel relationship that Said sees between imperialism as an attribute of British identity itself and the development of British aesthetics—here, the novel as the ultimate aesthetic tool of nineteenth-century representation. Wilde exposes the western canon and western aesthetics as codified discourses of British cultural identity. Riquelme, too, observes this parallel in Wilde when he discusses Walter Pater's original review of the novel

9. Riquelme, "Aesthetic Gothic," 618.
1. Like many critics of *Frankenstein*, I read Robert Walton as a double for Dr. Frankenstein, both in his search for a "perfect" discovery and his inability or unwillingness to stop his progression to the North Pole even when he is faced with the probable failure of his project. For a contemporary discussion of Shelley's illustrations of modernity in *Frankenstein* see Marc Redfield, "Frankenstein's Cinematic Dream" in *Romantic Circles Praxis Series/Frankenstein's Dream* (July 2003), http://www.rc.umd.edu/praxis/frankenstein/redfield/redfield.html.
2. Edward W. Said, *Culture and Imperialism* (New York, 1944), p. 71.

and the way that Pater underscored the novel's tense relationship with British culture:

> Pater makes the non-British character of the book and its author clear at the start and the end of the review. Besides closing by drawing attention to foreign models rather than one that is much closer to home, Pater begins with comments that situate Wilde prejudicially as an Irish writer. The book putatively produced on non-British patterns by an Irish writer is, not surprisingly, filled with anti-British sentiments. Wilde has turned the critical direction of the Gothic inward, toward England and toward art as an English writer presents it.[3]

As a leading voice of British aesthetics in the nineteenth century, Walter Pater, in his review of *Dorian Gray*, proves for Riquelme the magnitude of the novel's "anti-British sentiments." Instead of using the gothic motif to critique the fear of external threats, Wilde employs the gothic to show the cultural and aesthetic dangers of Britishness. Wilde was so successful that even Pater could see something non-British in the book—an emphasis on oral tradition, something that Pater could only mark as the production of an Irish writer: "We need only emphasise, once more, the skill, the real subtlety of art, the ease and fluidity withal of one telling a story by word of mouth, with which the consciousness of the supernatural is introduced into, and maintained amid, the elaborately conventional, sophisticated, disabused world Mr. Wilde depicts so cleverly, so mercilessly."[4]

Moreover, through the motif of the supernatural—a force that either reflects or consumes the fin-de-siècle British subject—Wilde's novel signifies a growing insecurity within both England's struggling imperial project and aesthetic narratives. Suddenly the threat to empire was at once inside and outside of British culture. Fin-de-siècle writers represented such insecurity through their gothic depictions of figures of Otherness, such as the vampire or Dorian's changing portrait. When the fictional Others of such novels confront the British subjects to whom they are a covert threat, they illustrate the dangers of a misguided colonial enterprise that claims to control the production of cultural modernity.

Wilde's critique of imperialism as a system that overlaps with both capitalism and Paterian aesthetics in *Dorian Gray* suggests that different ideologies of imperialism share what Seamus Deane refers to as an "expansionist economic system" that is generally "capitalist or

---

3. Riquelme, "Aesthetic Gothic," pp. 613–14.
4. Walter Pater, "A Novel by Mr. Oscar Wilde," *Bookman*, 1 (November 1891), 60.

communist."[5] Such a system "claims to have its roots in a universal human nature." Furthermore, such projects often "boast of possessing a wondrous cultural system that is either the inevitable consequence of the triumph of that economic system or one of the preconditions of its emergence." Within this framework, then, modernization is the effect of a strong, triumphant economic system that promises prosperity and civilization to peoples and countries that do not currently possess such characteristics. But, as Deane points out, the imperial growth of such versions of modernity depends on people "whose defeat, expropriation, enslavement, or extermination had to be justified in a series of theoretical formulations that relied on categories paraded as fundamental and universal."[6] To accomplish this justification, many categories that were maintained in the nineteenth century—such as race and class—had to be universalized and historicized according to the European view of an imperial destiny.

Such categorizations were particularly problematic within the British colonization of Ireland, which, in many ways, reached its climax during the nineteenth century. The late nineteenth century saw a dramatic shift in national sentiment in Ireland after the Famine. "The period from the 1880s," Kevin Whelan writes, "when the post-Famine generation took over, witnessed the creation of a series of radical responses to the Famine legacy, of which the Irish literary revival is one. Many other initiatives were also undertaken, inspired by people themselves born during the Famine. . . . They belonged to a generation that sought to reshape Ireland in fundamental ways following the Famine and the hollowing-out of indigenous Irish culture."[7] In response to the cultural devastation that followed the Famine, Irish nationalism emerged as an intimate counterpart to the imperial project, at times reinforcing many of the universalizing ideologies it sought to eliminate.[8] Deane points out that Ireland's "national independence movement was, from the beginning, closely involved with the production and recovery of a

5. Seamus Deane, "Imperialism/Nationalism" in *Critical Terms for Literary Study*, ed. Frank Lentricchia and Thomas McLaughlin (Chicago: U of Chicago P, 1995), p. 354.
6. Deane, p. 355.
7. Kevin Whelan, "The Cultural Effects of the Famine," in *The Cambridge Companion to Modern Irish Culture*, ed. Joe Cleary and Claire Connolly (Cambridge: Cambridge UP, 2005), p. 138.
8. In his discussion of hurling, Whelan fully explains this effect: "A national community must be nurtured, its identity carefully recuperated out of the shards of history, language and folklore. This new cultural vocabulary had then to be inserted into a grammar of political action. In its redefined form, national culture could be harnessed to political demands. . . . Janus-headed, [cultural nationalism] . . . simultaneously homogenised (stressing the unity of the Irish people) and differentiated (stressing their distinctiveness from the British people). Nationalism became a classifying protocol, which reordered relationships between peoples." Whelan, pp. 147–48.

national literature and the question of a revival of the national language. In the process, Ireland also produced some of the masterpieces of literary modernism, thereby clarifying in a previously unprecedented manner the nature of the relationships between imperialism, nationalism, and modernism."[9] Wilde wrote *Dorian Gray* at a time when Irish nationalistic and British imperialistic discourses were beginning to simultaneously challenge and echo each other—an echo that ultimately results in the various critiques of cultural modernity in Ireland by such Irish modernist writers as Joyce and Yeats.

Preceding the publication of *Dorian Gray,* Ireland was "modernized and Anglicized; it was also devastated by famine and repression to such a degree that its population was halved and its old Gaelic culture, already in retreat since the seventeenth century, was rendered almost extinct."[1] The Anglicization of Ireland not only fueled the nationalist movement from the late nineteenth into the twentieth century, but also initiated a nationalist aesthetic (specifically, the romanticized versions of Irish history, culture, and literature that emerged in the late nineteenth century and climaxed in Yeats' nostalgic portrayals of the Irish peasantry) that Irish modernist writers, after Wilde, find problematic. Richard Ellmann describes *Dorian Gray* as "the aesthetic novel *par excellence,* not in espousing the doctrine, but in exhibiting its dangers."[2]

In other words, the employment of aesthetics to personify Britishness in the nationalistic discourse of Ireland, both literary and political, is not the subject of *Dorian Gray* so much as is the excess of aesthetics itself—the danger of seeking perfection in representation. However, symbols of Irish nationalism both moonlight in much of Wilde's text and take center stage during scenes that underscore a degenerating British selfhood. Wilde implicates Ireland in his prophesy of British failure while also mourning the grave atrocities acted upon it by the same failing empire. Wilde's view of excess in *Dorian Gray* imagines Paterian aesthetics as a system closely resembling the imperial project in its quest for a perfect expression of youth, beauty and pleasure. By association, Wilde suggests that British aestheticism will self-destruct, by way of its dependence on excess and exploitation for the sake of a form of pure or perfect beauty.

Regenia Gagnier, in introducing *Critical Essays on Oscar Wilde,* claims that, in the late nineteenth century, "aestheticism was a protest against Victorian utility, rationality, and realism, or the reduction

9. Deane, p. 363.
1. Ibid., p. 363.
2. Richard Ellmann, *Oscar Wilde* (New York: Alfred A. Knopf, 1988), p. 315.

of human relations to utility and the market and the representation of this in bourgeois literature." In this way, aestheticism subtly
mirrors some of the basic principles of nationalism—an ideology
opposed to utility for the sake of bourgeois capitalism and a com-
petitive, imperial world market. As she builds her argument, Gagnier continues to define aestheticism in opposition to imperialism:

> Aestheticism represented a detachment from praxis indicating
> a break with imperialist society (Beardsley) and a preoccupa-
> tion with formal or technical qualities of artistic media (Dow-
> son and Johnson). Its function was to negate the means-end
> rationality of everyday middle-class life by theorizing art as an
> autonomous "useless" realm (Wilde). Its consequence was that
> art lacked overt political content, repeated archaic forms, and
> courted unproductiveness on the part of artists.[3]

Gagnier reads Wilde's aestheticism as an affront, in many ways, to the
commodifying project of capitalism and the rationality of "middle-
class life," but a much darker version of aesthetics permeates *Dorian
Gray*. Instead of challenging the mass-market, the aesthetics of the
novel participate in that market, and in the process, re-establish
and promote the class difference that supported that market to
begin with.

   Gagnier's explanation of aestheticism is both powerful and persuasive, especially in terms of Wilde's biographical role as a cultural
figure. Yet Wilde's project in *Dorian Gray* depicts an excessive aesthetics that is complicit in an imperial discourse. Both aestheticism
and imperialism reaffirm the Victorian categories of class and race
in order to maintain control of the imagination and the economy,
respectively. Ellmann captures Wilde's representation of aesthetic
excess in *Dorian Gray* when he describes the novel as a "tragedy of
aestheticism," suggesting that it uncovers "the life of mere sensation . . . as anarchic and self-destructive."[4] Gagnier's cultural posi-
tioning of Victorian aestheticism against the "rationality' that
supported both imperialism and capitalism convincingly underscores
Wilde's identification with dandyism as a form of political resistance.
But that political resistance is housed in the way that dandyism operates, as an ironic reflection of dominant culture.[5] Wilde's novel does
the very thing that Wilde sought to perform through his dandyism:

---

3. Reginia Gagnier, *Critical Essays on Oscar Wilde* (New York: G. K. Hall and Co., 1991), p. 3.
4. Ellmann, p. 315.
5. As Jerusha McCormack suggests: "Despising the society into which he seeks initiation,
   the dandy takes his revenge by creating himself in its image, miming its clothes, its
   manners and mannerisms. . . . Inherently exaggerated, such mimicry exposes the fis-
   sures of its own performance: the double standards on which it rests. . . . In effect, by
   means of his performance the dandy gets his audience to share his contempt for itself."
   McCormack, p. 89.

it overdramatically imitates British aesthetics, exposes the excess at the heart of it, and emphasizes its dependence on a gothic, colonial, and Irish Other.

Further, it has become increasingly common, as Maureen O'Connor points out, "to link Oscar Wilde's self-identification as Irish to his radically oppositional stance vis-à-vis late-Victorian Britain."[6] It is not Wilde who appears in his novel; instead, the hedonistic characters in *Dorian Gray* are saturated with a hyperbolic intensity that mocks not only the arrogance of ideal British autonomy, but also the belief that the aesthetic is only preoccupied with idealized beauty. In this sense, Wilde uses such hyperbolized images of the aesthetic to imagine the downfall of an international economic system that relies on the illusion of perfectionism and universalism to promote its colonial modernity.

As an ironic version of the bildungsroman, *Dorian Gray* tells the story of Dorian, a naive boy who falls under the influence of both Lord Henry Wotton, an aristocratic socialite whose wealth leaves him with an abundance of leisure time, and Basil Hallward, an artist who sees Dorian as the perfect specimen of beauty.[7] Basil paints a picture of Dorian that exquisitely portrays Dorian's youth, beauty, and innocence. After Lord Henry makes it clear that Dorian will not remain young forever—that age will eventually change him—Dorian wishes to trade his soul for a lifetime of youth and beauty:

> How sad it is! I shall grow old, and horrible, and dreadful. But this picture will remain always young. It will never be older than this particular day of June . . . If it were only the other way! If it were I who was to be always young, and the picture that was to grow old! For that—for that—I would give everything! Yes, there is nothing in the whole world I would not give! I would give my soul for that![8]

In this supernatural, Faustian exchange Dorian seals his fate by choosing his youthful exterior over an ethical life. Throughout the novel, Dorian's beauty turns into a dangerous vanity. He destroys

---

6. Maureen O'Connor, "*The Picture of Dorian Gray* as Irish National Tale," in *Writing Irishness in Nineteenth-century British Culture*, ed. Neil McCaw (Aldershot: Ashgate, 2003), p. 194.

7. Although Wilde devotes only one paragraph in chapter three to the history of Dorian's lineage, the story is illuminating. Dorian's father, a subaltern in the British army, was killed in a duel. The man who killed him was hired by Dorian's mother's father (Dorian's grandfather) to provoke his father's temper. Through his subaltern status and his unruly temper, Dorian's father illustrates what Joseph Valente calls "the double bind of Irish manhood." Dorian inherits the very thing that the novel suggests he is repressing throughout the story.

8. Oscar Wilde, *The Picture of Dorian Gray*, ed. Michael Patrick Gillespie (1891; New York: Norton, 2007 [rev. 2019]), pp. 25–26; hereafter cited parenthetically, thus: (*PDG* 25–26). [Page references have been updated to cite this Third Norton Critical Edition.—*Editor*]

anything that might threaten the appearance of perfection that he believes he has attained. Basil's painting of Dorian, however, supernaturally registers each act of selfishness, anger, and destruction; Dorian's outward appearance reflects only false innocence, false perfection.

Wilde parallels Dorian's story with the story of the Vane siblings, Sybil and James, who both encounter Dorian and are eventually destroyed by his influence in their lives. The working-class Vanes have made a living off of Sybil's acting career. Dorian falls in love with her talent and they become engaged; Sybil, however, can no longer perform on the stage once she has fallen in love. Dorian subsequently rejects her and their potential future together. Simultaneously, James Vane leaves England for the more manageable economy of Australia, and in time ends up as a British sailor in India. After Dorian's rejection, Sybil kills herself. James returns from India to avenge his sister's death. Although James is killed before the novel's close, his confrontations with Dorian lead to Dorian's eventual self-destruction and the end of the story, where Dorian reverses the supernatural curse by stabbing the painting and thereby killing himself.

In *Dorian Gray*, Wilde employs a framework of confrontation that creates different versions of Otherness, first for Dorian, who becomes the aesthetic creation of Lord Henry and Basil, then for the painting of Dorian that exchanges places with him as a work of art, and, finally, for the characters of Sybil and James Vane.[9] It is ultimately James Vane's accusations against and climactic encounter with Dorian that lead to Dorian's demise. Each confrontation is a moment of gothic doubling that borders on destruction, when the individual self of either a character or the painting is opposed and finally threatened by the Other. Because of their conjuring of uncanny recognitions that threaten to erase or absorb the original self within the novel—the self that is first the artist in the text, then the art itself, and finally the decadent, bourgeois culture of the London elite—the confrontations between "self" and "other" suggest a repressed cultural memory. Such memory is both colonial and Irish, as well as a representation of aesthetic beauty.[1] This beauty blinds most

9. The "framework of confrontation" here is based on Sedgwick's description of the "spatial model" of the gothic text. The role of the "self" is complicated by a presence "outside" of itself in Sedgwick's model: "The self and whatever it is that is outside have a proper, natural, necessary connection to each other, but one that the self is suddenly incapable of making. The inside life and the outside life have to continue separately, becoming counterparts rather than partners, the relationship between them one of parallels and correspondences rather than communication. This, though it may happen in an instant, is a fundamental reorganization, creating a doubleness where singleness should be. And the lengths there are to go to reintegrate the sundered elements—finally, the impossibility of restoring them to their original oneness—are the most characteristic energies of the Gothic novel." Sedgwick, *Gothic Conventions*, p. 13.

1. Levinas's explanation is especially helpful in understanding the Other: "The Other as Other is not only an alter ego: the Other is what I myself am not. The Other is this . . .

characters in *Dorian Gray,* particularly Lord Henry and Basil. Yet, it is James Vane, a working-class character complicit with the imperial project, who confronts and challenges Dorian's illusion; when he confronts Dorian, he becomes a reflection of Dorian's vanity and the vanity fueling British imperialism. When Dorian loses his signification as an aesthetically perfect image, he can no longer live in the world of the novel. If we accept that James Vane's role functions as the return of a repressed memory, then Kevin Whelan's explanation of the power of memory in the face of the pain and loss of the Irish past is crucial: "Radical memory in the post-Famine period deployed a prospective rather than an elegiac nostalgia, a nostalgia for the future, not the past. This dialogue of cultural memory and expectation keeps alive the memory of suffering and defeat against the obliterative force of the victors' narrative."[2]

In this sense, James Vane "keeps alive" the memory of his sister's death by appearing time and time again, before finally eliminating the force of Dorian's narrative. Through an identification with an Other who has the power to consume, reflect, and destroy the self (sometimes through memory), the aristocratic characters of Wilde's novel recognize both their own gothic tendencies and a fragile autonomy that exists not only outside of themselves, but also in the very thing they wished to possess or master. For many, recognizing the power of the Other proves fatal.

Dorian, the painting, and the Vane siblings—along with the aristocratic, but ignorant, attendees of various salons—are all products of a British sensibility that appears, through Wilde's portrayal, to be both disturbing and dangerous. Riquelme's comments on Wilde's gothic aesthetic suggest that this British sensibility would be especially apparent to Wilde as an Irish writer:

> In a typically modern transformation of gothic narrative, the threat in Wilde's novel comes from within culture and within British society, not from foreigners who can be treated as savages. As an Irish writer, Wilde would have been particularly aware of the distinctions the British tended to draw between themselves and ostensibly less civilized racial and national groups who might in some way pose a crude threat, Calibanlike, to British aspirations and identity.[3]

The threat posed in Wilde's novel takes the form of various gothic creations or projections of Otherness. Each maintains a rigorous

---

because of the Other's very alterity. The Other is, for example, the weak, the poor, 'the widow and the orphan,'" whereas I am the rich or the powerful." Emmanuel Levinas, *Time and the Other,* transl. Richard A. Cohen (Pittsburgh: Duquesne UP, 1987), p. 83.

2. Whelan, p. 152.
3. Riquelme, "Aesthetic Gothic," p. 618.

identity in the face of stereotypically British counterparts. The others participate in what O'Connor terms Wilde's "radical decentering of the self," where "the only identification possible is a necessarily impossible one with the *lost* and *fragmented*."[4] The self's impossible but necessary identification with the Other in *Dorian Gray* creates a sense of uncanny resemblance that certain characters eventually recognize. This sort of recognition leads to an identification that unhinges Dorian and drives him to try to kill the painting. It is exactly this type of impossible identification that carries the power to overwhelm, confuse, and, ultimately resist the dominant discourses of creation within the narrative—supplanting those discourses with a self-destructive nihilism.

When Basil describes the first time he met Dorian to Lord Henry, he expresses the feeling that he was somehow forced to expose his "soul" through that initial confrontation. Basil emphasizes the terror he felt:

> I turned half-way round, and saw Dorian Gray for the first time. When our eyes met, I felt that I was growing pale. A curious sensation of terror came over me. I knew that I had come face to face with some one whose mere personality was so fascinating that, if I allowed it to do so, it would absorb my whole nature, my whole soul, my very art itself. (*PDG* 10)

In *Dorian Gray*, personality is an aesthetic characteristic attributed to the power of appearance or beauty to fascinate a spectator during a confrontation such as this one. Dorian's personality, according to Basil, is the very thing that infuses the artist with terror and threatens to absorb, sponge-like, his artistic sensibility. The power of Dorian's stare lies in his ability to simultaneously represent pure beauty and reflect the artist's potential; he poses a danger to both Basil's "soul" and his "art." In Dorian, Basil sees "the one person who gives to my art whatever charm it possesses: my life as an artist depends on him" (*PDG* 16). Early in the story, we see Basil's artistic infatuation with Dorian as a presence that could potentially devastate and terrorize the forces of creation at play in the text. Dorian's early position as the aesthetic Other—a pure art form— paradoxically renders him both powerful and powerless against the influences of his masters or creators: Lord Henry, who "plays" Dorian like a violin, and Basil, who captures Dorian's beauty as a representation of artistic perfection, the combination of "body and soul." Ironically, it is Dorian's position as Other that allows him to acknowledge the reality of British decay at the end of the novel.

---

4. O'Connor, p. 456.

When Dorian visits the opium den, he realizes the significance of his aesthetic impressions. He suddenly feels that the

> ugliness that had once been hateful to him because it made things real, became dear to him now for that very reason. Ugliness was the one reality. The coarse brawl, the loathsome den, the crude violence of disordered life, the very vileness of thief and outcast, were more vivid, in their intense actuality of impression, than all the gracious shapes of Art, the dreamy shadows of Song.   (*PDG* 155)

Dorian identifies himself as an "outcast" at this point. His detailed depiction of the filth of London's reality occurs through the eyes not of a British aristocrat, but of someone trapped in the torturous position of stagnant, but pure beauty. Here Wilde suggests that ugliness, either in an aging, withering, and degenerate British aristocracy or in the excessive epidemic of British poverty, is a presence that the aesthetic Othering of the novel ignores and ultimately tries to erase in its idolatrous worship of beauty.

The aesthetic idolatry—art's obsession with the production of beauty—that Basil feels toward Dorian shifts when Basil describes the effects of his portrait to Dorian in the middle of the novel, in a scene that foreshadows Dorian's eventual murder of Basil. Basil's feelings about the painting have changed, because he no longer believes that his role as artist is reflected in the creation he has produced. The artist admits this view after the painting, unbeknownst to Basil, has supernaturally begun to reflect Dorian's deviant behavior.

Through *Dorian Gray*'s infamously frightful twist, the artistic creation that is the portrait assumes a dominant, autonomous position in the narrative based on its ability to reflect Dorian's soul—and in the process, critiques the depths of British decay. As in *Frankenstein*, the character of Dorian as a creation-turned-subject must kill Basil, his own creator, in order for his own autonomy to survive. Wilde posits art both as a confrontational Other on which the restoration or destruction of British aesthetics depends and as a purveyor of sublime terror, or the threat of pure beauty's eclipsing finality.

In this way, the painting is the strongest symbol of Wilde's careful critique of both British imperialism and the futile quest of empire toward a unified and Anglicized global culture—represented in the novel as pure beauty or a pure aesthetic—that could marginalize and eventually erase the cultural difference of the Other. Wilde's use of the painting resonates with with Sedgwick's characterization of the gothic as a literary form that is not necessarily dependent on a psychological model that values "the Gothic for its portrayal of 'depth'."[5]

---

5. Sedgwick, *Gothic Conventions*, p. 12.

Instead, Sedgwick shows that in gothic fiction, "the strongest energies inhere in the surface" or that which the self is separated from and struggles against. Ironically, Basil characterizes the artist as an abstraction within his own art:

> I cannot help feeling that it is a mistake to think that the passion one feels in creation is ever really shown in the work one creates. Art is always more abstract than we fancy. Form and colour tell us of form and colour—that is all. It often seems to me that art conceals the artist far more completely than it ever reveals him.   (*PDG* 96)

The portrait does not reveal Basil's soul, but rather, Dorian's; his "cruelty" slowly leads to murder and self-destruction during the course of the novel. Art cannot be wholly consumed or explained by the artist; it maintains its own identity, eventually surpassing the artist's vision. The portrait yokes the ideologies of art and empire and becomes the locus of power in the story of Dorian Gray's destruction. The painting refuses to reflect the artist. It serves instead as a constant memory of the degenerating forces that degrade and infect British life. The paradoxical relationship between what the painting, as a work of art, reveals as British corrosion and what it conceals in the gothic body of Dorian Gray suggests that an art that does not fail to represent, but instead represents absolutely, is the doppelganger for an empire that tries to eliminate cultural difference and vampirically regenerate itself through colonial assimilation. Such art seeks to erase autonomy rather than generate it.

In the middle of Wilde's 1891 dialogue *The Decay of Lying*, Cyril asks Vivian if he is serious in his suggestion that life is a mirror for art, thus rejecting the reduction of "genius to the position of a cracked looking-glass." Vivian famously responds "Paradox though it may seem—and paradoxes are always dangerous things—it is none the less true that Life imitates art far more than Art imitates life."[6] The concept that "art never expresses anything but itself" is the basis of Vivian's "new aesthetics," a critique of the realism that has begun to dominate the arts in the late nineteenth century.

Wilde opens the preface to *Dorian Gray* with the same notion of paradox personified in Caliban's reflection and, appropriately, it is life that is reduced to the cracked looking-glass, not art. If life is a mirror for art's "reality," as Cyril suggests in *Decay*, Wilde's sense of reality becomes more an expression of the artistic imagination than a diagnosis of late-Victorian degeneracy. Because Caliban is an

6. Oscar Wilde, "The Decay of Lying," *The Complete Writings of Oscar Wilde* (New York: Nottingham Society, 1909), p. 33.

artistic creation, it is ironic that art—as a figure for the ugly or real—looks in its own face in pursuit of reality and does not find it.

Wilde's depiction of reality would prove foundational for twentieth-century literary depictions of colonialism, particularly when Irish modernism employs Wilde's invocation of Caliban's reflection. Joyce explicitly employs Wilde's image of Caliban in *Ulysses* when Buck Mulligan quotes Wilde's reference, "the rage of Caliban at not seeing his face in a mirror," and exclaims to Stephen, "if Wilde were only alive to see you!"[7] Stephen's response that "It is a symbol of Irish art. The cracked lookingglass of a servant" reiterates Wilde's original suggestion in *Decay* that life—in this case, the life of a colonized Irish subject—imitates art, and for Joyce suggests that the mirror is a symbol for art, not the other way around. This, too, is Jerusha McCormack's argument in her introduction to *Wilde the Irishman*:

> Wilde's identification with Ireland had perhaps less to do ultimately with historical fact or party-political affiliation than a consistent cultural identification with what he called 'Celtic' . . . he was of the oppressed peoples which embodied all that was alien and rejected by the English . . . the Celt was heir to an ancient and rich race-experience. But to understand oneself in such terms, as Wilde evidently did, was also to reject terms of moral choice. Making one's life becomes a matter of fate: that of representing the master-race to itself, by embodying that secret self it has rejected or denied, to perform, with whatever degree of irony one could summon, the script already dictated by one's audience.[8]

Wilde's "cultural identification," then, is with the experiences of oppression and repression. The oppression of the Celt leads to the repression of that same space of Otherness in the cultural psyche of the "master-race." Echoing her arguments about Wilde's dandyism, McCormack's points here emphasize how important it was for Wilde to mirror the "secret self" of the master-race back to the imperial world. In *The Picture of Dorian Gray*, that secret self is an aesthetic creation that, while kept hidden, continues to imitate and reflect the grotesque behavior and attitude of both the British aristocracy and the imperial state.

As Wilde suggests in his opening references to Caliban, it is in the realm of the theater that imagination thrives in *Dorian Gray*. When life begins to fully reflect art—when the act of love expressed

---

7. James Joyce, *Ulysses*, ed. Hans Walter Gabler (New York: Vintage Books, 1986), p. 6. This occurs in the opening scene. Buck Mulligan and Stephen are on top of the Martello tower and already marginalized from the national politics of Dublin life.
8. McCormack, *Wilde the Irishman*, pp. 2–3.

on the stage becomes a reality for the actress, Sybil Vane—it no longer produces the "effect" desired by the hedonistic Dorian. For Dorian, Sybil's beauty lies in her ability to produce passion on the stage and to use her imagination to create and fashion images of love and romance. When love becomes a reality for Sybil and she falls in love with and becomes engaged to Dorian, she can no longer perform the acts of love that her theatrical roles demand.

When art becomes reality and Sybil's life really does begin to imitate the art she performs, it is her art that suffers. She is no longer beautiful to Dorian or to Dorian's friends, Lord Henry and Basil, who accompany him to the theater, upon his request, to witness Sybil's artistic talent. In this depiction, Wilde offers two intertwining observations. First, he suggests that life's paradoxical imitation of art is, as Vivian says in *Decay*, "dangerous," and, specifically, that such danger is magnified when the imitating life is neither a middle-class, nor an aristocratic life. Dorian naively believes that Sybil's artistic talent can transform the base lives of those who inhabit the theater community, making them cultivated spectators, similar to himself:

> she is divine beyond all living things. When she acts you will forget everything. These common, rough people, with their coarse faces and brutal gestures, become quite different when she is on the stage. They sit silently and watch her. They weep and laugh as she wills them to do. She makes them as responsive as a violin. She spiritualizes them, and one feels that they are of the same flesh and blood as one's self.   (*PDG* 70)

In Dorian's description, Sybil becomes the embodiment of a divine aesthetic, an artist who forces her spectators to respond to her talent like "spiritualized violins" who suddenly recognize their bourgeois potential.

In this way, Wilde positions Dorian as a double for the underprivileged audience—just as Lord Henry "plays" Dorian like a violin earlier, Sybil's onlookers also are manipulated. Through her art, they prove capable of cultivation and insight. However, through Sybil's status as a working-class actress who believes in "true" love the novel suggests that, were her union with Dorian to occur, she still would not survive the decadence surrounding Dorian's life. As Vivian declares in *Decay*, "Sooner or later one comes to that dreadful universal thing called human nature. Indeed, as any one who has ever worked among the poor knows only too well, the brotherhood of man is no mere poet's dream, it is a most depressing and humiliating reality."[9] In the England of Dorian Gray, there is no room for the

9. Wilde, "Decay of Lying," p. 33.

working class to imitate art in the reality of their lives off of the stage: they have neither the time, energy, or money to do so. Further, Sybil's artistic imitation (or imagination) depends on Dorian's recognition and support of her—he becomes her "Prince Charming," the man who will whisk her away from her degraded theatrical life.

But Sybil's separation from the theater (and partnership with Dorian) would also demand that she reject the lifestyle and people who comprise the lower-class world of the stage; Wilde will not allow her to occupy both economic spheres. Instead, he suggests that the cultural climate of the novel will maintain the class division at all costs. It is precisely this that leads Sybil's brother, James, to initially threaten Dorian's life: "'as sure as there is a God in heaven, if he ever does you any wrong, I shall kill him'" James says these words out of "jealousy . . . and a fierce murderous hatred of the stranger who, as it seemed to him, had come between them" (*PDG* 61). More than any other character, James realizes the danger of Sybil's relationship with Dorian: she must discard the world that created her if she is to imitate the art (Dorian, himself) that first taught her love. When Sybil leaves the symbolic world of the theater for Dorian, she loses the talent that kept her and her family economically secure. Once Dorian rejects her, she loses not only her talent, but also the world that was supposed to supplement that talent; she has nothing to imitate and no life to live.

Wilde's second observation in this section centers on Dorian's inability to experience love outside of theatrical performativity. Dorian only "loves" Sybil when her performance of classical, Shakespearian love is at its peak. Once she exchanges her acting for the reality of her feelings for Dorian, she can no longer perform the love that encourages Dorian's attention. Dorian is only capable of loving an art that is too real, not the life that imitates that art. And Sybil cannot be both artist and imitator once she falls in love with Dorian:

> The voice was exquisite, but from the point of view of tone it was absolutely false. It was wrong in colour. It took away all the life from the verse. It made the passion unreal. . . . She looked charming as she came out in the moonlight. That could not be denied. But the staginess of her acting was unbearable, and grew worse as she went on. Her gestures became absurdly artificial. She over-emphasized everything that she had to say.
>
> (*PDG* 71)

After she falls in love with Dorian Sybil's acting seems "unreal." She appears beautiful and sounds "exquisite," but she also appears stagy and artificial. When Dorian confronts her, astounded by her bad acting, Sybil explains that she has finally discovered "what reality really is":

> Dorian, Dorian . . . before I knew you, acting was the one real-
> ity of my life. It was only in the theatre that I lived. I thought
> that it was all true. . . . To-night, for the first time in my life, I
> saw through the hollowness, the sham, the silliness of the
> empty pageant in which I had always played. To-night, for the
> first time I became conscious . . . that the words I had to speak
> were unreal, were not my words, were not what I wanted to say.
> You had brought me something higher, something of which all
> art is but a reflection. You had made me understand what love
> really is.   (*PDG* 73)

Much as Lord Henry awakens Dorian's knowledge of himself in the
opening pages of the novel by suggesting that "the only way to get rid
of a temptation is to yield to it," Dorian has become Sybil's tree of
knowledge; once she bites the apple of Dorian's love, her eyes are
opened to the falsity of the theater. Ironically, the "true love" that
emancipates her from the false world of the stage is itself a fake emotion. Sibyl realizes that even if life does imitate art, art is not life itself.
   Dorian cannot grasp the conceptual separation between art and
life and, in response to Sybil's self-awakening, falls out of love with
her as quickly as he fell in:

> you have killed my love. You used to stir my imagination. Now
> you don't even stir my curiosity. You simply produce no effect.
> I loved you because you were marvelous, because you had genius
> and intellect, because you realized the dreams of great poets
> and gave shape and substance to the shadows of art. You have
> thrown it all away. You are shallow and stupid.   (*PDG* 74)

For Dorian, art is a reality and play performance is a form of living.
He hates Sybil Vane when she cannot act because she has "killed"
the love he maintained for the art she represented. Further, she kills
Dorian's image of genius, poetry, and "the shadows of art," threat-
ening his visions of beauty and perfection. Ironically, she kills
Dorian's reality only to then kill herself. Sybil's suicide foreshadows
Dorian's eventual destruction because she is Dorian's reality, the
reason he exists. When Dorian returns home after abandoning Sybil,
he finds that the painting has begun to display the corruption of his
soul: "The quivering, ardent sunlight showed him the lines of cruelty round the mouth as clearly as if he had been looking into a
mirror after he had done some dreadful thing" (*PDG* 77). The
supernatural elements of the novel force Dorian to confront his
soul's decay through artistic representation. When Sybil falls from
the pedestal upon which Dorian has placed her and becomes ugly
to him, the painting must grow ugly, too. For Wilde, art that could
somehow represent the truths of Dorian's reality would be ugly and
cruel—like Dorian, himself.

Wilde's staging of the vampiric tendencies of capitalism—the need for the rich to live off the lower classes—emerges in his illustration of Dorian and Sybil's relationship. Further, those who benefit from the excess of hedonistic, bourgeois lifestyles in the novel must face not only the poverty that feeds their economic structure, but also the imperial project that seeks to spread the infection of wealth and empire to other parts of the world. It is then no coincidence that Dorian's interaction with Sybil Vane leads to the only death that must be avenged in this novel—the suicide of Sibyl Vane. Dorian must come face-to-face with Sybil's counterpart, her brother, James Vane.

In Dorian's confrontation with James Vane—a working-class sailor forever displaced by the death of his sister—the violence of British aesthetics finally turns on itself and destroys both James and Dorian. Dorian returns home to find that the painting has begun its gothic transformation. Similarly, James returns from India to encounter Dorian in the gothic setting of the opium den. Both the painting and the opium den illustrate a cruel irresponsibility present in both Dorian's rejection of Sybil's aesthetic deficiency and England's mistreatment of its colonial enterprise. Notably, Dorian's confrontation with James occurs first at the opium den, a space where the subaltern and shunned Others in the tale congregate. As Dorian enters the opium den, he

> looked round at the grotesque things that lay in such fantastic postures on the ragged mattresses. The twisted limbs, the gaping mouths, the staring lusterless eyes, fascinated him. He knew in what strange heavens they were suffering and what dull hells were teaching them the secret of some new joy. They were better off than he was. He was prisoned in thought. Memory, like a horrible malady, was eating his soul away.   (*PDG* 157)

Such critics as Maureen O'Connor have noted the representations of Irishness in both the greenness of the opium that Dorian consumes and the colors of the Irish flag that constitute the décor greeting Dorian as he moves through the underworld of the opium den.

It is equally important to recognize the way that memory functions in this space. Wilde's declaration that memory is "eating" Dorian's soul, in combination with the descriptions of "twisted limbs," "gaping mouths," and "lusterless eyes" that pervade the atmosphere narrates the story of the Irish Famine in a highly mediated way. The Famine becomes an oblique subtext to the tragedy caused by Dorian's iniquities; it is a trauma so great that Wilde approaches it indirectly, through a fictional narrative. Dorian believes that those who inhabit the opium den, the victims of an irresponsible imperialism, are "better off than he was" because they are not imprisoned by their own memories. Many of the victims in the den have also been explicit victims of Dorian's sinful activities. Wilde's implied equation of Dorian's memory with a British memory, eaten alive by its production of the colonial atrocity of Famine and genocide, suggests that Dorian will be killed by that same memory.[1]

The memory that kills Dorian comes back in the form of James Vane. James waits in the opium den for the appearance of "Prince Charming," Dorian's alias during his relationship with Sibyl. When he first confronts Dorian, he demands "You had better confess your sin, for as sure as I am James Vane, you are going to die. . . . I give you one minute to make your peace—no more. I go on board tonight for India, and I must do my job first" (*PDG* 159). Here, the England that drives the failing and brutal imperial project in India comes face to face with the England whose desire for wealth and pleasure first inaugurated that project. In other words, Dorian's vanity is staring him in the face.

The problem diagnosed by the gothic in Wilde's text does, in fact, come from within Englishness itself. Although Dorian escapes James's first attempt on his life, he is unable to forget that confrontation—it leads to Dorian's intense paranoia and sickliness as the novel approaches its closing chapters. When Dorian and James meet again, it is through the "window of the conservatory" at Dorian's vacation home, against which James Vane's face is "pressed . . . like a white handkerchief . . . watching him" (*PDG* 166). When their eyes meet, James and Dorian mirror each other in a moment of gothic doubling that threatens to collapse the space between self and Other. The white handkerchief foreshadows the cloth that covers James's face when Dorian must identify his body after he is accidentally shot by an aristocratic friend of Dorian's, and suggests that James must surrender or sacrifice himself in order for the justice of the novel to finally occur. Dorian believes he is "safe" once James is dead and resolves to be "good," but he realizes that his attempts at goodness are grounded in his selfish desire to reverse the painting's aesthetic registration of his hideousness. Eventually, in an attempt to "kill the past," Dorian stabs the painting, hoping to "kill this monstrous soul-life" and free himself (*PDG* 184). Instead, Dorian is found dead on the floor next to the restored painting of his youthful

---

1. The extent to which the Famine was a natural disaster, and the extent to which it was a consequence of the mishandling of that disaster by British authorities, has been a persisting debate in Irish Studies. Writing of contemporary understandings of the Famine, Kevin Kenny—who provides a clear discussion of this controversy—observes that "one thing that reemerged quite forcefully from this new historiography on the famine is the extent to which Ireland was a colony in an empire rather than a genuinely equal and integrated part of the United Kingdom. . . . Most Irish people, on both sides of the Atlantic, have always found it difficult to believe that the British government would have responded to famine in England the way it did in Ireland." Kevin Kenny, *The American Irish: A History* (New York: Pearson Education Limited, 2000), p. 93.

image. The servants who find his body and the painting do not recognize him until they see the rings on his fingers.

At the end of the novel, through Dorian's death, the beauty of art is revealed to the working-class individuals who are disallowed such access throughout most of the story. The only things left marking their once-oppressed status are the metonymic jewels of aristocratic wealth that live on even after the self that exhibited them has been annihilated. Jed Esty points out that this is the "economic logic of Wilde's aesthetic" where "the soul who begins to live as a pure and ageless artwork ends up embodying the logic of pure commodification, hollowing out his will, and collapsing into a dead thing."[2] Dorian's dead body is rendered unrecognizable but for the art and wealth that survive him.

In *Culture and Imperialism*, Said suggests that we must read canonical British texts according to the postcolonial revisions that have identified sources of resistance in those texts "with an effort to draw out, extend, give emphasis and voice to what is silent or marginally present or ideologically represented in such works."[3] By representing the marginalized Other—India, Ireland, the working classes—in the subaltern locales of the theater and the opium den in *Dorian Gray*, Wilde holds accountable the British imperial project as well as a decadent British aesthetics associated with a privileged sense of hedonism. Strikingly, it is through his depiction of Dorian's memory as it is eating him alive that Wilde emphasizes the horrors of the Irish condition produced by British decadence: the haunting cultural memory of famine and starvation. *Dorian Gray* sharply illustrates Wilde's belief that the capitalist structures of Englishness have hindered the development of both great art and national culture: "For there can be no great sculpture without a beautiful national life, and the commercial spirit of England has killed that; no great drama without a noble national life, and the commercial spirit of England has killed that too."[4] The critical strength of Wilde's art is housed in the power of the gothic Other to reveal the hidden decay of nineteenth-century British culture, hold a mirror to imperial wealth, and, most significantly, to unsettle the wholeness of British identity and autonomy.

2. Jed Esty, *Unseasonable Youth: Modernism, Colonialism, and the Fiction of Development* (New York: Oxford UP, 2012), p. 103.
3. Said, *Culture and Imperialism*, p. 66.
4. Wilde, "The English Renaissance of Art" in *The First Collected Edition of the Works of Oscar Wilde, 1908–1922*, ed. Robert Ross (London: Dawsons of Pall Mall, 1969), p. 263.

Oscar Wilde: A Chronology

1854   Oscar Fingal O'Flahertie Wills Wilde is born in Dublin at 21 Westland Row on October 16. He is the second child of Dr. (later Sir) William Wilde, noted oculist (opthalmologist/optometrist), aural surgeon, and author of medical texts, travel books, and antiquarian studies of Irish folklore and custom, and Jane Francesca Elgee Wilde, fervent Irish nationalist who publishes under the pen name Speranza.

1857   Wilde's younger sister, Isola Francesca Emily Wilde, is born on April 2.

1864   William Wilde is given his knighthood.

1864–71   Wilde attends the Portora Royal School at Enniskillen. Upon leaving he is awarded the Portora Gold Medal as the best classical scholar.

1867   Wilde's younger sister, Isola, dies. Wilde writes the poem "Requiescat" to commemorate her passing.

1871–74   Wilde receives a scholarship to Trinity College, Dublin, where he wins the Berkeley Gold Medal for his study of Greek.

1874–78   After winning a scholarship to Oxford, Wilde enters Magdalen College, Oxford, in October of 1874. He studies with both Ruskin and Pater and distinguishes himself as a scholar, poet, and character.

1876   Wilde's father dies on April 19, and his mother moves to England.

1878   Wilde wins the Newdigate Prize for his poem "Ravenna." It is subsequently published by Thomas Shrimpton & Son, Oxford. He also completes his degree earning a rare double first in his final examinations.

1879   Wilde's flirtation with an academic career ends when his essay "The Rise of Historical Criticism" fails to win the Chancellor's Prize, which was not awarded that year, and he is not elected a fellow of the college. Wilde then settles in London and begins to work to secure a place in society, drawing attention to himself by loudly championing aesthetic pleasure.

1880	Wilde privately publishes his first play, *Vera, or the Nihilists.*
1881	Wilde privately publishes his first volume of verse, *Poems.* He also becomes the subject of a series of cartoons in *Punch* satirizing the "art for art's sake" movement. The Gilbert and Sullivan light opera *Patience,* produced that year, contains a character, Bunthorne, based on Wilde.
1882	Wilde arrives in New York on January 2 and begins a highly successful lecture tour of the United States and Canada. He departs for England on December 27.
1883	Wilde completes his second play, *The Duchess of Padua,* in Paris and has it privately printed. A production of *Vera* is staged in New York but withdrawn after one week.
1883–84	On September 24, 1883, he begins a successful lecture tour of the United Kingdom that will carry over into the next year.
1884	On May 29 Wilde marries Constance Lloyd, the daughter of a Dublin barrister and a woman with financial resources.
1885	On January 1 Wilde takes a house at 16 Tite Street, in Chelsea, an artistic section of London. His son Cyril is born on June 5. He becomes book review editor of the *Pall Mall Gazette.*
1886	His son Vyvyan is born on November 3. He begins a friendship with Robert Ross that will last for the rest of his life. Ross will subsequently act as Wilde's literary executor.
1887–89	Wilde edits *The Woman's World,* bringing a great deal of fame to the magazine by securing contributions from a number of well-known women.
1888	*The Happy Prince and Other Tales,* a collection of fairy tales that Wilde originally composed for his sons, appears.
1889	Wilde publishes "Pen, Pencil and Poison" in the *Fortnightly Review,* "The Decay of Lying" in *Nineteenth Century,* and "The Portrait of Mr. W. H." in *Blackwood's Edinburgh Magazine.*
1890	*The Picture of Dorian Gray* appears in novella form in the July issue of *Lippincott's Magazine.* It arouses a storm of controversy in the English press.
1891	Wilde publishes "The Soul of Man under Socialism" in the *Fortnightly Review* and a collection of essays, *Intentions.* Taken together they offer important insights into Wilde's aesthetic philosophy. He also brings out *Lord*

Arthur Savile's Crime and Other Stories and *A House of Pomegranates,* two collections of short stories, and a novel-length version of *The Picture of Dorian Gray* (which produces none of the uproar that the novella caused). Wilde also begins his doomed friendship with Lord Alfred Douglas, "Bosie."

1892   *Lady Windermere's Fan* is staged at the St. James's Theatre to great popular acclaim. Wilde writes (in French) *Salome.* The London production is prohibited because of the invocation of a little known and rarely enforced English law forbidding theatrical depiction of biblical characters.

1893   *A Woman of No Importance* is staged at the Theatre Royal. *Lady Windermere's Fan* and *Salome* (French version) are published.

1894   Wilde publishes *Salome* in English translation with illustrations by Aubrey Beardsley. He also publishes a long poem, *The Sphinx,* and the play *A Woman of No Importance.* He writes *The Importance of Being Earnest,* another play.

1895   *An Ideal Husband* opens on January 3 at the Haymarket Theatre, and *The Importance of Being Earnest* opens on February 14 at the St. James's Theatre. Both plays are popular and critical hits. Wilde's increasingly reckless behavior draws public criticism from the Marquess of Queensberry, Lord Douglas's father. Wilde sues for libel but loses the case. Evidence from this trial leads to Wilde's arrest for homosexual offenses. After a hung jury ends his first trial, Wilde is found guilty in a second. On May 25 he is sentenced to two years at hard labor. He is originally imprisoned in Pentonville. On November 20 he is transferred to H.M. Prison Reading.

1895–97 While in prison, Wilde writes *De Profundis,* a sometimes moving description of his spiritual progress and a sometimes violent castigation of Bosie's behavior during their affair. On his release from prison, Wilde goes to the Continent. For the next three years, he lives primarily in France, often subsisting on the charity of friends.

1898   Wilde anonymously publishes his best-known poem, *The Ballad of Reading Gaol,* on February 13. He also publishes two letters on prison reform. His wife, Constance, dies in Genoa on April 7.

1900   On November 30, after being received into the Roman Catholic Church, he dies of cerebral meningitis at the Hôtel d'Alsace in Paris. He is buried initially at Bagneux cemetery.

1909   At the direction of Robert Ross, Wilde's remains are removed to Père-Lachaise cemetery, Paris, to a tomb designed by Jacob Epstein.

Selected Bibliography

• indicates works included or excerpted in this Norton Critical Edition.

WORKS

Poems. London: Bogue; Boston: Roberts, 1881.

"L'Envoi." [Introduction.] *Rose Leaf and Apple Leaf.* By Rennell Rodd. Philadelphia: Stoddart, 1882.

The Happy Prince and Other Tales. London: Nutt; Boston: Roberts, 1888.

"The Portrait of Mr. W. H." *Blackwood's Edinburgh Magazine* 146 (July 1889): 1–21. Enl. ed. New York: Kennerley, 1921. Later ed. London: Methuen, 1958.

The Picture of Dorian Gray. Lippincott's Monthly Magazine 46 (July 1890): 3–100; London: Ward, Lock & Company, 1891.

The Picture of Dorian Gray. Ed. Wilfried Edener. Nurnburg: Carl, 1964.

The Picture of Dorian Gray. Ed. Isobel Murray. London: Oxford UP, 1974.

"The Soul of Man under Socialism." *Fortnightly Review* 49 (February 1891). Rpt. Arthur L. Humphreys, 1895, 1907, as *The Soul of Man;* and in 1912 intro. Robert Ross as *The Soul of Man under Socialism.*

Intentions. London: Osgood, McIlvaine; New York: Dodd, Mead, 1891.

Lord Arthur Savile's Crime and Other Stories. London: Osgood, McIlvaine; New York: Dodd, Mead, 1891.

A House of Pomegranates. London: Osgood, McIlvaine, 1891; New York: Dodd, Mead, 1892.

Lady Windermere's Fan. London: Mathews and Lane, Bodley Head, 1893. Opened at St. James's Theatre, London, in February 1892.

Salomé: drame en un acte. Paris: Librarie de l'Art Independent, 1893. Trans. Alfred Douglas. London: Mathews and Lane, Bodley Head, 1893. London: Mathews and Lane; Boston: Copeland and Day, 1894. Produced at Thèâtre de L'oeuvre, Paris, in February 1896.

The Sphinx. London: Mathews and Lane, Bodley Head; Boston: Copeland and Day, 1894.

A Woman of No Importance. London: Mathews and Lane, Bodley Head, 1894. Opened at Haymarket Theatre, London, in April 1893.

The Ballad of Reading Gaol [pseud. C.3.3.]. London: Smithers, 1898.

An Ideal Husband. London: Smithers, 1898. Opened at the Haymarket Theatre, London, in January 1895.

The Importance of Being Earnest. London: Smithers, 1899. Opened at the St. James's Theatre, London, in February 1895.

De Profundis. London: Methuen; New York: Putnam, 1905. The first of numerous incomplete texts of Wilde's famous letter from prison. The complete authoritative text appears in *Letters* (1962).

COLLECTED EDITIONS

First Collected Edition of the Works of Oscar Wilde. Ed. Robert Ross. Vols. 1–11, 13–24. London: Methuen, 1908; Boston: Luce, 1910. Vol. 12. Paris: Carrington, 1908. The *Second Collected Edition* appeared in 1909 (vols. 1–12), 1910 (vol. 13), and 1912 (vol. 14).
The Complete Works of Oscar Wilde. Rev. ed. Ed. Vyvyan Holland. London: Collins, 1966.
The Annotated Oscar Wilde. Ed. H. Montgomery Hyde. New York: Potter, 1982.

LETTERS

The Letters of Oscar Wilde. Ed. Rupert Hart-Davis. London: Hart-Davis; New York: Harcourt, 1962.
More Letters of Oscar Wilde. Ed. Rupert Hart-Davis. New York: Vanguard, 1985.

BIBLIOGRAPHIES

Fletcher, Ian, and John Stokes. "Oscar Wilde." *Recent Research on Anglo-Irish Writers.* Ed. Richard Finneran. New York: Modern Language Association, 1983.
Mason, Stuart [pseud. Christopher S. Millard]. *Bibliography of Oscar Wilde.* London: Laurie, 1914; rpt. London: Rota, 1967.
Mikhail, E. H. *Oscar Wilde: An Annotated Bibliography of Criticism.* Totowa, NJ: Roman, 1978.

BIOGRAPHIES

Byrne, Patrick. *The Wildes of Merrion Square.* London: Staples, 1953.
Croft-Cooke, Rupert. *The Unrecorded Life of Oscar Wilde.* London: Allen, 1972.
Douglas, Lord Alfred. *Oscar Wilde and Myself.* London: Long; New York: Duffield, 1914.
———. *My Friendship with Oscar Wilde.* New York: Coventry, 1932. First pub. as *The Autobiography of Lord Alfred Douglas.* London: Martin Secker, 1929.
———. *Without Apology.* London: Richards, 1938.
———. *A Summing Up.* London: Duckworth, 1940.
Ellmann, Richard. *Oscar Wilde.* New York: Knopf, 1988.
Harris, Frank. *The Life and Confessions of Oscar Wilde.* New York: Dell, 1960.
Hyde, H. Montgomery. *Oscar Wilde.* New York: Farrar, 1975.
Pearson, Hesketh. *Oscar Wilde.* New York: Harper, 1946.
Ricketts, Charles. *Recollections of Oscar Wilde.* London: Nonesuch, 1932.
Sherard, Robert H. *The Life of Oscar Wilde.* London: Laurie, 1906; New York: Kennerley, 1907.

CRITICISM

Beckson, Karl. *Oscar Wilde: The Critical Heritage.* New York: Barnes and Noble, 1970.
Bloom, Harold, ed. *Oscar Wilde.* New York: Chelsea, 1985.
• Carroll, Joseph. "Aestheticism, Homoeroticism, and Christian Guilt in *The Picture of Dorian Gray.*" *Philosophy and Literature* 29.2 (October 2005): 286–304.
Chamberlin, J. E. *Ripe Was the Drowsy Hour: The Age of Oscar Wilde.* New York: Seabury, 1977.

• Clausson, Nils. "'Culture and Corruption': Paterian Self-Development *versus* Gothic Degeneration in Oscar Wilde's *The Picture of Dorian Gray*." *Papers on Language and Literature* 39.4 (Fall 2003): 339–64.

Cohen, Ed. *Talk on the Wilde Side: Toward a Genealogy of a Discourse on Male Sexualities*. New York: Routledge, 1993.

Cohen, Philip. *The Moral Vision of Oscar Wilde*. Rutherford, NJ: Fairleigh Dickinson UP, 1978.

• Eells, Emily. "More Than a Coincidence? The Pre-Raphaelites and the Sibyl Vane Subplot of *The Picture of Dorian Gray*." *Anglo Saxonia* 2.26 (2008): 257–78.

Espey, John. "Resources for Wilde Studies at the Clark Library." In *Oscar Wilde: Two Approaches*. Los Angeles: Clark Library, 1977, pp. 25–48.

Gagnier, Regenia. *Idylls of the Marketplace: Oscar Wilde and the Victorian Public*. Stanford: Stanford UP, 1986.

• Gillespie, Michael Patrick. "Picturing Dorian Gray: Resistant Readings in Wilde's Novel." *English Literature in Transition, 1880–1920* 35.1 (1992): 7–25.

———. *The Picture of Dorian Gray: "What the World Thinks Me."* New York: Twayne, 1995.

———. *Oscar Wilde and the Aesthetics of Ambiguity*. Gainesville: UP of Florida, 1996.

———. "*The Picture of Dorian Gray* as a Post-Modern Work." *Études anglaises* 68 (January–March 2015): 19–31.

• Haslam, Richard. "The Hermeneutic Hazards of Hibernicizing Oscar Wilde's *The Picture of Dorian Gray*." *English Literature in Transition, 1880–1920* 57.1 (2014): 37–58.

• Hyde, H. Montgomery. *The Trials of Wilde*. London: Hodge, 1948; Enl. ed. pub. as *The Three Trials of Oscar Wilde*. New York: NYU P, 1956.

———. *Their Good Names*. London: Hamilton, 1970.

———. *The Cleveland Street Scandal*. New York: Coward, 1976.

Jones, John B. "In Search of Archibald Grosvenor: A New Look at Gilbert's *Patience*." *Victorian Studies* 3 (1965): 45–53.

Joyce, Simon. "Sexual Politics and the Aesthetics of Crime: Oscar Wilde in the Nineties." *ELH* 12.1 (Summer 2002): 501–23.

Kernahan, Coulson. *In Good Company*. London: Lane, 1917.

Koestenbaum, Wayne. "Wilde's Hard Labor and the Birth of Gay Reading." In *Engendering Men: The Question of Male Feminist Criticism*, ed. Joseph A. Boone and Michael Cadden. New York: Routledge, 1990, pp. 176–89.

• Lawler, Donald L. "Oscar Wilde's First Manuscript of *The Picture of Dorian Gray*." *Studies in Bibliography* 25 (1972): 125–35.

———. "Oscar Wilde in the *New Cambridge Bibliography of English Literature*." *Papers of the Bibliographical Society of America* 67.2 (1973): 172–88.

———. "The Revisions of *Dorian Gray*." *Victorian Institute Journal* 3 (1974): 21–36.

Lawler, Donald L., and Charles E. Knott. "The Context of Invention: Suggested Origins of *Dorian Gray*." *Modern Philology* 73 (1976): 389–98.

Liebman, Sheldon W. "Character Design in *The Picture of Dorian Gray*." *Studies in the Novel* 31.3 (Fall 1999): 296–316.

Lloyd, Lewis, and Henry Justin Smith. *Oscar Wilde Discovers America*. New York: Harcourt, 1936.

Nassaar, Christopher S. *Into the Demon Universe: A Literary Exploration of Oscar Wilde*. New Haven: Yale UP, 1974.

O'Connor, Maureen. "*The Picture of Dorian Gray* as Irish National Tale." In *Writing Irishness in 19th-Century British Culture*, ed. Neil McCaw. Burlington, VT: Ashgate, 2004, pp. 194–209.

Ragland-Sullivan, Ellie. "The Phenomenon of Aging in Oscar Wilde's *Picture of Dorian Gray*: A Lacanian View." In *Memory and Desire: Aging-Literature-Psychoanalysis*, ed. Kathleen Woodward and Murray M. Schwartz. Bloomington: Indiana UP, 1986, pp. 114–33.

Ransome, Arthur. *Oscar Wilde: A Critical Study*. London: Secker, 1912.

Riquelme, John Paul. "Oscar Wilde's Aesthetic Gothic: Walter Pater, Dark Enlightenment, and *The Picture of Dorian Gray*." *Modern Fiction Studies* 46.3 (Fall 2000): 610–31.

Sammells, Neil. *Wilde Style: The Plays and Prose of Oscar Wilde*. Harlow, Essex: Pearson Education Ltd., 2000.

Sandulescu, C. George, ed. *Rediscovering Oscar Wilde*. Gerrards Cross, Buckinghamshire: Smythe, 1994.

San Juan, Epifanio, Jr. *The Art of Oscar Wilde*. Princeton: Princeton UP, 1967.

• Scheible, Ellen. "Imperialism, Aesthetics, and Gothic Confrontation in *The Picture of Dorian Gray*." *New Hibernia Review* 18.4 (Winter 2014): 131–50.

Shewan, Rodney. *Oscar Wilde: Art and Egoism*. New York: Barnes and Noble, 1977.

Simpson, Colin, et al. *The Cleveland Street Affair*. Boston: Little, Brown, 1976.

Small, Ian. *Oscar Wilde Revalued: An Essay on New Materials & Methods of Research*. Greensboro, NC: ELT Press, 1993.

Symons, Arthur. *A Study of Oscar Wilde*. London: Sawyer, 1930.

Winwar, Francis. *Oscar Wilde and the Yellow Nineties*. New York: Harper, 1940.